Cranberry-Glazed Pork Loin, page 251;
Bourbon-Sweet Potato Stacks, page 246;
Frozen pumpkin pie with garnishes, page 276;
Garlic-Tarragon Green Beans, page 246

Meet the *Southern Living®* Foods Staff

D ozens of recipes go through our Test Kitchens each day, where they are evaluated on taste, appearance, practicality, and ease of preparation. On these pages, we invite you to match the names and faces of the people who test, photograph, and write about our favorites (left to right unless otherwise noted).

SUSAN DOSIER, *Executive Editor;*
SANDRA J. THOMAS, *Administrative Assistant;*
CHARLOTTE LIAPIS, *Editorial Assistant*

(sitting) ANGELA SELLERS, PAM LOLLEY, *Test Kitchens Staff;*
(standing) JAMES SCHEND, *Assistant Test Kitchens Director;*
REBECCA KRACKE GORDON, *Test Kitchens Staff*

ALYSSA PORUBCAN, VIE WARSHAW, *Test Kitchens Staff;*
Vanessa A. McNeil, *Test Kitchens Specialist/Food Styling;*
LYDA H. JONES *Test Kitchens Director*

(sitting) VICKI POELLNITZ, *Assistant Foods Editor:*
SHANNON SLITER SATTERWHITE, SHIRLEY HARRINGTON, *Associate Foods Editors;*
(standing) MARY ALLEN PERRY, JOY E. ZACHARIA, KATE NICHOLSON, *Associate Foods Editors*

Photographers and Photostylists:
(clockwise from top right) RALPH ANDERSON, LISA POWELL, ROSE NGUYEN,
MARY MARGARET CHAMBLISS, BETH DREILING, WILLIAM DICKEY,
CARI SOUTH, BUFFY HARGETT

SCOTT JONES, *Foods Editor;* DONNA FLORIO,
ANDRIA SCOTT HURST, *Senior Writers*

Lemon Curd Pound Cake,
page 278

Southern Living.

2004 ANNUAL RECIPES

Oxmoor House.

ISBN: 0-8487-2826-2
ISSN: 0272-2003

Printed in the United States of America
First printing 2004

To order additional publications, call 1-800-765-6400.

Congratulations!

As a buyer of *Southern Living 2004 Annual Recipes,* you have exclusive access to the *Southern Living* Web site on America Online. Simply go to **www.southernliving.com.**
   When prompted, log on with this Web site access code: **SLAR2826**
   Effective until December 31, 2005

Southern Living®
Executive Editor: Susan Dosier
Foods Editor: Scott Jones
Senior Writers: Donna Florio, Andria Scott Hurst
Associate Foods Editors: Shirley Harrington, Kate Nicholson, Mary Allen Perry, Shannon Sliter Satterwhite, Joy E. Zacharia
Assistant Foods Editor: Vicki Poellnitz
Assistant Recipe Editor: John McMillan
Test Kitchens Director: Lyda H. Jones
Assistant Test Kitchens Director: James Schend
Test Kitchens Specialist/Food Styling: Vanessa A. McNeil
Test Kitchens Staff: Rebecca Kracke Gordon, Pam Lolly, Alyssa Porubcan, Angela Sellers, Vie Warshaw
Administrative Assistant: Sandra J. Thomas
Editorial Assistant: Charlotte Liapis
Production and Color Quality Manager: Katie Terrell Morrow
Photography and Cover Art Director: Jon Thompson
Copy Chief: Dawn P. Cannon
Copy Assistants: Leah Dueffer, Stephanie Gibson Mims
Senior Foods Photographers: Ralph Anderson, Charles Walton IV
Photographers: Tina Cornett, William Dickey, Beth Dreiling
Assistant Photographer: Mary Margaret Chambliss
Senior Photo Stylist: Buffy Hargett
Photo Stylist: Rose Nguyen
Assistant Photo Stylists: Lisa Powell, Cari South
Photo Librarian: Tracy Duncan
Photo Assistant: Catherine Carr
Assistant Production Manager: Jamie Barnhart
Production Coordinators: Christy Coleman, Paula Dennis
Production Assistant: Allison Brooke Wilson

Oxmoor House, Inc.
Editor in Chief: Nancy Fitzpatrick Wyatt
Executive Editor: Susan Carlisle Payne
Art Director: Cynthia R. Cooper
Copy Chief: Allison Long Lowery

Southern Living® *2004 Annual Recipes*
Editor: Susan Hernandez Ray
Copy Editor: Donna Baldone
Editorial Assistant: Terri Laschober
Director of Production: Phillip Lee
Books Production Managers: Theresa L. Beste, Larry Hunter
Production Assistant: Faye Porter Bonner
Publishing Systems Administrator: Rick Tucker

Contributors
Designer: Nancy Johnson
Indexer: Mary Ann Laurens
Editorial Consultant: Jean Wickstrom Liles

Cover: Cream Cheese-Coconut-Pecan Pound Cake, page 280

Contents

Our Year at
Southern Living.

Dear Fellow Food Lovers,

Food is a hot topic these days—whether you're following a diet or craving your mom's meat loaf. This fascination with food works beautifully for the Southerner, who gleefully talks about eating as long as anyone will listen. (If you don't believe me, go check out the chat rooms at **southernliving.com!)**

We also know our Foods staff has plenty to say about the things we eat and cook—take a look at the new expanded tip boxes throughout the book called "Cook's Notes." In these tips, our editors and Test Kitchens professionals pass along the hints they've picked up at taste-testing, in research, and on photo shoots. Not only does this give us more opportunity to talk more about our favorite topic, but also we hope it gives you the inside scoop you need to get these recipes just right.

"We want those recipes that your friends are always asking for."

Food is also a hot topic for busy people. When we get together, I ask my girlfriends, "What have you made lately that's easy? And really good?" I scamper into their kitchens with pen in hand to copy down their latest "finds" in hopes of using them for the magazine (and for my family mealtimes). This very thought has inspired a new category for our 2005 Cook-Off called "Your Best Recipe." We want those recipes that your friends are always asking for. The offering may include a quick and easy "lifeline" dish—or it may be one that takes more effort, yielding results worth every minute. I hope you'll find a chance to log onto **www.southernlivingcookoff.com** and enter our 2005 contest—or drop an entry into the mail. Just remember to use one of the sponsor products listed on our Web site or in the magazine. I'd love to meet you onstage at next year's $100,000 *Southern Living* Cook-Off.

Until then, know that I love hearing YOU talk about food. Many of you have told me you're striving to eat and live well. We're reviewing lots of recipes now with an eye on health. I think you'll notice more light and healthy selections in this book . . . and even more are coming next year. But don't worry—we aren't budging an inch when it comes to flavor. Let me know what you think!

Cheers!

Susan Dosier

Executive Editor
susan_dosier@timeinc.com

Best Recipes of 2004

Our team of food professionals gathers almost every day to taste-test recipes and rate them based on taste, overall appeal, ease of preparation, and cost. Here we share this year's highest rated recipes.

Tropical Shake (page 21) Whip up an incredibly tasty—and nutritious—breakfast with a few fresh ingredients.

Golden Macaroni and Cheese (page 24) This mac 'n' cheese tastes terrific and is super easy. Just shake the ingredients in a jar for the rich cheese sauce instead of cooking the sauce separately.

Collard 'n' Black-Eyed Pea Stew (page 24) Frozen and canned products make it easy to simmer a potful of this delicious dinner.

Hot-Water Cornbread (page 25) These golden, crisp-edged corn cakes welcome pats of creamy butter. Four variations offer a choice of flavors to please any palate.

Bacon-Cheddar Hot-Water Cornbread (page 25) You'll love this variation that's flecked with bits of bacon and sharp Cheddar.

Southwestern Hot-Water Cornbread (page 25) This zesty variation of the original, filled with jalapeño, cilantro, and Mexican cheese, delivers a fiesta of flavors.

Country Ham Hot-Water Cornbread (page 25) Leftover smoky, salty ham gets put to good use in these crispy cakes.

Baked Hot-Water Cornbread (page 25) Enjoy the same great taste and texture of the original recipe—no skillet required. Easy oven procedure eliminates some of the hands-on cooking in batches.

Spoon Rolls (page 47) Savor every buttery bite of this Southern comfort food that boasts a wonderfully crisp crust.

Beef Tenderloin With Henry Bain Sauce (page 52) Make this crowd-pleasing dish the centerpiece of a lavish appetizer party. Serve alone or sandwiched in buns.

Blue Cheese Logs (page 53) A combination of three cheeses rolled in pecans and parsley makes this spread a sure party pleaser.

Memmie's Spoonbread (page (57) Cornmeal, butter, milk, and eggs are the main ingredients in this Southern classic that's so rich and creamy it requires a spoon.

Crab-and-Goat Cheese Poblanos With Mango Salsa (page 59) A salsa made from a few fresh ingredients adds such a refreshing flavor to this spicy-sweet dish that it received our highest rating along with the poblanos.

Beef Fajitas With Pico de Gallo (page 61) A zesty cilantro-inspired salsa with flank steak is one of our favorites.

Ice Cream-Toffee Dessert (page 82) This frozen treat gets incredible texture and flavor from a crust of ladyfingers and a sprinkling of chopped toffee candy bars.

Fruit Salad With Blackberry-Basil Vinaigrette (page 97) A variety of fruits mingle with salad greens and a tangy vinaigrette for a sensational play on flavors.

Buttermilk-Lime Ice Cream (page 103) This recipe, which hails from Texas cowboy Chef Grady Spears, is a refreshing and soothing treat.

Green Tomato-Tomatillo-Corn Pudding (page 103) The pairing of two cousins—green tomatoes and tomatillos—with fresh corn elevates corn casserole to a new level.

Pecan-Peach Cobbler (page 120) Two layers of fresh peaches sandwiched between a pastry made from piecrusts and pecans make the perfect ending to any meal.

Stuffed Focaccia With Roasted Pepper Vinaigrette (page 142) Wedges of focaccia bread drizzled with Roasted Pepper Vinaigrette encase goat cheese, pine nuts, roasted chicken, lettuce, and tomatoes for a gourmet sandwich.

Vidalia Onion Soufflé (page 167) Sweet onions sautéed in butter mix with bread cubes, evaporated milk, eggs, and cheese for a melt-in-your-mouth side-dish sensation.

Fried Okra Salad (page 167) Fried okra gives this hearty salad a new twist, and the tangy Lemon Dressing drizzled over lettuce leaves covered with tomato, onions, bell pepper, and bacon adds zing.

No-Cook Strawberry Ice Cream (page 179) This refreshing summertime treat boasts old-fashioned ice-cream flavor without the time-consuming task of making a traditional custard.

Saffron Butternut Squash Soup (page 187) A smidgen of saffron adds robust flavor and a vibrant orange-red color to this rich and creamy puree.

Apricot-Almond Coffee Cake (page 193) Who would guess that a packaged pound cake mix serves as the base for this breakfast treat that's topped with a swirl of tart apricot preserves, almonds, and a simple powdered sugar glaze?

Nectarine Cobbler With Blueberry Muffin Crust (page 200) Vanilla ice cream starts to melt the instant it's scooped over this dessert with a sweet nectarine filling and crispy blueberry-laced crust.

Apple-Pecan Pie Cobbler and **Pecan Pie Muffins** (page 200) A light pecan pie muffin batter stars in both of these top-rated recipes. Pour the batter over a fresh apple mixture for a scrumptious cobbler, or spoon it in miniature muffin pans for melt-in-your-mouth muffins.

Spiced Plum Muffins (page 201) Taste autumn in every bite of these little breads made with toasted pecans, ground allspice, and a container of plum baby food.

Oatmeal Muffins (page 201) Studded with oats and dates stirred into the batter, these tender and light muffins are irresistible.

Taquitos With Pork Picadillo (page 206) These spicy little meat-filled tacos are rolled and deep-fried. Cilantro, jalapeños, and red wine vinegar jazz up the flavor.

Pizza Crust (page 208) A quick roll of the dough turns Italian Bread into a tender and crusty base for pizza.

Whole Wheat Date-Nut Bread, Whole Wheat Raisin-Nut Bread, and **Whole Wheat Nut Bread** (page 208) Several variations of this hearty bread produce moist and tender loaves that are perfect anytime of day.

Homemade Biscuits, Sour Cream Biscuits, and **Ham-and-Swiss Cheese Biscuits** (page 209) It takes less than 30 minutes to whip up a dozen of these light and fluffy biscuits. Bet'cha can't eat just one!

Parmesan Cheese Muffins and **Breakfast Muffins** (page 209) Parmesan cheese perks up these mouthwatering quick breads. Breakfast Muffins are a bit heartier because they contain ground pork sausage.

Muscadine Sauce (page 231) Gravy's great, but spice up your holiday with muscadine grapes, cider vinegar, and spices in a scrumptious sauce that pairs perfectly with turkey.

Miss Kitty's Chili Sauce (page 231) Miss Kitty proportions the peppers and seasonings just right in this favorite condiment that Southerners like to lavish over cooked greens and meats.

Sweet Potato-Apple Cobbler (page 232) With a dollop of Bourbon Whipped Cream on the crunchy pecan crust, this dessert is love at first bite.

Toffee-Coffee Ice-Cream Torte (page 234) Coffee ice cream combined with toffee candy bars and spread inside a ladyfinger crust make an incredible ending to a special dinner.

Mildred's Toffee (page 235) No one will guess how easy it is to make this crunchy candy. Once you tackle the basic version, you'll be eager to try the bourbon and nut variations.

Cream Cheese-and-Olive Biscuits With Olive-Parsley Spread (page 238) Split the homemade biscuits and top them with goat cheese and the olive spread. Then devour joyfully.

Chipotle-Marinated Quail (page 240) Pan-roasting the spices in this dish gives it an intense flavor and aroma that makes the quail spectacular.

Chile-Blue Cheese Grits (page 240) A mellow blue cheese makes these creamy grits a perfect partner for poultry.

Rudolph's Chocolate Truffle Cake (page 253) This decadent chocolate fantasy sandwiched with a Chocolate Truffle Filling caught our attention with its richness.

Pecan Squares (page 271) Save room to enjoy this rich and crunchy bar cookie with a honey flavor and a buttery crust.

Cupcake Cookies (page 273) Oh, what fun to nibble—a merry mix of pecans, walnuts, chocolate, and graham cracker crumbs are rolled into bite-size treats.

Red Velvet Cheesecake (page 292) A deep red filling covered with a snowy topping ensures that you won't be able to stop at one bite of this dramatically delicious dessert.

Taste of the South

This regular column showcases Southern classics.
Check out these recipes rich in tradition.

Muffulettas (page 27) These olive-based sandwiches remain enduring standards of the New Orleans food scene.

Down-Home Spoonbread (page 57) Few foods are as comforting as this baked blend of cornmeal, butter, milk, and eggs.

Refrigerator Rolls (page 70) Sunday dinner wouldn't be complete without a basketful of these yeast rolls.

Squash Casserole (page 126) A cheesy yellow squash topped with a buttery crumb topping scores high marks every time. Don't miss these two renditions.

Classic Gumbo (page 213) A rich and browned roux forms the hearty base for this classic stew.

Ambrosia (page 233) Discover different ways to create this holiday classic.

Quick & Easy

Busy cooks need simple recipes that taste great.
Our readers and staff frequently flock to this menagerie of ideas.

■ The original one-dish meal, soups offer slow-simmered flavor in these recipes without the long wait (page 26).

■ Your family will add cabbage to its list of favorites once they taste these easy, flavorful sides (page 62).

■ Pull out a bottle of Ranch dressing for an easy way to jazz up your cooking (page 91).

■ What could be simpler than using these delicious marinades to flavor both meats and salads (page 123)?

■ Whip up this scrumptious sauce, and you'll have the base for two great shrimp suppers (page 147).

■ Get out your knife and fork to dive into open-faced sandwiches piled high with a variety of toppings (page 170).

■ Wow everybody at a moment's notice with easy, portable appetizers (page 196).

■ No one will ever guess that these sides were made from refrigerated, ready-to-put-in-the-pan potatoes (page 214).

■ Tired of turkey sandwiches? Savor these delicious ways to use your Thanksgiving leftovers (page 232).

■ Spice up your weeknight meals with a few of these Creole favorites (page 288).

What's for Supper?

We hope these streamlined weeknight favorites ease the pace
and please the palate as you get dinner on the table.

■ These easy ideas for baking and grilling pork chops give juicy results every time (page 44).

■ Plug in an indoor electric grill to cook up two speedy meals (page 61).

■ A few shortcuts help you get an oven-fried chicken supper on the table in a hurry (page 81).

■ Forget the drive-through—enjoy juicy homemade burgers and fries in no time (page 127).

■ Start with pork tenderloin for a simple weeknight menu from the grill. Grill squash halves alongside the pork (page 138).

■ Stock your freezer with his delicious chicken-and-rice casserole that offers convenient portioning variations (page 182).

■ Make a variety of meals from one sensational meat loaf recipe (page 188).

■ These recipes for meal-in-one packets deliver dinners with minimal cleanup and please-everyone ease (page 222).

Healthy and Light

*Each month we focus on different foods and timely concepts
to help you make healthy choices for your family.*

❤ Garlic adds tons of flavor and aroma without extra calories and fat in this medley of dishes (page 16).

❤ These scrumptious recipes start with olive oil, which lends great taste as well as health benefits (page 46).

❤ Enjoy two delicious ways to incorporate cheese into your healthy eating plan (page 58).

❤ Limes provide plentiful possibilities for zesty meals (page 88).

❤ Whip up speedy dinners packed with personality using refrigerated pasta (page 128).

❤ Explore new ingredients to freshen up humdrum fare (page 134).

❤ Turn up the heat with a generous splash of hot sauce in these mealtime marvels (page 183).

❤ These great-tasting recipes will help you relive the days of dinnertime without the care of calories (page 202).

❤ Robust appetizers and main dishes will change your view of yogurt forever (page 216).

❤ Fresh herbs, as well as citrus and other fruits, perk up the flavor of simple ingredients to make a truly luscious meal (page 236).

❤ Juicy slices of turkey anchor this Mediterranean menu that will be a welcome change to the dinner table (page 282).

Top-Rated Menus

*This popular column features hard working menus using award-winning
classics from the* Southern Living *Recipe Hall of Fame.*

■ Throw an **Elegant Couples' Party** with this delicious, mostly make-ahead appetizer menu. Guests will rave over Garlic-and-Rosemary Shrimp, Beef Tenderloin With Henry Bain Sauce, Steamed Asparagus With Tomato-Basil Dip, and Blue Cheese Logs with crackers (page 52).

■ Celebrate an anniversary or a birthday with **A Special Dinner.** Grilled Port Tenderloins With Rosemary Pesto, Lemon Rice Pilaf, and Ice Cream-Toffee Dessert are not only delicious, but can also be made ahead to leave you more time with your guests (page 82).

■ Enjoy a summer supper outdoors with a **Starlight Picnic.** Fill your gourmet basket with Stuffed Focaccia With Roasted Pepper Vinaigrette, Green Bean-Potato Salad, and Amaretto-Walnut Brownies (page 142).

■ Set up a table in an unexpected place, and **Enjoy Dinner Outside.** Your family and friends will rave about a casual menu of Grilled Maple Chipotle Pork Chops on Smoked Gouda Grits and, for dessert, Mocha-Chocolate Shortbread (page 172).

■ Nothing says **It's Grilling Time** like burgers in the backyard. Barbara's Big Juicy Burgers loaded with Sweet-Hot Ketchup are sure to be some of the best you've ever tasted. Throw Grilled Corn With Jalapeño-Lime Butter and Grilled Tomatoes on the grill for a fun and fabulous dinner (page 178).

■ **Let's Do Italian** for a meal that's festive yet easy. Convenience products are the scrumptious secret behind a menu of Tapenade, Spicy Vegetables With Penne Pasta, and Tiramisù Toffee Trifle Pie (page 194).

■ Take in the cool crisp autumn air with a **Fall Porch Party.** Show off this easy harvest menu of Steak-and-Vegetable Kebabs, Orphan's Rice, and Apple-Gingerbread Cobbler (page 218).

■ Set aside a quiet evening to savor **Quail and Cheese Grits.** Start the evening with a refreshing Lemon-Rum Slush made from frozen lemonade and pineapple juice. Follow it with Chipotle-Marinated Quail and Chile-Blue Cheese Grits, and cap the evening with make-ahead Almond-Orange Flan (page 240).

Gotta Have Garlic

Improve your health and your cuisine by adding garlic to your grocery list. These main dishes all contain garlic and are certain to receive rave reviews.

Ever walked into a home while garlic is either sizzling in a skillet or roasting in the oven? The scent is one of the most mouthwatering imaginable. Garlic, fresh or roasted, is great for seasoning lighter recipes because it imparts flavor and aroma without adding fat and calories. We think you'll love these savory choices.

CREAMY TOMATO-STUFFED CHICKEN

family favorite

Prep: 20 min., Bake: 45 min., Stand: 10 min.

This creamy dish is simple yet impressive enough for entertaining.

1 pound skinned and boned chicken breasts (4 breasts)
½ teaspoon salt, divided
½ teaspoon pepper, divided
½ (8-ounce) package ⅓-less-fat cream cheese, softened
3 garlic cloves, minced and divided
¼ cup chopped dried tomatoes (not in oil)
½ cup chopped fresh basil, divided
¼ cup shredded Parmesan cheese
Vegetable cooking spray
6 plum tomatoes, chopped
2 teaspoons olive oil
2 teaspoons red wine vinegar

PLACE chicken between 2 sheets of heavy-duty plastic wrap, and flatten to ¼-inch thickness using a meat mallet or rolling pin. Sprinkle evenly with ¼ teaspoon salt and ¼ teaspoon pepper.

STIR together cream cheese, two-thirds of minced garlic, and dried tomatoes. Spread cream cheese mixture evenly over 1 side of each chicken breast, leaving a ¼-inch border. Sprinkle ¼ cup basil and Parmesan cheese evenly over breasts; roll up, jellyroll fashion, and secure with wooden picks, if necessary. Arrange in an 8-inch square baking dish coated with cooking spray.

BAKE at 350° for 30 to 45 minutes or until chicken is done. Remove from oven, and let stand 10 minutes.

STIR together plum tomatoes, olive oil, vinegar, remaining ¼ teaspoon salt, remaining ¼ teaspoon pepper, remaining one-third garlic, and remaining ¼ cup basil.

CUT chicken into slices. Serve with tomato mixture. **MAKES** 4 servings.

NOTE: Fresh tomato mixture may also be served with toasted or grilled French bread slices.

Calories 262 (34% from fat); Fat 9.9g (sat 4.7g, mono 2.5g, poly 0.7g); Protein 32.3g; Carb 9.5g; Fiber 1.8g; Chol 83mg; Iron 1.8mg; Sodium 662mg; Calc 133mg

ROASTED GARLIC-ROSEMARY BREAD

family favorite

Prep: 20 min.; Bake: 1 hr., 10 min.; Rise: 2 hrs.

1 garlic bulb
1 tablespoon water
1 teaspoon grated lemon rind
1 teaspoon fresh lemon juice
1 teaspoon dried rosemary
½ teaspoon salt
½ teaspoon pepper
½ (32-ounce) package frozen bread dough, thawed
1 large egg, lightly beaten
1 teaspoon kosher salt

CUT off pointed end of garlic; place garlic on a piece of aluminum foil, and drizzle with 1 tablespoon water. Fold foil to seal.

BAKE at 350° for 45 to 50 minutes or until garlic is tender. Reduce oven temperature to 200°. Remove garlic from oven, and let cool. Squeeze pulp from garlic cloves into a small bowl, and mash pulp with a fork until smooth. Stir in lemon rind and next 4 ingredients.

ROLL dough into a 12-inch square on a lightly floured surface. Spread garlic mixture over dough; roll up, jellyroll fashion. Place dough roll on a parchment paper-lined baking sheet; bring ends together forming a ring, and pinch ends to seal. Cut 1-inch slits along top of dough. Turn oven off; place dough ring in oven. Let rise 1½ to 2 hours or until doubled in bulk. Remove from oven; brush dough with egg, and sprinkle with kosher salt. Increase oven temperature to 375°. Using a water bottle, spray each interior wall of oven 2 or 3 times before closing oven door. (Do not spray dough.)

BAKE at 375° for 18 to 20 minutes or until golden. **MAKES** 16 servings.

Calories 86 (17% from fat); Fat 1.6g (sat 0.1g, mono 0.1g, poly 0g); Protein 3.5g; Carb 15.3g; Fiber 1g; Chol 13mg; Iron 1.2mg; Sodium 352mg; Calc 12.6mg

RED SAUCE AND MEATBALLS

freezeable • make ahead

Prep: 30 min., Bake: 10 min., Cook: 45 min.

Spray your hands with a little cooking spray for perfectly round meatballs that don't stick to your hands.

- **1½ pounds extra-lean ground beef**
- **1 cup Italian-seasoned breadcrumbs**
- **1 large egg**
- **½ small onion, grated**
- **½ cup water**
- **¼ cup grated Parmesan cheese**
- **6 garlic cloves, minced and divided***
- **2 tablespoons dried basil, divided**
- **2 tablespoons dried parsley, divided**
- **1 tablespoon dried oregano, divided**
- **¾ teaspoon salt, divided**
- **1 teaspoon pepper, divided**
- **Vegetable cooking spray**
- **1 medium onion, chopped**
- **1 cup red wine**
- **3 (28-ounce) cans crushed tomatoes****
- **1 tablespoon sugar**
- **1 (16-ounce) package linguine**

COMBINE first 6 ingredients, half of minced garlic, 1 tablespoon each of basil and parsley, 1½ teaspoons oregano, ¼ teaspoon salt, and ½ teaspoon pepper in a large bowl. Shape mixture into 32 (1-inch) balls.

PLACE a rack coated with cooking spray in an aluminum foil-lined broiler pan. Arrange meatballs on rack.

BAKE at 400° for 10 minutes or until meatballs are browned.

SAUTÉ chopped onion and remaining half of garlic in a Dutch oven coated with cooking spray over medium-high heat 5 minutes or until onion is tender. Add red wine, tomatoes, sugar, and remaining 1 tablespoon each of basil and parsley, 1½ teaspoons oregano, ½ teaspoon salt, and ½ teaspoon pepper. Bring to a boil; reduce heat, and add meatballs. Simmer, stirring occasionally, 30 minutes.

COOK pasta according to package directions, omitting salt and oil. Serve tomato sauce with meatballs over hot linguine.

MAKES 10 servings.

NOTE: Red sauce and meatballs can be prepared ahead and refrigerated for a day or frozen for up to a month.

*****You can substitute bottled minced garlic: ½ teaspoon equals 1 clove.

******To reduce sodium, choose low-sodium canned tomato products and omit added salt.

FRANK PELLEGRINO
PORT ORANGE, FLORIDA

Calories 433 (19% from fat); Fat 8.9g (sat 3.2g, mono 3.2g, poly 1g); Protein 27.2g; Carb 61g; Fiber 6.8g; Chol 48mg; Iron 5.6mg; Sodium 1147mg**; Calc 180mg

SWEET PORK WITH GARLIC

family favorite

Prep: 10 min., Bake: 30 min., Stand: 10 min.

Serve tender Sweet Pork With Garlic with steamed broccoli and fluffy rice.

- **4 garlic cloves, minced**
- **1 tablespoon hoisin sauce**
- **1 tablespoon Dijon mustard**
- **1 tablespoon ketchup**
- **2 tablespoons lite soy sauce, divided**
- **6 teaspoons honey, divided**
- **1 (¾-pound) pork tenderloin**
- **Vegetable cooking spray**
- **2 teaspoons rice vinegar**
- **1 teaspoon sesame oil**
- **1 teaspoon chili garlic sauce**
- **½ cup chopped green onions**
- **¼ cup chopped fresh cilantro**
- **Garnish: fresh cilantro sprigs**

STIR together first 4 ingredients, 1 tablespoon soy sauce, and 2 teaspoons honey.

SPOON garlic mixture evenly over pork, rubbing well into pork.

PLACE pork on a rack coated with cooking spray in an aluminum foil-lined roasting pan.

BAKE at 350° for 30 minutes or until a meat thermometer inserted into thickest portion registers 155°. Remove from oven; cover pork loosely with aluminum foil, and let stand 10 minutes.

CUT pork diagonally into slices. Place slices on a serving platter.

WHISK together vinegar, sesame oil, chili garlic sauce, remaining 1 tablespoon soy sauce, and remaining 4 teaspoons honey. Drizzle evenly over pork. Sprinkle evenly with green onions and chopped cilantro. Garnish, if desired. **MAKES** 4 servings.

TINA SHIFFLETT
ATLANTA, GEORGIA

Calories 197 (31% from fat); Fat 6.9g (sat 2g, mono 2.7g, poly 1.1g); Protein 19.2g; Carb 14.2g; Fiber 0.9g; Chol 58mg; Iron 1.2mg; Sodium 301mg; Calc 18mg

---

Garlic Gotta-Know

- Garlic bulbs or heads are made up of sections called cloves.
- Purchase firm bulbs with dry skins. Avoid bulbs with soft or shriveled cloves or those with green shoots sprouting from the top.
- Store fresh garlic in an open container, such as a basket (away from other foods) in a cool, dark place.
- Garlic will burn and turn bitter quickly when cooked at high heat. If you're sautéeing other veggies such as peppers or onions for the same dish, add the garlic last and sauté briefly (30 seconds to 1 minute).
- Two medium cloves equal about 1 teaspoon minced garlic (depending on clove size). Minced garlic in jars can be substituted for fresh, but jarred garlic tends to be stronger in flavor and aroma. Start with less than your recipe calls for and increase according to your liking. The longer minced garlic is stored in your fridge, the stronger it gets.
- Garlic powder may be substituted for fresh garlic, but the flavor will be different. Use ⅛ teaspoon for each garlic clove.

New Year's Eve Appetizers

These easy recipes are perfect for year-round entertaining.

Offer these finger foods at a gathering on New Year's Eve or anytime. Everything can be made ahead—the Black-Eyed Pea Dip is heated in the microwave just before serving, and the shrimp taste even better once they've soaked up all the wonderful flavors. Serve with your favorite chilled Champagne.

TANGY SHRIMP

make ahead

Prep: 20 min., Chill: 6 hrs.

If time allows, use fresh boiled shrimp and peel, leaving just the tail intact.

- 1 (2-pound) package medium-size frozen cooked shrimp with tails, thawed and drained
- 1 cup safflower oil
- ⅓ cup white vinegar
- 1 medium-size sweet onion, thinly sliced
- 3 tablespoons capers with juice
- 1 tablespoon hot sauce
- 1 teaspoon salt
- 1 teaspoon celery salt
- 1½ teaspoons grated lemon rind
- 1 tablespoon fresh lemon juice
- 7 bay leaves

COMBINE all ingredients in a large bowl. Cover and chill at least 6 hours or up to 2 days. Remove and discard bay leaves before serving. **MAKES** 8 to 10 appetizer servings.

SHIRLEY CARTER
WALLS, MISSISSIPPI

BLACK-EYED PEA DIP

fast fixin's • make ahead

Prep: 15 min.

- 1 (15-ounce) can black-eyed peas, rinsed and drained
- 1 (8-ounce) package pasteurized prepared cheese product, cubed
- ¼ cup butter
- 6 to 10 pickled jalapeño slices, minced
- 6 green onions, chopped
- 1 teaspoon garlic powder
- Corn chips

MASH peas coarsely with a fork or potato masher in a microwave-safe bowl. Stir in cheese and next 4 ingredients; microwave at MEDIUM-HIGH (70% power) about 2½ minutes, stirring every 30 seconds until melted. Serve with corn chips. **MAKES** about 3 cups.

PEGGY SHARPE
MICHIGAN CITY, MISSISSIPPI

BLUE CHEESE PUFFS

make ahead

Prep: 15 min., Cook: 2 min., Stand: 15 min., Bake: 30 min.

- ¼ cup butter
- ¾ cup water
- ¾ cup all-purpose flour
- ⅛ teaspoon ground red pepper
- 3 large eggs
- 1 (4-ounce) container crumbled blue cheese

BRING butter and ¾ cup water to a boil in a heavy saucepan.

REMOVE from heat. Add flour and pepper, beating with a rubber spatula or wooden spoon until mixture leaves sides of pan and forms a smooth ball. Add eggs, 1 at a time, beating well after each addition.

STIR in cheese, and let mixture stand 15 minutes.

DROP dough by rounded tablespoonfuls 2 inches apart onto buttered baking sheets.

BAKE at 400° for 30 minutes or until golden. Serve either warm or at room temperature. **MAKES** about 2 dozen.

ELAINE JACKAMORE
OKEECHOBEE, FLORIDA

EGGS STUFFED WITH CRABMEAT

fast fixin's • make ahead

Prep: 20 min.

Canned crabmeat, smoked salmon, or shrimp are good alternatives to fresh crabmeat.

- 6 hard-cooked eggs
- ¾ cup fresh crabmeat
- ⅓ cup mayonnaise
- 2 celery ribs, minced (½ cup)
- 1 teaspoon dry mustard
- ½ teaspoon salt
- ⅛ teaspoon ground red pepper
- Paprika
- Lettuce (optional)

CUT eggs in half lengthwise. Carefully remove yolks, and mash. Set egg whites aside.

DRAIN and flake crabmeat, removing any bits of shell. Combine mashed egg yolks, crabmeat, mayonnaise, and next 4 ingredients, stirring well.

SPOON mixture into egg whites. Sprinkle with paprika. Cover and chill until ready to serve. Serve on a bed of lettuce, if desired. **MAKES** 1 dozen.

MARIANNE CHALIFOUX
WINFIELD, ILLINOIS

A New Look for Hoppin' John

This timeless good-luck combination of rice, black-eyed peas, and pork gets a creative update in these easy recipes.

Hoppin' John is a popular New Year's Day staple for its comforting flavors, stick-to-your-ribs heartiness, and, of course, good luck. This year, consider one of these unique variations on the classic dish. We've kept prep time to a minimum by using canned black-eyed peas. If you're looking to really shake things up at the table, make Hoppin' John's often underappreciated sister, Limpin' Susan, by substituting okra for black-eyed peas.

BLACK-EYED PEA STEW WITH RICE

Prep: 30 min.; Cook: 1 hr., 22 min.

- **2 pounds boneless pork loin chops, cut into cubes**
- **2 tablespoons olive oil, divided**
- **1 large onion, chopped**
- **4 celery ribs, chopped**
- **1 large red bell pepper, chopped**
- **1 small jalapeño pepper, seeded and finely chopped**
- **2 garlic cloves, minced**
- **1 teaspoon dried oregano**
- **½ teaspoon dried thyme**
- **3 (15-ounce) cans black-eyed peas, rinsed and drained**
- **1 (32-ounce) container chicken broth**
- **1 bay leaf**
- **1 (28-ounce) can crushed tomatoes**
- **1 teaspoon salt**
- **1 teaspoon ground black pepper**
- **1 teaspoon hot sauce**
- **¼ teaspoon ground red pepper**
- **Hot cooked rice**

SAUTÉ pork in 1 tablespoon hot oil in a Dutch oven over medium-high heat 8 to 10 minutes. Remove pork; set aside.
ADD remaining 1 tablespoon oil to Dutch oven. Sauté onion and next 4 ingredients in hot oil 5 minutes. Stir in oregano and thyme; cook, stirring often, 2 minutes.
ADD peas, broth, and bay leaf; bring to a boil. Cover, reduce heat, and simmer, stirring occasionally, 45 minutes.
STIR in tomatoes; simmer, stirring occasionally, 20 minutes. Stir in reserved pork, salt, and next 3 ingredients. Remove and discard bay leaf. Serve stew over rice. **MAKES** 10 cups.

Here's to Good Luck

Over the years, many of the traditional foods we enjoy on New Year's Day have taken on meanings above and beyond their great tastes.

■ **Black-eyed peas and collard greens:** Thought to bring wealth because they look like tiny coins and dollar bills, respectively.
■ **Rice:** Signifies abundance for the coming year.
■ **Pork:** Hogs root forward, so pork represents the future. Poultry, on the other hand, isn't recommended, because chickens scratch backwards, conjuring up thoughts of the past.

HOPPIN' JOHN WAFFLE STACK

Prep: 10 min., Cook: 30 min.

- **1 (1-pound) package andouille sausage, sliced**
- **2 (15-ounce) cans black-eyed peas, rinsed and drained**
- **2 (10-ounce) cans hot diced tomatoes and green chiles**
- **½ teaspoon garlic powder**
- **2 (6-ounce) packages cornbread mix**
- **½ cup cooked rice**
- **½ teaspoon rubbed sage**
- **½ teaspoon onion powder**
- **3 tablespoons butter or margarine, softened**
- **Toppings: shredded Cheddar cheese, chopped tomato, sliced green onions, crumbled cooked bacon**

COOK sausage in a large skillet over medium-high heat 5 minutes or until lightly browned; drain and return sausage to skillet.
ADD black-eyed peas, tomatoes and green chiles, and garlic powder to skillet, and simmer 5 minutes. Remove from heat; cover and keep warm.
PREPARE cornbread mix according to package directions, adding cooked rice, sage, and onion powder.
COOK ⅓ cup cornbread mixture in a preheated, oiled waffle iron until golden brown. Spread waffles evenly with butter, and place on a wire rack in a jelly-roll pan. Keep warm in a 200° oven. Repeat with remaining batter.
PLACE waffles on individual serving plates; top evenly with black-eyed pea mixture, and serve with desired toppings. **MAKES** 8 servings.

ANNE TEAGUE
MESQUITE, TEXAS

Good Food for Busy Families

This mom makes healthy menus her number one priority.

When Associate Foods Editor Joy Zacharia talked to Jamie Baldwin of Acworth, Georgia, Jamie was ready for a family nutrition makeover. Two kids, a full-time job, and a long commute make it difficult for her to prepare tasty, wholesome entrées that everyone will eat. "My biggest problem is meal planning. We tend to eat whatever is fast," Jamie says. She's out the door by 6 a.m. and home after 5 p.m. By then, everyone's hungry. For Jamie, that translates into dining out, picking up something on the way home, or tossing together something quick in the kitchen. Sound familiar? Here's what Joy proposed to help her.

The Problem

Many restaurant options are high in calories and fat and come in large portions that distort our notion of normal serving sizes. Quick-cooking meals, such as ramen noodles, boxed macaroni and cheese, and fettuccine Alfredo, can sabotage a good plan. Another challenge for Jamie and her husband is feeding their choosy son.

Smart Solutions

■ Plan and shop for at least two home-cooked meals on Saturday or Sunday for the following week's suppers. Make double batches of casseroles; freeze one for another night. Grill or bake extra servings of marinated chicken or lean beef, and freeze them for an upcoming dinner.

Joy gave Jamie a binder of family-friendly, healthy recipes for quick access to easy weeknight meals. Start collecting nutritious recipes that you think your family will enjoy, and place them in plastic sheet protectors inside a binder. Review them while making your grocery list.

■ Limit dining out to one or two times per week, and order good-for-you items from the menu. Choose grilled, baked, or broiled lean beef, pork, chicken, and seafood (fish, scallops, shrimp, and oysters). Ask the server how sautéed dishes are prepared. (They may use generous amounts of oil or butter.) Avoid fried selections and dishes in butter or cream sauces. Stay away from all-you-can-eat restaurants—period.

■ Split entrées with your spouse or kids. In many restaurants, one entrée can feed two to four people.

■ Eating at home? Well-balanced meals include a lean protein (fish, chicken, lean pork or beef); a nonstarchy veggie (collard greens, green beans, carrots, tossed salad, broccoli, yellow squash); and whole grains (brown rice, whole wheat pasta) or starchy veggies (sweet potatoes, corn). Dry or fresh beans, such as kidney, lima, black, and black-eyed peas, are excellent sources of protein, complex carbohydrates, and soluble fiber and may be substituted for lean meats.

■ Read Nutrition Facts labels on food packages carefully. Serving sizes can often be misleading. For example, the nutritional information on a 20-ounce cola says it contains 2½ (8-ounce) servings, but that size soft drink is rarely shared. So instead of 100 calories, you get 250 calories.

■ Make exercise a priority. Begin by walking 15 to 20 minutes two or three times per week. Work up to a challenging pace and eventually 30 minutes every day. Other good choices include biking, hiking, dancing, and swimming. For weight loss, getting one hour of exercise on most days is ideal.

SWEET SKILLET SIRLOIN

family favorite

Prep: 15 min., Chill: 30 min., Cook: 10 min.

> 3 green onions, minced
> 2 tablespoons lite soy sauce
> 1 tablespoon honey
> 1 teaspoon dark sesame oil
> ½ teaspoon dried crushed red pepper
> 3 garlic cloves (about 3 teaspoons), minced and divided
> 1 pound beef sirloin, thinly sliced
> 1 teaspoon vegetable oil
> Hot cooked brown rice (optional)
> Cooked frozen mixed vegetables (optional)

COMBINE first 5 ingredients and 2 teaspoons minced garlic in a large zip-top freezer bag; add beef. Seal and shake to coat. Chill 30 minutes.

SAUTÉ remaining 1 teaspoon minced garlic in hot oil in a large skillet over medium-high heat until tender. Add beef mixture; cook over medium-high heat 3 to 5 minutes or to desired degree of doneness. (Do not overcook or beef will burn.) Serve with rice and vegetables, if desired. **MAKES** 4 servings.

Calories (including ½ cup brown rice and 1 cup cooked frozen vegetable medley) 352 (25% from fat); Fat 9.6g (sat 2.9g, mono 4g, poly 1.6g); Protein 30g; Carb 35g; Fiber 5.5g; Chol 67mg; Iron 3.2mg; Sodium 503mg; Calc 54mg

CRUNCHY CATFISH FINGERS WITH CURRIED RICE

family favorite

Prep: 20 min., Bake: 22 min.

> 8 (4-ounce) catfish fillets
> ¾ teaspoon seasoned salt, divided
> 1½ cups fat-free milk
> 2 tablespoons Dijon mustard
> 2 cups crushed crispy corn cereal squares (about 5 cups uncrushed)
> ¼ cup cornstarch
> ½ teaspoon pepper
> Vegetable cooking spray
> Curried Rice

CUT each fillet lengthwise into 3 strips; sprinkle with ½ teaspoon seasoned salt. **WHISK** together milk and mustard. Combine crushed cereal, cornstarch, pepper, and remaining ¼ teaspoon seasoned salt. Dip fish in milk mixture; dredge in cereal mixture. Arrange fish fingers on a rack coated with cooking spray. Place rack in an aluminum foil-lined broiler pan. Lightly coat fish with cooking spray.

BAKE at 375° for 20 to 22 minutes or until fish flakes with a fork. Serve with Curried Rice. **MAKES** 8 servings.

NOTE: For testing purposes only, we used Corn Chex cereal.

Curried Rice:
Prep: 20 min., Cook: 25 min.

- 1 cup uncooked long-grain white rice
- 1 small onion, chopped
- 1 apple, peeled and chopped
- 1 tablespoon curry powder
- 1 teaspoon minced garlic
- 2 teaspoons olive oil
- 2 cups fat-free reduced-sodium chicken broth
- ¼ teaspoon salt
- ¼ cup golden raisins
- ¼ cup sliced green onions
- 2 tablespoons slivered almonds, toasted

SAUTÉ first 5 ingredients in hot oil in a large saucepan coated with cooking spray 5 minutes. (Do not brown.) Stir in broth and salt; bring to a boil. Cover, reduce heat, and simmer 20 minutes or until liquid is absorbed. Stir in raisins, green onions, and toasted almonds. **MAKES** about 3½ cups.

Calories (including ½ cup cooked rice) 411 (26% from fat); Fat 11.9g (sat 2.4g, mono 5.8g, poly 2.3g); Protein 24g; Carb 51g; Fiber 2.5g; Chol 54mg; Iron 7.9mg; Sodium 691mg; Calc 162mg

Simple Breakfast

Making time for breakfast needn't be as complicated as getting the dog walked, lunches packed, and the family out the door. These morning meals can easily fit into your schedule.

Try these fast-forward planning tips. Bake a batch of muffins at the beginning of the week, and freeze them; a quick reheat in the microwave will turn out pastries that beat toaster snacks any day. Also, keep a variety of fresh or sliced refrigerated fruit on hand for recipes and healthy snacks. Such smart starts will give your body the necessary fuel to tackle the busy day ahead.

TROPICAL SHAKE

family favorite

Prep: 10 min.; Freeze: 1hr., 30 min.

You can make this drink at a moment's notice when you have a handy supply of banana slices in your freezer. Simply toss fresh slices in lemon juice, and freeze up to six months in zip-top freezer bags.

- 1 medium-size ripe banana, cut into 1-inch slices
- 2 teaspoons lemon juice
- 1 medium mango, peeled and cut into pieces
- 1½ cups pineapple-orange juice, chilled
- 1 (8-ounce) container nonfat vanilla yogurt

TOSS banana with lemon juice; drain, reserving lemon juice. Place banana slices on a baking sheet, and freeze 1 hour and 30 minutes.

PROCESS frozen banana slices, reserved lemon juice, mango, 1½ cups pineapple-orange juice, and yogurt in a blender until smooth, stopping to scrape down sides. Pour into chilled glasses; serve immediately. **MAKES** 4 cups.

Calories (per 1-cup serving) 154 (2% from fat); Fat 0.4g (sat 0.2g, mono 0.1g, poly 0.1g); Protein 4g; Carb 36g; Fiber 1.8g; Chol 0.9mg; Iron 0.4mg; Sodium 41mg; Calc 116mg

BANANA-PRALINE MUFFINS

fast fixin's • freezeable

Prep: 10 min., Bake: 20 min.

Grab a muffin for a breakfast on the go.

- ⅓ cup chopped pecans, toasted
- 3 tablespoons brown sugar
- 1 tablespoon light sour cream
- 3 small ripe bananas
- 1 large egg
- 1½ cups pancake mix
- ½ cup granulated sugar
- 2 tablespoons vegetable oil
- Vegetable cooking spray

STIR together pecans, brown sugar, and sour cream. Set aside.

MASH bananas in a medium bowl; add egg and next 3 ingredients, stirring just until dry ingredients are moistened.

PLACE paper baking cups in muffin pans, and coat cups with cooking spray.

SPOON batter into muffin cups, filling three-fourths full. Carefully spoon pecan mixture evenly in center of each muffin.

BAKE at 400° for 18 to 20 minutes or until golden. Remove from pans immediately, and cool on wire racks. **MAKES** 1 dozen.

NOTE: You can freeze muffins, if desired. To reheat, microwave at HIGH 1 minute.

COLEY L. BAILEY
COFFEEVILLE, MISSISSIPPI

Calories per serving 181 (31% from fat); Fat 6.2g (sat 0.8g, mono 3.2g, poly 1.8g); Protein 2.8g; Carb 30g; Fiber 1.5g; Chol 22mg; Iron 0.8mg; Sodium 205mg; Calc 49mg

Eating Right: Just the Facts

Want to feel better? Start by incorporating these nourishing foods into your life.

Imagine choosing foods because they can reduce anxiety, make you more alert, and give you the energy to leap tall buildings in a single bound. There just might be a little truth to the old adage, "You are what you eat."

Numerous foods can affect the way we function throughout the day—mentally and physically. In fact, what we eat drives our daily performance, social interactions, and emotional well-being.

Stay balanced with these energizing and mood-boosting recipes that provide important nutrients to keep your mind and body in sync. Start the morning with Fruit-and-Bran Muffins. A good breakfast can improve your brain power and keep you motivated. Or for a quick lift, try Banana-Peach Buttermilk Smoothie anytime of the day. Rest assured, all these rejuvenating recipes will keep you on your toes.

FRUIT-AND-BRAN MUFFINS

family favorite

Prep: 15 min., Stand: 5 min., Bake: 20 min.

These muffins serve up a good dose of fiber.

- **1 cup fat-free milk**
- **2 cups O-shaped sweetened oat-and-wheat bran cereal**
- **1 large Granny Smith apple, peeled and diced**
- **1¼ cups uncooked oat bran hot cereal**
- **⅓ cup golden raisins**
- **¼ cup firmly packed dark brown sugar**
- **¼ cup egg substitute**
- **1 tablespoon baking powder**
- **½ teaspoon ground cinnamon**
- **¼ teaspoon ground nutmeg**
- **3 tablespoons applesauce**
- **Vegetable cooking spray**

BRING milk to a boil in a large saucepan; remove from heat, and stir in O-shaped cereal. Let stand 5 minutes or until cereal is softened.

STIR in apple and next 8 ingredients until blended.

PLACE paper baking cups in muffin pans, and lightly coat with cooking spray. Spoon batter evenly into cups.

BAKE at 375° for 18 to 20 minutes or until a wooden pick inserted in center comes out clean. **MAKES** 12 muffins.

NOTE: For testing purposes only, we used Cracklin' Oat Bran Cereal for sweetened cereal and Hodgson Mill Oat Bran Hot Cereal for uncooked cereal.

Calories (per muffin) 150 (17% from fat); Fat 2.9g (sat 0.6, mono 1.08, poly 0.36); Protein 5.2g; Carb 27.3g; Fiber 4.1g; Chol .5mg; Iron 1.9mg; Sodium 158mg; Calc 118mg

BANANA-PEACH BUTTERMILK SMOOTHIE

fast fixin's

Prep: 8 min.

Cultured dairy products—such as buttermilk and yogurt—are good for maintaining a healthy digestive tract.

- **2 large ripe bananas, sliced and frozen**
- **2 cups frozen peaches**
- **1 cup fat-free buttermilk**
- **¼ cup fresh orange juice**
- **1 tablespoon honey**

PROCESS all ingredients in a blender until smooth, stopping to scrape down sides. Serve immediately. **MAKES** 4 cups.

RUBLELENE SINGLETON
SCOTTS HILL, TENNESSEE

Calories (per 1-cup serving) 221 (4% from fat); Fat 1.1g (sat 0.5g, mono 0.1g, poly 0.1g); Protein 3.7g; Carb 52.6g; Fiber 3.3g; Chol 3.8mg; Iron 0.7mg; Sodium 76mg; Calc 72mg

Eating and Your Mood

Did you know that foods can affect your emotions?
- Eating breakfast may increase memory and calmness.
- A cup of hot tea can have a soothing effect. Green and black teas are thought to have protective properties against heart disease and a few types of cancer.
- If you're a chocolate junkie, here's good news: Some research suggests that chocolate may actually improve your mood and cause the brain to produce serotonin, which is a natural antidepressant.
- Dairy products, particularly milk, tend to be relaxing (reaction is similar to that of tea). Dairy and other high-protein foods may also increase alertness.

SALMON WITH ALMONDS AND TOMATO-LEMON SAUCE

Prep: 30 min., Bake: 6 min., Cook: 26 min., Broil: 10 min.

- ½ cup sliced almonds
- 1 small onion, sliced
- 1 tablespoon olive oil
- 2 garlic cloves, minced
- 1 (28-ounce) can diced tomatoes, drained
- 1½ tablespoons honey
- 1 teaspoon grated lemon rind
- ¾ teaspoon ground cumin
- 1½ teaspoons fresh lemon juice
- ¾ teaspoon salt, divided
- ½ teaspoon ground black pepper, divided
- 6 (4-ounce) salmon fillets
- ⅛ teaspoon ground red pepper
- Garnish: fresh cilantro sprigs

BAKE almonds in a shallow pan at 350°, stirring occasionally, 5 to 6 minutes or until toasted. Set aside.

SAUTÉ onion in hot oil in a skillet 10 minutes or until golden. Add garlic; sauté 1 minute. Stir in tomatoes and next 3 ingredients; reduce heat, and simmer, stirring occasionally, 15 minutes. Stir in lemon juice and ¼ teaspoon each of salt and black pepper; keep warm.

SPRINKLE salmon fillets with red pepper, remaining ½ teaspoon salt, and remaining ¼ teaspoon black pepper. Place on a lightly greased rack in a broiler pan.

BROIL 6 inches from heat 10 minutes or until fish flakes with a fork. Serve with tomato mixture; sprinkle with almonds. Garnish, if desired. **MAKES** 6 servings.

HELEN H. MAURER
CLERMONT, GEORGIA

Calories 354 (47% from fat); Fat 18.6g (sat 2g, mono 10.3g, poly 4.8g); Protein 30.8g; Carb 16.2g; Fiber 4.6g; Chol 65mg; Iron 1.5mg; Sodium 528mg; Calc 107mg

TOMATO-SPINACH SAUTÉ

fast fixin's

Prep: 10 min., Cook: 5 min.

Popeye was right—spinach makes you strong. It's a good source of fiber and calcium. Sauté it with fresh garlic, which is believed to help control blood pressure and lower the risk of cancer.

- 1 (16-ounce) package fresh spinach
- 1 tablespoon olive oil
- ½ teaspoon salt, divided
- ½ teaspoon coarsely ground pepper, divided
- 2 garlic cloves, minced
- 1 medium tomato, chopped
- 1 tablespoon balsamic vinegar (optional)
- Salt to taste (optional)

SAUTÉ spinach in hot olive oil in a non-stick skillet over medium-high heat 2 minutes or until wilted. Stir in ¼ teaspoon each of salt and pepper. Transfer to a serving platter.

ADD garlic to skillet, and sauté 1 minute. Stir in chopped tomato, and sauté until thoroughly heated. Stir in remaining ¼ teaspoon each of salt and pepper. Spoon mixture over spinach. Drizzle with vinegar, if desired, and serve immediately. Lightly salt to taste, if desired. **MAKES** 4 servings.

DINA SKINNER
NEW ORLEANS, LOUISIANA

Calories (not including salt to taste) 69 (50% from fat); Fat 3.9g (sat 0.5g, mono 2.5g, poly 0.3g); Protein 3.6g; Carb 7g; Fiber 1.4g; Chol 0mg; Iron 3.3mg; Sodium 383mg; Calc 122mg

" Cook's Notes "

"We've wanted to do this story for a while because there are so many misconceptions about what we should or shouldn't eat, especially with all the popular fad diets out there," says Associate Foods Editor **Shannon Satterwhite**. The truth is, there are no bad foods, just bad choices. Apple pie, for instance, is not a bad food. It contains nutrient-rich apples. Eating the whole pie, however, is a bad choice! By defining the functions and benefits of certain foods, we hope to encourage good eating choices.

Top-Rated Sides

When it comes to Southern food, it's hard to beat these down-home dishes.

For this collection we've chosen some all-time favorites as well as a new recipe for the beloved mac and cheese—this one coming from Editor-in-Chief John Floyd's late mother, Louise Floyd, of Potters Station, Alabama. Her version received our highest rating. We loved her easy method for making the thickener for the cheese sauce. You simply shake the ingredients in a jar. You'll find more shortcuts in our other recipes: Turnip Greens Stew and Collard 'n' Black-Eyed Pea Stew use frozen and canned products, and the coleslaw uses packaged shredded cabbage.

GOLDEN MACARONI AND CHEESE

family favorite

Prep: 10 min., Cook: 15 min., Bake: 45 min.

For a divine main dish, stir in chopped cooked ham before baking. Sprinkle top with chopped cooked bacon before serving. *(pictured on page 39)*

- 1 (8-ounce) package elbow macaroni (about 2 cups uncooked macaroni)
- 2 cups milk
- ¼ cup all-purpose flour
- 1 teaspoon onion salt
- 2 (10-ounce) blocks sharp Cheddar cheese, shredded (about 4½ cups) and divided*
- 1 cup soft breadcrumbs (4 slices, crusts removed)
- ¼ cup butter or margarine, melted

COOK macaroni according to package directions; drain well. Set aside.
PLACE milk, flour, and onion salt in a quart jar; cover tightly, and shake vigorously 1 minute.

STIR together flour mixture, 3½ cups cheese, and macaroni.
POUR macaroni mixture into a lightly greased 13- x 9-inch baking dish or 2 (11-inch) oval baking dishes. Sprinkle evenly with breadcrumbs and remaining 1 cup cheese; drizzle evenly with melted butter.
BAKE at 350° for 45 minutes or until golden brown. **MAKES** 8 servings.

NOTE: For testing purposes only, we used Kraft Cracker Barrel Sharp Cheddar Cheese.

*Substitute 20 ounces loaf pasteurized prepared cheese product, shredded or cut into small cubes, if desired. Omit breadcrumbs if using prepared cheese product.

❝ Cook's Notes ❞

There are no shortages of opinions among the *Southern Living* Foods staff when it comes to the perfect mac and cheese. Serious debates have gone on for years. "But when it came to Louise Floyd's Golden Macaroni and Cheese, the entire group easily agreed that it was truly one of the best ever to grace our taste testing table," says Associate Foods Editor **Kate Nicholson**.

TURNIP GREENS STEW

Prep: 5 min., Cook: 30 min.
(pictured on page 38)

- 2 cups chopped cooked ham
- 1 tablespoon vegetable oil
- 3 cups chicken broth
- 2 (16-ounce) packages frozen chopped turnip greens
- 1 (10-ounce) package frozen diced onion, red and green bell peppers, and celery
- 1 teaspoon sugar
- 1 teaspoon seasoned pepper

SAUTÉ ham in hot oil in a Dutch oven over medium-high heat 5 minutes or until lightly browned. Add broth and remaining ingredients; bring to a boil. Cover, reduce heat to low, and simmer, stirring occasionally, 25 minutes. **MAKES** 6 to 8 servings.

NOTE: For testing purposes only, we used McKenzie's Seasoning Blend for frozen diced onion, red and green bell peppers, and celery. You can substitute 1 chopped onion, 1 chopped red bell pepper, 1 chopped green bell pepper, and 1 chopped celery rib.

COLLARD 'N' BLACK-EYED PEA STEW: Substitute 1 (16-ounce) package frozen chopped collard greens for turnip greens. Prepare stew as directed, and cook for 15 minutes. Add 1 (16-ounce) can black-eyed peas, drained, and cook 10 more minutes.

BUTTERMILK DRESSING COLESLAW

family favorite • make ahead

Prep: 15 min., Chill: 2 hrs.

- ½ cup sugar
- ½ cup mayonnaise
- ¼ cup milk
- ¼ cup buttermilk
- 2½ tablespoons lemon juice
- 1½ tablespoons white vinegar
- ½ teaspoon salt
- ⅛ teaspoon pepper
- 2 (10-ounce) packages finely shredded (angel hair) cabbage
- 1 carrot, shredded

WHISK together first 8 ingredients in a large bowl until blended. Add cabbage and carrot to bowl, and toss to coat. Cover and chill at least 2 hours. **MAKES** 8 to 10 servings.

DYLAN PEACOCK
BIRMINGHAM, ALABAMA

HOT-WATER CORNBREAD

family favorite • fast fixin's

Prep: 5 min., Cook: 18 min.

Prepare this cornbread at the last minute so you can serve it piping hot. *(pictured on page 38)*

- 2 cups white cornmeal
- ¼ teaspoon baking powder
- 1¼ teaspoons salt
- 1 teaspoon sugar
- ¼ cup half-and-half
- 1 tablespoon vegetable oil
- ¾ cup to 1¼ cups boiling water
- Vegetable oil
- Softened butter

COMBINE first 4 ingredients in a bowl; stir in half-and-half and 1 tablespoon oil. Gradually add boiling water, stirring until batter is the consistency of grits.

POUR oil to a depth of ½ inch into a large heavy skillet; place over medium-high heat. Scoop batter into a ¼-cup measure; drop into hot oil, and fry in batches 3 minutes on each side or until golden. Drain well on paper towels. Serve immediately with softened butter. **MAKES** 8 patties.

NOTE: Stone ground (coarsely ground) cornmeal requires more liquid.

BACON-CHEDDAR HOT-WATER CORN-BREAD: Stir in 8 slices cooked and crumbled bacon, 1 cup shredded sharp Cheddar cheese, and 4 minced green onions after adding boiling water.

SOUTHWESTERN HOT-WATER CORN-BREAD: Stir in 1 seeded and minced jalapeño pepper; 1 cup Mexican cheese blend; 1 cup frozen whole kernel corn, thawed; and ¼ cup minced fresh cilantro after adding boiling water.

COUNTRY HAM HOT-WATER CORN-BREAD: Stir in 1 to 2 cups finely chopped country ham after adding boiling water.

BAKED HOT-WATER CORNBREAD: Omit skillet procedure. Pour ⅓ cup vegetable oil into a 15- x 10-inch jellyroll pan, spreading to edges. Drop batter as directed onto pan. Bake at 475° for 12 to 15 minutes. Turn cakes, and bake 5 more minutes or until golden brown.

What's for Supper?

Super Spuds

Once college bowl games wrap up and the Super Bowl rolls around, you might be ready to sideline chip-and-dip dinners for real food. Here's a winning game plan to follow. Prepare Cheddar, Broccoli, and Ham Stuffed Potatoes the day before friends gather to watch the game; then pop them in the oven during a time-out. Kick in a green salad, and you have a winning dinner.

CHICKEN FAJITA SPUDS WITH BLACK BEAN SALSA

Prep: 10 min., Chill: 2 hrs., Cook: 16 min.

- 2 pounds skinned and boned chicken breasts, cut into 2- x ½-inch strips
- 2 tablespoons olive oil
- 1¼ teaspoons fajita seasoning
- ½ teaspoon chipotle chile pepper seasoning
- 1 yellow onion, cut into strips
- 1 large green bell pepper, cut into strips
- 2 tablespoons fresh lime juice
- 8 to 10 baked potatoes
- Black Bean Salsa
- Toppings: shredded Monterey Jack cheese with peppers or Mexican four-cheese blend, sour cream, tomato, salsa, guacamole

TOSS together first 4 ingredients in a bowl; cover and chill 2 hours.

COOK chicken and marinade in a large skillet over medium-high heat 8 to 10 minutes or until chicken is no longer pink, stirring occasionally. Remove chicken, and keep warm.

RETURN skillet to heat, and add onion and pepper. Sauté 5 to 6 minutes or until tender. Return chicken to skillet, and stir in lime juice. Serve over baked potatoes with Black Bean Salsa and desired toppings. **MAKES** 8 to 10 servings.

Black Bean Salsa:

Prep: 10 min., Chill: 1 hr.

- 1 (15-ounce) can black beans, rinsed and drained
- 1 cup frozen white kernel corn, thawed
- 1 small red onion, chopped (½ cup)
- 1 tablespoon chopped fresh cilantro
- ¼ cup fresh lime juice
- 1 jalapeño pepper, seeded and diced
- 1 garlic clove, minced
- 1 teaspoon fajita seasoning

COMBINE all ingredients. Cover and chill at least 1 hour. **MAKES** 2¾ cups.

NOTE: For testing purposes only, we used McCormick Southwest Flavor Fajita Seasoning and McCormick Gourmet Collection Chipotle Chile Pepper.

Bake the Perfect Potato

Scrub 4 baking potatoes with a vegetable brush; pat dry.

Pierce each potato 3 or 4 times with a fork, and rub with butter or olive oil for a crisper skin.

Roll in salt or sea salt, if desired. (Do not wrap in foil. This holds in moisture, causing a texture similar to a boiled potato. If you like soft skin, wrap potatoes in foil after baking, and let stand 10 minutes.)

Bake potatoes directly on the oven rack at 450° for 1 hour and 10 minutes. If baking more than 4 potatoes, add 5 minutes to the bake time for every additional potato.

Cheddar, Broccoli, and Ham Stuffed Potatoes

family favorite • make ahead

Prep: 25 min., Cook: 5 min., Bake: 50 min.

If you prepare these potatoes the day before, cover them and refrigerate. Let stand 30 minutes at room temperature before baking as directed. We found the few minutes it takes to chop thawed broccoli florets worth it—the appearance was much better than using frozen chopped broccoli.

- 4 large baked potatoes, cooled slightly
- 2 tablespoons butter or margarine, softened and divided
- 1 small red bell pepper, chopped (½ cup)
- 3 green onions, sliced
- 1 cup chopped cooked ham
- ¾ cup sour cream
- ¾ teaspoon salt
- ½ teaspoon pepper
- 1 (10-ounce) package frozen broccoli florets, thawed and coarsely chopped
- 1 cup (4 ounces) shredded sharp Cheddar cheese

CUT a 2- to 3-inch-wide strip from top of each baked potato. Carefully scoop out pulp, leaving shells intact. Place pulp in a large mixing bowl; set pulp and shells aside.

MELT 1 tablespoon butter in a small skillet over medium-high heat; add red bell pepper and green onions, and sauté 3 to 4 minutes or until vegetables are tender.

STIR together potato pulp, remaining 1 tablespoon butter, green onion mixture, ham, and next 3 ingredients, blending well. Gently fold in broccoli. Spoon mixture into potato shells, and place on a baking sheet.

BAKE at 350° for 40 minutes. Sprinkle with cheese, and bake 10 more minutes. Serve immediately. **MAKES** 4 servings.

Simply Satisfying Soups

Enjoy slow-simmered flavors without the long wait.

Soup is the original one-dish meal. There is little better than a potful of body-warming broth with chunky cuts of meat and vegetables. All the recipes featured here start with basic frozen and pantry items and finish with a few additional fresh ingredients. Stock up on supplies on your next trip to the grocery store, and you'll have everything you need to take the chill off this winter.

Tortilla Soup

family favorite

Prep: 15 min., Cook: 20 min.

Don't let this long list of ingredients stop you—most of these items are in your pantry or fridge.

- 2 (14½-ounce) cans chicken broth
- 1 (14½-ounce) can Cajun-style stewed tomatoes
- 3 tablespoons fresh lemon juice
- 3 garlic cloves, pressed
- 2 teaspoons chili powder
- ½ teaspoon ground cumin
- ¼ teaspoon ground red pepper
- 1½ cups chopped cooked chicken
- 1 cup frozen corn kernels
- 1 (15-ounce) can black beans, rinsed and drained
- 2 tablespoons half-and-half
- 1 green onion, thinly sliced
- Tortilla chips
- 1 cup (4 ounces) shredded Mexican four-cheese blend (optional)
- Sliced green onions (optional)

BRING first 7 ingredients to a boil. Reduce heat; add chicken and next 4 ingredients, and simmer 20 minutes. Serve with tortilla chips and, if desired, cheese and green onions. **MAKES** 6 cups.

LEANNE POINDEXTER
POTOMAC FALLS, VIRGINIA

Chicken-and-Wild Rice Soup

family favorite

Prep: 20 min., Cook: 15 min.

If you don't have cooked chicken, bone and chop a deli-roasted chicken. One deli-roasted chicken will yield about 3 cups chopped cooked chicken—freeze 1 cup for another use.

- 1 small onion, chopped
- 1 cup shredded carrots
- 5 cups water
- 1 (6.2-ounce) package fast-cooking long-grain and wild rice mix
- 1 (10-ounce) package frozen chopped broccoli
- 2 cups chopped cooked chicken
- 1 (8-ounce) loaf pasteurized prepared cheese product, cubed
- 1 (10¾-ounce) can cream of chicken soup, undiluted

SAUTÉ onion and carrots in a lightly greased Dutch oven over medium heat 5 minutes. Add 5 cups water, seasoning packet from rice, broccoli, and chicken. **BRING** to a boil, and stir in rice; reduce heat, cover, and cook 5 minutes. Add cheese and soup; cook, stirring constantly,

5 minutes or until cheese melts. Serve immediately. **MAKES** about 10 cups.

NOTE: For testing purposes only, we used Uncle Ben's Long Grain & Wild Rice Fast Cook Recipe.

CAROL MICHAEL
HEWITT, TEXAS

QUICK SHRIMP CHOWDER

family favorite

Prep: 15 min., Cook: 20 min.

We've streamlined this favorite dish by using canned soup as the base.

- **2 tablespoons butter or margarine**
- **1 medium onion, chopped**
- **2 (10¾-ounce) cans cream of potato soup, undiluted**
- **3½ cups milk**
- **¼ teaspoon ground red pepper**
- **1½ pounds medium-size fresh shrimp, peeled***
- **1 cup (4 ounces) shredded Monterey Jack cheese**
- **Garnish: chopped fresh parsley**
- **Oyster crackers (optional)**

MELT butter in a Dutch oven over medium heat; add onion, and sauté 8 minutes or until tender.

STIR in soup, milk, and pepper; bring to a boil.

ADD shrimp; reduce heat, and simmer, stirring often, 5 minutes or just until shrimp turn pink.

STIR in cheese until melted. Garnish, if desired. Serve immediately. Serve with oyster crackers, if desired. **MAKES** 12 cups.

*Substitute 1½ pounds frozen shrimp, thawed; 1½ pounds peeled crawfish tails; or 3 cups chopped cooked chicken, if desired.

CYNTHIA J. STRICKLAND
BETHEL, NORTH CAROLINA

Taste of the South

Muffulettas

Take a bite of a well-prepared muffuletta, and you'll know why these large, round sandwiches remain enduring standards of the New Orleans food scene. Filled with layers of salami, ham, cheese, and olive salad, muffulettas are cold-cut competitors of the po'boy. The flavors are bold, and the servings are generous.

Who created the first muffuletta is a matter of dispute, but food critic and historian Gene Bourg uncovered a likely scenario. He interviewed elderly Sicilians who lived in the French Quarter for many years. "They told me vendors used to sell them on the streets, as did Italian groceries," he says. "The name refers to the shape of the bread. 'Muffuletta' means 'little muffin.' Italian bakers made muffuletta loaves and sold them to Italian delis. The delis then wrapped the sandwiches in the same paper the bread came in, so the sandwich took on the name."

You'll find many places to enjoy a muffuletta in New Orleans, but two favorites reside on Decatur Street. Lines begin to form outside Central Grocery by midmorning. Luigi's Fine Food, two doors down, offers an excellent sandwich without the wait. Or try the warm muffuletta at Napoleon House Bar & Cafe on the corner of Chartes and St. Louis streets.

If the Big Easy isn't in your travel plans, don't despair. Read on for our favorite muffuletta. You can also order a tasty version of olive salad from **www.cajuncreations.com.**

MUFFULETTA

fast fixin's

Prep: 10 min.

- **1 (10-inch) round Italian bread loaf**
- **2 cups Olive Salad**
- **½ pound sliced hard salami**
- **½ pound sliced cooked ham**
- **6 Swiss cheese slices**
- **6 thin provolone cheese slices**

CUT bread loaf in half horizontally; scoop out soft bread from both halves, leaving a 1-inch-thick shell. Reserve soft bread centers for another use, if desired.

SPOON 1 cup Olive Salad evenly into bottom bread shell; top with salami, ham, cheeses, and remaining 1 cup Olive Salad. Cover with bread top, and cut crosswise into wedges or quarters. **MAKES** 4 servings.

Olive Salad:

Prep: 15 min., Chill: 8 hrs.

- **1 (1-quart) jar mixed pickled vegetables**
- **1 red onion, quartered**
- **1 (16-ounce) jar pitted green olives, drained**
- **1 (6-ounce) can medium pitted ripe olives, drained**
- **¼ cup sliced pepperoncini salad peppers**
- **2 tablespoons capers**
- **1 tablespoon minced garlic**
- **½ cup olive oil**
- **1½ teaspoons dried parsley flakes**
- **1 teaspoon dried oregano**
- **1 teaspoon dried basil**
- **½ teaspoon ground black pepper**
- **1 (7.25-ounce) jar roasted red bell peppers, drained and coarsely chopped (optional)**

DRAIN pickled vegetables, reserving ¼ cup liquid.

PULSE pickled vegetables 4 times in a food processor or until coarsely chopped; pour into a large bowl. Pulse onion 4 times in food processor or until coarsely chopped; add to pickled vegetables in bowl. Pulse olives and salad peppers in food processor 4 times or until coarsely chopped; add to vegetable mixture. Stir in capers, next 6 ingredients, reserved ¼ cup pickled vegetable liquid, and, if desired, chopped red bell peppers. Cover and chill 8 hours. Chill leftover mixture up to 2 weeks. **MAKES** 6 cups.

NOTE: We used mixed pickled vegetables that contained cauliflower, onions, carrots, peppers, and celery.

Easy-as-Pie Cobblers

Savor home-style desserts all year long with these time-saving recipes.

Sweet, bubbling cobbler—right out of the oven—makes Assistant Foods Editor Shannon Sliter Satterwhite happy. Though usually a summer indulgence, there's nothing quite as cozy on a chilly day. Your grandma's version was likely an all-day event that involved preparing fresh produce and rolling homemade dough. These cobblers are just as gratifying, but they won't leave you confined to the kitchen or limited by a lack of fresh summer fruit. Instead, we offer the convenience of frozen berries, canned fillings, refrigerated crusts, and baking mixes so you can enjoy these simple recipes year-round. You can even choose your favorite filling and topping to create your own variation. Serve them warm with a generous dollop of ice cream or sweetened whipped cream—whatever makes you happy.

CRAN-BLUEBERRY COBBLER

family favorite

Prep: 15 min., Cook: 5 min., Bake: 25 min.

A drop dough made from baking mix bakes into golden "cobbles" atop this double-berry delight.

- 2 tablespoons cornstarch
- ¾ cup sugar
- 3 cups frozen blueberries, unthawed
- 1 cup frozen cranberries, unthawed
- 1 teaspoon lemon juice
- 1 teaspoon vanilla extract
- 1½ cups all-purpose baking mix
- 2 tablespoons sugar
- ¼ cup butter or margarine, softened
- 1 large egg, lightly beaten
- ¼ cup milk
- Vanilla ice cream or sweetened whipped cream (optional)

STIR together cornstarch and ¾ cup sugar in a large saucepan. Add frozen berries, lemon juice, and vanilla, and bring to a boil, stirring constantly; boil 1 minute. Pour into a lightly greased 2-quart baking dish.

COMBINE baking mix and 2 tablespoons sugar. Cut in softened butter with a fork or pastry blender until mixture is crumbly; stir in egg and milk. Drop by 2 tablespoonfuls onto hot berry mixture.

BAKE at 400° for 20 to 25 minutes or until cobbler is golden and bubbly. Serve warm with vanilla ice cream or sweetened whipped cream, if desired. **MAKES** 6 to 8 servings.

LESLIE MEADOWS
MONTGOMERY, ALABAMA

TOO-EASY CHERRY COBBLER

family favorite

Prep: 15 min., Bake: 45 min.

Too-Easy Cherry Cobbler is topped with white bread slices and drizzled with a sweet butter mixture for a melt-in-your-mouth crust. Save time by using store-bought crustless white bread for the topping. *(pictured on page 40)*

- 2 (21-ounce) cans cherry pie filling
- 1 (15-ounce) can pitted dark sweet cherries in heavy syrup, drained
- ¼ cup all-purpose flour, divided
- ½ teaspoon almond extract
- 5 white bread slices
- 1¼ cups sugar
- ½ cup butter or margarine, melted
- 1 large egg
- 1½ teaspoons grated lemon rind

STIR together pie filling, cherries, and 2 tablespoons flour. Stir in almond extract. Place in a lightly greased 8-inch square baking dish.

TRIM crusts from bread slices; cut each slice into 5 strips. Arrange bread strips over fruit mixture.

STIR together remaining 2 tablespoons flour, sugar, and next 3 ingredients; drizzle over bread strips.

BAKE at 350° for 35 to 45 minutes or until golden and bubbly. **MAKES** 4 to 6 servings.

TOO-EASY PEACH COBBLER: Substitute 2 (16-ounce) packages frozen peaches, thawed and drained, for cherry pie filling and canned cherries. Omit almond extract and grated lemon rind. Proceed as directed.

TOO-EASY BERRY COBBLER: Substitute 1 (21-ounce) can blueberry pie filling and 2 (10-ounce) packages frozen whole strawberries, unthawed, for cherry pie filling and canned cherries. Omit almond extract; add 1 teaspoon vanilla extract and 1 teaspoon lemon juice. Proceed as directed.

VERA PIRTLE
DECATUR, ALABAMA

Prep: 15 min., Bake: 1 hr.

Refrigerated piecrust lets you create a double crust lattice-topped cobbler in no time.

- 1 (12-ounce) package frozen blackberries, unthawed
- 1 (12-ounce) package frozen raspberries, unthawed
- 1 (12-ounce) package frozen blueberries, unthawed
- 1½ cups sugar
- ½ cup all-purpose flour
- ¼ cup butter or margarine, melted
- 1 teaspoon vanilla extract
- 1 (15-ounce) package refrigerated piecrusts
- 1 large egg, lightly beaten
- 1 tablespoon sugar

STIR together first 7 ingredients in a large bowl, stirring just until combined. Spoon into a lightly greased 13- x 9-inch baking dish.

ROLL 1 piecrust to fit baking dish; place on berry mixture. Cut remaining piecrust into ½-inch strips. Arrange strips in a lattice design over piecrust. Brush with egg, and lightly sprinkle with 1 tablespoon sugar.

BAKE at 400° for 55 to 60 minutes or until golden and bubbly. **MAKES** 6 to 8 servings.

MELODY LEE
DOTHAN, ALABAMA

Cook's Notes

- Wally Sliter, Associate Foods Editor **Shannon Sliter Satterwhite**'s grandmother who lives in Colorado, is a self-taught gardener and cook. She used to grow her own fruits and berries for all kinds of homemade pies and cobblers. She was always in the kitchen cooking up something yummy, and she was Shannon's inspiration for writing this story.
- Shannon prefers fresh-from-the-oven taste from her cobblers so she always reheats her leftover cobbler. She also requires a generous dollop of ice cream to melt over her warm cobbler.
- Shannon says that the **Too-Easy Cherry Cobbler** and the variations that follow have a crust that literally melts in your mouth. It's just white bread slices drizzled with butter and sprinkled with sugar. So divine!
- You could also use fresh berries instead of frozen in **Cran-Blueberry Cobbler**. Since the fruits aren't fresh at the same time of year, buy them during season and just freeze the container in a zip-top freezer bag.

APPLE DUMPLING COBBLER

family favorite

Prep: 20 min., Cook: 5 min., Bake: 25 min.

Crescent roll dough makes a quick wrap for apple dumplings drizzled with a cinnamon-orange syrup and baked into a cobbler.

- 1 (8-ounce) can refrigerated crescent rolls
- 2 large Granny Smith apples, peeled and quartered
- 1 cup orange juice
- ⅔ cup sugar
- ½ cup butter or margarine
- 2 teaspoons sugar
- 1 teaspoon ground cinnamon

UNROLL crescent rolls, and separate. Wrap each apple quarter with crescent roll dough, and place in a lightly greased 13- x 9-inch baking dish.

BRING orange juice, ⅔ cup sugar, and butter to a boil in a saucepan. Pour over apple dumplings. Stir together 2 teaspoons sugar and cinnamon; sprinkle over dumplings.

BAKE at 350° for 25 minutes or until golden and bubbly. **MAKES** 8 servings.

VIVIAN ABBOTT
MOLINO, FLORIDA

CINNAMON-APPLE BAKE

family favorite

Prep: 10 min., Bake: 55 min.

Cobbler crusts don't come much easier than sprinkling dry cake mix on the top of the fruit and drizzling the whole thing with melted butter. It bakes with a golden and pebbly crust.

- 2 (20-ounce) cans sliced apples, undrained
- 1 to 2 teaspoons ground cinnamon
- 1 cup firmly packed light brown sugar
- 1 (9-ounce) package yellow cake mix
- ½ cup butter, melted

SPREAD apples in a lightly greased 13- x 9-inch baking dish. Sprinkle with cinnamon and brown sugar. Top with dry cake mix, and drizzle with melted butter.

BAKE at 350° for 50 to 55 minutes or until golden and bubbly. **MAKES** 8 to 10 servings.

NOTE: For testing purposes only, we used Jiffy Golden Yellow Cake Mix.

CHERRY-APPLE BAKE: Add ¾ cup dried cherries to baking dish with sliced apples, and proceed with recipe as directed.

AMY PATILLO
HOOVER, ALABAMA

from our kitchen

Mâche: The Best of the Bunch

Once exclusive to European markets and upscale restaurants, this heirloom variety of lamb's lettuce, marketed under its French name of *mâche,* is now being grown commercially in California's Salinas Valley. High in vitamins and antioxidants, the delicate rosettes of tender round leaves have a slightly sweet, nutty flavor and buttery texture unlike any other salad green. Lightly dressed with Fresh Lemon Vinaigrette (see recipe below, right) and paper-thin slivers of Parmesan cheese, it received our Test Kitchens' highest rating.

Available prewashed in 4-ounce packages, mâche is somewhat pricier than other ready-to-eat specialty salads, but well worth the indulgence. One 3-ounce serving has no fat and only 20 calories, but it tips the nutritional scales with 2 grams of protein and fiber, 100% of the daily requirement of vitamin A, 50% of vitamin C, 20% of iron, and 8% of calcium. It even has more potassium than bananas. If your local grocer doesn't already carry mâche, ask the manager to order it for you. For additional recipes and information, visit **www.epicroots.com.**

Home Brew

Whip up a frothy topping for cappuccinos and lattes with a battery-powered Bon-Jour Caffé Froth Turbo ($14.99). BonJour offers quite a variety of French coffee presses, cooktop espresso makers, and some other creative culinary products. To locate a retailer in your area, visit **www.bonjourproducts.com.**

Five-a-Day Fruits and Vegetables

Fresh salsas and main-dish salads are a terrific way to add more fruits and vegetables to your diet, even during the winter months. We usually think of heartier fare, such as collards simmered with the restorative powers of pork-rich pot liquor in January. Not that we're willing to forego such cold-weather comforts, but there is a bigger bounty of produce out there.

Winter is peak season for citrus fruits, and fresh oranges and grapefruit play a starring role in many of our top-rated salads. Try replacing canned Mandarin oranges with fresh varieties such as tangerines or clementines. Chilean stone fruits such as peaches, plums, and nectarines will be arriving soon, and although they lack the memorable flavor of our Southern peaches and nectarines, they're quite good in salsa.

Tips and Tidbits

- Fresh cranberries won't be around for long after the first of the year, but when sealed in airtight containers, they will keep for up to 12 months in the freezer. For optimum flavor and texture, add them to recipes while still frozen. Like raspberries, the red plant pigments in cranberries can turn blue when mixed with alkaline ingredients such as baking soda. So when using them in muffins or quick breads, be sure to toss them with a sprinkling of fresh lemon juice to prevent discoloration.

- OSO onions, grown in the rich volcanic soil of South America, have a crunchy sweetness that rivals Vidalias. OSO onions are available in supermarkets from January through March. Look for firm, plump onions with shiny skin and a delicate aroma. A high sugar content makes them perfect for caramelizing. **To make Caramelized Onions:** Heat 1 tablespoon olive oil in a large skillet over medium heat. Add 6 large sweet onions, coarsely chopped, and 1 tablespoon sugar. Cook, stirring often, 25 to 30 minutes or until onions are a deep golden brown. Cool and store in an airtight container; chill up to 1 week, or, if desired, freeze up to 2 months. Makes about 3 cups.

Fresh Lemon Vinaigrette

Whisk together ¼ cup fresh lemon juice; 1 teaspoon Dijon mustard; 1 large garlic clove, pressed; ¼ teaspoon salt; and ¼ teaspoon freshly ground black pepper. Gradually add ½ cup olive oil in a steady stream, whisking until blended. Store in refrigerator for up to 1 week; bring to room temperature, and whisk before serving. Makes about ¾ cup.

February

Make It Casual

Weekend company coming?
Our timeline and do-ahead recipes
inspire fuss-free entertaining.

Welcoming guests into your home for several days can be supereasy when you have a game plan. You want to be able to enjoy spending time with your guests instead of spending hours in the kitchen. Accomplish as much as you can ahead, and then follow our step-by-step make-ahead suggestions for sure success. Try this great menu for a weekend that your guests will rave about! The Make-Ahead Preparation Timeline on the facing page helps you get as much ready in advance as possible.

In addition to cooking, there are other things to consider. There's more cleaning involved for an overnight guest than a drop-by guest. Also, you want to be sure to have ample supplies so that your company will feel at home. Then there are those small touches such as decorating and entertaining. See our Make It Look Effortless tips on the facing page. And, most of all, enjoy yourself, and your guests are sure to follow suit.

EASY BURRITOS

Prep: 30 min.; Cook: 5 hrs., 30 min.

Wrap up Easy Burritos, which start with a slow cooker, for a tasty, manageable Friday night supper. If your company runs late, the meat for the burritos will hold for quite a while. Keep warm on low in the slow cooker, if necessary.

- **1 large onion, sliced into rings**
- **1 (3- to 4-pound) sirloin beef roast**
- **½ cup water**
- **2 (1.25-ounce) envelopes taco seasoning mix, divided**
- **16 (6-inch) flour tortillas**
- **Toppings: diced tomatoes, diced onions, sliced jalapeño peppers, sour cream, black beans**
- **4 cups (16 ounces) shredded Cheddar or Monterey Jack cheese**
- **Pico de Gallo**

PLACE onion in a 5-quart slow cooker; add roast and ½ cup water. Sprinkle 1 package taco seasoning mix over top of roast.

COVER and cook on HIGH 5 hours. Remove roast, and shred with 2 forks; return to slow cooker, and stir in remaining package of taco seasoning mix. Cover and cook on HIGH 30 more minutes or until boiling.

HEAT tortillas according to package directions. Using a slotted spoon, spoon beef mixture evenly down center of each tortilla; top with desired toppings and cheese, and roll up. Serve with Pico de Gallo. **MAKES** 8 to 10 servings.

TATIA WILLIAMS
SUMMERVILLE, SOUTH CAROLINA

Pico de Gallo:

Prep: 10 min.

- **3 cups diced plum tomatoes**
- **½ cup diced red onion**
- **6 tablespoons chopped fresh cilantro**
- **4 to 6 tablespoons diced jalapeño peppers**
- **⅓ cup fresh lime juice**
- **½ teaspoon olive oil**
- **¼ teaspoon salt**
- **¼ teaspoon pepper**

STIR together all ingredients in a medium bowl. Cover and chill until ready to serve. **MAKES** about 3 cups.

Weekend Menus for Feasting With Friends
Serves 8

Friday Supper
- Easy Burritos with toppings
- Pico de Gallo
- purchase brownies with ice cream

Saturday Breakfast
- Pound Cake French Toast
- Maple-Mint Cream
- Raspberry Sauce
- juice and fresh fruit (Buy extra.)

Saturday Lunch
- Go out to lunch.

Saturday Supper
- Chicken Marbella (Look for sales to stock up on chicken

pieces in the weeks before guests arrive. Freeze and thaw in refrigerator when needed.)
- wild rice (Use your favorite mix. For extra flavor, substitute chicken broth for water; cook according to package directions.)
- tossed salad (Use bag salad, precut veggies or fruits, and prepared dressing.)
- crusty French bread
- purchased dessert

Sunday Lunch
- purchased baked ham
- Colorful Vegetable Salad
- purchased rolls

POUND CAKE FRENCH TOAST

family favorite • fast fixin's

Prep: 5 min., Cook: 5 min. per batch

Purchase pound cake from a bakery or a frozen loaf pound cake to save time. Or bake your favorite, and freeze it the weekend before. Thaw frozen cake in refrigerator overnight.

3 large eggs
1½ cups milk
16 (½-inch) pound cake slices
Maple-Mint Cream (optional)
Raspberry Sauce (optional)
Garnish: fresh mint sprigs

STIR together eggs and milk in a shallow dish.
DIP pound cake slices in egg mixture, evenly coating both sides. Cook pound cake slices, in batches, in a lightly greased large nonstick skillet over medium heat 2½ minutes on each side or until golden brown.
SERVE with Maple-Mint Cream and Raspberry Sauce, if desired. Garnish, if desired. **MAKES** 8 servings.

Maple-Mint Cream:

Prep: 5 min.

1 cup whipping cream
1½ teaspoons plain yogurt
1½ teaspoons maple syrup
¼ teaspoon mint extract

BEAT cream at high speed with an electric mixer until soft peaks form. Add yogurt, syrup, and mint extract, beating until blended. **MAKES** 2 cups.

LIZ GIPSON
LOVELAND, COLORADO

Raspberry Sauce:

Prep: 5 min.

3 (12-ounce) bags frozen
raspberries, thawed
3 tablespoons sugar

PROCESS raspberries and sugar in a blender or food processor until smooth, stopping to scrape down sides. Pour mixture through a wire-mesh strainer into a bowl, discarding seeds. **MAKES** 2 cups.

Make It Look Effortless

Write down everything that needs to be completed, from cleaning to buying groceries. It feels great to cross off items on your to-do list.

Cleaning the House
This is a chore that can take up a large portion of time. Do heavy cleaning the week before or consider a cleaning service.
■ Wash linens and towels.
■ Make room in the hall closet for extra coats.
■ Clean out the refrigerator.
■ Clean the oven.

Supplies
■ Choose dishes, glasses, and flatware to be used. Decide if you will use any paper products, plastic flatware, and disposable cups; if so, add them to the shopping list.
■ Restock a variety of plastic bags, aluminum foil, paper towels, bathroom tissue, cleaning products, and garbage bags.
■ Borrow a baby bed or portable crib, if necessary.
■ Make a grocery list from recipes you plan to use. List similar ingredients together to save time. For example, group all frozen items under one heading; list all condiments together, etc.

In-house Planning
■ If you don't have the luxury of a guest room, figure out where everyone will sleep and inform family members before the weekend.
■ Determine how involved family members and your guests will be with cleaning and chores during the weekend. Be sure to make job assignments ahead.

Decorate on a Budget
■ Buy inexpensive blooming plants in small pots to easily tuck into decorative containers and scatter them around the house. Primroses and ivy work well this time of year. Group several pots in a basket or a large bowl to create a centerpiece.

Activities for All Ages
■ Decide on how you'll keep busy during the visit. Have both rain and fair-weather plans. Determine if the group will do everything together. Plan schedules that are compatible with the group's stamina and ages. Talk this over with your family to avoid possible conflicts.

Make-Ahead Preparation Timeline

Friday morning
■ Slow-cook roast for burritos.
■ Prepare Pico de Gallo, Maple-Mint Cream, and Raspberry Sauce; cover and chill.

Friday late afternoon
■ Prepare toppings for burritos.
■ Thaw cake in refrigerator for Pound Cake French Toast.
■ Combine ingredients for Chicken Marbella; cover and chill overnight. You can also assemble this as you clean up the kitchen after supper.

Saturday afternoon
■ Prepare Colorful Vegetable Salad; cover and chill.
■ Purchase ham and bakery rolls. (If you have enough refrigerator space, buy ham ahead or pick it up Friday afternoon.)

CHICKEN MARBELLA

family favorite • make ahead
Prep: 10 min., Chill: 8 hrs., Bake: 1 hr.

Chicken Marbella, a marinated chicken baked with olives, capers, oregano, and dried plums, is the perfect choice for a hearty yet stylish meal. This recipe has a long ingredient list, but it's always a hit, even with kids. Choose a mixture of everyone's favorite cuts of chicken—such as one package each of bone-in breasts, legs, thighs, and wings—or purchase pick-of-the-chick packages or chicken quarters to equal 8 pounds.

  1 (12-ounce) package pitted,
    bite-size dried plums
  1 (3.5-ounce) jar capers, drained
  1 (0.5-ounce) bottle dried oregano
  6 bay leaves
  1 garlic bulb, minced (about
    1 tablespoon)
  1 cup pimiento-stuffed olives
  ½ cup red wine vinegar
  ½ cup olive oil
  1 tablespoon coarse sea salt
  2 teaspoons pepper
  8 pounds mixed chicken pieces
  1 cup firmly packed brown sugar
  1 cup dry white wine
  ¼ cup fresh parsley, chopped

COMBINE first 10 ingredients in a large zip-top freezer bag or a large bowl. Add chicken pieces, turning to coat well; seal or cover and chill for at least 8 hours (overnight is best), turning chicken occasionally.

ARRANGE chicken in a single layer in 1 or 2 (13- x 9-inch) baking pan(s). Pour marinade evenly over chicken, and sprinkle evenly with brown sugar; pour wine around pieces.

BAKE at 350° for 50 minutes to 1 hour, basting often.

REMOVE chicken, dried plums, capers, and olives to a serving platter. Drizzle with ¾ cup pan juices; sprinkle parsley evenly over top. Discard bay leaves. Serve with remaining pan juices. **MAKES** 8 to 10 servings.

JAN KIMBELL
VESTAVIA HILLS, ALABAMA

COLORFUL VEGETABLE SALAD

family favorite • make ahead
Prep: 15 min., Cook: 5 min., Stand: 30 min., Chill: 8 hrs.

This dump-and-stir recipe is a make-ahead timesaver. It's great for a potluck gathering.

  ¼ cup sugar
  ½ cup cider vinegar
  ½ cup vegetable oil
  1 teaspoon salt
  1 teaspoon paprika
  2 (14.5-ounce) cans French-style
    green beans, drained
  2 (15.5-ounce) cans black-eyed
    peas, drained
  2 (15.4-ounce) cans small green
    peas, drained
  2 (4-ounce) jars diced pimientos,
    drained
  1 bunch green onions, sliced (about
    1 cup)
  1 (16-ounce) package frozen
    shoepeg corn, thawed
  1 green bell pepper, diced
  1 cup diced celery

BRING first 5 ingredients to a boil in a small saucepan over medium heat, stirring often, 5 minutes or until sugar dissolves. Remove from heat, and let stand 30 minutes to cool.

STIR together green beans and next 7 ingredients in a large bowl; gently stir in dressing. Cover and chill 8 hours. Serve with a slotted spoon. **MAKES** 8 to 10 servings.

MARY BRUCE ALLEN
BERTRAM, TEXAS

Simple Sides

Complement an entrée with one of these flavorful side-dish recipes. While we often neglect sides, they can add color, texture, taste, and nutrition that only make the meal better. So try these creative sides to prevent mealtime monotony. We promise that these tasty side dishes will warm up a wintertime meal.

PEPPERY PEAS O' PLENTY

Prep: 15 min., Cook: 40 min.

  4 hickory-smoked bacon slices
  1 large onion, chopped
  1 cup frozen black-eyed peas
  1 cup frozen purple hull peas
  1 cup frozen crowder peas
  1 cup frozen butter peas
  1 cup frozen field peas with snaps
  1 (32-ounce) container chicken broth
  1 tablespoon Asian garlic-chili sauce
  ¾ to 1 teaspoon salt
  1 tablespoon freshly ground pepper

COOK bacon in a Dutch oven until crisp; remove bacon, and drain on paper towels, reserving drippings in pan. Crumble bacon.

SAUTÉ onion in hot drippings in Dutch oven over medium-high heat 8 minutes or until translucent. Add black-eyed peas and next 8 ingredients, and cook 20 to 25 minutes, uncovered. Top with crumbled bacon. **MAKES** 4 to 6 servings.

NOTE: For testing purposes only, we used Bryan Sweet Hickory Smoked Bacon and A Taste of Thai Garlic Chili Pepper Sauce.

WILLIAM DICKEY
BIRMINGHAM, ALABAMA

SUPPERTIME TURNIP GREENS

Prep: 20 min., Cook: 45 min.

  2 (1-pound) packages fresh turnip
    greens
  4 cups water
  1 bacon slice
  1 teaspoon seasoned salt
  ½ teaspoon sugar
  ½ teaspoon garlic powder
  ½ teaspoon ground red pepper

REMOVE and discard stems from greens. Coarsely chop leaves.

BRING 4 cups water and bacon slice to a boil in a large Dutch oven. Add greens, seasoned salt, and remaining ingredients. Cook over medium heat 35 to 45 minutes or until tender. **MAKES** 4 servings.

OLIVIA WILLIAMS
FORT WORTH, TEXAS

Easy Home Baking

Fresh bread is a breeze when you use these recipes to dress up frozen and refrigerated dough.

Most folks are too busy for from-scratch baking, especially on weeknights. The next best thing is enjoying just-baked flavor without dusting up the kitchen. We used frozen bread dough, refrigerated canned biscuits, and refrigerated pizza dough to serve as blueprints for fast, simple, seasoned breads. So turn on the oven, but leave the kneading for leisurely weekends.

POPPY-ONION LOAF

family favorite

Prep: 10 min., Bake: 30 min., Cool: 10 min.

Perfectly browned and buttery Poppy-Onion Loaf starts with canned buttermilk biscuits.

- ¼ cup butter, melted
- 2 tablespoons dried minced onion
- 1 tablespoon poppy seeds
- 2 (12-ounce) cans refrigerated buttermilk biscuits

STIR together melted butter, onion, and poppy seeds.

SEPARATE biscuits, and dip each biscuit in butter mixture, turning to coat. Arrange biscuits, standing on edge, in a 9- x 5-inch loafpan, arranging in 2 rows. Brush with remaining butter mixture.

BAKE at 350° for 25 to 30 minutes or until golden. Cool in pan 10 minutes. **MAKES** 1 loaf.

JANE PARISH
MATTHEWS, NORTH CAROLINA

ITALIAN HERB BREADSTICKS

family favorite

Prep: 25 min., Rise: 20 min., Bake: 15 min., Cool: 10 min.

Serve with soups, salads, or spaghetti.

- 4 tablespoons grated Parmesan cheese
- 2½ teaspoons dried Italian seasoning
- 1 teaspoon garlic powder
- 1 pound frozen bread dough, thawed
- 2 tablespoons melted butter or margarine
- 1 tablespoon kosher salt*

COMBINE first 3 ingredients.

CUT dough into 24 pieces. Roll each piece into a 12-inch rope. Sprinkle evenly with Parmesan mixture.

PLACE ropes, 1 inch apart, on lightly greased baking sheets. Cover with plastic wrap, and let rise at room temperature for 20 minutes.

BAKE at 350° for 15 minutes or until golden. Brush breadsticks with melted butter, and sprinkle with kosher salt. Cool on wire racks 10 minutes. **MAKES** 24 servings.

*Kosher salt has a coarser texture than regular iodized salt. Kosher salt can be found near other salts in the supermarket. Substitute 1½ teaspoons iodized salt, if desired.

CHARLOTTE BRYANT
GREENSBURG, KENTUCKY

PIZZA BREAD ROLLUPS

family favorite

Prep: 10 min., Bake: 35 min.

Cooking the pepperoni between layers of paper towels helps avoid a greasy mess.

- 1 (3.5-ounce) package sliced turkey pepperoni
- 1 (10-ounce) package refrigerated pizza dough
- 1 large egg, lightly beaten and divided
- 1 cup (4 ounces) shredded sharp Cheddar cheese
- 1 teaspoon dried Italian seasoning
- Pasta sauce (optional)

COOK pepperoni slices between layers of paper towels in microwave at HIGH for 1 minute.

UNROLL dough onto a 15- x 10-inch jellyroll pan to ¼-inch thickness. Brush lightly with egg. Sprinkle with cheese and pepperoni. Roll up, jellyroll fashion.

PLACE dough on a lightly greased baking sheet. Curl dough into a circle, pinching edges together to seal. Brush with egg, and sprinkle with Italian seasoning.

BAKE at 375° for 30 to 35 minutes or until golden. Cut into 2-inch-thick slices. Serve with warm pasta sauce, if desired. **MAKES** 4 to 6 servings.

MARGARET L. HARPER
OTTAWA, ONTARIO, CANADA

" Cook's Notes "

■ According to Associate Foods Editor **Joy Zacharia, Poppy-Onion Loaf** makes a nice knife-free bread since the biscuits are placed side by side in the loafpan. Joy adds a little ground red pepper to the butter mixture for a kicked up boost.

■ **"Pizza Bread Rollups** are great for folks who love homemade bread but are scared to death of yeast," says Joy. We tried regular pepperoni but found it too greasy.

■ Use grated Parmesan cheese from a can rather than shredded from the cheese section for **Italian Herb Breadsticks.**

The Kitchen: Heart of the Home

The kitchen is where your day begins and ends, so make the most of it.

We've teamed up to bring you great ideas for decorating, entertaining, and just everyday living in the kitchen. A few homeowners share their tried-and-true recipes, and some great organizing tips. See how well an efficient kitchen and delicious recipes go hand-in-hand.

Room for All Ages

An Austin, Texas, couple adds a space for cooking, entertaining, and living with their three children.

Bari and Ned Furst have hectic work schedules. Both are anesthesiologists, and they're also busy parents. For them, cooking is a form of relaxation. "When we redesigned the kitchen, we went for the bigger range for Ned," says his wife. It's perfect for making Grilled Chicken Quesadillas. The Fursts prefer family-friendly fare during the week, but on weekends they gravitate toward the bold flavors of Tex-Mex. They are particularly fond of brunch, which gives them a chance to leisurely prepare dishes. "Saturday morning is an opportunity for us to really bond as a family," says Bari.

GRILLED CHICKEN QUESADILLAS

family favorite

Prep: 20 min., Chill: 2 hrs., Grill: 8 min., Cook: 6 min. per batch

This is a Furst brunch favorite, but the recipe is also perfect for lunch or supper. Homemade Salsa Picante packs lots of flavor.

- 1/3 cup lime juice
- 2 tablespoons olive oil
- 1 tablespoon minced fresh marjoram or 1 teaspoon dried
- 1 teaspoon salt
- 1 teaspoon pepper
- 1½ pounds skinned and boned chicken breasts
- 12 (6-inch) flour tortillas
- Cilantro-Pecan Pesto
- 1 cup (4 ounces) shredded Mexican four-cheese blend
- Toppings: Salsa Picante, sour cream, chopped cilantro

COMBINE first 5 ingredients in a shallow dish or zip-top freezer bag; add chicken. Cover or seal, and chill 2 hours. Remove chicken from marinade, discarding marinade.

GRILL chicken, covered with grill lid, over medium-high heat (350° to 400°) 4 minutes on each side or until done. Cut chicken into thin strips.

TOP 1 side of 6 tortillas evenly with Cilantro-Pecan Pesto, cheese, and chicken. Top with remaining tortillas.

COOK quesadillas in a lightly greased skillet or griddle over medium-high heat 2 to 3 minutes on each side or until browned. Cut each quesadilla into quarters. Serve with desired toppings. **MAKES** 6 servings.

Cilantro-Pecan Pesto:
freezeable • make ahead
Prep: 5 min.

- 1½ cups fresh cilantro leaves
- 2 garlic cloves, chopped
- 1/3 cup olive oil, divided
- 2 tablespoons pecans, chopped
- 2 tablespoons pine nuts
- ¼ cup shredded Parmesan cheese

PROCESS cilantro, garlic, and 2 tablespoons olive oil in a food processor until a rough paste forms. Add pecans, pine nuts, and cheese, and process until blended, stopping to scrape down sides. With processor running, pour remaining oil through food chute in a slow, steady stream; process until smooth. Cover and chill up to 5 days or freeze up to 1 month, if desired. **MAKES** about ¾ cup.

NED AND BARI FURST
AUSTIN, TEXAS

CREAMY CAULIFLOWER SALAD

fast fixin's

Prep: 15 min.

- 1 head cauliflower
- 4 green onions, sliced
- 2 celery ribs, diced
- 1 cup (4 ounces) shredded sharp Cheddar cheese
- 1 cup Ranch-style dressing
- 3 tablespoons chopped fresh parsley
- Cooked and crumbled bacon (optional)

SEPARATE 1 head of cauliflower into florets, and coarsely chop. Combine florets, green onions, and next 4 ingredients. Toss with bacon, if desired. **MAKES** 4 servings.

NOTE: To lighten, use 2% reduced-fat Cheddar cheese and low-fat dressing, and omit bacon.

Aunt Mary's Pot Roast, page 47

Turnip Greens Stew, page 24;
Hot-Water Cornbread, page 25

38

Golden Macaroni and Cheese, page 24

Too-Easy Cherry Cobbler, page 28

SALSA PICANTE

family favorite • make ahead

Prep: 15 min., Chill: 8 hrs.

This is delicious by itself with tortilla chips, or try it with Grilled Chicken Quesadillas or in Southwestern Quiche.

- **4 plum tomatoes, diced**
- **1 (28-ounce) can crushed tomatoes, undrained**
- **2 (3-ounce) cans diced green chiles**
- **1 bunch green onions, chopped**
- **½ cup chopped fresh cilantro**
- **1 tablespoon chopped fresh oregano**
- **1 tablespoon white vinegar**
- **2 teaspoons salt**
- **2 teaspoons pepper**
- **1 teaspoon sugar**
- **2 teaspoons lite soy sauce**
- **1 teaspoon lime juice**

COMBINE all ingredients in a bowl, mixing well. Cover and chill 8 hours. **MAKES** 1½ quarts.

LAURIE LOCKE
GEORGETOWN, TEXAS

CHOCOLATE-SWIRL BREAKFAST CAKE

family favorite

Prep: 15 min., Bake: 25 min.

- **2 cups all-purpose baking mix**
- **¾ cup milk**
- **½ cup sugar**
- **1 large egg**
- **2 tablespoons butter or margarine, melted**
- **⅔ cup semisweet chocolate morsels**
- **2 tablespoons milk**
- **Coconut-Pecan Topping**

STIR together first 5 ingredients. Pour batter into a lightly greased 9-inch square pan.

MICROWAVE morsels and 2 tablespoons milk in a 2-cup glass measuring cup at HIGH 1½ minutes or until melted, stirring twice.

SWIRL melted chocolate mixture gently through batter with a knife to create a marbled effect. Sprinkle Coconut-Pecan

Topping on top of batter. Bake at 350° for 20 to 25 minutes or until golden brown. **MAKES** 6 servings.

Coconut-Pecan Topping:

Prep: 5 min.

- **⅓ cup sweetened flaked coconut**
- **⅓ cup chopped pecans, toasted**
- **⅓ cup sugar**
- **2 tablespoons butter or margarine, melted**

STIR together all ingredients. **MAKES** about 1 cup.

NOTE: For testing purposes only, we used Bisquick All-Purpose Baking Mix.

NADINE BRISSEY
JENKS, OKLAHOMA

SOUTHWESTERN QUICHE

family favorite

Prep: 20 min., Bake: 1 hr., Cook: 5 min., Stand: 10 min.

You can use Salsa Picante in place of the store-bought sauce in this recipe.

- **1 (15-ounce) package refrigerated piecrusts**
- **2 cups sliced fresh mushrooms**
- **2 teaspoons vegetable oil**
- **½ cup (2 ounces) shredded mozzarella cheese**
- **½ cup (2 ounces) shredded Swiss cheese**
- **½ cup (2 ounces) shredded Cheddar cheese**
- **5 large eggs, lightly beaten**
- **½ cup half-and-half**
- **½ cup picante sauce**
- **1 tablespoon all-purpose flour**
- **½ small green bell pepper, chopped**
- **¼ cup ripe olives, chopped**

UNFOLD and stack 2 piecrusts; gently roll or press piecrusts together. Fit piecrusts into a 9-inch pieplate according to package directions; fold edges under, and crimp. Line pie shell with aluminum foil; fill with pie weights or dried beans.

BAKE on lowest oven rack at 425° for 15 minutes. Remove weights and foil; cool.

SAUTÉ mushrooms in hot oil over medium-high heat 5 minutes or until golden brown and liquid is absorbed.

COMBINE cheeses; set aside.

STIR together eggs and next 3 ingredients in a bowl; add mushrooms, bell pepper, and olives.

POUR half of egg mixture into prepared crust. Sprinkle evenly with two-thirds cheese mixture. Top with remaining egg mixture, and sprinkle with remaining cheese mixture.

BAKE at 375° for 40 to 45 minutes or until set, shielding edges with aluminum foil to prevent excessive browning. Let stand 10 minutes before serving. **MAKES** 8 servings.

LAURIE LOCKE
GEORGETOWN, TEXAS

A Decorative Touch

Glass cabinet doors are a great way to display a collection of china. But if your china is white and the cabinets are too, the look is lost. Adding some subtle color to the inside of the cabinets picks up the warmth of the walls and calls attention to the dishes.

Urban Entertaining

It can be easy and affordable to spruce up a dated space for great get-togethers.

When Kelly Pinion-Smith and Alfred Smith purchased their home, they knew the kitchen would rank high on their priority list for a makeover. Devising a plan of action, the couple tackled one task at a time, added funky details and splashes of color, and discovered how rewarding a do-it-yourself project can be. Now Kelly and Alfred have the perfect space to host casual gatherings with a hearty soup party menu. Just provide an assortment of breads and crackers to round out the meal. For a sweet and easy ending, assemble an ice cream bar.

Tomato-Beef-Wild Rice Soup

Prep: 20 min.; Cook: 1 hr., 10 min.

We used regular wild rice in this soup rather than a mixture of long-grain and wild rice.

    1 pound beef tips
    2 tablespoons olive oil
    4 celery ribs, chopped (about 1 cup)
    2 large onions, sliced (about 2½ cups)
    2 garlic cloves, minced
    1 tablespoon dried Italian seasoning
    3 (14-ounce) cans beef broth
    1 (6-ounce) package wild rice
    1 (14-ounce) can diced tomatoes
    1 cup sliced fresh mushrooms
    ¼ teaspoon hot sauce
    ½ to 1 teaspoon salt
    1 teaspoon pepper
    1 bay leaf

SAUTÉ beef, in batches, in hot oil in a Dutch oven over medium-high heat until brown. Add celery and next 3 ingredients; sauté 5 minutes or until vegetables are tender.

STIR in beef broth and remaining ingredients; bring to a boil. Reduce heat, and simmer 30 minutes. Cover and simmer 30 more minutes or until rice is tender. Discard bay leaf before serving. **MAKES** 8 cups.

KATHY LUECKERT
PLYMOUTH, MINNESOTA

Cream of Squash and Leek Soup

Prep: 15 min.; Cook: 1 hr., 5 min.; Cool: 10 min.

    2 small leeks
    ⅓ cup butter or margarine
    2 medium butternut squash (about 4
        pounds), peeled, seeded, and
        cubed
    6 cups chicken broth
    1½ teaspoons salt
    ¼ teaspoon dried thyme
    ¼ teaspoon pepper
    1 cup whipping cream
    1 cup milk
    Toppings: shredded Parmesan
        cheese, chopped fresh chives or
        parsley

DISCARD roots and green tops of leeks. Cut leeks in half lengthwise; rinse well, and chop.

MELT butter in a Dutch oven over medium heat; add leeks, and sauté 4 minutes or until tender. Stir in squash and next 4 ingredients; bring to a boil. Cover, reduce heat, and simmer 40 minutes or until squash is tender. Remove from heat, and cool 10 minutes.

PROCESS squash mixture, in batches, in a food processor or blender until smooth, stopping to scrape down sides. Return mixture to Dutch oven; stir in whipping cream and milk, and simmer, stirring occasionally, 20 minutes or until thoroughly heated. (Do not boil.) Serve with desired toppings. **MAKES** 3 quarts.

SHERYL DAVIDSON
ATLANTA, GEORGIA

Save Time and Space

An organized pantry is essential. Use these tips from Mona Williams, senior merchandise director for The Container Store.
■ Store rarely used appliances on top shelves.
■ Reserve the most convenient shelves for items that you use every day.
■ Use turntables and tiered shelves to maximize shelf space.
■ Bundle small items in bins or baskets.
■ Use clear containers to store flour, sugar, and pasta. Canisters that stack work well.
■ Keep a step stool nearby so you can easily access high shelves in the pantry.

Quick Update

In six weeks and on a modest budget, a couple turned their kitchen from outdated to fresh and stylish.

Andy and Paula Hughes were in their new home for only a few months when they undertook the mighty task of updating a kitchen that hadn't changed in four decades. This cozy, sunny room is a great place to cook some of their favorite recipes, which they shared with us along with some organizing tips.

Chicken Parmesan

family favorite

Prep: 10 min., Cook: 6 min., Bake: 20 min.

    1 cup Italian-seasoned breadcrumbs
    2 tablespoons all-purpose flour
    ½ teaspoon ground red pepper
    2 skinned and boned chicken breasts
    2 egg whites, lightly beaten
    1 tablespoon olive oil
    Tomato Sauce
    1 cup (4 ounces) shredded
        mozzarella cheese
    ¼ cup freshly grated Parmesan
        cheese

COMBINE first 3 ingredients in a small bowl, and set aside.

PLACE chicken between 2 sheets of heavy-duty plastic wrap, and flatten to ¼-inch thickness, using a meat mallet or rolling pin.

DIP 1 chicken breast in egg whites, and coat with breadcrumb mixture. Dip again in egg whites, and coat again in breadcrumb mixture.

REPEAT procedure with remaining chicken breast.

COOK chicken in hot oil over medium heat 2 to 3 minutes on each side or until done.

PLACE chicken breasts in a single layer in a lightly greased 8-inch square baking dish. Top evenly with Tomato Sauce and cheeses.

BAKE at 350° for 20 minutes or until cheeses melt. **MAKES** 2 servings.

Tomato Sauce:

Prep: 5 min., Cook: 27 min.

Paula serves this simple and delicious sauce with Chicken Parmesan or over whole wheat pasta for meatless spaghetti.

- ½ small onion, chopped
- 2 garlic cloves, minced
- 1 tablespoon olive oil
- 1 (14½-ounce) can diced tomatoes with basil, garlic, and oregano
- ¼ cup red wine
- ½ teaspoon ground red pepper
- ½ teaspoon salt
- ¼ cup chopped fresh basil

SAUTÉ onion and garlic in hot oil over medium heat 5 to 7 minutes or until tender. Add tomatoes, wine, and red pepper; simmer 20 minutes or until thoroughly heated. Add salt and basil. **MAKES** 1½ cups.

PAULA AND ANDY HUGHES
HOMEWOOD, ALABAMA

WHITE CHOCOLATE CHIP-OATMEAL COOKIES

family favorite

Prep: 15 min., Bake: 12 min. per batch

- 1 cup butter or margarine, softened
- 1 cup firmly packed light brown sugar
- 1 cup granulated sugar
- 2 large eggs
- 2 teaspoons vanilla extract
- 3 cups all-purpose flour
- 1 teaspoon baking soda
- 1 teaspoon baking powder
- 1 teaspoon salt
- 1½ cups uncooked regular oats
- 2 cups (12 ounces) white chocolate morsels
- 1 cup coarsely chopped pecans

BEAT butter at medium speed with an electric mixer until creamy; gradually add sugars, beating well. Add eggs, 1 at a time, beating just until yellow disappears after each addition. Stir in vanilla.

COMBINE flour and next 3 ingredients; gradually add to butter mixture, beating until blended. Stir in oats, chocolate morsels, and pecans. Drop by tablespoonfuls onto greased baking sheets. **BAKE** at 350° for 12 minutes. Cool on baking sheets 3 minutes; remove to wire racks to cool completely. **MAKES** about 5 dozen.

PAULA AND ANDY HUGHES
HOMEWOOD, ALABAMA

Sweet Citrus Dessert

We know you love hearing the "yum" when you present your guests with an impressive end to the meal. We're sure this gorgeous tart will do you proud. It starts with a buttery shortbread crust made from commercial cookies followed by a smooth-as-silk red grapefruit custard. The arrangement of colorful fruit sections on top may look a little challenging, but Test Kitchens professional Rebecca Gordon assures us that it's a cinch. Her grapefruit sectioning hints in "From Our Kitchen" on page 48 make this dessert as easy as pie—or, tart, that is.

> **❝ Cook's Notes ❞**
>
> "This was a fun story for me to work on because it reminded me of the days I used to develop recipes and plate desserts in restaurants," says Test Kitchens' Staffer **Rebecca Gordon.** The simplicity of the recipe is very appealing to her. It takes less than 10 minutes to squeeze 2 cups of fresh grapefruit juice. To save time, omit 3 red grapefruit. Instead, top Grapefruit Tart as directed with 2 (24-ounce) jars of drained red grapefruit sections. They can be found refrigerated in the produce section of the grocery store.

GRAPEFRUIT TART

Prep: 40 min.; Bake: 12 min.; Cook: 12 min.; Chill: 2 hrs., 30 min.

- 1 (5.3-ounce) package pure butter shortbread
- 3 tablespoons sugar
- 2 tablespoons butter, melted
- ½ cup sugar
- 6 tablespoons cornstarch
- ⅛ teaspoon salt
- 2 cups fresh red grapefruit juice
- 4 egg yolks
- 3 tablespoons butter
- 2 teaspoons grated red grapefruit rind
- 3 red grapefruit, peeled and sectioned
- 2 tablespoons sugar

PROCESS shortbread in a blender or food processor until graham cracker crumb consistency (about 1⅓ cups of crumbs).

STIR together shortbread crumbs, 3 tablespoons sugar, and 2 tablespoons melted butter in a small bowl. Press mixture lightly into a greased 9-inch tart pan.

BAKE at 350° for 10 to 12 minutes or until lightly browned. Set aside.

COMBINE ½ cup sugar, cornstarch, and salt in a medium-size heavy saucepan. Whisk in juice and egg yolks. Cook over medium-high heat, whisking constantly, 10 to 12 minutes or until mixture thickens and boils. Remove from heat; stir in 3 tablespoons butter and rind. Pour filling into prepared shell. Cover surface of filling with plastic wrap. Chill 2½ hours.

PLACE grapefruit sections in an 8-inch square baking dish. Sprinkle with 2 tablespoons sugar, and chill until ready to assemble. Drain grapefruit.

ARRANGE segments, with outer part of segments facing the edge, around border of tart. Arrange remaining segments around tart, slightly overlapping to cover filling completely. Serve immediately. Chill leftovers. **MAKES** 8 servings.

NOTE: For testing purposes only, we used Walkers Pure Butter Shortbread and TexaSweet Ruby Red Texas grapefruit.

TO MAKE AHEAD: Prepare the crust and filling up to 2 days ahead, but do not top with fruit. Top with grapefruit just before serving.

Pork Chops, Family Style

These tender, juicy favorites make great meals.

Pass the plate—it's time for a pork chop supper! Baking and grilling give these recipes juicy results. When grocery shopping, look for the family pack.

FLAVORFUL CRUSTED PORK CHOPS

family favorite

Prep: 25 min., Cook: 20 min., Bake: 12 min.

Serve these crumb-crusted pork chops with mushroom-tomato sauce on a bed of couscous.

- 4 (1-inch-thick) bone-in pork chops
- ½ teaspoon salt
- ½ teaspoon pepper
- 3 tablespoons olive oil, divided
- 2 tablespoons Dijon mustard
- 1 cup soft breadcrumbs
- ¼ cup minced parsley
- 2 garlic cloves, minced
- ¼ cup minced onion
- ½ (8-ounce) package sliced fresh mushrooms
- 1½ tablespoons all-purpose flour
- ½ cup dry white wine
- 1 teaspoon tomato paste
- 1 (14½-ounce) can reduced-sodium beef broth

SPRINKLE both sides of pork chops evenly with salt and pepper.

COOK chops in 1 tablespoon hot oil in a nonstick ovenproof skillet over medium-high heat 2 to 3 minutes on each side. Remove skillet from heat. Brush tops of pork chops evenly with Dijon mustard.

COMBINE breadcrumbs, parsley, garlic, and remaining 2 tablespoons olive oil in a medium bowl. Press crumb mixture evenly over tops and sides of pork chops. **BAKE** at 400° for 10 to 12 minutes or until done. Remove skillet from oven; remove pork chops, and keep warm.

SAUTÉ onion and mushrooms in skillet over high heat 7 to 8 minutes. Reduce heat to medium low; add flour, and cook, whisking constantly, 1 minute. Whisk together wine and tomato paste. Add to skillet, whisking constantly. Whisk in broth, and cook, whisking constantly, 5 minutes or until mixture is thickened. Arrange pork chops on individual plates, and spoon sauce on top. **MAKES** 4 servings.

GILDA LESTER
WILMINGTON, NORTH CAROLINA

BOURBON-GLAZED PORK CHOPS

family favorite

Prep: 10 min., Chill: 30 min., Grill: 12 min., Cook: 2 min.

- ½ cup firmly packed light brown sugar
- 3 tablespoons Dijon mustard
- 2 tablespoons soy sauce
- 2 tablespoons bourbon
- ½ teaspoon salt
- ¼ teaspoon pepper
- 6 (1-inch-thick) bone-in pork chops

STIR together first 6 ingredients in a shallow dish or large zip-top freezer bag; add pork chops. Cover or seal, and chill 30 minutes, turning once.

REMOVE pork from marinade, reserving marinade.

GRILL pork, covered with grill lid, over medium-high heat (350° to 400°) about 10 to 12 minutes or until a meat thermometer inserted into thickest portion registers 160°, turning once.

BRING reserved marinade to a boil in a small saucepan, and cook, stirring occasionally, 2 minutes. Pour over chops before serving. **MAKES** 6 servings.

NANCY MATTHEWS
GRAYSON, GEORGIA

GREEK-STYLE BAKED PORK CHOPS

family favorite

Prep: 20 min., Cook: 4 min., Bake: 10 min.

- ½ cup bottled diced roasted red bell peppers
- 1 tablespoon chopped fresh parsley
- 2 tablespoons olive oil
- 2 teaspoons grated lemon rind
- 1 tablespoon fresh lemon juice
- 2 teaspoons minced garlic
- ½ teaspoon dried oregano
- ¼ cup all-purpose flour
- 1 teaspoon coarsely ground pepper
- 4 (¾-inch-thick) center-cut pork chops
- ½ cup crumbled feta cheese
- ⅓ cup kalamata olives, chopped

STIR together first 7 ingredients.

STIR together flour and pepper. Coat both sides of pork chops evenly with flour mixture. Cook pork chops in a lightly greased ovenproof skillet over medium heat 2 minutes on each side. Spoon red bell pepper mixture over pork chops.

BAKE, covered, at 400° for 5 minutes. Combine feta cheese and olives in a small bowl. Spoon mixture evenly over pork chops, and bake, covered, 5 more minutes. **MAKES** 4 servings.

JANE ALVARADO
DALLAS, TEXAS

Salads for Winter

These colorful side dishes will brighten your meals this month.

These delicious recipes prove that salads aren't just for summer. Fresh watercress or baby spinach gets all dressed up with juicy orange segments and rich crumbled blue cheese. Not sure what to do with butternut squash or parsnips? Try Baked Winter Vegetable Salad. It's a sweet, glazed, and tender medley.

WATERCRESS-ORANGE SALAD WITH BLUE CHEESE

fast fixin's

Prep: 10 min.

If you can't find watercress, 1 (6-ounce) package of prewashed baby spinach will be just as delicious. For milder onion flavor, rinse onion slices, pat dry, and then add to salad.

- 1 bunch watercress
- 2 navel oranges, peeled and sectioned
- ½ medium-size red onion, thinly sliced (about ¼ cup sliced)
- ¼ cup vegetable oil
- 2 tablespoons red wine vinegar
- 1 teaspoon Dijon mustard
- ½ teaspoon sugar
- ¼ teaspoon salt
- ¼ teaspoon pepper
- ¼ teaspoon dried tarragon
- ½ (4-ounce) package crumbled blue cheese

REMOVE and discard tough stems from watercress. Place watercress, oranges, and onion in a large bowl.
WHISK together oil and next 6 ingredients. Drizzle over watercress mixture, and toss to coat. Sprinkle with blue cheese, and serve immediately. **MAKES** 4 servings.

BAKED WINTER VEGETABLE SALAD

Prep: 25 min., Bake: 45 min.

Wear latex gloves to avoid staining your hands with beets.

- 2 medium-size red onions
- 2 beets, peeled
- 2 parsnips, peeled
- 1 medium butternut squash, peeled and seeded
- 3 tablespoons olive oil, divided
- 1 teaspoon salt, divided
- ½ teaspoon freshly ground pepper, divided
- 2 tablespoons maple syrup
- 6 cups torn mixed salad greens
- ¼ cup walnuts, coarsely chopped and toasted

CUT first 4 ingredients into 1-inch cubes. Line 2 (13- x 9-inch) pans with aluminum foil.
TOSS together onions, beets, 1 tablespoon olive oil, ½ teaspoon salt, and ¼ teaspoon pepper in 1 lined pan, and set aside.
TOSS together parsnips, squash, remaining 2 tablespoons olive oil, remaining ½ teaspoon salt, remaining ¼ teaspoon pepper, and maple syrup in empty lined pan.
BAKE both pans of vegetables at 350° for 45 minutes or until vegetables are tender, shielding with aluminum foil, if necessary, to prevent any excessive browning.
COMBINE all baked vegetables. Add salad greens, and toss. Arrange on a serving platter, and sprinkle with walnuts. Serve immediately. **MAKES** 4 to 6 servings.

CAROLINE KENNEDY
LIGHTHOUSE POINT, FLORIDA

AVOCADO-APPLE SALAD WITH MAPLE-WALNUT VINAIGRETTE

fast fixin's

Prep: 20 min.

Group the colorful ingredients for Avocado-Apple Salad in a large bowl, and drizzle with Maple-Walnut Vinaigrette just before serving.

- 6 cups mixed baby greens
- 2 Gala or Fuji apples, sliced into thin wedges (about 2 cups sliced)
- 1 cup thinly sliced jícama (about ½ medium jícama)
- 1 cup cubed Monterey Jack cheese
- 3 tablespoons chopped red onion
- 1 large avocado, cut into 1-inch cubes
- ⅔ cup coarsely chopped pecans, toasted
- Maple-Walnut Vinaigrette

PLACE greens in a large bowl. Top with apples and next 4 ingredients, arranging them in clusters, if desired. Sprinkle with ⅓ cup pecans. Drizzle with Maple-Walnut Vinaigrette just before serving. Sprinkle with remaining ⅓ cup pecans. **MAKES** 4 to 6 servings.

Maple-Walnut Vinaigrette:

Prep: 5 min.

Walnut oil has a distinctively nutty flavor and fragrance. If you can't find walnut oil, use peanut oil or whichever vegetable oil you have on hand.

- ½ cup walnut oil
- ¼ cup sherry vinegar
- ¼ cup maple syrup
- 1 tablespoon Dijon mustard
- ½ teaspoon salt
- ¼ teaspoon pepper
- ⅛ teaspoon ground nutmeg

WHISK together all ingredients. Store in refrigerator up to 1 week. **MAKES** 1 cup.

MARIE RIZZIO
TRAVERSE CITY, MICHIGAN

Flavored With Olive Oil

Try it for great taste and a boost to health.

Want to serve a scrumptious dish? Start with olive oil. Keep two types on hand: light-colored or Gentile olive oil for sautéing or for use with delicate flavors, and extra-virgin for rich taste and full body. Olive oil is good for you. See "From Our Kitchen" on page 48 for information on different grades of olive oil.

BROILED SALMON WITH LEMON AND OLIVE OIL

Prep: 20 min., Chill: 30 min., Broil: 12 min.

This dish is a highly nutritious choice. Monounsaturated fat from olive oil, omega-3 fatty acids from salmon, and fiber from brown rice together spell heart health.

- 4 (6-ounce) salmon fillets
- ½ teaspoon salt
- ½ teaspoon coarsely ground pepper
- 1 teaspoon grated lemon rind
- 3 tablespoons fresh lemon juice, divided
- 2 tablespoons extra-virgin olive oil, divided
- 1 teaspoon fresh or dried rosemary
- Vegetable cooking spray
- 2 cups hot cooked brown rice
- 4 cups arugula or uncooked baby spinach
- Garnishes: lemon slices, fresh rosemary sprigs

SPRINKLE salmon fillets evenly with salt and pepper.
PLACE fillets, lemon rind, 1 tablespoon lemon juice, 1 tablespoon oil, and 1 teaspoon rosemary in a large zip-top freezer bag. Seal and turn to coat. Chill 30 minutes.
REMOVE fillets from marinade, discarding marinade. Place fillets, skin side down, on a rack coated with cooking spray in an aluminum foil-lined broiler pan.
BROIL fish 5½ inches from heat 10 to 12 minutes or until fillets flake with a fork.
ARRANGE rice and arugula on a serving platter; top with fillets.
WHISK together remaining 2 tablespoons lemon juice and 1 tablespoon oil; drizzle evenly over fillets. Garnish, if desired. **MAKES** 4 servings.

CHELSEY BLANCHARD
BIRMINGHAM, ALABAMA

Calories including arugula and rice: 457 (40% from fat); Fat 20.4g (sat 3.1g, mono 9.8g, poly 6g); Protein 41.6g; Carb 24.6g; Fiber 2.4g; Chol 107mg; Iron 2.4mg; Sodium 386mg; Calc 71mg

CREAMY LIME DRESSING

fast fixin's

Prep: 10 min.

Serve as a delicious dip for raw vegetables or baked chips, as a salad dressing, or as a sandwich spread.

- 1 (16-ounce) package firm tofu, drained
- ½ cup chopped fresh parsley*
- ½ cup fresh lime juice
- ½ cup olive oil
- ¼ cup tahini
- 2 tablespoons lite soy sauce
- 1 teaspoon garlic powder
- ½ teaspoon salt

PROCESS all ingredients in a blender or food processor until smooth, stopping to scrape down sides. Cover and chill until ready to serve. **MAKES** about 2½ cups.

NOTE: Tofu is made from soybeans, making it an excellent source of protein and cancer-fighting antioxidants. Look for brands fortified with calcium.

*Substitute ½ cup chopped fresh basil, if desired.

SU ABBOTT
ATLANTA, GEORGIA

Calories per 2 tablespoons: 70 (79% from fat); Fat 6.2g (sat 0.9g, mono 3.5g, poly 1.6g); Protein 3g; Carb 1.7g; Fiber 0.5g; Chol 0mg; Iron 1.8mg; Sodium 85mg; Calc 112mg

OLIVE OIL-BALSAMIC DIPPING SAUCE

fast fixin's

Prep: 10 min., Bake: 15 min.

For a fresh, quick appetizer, layer plum tomatoes, thinly sliced red onion, and part-skim mozzarella cheese cubes in a shallow dish, and drizzle with sauce. Or serve it with crusty whole grain bread, which is a good source of fiber.

- 3 tablespoons freshly grated Parmesan cheese
- 1 garlic clove, minced
- ½ teaspoon dried Italian seasoning
- ½ teaspoon salt
- ½ teaspoon freshly ground pepper
- ¼ cup extra-virgin olive oil
- 2 tablespoons balsamic vinegar
- 1 (16-ounce) unsliced multigrain bread loaf

STIR together first 5 ingredients in a shallow bowl. Drizzle oil and vinegar evenly over cheese mixture, and stir.
PLACE bread loaf directly on lower oven rack. Bake at 350° for 15 minutes or until heated. Cut bread into 1-inch slices. Dip bread into sauce. **MAKES** 6 servings.

CARLY DRUDA
CLEARWATER, FLORIDA

Calories including bread: 214 (39% from fat); Fat 9.3g (sat 1.3g, mono 5.6g, poly 1.8g); Protein 6.6g; Carb 27.5g; Fiber 3.5g; Chol 1.5mg; Iron 1.7mg; Sodium 390mg; Calc 202mg

Gnocchi With Olive Oil, Tomato, and Parmesan

Prep: 20 min., Bake: 1 hr., Cook: 5 min.

Save time by roasting the garlic bulb ahead or using roasted garlic from a jar. The jar provides conversion information for using it instead of fresh roasted. We tested this dish with extra-virgin olive oil, but any type will work.

- 1 garlic bulb
- 2 tablespoons extra-virgin olive oil
- 10 to 12 fresh sage leaves
- 1 (16-ounce) package gnocchi
- 1 (32-ounce) container fat-free reduced-sodium chicken broth
- 4 plum tomatoes, chopped
- ¼ to ½ teaspoon coarsely ground black pepper
- 2 tablespoons freshly shaved Parmesan or Romano cheese

CUT off pointed end of garlic; place garlic on a piece of aluminum foil. Fold foil to seal.
BAKE at 375° for 1 hour; cool. Squeeze pulp from garlic cloves into a bowl, and mash with a fork; set aside.
STIR together oil and sage in a small skillet, and cook over medium-low heat 2 to 3 minutes or until fragrant and crisp. Remove leaves, and drain on a paper towel; reserve oil and sage leaves.
PREPARE gnocchi according to package directions, substituting chicken broth for water. Drain, reserving ¼ cup broth. Add gnocchi and reserved oil to roasted garlic in bowl. Add reserved ¼ cup chicken broth, chopped tomatoes, and pepper, tossing to coat. Sprinkle with cheese and sage leaves; serve immediately. **MAKES** 4 servings.

Calories 420 (34% from fat); Fat 16g (sat 6.3g, mono 7.9g, poly 1.1g); Protein 9.1g; Carb 61.2g; Fiber 1.9g; Chol 23mg; Iron 1.3mg; Sodium 692mg; Calc 75mg

Home-Cooked Comfort

Use cast-iron cookware to make these favorites.

Aunt Mary's Pot Roast

family favorite

Prep: 10 min., Cook: 10 min., Bake: 3 hrs.

To reduce the fat in this recipe, substitute an eye of round roast for the chuck roast. Both cuts of meat become fall-apart tender when cooked with slow, moist heat. Long before the advent of electricity, pioneers were using cast-iron Dutch ovens as "slow cookers." *(pictured on page 37)*

- 1 (3- to 4-pound) chuck roast
- 1 (12-ounce) can beer
- 1 (0.7-ounce) envelope Italian dressing mix
- Roasted Vegetables (optional)
- Garnish: fresh thyme sprigs

BROWN roast on all sides in a lightly oiled 5-quart cast-iron Dutch oven over high heat. Remove from heat, and add beer and dressing mix.
BAKE, covered, at 300° for 3 hours or until tender, turning once. Serve with Roasted Vegetables, and garnish, if desired. **MAKES** 6 servings.

Roasted Vegetables:

Prep: 10 min., Bake: 45 min.

Slow roasting in a cast-iron skillet accentuates the natural sweetness of these vegetables. You can omit the olive oil and add vegetables to the Dutch oven with the pot roast during the last hour of baking.

- 1½ pounds new potatoes, cut in half
- 1 (16-ounce) bag baby carrots
- 2 medium onions, quartered
- 1 tablespoon olive oil
- Salt and pepper to taste

TOSS potatoes, carrots, and onions with oil; season to taste with salt and pepper.
BAKE at 300° in a large cast-iron skillet for 45 minutes, stirring once. **MAKES** 6 servings.

VIRGINIA ENGLAND
A SKILLET FULL OF TRADITIONAL SOUTHERN LODGE CAST IRON RECIPES & MEMORIES
LODGE PRESS, 2003
SOUTH PITTSBURG, TENNESSEE

Spoon Rolls

Prep: 10 min., Stand: 5 min., Bake: 20 min.

These can be baked in a well-greased muffin pan. As with cornbread, the cast iron creates a wonderfully crisp crust. If you're a fan of muffin tops, bake these in a drop biscuit pan (see page 48).

- 1 (¼-ounce) envelope active dry yeast
- 2 cups lukewarm water (100° to 110°)
- 4 cups self-rising flour
- ¼ cup sugar
- ¾ cup butter or margarine, melted
- 1 large egg, lightly beaten

COMBINE yeast and 2 cups lukewarm water in a large bowl; let stand 5 minutes.
STIR in flour and remaining ingredients until blended. Spoon into well-greased cast-iron muffin pans, filling two-thirds full, or into well-greased cast-iron drop biscuit pans, filling half full.
BAKE at 400° for 20 minutes or until rolls are golden brown. **MAKES** 14 rolls.

NOTE: Store unused batter in an airtight container in the refrigerator up to 1 week.

SARAH KIRKWOOD LODGE AND
BILLIE CLINE HILL
A SKILLET FULL OF TRADITIONAL SOUTHERN LODGE CAST IRON RECIPES & MEMORIES
LODGE PRESS, 2003
SOUTH PITTSBURG, TENNESSEE

from our kitchen

Cast-Iron Cookware

We had great fun testing the recipes for "Home-Cooked Comfort" on page 47 and experimenting with the different types of cast-iron cookware, from grill skillets and drop biscuit pans to Dutch ovens and casserole dishes.

Cast-iron cookware has been the touchstone of Southern food and hospitality for generations. Aside from being virtually indestructible, it has the remarkable ability to evenly distribute and maintain heat, creating perfectly fried chicken and cornbread so crisp you can hear it crackle when cut.

The most treasured pieces of cast-iron cookware are those well-seasoned windfalls we're fortunate enough to inherit from a much-loved relative or friend. With proper care, these will last for years longer. Even that rare flea market find, splattered with rust, can be scoured with a steel wool soap pad and reseasoned.

If you've never purchased a new piece of cast-iron cookware, you might be surprised by its gray color. During the seasoning process, oil is absorbed into the pores of the iron, creating a slick, black surface that only improves with age. To learn more about seasoning cast-iron cookware, visit **southernliving.com/features.**

Lodge Manufacturing Company also offers seasoned cast iron that's ready for use. To view the different types of available cookware or to order a copy of *A Skillet Full of Traditional Southern Lodge Cast Iron Recipes & Memories* (Lodge Press, 2003), visit **www.lodgemfg.com.**

Grades of Olive Oil

■ **Extra-virgin olive oil**—the best grade of olive oil. It's unprocessed (produced without the use of heat), and its acidity level doesn't exceed 1%. It will have the most intense flavor and is usually the most expensive. Reserve this for dipping, drizzling, or salad dressings.
■ **Virgin olive oil**—also unprocessed, with an acidity level no higher than 2%. This type of oil is still quite flavorful and can be used for dipping and salad dressings.
■ **Pure olive oil**—a blend of refined and virgin olive oils. Its acidity is no higher than 1.5%, and it adds flavor and color. It's milder than virgin olive oil and great for cooking and sautéing.

Sectioning 1-2-3

For picture-perfect grapefruit segments (such as those Test Kitchens professional Rebecca Gordon used to make the Grapefruit Tart on page 43), just follow these easy steps.
■ Using a sharp, thin-bladed knife, cut a ¼-inch-thick slice from each end of the grapefruit.
■ Place a flat end down on a cutting board, and remove the peel in strips, cutting from top to bottom following the curvature of the fruit. Remove any remaining bitter white pith.
■ Holding the peeled grapefruit in the palm of one hand, slice between the membranes, and gently remove the whole segments.

In the Groove

Kuhn Rikon's Julienne Peeler ($12.99) works as quickly and safely as a traditional swivel peeler, creating thin, colorful strips of vegetables for festive salads and side dishes. Look for it in specialty stores and cookware catalogs. For more information visit **www.kuhnrikon.com.**

Spring Salads

These easy entrées offer endless possibilities for family meals or entertaining.

The secret to a really good salad is fresh ingredients—simply prepared and well seasoned. Greens should be crisp and cold. Fruits, cheeses, and vinaigrettes are best at room temperature.

Tropical Spinach Salad With Grilled Shrimp, for example, is just as delicious when prepared with chicken or pork. Substitute fresh peaches for mangoes, feta for goat cheese, or pine nuts for pistachios. Add a little crumbled blue cheese to Strawberry Chicken Salad, or replace the diced onion with a handful of fresh chives. And, for a clever serving bowl idea, see "From Our Kitchen" on page 64 to learn how to create the bread basket bowl pictured on page 74 from refrigerated breadstick dough.

SHRIMP-AND-ARTICHOKE SALAD

fast fixin's • make ahead

Prep: 30 min.

For a special occasion, serve this in whole steamed artichokes garnished with lemon wedges and edible flowers. To prepare fresh artichokes, see page 53. *(pictured on page 75)*

- **2½ pounds unpeeled, medium-size fresh shrimp, cooked**
- **½ cup mayonnaise***
- **½ cup sour cream***
- **½ cup chopped fresh parsley**
- **5 green onions, thinly sliced**
- **1 tablespoon grated lemon rind**
- **2 teaspoons dry Italian dressing mix**
- **1 teaspoon hot sauce**
- **½ teaspoon Creole seasoning**
- **1 (14-ounce) can artichoke hearts, drained and quartered**

PEEL shrimp; devein, if desired.
WHISK together mayonnaise and next 7 ingredients. Stir in artichoke hearts and shrimp. Cover and chill until ready to serve. **MAKES** 8 servings.

NOTE: When selecting canned artichoke hearts, look on the label for a count of 10 to 12. Not only are these whole artichoke hearts less expensive, they are consistently more tender than either the larger sizes or the quartered ones.

*Substitute reduced-fat mayonnaise and sour cream, if desired.

ANNE Y. FITZGERALD
CHENEYVILLE, LOUISIANA

STRAWBERRY-CHICKEN SALAD

family favorite

Prep: 30 min., Chill: 1 hr., Grill: 8 min., Stand: 10 min.

You can omit the chicken, add a sprinkling of blue cheese, and serve this as a side salad with grilled steaks. *(pictured on page 74)*

- **4 skinned and boned chicken breasts**
- **Raspberry Vinaigrette, divided**
- **8 cups mixed salad greens**
- **1 quart strawberries, sliced**
- **2 pears, sliced**
- **2 avocados, peeled and sliced**
- **½ small sweet onion, diced**
- **½ cup pecan halves, toasted**

COMBINE chicken and ½ cup Raspberry Vinaigrette in a large zip-top freezer bag. Seal and chill 1 hour.
REMOVE chicken from marinade, discarding marinade.
GRILL, covered with grill lid, over medium-high heat (350° to 400°) 4 minutes on each side or until done. Let chicken stand 10 minutes; slice.
PLACE salad greens and next 5 ingredients in a large bowl, and gently toss. Divide mixture evenly among 4 serving plates; top with grilled chicken slices. Serve with remaining Raspberry Vinaigrette. **MAKES** 4 servings.

Raspberry Vinaigrette:
fast fixin's • make ahead
Prep: 5 min.

- **¾ cup pear nectar**
- **⅓ cup vegetable oil**
- **⅓ cup raspberry vinegar**
- **3 tablespoons chopped fresh basil**
- **1 tablespoon Dijon mustard**
- **1 tablespoon sesame oil**
- **½ teaspoon freshly ground pepper**
- **¼ teaspoon salt**

PLACE all ingredients in a screw-top jar; cover tightly, and shake vigorously until blended. Store in refrigerator for up to 2 weeks, shaking before serving. **MAKES** 1½ cups.

MITZI ADKINSON
INDIANAPOLIS, INDIANA

HONEY CHICKEN SALAD

fast fixin's

Prep: 20 min.

The mayonnaise-and-honey mixture that dresses this salad is reminiscent of poppy seed dressing. Reduce the amount of honey for a less sweet taste. *(pictured on page 75)*

- **4 cups chopped cooked chicken**
- **3 celery ribs, diced (about 1½ cups)**
- **1 cup sweetened dried cranberries**
- **½ cup chopped pecans, toasted**
- **1½ cups mayonnaise**
- **⅓ cup orange-blossom honey**
- **¼ teaspoon salt**
- **¼ teaspoon pepper**
- **Garnish: chopped toasted pecans**

STIR together first 4 ingredients.
WHISK together mayonnaise and next 3 ingredients. Add to chicken mixture, stirring gently until combined. Garnish, if desired. **MAKES** 4 servings.

TERESA MOSHER
BRADENTON, FLORIDA

TROPICAL SPINACH SALAD WITH GRILLED SHRIMP

Prep: 30 min., Chill: 1 hr., Soak: 30 min., Grill: 4 min.

This recipe provides a variety of options. You can omit the shrimp and serve this as a side salad, or try one of the chicken or pork variations that follow the recipe. *(pictured on page 75)*

- **2 pounds unpeeled, large fresh shrimp**
- **Citrus Marinade**
- **8 (12-inch) wooden skewers**
- **2 (6-ounce) bags fresh baby spinach**
- **2 mangoes, peeled and sliced**
- **1 medium-size red onion, sliced**
- **1 (3-ounce) package goat cheese, crumbled**
- **1 cup fresh raspberries**
- **½ cup chopped pistachio nuts**
- **Fresh Basil Vinaigrette**

PEEL shrimp; devein, if desired.
PLACE shrimp in a large zip-top freezer bag, and add Citrus Marinade. Seal and shake to coat. Chill 1 hour.

SOAK wooden skewers in water to cover 30 minutes.
REMOVE shrimp from marinade, discarding marinade. Thread shrimp onto skewers.
GRILL, covered with grill lid, over medium-high heat (350° to 400°) 2 minutes on each side or just until shrimp turn pink. Remove shrimp from skewers.
ARRANGE baby spinach on a large serving platter. Top baby spinach evenly with mango slices, onion slices, and grilled shrimp. Sprinkle with crumbled goat cheese, raspberries, and chopped pistachio nuts. Serve salad with Fresh Basil Vinaigrette. **MAKES** 6 servings.

Citrus Marinade:
fast fixin's • make ahead
Prep: 5 min.

- **¾ cup fresh orange juice**
- **2 tablespoons chopped fresh basil**
- **2 tablespoons lime juice**
- **2 tablespoons extra-virgin olive oil**
- **1 garlic clove, crushed**
- **½ teaspoon dried crushed red pepper**
- **¼ teaspoon salt**

WHISK together all ingredients. Cover and chill until ready to use. **MAKES** 1 cup.

Fresh Basil Vinaigrette:
fast fixin's • make ahead
Prep: 5 min.

- **¼ cup chopped fresh basil**
- **¼ cup raspberry vinegar**
- **1 teaspoon Dijon mustard**
- **1 garlic clove, chopped**
- **¼ teaspoon salt**
- **¼ teaspoon pepper**
- **¾ cup extra-virgin olive oil**

PROCESS first 6 ingredients in a blender until smooth. With blender running, gradually add oil in a slow, steady stream; process until smooth. Cover and chill until ready to serve. **MAKES** 1 cup.

TROPICAL SPINACH SALAD WITH GRILLED PORK TENDERLOIN: Substitute 2 (1-pound) pork tenderloins for shrimp. Grill, covered with grill lid, over medium-high heat (350° to 400°) 10 to 12 minutes on each side or until a meat thermometer inserted into thickest portion registers 155°. Let stand 10 minutes. Slice and serve as directed.

TROPICAL SPINACH SALAD WITH GRILLED CHICKEN: Substitute 6 skinned and boned chicken breasts for shrimp. Grill, covered with grill lid, over medium-high heat (350° to 400°) 4 minutes on each side or until done. Let stand 10 minutes. Slice and serve as directed.

STACEY LILLY
DALLAS, TEXAS

Entertaining Touches

If a hectic schedule keeps you out of the kitchen, order an assortment of salads and tea sandwiches from a favorite cafe or delicatessen, and focus on a festive presentation. A colorful collection of teacups and pretty silverware can transform the simplest of salads into an elegant luncheon. Cream pitchers and sugar bowls make terrific containers for dressings and croutons.

Flavor softened butter with finely chopped herbs or fruit preserves, and serve with a basket of hot cornbread and homemade rolls or miniature muffins and biscuits.

Elegant Couples' Party

Throw a shower—or any type of gathering—

with this sensational menu.

Menu

Serves 12

Garlic-and-Rosemary Shrimp

Beef Tenderloin With Henry Bain Sauce and rolls

Steamed Asparagus With Tomato-Basil Dip

Blue Cheese Logs and crackers

Purchased cheesecake

Wedding showers used to be for ladies only, but the trend these days is to throw a couples' party for the bride and groom together. Consider this delicious and impressive menu for such an occasion (or for your next supper club). Most of these recipes can be prepared ahead, making the event that much easier. Help guests bring the perfect gift by providing a fun theme on the shower invitation. With our menu and decorating tips, you can entertain 12 guests with ease.

GARLIC-AND-ROSEMARY SHRIMP

Prep: 25 min., Cook: 25 min.

- **3 pounds unpeeled, medium-size fresh shrimp**
- **¼ cup butter or margarine**
- **¼ cup extra-virgin olive oil**
- **1 large garlic bulb**
- **1 cup dry white wine**
- **¼ cup white wine vinegar**
- **¼ cup lemon juice**
- **4 dried red chile peppers**
- **3 bay leaves**
- **¾ teaspoon salt**
- **1 tablespoon chopped fresh rosemary**
- **1 teaspoon dried oregano**
- **½ teaspoon dried crushed red pepper**

PEEL shrimp, leaving tails on; devein, if desired, and set aside.

MELT butter with oil in a large skillet over medium-high heat. Separate and peel garlic cloves. Add to butter mixture, and sauté 2 minutes.

STIR in wine and next 8 ingredients; bring to a boil. Boil, stirring occasionally, 8 to 10 minutes or until reduced by half and thoroughly heated.

ADD half of shrimp. Cook 5 to 6 minutes or just until shrimp turn pink; remove with a slotted spoon. Cook remaining shrimp 5 to 6 minutes or just until shrimp turn pink. Discard bay leaves. Serve shrimp with warm broth. **MAKES** 12 appetizer servings.

BEEF TENDERLOIN WITH HENRY BAIN SAUCE

family favorite

Prep: 10 min., Chill: 2 hrs., Bake: 35 min., Stand: 15 min.

Henry Bain Sauce was originated by the head waiter at the Pendennis Club in Louisville. Freeze any leftover sauce for later use.

- **1 (9-ounce) bottle chutney**
- **1 (14-ounce) bottle ketchup**
- **1 (12-ounce) bottle chili sauce**
- **1 (10-ounce) bottle steak sauce**
- **1 (10-ounce) bottle Worcestershire sauce**
- **1 teaspoon hot sauce**
- **¼ cup butter or margarine, softened**
- **2 teaspoons salt**
- **1 teaspoon freshly ground pepper**
- **1 (4½- to 5-pound) beef tenderloin, trimmed**
- **Rolls**

PROCESS chutney in a food processor until smooth. Add ketchup and next 4 ingredients, and process until blended. Chill sauce at least 2 hours.

STIR together butter, salt, and pepper; rub over tenderloin. Place on a lightly greased rack in a jellyroll pan. (Fold under narrow end of meat to fit on rack.)

BAKE at 500° for 30 to 35 minutes or until a meat thermometer inserted into thickest portion registers 145° (medium rare). Loosely cover tenderloin with aluminum foil, and let stand 15 minutes before slicing. Serve tenderloin with sauce and rolls. **MAKES** 3 dozen appetizer or 12 main-dish servings.

NOTE: For testing, we used Major Grey's Chutney and A.1. Steak Sauce.

Cooking Whole Artichokes

Baffled by artichokes? Don't just buy a can of hearts, try them whole. They can be used as an edible centerpiece. When eating an artichoke, start by plucking the leaves, one at a time, beginning at the base; dip the meaty end of each leaf into our Creamy Herb Dip or Garlic-Lemon Butter. Draw each leaf between your teeth, scraping off the meat. Discard leaves on a plate or in a large bowl.

STEAMED ASPARAGUS WITH TOMATO-BASIL DIP

fast fixin's • make ahead

Prep: 20 min., Cook: 3 min.

- 1 cup mayonnaise
- ½ cup sour cream
- ½ cup chopped fresh basil
- 1 tablespoon tomato paste
- 1 tablespoon grated lemon rind
- 4 pounds fresh asparagus

WHISK together first 5 ingredients. Cover and chill up to 2 days, if desired. SNAP off tough ends of asparagus. Cook in boiling salted water to cover 3 minutes or until crisp-tender; drain. Plunge asparagus into ice water to stop the cooking process; drain. Cover and chill, if desired. Serve with dip. MAKES 12 to 15 servings.

BLUE CHEESE LOGS

freezeable • make ahead

Prep: 15 min., Chill: 1 hr.

- 2 (8-ounce) packages cream cheese, softened
- 8 ounces sharp Cheddar cheese, cubed
- 2 (4-ounce) packages crumbled blue cheese
- ½ small onion, diced
- 1½ tablespoons Worcestershire sauce
- ½ teaspoon ground red pepper
- 2 cups finely chopped pecans, toasted and divided
- 2 cups finely chopped fresh parsley, divided
- Crackers

PROCESS first 6 ingredients in a food processor 1 to 2 minutes until combined, stopping to scrape down sides.
STIR together cheese mixture, 1 cup pecans, and ½ cup parsley. Cover and chill 1 hour.
SHAPE mixture into 4 (7-inch) logs.
COMBINE remaining 1 cup pecans and 1½ cups parsley. Roll logs in parsley mixture; cover and chill until ready to serve. Serve with crackers. MAKES about 24 appetizer servings.

NOTE: For testing purposes only, we used Cracker Barrel cheese for Cheddar cheese. Cheese logs can be prepared ahead and frozen, if desired. Thaw in refrigerator overnight.

WHOLE COOKED ARTICHOKES

Prep: 15 min., Cook: 35 min.

- 4 large artichokes
- Lemon wedge
- 3 tablespoons lemon juice

WASH artichokes by plunging up and down in cold water. Cut off stem ends, and trim about ½ inch from top of each artichoke. Remove any loose bottom leaves. Trim one-fourth off top of each outer leaf with scissors, and rub cut edges with lemon wedge.
ARRANGE artichokes in a Dutch oven; cover with water, and add lemon juice.
BRING to a boil; cover, reduce heat, and simmer 35 minutes or until lower leaves pull out easily. Drain. MAKES 4 servings.

MICROWAVE DIRECTIONS: Stand artichokes in an 11- x 7-inch baking dish; add 1 cup water to dish. Cover dish with heavy-duty plastic wrap. Microwave at HIGH 15 to 20 minutes, giving dish a quarter turn halfway through cooking time. Let stand 5 minutes. (When done, petals near the center will pull out easily). Prep: 15 min., Cook: 20 min., Stand: 5 min.

GARLIC-LEMON BUTTER

fast fixin's

Prep: 10 min., Cook: 3 min.

- ½ cup butter or margarine, softened
- 1 garlic clove, minced
- 2 teaspoons grated lemon rind
- 1 teaspoon minced fresh parsley
- ¼ teaspoon salt
- ¼ teaspoon freshly ground black pepper

COOK all ingredients in a saucepan over low heat, stirring until butter melts and mixture is thoroughly heated. Serve with cooked artichokes. **MAKES** about ½ cup.

ESTHER HARMON
BANNER ELK, NORTH CAROLINA

CREAMY HERB DIP

fast fixin's • make ahead

Prep: 10 min.

Also try serving this dip with your favorite raw vegetables.

- ¾ cup sour cream
- ¾ cup mayonnaise
- 1 tablespoon minced fresh parsley
- 1 tablespoon minced fresh chives
- 1 teaspoon minced fresh dill
- 1 teaspoon grated lemon rind
- 1 tablespoon fresh lemon juice

STIR together all ingredients. Cover and chill until ready to serve. Serve with cooked artichokes. **MAKES** 1½ cups.

NANCY RIERSON
WINSTON-SALEM, NORTH CAROLINA

Secrets from the Cake (Mix) Doctor

These traditional Southern cakes are so good, no one will guess they're not made from scratch.

Wish you had the time and talent to make great cakes like your mother or aunt? Then take some advice from Nashville food writer Anne Byrn, aka The Cake Mix Doctor. Her books offer great ways to enhance mixes to make them as good—or better—than cakes made from scratch.

Her books, *The Cake Mix Doctor* and *Chocolate From the Cake Mix Doctor,* offer updated versions of a number of favorite Southern cakes that have graced family dinners and covered-dish suppers for a generation.

"I wrote a story for *The Tennessean* in Nashville in June 1998, sharing cake mix recipes my family had doctored," Anne explains. "The reaction was so strong, I asked readers to send in their own favorites. I got 500 recipes within one week. I quickly realized this should be a book."

The Cake Mix Doctor (Workman Publishing Company, Inc., 1999) was a runaway success. Anne soon had a Web site, **www.cakemixdoctor.com,** and a second book. She most recently turned her surgical skills to savory foods with *The Dinner Doctor* (Workman Publishing Company, Inc., 2003). Of course, the book includes her signature cakes as well.

Her efforts have helped other time-pressed cooks produce delicious desserts. Anne says, "The Cake Mix Doctor has made baking accessible to an awful lot of people who hadn't had any luck with it before." Whip up your own excellent confection with one of these favorites adapted from *The Cake Mix Doctor.*

❝ Cook's Notes ❞

"Anne came to the Test Kitchens one day to make cakes with us," says Test Kitchens Director **Lyda Jones.** "And we all learned so much from her. The strawberry cake is one of my favorites because I have had a strawberry cake every year for my birthday since I was a child."

Lyda also is wild about the **Quick Caramel Frosting** because it's so doable that even a novice cook can make it. "It's Anne's mother's recipe—so just like us, Anne cooks some of her family favorites," says Lyda.

TRIPLE-DECKER STRAWBERRY CAKE

freezeable • make ahead

Prep: 25 min., Bake: 23 min.

We doubled the frosting called for in Anne's original recipe to add extra richness to this cake. It keeps best in the refrigerator.

- 1 (18.25-ounce) package white cake mix
- 1 (3-ounce) package strawberry gelatin
- 4 large eggs
- ½ cup sugar
- ¼ cup all-purpose flour
- ½ cup finely chopped fresh strawberries
- 1 cup vegetable oil
- ½ cup milk
- Strawberry Buttercream Frosting
- Garnish: whole strawberries

BEAT first 8 ingredients at low speed with an electric mixer 1 minute. Scrape down sides, and beat at medium speed 2 more minutes, stopping to scrape down sides, if needed. (Chopped strawberries should be well blended into batter.)

POUR batter into 3 greased and floured 9-inch cakepans.

BAKE at 350° for 23 minutes or until cakes spring back when lightly pressed with a finger.

COOL in pans on wire racks for 10 minutes. Remove from pans; cool completely on wire racks.

SPREAD Strawberry Buttercream Frosting between layers and on top and sides of cake. Store in refrigerator. Garnish, if desired. MAKES 16 servings.

Strawberry Buttercream Frosting:

fast fixin's

Prep: 10 min.

- 1 cup butter, softened
- 2 (16-ounce) packages powdered sugar, sifted
- 1 cup finely chopped fresh strawberries

BEAT butter at medium speed with an electric mixer 20 seconds or until fluffy. Add sugar and strawberries; beat at low speed until creamy. (Add more sugar if frosting is too thin, or add strawberries if too thick.) MAKES 2½ cups.

NOTE: For testing purposes only, we used Duncan Hines Moist Deluxe Classic White Cake Mix without pudding.

TO MAKE AHEAD: Place finished cake in the refrigerator, uncovered, and chill for 20 minutes or until the frosting sets. Cover frosted cake well with wax paper, and store in the refrigerator for up to 1 week. To freeze, wrap chilled cake with aluminum foil, and freeze up to 6 months. Thaw cake overnight in the refrigerator.

TRIPLE-LAYER TENNESSEE JAM CAKE

family favorite

Prep: 25 min., Bake: 23 min., Stand: 10 min.

We especially love this luscious caramel frosting, which is easier and quicker than others we've tried.

- 1 (18.25-ounce) package spice cake mix
- 1 cup buttermilk
- ⅓ cup sweetened applesauce
- ⅓ cup vegetable oil
- 3 large eggs
- ¼ teaspoon ground cinnamon
- 1 cup blackberry jam
- Quick Caramel Frosting

BEAT first 6 ingredients at low speed with an electric mixer for 1 minute. Scrape down sides, and beat at medium speed 2 more minutes until well blended, stopping to scrape down sides, if needed.

POUR batter evenly into 3 greased and floured 9-inch round cakepans.

BAKE at 350° for 20 to 23 minutes or until cakes are light brown and spring back when lightly pressed with a finger.

COOL in pans on wire racks for 10 minutes. Remove from pans; cool completely on wire racks.

PLACE 1 layer on a serving platter. Spread with ½ cup blackberry jam, leaving a ½-inch border. Spread a smooth, thin layer of warm Quick Caramel Frosting over jam. Repeat layers. Top with third cake layer. Spread top and sides of cake with remaining Quick Caramel Frosting, working quickly before the frosting hardens. (If frosting becomes too hard to spread, place it over low heat for 1 minute, stirring constantly.) Let cake stand 10 minutes. MAKES 16 servings.

Quick Caramel Frosting:

fast fixin's

Prep: 10 min., Cook: 12 min.

- ½ cup butter or margarine
- ½ cup firmly packed light brown sugar
- ½ cup firmly packed dark brown sugar
- ¼ cup milk
- 2 cups powdered sugar, sifted
- 1 teaspoon vanilla extract

BRING first 3 ingredients to a boil in a 3½-quart saucepan over medium heat, whisking constantly, about 2 minutes.

STIR in milk, and bring to a boil; remove from heat. Add powdered sugar and vanilla, stirring with a wooden spoon until smooth. Use immediately. MAKES 3 cups.

TENNESSEE JAM CAKE: Pour batter evenly into 2 (9-inch) round cakepans. Bake at 350° for 26 to 28 minutes or until cakes are light brown and spring back when pressed with a finger. Place 1 layer on a serving platter, and spread ½ cup blackberry jam on top of layer. Spread warm Quick Caramel Frosting smoothly over jam. Top with remaining layer; proceed as directed.

NOTE: For testing purposes only, we used Knott's Berry Farm Blackberry Jam.

Jazzed-Up Chicken

Looking for something new? These recipes will inspire you to cook a great supper tonight.

Just about everybody keeps a package of chicken in the freezer or fridge, but we tend to make the same recipes over and over. If you love chicken but are bored with the expected flavors, try these great new supper options. You probably already have most of the ingredients.

CHICKEN-CHEESE BURGERS

freezeable • make ahead

Prep: 20 min., Chill: 30 min., Cook: 15 min. per batch

These patties can be shaped ahead, wrapped in plastic wrap, and stored in zip-top freezer bags in the freezer for up to 3 months. Chicken thighs mixed with chicken breasts make the burgers tender and juicy.

- 1 pound skinned and boned chicken breasts, cut into 2-inch pieces
- 1 pound skinned and boned chicken thighs, cut into 2-inch pieces
- 1 large egg, lightly beaten
- 10 saltine crackers, finely crushed
- 3 to 4 green onions, sliced (about ½ cup)
- 2½ teaspoons salt
- 1 teaspoon fresh or dried rosemary
- ¾ teaspoon pepper
- ½ teaspoon garlic powder
- 8 mozzarella cheese slices
- 8 onion buns, split
- Tomato slices
- Lemon Mayonnaise
- Lettuce leaves

PROCESS chicken in a food processor until consistency of ground beef; spoon into a large bowl.

ADD egg and next 6 ingredients to ground chicken in bowl; stir until blended. Shape chicken mixture into 8 patties (about 6 ounces each). Chill 30 minutes or until firm.

COOK chicken patties, in batches, in a lightly greased nonstick skillet over medium-high heat 5 to 7 minutes on each side or until done. Top each patty with 1 cheese slice. Cover and cook 1 minute or until cheese melts.

TOP bottom halves of buns with tomato slices. Spread Lemon Mayonnaise evenly on tomato slices. Top with chicken patties and lettuce, and cover with tops of buns. **MAKES** 8 servings.

Lemon Mayonnaise:
fast fixin's
Prep: 5 min.

- 1 cup light mayonnaise
- ½ teaspoon grated lemon rind
- 1 tablespoon fresh lemon juice
- ¼ teaspoon pepper

STIR together all ingredients. Cover and chill until ready to serve. **MAKES** about 1 cup.

STUFFED ALFREDO CHICKEN

family favorite

Prep: 25 min., Cook: 10 min., Bake: 1 hr., Stand: 10 min.

This is wonderful alongside egg noodles and crisp-tender green beans or asparagus.

- 4 skinned and boned chicken breasts
- 8 ounces mild ground Italian pork sausage
- 1 (1.25-ounce) envelope Alfredo sauce mix
- 1 cup (4 ounces) shredded mozzarella cheese
- 1 cup (4 ounces) shredded Parmesan cheese
- 1 (10-ounce) package frozen chopped spinach, thawed and drained
- ½ cup ricotta cheese
- 2 plum tomatoes, diced

PLACE chicken between 2 sheets of heavy-duty plastic wrap, and flatten to ¼-inch thickness using a meat mallet or rolling pin. Set aside.

COOK sausage in a large skillet over medium-high heat 10 minutes, stirring until it crumbles and is no longer pink; drain and set aside.

PREPARE Alfredo sauce according to package directions; set aside.

COMBINE shredded mozzarella and Parmesan cheeses.

STIR together sausage, spinach, ricotta cheese, and ½ cup mozzarella cheese mixture. Spoon mixture evenly down center of each chicken breast, and roll up, jellyroll fashion. Arrange chicken rolls, seam side down, in a lightly greased 2-quart baking dish. Pour Alfredo sauce over chicken, and sprinkle evenly with remaining 1½ cups mozzarella cheese mixture.

BAKE at 350° for 50 minutes to 1 hour or until chicken is done. Let stand 10 minutes. Cut chicken rolls into slices. Serve with sauce; sprinkle evenly with diced tomatoes just before serving. **MAKES** 4 servings.

NOTE: For testing purposes only, we used McCormick Creamy Garlic Alfredo Pasta Sauce Blend.

CHRISTINA VALENTA
FRIENDSWOOD, TEXAS

PEPPERY CHICKEN FRIED CHICKEN

family favorite

Prep: 30 min., Fry: 15 min. per batch,
Cook: 12 min.

Cut leftover chicken into strips, and serve over salad greens. Drizzle with creamy Ranch or blue cheese dressing. *(pictured on page 73)*

- 8 (6-ounce) skinned and boned chicken breasts
- 4½ teaspoons salt, divided
- 2½ teaspoons freshly ground black pepper, divided
- 76 saltine crackers (2 sleeves), crushed
- 2½ cups all-purpose flour, divided
- 1 teaspoon baking powder
- 1 teaspoon ground red pepper
- 8 cups milk, divided
- 4 large eggs
- Peanut oil

PLACE chicken breasts between 2 sheets of heavy-duty plastic wrap, and flatten to ¼-inch thickness using a meat mallet or rolling pin.

SPRINKLE ½ teaspoon salt and ½ teaspoon black pepper evenly over chicken. Set aside.

COMBINE cracker crumbs, 2 cups flour, baking powder, 1½ teaspoons salt, 1 teaspoon black pepper, and red pepper.

WHISK together 1½ cups milk and eggs. Dredge chicken in cracker crumb mixture; dip in milk mixture, and dredge in cracker mixture again.

POUR oil to a depth of ½ inch in a 12-inch skillet (do not use a nonstick skillet). Heat to 360°. Fry chicken, in batches, 10 minutes, adding oil as needed. Turn and fry 4 to 5 more minutes or until golden brown. Remove to a wire rack in a jellyroll pan. Keep chicken warm in a 225° oven. Carefully drain hot oil, reserving cooked bits and 2 tablespoons drippings in skillet.

WHISK together remaining ½ cup flour, remaining 2½ teaspoons salt, remaining 1 teaspoon black pepper, and remaining 6½ cups milk. Pour mixture into reserved drippings in skillet; cook over medium-high heat, whisking constantly, 10 to 12 minutes or until thickened. Serve gravy with chicken. **MAKES** 8 servings.

LIGHT KING RANCH CHICKEN CASSEROLE

freezeable • make ahead

Prep: 15 min., Cook: 5 min., Bake: 35 min.

Serve with a veggie-loaded salad and vinaigrette. For added Southwest flavor, whisk a few dashes of hot sauce into the dressing.

- 1 large onion, chopped
- 1 large green bell pepper, chopped
- Vegetable cooking spray
- 2 cups chopped cooked chicken breasts
- 1 (10-ounce) can fat-free cream of chicken soup, undiluted
- 1 (10-ounce) can fat-free cream of mushroom soup, undiluted
- 1 (10-ounce) can diced tomato and green chiles
- 1 teaspoon chili powder
- ½ teaspoon pepper
- ¼ teaspoon garlic powder
- 12 (6-inch) corn tortillas
- 1 (8-ounce) block reduced-fat Cheddar cheese, shredded

SAUTÉ onion and bell pepper in a large skillet coated with cooking spray over medium-high heat 5 minutes or until tender.

STIR in chicken and next 6 ingredients; remove from heat.

TEAR tortillas into 1-inch pieces; layer one-third tortilla pieces in a 13- x 9-inch baking dish coated with cooking spray. Top with one-third chicken mixture and one-third cheese. Repeat layers twice.

BAKE at 350° for 30 to 35 minutes or until bubbly. **MAKES** 8 servings.

NOTE: Freeze casserole up to 1 month, if desired. Thaw in refrigerator overnight, and bake as directed.

Calories 282 (32% from fat); Fat 9.9g (sat 5g, mono 0.5g, poly 0.7g); Protein 21g; Carb 26.4g; Fiber 3.1g; Chol 54.4mg; Iron 0.7mg; Sodium 947mg; Calc 248mg

Taste of the South

Down-Home Spoonbread

What could be more comforting and Southern than this freshly baked concoction that's made from cornmeal, butter, milk, and eggs—so light, yet so rich and creamy that it requires a spoon? If you've never prepared spoonbread, now is the time. It's surprisingly easy; just be sure to start with plain cornmeal, not a mix, which may contain baking soda.

One bite and this soufflélike dish could become a new favorite. Serve it warm from the oven to keep it from becoming too dense. Spoonbread invites a host of accompaniments—our favorite being any braised meat smothered in gravy, especially when flavored with smoked bacon drippings. It's great for breakfast, lunch, or dinner. Also try it warmed up in the microwave with just a kiss of real butter and a crack of fresh black pepper.

MEMMIE'S SPOONBREAD

Prep: 15 min., Stand: 10 min., Bake: 50 min.

We used Quaker yellow cornmeal for a smooth, creamy texture.

- 3 cups boiling water
- 2 cups cornmeal
- 2 teaspoons salt
- ½ cup butter or margarine, cut up
- 2 cups milk
- 4 large eggs, lightly beaten
- 1 tablespoon baking powder

POUR 3 cups boiling water gradually over cornmeal in a large bowl, stirring until smooth. Add salt and butter, stirring until well blended; let stand 10 minutes. Gradually stir in milk and eggs. Stir in baking powder. Pour mixture into a lightly greased 13- x 9-inch baking dish.

BAKE at 375° for 45 to 50 minutes or until lightly browned. **MAKES** 10 to 12 servings.

SPOONBREAD

chef recipe

Prep: 25 min., Cook: 8 min., Stand: 30 min.,
Bake: 30 min.

Pawley's Island chef Louis Osteen's version of spoonbread is one of our favorites due to the delicious addition of Parmesan cheese and fresh chives. This recipe is adapted from *Louis Osteen's Charleston Cuisine* (Algonquin Books, 1999).

- 1¾ cups milk
- 1 cup whipping cream
- ⅓ cup buttermilk
- 1⅓ tablespoons unsalted butter
- 1 cup stone-ground white cornmeal
- ⅓ cup freshly grated Parmesan cheese
- 1⅓ teaspoons baking powder
- ⅔ teaspoon baking soda
- 4 large eggs, separated
- 4 teaspoons chopped fresh chives
- 2 teaspoons sugar
- ⅔ teaspoon salt

HEAT first 4 ingredients in a heavy saucepan over medium-high heat 6 to 8 minutes (do not boil). Remove from heat. (Mixture will curdle.)

COMBINE cornmeal and Parmesan cheese in a large bowl. Pour milk mixture over cornmeal mixture, whisking until smooth. Let stand 30 minutes or until lukewarm. Stir in baking powder and baking soda.

BEAT egg yolks lightly, and stir into cornmeal mixture. Fold in chives.

BEAT egg whites, sugar, and salt at high speed with an electric mixer until stiff peaks form. Carefully fold into cornmeal mixture.

POUR into a buttered 13- x 9-inch baking dish.

BAKE at 350° for 30 minutes or until top is golden and a wooden pick inserted in center comes out clean. Serve spoonbread immediately. **MAKES** 8 servings.

LOUIS OSTEEN
PAWLEY'S ISLAND, SOUTH CAROLINA

Healthy & Light

Cooking With Cheese

Preparing great-tasting dishes is easy when they're complemented with this favorite ingredient.

Who doesn't love cheese? The problem (or so you might think) is that it isn't healthy, right? Wrong. It boasts generous amounts of calcium, protein, and riboflavin.

Let these delicious recipes inspire you to incorporate cheese into your healthy eating plan.

FRESH MOZZARELLA AND BASIL PIZZA

family favorite

Prep: 30 min., Rise: 20 min., Bake: 10 min.

If you don't have time to prepare fresh dough, some supermarkets sell uncooked pizza dough on request from the bakery department. Bake pizza on a pizza stone or heavy baking sheet that withstands high baking temperatures. (High heat makes the crust crispy.) For a lighter meal, enjoy half a pizza with a tossed salad drizzled with fresh lemon juice and olive oil.

- 1 (4-ounce) portion Pizza Dough
- ½ teaspoon extra-virgin olive oil
- 1 large plum tomato, thinly sliced
- 1 tablespoon sliced fresh basil
- 4 thin slices (2 ounces) fresh mozzarella
- 1 (1-ounce) slice country ham or smoked ham, cut into thin strips
- ¼ teaspoon pepper

PREHEAT oven to 450°. Shape Pizza Dough ball into a 6- to 8-inch circle on a lightly floured surface. (Dough doesn't need to be perfectly round.) Place dough on a piece of parchment paper. Fold up edges of dough, forming a 1-inch border. Brush oil evenly over dough using a pastry brush. (If you don't have a pastry brush, drizzle oil evenly over dough.)

COVER pizza dough circle loosely with plastic wrap, and let rise in a warm place (85°), free from drafts, 15 to 20 minutes. Heat pizza stone or heavy baking sheet 10 to 12 minutes in oven.

REMOVE and discard plastic wrap from dough. Layer tomato and next 3 ingredients evenly. Sprinkle with pepper. Carefully transfer dough on parchment paper to pizza stone.

BAKE at 450° for 10 minutes or until crust is golden. **MAKES** 1 pizza.

Pizza Dough:

freezeable • make ahead

Prep: 15 min.; Stand: 7 min.; Rise: 1 hr., 30 min.

Dough can be frozen up to 1 month. To freeze, wrap each portion in plastic wrap, and place in zip-top freezer bags. Thaw in refrigerator overnight, or let stand at room temperature 4 hours.

- 1 cup warm water (100° to 110°)
- ⅛ teaspoon sugar
- 1 (¼-ounce) envelope active dry yeast
- 3 to 3½ cups all-purpose flour
- 1½ teaspoons salt
- 1 tablespoon extra-virgin olive oil
- Vegetable cooking spray

STIR together 1 cup warm water and sugar in a 2-cup glass measuring cup. Sprinkle with yeast, and let stand 5 to 7 minutes or until mixture is bubbly; stir until blended.

PLACE 3 cups flour and salt in a food processor. With motor running, add yeast mixture and olive oil; process mixture until dough forms. (If dough is too sticky, add more flour, 2 tablespoons at a time.) Place dough in a large bowl coated with cooking spray; lightly coat dough with cooking spray. Cover with a clean cloth, and let rise in a warm place (85°), free from drafts, 1 hour or until doubled in bulk.

PUNCH dough down. Turn dough in bowl, and coat with cooking spray; cover with cloth, and let rise in a warm place (85°), free from drafts, 30 minutes or until doubled in bulk. Cut dough into 6 equal portions, shaping each portion into a 3-inch ball. **MAKES** 6 individual dough rounds.

JULIE JOHNSON
PONTE VEDRA BEACH, FLORIDA

Calories per pizza 508 (38% from fat); Fat 21.4g (sat 10.2g, mono 5.4g, poly 1.2g); Protein 23.4g; Carb 52.8g; Fiber 2.9g; Chol 60mg; Iron 4mg; Sodium 1063mg; Calcium 346mg

CRAB-AND-GOAT CHEESE POBLANOS WITH MANGO SALSA

Prep: 30 min., Broil: 10 min., Stand: 10 min., Bake: 30 min.

Rinse canned crabmeat to freshen the taste; drain well before combining with other ingredients. Goat cheese adds tangy flavor to this spicy-sweet dish.

8 poblano chile peppers
2 egg whites
1 (8-ounce) block part-skim mozzarella cheese, shredded
1 (4-ounce) package goat cheese
2 garlic cloves, minced
1 teaspoon ground cumin
½ to 1 teaspoon freshly ground black pepper
¼ to ½ teaspoon dried red pepper flakes
1 (6-ounce) can lump crabmeat, rinsed and drained
1 cup frozen whole kernel corn, thawed
⅓ cup chopped fresh cilantro
1 tablespoon fresh lime juice
Vegetable cooking spray
Mango Salsa
Garnish: chopped fresh cilantro

BROIL chile peppers on an aluminum foil-lined baking sheet 5 inches from heat 5 minutes on each side or until peppers look blistered.

PLACE peppers in a large zip-top freezer bag; seal and let stand 10 minutes to loosen skins. Peel peppers. Carefully cut peppers open lengthwise on 1 side, keeping stems intact; discard seeds. Set peppers aside.

PROCESS egg whites in a food processor until foamy. Add mozzarella cheese and next 5 ingredients, processing until blended.

PLACE cheese mixture in a large bowl. Stir in crabmeat and next 3 ingredients.

SPOON crabmeat mixture evenly into peppers, pinching cut edges together to seal. Arrange stuffed peppers, seam side down, in a 13- x 9-inch baking dish coated with cooking spray.

BAKE, covered, at 375° for 25 to 30 minutes or until thoroughly heated. Top with Mango Salsa, and garnish, if desired. **MAKES** 8 servings.

Mango Salsa:
fast fixin's
Prep: 15 min.

Purchase jarred mango, found in the produce section of the supermarket, if you can't find ripe mangoes.

1 mango, peeled and chopped
⅓ cup diced red onion
⅓ cup chopped fresh cilantro
1 tablespoon fresh lime juice

STIR together all ingredients. Cover and chill until ready to serve. **MAKES** about 1½ cups.

ELIZABETH CARRERA
SUWANEE, GEORGIA

Calories (including ¼ cup salsa) 229 (39% from fat); Fat 9.8g (sat 5.4g, mono 2.3g, poly 1.2g); Protein 17.5g; Carb 20.6g; Fiber 5g; Chol 36mg; Iron 2.7mg; Sodium 277mg; Calc 264mg

Regional Cheeses

Cheese-making in the South? That's right, y'all. Try some of our favorite purveyors.

■ **Cheesemakers, Inc.,** in Cleveland, Texas, offers Jaimito Mexican-style cheeses, such as Queso Quesadilla, a rich, melting-type cheese perfect for quesadillas. Visit **www.cheesemakers.com.**

■ **Fromagerie Belle Chèvre's** Fromage Blanc, a creamy white cheese, is delicious when served with pear or apple slices. Call 1-800-735-2238, or visit Fromagerie Belle Chèvre at 26910 Bethel Road in Elkmont, Alabama.

■ **Goat Lady Dairy** in Climax, North Carolina, makes a variety of goat cheeses. Chèvre Taleggio, a soft, pungent cheese, tastes divine with toasty bread and fresh figs. Call (336) 824-2163, or visit **www.goatladydairy.com.**

■ **Meadow Creek Dairy** in Galax, Virginia, sells its cheeses (such as Rosemary Jack) in stores throughout the state, or you can mail-order by calling (276) 236-2776 or 1-888-236-0622 or visiting **www.meadowcreekdairy.com.**

■ **Sweet Grass Dairy** in Thomasville, Georgia, offers Georgia Pecan Chèvre, which is just amazing with dried fruit and a glass of Chardonnay. Call (229) 227-0752, or visit **www.sweetgrassdairy.com.**

Veggie Sides

The fresh flavors of these dishes perk up any meal.

We tested these delicious vegetables in hopes of perfecting the ultimate spring menu. We're sure you'll love the results, which will complement any type of entrée you serve this season. The Super Special Spinach Pie and the Roasted Asparagus-and-Hazelnut Couscous can also be enjoyed as main courses with a salad and dessert of sliced fresh fruit.

SUPER SPECIAL SPINACH PIE

Prep: 10 min., Cook: 5 min., Bake: 25 min., Stand: 10 min.

This is a creamy quichelike pie without the crust.

- 2 (6-ounce) packages fresh baby spinach
- ¼ cup butter
- 3 tablespoons all-purpose flour
- ¼ teaspoon salt
- ¼ teaspoon pepper
- ¼ teaspoon garlic powder
- 4 large eggs, lightly beaten
- ¾ cup whipping cream
- ½ cup (2 ounces) shredded Parmesan cheese

RINSE spinach well; drain.
MELT butter in a large skillet over medium heat. Add spinach, and cook just until wilted.
COMBINE flour, salt, pepper, and garlic powder in a large bowl. Add spinach, eggs, whipping cream, and Parmesan cheese, stirring well. Pour mixture into a lightly greased 9-inch pieplate.
BAKE at 350° for 25 minutes or until pie is set. Let stand 10 minutes. Cut pie into wedges. **MAKES** 8 servings.

GLORIA T. BOVE
BETHLEHEM, PENNSYLVANIA

GREEN PEAS WITH CRISPY BACON

Prep: 20 min., Cook: 18 min.

Mint and orange really brighten this often under-rated legume, while the bacon lends a smoky flavor. When in season, use fresh sweet green peas.

- 2 smoked bacon slices
- 1 shallot, sliced
- ½ teaspoon grated orange rind
- ½ cup fresh orange juice
- ½ teaspoon pepper
- ¼ teaspoon salt
- 1 (16-ounce) bag frozen sweet green peas, thawed*
- 1 teaspoon butter or margarine
- 1 tablespoon chopped fresh mint
- Garnishes: fresh mint sprig, orange rind curl

COOK bacon in a medium skillet until crisp; remove bacon, and drain on paper towels, reserving 1 teaspoon bacon drippings in skillet. Crumble bacon, and set aside.
SAUTÉ shallot in hot bacon drippings over medium-high heat 2 minutes or until tender. Stir in orange rind, orange juice, pepper, and salt. Cook, stirring occasionally, 5 minutes or until reduced by half. Add peas, and cook 5 more minutes; stir in butter and mint.
TRANSFER peas to a serving dish, and sprinkle with crumbled bacon. Garnish, if desired. **MAKES** 6 servings.

*Substitute 3 cups shelled fresh sweet green peas for frozen, if desired. Cook peas in boiling water 5 minutes, and proceed with recipe.

DEBRA HOPPE
SLIDELL, LOUISIANA

ROASTED ASPARAGUS-AND-HAZELNUT COUSCOUS

Prep: 15 min., Bake: 10 min., Cook: 5 min., Stand: 10 min.

This makes a beautiful presentation alongside roast chicken or pork.

- 1 pound fresh asparagus
- 1 tablespoon olive oil
- 1 (14.5-ounce) can fat-free roasted garlic-seasoned chicken broth
- 1 teaspoon dried Italian seasoning
- 1 cup couscous, uncooked
- ⅓ cup chopped hazelnuts or pecans, toasted
- ½ teaspoon salt
- ¼ teaspoon pepper

SNAP off tough ends of asparagus, and cut into 1-inch pieces. Place in a 13- x 9-inch roasting pan. Drizzle with oil, tossing to coat.
BAKE at 450° for 8 to 10 minutes or just until asparagus is tender. Set aside, and keep warm.
BRING broth and Italian seasoning to a boil over medium-high heat. Stir in couscous; cover, remove from heat, and let stand 10 minutes.
ADD asparagus and hazelnuts to couscous, and toss. Stir in salt and pepper.
MAKES 6 servings.

NOTE: For testing purposes only, we used Swanson Seasoned Chicken Broth with Roasted Garlic.

CAMILLA V. SAULSBURY
BLOOMINGTON, INDIANA

Beef, Grilled Indoors

Plug in a countertop electric grill for our two speedy meals.

Don't let a rain shower or cold snap rule out a grilled supper. Try our recipes cooked on an indoor grill. (Grilling purists, before you faint, we've included outdoor grill directions.) We used a two-sided contact indoor electric grill, which cuts cooking time in half.

BEEF FAJITAS WITH PICO DE GALLO

family favorite

Prep: 5 min., Chill: 8 hrs., Grill: 10 min., Stand: 5 min.

    1 (8-ounce) bottle zesty Italian
        dressing
    3 tablespoons fajita seasoning
    2 (1-pound) flank steaks
    12 (6-inch) flour tortillas, warmed
    Shredded Cheddar cheese
    Pico de Gallo
    Garnishes: lime wedges, fresh
        cilantro sprigs

COMBINE Italian dressing and fajita seasoning in a shallow dish or zip-top freezer bag; add steak. Cover or seal, and chill 8 hours, turning occasionally. Remove steak from marinade, discarding marinade.

PREHEAT a two-sided contact indoor electric grill according to manufacturer's instructions on HIGH. Place steaks on food grate, close lid, and grill 10 minutes (medium rare) or to desired degree of doneness. Remove steaks, and let stand 5 minutes.

CUT steaks diagonally across the grain into very thin slices, and serve with tortillas, cheese, and Pico de Gallo. Garnish, if desired. **MAKES** 6 servings.

NOTE: When using an outdoor gas or charcoal grill, grill steaks, covered with grill lid, over medium-high heat (350° to 400°) for 8 minutes. Turn and grill 5 more minutes or to desired degree of doneness. Proceed as directed. For testing purposes only, we used McCormick Fajita Seasoning.

Pico de Gallo:

Prep: 25 min., Chill: 1 hr.

    1 pint grape tomatoes, chopped*
    1 green bell pepper, chopped
    1 red bell pepper, chopped
    1 avocado, peeled and chopped
    ½ medium-size red onion, chopped
    ½ cup chopped fresh cilantro
    1 garlic clove, pressed
    ¾ teaspoon salt
    ½ teaspoon ground cumin
    ½ teaspoon grated lime rind
    ¼ cup fresh lime juice

STIR together all ingredients; cover and chill 1 hour. **MAKES** about 3 cups.

*Substitute 2 large tomatoes, chopped, if desired.

ITALIAN SIRLOIN STEAKS

family favorite

Prep: 15 min., Chill: 2 hrs., Grill: 9 min.

Serve pasta and a salad to complete the meal.

    4 garlic cloves, pressed
    ¼ cup olive oil
    2 teaspoons dried basil
    2 teaspoons dried oregano
    2 teaspoons dried parsley
    1 teaspoon dried rosemary
    2 (¾-inch-thick) top sirloin steaks
        (about 2 pounds)
    1¼ teaspoons salt, divided
    1 teaspoon pepper

STIR together first 6 ingredients in a small bowl.

SPRINKLE steaks evenly with 1 teaspoon salt and pepper; rub with garlic mixture. Cover and chill steaks at least 2 hours.

SPRINKLE steaks evenly with remaining ¼ teaspoon salt.

PREHEAT a two-sided contact indoor electric grill according to manufacturer's instructions on HIGH. Place steaks on food grate, close lid; grill 7 to 9 minutes (medium rare) or to desired degree of doneness. Cut steaks in half. **MAKES** 4 servings.

NOTE: When using an outdoor gas or charcoal grill, grill steaks, covered with grill lid, over medium-high heat (350° to 400°) 7 minutes on each side or to desired degree of doneness.

 Cook's Notes

About Indoor Electric Grills
We tested our recipes with a George Foreman Jumbo Size Plus electric grill, which grilled all the beef called for in the recipe at one time. If you already own a smaller version of this appliance, cook the beef in batches, wrap in foil, and keep warm while the remainder cooks. Be sure to read the manufacturer's instruction book and safety guidelines first.

Not Your Average Cabbage

From sides to one-dish meals, this simple, adaptable vegetable covers it all.

If you remember cabbage as an over-cooked, smelly side dish from your childhood, take another look. With these easy, flavorful recipes, cabbage may even become a family favorite. Short cooking times help reduce odor and retain nutrients such as vitamins C and A, calcium, magnesium, and iron. Both green and red cabbages are found year-round in the grocery produce department and can be used interchangeably in recipes. Look for well-rounded, even-colored spheres that are heavy for their size. Packages of shredded or chopped cabbage are great alternatives to whole heads and save time too.

Cabbage With Garlic

Prep: 5 min., Cook: 10 min., Bake: 25 min.

- 1 small cabbage (about 2 pounds)
- 6 garlic cloves, finely sliced
- 3 tablespoons olive oil
- ½ cup chicken broth
- 1 teaspoon coarse or kosher salt
- Freshly ground pepper to taste

REMOVE outside leaves and stalk from cabbage; cut into 4 wedges.

SAUTÉ garlic in hot oil in an ovenproof skillet over medium heat 1 to 2 minutes or until golden. Add cabbage to skillet, cut sides down; cook 5 minutes. Turn to other cut sides, and cook 2 to 3 minutes. Stir in broth, and sprinkle evenly with salt.

BAKE at 350° for 20 to 25 minutes or until crisp-tender. Sprinkle evenly with pepper. Serve immediately. **MAKES** 4 to 5 servings.

CAROLINE W. KENNEDY
LIGHTHOUSE POINT, FLORIDA

Spicy Chicken Salad With Cabbage Wraps

Prep: 20 min., Cook: 10 min., Chill: 30 min.

Cabbage leaves are a great substitute for bread to hold the chicken salad.

- 1 pound skinned and boned chicken breasts, cut into large cubes
- 1½ tablespoons thinly sliced fresh ginger
- ½ red onion, thinly sliced
- 4 green onions, thinly sliced
- 3½ tablespoons Asian fish sauce
- 1 teaspoon grated lime rind
- ¼ cup fresh lime juice
- 1 small jalapeño pepper, minced
- 2 teaspoons sesame oil
- ¾ teaspoon ground red pepper
- ½ cup dry-roasted unsalted peanuts, coarsely chopped
- 1 small green cabbage, cut into wedges
- Toppings: baby carrot slices, cucumber slices, radish slices

PROCESS chicken breasts in a food processor until the consistency of ground beef.

COOK chicken in a lightly greased large skillet over medium-high heat 10 minutes or until done, stirring often. Drain and place in a large bowl.

CUT sliced ginger into thin strips.

STIR ginger and next 8 ingredients into chicken. Cover and chill 15 to 30 minutes or until ready to serve, stirring in peanuts during last 5 minutes.

SPOON chicken salad onto individual cabbage wedge leaves. Serve cabbage wraps with desired toppings. **MAKES** 4 to 6 servings.

Cabbage Stir-Fry

fast fixin's

Prep: 20 min., Cook: 10 min.

The beautiful color and fresh flavor of this dish will entice even picky eaters. Chopped fresh cilantro and lime juice give it a bit of a Southwestern kick.

- 2 tablespoons vegetable oil
- ½ red cabbage, thinly sliced
- 1 green bell pepper, thinly sliced
- 1 small onion, thinly sliced
- ¾ cup chopped fresh cilantro
- 1 tablespoon lime juice
- 1 teaspoon salt
- ½ teaspoon pepper

HEAT oil in a large skillet or wok at high heat 3 to 4 minutes. Add cabbage, bell pepper, and onion, and stir-fry 7 to 10 minutes or until crisp-tender or to desired degree of doneness. Stir in cilantro and remaining ingredients. **MAKES** 4 to 6 servings.

SPICY CABBAGE STIR-FRY: Stir in 3 tablespoons jalapeño jelly with cabbage, bell pepper, and onion. Proceed as directed.

SANDRA KIMMEY
KERRVILLE, TEXAS

SPICY COLESLAW REUBENS

fast fixin's

Prep: 15 min., Cook: 13 min.

- 1 (10-ounce) package finely shredded cabbage
- 4 green onions, sliced
- 1 teaspoon olive oil
- ½ cup Thousand Island dressing
- 3 tablespoons spicy brown mustard
- 12 sourdough sandwich bread slices
- 6 (1-ounce) Monterey Jack cheese with peppers slices
- 1 pound thinly sliced corned beef

SAUTÉ cabbage and green onions in hot oil in a large nonstick skillet over medium-high heat 3 to 5 minutes or until cabbage is wilted. Remove from heat, and stir in dressing.

SPREAD mustard evenly on 1 side of 6 bread slices. Layer evenly with cheese slices, corned beef, and cabbage mixture. Top with remaining bread slices.

COOK sandwiches on a lightly greased nonstick griddle or skillet 3 to 4 minutes on each side or until golden brown. **MAKES** 6 servings.

BETTY MAE STAFFORD
GULFPORT, MISSISSIPPI

Flavored Iced Tea

As any Southerner knows, there's nothing more refreshing than a glass of iced tea. Give this popular drink a special twist with these flavorful ideas. Fresh mint sprigs are steeped to create the soothing taste of Mint Tea Punch, while cinnamon and cloves add a kick to Cranberry Tea. Fruit juices make each recipe uniquely delicious.

STRAWBERRY TEA SLUSH

Prep: 15 min., Steep: 5 min., Chill: 1 hr.

- 2 cups boiling water
- 4 regular-size tea bags
- 1½ cups frozen strawberries
- 1 (6-ounce) can frozen lemonade concentrate
- 1 cup ice cubes
- ¼ cup powdered sugar

POUR 2 cups boiling water over tea bags. Cover and steep 5 minutes. Remove tea bags. Cover and chill at least 1 hour.
PROCESS chilled tea, frozen strawberries, and remaining ingredients in a blender until smooth and slushy. Serve immediately. **MAKES** 1½ quarts.

BEBE MAY
PENSACOLA, FLORIDA

MINT TEA PUNCH

fast fixin's

Prep: 10 min., Steep: 10 min.

- 5 cups boiling water
- 5 regular-size tea bags
- 8 mint sprigs, crushed
- 1 cup sugar
- 1 (12-ounce) can frozen orange juice concentrate, thawed and undiluted
- 1 (12-ounce) can frozen lemonade concentrate, thawed and undiluted
- 6¾ cups water
- Garnishes: fresh mint sprigs, lemon slices

POUR 5 cups boiling water over tea bags; add 8 mint sprigs. Cover and steep 5 minutes. Stir in sugar, and steep 5 more minutes.
REMOVE tea bags. Pour tea through a fine wire-mesh strainer into a pitcher, discarding mint sprigs. Stir in concentrates and 6¾ cups water. Cover and chill. Serve over ice. Garnish, if desired. **MAKES** 3½ quarts.

LORI COOK
WICHITA FALLS, TEXAS

PASSION TEA

Prep: 10 min., Steep: 3 min., Chill: 1 hr.

Orange pekoe tea is not flavored with orange. The name actually refers to the grade of tea, with orange pekoe consisting of leaves that are smaller than medium-size, coarser pekoe leaves.

- 6¼ cups boiling water
- 3 family-size orange pekoe tea bags
- ⅓ cup sugar
- 1 cup cranberry juice cocktail
- 1 cup frozen passion-fruit juice concentrate, thawed and undiluted

POUR 6¼ cups boiling water over tea bags. Cover and steep 3 minutes. Remove tea bags. Stir in sugar until dissolved. Cover and chill 1 hour.
STIR together chilled tea, cranberry juice, and juice concentrate. Serve over ice. **MAKES** 2 quarts.

M. B. QUESENBERRY
DUGSPUR, VIRGINIA

CRANBERRY TEA

Prep: 5 min., Steep: 3 min., Chill: 1 hr.

- 1 quart water
- 12 whole cloves
- 2 (3-inch) cinnamon sticks
- ⅓ cup sugar
- 4 regular-size tea bags
- 1 (12-ounce) can frozen cranberry juice concentrate, thawed and undiluted

BRING first 4 ingredients to a boil in a large saucepan. Pour boiling mixture over tea bags; cover and steep 3 minutes. Remove tea bags. Pour tea through a fine wire-mesh strainer into a pitcher, discarding spices. Stir in juice concentrate. Cover and chill at least 1 hour. Serve over ice. **MAKES** about 1 quart.

SUZAN L. WIENER
SPRING HILL, FLORIDA

from our kitchen

Serving With Style

Creating a serving basket from refrigerated breadstick dough may look complicated, but it's surprisingly simple. In fact, when we were planning the photography for our spring salad story on page 50, Senior Photo Stylist Cindy Manning Barr suggested that we make two baskets and use one as a lid. Just follow these instructions and use the photos to make one basket—it's as easy as pie!

Unroll the dough from 2 (11-ounce) packages of refrigerated breadsticks, and separate at perforations. Reserve and set aside 6 strips. Gently press and stretch each of the remaining 18 strips to a length of 12 inches.

Wrap the outside of a 4-quart stainless steel mixing bowl with nonstick aluminum foil, and invert onto a lightly greased baking sheet. Arrange strips in a lattice pattern over the top and sides of the bowl, trimming excess as needed. (To weave a lattice pattern, place 4 or 5 strips of dough across the bowl in one direction; fold back alternating strips as each crisscross strip is added [photo 1].)

Whisk together 1 large egg and 1 tablespoon water; brush lightly over strips, reserving remaining egg mixture.

Roll each of the 6 reserved strips into a 20-inch rope; pinch 3 of the ropes together at 1 end to seal, and braid. Repeat procedure with remaining 3 ropes. Gently press the 2 braided ropes around the rim of the bowl, pinching together at both ends to seal (photo 2). Brush lightly with reserved egg mixture, discarding any remaining mixture.

Bake at 375° for 30 minutes or until evenly browned. Shield top of bowl with aluminum foil after 20 minutes to prevent overbrowning. Remove from oven, and cool completely on a wire rack. Gently remove basket from bowl. (The inside of the basket will be pale in color.)

If you plan on eating the basket, it's best prepared the same day. If not, prepare it up to a week ahead, and store in a cool, dry place until ready to use.

NOTE: We used Reynolds Release Non-Stick Aluminum Foil. It's also terrific for lining baking dishes and pans, or for covering casseroles.

A Light Side of Pasta

The classic version of Fettuccine Alfredo is quick and easy to make, but it's loaded with fat and calories. In experimenting with healthier options, we discovered a delicious light alternative that combines a rich and creamy frozen pasta with fresh spring vegetables. Prepare and sauté the additional ingredients while the pasta is in the microwave, and this dish is ready for the table in less than 15 minutes. Here's the recipe.

Fettuccini Primavera: Microwave 3 (9.25-ounce) packages of Stouffer's Lean Cuisine Fettuccini Alfredo according to package directions. Sauté 3 ounces chopped prosciutto and 1 (8-ounce) package sliced fresh mushrooms in 2 teaspoons hot oil in a large nonstick skillet over medium-high heat 3 to 5 minutes or until the mushrooms are tender. Add ½ cup white wine, stirring to loosen particles from bottom of skillet. Add ½ pound fresh asparagus, trimmed and cut into 2-inch pieces, and 1 cup baby green peas. Cook, stirring often, 3 minutes or until vegetables are tender. Stir in the hot Fettuccini Alfredo and ½ cup shredded Parmesan cheese. Serve immediately. If desired, garnish with additional steamed asparagus and shredded Parmesan cheese. Three ounces baked ham and ½ cup reduced-sodium chicken broth may be substituted for the prosciutto and white wine. Makes 4 to 6 servings. Prep: 10 min., Cook: 8 min.

A Taste of Summer

The spring months are peak season for fresh Supersweet Corn (**www.freshsupersweetcorn.com**). Yellow, white, and bicolor varieties are harvested year-round in Florida, almost year-round in Georgia, and during warmer months in Alabama. The crisp, plump kernels are incredibly sweet and tender, and they cook in mere minutes.

April

In the Courtyard of Commander's Palace

Enjoy brunch with the grand dames of New Orleans.

Sunday Brunch

Serves 8

Rémoulade Sauce and shrimp

Garden District Eggs with asparagus

Pain Perdu

Bloody Marys

For Ella and Dottie Brennan, owners of New Orleans' famed Commander's Palace, the restaurant's courtyard is an ideal spot for a Sunday brunch with friends. Friends welcome the opportunity to share delicious food and conversation with the Brennan sisters.

Ella worked with her family at Brennan's for 28 years before moving to Commander's Palace 30 years ago. Dottie joined her big sister after the Korean War, and the two have worked together ever since. Now their niece, Lally, and Ella's daughter, Ti (pronounced Tee) Martin, oversee the day-to-day operations of the restaurant.

"The ladies," as they are affectionately called, ensure that Commander's is consistently named one of the best restaurants in the world for both food and service.

Serve your own New Orleans-style brunch with these recipes and those on page 68. Most are adapted from *Commander's Kitchen* (Broadway, 2000) by Ti Adelaide Martin and Jamie Shannon.

RÉMOULADE SAUCE

chef recipe • make ahead

Prep: 20 min.

Make this sauce up to several days ahead to serve with peeled, boiled shrimp. Leftover sauce will keep in the refrigerator for 2 weeks and is delicious on sandwiches, chicken or crab cakes, or salad.

- 6 garlic cloves, peeled
- 3 celery ribs, chopped
- 1/3 cup white vinegar
- 1/2 cup egg substitute
- 1/4 cup ketchup
- 1/4 cup prepared horseradish
- 1/4 cup Creole mustard
- 1/4 cup yellow mustard
- 2 tablespoons mild paprika
- 2 tablespoons Worcestershire sauce
- 1 tablespoon hot sauce (or to taste)
- 1 teaspoon ground red pepper
- 1 1/2 cups vegetable oil
- 6 green onions, sliced
- Kosher salt and black pepper to taste

PROCESS first 12 ingredients in a blender or food processor until smooth. With blender running, pour oil in a slow, steady stream until thickened. Stir in green onions, salt, and black pepper; cover and chill until ready to serve. **MAKES** 5 cups.

RECIPE ADAPTED FROM
COMMANDER'S KITCHEN
BROADWAY, 2000

GARDEN DISTRICT EGGS

chef recipe • make ahead

Prep: 1 hr., Cook: 1 hr., Chill: 8 hrs.

You don't need a platoon of chefs to prepare this recipe, so don't be intimidated. Use our timeline on facing page to produce a dish that's sure to dazzle. Steamed asparagus makes a colorful accompaniment to this delicious dish. *(pictured on page 76)*

- 1 cup butter
- 1 medium onion, finely chopped
- 1 medium-size green bell pepper, finely chopped
- 1 medium-size red bell pepper, finely chopped
- 7 garlic cloves, minced
- 1/2 pound wild mushrooms, sliced
- 1 pound fresh mushrooms, sliced
- 1 (16-ounce) French bread loaf, cut into 1-inch cubes
- 4 large eggs, lightly beaten
- 1 cup fine, dry breadcrumbs
- 1 (32-ounce) container chicken broth
- 1/3 cup each of chopped fresh basil, thyme, and oregano
- 2 bunches green onions, chopped
- 1 teaspoon salt
- 1 teaspoon pepper
- Vegetable cooking spray
- 2 (6-ounce) packages fresh baby spinach
- 1 tablespoon water
- 16 poached eggs
- Tasso Hollandaise
- Steamed asparagus (optional)
- Garnishes: finely chopped red bell pepper, chopped fresh parsley

MELT butter in a Dutch oven over medium heat. Add onion, peppers, and garlic; sauté 10 minutes or until tender. **ADD** mushrooms; cook 30 minutes or until liquid evaporates. Stir in bread cubes, lightly beaten eggs, and bread-crumbs. Gradually stir in chicken broth until mixture resembles stuffing. Stir in herbs, green onions, salt, and pepper. Cover and chill 8 hours.

SHAPE mixture into 16 patties, using about ¾ cup mixture for each patty. Cook in batches on a nonstick griddle or a large nonstick skillet coated with cooking spray over medium-high heat 4 minutes on each side or until golden. Place cakes on a wire rack in a jellyroll pan, and keep warm in a 200° oven.

COOK spinach and 1 tablespoon water in a large nonstick skillet over medium heat 5 minutes or until wilted, stirring once; drain well. Place ¼ cup spinach on each of 8 serving plates; top with two mushroom cakes. Top with 2 poached eggs and Tasso Hollandaise. Serve with asparagus, if desired. Garnish, if desired. **MAKES** 8 servings.

Tasso Hollandaise:

Prep: 10 min., Cook: 12 min.

- **8 egg yolks**
- **¼ cup fresh lemon juice**
- **2 tablespoons white wine**
- **2 cups butter, melted**
- **½ teaspoon salt**
- **⅛ teaspoon ground red pepper**
- **½ cup finely chopped tasso ham (about 6 ounces)***

WHISK yolks in top of a double boiler; gradually whisk in lemon juice and wine. Place over hot water (do not boil). Add butter, ⅓ cup at a time, whisking until smooth; whisk in salt and red pepper. Cook, whisking constantly, 10 minutes or until thickened and a thermometer registers 160°. Stir in tasso. Serve immediately. **MAKES** 3 cups.

*Substitute ½ cup diced cooked andouille sausage, if desired.

KITCHEN EXPRESS: Prepare 2 (0.9-ounce) packages hollandaise sauce mix according to package directions; stir in tasso. For testing purposes only, we used Knorr Hollandaise Sauce Mix.

RECIPE FROM CHEF TORY MCPHAIL
OF COMMANDER'S PALACE

Garden District Eggs Timeline

We've streamlined this dish into several make-ahead steps. If you're reluctant to poach the eggs, you can scramble or fry them instead.

Two days ahead:
- Chop the vegetables and mushrooms, place in zip-top plastic bags, and chill.
- Cube the bread, and store in a zip-top plastic bag.

One day ahead:
- Make mushroom cake mixture, and chill.

Day of brunch:
- Cook mushroom cakes up to 1 hour ahead; cover loosely, and keep warm in a 200° oven.
- Make the Tasso Hollandaise; keep warm in a thermos or very clean insulated coffee carafe.
- Steam the asparagus, if serving.
- Cook the spinach. Cover and keep warm.
- Poach the eggs. To poach eggs, pour water to a depth of 3 inches in a large saucepan. Bring to a boil; reduce heat, and maintain at a light simmer. Add ½ teaspoon white vinegar. Break eggs, 1 at a time, and slip into water as close as possible to the surface of the water. Simmer 3 to 5 minutes or until done. Remove eggs with a slotted spoon. Trim edges, if desired.
- Assemble the egg dish; serve asparagus on the side.

PAIN PERDU

chef recipe

Prep: 20 min., Stand: 30 min., Cook: 35 min.

The French call French toast *pain perdu*, or "lost bread," because it's made from stale bread. Whipping cream gives Pain Perdu its rich flavor. *(pictured on page 77)*

- **2 (16-ounce) French bread loaves**
- **8 large eggs**
- **4 cups whipping cream**
- **1 cup sugar**
- **½ to 1 tablespoon ground cinnamon**
- **1½ teaspoons ground nutmeg**
- **4 teaspoons vanilla extract**
- **1½ cups Champagne**
- **2 cups cane syrup**
- **4 cups raspberries and blueberries**
- **4 tablespoons cream cheese (optional)**
- **Garnish: powdered sugar**

CUT bread into 24 (¾-inch-thick) diagonal slices.

WHISK together eggs and next 5 ingredients until well blended.

PLACE bread slices in a 13- x 9-inch baking dish; pour egg mixture evenly over slices. Let stand 30 minutes or until liquid is absorbed.

REMOVE bread slices from egg mixture, letting excess drip off. Cook bread slices, in batches, in a lightly greased nonstick skillet or griddle over medium-high heat 2 minutes on each side or until golden.

PLACE bread slices on baking sheets; keep warm in a 200° oven.

COOK Champagne in a large saucepan over high heat until reduced by half. Gradually stir in syrup; cook over low heat until blended and warm.

ARRANGE bread slices on serving plates; top with raspberries, blueberries, and, if desired, cream cheese. Drizzle bread slices evenly with syrup mixture. Garnish, if desired. **MAKES** 8 to 12 servings.

RECIPE FROM CHEF TORY MCPHAIL
OF COMMANDER'S PALACE

Bloody Marys

chef recipe • fast fixin's

Prep: 10 min.

Bartenders at Commander's Palace skewer the garnish on a stick of sugarcane, but a wooden skewer works too. *(pictured on page 77)*

- **1½ cups chilled vodka**
- **8 teaspoons prepared horseradish**
- **8 teaspoons Worcestershire sauce**
- **14 drops hot sauce**
- **4 cups vegetable or tomato juice**
- **Garnishes: pickled okra, cherry peppers**

WHISK together first 5 ingredients in a large pitcher until well blended. Place ice cubes in 8 old-fashioned glasses, filling ⅔ full. Pour mixture evenly into glasses. Garnish, if desired. **MAKES** 8 servings.

NOTE: For testing purposes only, we used Crystal Hot Sauce.

RECIPE ADAPTED FROM
COMMANDER'S KITCHEN
BROADWAY, 2000

Cook's Notes

"Meeting and working with the Brennan women was a real thrill for me," says Senior Writer **Donna Florio**. "They are legends in New Orleans and in the restaurant business nationally. Despite their fame, they are all lovely, genuine, funny women. Ella and Dottie, who live together next door to Commander's Palace, get to enjoy 'room service' from one of the world's best restaurants. Naturally, they don't bother to cook much. In fact, Dottie jokes that she and Ella could nail their kitchen door closed, and no one would be the wiser! They know absolutely everyone in town and could probably offer a complete oral history of everything that's happened in New Orleans in the last 50 years, and who was involved."

New Orleans Favorites

The chefs at Commander's Palace are experts at making haute Creole cuisine.

Catfish Pecan With Lemon-Thyme-Pecan Butter

chef recipe

Prep: 25 min., Cook: 28 min.

This is one of our favorite catfish dishes ever.

- **1½ cups pecan halves, divided**
- **¾ cup all-purpose flour**
- **1½ teaspoons Creole seasoning**
- **1 large egg**
- **1 cup milk**
- **8 (6-ounce) catfish, flounder, redfish, or bass fillets**
- **1 cup butter, divided**
- **2 large lemons, halved**
- **1 tablespoon Worcestershire sauce**
- **6 large fresh thyme sprigs**
- **Kosher salt and pepper to taste**
- **Garnishes: fresh thyme, lemon slices**

PROCESS ¾ cup pecans, flour, and 1 teaspoon Creole seasoning in a food processor until finely ground; place pecan mixture in a large shallow bowl. **WHISK** together egg and milk in a large bowl, and set aside.

SPRINKLE both sides of fillets evenly with remaining ½ teaspoon Creole seasoning. **DIP** fillets in egg mixture, draining off excess; dredge in pecan mixture, coating both sides, and shake off excess.

MELT 2 tablespoons butter in a large nonstick skillet over medium heat until butter starts to bubble. Place 2 fillets in skillet; cook 2 to 3 minutes on each side or until golden. Drain on a wire rack in a jellyroll pan; keep warm in a 200° oven. Wipe skillet clean; repeat procedure with remaining fillets.

WIPE skillet clean. Melt remaining ½ cup butter in skillet over high heat; add remaining ¾ cup pecans, and cook, stirring occasionally, 2 to 3 minutes or until toasted. Squeeze juice from lemon halves into skillet; place halves, cut side down, in skillet. Stir in Worcestershire sauce, thyme sprigs, salt, and pepper, and cook 30 seconds or until thyme wilts and becomes very aromatic. Discard lemon halves and wilted thyme.

PLACE fish on a serving platter; spoon pecan mixture over fish. Garnish, if desired. **MAKES** 8 servings.

RECIPE ADAPTED FROM
COMMANDER'S KITCHEN
BROADWAY, 2000

Iced Coffee

chef recipe

Prep: 5 min.

Make a batch of concentrate to keep in the refrigerator for hot or cold coffee. If you purchase coffee beans, grind them to percolator coarseness.

- **¼ cup Coffee Concentrate**
- **¼ cup water**
- **Milk (optional)**
- **Sugar (optional)**

STIR together ¼ cup each of Coffee Concentrate and water, and, if desired, stir in desired amounts of milk and sugar. Serve over ice. **MAKES** ½ cup.

Coffee Concentrate:

Prep: 30 min., Stand: 12 hrs.

- **½ pound ground coffee with chicory or dark roast ground coffee**
- **7 cups cold water**
- **1½ teaspoons vanilla extract**

STIR together ground coffee and 7 cups cold water in a pitcher until all ground coffee is wet; let coffee mixture stand 12 hours at room temperature.

POUR coffee mixture through a large fine wire-mesh strainer, discarding grounds. Clean strainer; place a coffee filter or double layer of cheesecloth in strainer, and pour coffee mixture through lined strainer. Add vanilla; cover and store in the refrigerator up to 1 month. **MAKES** about 1¾ quarts.

RECIPE ADAPTED FROM
COMMANDER'S KITCHEN
BROADWAY, 2000

Appetizers in a Snap

If you don't have all day to make tonight's nibbles, these scrumptious recipes are for you.

Don't cancel tonight's gathering just because you're short on time. These easy recipes call for a short prep or can be made ahead. Most start with stuff you already have, so check your pantry and fridge and start stirring.

LAYERED CRABMEAT SPREAD

make ahead

Prep: 20 min., Chill: 20 min.

For a lighter version, use ⅓-less-fat cream cheese, light mayonnaise, and 2% reduced-fat Monterey Jack cheese. This appetizer requires no cooking and can be prepared ahead. Try it with assorted crackers and cool, crunchy vegetables.

- 1 (8-ounce) package cream cheese, softened
- 2 tablespoons lemon juice
- 1 tablespoon mayonnaise
- ½ teaspoon seasoned salt
- ½ teaspoon lemon pepper
- ¼ teaspoon Worcestershire sauce
- ¾ cup cocktail sauce
- 1 (16-ounce) container lump crabmeat, drained
- 2 cups (8 ounces) shredded Monterey Jack cheese
- 3 green onions, chopped
- ½ green bell pepper, chopped
- ½ cup sliced ripe olives
- Assorted crackers and fresh vegetables

BEAT cream cheese at medium speed with an electric mixer until smooth; add lemon juice and next 4 ingredients, beating until blended. Spoon mixture into a 9-inch serving dish. Cover and chill at least 20 minutes.
SPREAD cocktail sauce evenly over cream cheese mixture. Top with crabmeat; sprinkle with cheese, green onions, bell pepper, and ripe olives. Serve spread with crackers and fresh vegetables. **MAKES** 12 to 15 appetizer servings.

VELDA KAY HUGHES
GREENVILLE, SOUTH CAROLINA

ROASTED RED PEPPER-FETA CROSTINI

Prep: 30 min., Bake: 37 min.

- 1 garlic bulb
- 5 tablespoons olive oil, divided
- 1 (15.8-ounce) can great Northern beans, rinsed and drained
- ½ (16-ounce) jar roasted red bell peppers, drained
- 1 tablespoon red wine vinegar
- ½ teaspoon salt
- ½ teaspoon pepper
- 1 (4-ounce) package crumbled feta cheese, divided
- 1 French baguette

CUT off pointed end of garlic bulb; place garlic on a piece of aluminum foil, and drizzle with 1 tablespoon oil. Fold foil to seal.
BAKE at 425° for 30 minutes; cool. Squeeze pulp from garlic.
PROCESS garlic pulp, 2 tablespoons oil, beans, and next 4 ingredients in a food processor until smooth. Add half of cheese, and pulse 5 or 6 times or until combined.
CUT bread, at a diagonal, into 24 (¼-inch) slices. Arrange on a baking sheet; brush evenly with remaining 2 tablespoons oil.
SPREAD 2 tablespoons bean mixture onto 1 side of each bread slice, and sprinkle bread slices with remaining feta cheese.
BAKE at 350° for 5 to 7 minutes. **MAKES** about 12 appetizer servings.

CHILI CON QUESO

fast fixin's

Prep: 5 min., Cook: 15 min.

Dotty says chicken broth mellows the flavor of this cheese dip and gives it a smoother texture. Keep warm in a 1-quart stockpot or fondue pot.

- 1 small onion, chopped
- ½ to ¾ cup chicken broth, divided
- 1 (16-ounce) loaf pasteurized prepared cheese product, cubed
- 1 (10-ounce) can tomatoes and green chiles, drained
- Tortilla chips

COOK onion in 1 tablespoon chicken broth in a large saucepan over low heat 5 minutes or until tender, stirring often. Stir in cheese and tomatoes until cheese begins to melt; stir in remaining chicken broth, ¼ cup at a time, until dip is desired consistency. Serve with tortilla chips. **MAKES** about 4 cups.

NOTE: For testing purposes only, we used Velveeta for pasteurized prepared cheese product.

RECIPE ADAPTED FROM
DOTTY GRIFFITH'S
THE TEXAS HOLIDAY COOKBOOK
GULF PUBLISHING, 1997

LIMA BEAN-AND-FRESH HERB PÂTÉ

make ahead

Prep: 15 min., Chill: 8 hrs.

This spread is nicely flavored with fresh herbs. Be sure to chill it overnight. Serve with crackers or crusty bread.

- **1 (15-ounce) can lima beans, rinsed and drained**
- **2 garlic cloves**
- **1 cup ricotta cheese**
- **3 tablespoons fresh lemon juice**
- **2 tablespoons extra-virgin olive oil**
- **¾ teaspoon salt**
- **¼ teaspoon pepper**
- **2 tablespoons chopped fresh chives**
- **2 tablespoons chopped fresh parsley**
- **2 to 3 teaspoons chopped fresh dill**

PROCESS first 7 ingredients in a food processor until smooth, stopping to scrape down sides. Add chives, parsley, and dill; process until combined.

SPOON mixture into a lightly greased 2-cup bowl lined with plastic wrap. Cover and chill 8 hours.

UNMOLD pâté, discarding plastic wrap; place on a serving dish. **MAKES** about 2 cups.

BROWN SUGAR BACON

family favorite

Prep: 5 min., Bake: 25 min., Stand: 3 min.

Try these sweet-salty strips in a BLT, a grilled cheese-apple slice sandwich, or crumble over salads. We recommend using only the oven for this recipe because we couldn't get the same results in the microwave.

- **1 pound thick bacon slices**
- **1½ cups firmly packed dark brown sugar**

ARRANGE bacon in a single layer in an aluminum foil-lined broiler pan. Cover evenly with brown sugar.

BAKE at 425° for 25 minutes or until done. Quarter each slice; let stand 2 to 3 minutes or until sugar is set. **MAKES** 12 servings.

BLACK PEPPER-BROWN SUGAR BACON: Press ¼ cup cracked black pepper onto bacon slices before covering with brown sugar. Proceed with recipe as directed.

JACKIE SINEATH
SAFETY HARBOR, FLORIDA

Taste of the South

Refrigerator Rolls

Okay, let's admit it—Southerners bake the best homemade breads, hands down. We take the process seriously, and these yeast rolls are worthy of being Sunday dinner's featured attraction.

If you consider making yeast bread a chore, this recipe will change your mind. The beauty of our rolls is you don't have to bake them all the same day. Simply make the dough, and keep it tightly covered in the refrigerator for up to five days. Pinch off the amount you need, and save the rest for later.

This recipe is convenient and absolutely scrumptious. You owe it to yourself to make these rolls. Trust us, you'll be glad you did.

What's in a Name?

Icebox Rolls get their name from a large container used for cooling many years before the advent of the electric refrigerator. Similar to today's ice chests, this insulated unit held a huge block of ice to keep foods cold. The modern refrigerator is still sometimes nostalgically referred to as an icebox.

ICEBOX ROLLS

family favorite • make ahead

Prep: 15 min.; Stand: 35 min.; Chill: 12 hrs.; Rise: 1 hr., 30 min.; Bake: 15 min. per batch

In some editions of the April 2004 issue, the method of combining the shortening and water was incorrect. The following recipe has been corrected.

- **1 cup boiling water**
- **½ cup shortening**
- **1 (¼-ounce) envelope active dry yeast**
- **½ cup warm water (100° to 110°)**
- **1 teaspoon sugar**
- **2 large eggs**
- **½ cup sugar**
- **1 teaspoon salt**
- **5 cups bread flour**
- **¼ to ½ cup butter, melted**

POUR 1 cup boiling water over shortening in a large bowl, stirring to melt shortening. Let stand 30 minutes or until completely cooled.

STIR together yeast, ½ cup warm water, and 1 teaspoon sugar in a glass measuring cup, and let mixture stand 5 minutes.

BEAT eggs at medium speed using a heavy-duty stand mixer; add ½ cup sugar and 1 teaspoon salt. Add shortening mixture and yeast mixture. Reduce speed to low, and gradually add 5 cups flour, beating until blended.

COVER and chill dough 12 hours or up to 5 days.

TURN dough out on a lightly floured surface, and roll to ¼-inch thickness. Cut with a lightly floured 2½-inch round cutter. Make a crease across the middle of each dough round with a knife, and fold in half; gently press edges to seal. Place rolls on lightly greased baking sheets.

COVER and let rise in a warm place (85°), free from drafts, 1½ hours or until doubled in bulk. Brush rolls evenly with melted butter.

BAKE at 400° for 15 minutes or until golden brown. Brush again with melted butter, if desired. **MAKES** 3 to 4 dozen.

Front Porch Gathering

Choose these simple, mostly make-ahead recipes for a relaxed get-together.

Keep It Casual

Serves 6

Zesty Feta Dip

Marinated Olives and Peppers

Crunchy Tuna-and-Almond Salad with crackers or multigrain bread

Peanutty Spicy Noodle Salad

Banana Pudding With Sugar Biscuits

Iced Hibiscus Tea

ZESTY FETA DIP

chef recipe • make ahead

Prep: 15 min., Bake: 30 min., Chill: 2 hrs.

Also try this as a creamy, bold spread for rolled-up sandwiches made with flour tortillas.

- **1 garlic bulb**
- **1 tablespoon olive oil**
- **4 cups (16 ounces) crumbled feta cheese**
- **⅔ cup plain yogurt**
- **½ cup sour cream**
- **¼ teaspoon salt**
- **¼ teaspoon pepper**
- **Garnish: chopped green onions**
- **Miniature pita rounds**
- **Fresh sugar snap peas, baby carrots, radishes, broccoli and cauliflower florets, cucumber slices, green onions**

CUT off pointed end of garlic; place garlic on piece of aluminum foil, and drizzle with oil. Fold foil to seal.
BAKE at 425° for 30 minutes; cool. Squeeze pulp from garlic cloves.
PROCESS garlic pulp, cheese, and next 4 ingredients in a food processor until smooth, stopping to scrape down sides. Cover and chill at least 2 hours (mixture will thicken as it chills). Garnish, if desired. Serve with miniature pita rounds and raw vegetables. **MAKES** 3 cups.

CHEF BART HOSMER
SPOODLES AT DISNEY BOARDWALK RESORT

MARINATED OLIVES AND PEPPERS

make ahead

Prep: 15 min., Stand: 1 hr.

This flavorful combination can be stored in the refrigerator up to 1 week; let stand at room temperature 1 hour before serving.

- **1 cup olive oil**
- **½ cup red wine vinegar**
- **1 garlic clove, minced**
- **1 tablespoon chopped fresh or ¾ teaspoon dried oregano**
- **½ teaspoon coarsely ground pepper**
- **¼ teaspoon ground cinnamon**
- **1 (12-ounce) jar colossal pimiento-stuffed olives, drained**
- **1 (12-ounce) jar roasted red bell peppers, drained and sliced**
- **2 tablespoons small capers, drained**
- **1 (10-ounce) jar kalamata olives, drained**

WHISK together first 6 ingredients.
LAYER 1 (1½-quart) jar or 2-quart bowl evenly with stuffed olives and next 3 ingredients. Pour marinade over olive mixture in jar. Tightly seal jar or cover bowl, and let stand 1 hour before serving. **MAKES** 6 cups.

❝ Cook's Notes ❞

Associate Foods Editor **Joy Zacharia** offers several savory ideas.

- ▪ "**Zesty Feta Dip** is also good as a dip for boiled shrimp," says Joy. "If it's too thick, dilute it with a few tablespoons of water."
- ▪ For a fun serving idea, freeze some of the **Iced Hibiscus Tea** in ice cube trays and serve the remaining tea over the cubes so that your tea won't taste diluted.
- ▪ If you're not a big tuna fan, use chopped shrimp, canned salmon, or finely chopped chicken in the **Crunchy Tuna-and-Almond Salad.**
- ▪ For a fabulous Italian-style sandwich, chop some of the **Marinated Olives and Peppers** and spoon over salami, ham, or provolone, and drizzle with the marinade.

CRUNCHY TUNA-AND-ALMOND SALAD

fast fixin's

Prep: 10 min.

- ¾ cup light mayonnaise
- 1 teaspoon grated lemon rind
- 1 tablespoon fresh lemon juice
- ½ teaspoon curry powder
- ⅛ teaspoon garlic powder
- 1 (13-ounce) can solid white tuna in spring water, drained and flaked
- ½ (10-ounce) package frozen peas, thawed
- 2 celery ribs, chopped
- ¼ teaspoon salt
- ⅛ teaspoon pepper
- 1 (10-ounce) package mixed salad greens
- ¼ cup slivered almonds, toasted
- ½ cup chow mein noodles

STIR together first 5 ingredients in a large bowl until blended. Add tuna and next 4 ingredients; toss gently to coat. Serve over greens. Sprinkle salad with almonds and noodles. MAKES 6 servings.

SUSAN AMERIKANER
SAN LUIS OBISPO, CALIFORNIA

PEANUTTY SPICY NOODLE SALAD

fast fixin's

Prep: 20 min.

- 8 ounces uncooked linguine
- 1 red bell pepper
- 1 cucumber, peeled and seeded
- ¼ cup peanut butter
- ¼ cup reduced-sodium fat-free chicken broth
- ¼ cup rice wine vinegar
- 1 tablespoon light soy sauce
- 1 tablespoon vegetable oil
- 1½ teaspoons sugar
- 2 teaspoons minced fresh ginger
- 2 teaspoons chili-garlic sauce
- 1 garlic clove, minced
- ½ (10-ounce) package broccoli slaw
- 4 green onions, thinly sliced
- 1 tablespoon chopped dry-roasted peanuts
- Garnish: green onions

PREPARE pasta according to package directions. Rinse and drain; set aside.
CUT bell pepper and cucumber into thin strips.
STIR together peanut butter and next 8 ingredients in a large bowl. Add pasta, bell pepper, cucumber, and broccoli slaw, tossing to coat. Sprinkle with sliced green onions and chopped peanuts. Garnish, if desired. MAKES 8 servings.

BANANA PUDDING WITH SUGAR BISCUITS

make ahead

Prep: 20 min., Cook: 10 min., Chill: 8 hrs.

You'll find that this easy-to-make dessert provides a delicious ending to a relaxed outdoor gathering.

- ¾ cup granulated sugar
- ¼ cup cornstarch
- ⅛ teaspoon salt
- 3 egg yolks
- 4 cups milk
- 3 tablespoons butter
- 1½ teaspoons vanilla extract
- 3 bananas, sliced
- 1 cup whipping cream
- ½ cup powdered sugar
- Sugar Biscuits

WHISK together first 5 ingredients in a large saucepan. Cook over medium heat, whisking constantly, until mixture boils. Boil, whisking constantly, 1 minute. Remove from heat, and stir in butter and vanilla.
LINE bottom of a trifle bowl or large clear bowl with one-third banana slices and one-third pudding. Repeat layers twice, ending with pudding. Cover and chill 8 hours.
BEAT whipping cream at medium speed with an electric mixer until foamy; gradually add powdered sugar, beating until soft peaks form. Spread evenly over pudding. Serve with Sugar Biscuits. MAKES 8 to 10 servings.

Sugar Biscuits:

fast fixin's

Prep: 10 min., Bake: 20 min.

- 2 cups baking mix
- ½ cup sugar
- ½ teaspoon ground cinnamon
- ¼ cup butter or margarine
- ½ cup milk

STIR together first 3 ingredients in a large bowl; cut in butter with a pastry blender until crumbly. Add milk, stirring until dry ingredients are moistened. Drop mixture into 12 mounds on a lightly greased baking sheet.
BAKE at 425° for 15 to 20 minutes or until lightly browned. Cool. MAKES 12 biscuits.

ICED HIBISCUS TEA

fast fixin's

Prep: 5 min., Cook: 7 min.

Iced Hibiscus Tea offers a tangy-sweet, refreshing change from regular iced tea.

- 7 cups water, divided
- 1 cup firmly packed hibiscus flowers*
- 1 cup sugar

BRING 6 cups water and hibiscus flowers to a boil in a large saucepan. Reduce heat to low, and simmer 5 minutes. Remove from heat, and stir in sugar.
POUR mixture through a wire-mesh strainer into a pitcher, discarding hibiscus flowers. Stir in remaining 1 cup water. Serve hibiscus tea over ice. MAKES 2 quarts.

*Substitute 6 regular-size Red Zinger tea bags for 1 cup hibiscus flowers, if desired.

NOTE: Look for hibiscus flowers in Mexican or Latin supermarkets. Use only flowers that are labeled for consumption and that you know are pesticide-free.

Peppery Chicken Fried Chicken, page 57

Strawberry-Chicken Salad, page 50

Shrimp-and-Artichoke
Salad, page 50

Honey Chicken Salad and Tropical Spinach Salad, page 51

Garden District Eggs, page 66

Pain Perdu, page 67

Bloody Marys, page 68

Roasted New Potato Salad, page 91

Mexican Deviled Eggs, page 93

Smoky Chipotle Baby Back Ribs, page 87

Eggshell Vases and
Candy Dishes, page 94

Woodland centerpiece
with Sugared Rabbits,
page 94

Oven-Fried Chicken

We take a few shortcuts but don't scrimp on flavor.

Here's a schedule to help you get each dish in this menu on the table at the same time. Once the chicken is in the oven, you have about 10 minutes to clean up those prep dishes before you start the mashed potatoes. We used frozen mashed potatoes and cooked them in the microwave. Before you stir in the cheese and seasoning, get the sugar snap peas cooking in the microwave, and then add the extra ingredients to the potatoes. (Cover with foil, and keep warm if you're ahead of schedule.) When the timer rings on the chicken, you're ready to serve plates and enjoy.

Easy Chicken Supper

Serves 4

Oven-Fried Chicken Cutlets

Speedy Garlic Mashed Potatoes

Steamed sugar snap peas
(Prepare 1 [10-ounce] package
frozen sugar snap peas according
to package directions. Stir in 1 tablespoon butter, 2 teaspoons lemon
juice, and ½ teaspoon salt.)

Pudding-and-Cookie Cups

OVEN-FRIED CHICKEN CUTLETS

family favorite

Prep: 15 min., Bake: 30 min.

Chicken cutlets are skinned and boned chicken breasts that have been sliced to a thin, even thickness, and then packaged for sale. This convenience saves you the time of pounding chicken breasts to flatten, but will cost more. For a crispy coating, do not crowd chicken on baking sheet.

- **⅓ cup butter or margarine, melted**
- **1 tablespoon Dijon mustard**
- **¼ teaspoon garlic powder**
- **¼ teaspoon salt**
- **¼ teaspoon pepper**
- **1 cup round buttery cracker crumbs (about 44 crackers)**
- **½ cup grated Parmesan cheese**
- **4 chicken breast cutlets (about 1¼ pounds)**
- **Garnish: chopped fresh parsley**

STIR together first 5 ingredients in a medium bowl. Combine cracker crumbs and cheese in a shallow bowl.
DIP chicken in butter mixture; dredge in cracker crumb mixture. Place on an aluminum foil-lined baking sheet.
BAKE at 400° for 25 to 30 minutes or until chicken is brown and done. Garnish, if desired. **MAKES** 4 servings.

MELANIE WINTERNHEIMER
SANFORD, FLORIDA

SPEEDY GARLIC MASHED POTATOES

family favorite • fast fixin's

Prep: 5 min., Cook: 13 min.

- **1 (22-ounce) package frozen mashed potatoes**
- **1¾ cups milk**
- **1 (4-ounce) container garlic-and-herb spreadable cheese***
- **½ to 1 teaspoon salt**
- **½ teaspoon pepper**

STIR together mashed potatoes and milk in a large glass bowl.
MICROWAVE, uncovered, at HIGH 11 to 13 minutes. Add cheese and remaining ingredients, stirring until cheese is melted. **MAKES** 4 to 6 servings.

NOTE: For testing purposes only, we used Alouette Garlic & Herbs Spreadable Cheese.

*Substitute 1 (3-ounce) package cream cheese, softened and cubed; 3 tablespoons butter; and 1 minced garlic clove, if desired.

JULIA MITCHELL
LEXINGTON, KENTUCKY

Pudding-and-Cookie Cups

Make your family's favorite pudding, and layer it with thawed whipped topping in parfait dishes. To save on cleanup, use disposable clear plastic cups. To make the day before, cover with plastic wrap and refrigerate. Just before serving, tuck in a couple of cookies. (Use smaller cookies for kid-size servings.)

A Special Dinner

Celebrate an anniversary or a birthday with this simple yet tasteful and elegant menu.

Cozy Celebration

Serves 6

Grilled Pork Tenderloins With Rosemary Pesto

Lemon Rice Pilaf

Steamed green beans

Ice Cream-Toffee Dessert

This menu leaves you time to spend with others. The tenderloins can be prepared and assembled ahead. While the meat is grilling, prepare lightly scented Lemon Rice Pilaf. Ice Cream-Toffee Dessert can be made ahead and creates an easy ending.

GRILLED PORK TENDERLOINS WITH ROSEMARY PESTO

make ahead

Prep: 30 min.; Grill: 1 hr., 30 min.; Stand: 10 min.

Smoke from grilling the meat gives the outer edge a pink color.

- **½ cup walnuts, toasted**
- **¼ cup chopped fresh rosemary (about 4 sprigs)**
- **3 tablespoons Creole mustard**
- **3 garlic cloves, chopped**
- **½ cup olive oil, divided**
- **4 (½- to ¾-pound) pork tenderloins**
- **Kitchen string**
- **1 teaspoon salt**
- **½ teaspoon black pepper**

PROCESS first 4 ingredients in a food processor until smooth, stopping to scrape down sides. With processor running, pour ¼ cup oil through food chute in a slow stream; process until smooth.

PLACE tenderloins between 2 sheets of heavy-duty plastic wrap, and flatten to a ½- to ¾-inch thickness, using a meat mallet or rolling pin. Spread rosemary mixture evenly over top of 2 tenderloins; top with remaining tenderloins, and tie together with kitchen string.

RUB remaining ¼ cup oil over pork; sprinkle with salt and pepper.

PREPARE a hot fire by piling charcoal on 1 side of grill, leaving other side empty. (For gas grills, light only 1 side.) Place food grate on grill. Arrange pork over unlit side.

GRILL, covered with grill lid, 1 hour and 30 minutes or until a meat thermometer inserted into thickest portion registers 155°. Let stand 10 minutes or until thermometer registers 160°. **MAKES** 10 to 12 servings.

LEMON RICE PILAF

Prep: 15 min., Cook: 30 min.

- **¼ cup butter or margarine**
- **4 celery ribs, sliced**
- **6 green onions, sliced**
- **2 cups uncooked long-grain rice**
- **1 (32-ounce) container chicken broth**
- **2 tablespoons grated lemon rind**
- **½ teaspoon salt**
- **¼ teaspoon pepper**

MELT ¼ cup butter in a large skillet over medium-high heat; add celery and green onions, and sauté until celery is tender. Stir in rice, and sauté 2 minutes or until golden brown. Stir in broth, and bring to a boil. Cover, reduce heat, and simmer 20 minutes or until rice is tender. Stir in lemon rind, salt, and pepper. **MAKES** 6 servings.

ICE CREAM-TOFFEE DESSERT

make ahead

Prep: 20 min., Freeze: 8 hrs., Stand: 30 min.

Bits of toffee sprinkled throughout the ice-cream mixture give this delicious dessert a crunchy texture.

- **2 (3-ounce) packages ladyfingers**
- **2 tablespoons instant coffee granules**
- **¼ cup hot water**
- **6 (1.4-ounce) toffee candy bars, divided**
- **½ gallon vanilla ice cream, softened***
- **3 tablespoons coffee liqueur (optional)**
- **1 (8-ounce) container frozen whipped topping, thawed**

STAND ladyfingers around edge of a 9-inch springform pan; line bottom of pan with remaining ladyfingers, and set aside.

COMBINE coffee granules and ¼ cup hot water in a small bowl, stirring until dissolved; let cool completely.

CHOP 5 candy bars into small pieces. Stir chopped candy and coffee into ice cream. Spoon into prepared pan. Cover mixture with plastic wrap, and freeze 8 hours.

STIR liqueur into whipped topping, if desired. Dollop whipped topping around edge of ice-cream mixture.

CHOP remaining candy bar; sprinkle evenly over top. Gently run a knife around edge of ice cream to release sides. Let stand 30 minutes before serving. **MAKES** 8 servings.

*Substitute ½ gallon coffee ice cream for vanilla, if desired.

NOTE: For testing purposes only, we used Skor English Toffee candy bars.

Pretty Teapot Cake

Guests at Rebecca Edgar's annual springtime tea party (see the following page) in Opp, Alabama, delight in the centerpiece: a yummy teapot cake. Preparation is not as hard as it looks. You don't even need special pans—just 2 (1.5-liter) ovenproof bowls. If you love the idea but aren't into cake baking, take the recipe to your favorite bakery.

TEAPOT CAKE

Prep: 1 hr.; Bake: 1 hr., 15 min.

Though the butterflies are made of fondant, the finished versions contain plastic stamens and should not be eaten.

  1 recipe Pound Cake Batter (page 84)
  Violet food-coloring paste
  Creamy Frosting, divided
  Lime green food-coloring paste
  3 (6-inch) wooden skewers
  Fondant Teapot Spout
  Fondant Teapot Handle
  Fondant Daisies
  Fondant Butterflies

POUR batter evenly into 2 (1.5-liter) greased and floured ovenproof bowls.
BAKE at 325° for 1 hour and 5 minutes to 1 hour and 15 minutes or until a wooden pick inserted in center comes out clean. Cool in bowls on wire racks 10 minutes. Remove from bowls; let cool completely on wire racks, large flat sides down. Using a serrated knife, cut domed tops (about ¾ to 1 inch) off each cake to make level. Cut 1 cake top with a 3-inch round cutter, and reserve for teapot lid.
STIR together violet food-coloring paste and 3 cups Creamy Frosting until well blended, and set aside.
STIR together lime green food-coloring paste and remaining 1 cup Creamy Frosting until well blended; set aside.
TRANSFER 1 cake half, large flat side up, to a serving platter; spread sides with 1 cup violet frosting, and spread top with ½ cup violet frosting. Top with remaining cake, large flat side down. Spread top and sides with 1¼ cups violet frosting. Place reserved round cake lid on top of cake. Spread with ¼ cup violet frosting.
INSERT 1 wooden skewer halfway horizontally into middle side of cake; attach Teapot Spout, pressing gently. Insert 2 wooden skewers, 3 inches apart, on opposite side of spout; attach Teapot Handle, pressing gently. Pipe border of dots around bottom edge of cake and cake lid with lime green frosting. Press Fondant Daisies and Butterflies onto cake as desired. **MAKES** 12 servings.

Creamy Frosting:
fast fixin's
Prep: 5 min.

  1 cup butter, softened
  1 cup shortening
  2 (16-ounce) packages powdered
    sugar
  ⅓ cup milk
  2 teaspoons vanilla extract

BEAT butter and shortening at medium speed with an electric mixer until creamy; gradually add powdered sugar alternately with milk, and beat until smooth. Stir in vanilla. **MAKES** 4 cups.

SHIRLEY D. CULBERTSON
HARTFORD, ALABAMA

Fondant Teapot Spout, Handle, Daisies, and Butterflies:
Prep: 2 hrs., Dry: 2 hrs.

  Yellow food-coloring paste
  ½ (24-ounce) package rolled fondant
  Regular white stamens

DIP half of a wooden pick in yellow food-coloring paste, and smear on fondant. Knead color into fondant until evenly blended and distributed. Repeat procedure until desired shade is reached. Divide tinted fondant into 4 equal portions. Shape 1 portion into a spout. (Keep remaining portions moist by placing in a sealed zip-top plastic bag until ready to use.)
ROLL another portion into a 4- x 1-inch strip; shape into a handle. Place handle and spout on a wax paper-lined baking sheet, and let stand 2 hours at room temperature or until dry. (For assembly purposes, it's important that the handle and spout remain somewhat pliable, yet they need to be firm enough to hold their shape when attached to the sides of the cake.)
ROLL another tinted fondant portion to ⅛-inch thickness, and cut with a 1½-inch daisy-shaped cutter. Roll and shape trimmings into pea-sized balls; press into flower centers. Let flowers stand on a wax paper-lined baking sheet at room temperature 2 hours or until dry. (For a three-dimensional effect, pinch center of bottom side of each flower to create an inverted center; press fondant balls in center of flowers.)
ROLL remaining tinted fondant portion to ⅛-inch thickness, and cut with a ¾-inch heart-shaped cutter. Roll and shape pea-sized pieces of trimmings into about 1½-inch long pieces, forming body of butterfly.
ATTACH 2 fondant hearts, point to point, pressing slightly to seal. Place fondant body of butterfly, lengthwise, down center of attached hearts; pressing slightly to seal. Lift outer sides, forming butterfly wings. Cut 1 stamen in half; insert halves into 1 end of body, forming butterfly antennae. Let butterflies stand on a wax paper-lined baking sheet at room temperature 2 hours or until dry.

NOTE: Daisies and butterflies can be made up to 1 month ahead and stored at room temperature until ready to use. For testing purposes only, we used Wilton Ready-To-Use Pure White Rolled Fondant. Daisy- and heart-shaped cutters, as well as the fondant, can be purchased from **www.wilton.com.**

Let's Have a Tea Party

Spring frills along with whimsical food brighten this special day.

Decorated hats bob in the midday sunshine as a chorus of little girl laughter fills the air. Rebecca Edgar, affectionately known as "Dollbaby," began an annual spring tea party at her home in Opp, Alabama, five years ago to entertain her granddaughters and their friends. The main attraction is nibbling and socializing at tiny tables adorned with elegant tablecloths and fresh flowers. Good friend Shirley Culbertson prepares the sweets including a magnificent Teapot Cake centerpiece (see recipe on previous page).

COLORFUL CAKES ON A STICK

Prep: 1 hr.; Bake: 10 min.; Freeze: 1 hr., 10 min.

These cakes can be made using any pound cake batter, but to streamline, we started with a pound cake mix. Cake on a Stick pans can be ordered from **www.brylanekitchen.com.**

- **Pound Cake Batter**
- **46 wooden craft sticks**
- **Vanilla Glaze**
- **Decorations: candy sprinkles, candy dots, colored decorator icing**

SPOON 2 tablespoons Pound Cake Batter into each of 46 well-greased cake-on-a-stick pan molds. Level batter with a small spatula.

BAKE at 350° for 8 to 10 minutes or until a wooden pick inserted in center comes out clean. Cool in pans on wire racks 5 minutes. Remove cakes to wire racks, and let cool completely. Freeze cakes 1 hour.

INSERT 1 wooden craft stick in center of flat side of each cake. Dip each cake in Vanilla Glaze, and place on wire racks.

Decorate as desired, and freeze 10 minutes or until Vanilla Glaze is firm. Remove cakes from freezer. Serve at room temperature. (Store any remaining cakes at room temperature.) **MAKES** 46 servings.

Pound Cake Batter:
fast fixin's
Prep: 5 min.

- **2 (16-ounce) packages pound cake mix**
- **1½ cups buttermilk**
- **4 large eggs**
- **3 tablespoons fresh lemon juice**

BEAT all ingredients at low speed with an electric mixer until combined. Increase speed to medium, and beat 3 minutes or until light and fluffy. **MAKES** about 3¾ cups.

Vanilla Glaze:
fast fixin's
Prep: 5 min.

- **1 (24-ounce) package vanilla bark coating squares**
- **1 cup whipping cream**
- **1 teaspoon white coloring**

MICROWAVE chocolate and whipping cream at HIGH 5 minutes or until mixture is smooth, stirring every 30 seconds. Stir in white coloring. **MAKES** about 3½ cups.

NOTE: For testing purposes only, we used Wilton's White-White Icing Color for white coloring. It's sold at crafts stores.

BIRDS' NESTS

Prep: 25 min., Cook: 8 min.

You can substitute jelly beans for the chocolate pieces.

- **⅓ cup corn syrup**
- **3 cups miniature marshmallows**
- **2 tablespoons butter**
- **5 cups crisp rice cereal**
- **Pastel-colored candy-coated chocolate pieces**

STIR together first 3 ingredients in a Dutch oven over low heat, and cook, stirring often, 8 minutes or until marshmallows melt. Add cereal, stirring until well blended.

SPOON mixture evenly into 16 lightly greased muffin pan cups. Press with wax paper to compact. Press an indentation in centers, forming a nest, and let cool completely. Remove nests, and fill centers with pastel chocolate pieces. **MAKES** 16.

PEANUT-BUTTER BIRDS' NESTS: Reduce marshmallows to 2 cups, and substitute ½ cup creamy peanut butter for butter. Proceed as directed.

TEA CAKE HAT COOKIES

Prep: 1 hr., Bake: 14 min. per batch

- **½ cup shortening**
- **½ cup butter**
- **2 cups sugar**
- **2 large eggs**
- **3 tablespoons milk**
- **1 teaspoon vanilla extract**
- **3½ cups all-purpose flour**
- **2 teaspoons baking powder**
- **¼ teaspoon salt**
- **2 recipes Creamy Frosting (recipe on page 83)**
- **Assorted food-coloring pastes**

BEAT shortening and butter at medium speed with an electric mixer until mixture is creamy. Gradually add sugar, and beat mixture until light and fluffy. Add eggs, milk, and vanilla, and beat until blended.

COMBINE flour, baking powder, and salt. Gradually add to shortening mixture, beating until smooth. Turn dough out onto a lightly floured surface.

PAT or roll dough to ¼-inch thickness; cut 30 circles with a 1¾-inch round cutter. Reroll excess dough, and cut 30 circles with a 3¼-inch round cutter. Place dough circles on lightly greased baking sheets.

BAKE at 350° for 11 to 14 minutes per batch or until lightly browned on edges. Cool 5 minutes; remove cookies to wire racks, and let cool completely.

PLACE a small dollop of Creamy Frosting in center of each large round cookie; top with 1 small round cookie. Divide remaining Creamy Frosting, and tint with desired food-coloring pastes. Spoon tinted icing into small zip-top freezer bags, and seal. Snip a tiny hole in 1 corner of each bag, and pipe desired decorative designs on cookies. **MAKES** 30 cookies.

SHIRLEY D. CULBERTSON
HARTFORD, ALABAMA

Sweets for the Season

This Virginia cook's Passover desserts are guaranteed to please for any occasion.

Ronnie Mand of Danville, Virginia, serves wonderful treats as she celebrates Passover. We like the extra crunch of the crushed matzo in her cheesecake crust. If you haven't tried matzo, this is a delicious way to do so. Whether you observe this holiday or not, you and your family will love these recipes.

CHOCOLATE ROLL

family favorite

Prep: 20 min., Bake: 15 min.

Garnish Chocolate Roll with fresh berries, unsweetened cocoa, and powdered sugar for a beautiful presentation.

Unsweetened cocoa
6 large eggs, separated
¾ cup granulated sugar, divided
¾ cup unsweetened cocoa, divided
2½ teaspoons vanilla extract, divided
Pinch of salt
2 tablespoons unsweetened cocoa
1½ cups whipping cream
½ cup powdered sugar
Garnishes: powdered sugar, mixed fresh berries

GREASE bottom and sides of a 15- x 10-inch jellyroll pan; line with wax paper. Grease wax paper and dust with cocoa. Set prepared pan aside.

BEAT egg yolks at high speed with an electric mixer until foamy. Gradually add ¼ cup granulated sugar, beating until thick and pale. Gradually stir in

½ cup cocoa, 1½ teaspoons vanilla, and pinch of salt, beating until well blended.

BEAT egg whites until soft peaks form; gradually add remaining ½ cup granulated sugar, beating until stiff peaks form. Fold gently into cocoa mixture. Spread batter evenly into prepared jellyroll pan.

BAKE at 375° for 12 to 15 minutes or until a wooden pick inserted in center comes out clean.

SIFT 2 tablespoons cocoa in a 15- x 10-inch rectangle onto a cloth towel. Remove cake from oven, run a knife around edges of pan to loosen cake, and turn cake out onto prepared towel.

PEEL off wax paper; trim cake edges, and discard. Starting at a short end, roll up cake and towel together; place seam side down on a wire rack to cool.

BEAT whipping cream at low speed with electric mixer until foamy; add ½ cup powdered sugar, remaining ¼ cup cocoa, and remaining 1 teaspoon vanilla. Beat at high speed until soft peaks form.

UNROLL cake, and spread evenly with whipped cream mixture, leaving a 1-inch border around edges. Reroll cake without towel, and place seam side down on a serving platter; garnish, if desired. **MAKES** 8 servings.

PASSOVER CHEESECAKE

family favorite

Prep: 15 min., Bake: 45 min., Chill: 8 hrs.

Matzo is a flat, brittle bread made from only flour and water and baked without leavening. Find it on the ethnic food aisle of your local supermarket.

- ¾ **cup crushed matzo**
- ¼ **cup butter, melted**
- ¼ **cup sugar**
- 3 **(8-ounce) packages cream cheese, softened**
- 1 **cup sugar**
- 3 **large eggs**
- ½ **teaspoon grated lemon rind**
- 1 **tablespoon fresh lemon juice**

STIR together first 3 ingredients in a bowl. Press mixture into bottom and 1 inch up sides of a lightly greased 9-inch springform pan.

BEAT cream cheese at medium speed with an electric mixer until smooth. Gradually add 1 cup sugar, beating until blended.

ADD eggs, 1 at a time, beating until blended after each addition. Beat in lemon rind and juice. Pour mixture into prepared crust.

BAKE at 375° for 45 minutes or until set. Remove cheesecake from the oven; cool on a wire rack. Cover and chill 8 hours. To serve, gently run a knife around edge of cheesecake to release sides of pan.

MAKES 10 to 12 servings.

Food and Hospitality

Sweet-to-the-Bone Ribs, ASAP

You'll be licking your fingers quicker than you think—we promise.

Cooking ribs doesn't have to be an all-day affair. You can have them on the table in three hours flat. Buy baby back ribs—they're meatier and more tender than spare ribs and worth the extra money. Then select a rub-and-sauce combination from our two flavor options. Just four ingredients make up the rubs while bottled products are the base for the sauces. Grill the ribs upright in a rib rack (about a $15 investment). So, can ribs be easy and awesome? You bet.

BABY BACK RIBS

family favorite

Prep: 15 min., Chill: 8 hrs., Stand: 40 min., Grill: 2½ hrs.

Plug one of our flavorful rub-and-sauce combinations (Smoky Chipotle or Sweet-and-Sour) into these simple directions for grilling ribs.

- 3 **slabs baby back pork ribs (about 5½ pounds)**
- 2 **citrus fruits, halved**
- 1 **recipe desired rub**
- 1 **recipe desired 'cue sauce**

RINSE and pat ribs dry. If desired, remove thin membrane from back of ribs by slicing into it with a knife and then pulling it off (this will make ribs more tender).

RUB meat with cut sides of citrus fruit, squeezing as you rub. Massage rub into meat, covering all sides. Wrap tightly with plastic wrap, and place in a zip-top freezer bag or 13- x 9-inch dish; chill 8 hours. Let ribs stand at room temperature 30 minutes before grilling. Remove plastic wrap.

TO GRILL ON A CHARCOAL GRILL: Prepare hot fire by piling charcoal on 1 side of grill, leaving the other side empty. Place food grate on grill; position rib rack on grate over unlit side. Place slabs in rack. Grill, covered with grill lid, over medium-high heat (350° to 400°) 1 hour. Reposition rib slabs, placing the ones closest to the heat source away from heat, moving other slabs closer. Grill ribs 1 more hour or until meat is tender. Grill 30 more minutes over medium heat (325° to 350°), basting with half of 'cue sauce. Remove ribs from grill, and let stand 10 minutes. Cut ribs, slicing between bones. Serve with remaining sauce.

TO GRILL ON A GAS GRILL: Light only 1 side. Coat food grate with vegetable cooking spray, and place on grill; position rib rack on grate over unlit side. Place rib slabs in rack. Grill, covered with grill lid, over medium-high heat (350° to 400°) 1 hour. Reposition rib slabs, placing the ones closet to the heat source away from heat and moving other slabs closer. Grill 1 more hour or until meat is tender. Lower temperature to medium heat (325° to 350°), and cook ribs 30 more minutes, basting with half of 'cue sauce. Remove ribs from grill, and let stand 10 minutes. Cut ribs, slicing between bones. Serve ribs with remaining 'cue sauce. **MAKES** 6 servings.

JOE BATRIC
BIRMINGHAM, ALABAMA

SMOKY CHIPOTLE BABY BACK RIBS

family favorite

(pictured on page 79)

PREPARE ribs as directed using 4 oranges halves, Chipotle Rub, and Smoky Chipotle 'Cue Sauce.

Chipotle Rub:

Prep: 5 min.

CHOP 2 to 3 canned chipotle chile peppers; stir together peppers, ¼ cup firmly packed brown sugar, 1 tablespoon chili powder, and 1 teaspoon salt to form a paste. **MAKES** ⅓ cup.

Smoky Chipotle 'Cue Sauce:

Prep: 5 min., Cook: 35 min.

PROCESS 2 (18-ounce) bottles barbecue sauce, 2 canned chipotle chile peppers, 2 tablespoons brown sugar, and 1 teaspoon chili powder in a blender until smooth. Pour into a saucepan, and bring to a boil over medium-high heat. Reduce heat, and simmer 30 minutes. **MAKES** about 2½ cups.

NOTE: For testing purposes only, we used Stubb's Original Bar-B-Q Sauce.

JOE BATRIC
BIRMINGHAM, ALABAMA

SWEET-AND-SOUR BABY BACK RIBS

family favorite

PREPARE ribs as directed using 4 lime halves, Ginger Rub, and Sweet-and-Sour 'Cue Sauce. Garnish ribs with sesame seeds and green onions, if desired.

Ginger Rub:

Prep: 5 min.

COMBINE 2 tablespoons ground ginger, ½ teaspoon dried crushed red pepper, 1 teaspoon salt, and 1 teaspoon black pepper. **MAKES** about 3 tablespoons.

Sweet-and-Sour 'Cue Sauce:

Prep: 5 min., Cook: 35 min.

STIR together 2 (10-ounce) bottles sweet-and-sour sauce, 2 cups ketchup, ½ cup cider vinegar, ½ teaspoon ground ginger, and 2 teaspoons hot sauce in a saucepan over medium-high heat. Bring mixture to a boil; reduce heat, and simmer sauce 30 minutes. **MAKES** 3½ cups.

NOTE: For testing purposes only, we used Ty Ling Sweet & Sour Sauce for sweet-and-sour sauce.

How to Grill Baby Back Ribs

Test Kitchens' professional **Vanessa McNeil** shares tips for grilling ribs using the Smoky Chipotle Baby Back Ribs recipe.

■ Don't skip rubbing the ribs with citrus fruit halves; the juice adds a perky zip to the flavor. You'll find the canned chipotle chile peppers at the grocery store alongside other ethnic ingredients.

■ Remove the thin membrane on the back, or bone side, of each rib rack if you want the meat to almost fall off. Leave it on if you like the crispy texture that results while grilling or want to save prep time.

■ For best flavor, wrap seasoned ribs in plastic wrap to hold rub mixture close to the meat. Place each slab in a separate 2-gallon-size zip-top freezer bag, and refrigerate overnight. When ready to grill, unwrapping the ribs can be messy, so hang a zip-top freezer bag on the grill handle, being careful that it doesn't touch the hot grill. Unwrap ribs over the bag, discarding plastic wrap into bag. Slide ribs into rib rack (photo 1). Immediately remove bag from handle, and discard. (For testing purposes only, we used a Weber Rib Rack.) Vanessa says that ribs also can be placed directly on the food grate; however, expect to turn the ribs and manage the fire more often. Place an oven thermometer on the unlit cooking area of the grill. To maintain temperature, stoke the fire, and make sure vents are open.

■ When the meat is tender and done, bones should wiggle easily when moved, and the meat will be shrunk down from the bones. Slow the fire by partially or fully closing vents before basting. Pour sauce over ribs, guiding it to cover with a grill brush (photo 2).

Perked Up With Limes

You're one squeeze away from zestier, healthier food.

The juice of limes along with their rinds lends so much fresh flavor and citrus aroma that you don't need to add a lot of oil or butter to prepare recipes everyone will rave about.

Try lime juice squeezed over raw vegetables, grilled corn on the cob, or meaty soft tacos. Keep your mind open to this fruit's plentiful possibilities.

LIME CHICKEN WITH GRILLED PINEAPPLE

family favorite

Prep: 25 min., Chill: 2 hrs., Grill: 18 min., Stand: 5 min.

- **6 skinned and boned chicken breasts**
- **1 teaspoon salt, divided**
- **1 teaspoon pepper, divided**
- **1 cup fresh lime juice, divided**
- **2 jalapeño peppers, seeded, minced, and divided**
- **½ cup pineapple juice**
- **2 garlic cloves, minced**
- **½ cup tequila (optional)**
- **1 pineapple, peeled, cored, and cut horizontally in half**
- **1 orange, sliced (¼ inch thick)**
- **2 tablespoons honey**
- **½ teaspoon grated lime rind**

PLACE chicken between 2 sheets of plastic wrap, and flatten to a ¼-inch thickness, using a meat mallet or rolling pin. Sprinkle evenly with ½ teaspoon salt and ½ teaspoon pepper.

WHISK together remaining ½ teaspoon salt, remaining ½ teaspoon pepper, ¾ cup lime juice, 1 minced jalapeño pepper, pineapple juice, garlic, and, if desired, tequila in a medium bowl.

PLACE chicken and lime mixture in a shallow bowl or a large zip-top freezer bag. Cover or seal, and chill 2 hours. Drain chicken, discarding marinade.

GRILL, covered with grill lid, over medium-high heat (350° to 400°) 4 minutes on each side or until done. Let stand 5 minutes before serving.

GRILL pineapple and orange slices 5 minutes on each side, watching to prevent burning; coarsely chop pineapple, and place in a medium bowl. Stir in remaining ¼ cup lime juice, remaining 1 minced jalapeño, honey, and lime rind. Serve with chicken and grilled orange slices. **MAKES** 6 servings.

URSULA SPACKMAN
COOKEVILLE, TENNESSEE

Calories 215 (8% from fat); Fat 1.9g (sat 0.4g, mono 0.4g, poly 0.5g); Protein 28g; Carb 20g; Fiber 1.7g; Chol 68mg; Iron 1.3mg; Sodium 369mg; Calc 32mg

ROASTED LIME-CILANTRO EYE OF ROUND ROAST

family favorite

Prep: 15 min.; Chill 8 hrs.; Bake 3 hrs., 15 min.; Stand: 10 min.

We enjoyed this spice-and-herb-seasoned shredded roast with warm tortillas, fat-free sour cream, Pico de Gallo, Citrus Onions, and an extra squeeze of fresh lime juice. It cooks for a while, but it's hands-off cooking.

- **8 garlic cloves**
- **1 jalapeño pepper, seeded**
- **¼ cup chopped fresh cilantro**
- **¼ cup lime juice**
- **1 tablespoon coriander seeds**
- **1 tablespoon cumin seeds**
- **1 tablespoon coarse-grain salt**
- **1 tablespoon olive oil**
- **1 (4.5-pound) eye of round roast**
- **Garnishes: fresh cilantro sprigs, lime wedges**
- **Corn tortillas (optional)**
- **Fat-free sour cream (optional)**
- **Pico de Gallo (optional)**
- **Citrus Onions (optional)**

PROCESS first 8 ingredients in a food processor until a thick paste forms, stopping to scrape down sides.

MAKE 3 to 4 (1-inch) cuts in each side of roast with a sharp knife. Fill each cut with about 1 teaspoon paste. Spread remaining paste over beef. Wrap tightly with plastic wrap; chill at least 8 hours or up to 24 hours. Unwrap roast; place in a 13- x 9-inch pan.

BAKE, covered, at 325° for 3 hours and 15 minutes or until meat shreds and a meat thermometer inserted into thickest portion registers 180°. (Meat will not shred below this temperature.) Let stand 10 minutes before shredding or chopping. Garnish, if desired. Serve with corn tortillas, sour cream, Pico de Gallo, and Citrus Onions, if desired. **MAKES** 12 servings.

Calories (meat only) 231 (29% from fat); Fat 7.4g (sat 2.3g, mono 3.6g, poly 0.3g); Protein 37.2g; Carb 2g; Fiber 0.4g; Chol 88mg; Iron 3mg; Sodium 551mg; Calc 19.4mg

Pico de Gallo:

Prep: 15 min., Chill: 1 hr.

2 medium tomatoes, chopped
1 medium onion, diced
1 jalapeño pepper, seeded and minced
2 tablespoons chopped fresh cilantro
3 tablespoons fresh lime juice
¼ teaspoon salt

STIR together all ingredients. Chill until ready to serve. **MAKES** about 1½ cups.

Calories (per 2 tablespoons) 12.8 (0% from fat); Fat 0.1g (sat 0g, mono 0g, poly 0g); Protein 0.5g; Carb 3g; Fiber 0.6g; Chol 0mg; Iron 0.2mg; Sodium 52mg; Calc 5.5mg

Citrus Onions:

fast fixin's

Prep: 5 min.

1 medium-size sweet onion, thinly sliced
⅓ cup fresh lime juice*

COMBINE onion and juice in a small glass bowl. Use immediately, or cover and chill until ready to serve. **MAKES** about 1½ cups.

*Substitute fresh lemon juice, if desired.

Calories 6.7 (0% from fat); Fat 0g (sat 0g, mono 0g, poly 0g); Protein 0.2g; Carb 1.8g; Fiber 0.3g; Chol 0mg; Iron 0mg; Sodium 0.5mg; Calc 3.8mg

CREAMY LIME CAKES

family favorite

Prep: 25 min., Bake: 30 min.

Roxana Lambeth prepares this dessert with lemons. Either fruit offers fabulous flavor. For a sweet-tart taste combination, top custardlike Creamy Lime Cakes with fresh blueberries.

Vegetable cooking spray
⅔ cup sugar
¼ cup all-purpose flour
2 teaspoons grated lime rind
5 tablespoons fresh lime juice
2 tablespoons butter, melted
3 large eggs, separated
1½ cups fat-free milk
⅛ teaspoon cream of tartar
3 tablespoons sugar
Garnishes: fresh blueberries, lime slices

COAT 6 (10-ounce) custard cups evenly with cooking spray. Place cups in a baking pan.
STIR together ⅔ cup sugar and next 4 ingredients in a bowl until blended.
BEAT egg yolks in a large bowl at medium speed with an electric mixer until thick and pale. Add 1½ cups milk, beating until blended. Stir in sugar mixture, beating until blended.
BEAT egg whites at medium speed until foamy. Add cream of tartar, beating until soft peaks form. Add 3 tablespoons sugar, and beat until stiff. Gently fold into egg yolk mixture. Spoon batter evenly into prepared custard cups, filling three-fourths full. Fill baking pan with hot water to a depth of 1 inch.
BAKE at 350° for 30 minutes or until cakes are set and tops are golden. Remove cups to wire racks to cool. Serve warm or chilled. Garnish, if desired. **MAKES** 6 servings.

ROXANA LAMBETH
MORENO VALLEY, CALIFORNIA

Calories 226 (25% from fat); Fat 6.4g (sat 3.1g, mono 2.1g, poly 0.5g); Protein 6g; Carb 37.3g; Fiber 0.3g; Chol 118mg; Iron 0.6mg; Sodium 103mg; Calc 91.5mg

Paella for Supper

If you like rice dishes, then you'll love paella. Pronounced *pie-AY-yuh,* this staple that hails from Spain is a flavorful combination of rice, meat, seafood, and seasonings. The traditional version includes clams, mussels, lobster or shrimp, and perhaps a Spanish spicy sausage called chorizo.

Here, we offer a roasted-vegetable version so delicious you won't even miss the meat and seafood, but you can add them in if you'd like. Paella is such an adaptable concoction that it's hard to go wrong with whatever ingredients you may want to include.

Try any combination of seafood and chorizo or cubed ham in paella. If you don't have a paella pan, don't worry—a large ovenproof skillet or Dutch oven will work just fine.

ROASTED-VEGETABLE PAELLA

Prep: 15 min.; Cook: 1 hr., 25 min.;
Bake: 30 min.

Serve with a tossed salad or gazpacho.

3 cups chicken broth
1¼ teaspoons saffron threads
1 large red bell pepper, cut into strips
1 large green bell pepper, cut into strips
½ pound zucchini, sliced
2 tablespoons olive oil, divided
1 teaspoon dried oregano
1 teaspoon dried thyme
1 large onion, chopped
3 garlic cloves, chopped
1 jalapeño pepper, seeded and chopped
3 plum tomatoes, chopped
1½ cups uncooked Arborio rice
Lemon wedges (optional)

BRING chicken broth and saffron threads to a boil over medium-high heat; reduce heat, and simmer 20 minutes.
TOSS together bell pepper strips, sliced zucchini, and 1 tablespoon oil; place in an even layer in a 15- x 10-inch jellyroll pan. Sprinkle evenly with oregano and thyme.
BAKE at 400° for 25 to 30 minutes or until tender, stirring once.
SAUTÉ onion, garlic, and jalapeño in remaining 1 tablespoon hot oil in a large skillet over medium heat 20 to 25 minutes or until onion is caramelized. Add tomatoes, and cook, stirring often, 3 to 5 minutes or until liquid is absorbed.
ADD uncooked rice and chicken broth mixture to skillet; bring to a boil. Cover, reduce heat, and simmer 20 to 30 minutes, stirring once after 15 minutes. Stir in bell pepper and zucchini, and cook 5 minutes. Serve with lemon wedges, if desired. **MAKES** 4 to 6 servings.

DEBRA NELSON-HOGAN
NEW YORK, NEW YORK

Laid-Back Supper Club

This tasty mix of recipes shows how easy it is to share a little Southern hospitality.

Company Supper

Serves 6

East-West Flank Steak

Asparagus Pasta With Toasted Pecans

Crusty French bread

Pineapple-Cherry Dump Cake

Iced tea

Readers from all over find great food, fun, and friendship through supper clubs. When we covered them in a story a couple of years ago, we found that for many of you, these gatherings have become less formal. However, one thing has certainly not changed: the need for delicious recipes that require minimal effort.

The following dishes are sure winners. If you're new to dump cake, few desserts are easier to make. And this one uses light cherry pie filling without sacrificing a lick of flavor.

EAST-WEST FLANK STEAK

Prep: 10 min., Chill: 8 hrs., Grill: 20 min., Stand: 5 min.

Serve sliced flank steak with rice or beans and Mexican-style corn.

- ½ cup vegetable oil
- ¼ cup soy sauce
- 2 tablespoons brown sugar
- 2 tablespoons lime juice
- 1 tablespoon grated fresh ginger
- 1 teaspoon dried crushed red pepper
- 1 teaspoon ground black pepper
- 2 garlic cloves, chopped
- 4 green onions, finely chopped
- 1 (2-pound) flank steak, trimmed

COMBINE first 9 ingredients in a shallow dish or large zip-top freezer bag; add steak. Cover or seal, and chill 8 hours, turning occasionally.

REMOVE steak from marinade, discarding marinade.

GRILL, covered with grill lid, over medium-high heat (350° to 400°) 10 minutes on each side or to desired degree of doneness. Let stand 5 minutes; cut into thin slices diagonally across the grain. **MAKES** 4 to 6 servings.

NOTE: To reheat, place slices of steak in a single layer on an aluminum foil-lined baking sheet. Cover baking sheet with foil, and seal edges. Allow to stand for 10 minutes. Bake at 425° for 9 minutes. (Do not overcook.)

SUSAN FRANCO
ATLANTA, GEORGIA

ASPARAGUS PASTA WITH TOASTED PECANS

fast fixin's

Prep: 15 min., Cook: 10 min.

This recipe can work as either a main or side dish. You might be tempted to drain off the chicken broth after cooking the asparagus, but we found that's one of the keys to the recipe's flavor.

- 1 (16-ounce) package penne pasta
- 1 bunch fresh asparagus (about 1 pound)
- 2 tablespoons olive oil
- 1 red bell pepper, seeded and chopped (about ¾ cup)
- 1 tablespoon minced garlic
- 1 cup low-sodium chicken broth
- 1 teaspoon salt
- ½ teaspoon pepper
- 3 tablespoons chopped fresh basil
- ¾ cup shredded Parmesan cheese, divided
- 2 tablespoons butter
- 1 cup pecan halves, toasted and divided
- Garnishes: freshly grated Parmesan cheese, freshly ground pepper

PREPARE pasta according to package directions; drain and keep warm.

SNAP off tough ends of asparagus, and cut into 2-inch pieces.

SAUTÉ asparagus in hot oil in a large skillet over medium heat 4 minutes. Stir in red bell pepper and garlic; cook, stirring occasionally, 2 minutes. Stir in chicken broth. Bring to a boil. Reduce heat, and simmer 2 minutes or until asparagus is crisp-tender. Stir in salt and pepper.

TOSS together pasta, asparagus mixture, basil, ½ cup cheese, butter, and ½ cup pecans. Sprinkle evenly with remaining ¼ cup cheese and ½ cup pecans. Garnish, if desired. **MAKES** 6 servings.

JACK PERKINS
HOLLANDALE, MISSISSIPPI

PINEAPPLE-CHERRY DUMP CAKE

Prep: 15 min., Bake: 50 min.

Go ahead and have a second helping—this lip-smacking dessert uses light pie filling.

- 1 (15¼-ounce) can unsweetened crushed pineapple, undrained
- 1 (20-ounce) can light cherry pie filling
- 1 (18.25-ounce) package white cake mix
- 1 cup water
- ¼ cup canola oil
- ¼ cup chopped pecans

SPREAD crushed pineapple evenly into a lightly greased 13- x 9-inch baking dish. Spread cherry pie filling over pineapple.

STIR together cake mix, 1 cup water, and oil just until blended. (Batter will be lumpy.) Pour over cherry filling. Sprinkle with pecans.

BAKE at 350° for 40 to 50 minutes or until cake is golden. **MAKES** 12 servings.

LINDA VAGNIER
DUBLIN, OHIO

Start With Ranch

Season supper in surprising ways with flavorful salad dressing.

We've rounded up a great group of recipes using bottled Ranch dressing and dry dressing mix to save time in the kitchen. One secret to quick, economical meals is using ingredients on hand in your refrigerator or pantry, so pull out the Ranch and begin a great meal.

ROASTED NEW POTATO SALAD

family favorite

Prep: 15 min., Bake: 35 min.

If you like your potatoes crispier, bake about 10 minutes longer, stirring once. Don't forget to schedule the extra time when planning your meal. *(pictured on page 78)*

- 2 tablespoons olive oil
- 2 pounds small red potatoes, diced
- ½ medium-size sweet onion, chopped
- 2 teaspoons minced garlic
- 1 teaspoon coarse salt
- ½ teaspoon freshly ground pepper
- 8 to 10 cooked crisp bacon slices, crumbled
- 1 bunch green onions, chopped
- ¾ cup prepared Ranch dressing
- Salt and pepper to taste

PLACE oil in a 15- x 10-inch jellyroll pan; add potatoes and next 4 ingredients, tossing to coat. Arrange potato mixture in a single layer.

BAKE at 425° for 30 to 35 minutes or until potatoes are tender, stirring occasionally. Transfer to a large bowl.

TOSS together potatoes, bacon, green onions, and dressing. Add salt and pepper to taste. Serve immediately, or cover and chill until ready to serve. **MAKES** 4 to 6 servings.

FRANK NOWICKI
MOUNTAIN BROOK, ALABAMA

GREEN-AND-GOLD SALAD WITH FRESH CITRUS RANCH DRESSING

family favorite • fast fixin's

Prep: 20 min.

Use refrigerated fruit slices to save on prep.

- 3 cups chopped fresh broccoli
- 1½ cups diced mango
- 1 large navel orange, sectioned and chopped
- ½ cup pecans, toasted
- 1 (6-ounce) package fresh baby spinach
- Fresh Citrus Ranch Dressing

COMBINE first 5 ingredients in a large bowl. Toss with Fresh Citrus Ranch Dressing. **MAKES** 4 to 6 servings.

Fresh Citrus Ranch Dressing:
fast fixin's

Prep: 5 min.

- ¾ cup low-fat buttermilk-Ranch dressing
- 2 teaspoons grated orange rind
- 3 tablespoons fresh orange juice

WHISK together all ingredients. Cover and chill until ready to serve. **MAKES** about 1 cup.

JUDY WHITELEATHER
CAMBRIDGE, OHIO

VEGETABLE PATCH CHICKEN SALAD

family favorite • make ahead

Prep: 15 min., Chill: 30 min.

- 3 cups chopped cooked chicken
- ½ cup prepared cucumber-Ranch dressing
- ½ cup frozen tiny green sweet peas, thawed
- ¼ cup seeded, chopped cucumber
- 2 tablespoons minced onion
- 2 tablespoons minced red bell pepper
- 2 tablespoons minced fresh parsley
- 1 tablespoon fresh lemon juice

STIR together all ingredients in a large bowl. Cover and chill at least 30 minutes before serving. **MAKES** 4 servings.

CAROL S. NOBLE
BURGAW, NORTH CAROLINA

MAKE-AHEAD SNACK MIX

family favorite • make ahead

Prep: 15 min., Cool: 30 min.

- 3 cups crisp oat cereal squares
- 3 cups corn-and-rice cereal
- 3 cups crisp wheat cereal squares
- 1 (11.5-ounce) can lightly salted mixed nuts
- 2 (1-ounce) envelopes Ranch dressing mix
- ½ cup vegetable oil

STIR together all ingredients in a large glass bowl, tossing to coat.
MICROWAVE cereal mixture at HIGH 2 minutes, and stir well. Microwave at HIGH 2 more minutes, and stir. Spread mixture in a single layer on wax paper, and let cool 30 minutes. **MAKES** about 10½ cups.

ANNE STINSON
MONTGOMERY, ALABAMA

Update Your Deviled Eggs

Grace your next spring gathering with different versions of these down-home delights.

Whether deviled, served in salads, or even eaten out of hand, hard-cooked eggs are a true staple in the Southern kitchen. Follow our tips for perfect hard-cooked eggs every time, and we guarantee your guests will beg for these recipes.

Always remember to start eggs in cold water—adding cold eggs to boiling water can cause them to crack. However, if they do crack, add a pinch of salt or dash of vinegar to the water, which will help the egg whites coagulate. Once eggs are cooked and drained, Associate Foods Editor Kate Nicholson recommends adding about an inch of cold water and several ice cubes to the saucepan to make peeling the eggs much easier. To peel them immediately after cooking, "Cover the pot and shake vigorously so that the eggs crack all over. Then peel them under cold, running water, starting at the large end—the air pocket will give you something to grip," Kate says. (If you don't intend to use them right away, refrigerate hard-cooked eggs in their shells for up to a week.)

Foods Editor Scott Jones's favorite trick for transporting deviled eggs is to store the filling and eggs in separate zip-top freezer bags. When you're ready to serve, simply snip one of the bottom corners of the bag containing the filling, and squeeze into the egg halves.

" Cook's Notes "

■ Associate Foods Editor **Mary Allen Perry** recommends adding potato flakes to deviled eggs. It's a little tip she learned from a cake decorator with whom she once worked. Deviled eggs, like egg salad, have a tendency to "water out" and the potato flakes absorb the extra moisture, enabling the eggs to be made ahead. The potato flakes also have a similar texture to the mashed egg yolks and will increase the yield of the filling, allowing for ample "stuffing" to be piped or spooned into the egg whites.
■ And here's a great serving tip: Cut a small slice along the bottom of each egg half to keep it from sliding around on the platter or plate.

No More Green Ring

The secret to preventing a greenish ring around the yolk of hard-cooked eggs is not to overcook them. The best way to cook them is to place the eggs in a single layer in a saucepan and add enough water to cover 1 inch above the eggs. Bring them to a boil; then immediately cover and remove from the heat. Let the eggs sit, covered, for 15 minutes. Pour off the water, and immediately place the hard-cooked eggs under cold, running water or use the ice cube trick described at left.

PECAN-STUFFED DEVILED EGGS

fast fixin's

Prep: 15 min.

Top with fresh parsley sprigs and sliced pimientos or chopped pecans for a festive presentation. You might be tempted to use chopped onion, but we found that grating the onion gives the filling a better texture.

6 hard-cooked eggs
¼ cup mayonnaise
1 teaspoon grated onion
1 teaspoon white vinegar
½ teaspoon chopped fresh parsley
½ teaspoon dry mustard
⅛ teaspoon salt
⅓ cup coarsely chopped pecans

CUT eggs in half lengthwise, and carefully remove yolks.
MASH yolks in a small bowl. Stir in mayonnaise and next 5 ingredients, and blend well. Stir in pecans.
SPOON or pipe yolk mixture evenly into egg-white halves. **MAKES** 6 servings.

ALANA CHANDLER
RICHARDSON, TEXAS

MEXICAN DEVILED EGGS

fast fixin's

Prep: 10 min.

Although these eggs are not too spicy, prepare a milder version by reducing the amount of minced jalapeños. *(pictured on page 78)*

6 hard-cooked eggs
¼ cup mayonnaise
2 tablespoons pickled jalapeño slices, minced
1 tablespoon prepared mustard
¼ teaspoon ground cumin
⅛ teaspoon salt
Garnishes: chili powder, fresh parsley sprigs

CUT eggs in half lengthwise, and carefully remove yolks.
MASH egg yolks in a small bowl. Stir in mayonnaise and next 4 ingredients, and blend well.
SPOON or pipe yolk mixture evenly into egg-white halves. Garnish, if desired.
MAKES 6 servings.

EDIE BULLARD
DETROIT, MICHIGAN

Cook's Corner

Spring is off to a good start with these publications from The National Honey Board, the National Chicken Cooking Contest, and The National Onion Association.

■ "In the Garden with Honey," from the National Honey Board, is a free brochure just buzzing with information. It includes delicious recipes, directions for infusing honey with herbs and citrus flavors, homemade food gift ideas, all-natural soothing beauty treatments, and a helpful chart describing the flavor characteristics of selected varieties of honey.

Visit **www.honeylocator.com** to find retail outlets, local sources, or specialty shops that carry some of the 300 varieties of honey available in the U.S.

This brochure needs no envelope, so simply e-mail your request to **garden@nhb.org** or send to National Honey Board, 390 Lashley Street, Longmont, CO 80501.

■ The National Chicken Council and the U.S. Poultry & Egg Association are offering *The Chicken Cookbook,* a 128-page cookbook from the 45th National Chicken Cooking Contest. It features the $25,000 grand-prize recipe, Pacific Rim Chicken Burgers with Ginger Mayonnaise, and four other top winners, as well as recipes from the 51 finalists (one from each state and the District of Columbia).

Sections of the book feature spicy chicken recipes, regional varieties, holidays or special occasions, outdoor dining, and time-savers using convenient diced, cut up, marinated, or precooked products.

To order, send a check or money order (no cash, please) for $2.95 (includes postage) payable to Chicken Cookbook with your name and address to Chicken Cookbook, Department NCC, Box 307W, Coventry, CT 06238. For other great recipes, tips, and information, visit **www.eatchicken.com.**

■ It's that time of year again for every Southerner's favorite—sweet onions. The National Onion Association offers two helpful brochures to take advantage of the season.

"Onions for Your Health" contains nutritional facts and valuable data concerning possible prevention of chronic diseases and links to lowering blood pressure and cholesterol levels. A sprinkling of recipes includes Caramelized Onions and a spicy Onion-Peach Salsa.

"Favorite Onion Recipes" highlights updated classic tastes such as onion soup, onion rings, and even a healthy baked version of the popular fried onion bloom.

To receive these offers, send a self-addressed, stamped business-sized envelope (one envelope for each brochure) to National Onion Association, Dept. SL, 822 Seventh Street, Suite 510, Greeley, CO 80631. Visit **www.onions-usa.org** for a variety of recipes and facts.

from our kitchen

Delightfully simple and inexpensive table decorations are sure to charm your guests on Easter. Create a magical woodland centerpiece (pictured on page 80) by filling a moss-covered basket with fresh flowers and sugared white chocolate rabbits, or use mismatched eggcups to display miniature eggshell vases and candy dishes. We used small cell packs (four to six plants per pack) of pansies, violas, and variegated ivy, but any assortment of fresh flowers and foliage will work well. Plus, they can all be planted outdoors after the holiday. Just select a color scheme that will complement your china and table linens, and then follow the easy directions below.

Sugared Rabbits

Whisk together 2 tablespoons of water and 2 teaspoons of meringue powder until light and foamy. Brush a thin, even layer over white chocolate rabbits, and sprinkle with granulated sugar. Let dry completely on wax paper. Tie with bits of colored ribbon, if desired.

NOTE: Meringue powder is available at crafts stores and Wal-Mart stores that sell cake-decorating supplies, or you can order it online from the Wilton Web site at **www.wilton.com.** We use it often in dessert recipes such as chilled soufflés or mousses that call for uncooked egg whites. Made from pasteurized powdered egg whites, it's free of salmonella. After opening, it can be stored in a cool, dry place for up to two years and used as an egg-white substitute in cakes and candies as well as royal icings and frostings (2 teaspoons of meringue powder whisked with 2 tablespoons of water equals 1 egg white). Meringue powder also contains small amounts of cornstarch and cream of tartar that work as stabilizers, creating exceptionally crisp baked meringues and pie shells. For more information and recipes visit **www.wilton.com.**

Eggshell Vases and Candy Dishes
(pictured on page 80)

Prepare egg dye according to package directions. Color extra-large raw eggs as desired, and let dry. Pierce the narrow end of each egg with a sturdy pin or sewing needle. Using a small pair of sharp, pointed scissors, carefully snip away the top third of each eggshell. Empty out the white and yolk, and reserve for another use. Gently rinse the eggshells, and invert onto paper towels to dry. Place eggshells in eggcups, and fill with water and fresh flowers or assorted pastel candies and trinkets.

Tips and Tidbits

■ Pop a container of the new Baker's Dipping Chocolate (available in dark and milk chocolate) in the microwave for a quick and easy fondue, or create an amazing array of fanciful desserts and petits fours by coating cubes of pound cake, cookies, candies, pretzels, and fruits. To harden the chocolate coating, place the dipped treats on a wax paper-lined tray and refrigerate 10 to 15 minutes or until set. Excess moisture can cause the chocolate to clump together, so be sure to pat fresh fruits dry with a paper towel before dipping. Left-over chocolate can be refrigerated up to two weeks and remelted. For more information visit **www.bakerschocolate.com.**

■ Brighten a spring buffet with a festive bowl of Easter Egg Potatoes from Wood Prairie Farms. This colorful collection of baby egg-shaped organic potatoes is delicious roasted with a sprinkling of olive oil and fresh herbs or boiled and tossed with your favorite condiments for potato salad. They're available in 2- to 20-pound boxes ($9.95 to $69.95) from **www.woodprairie.com.**

Mint Juleps

The Brown Hotel in Louisville surrendered the following Mint Julep recipe to us for you to try at home.

Make mint simple syrup using 1 cup granulated sugar and 1 cup water; bring to a boil. Add fresh mint sprigs (about 12); cool and discard leaves. Pack a 10-ounce glass with crushed ice; add 1 tablespoon simple syrup and $2\frac{1}{4}$ teaspoons Kentucky bourbon. Add water to fill glass; stir once. Garnish with mint sprigs, and sprinkle with powdered sugar. Serve with a short straw. (Makes one 10-ounce serving.)

Test Kitchens' Speedy Suppers

Snag one of these ideas for a quick-to-fix meal.

Even people who enjoy spending time in the kitchen value a clever shortcut—especially on busy days when they're craving the comfort of a home-cooked meal or needing an impressive menu for last-minute entertaining. *Southern Living* Test Kitchens' professionals are no exception. These top-rated recipes combine the ease of our favorite convenience products with fresh ingredients to deliver a great-tasting meal in a matter of minutes.

CHICKEN SCALOPPINE WITH LINGUINE ALFREDO

family favorite • fast fixin's
Prep: 5 min., Cook: 6 min.

The secret to sautéing thinly sliced cutlets is to have the pan and oil hot enough to sear the meat—the food should hiss as soon as it hits the pan.

- **½ cup all-purpose flour**
- **1 teaspoon salt**
- **¾ teaspoon seasoned pepper**
- **1½ pounds chicken cutlets**
- **2 tablespoons olive oil**
- **1 cup white wine**
- **Garnish: fresh parsley sprigs**
- **Linguine Alfredo**

COMBINE first 3 ingredients in a shallow dish; dredge chicken cutlets in flour mixture.
COOK chicken in hot oil in a large skillet over medium-high heat 1 to 2 minutes

on each side or until done. Remove from skillet, and keep warm.
ADD wine to skillet; cook chicken 1 to 2 minutes or until liquid is reduced by half, stirring to loosen particles from bottom of skillet.
ARRANGE cutlets on a serving platter, and drizzle with sauce. Garnish, if desired. Serve with Linguine Alfredo. **MAKES** 4 servings.

Linguine Alfredo:
fast fixin's
Prep: 5 min., Cook: 3 min.

- **1 (10-ounce) container refrigerated light Alfredo sauce**
- **½ cup chopped fresh parsley**
- **½ cup white wine**
- **3 tablespoons reduced-fat sour cream**
- **1 garlic clove, sliced**
- **1 (8-ounce) package refrigerated linguine**

PROCESS first 5 ingredients in a blender or food processor until smooth, stopping to scrape down sides.
PREPARE linguine according to package directions; drain and return to pan. Stir in Alfredo sauce mixture, and serve immediately. **MAKES** 4 servings.

NOTE: For testing purposes only, we used Buitoni Light Alfredo Sauce.

SPICY GRILLED PORK TENDERLOIN

family favorite
Prep: 5 min., Grill: 20 min., Stand: 10 min.

Caribbean seasoning adds a touch of sweet heat to these grilled tenderloins. If you're in search of an easy entrée that can go from everyday to gourmet, this is it. *(pictured on page 115)*

- **2 (16-ounce) pork tenderloins**
- **1 tablespoon olive oil**
- **1½ tablespoons Caribbean jerk seasoning**

BRUSH tenderloins with olive oil, and rub evenly with seasoning.
GRILL, covered with grill lid, over medium-high heat (350° to 400°) 10 minutes on each side or until a meat thermometer inserted in thickest portion of tenderloins registers 155°. Remove from grill, and let stand 10 minutes or until temperature registers 160°. **MAKES** 6 servings.

NOTE: For testing purposes only, we used McCormick Caribbean Jerk Seasoning.

CHICKEN ENCHILADAS

family favorite
Prep: 15 min., Bake: 30 min.

It's fun to set up a buffet line with the desired toppings and let guests take their choice.

- **3 cups chopped cooked chicken**
- **2 cups (8 ounces) shredded Monterey Jack cheese with peppers**
- **½ cup sour cream**
- **1 (4.5-ounce) can chopped green chiles, drained**
- **⅓ cup chopped fresh cilantro**
- **8 (8-inch) flour tortillas**
- **Vegetable cooking spray**
- **1 (8-ounce) container sour cream**
- **1 (8-ounce) jar tomatillo salsa**
- **Toppings: diced tomatoes, chopped avocado, chopped green onions, sliced ripe olives**

STIR together first 5 ingredients. Spoon chicken mixture evenly down center of each tortilla, and roll up. Arrange seam side down in a lightly greased 13- x 9-inch baking dish. Coat tortillas with cooking spray.

BAKE at 350° for 30 minutes or until golden brown.

STIR together 8-ounce container sour cream and salsa. Spoon over hot enchiladas; sprinkle with desired toppings.

MAKES 4 servings.

TWICE-BAKED MASHED POTATOES

family favorite

Prep: 15 min., Bake: 20 min.

You'll find that these potatoes are just as delicious when you substitute reduced-fat dairy products. The potatoes can also be served family style in a 2-quart baking dish. *(pictured on page 115)*

- 1 (22-ounce) package frozen mashed potatoes
- ½ (8-ounce) package cream cheese, softened
- ½ cup sour cream
- ¼ cup chopped fresh chives
- 4 bacon slices, cooked and crumbled
- ½ teaspoon seasoned pepper
- ¼ teaspoon salt
- ½ cup (2 ounces) shredded Cheddar cheese

PREPARE potatoes according to package directions.

STIR in cream cheese and next 5 ingredients. Divide mixture evenly between 6 (6-ounce) lightly greased ramekins or custard cups. Sprinkle evenly with Cheddar cheese.

BAKE at 350° for 20 minutes or until thoroughly heated. **MAKES** 6 servings.

NOTE: For testing purposes only, we used Ore-Ida Frozen Mashed Potatoes.

The Hot List of Time-Saving Tips

- **Rotisserie chicken:** It's terrific when you need chopped cooked chicken for a recipe. Remove the meat from the bones while chicken is still warm, and freeze in a zip-top freezer bag. One rotisserie chicken will yield about 3 cups of chopped meat.
- **9-1-1 Pot Roast:** Purchase sliced beef brisket by the pound from your favorite barbecue restaurant. Arrange in a baking dish, and cover with equal parts barbecue sauce and beef broth. Bake, covered, at 350° for 30 minutes or until thoroughly heated.
- **Frozen mashed potatoes:** You might be skeptical at first, but these are absolutely delicious. Prepare 1 (22-ounce) bag according to package directions, and then stir in 4 ounces of softened cream cheese, ½ teaspoon seasoned pepper, and ¼ teaspoon salt. It's as simple as that. The trick is in the cream cheese, and ⅓-less-fat works as well as regular—you don't even need to add butter.
- **Refrigerated pasta:** It comes in a wide variety of shapes and flavors and cooks in boiling water in only 2 to 3 minutes.
- **Spice blends:** Instead of purchasing separate jars of dried herbs and spices, invest in a few versatile seasoning blends. A word of caution: Flavor profiles and salt content can vary dramatically according to brand, so read the label. Ingredients are always listed in descending order according to weight.

FRUIT SALAD WITH BLACKBERRY-BASIL VINAIGRETTE

family favorite • fast fixin's

Prep: 10 min.

Look for refrigerated jars of sliced mango and pink grapefruit segments in the produce section of the supermarket. *(pictured on page 115)*

- 8 cups gourmet mixed salad greens
- 1½ cups sliced mango
- 1½ cups pink grapefruit segments
- 1½ cups sliced fresh strawberries
- 1 cup fresh blackberries
- 1 large avocado, sliced
- Blackberry-Basil Vinaigrette

PLACE first 6 ingredients in a large bowl, and gently toss. Serve immediately with Blackberry-Basil Vinaigrette. **MAKES** 6 servings.

Blackberry-Basil Vinaigrette:
fast fixin's

Prep: 5 min.

- ½ (10-ounce) jar seedless blackberry preserves
- ¼ cup red wine vinegar
- 6 fresh basil leaves
- 1 garlic clove, sliced
- ½ teaspoon salt
- ½ teaspoon seasoned pepper
- ¾ cup vegetable oil

PULSE first 6 ingredients in a blender 2 or 3 times until blended. With blender running, pour vegetable oil through food chute in a slow, steady stream; process until smooth. **MAKES** 1 cup.

Grains of Gold

Rice has been a staple in our dishes and culture for generations.

Robert Petter, Jr., and his brother, David, of Stuttgart, Arkansas, cultivate rice on the land their family has farmed for over a century. Their spread is one of roughly 4,200 Arkansas farms that together produce half the U.S. rice harvest of 458 million bushels. This country's first rice harvest was grown in the South Carolina Lowcountry in the late 17th century.

Wherever it's grown, rice is one of the South's most sustaining and versatile grains. It's an admirable complement to any entrée that includes gravy or sauce, and can be used as a base for pudding and patties.

" Cook's Notes "

As a Charlestonian, Senior Writer **Donna Florio** grew up with rice on the table every day—it was simply a fact of life. "Only as I grew older did I realize this was not the case for most of the rest of the country," says Donna. "Because the Low-country was the entry point for rice in America, I've always taken a pro-prietary interest in the grain and its historic value to the community. Without rice and the labor of the slaves that produced it, Charleston as we know it wouldn't exist." She was fascinated to learn how the rice culture moved west after the Civil War and how people are keep-ing it alive in South Carolina. Natu-rally, Donna got to taste a lot of great rice dishes as we followed the trail of golden grains.

ENGLISH RICE PUDDING

family favorite

Prep: 5 min., Bake: 1 hr.

Shirley Petter got this recipe from her mother, Kitty Stipp.

- **3 cups cooked long-grain rice**
- **2 cups hot milk**
- **2 cups hot whipping cream**
- **4 eggs, lightly beaten**
- **1½ cups sugar**
- **1 cup raisins**
- **1 teaspoon vanilla extract**
- **¼ teaspoon salt**
- **2 tablespoons butter or margarine, cut up**
- **¼ teaspoon ground nutmeg**
- **Lemon Sauce (optional)**

STIR together first 8 ingredients until thoroughly blended. Pour into a greased 13- x 9-inch baking dish; dot with butter, and sprinkle evenly with nutmeg. Place baking dish in a large pan; add hot water to pan to a depth of 1 inch.
BAKE at 350° for 1 hour or until lightly browned and set. Cool slightly, and cut into squares. Serve with Lemon Sauce, if desired. **MAKES** 18 servings.

Lemon Sauce:
fast fixin's
Prep: 5 min., Cook: 5 min.

- **1 cup water**
- **½ cup sugar**
- **2 tablespoons cornstarch**
- **⅛ teaspoon salt**
- **1 tablespoon butter or margarine**
- **1 tablespoon grated lemon zest**
- **½ cup fresh lemon juice**

STIR together first 4 ingredients in a small saucepan until smooth. Cook, stir-ring constantly, over medium heat 5 minutes or until thickened. Remove from heat, and stir in butter, zest, and lemon juice. Serve warm or cold. **MAKES** about 1½ cups.

SHIRLEY PETTER
TOLLVILLE, ARKANSAS

Rice Cooking Basics

We cooked rice in a cooktop steamer, an electric steamer, and a heavy pot with a tight-fitting lid. All methods yielded similar results. *For the steamers,* we used the amounts of liquid and cooking methods recommended in the direc-tions. *For the pot method:* Bring 2 cups of water and ½ teaspoon salt to a boil. Add 1 cup long-grain rice; reduce heat, and cook, covered (no peeking), for 20 minutes. Let stand, covered, 5 minutes, and fluff with a fork. Makes 3 cups.

Some cooks suggest washing the grains before cooking for a fluffier finished product, but we found the washed rice to be stickier than the batch that we didn't wash.

Purchase electric rice steamers at cookware stores and Asian markets. Order cooktop rice steamers from Charleston Hardware, (843) 556-0220.

CHICKEN-AND-HAM JAMBALAYA WITH SHRIMP

family favorite

Prep: 25 min.; Cook: 1 hr., 50 min.

This one-dish meal is adapted from *Eula Mae's Cajun Kitchen* (Harvard Common Press, 2002) by Eula Mae Doré and Marcelle Bienvenu.

- ¾ **pound skinned and boned chicken thighs, cut into 1-inch cubes**
- ¾ **pound skinned and boned chicken breasts, cut into 1-inch cubes**
- 1 **teaspoon salt**
- ⅛ **teaspoon ground black pepper**
- ⅛ **teaspoon ground red pepper**
- 2 **tablespoons vegetable oil**
- ½ **pound cooked ham, cut into ½-inch cubes**
- 2 **medium-size yellow onions, chopped (about 2 cups)**
- 1 **large green bell pepper, seeded and chopped**
- 1½ **celery ribs, chopped (about 1 cup)**
- 4 **whole garlic cloves**
- 1 **(16-ounce) can diced tomatoes, undrained**
- 3 **cups chicken broth**
- 2 **pounds unpeeled, medium-size fresh shrimp**
- ½ **cup chopped green onions tops**
- 2 **tablespoons chopped fresh parsley**
- 1 **teaspoon hot pepper sauce**
- 2 **cups uncooked long-grain rice, rinsed and drained**

SPRINKLE chicken evenly with salt and ground peppers.
COOK chicken in hot oil in a Dutch oven over medium heat 8 to 10 minutes or until brown on all sides. Remove chicken with a slotted spoon to a large bowl.
ADD ham to Dutch oven, and cook, stirring constantly, 5 minutes or until lightly browned. Add ham to chicken; set aside.
ADD yellow onions and next 3 ingredients to Dutch oven, and cook 5 minutes, stirring to loosen any browned bits.
DRAIN diced tomatoes, reserving liquid; set tomatoes aside. Stir reserved tomato liquid and chicken broth into Dutch oven. Add chicken and ham; cover and cook over low heat 45 minutes.

PEEL shrimp; devein, if desired.
MASH cooked garlic against side of Dutch oven, and blend into mixture. Add drained tomatoes, shrimp, green onions, and remaining ingredients, and bring to a boil. Cover and reduce heat to medium low; simmer, stirring occasionally, 25 minutes or until rice is tender and liquid is absorbed. **MAKES** 6 to 8 servings.

EULA MAE DORÉ
AVERY ISLAND, LOUISIANA

JOURNEY CAKES

fast fixin's

Prep: 5 min., Fry: 4 min. per batch

These cakes were an early version of road food. Workers in the field or travelers would tuck several into their pockets for a simple meal.

- 2 **cups cold, cooked aromatic rice***
- 2 **large eggs, lightly beaten**
- 2 **cups milk**
- 2 **cups all-purpose flour**
- 1½ **tablespoons butter, melted**
- 2 **teaspoons salt**
- **Peanut oil**

STIR together first 6 ingredients.
POUR oil to a depth of ¼ inch into a large heavy skillet; heat to 350°.
DROP batter by ¼ cupfuls into hot oil; fry in batches 2 minutes on each side or until golden. Drain on wire racks over paper towels. Serve immediately. **MAKES** 20 cakes.

ROSEMARY-GARLIC JOURNEY CAKES: Add ¼ cup finely chopped fresh or dried rosemary and 1 tablespoon finely chopped garlic to batter. Proceed as directed. **MAKES** 20 cakes. Prep: 5 min., Fry: 4 min per batch.

TOMATO, PARMESAN, AND KALAMATA OLIVE JOURNEY CAKES: Add 1 tomato, seeded and finely chopped; ½ cup shredded Parmesan cheese; and ¼ cup minced kalamata olives to rice mixture. Proceed as directed. **MAKES** 20 cakes. Prep: 10 min., Fry: 4 min. per batch.

*Basmati and jasmine are two types of long-grain rice that are fragrant and have a nutlike flavor.

MEREDITH COXE
DARLINGTON, SOUTH CAROLINA

Which Rice?

Here are some definitions of the most common varieties of rice.
- **Long-grain rice** has long, slender kernels that cook up separate, light, and fluffy.
- **Medium-grain rice** is slightly shorter and wider than long-grain rice. Cooked kernels are moist, tender, and slightly sticky.
- **Short-grain rice** kernels are almost round and stick together when cooked. Short-grain rice has a higher starch content than other types.
- **Brown rice** has the outer hull removed, but retains the bran layers that give it a tan color, chewy texture, and nutlike flavor. Brown rice has more minerals, vitamins, and fiber than white rice.
- **Parboiled rice** is soaked, steamed, and dried to remove the outer hull. Grains are firmer and more separate and retain more nutrients than regular rice.

Where to Find It

- Carolina Gold is a delicate rice with grains that break easily, making it great in creamy, stirred dishes. You can order it from **www.charlestonfavorites.com,** 1-800-538-0003.
- You can order Carolina Plantation Aromatic Rice from **www.carolinaplantationrice.com,** (843) 393-1812.

Our Favorite Catfish Feast

Pull up a chair for an authentic Southern fish fry.

Down-Home Dinner

Serves 8 to 10

Fried Catfish

Best Barbecue Coleslaw

Potato Salad With Roasted Red Peppers

Double-Chocolate Brownies

FRIED CATFISH

chef recipe • fast fixin's

Prep: 10 min., Fry: 6 min. per batch

Originally appearing in 1996, this staff favorite is rolled in cornmeal and fried to crunchy perfection. Fry in batches to prevent the oil temperature from dropping too low. *(pictured on page 113)*

- 1 cup all-purpose flour
- 1 tablespoon salt
- 2 teaspoons ground black pepper
- 2 teaspoons ground red pepper
- 1 cup buttermilk
- 1 large egg
- 2½ cups self-rising yellow cornmeal
- 1 tablespoon garlic powder
- 2 tablespoons dried thyme
- 10 (6- to 8-ounce) farm-raised catfish fillets
- Peanut oil
- Lemon wedges

COMBINE first 4 ingredients in a shallow dish. Stir together buttermilk and egg in a bowl. Combine cornmeal, garlic powder, and thyme in a zip-top freezer bag.
DREDGE catfish in flour mixture, and dip in buttermilk mixture, allowing excess to drip off. Place catfish in cornmeal mixture; seal bag, and shake to coat.
POUR oil to a depth of 1½ inches into a large cast-iron skillet; heat to 360°. Fry catfish, in batches, 3 minutes on each side or until golden. Drain on wire racks over paper towels. Serve immediately with lemon wedges. **MAKES** 10 servings.

FRONT PORCH RESTAURANT
YELLVILLE, ARKANSAS

BEST BARBECUE COLESLAW

family favorite • make ahead

Prep: 10 min., Chill: 2 hrs.
(pictured on page 113)

- ½ cup sugar
- ½ cup mayonnaise
- ¼ cup milk
- ¼ cup buttermilk
- 2½ tablespoons lemon juice
- 1½ tablespoons white vinegar
- ½ teaspoon salt
- ⅛ teaspoon pepper
- 2 (10-ounce) packages finely shredded cabbage
- 1 carrot, shredded

WHISK together first 8 ingredients in a large bowl; add vegetables, tossing to coat. Cover and chill at least 2 hours. **MAKES** 8 to 10 servings.

POTATO SALAD WITH ROASTED RED PEPPERS

family favorite

Prep: 20 min., Cook: 30 min.
(pictured on page 113)

- 3 pounds Yukon gold or red potatoes
- 1 teaspoon salt
- 1 (12-ounce) jar roasted red bell peppers, drained
- 7 green onions, sliced
- ½ cup chopped fresh cilantro or parsley
- ⅓ cup fresh lime juice
- ¾ teaspoon salt
- ½ teaspoon pepper
- 2 tablespoons olive oil

BRING potatoes, 1 teaspoon salt, and water to cover to a boil in a Dutch oven; cook 30 minutes or until potatoes are tender. Drain; cool slightly, and peel. Cut into cubes.
COMBINE potatoes, roasted peppers, green onions, and cilantro in a large bowl. Stir together lime juice and next 3 ingredients; pour over potato mixture, tossing gently to coat. Cover and chill until ready to serve. **MAKES** 8 to 10 servings.

DOUBLE-CHOCOLATE BROWNIES

Prep: 10 min., Bake: 35 min.

Two kinds of chocolate will lure you to try these rich brownies.

- 1 cup butter or margarine, softened
- 2 cups sugar
- 4 large eggs
- 1 cup unsweetened cocoa
- 1 teaspoon vanilla extract
- 1 cup all-purpose flour
- 1 cup chopped pecans
- ⅔ cup white chocolate or semisweet chocolate morsels

BEAT butter at medium speed with an electric mixer until creamy; gradually add sugar, beating well. Add eggs, 1 at a time, beating just until blended.

ADD cocoa and vanilla; beat at low speed 1 minute or until blended. Gradually add flour, beating well.

STIR in pecans and morsels. Pour batter into a greased 13- x 9-inch pan.

BAKE at 350° for 30 to 35 minutes or until done. Cool and cut into squares. **MAKES** 2 dozen.

STACEY ATTANASIO
LOS ANGELES, CALIFORNIA

Pick a Pesto

Use that abundant fresh basil in your garden to make flavorful pesto. This easy Italian sauce requires only a few ingredients and a food processor. Here we offer the traditional as well as some new and different versions, including one with dried tomatoes and one that replaces the basil with poblano chile peppers and fresh cilantro. Any of these recipes can be spread on sandwiches, pizzas, or even on meat before grilling. Or you can simply serve them as dips for bread. We've also included a recipe for a flank steak-and-pasta dish that's great for grilling.

DRIED TOMATO-BASIL PESTO

fast fixin's

Prep: 5 min.

> **¼ cup dried tomatoes in oil**
> **¾ cup Basil Pesto (see following recipe)**

DRAIN tomatoes well, pressing between paper towels.

PROCESS dried tomatoes in a food processor 30 seconds or until coarsely chopped; add Basil Pesto, and process until smooth, stopping to scrape down sides. Store pesto in refrigerator up to 5 days. **MAKES** 1½ cups.

BASIL PESTO

fast fixin's

Prep: 5 min.

> **2 cups loosely packed fresh basil leaves**
> **½ cup shredded Parmesan cheese**
> **½ cup pine nuts, toasted**
> **½ cup olive oil**
> **3 large garlic cloves**
> **⅛ teaspoon salt**

PROCESS all ingredients in a food processor until smooth, stopping to scrape down sides. Store pesto in refrigerator up to 5 days. **MAKES** 1 cup.

ANNE SLITER
MONTGOMERY, ALABAMA

FLANK STEAK AND DRIED TOMATO-BASIL PESTO LINGUINE

Prep: 10 min., Cook: 35 min., Grill: 20 min., Stand: 10 min.

> **1 (16-ounce) package linguine**
> **1 (1½-pound) flank steak**
> **2 tablespoons olive oil**
> **½ teaspoon salt**
> **1 cup Dried Tomato-Basil Pesto (recipe at left)**
> **4 cups loosely packed fresh spinach leaves**
> **1 teaspoon freshly ground pepper**
> **1 teaspoon dried crushed red pepper**

COOK pasta according to package directions; drain and set aside.

BRUSH both sides of flank steak evenly with olive oil, and sprinkle with salt.

GRILL steak, covered with grill lid, over medium-high heat (350° to 400°) 8 to 10 minutes on each side or to desired degree of doneness. Let stand 10 minutes before slicing. Cut diagonally across the grain into thin strips.

HEAT ½ cup Dried Tomato-Basil Pesto in a large nonstick skillet over medium heat. Add beef strips, and cook, stirring often, 2 to 3 minutes. Add spinach, and cook, stirring often, 3 minutes or just

until wilted. Add cooked pasta and remaining ½ cup Dried Tomato-Basil Pesto, and cook, stirring occasionally, 2 minutes or until thoroughly heated. Sprinkle with ground pepper and red pepper, and serve immediately. **MAKES** 8 servings.

CENTRAL MARKET'S POBLANO-CILANTRO PESTO

chef recipe

Prep: 10 min., Broil: 10 min., Stand: 10 min.

Central Market is headquartered in Austin. You can also find locations in Dallas, Fort Worth, Houston, Plano, and San Antonio. This unique pesto is fabulous served in or as a topping for fajitas or quesadillas.

> **4 poblano chile peppers**
> **¾ cup freshly grated Parmesan cheese**
> **½ cup fresh cilantro**
> **¼ cup chopped walnuts**
> **¾ cup olive oil**
> **3 garlic cloves**
> **3 tablespoons fresh lime juice**
> **1 teaspoon salt**

PLACE peppers on an aluminum foil-lined baking sheet.

BROIL 5 inches from heat about 5 minutes on each side or until blistered.

PLACE peppers in a zip-top freezer bag; seal and let stand 10 minutes to loosen skins. Peel peppers; remove and discard seeds.

PROCESS peppers and remaining ingredients in a food processor until smooth, stopping to scrape down sides. Store pesto in refrigerator up to 1 week. **MAKES** 1¾ cups.

NOTE: Poblano peppers are dark green, tapered chile peppers, about 3 inches wide and 4 to 5 inches long. You can find them in the produce section of your grocery store.

CENTRAL MARKET
AUSTIN, TEXAS

Restaurant Recipes We Love

Great Southern chefs share some favorite dishes, which are all easy enough to make at home.

Southerners are known for good home cooking. But we also love to dine out, especially in urban hot spots. We're fortunate to live in a region offering a wealth of incredible dining establishments. There are so many great places, from family-run eateries to world-class restaurants, it was difficult to choose our favorites, but we narrowed it down to these exceptional dishes.

COMMUNE'S MAPLE-GLAZED PORK CHOPS WITH PECANS AND APPLES

chef recipe

Prep: 25 min., Cook: 3 min., Grill: 22 min.

Commune, in midtown Atlanta, is known for its popular outdoor movie series as well as its fabulous food. Innovative cuisine is enjoyed by diners seated in a community atmosphere.

- 1 cup maple syrup
- 4 teaspoons balsamic vinegar
- 4 teaspoons brown sugar
- ¼ teaspoon ground cinnamon
- ¾ cup pecan halves, toasted
- 4 (1-inch-thick) pork chops
- ¾ teaspoon salt
- ½ teaspoon freshly ground pepper
- 2 tablespoons olive oil, divided
- 2 green apples, cut into (¾-inch) slices
- ½ teaspoon salt
- ¼ cup finely diced crystallized ginger (optional)

WHISK together first 4 ingredients in a medium bowl.

STIR together pecans and 2 tablespoons maple syrup mixture in a skillet over medium heat, stirring to coat pecans. Cook, stirring often, 3 minutes or until pecans are glazed. Arrange pecans in an even layer on wax paper; let cool. Coarsely chop, and set aside.

SPRINKLE pork chops evenly with ¾ teaspoon salt and pepper; brush with 1 tablespoon olive oil.

GRILL chops, covered with grill lid, over medium-high heat (350° to 400°) 8 minutes on each side or until a meat thermometer inserted in thickest portion registers 160°, basting with ½ cup maple syrup mixture during last 5 minutes of cooking. (If glazed earlier, glaze will burn.) Transfer to a serving platter. Cover and keep warm.

SPRINKLE apple slices evenly with ½ teaspoon salt; brush with remaining 1 tablespoon oil.

GRILL apples, without grill lid, over medium-high heat 4 to 6 minutes, turning occasionally and brushing with ¼ cup syrup mixture.

SPOON remaining maple syrup mixture over pork chops. Sprinkle with chopped pecans and, if desired, crystallized ginger. Serve with grilled apples. **MAKES** 4 servings.

EXECUTIVE CHEF THOMAS RICCI
COMMUNE
ATLANTA, GEORGIA

CROOK'S CORNER SHRIMP AND GRITS

chef recipe

Prep: 30 min., Cook: 30 min.

The late Bill Neal has influenced young chefs across the South, and diners still enjoy his inspired recipes at this landmark restaurant in Chapel Hill. Executive Chef Bill Smith has added some creative touches to the menu, such as Warm Goat Cheese Salad With Roasted Beets and Pumpkin Seeds and Hangar Steak With Bourbon Brown Sauce, but Shrimp and Grits is still a Crook's Corner classic. *(pictured on page 114)*

- 2 cups water
- 1 (14-ounce) can chicken broth
- ¾ cup half-and-half
- ¾ teaspoon salt
- 1 cup uncooked regular grits
- ¾ cup (3 ounces) shredded Cheddar cheese
- ¼ cup grated Parmesan cheese
- 2 tablespoons butter
- ½ teaspoon hot sauce
- ¼ teaspoon ground white pepper
- 3 bacon slices
- 1 pound medium-size fresh shrimp, peeled and deveined
- ¼ teaspoon black pepper
- ⅛ teaspoon salt
- ¼ cup all-purpose flour
- 1 cup sliced mushrooms
- ½ cup chopped green onions
- 2 garlic cloves, minced
- ½ cup low-sodium, fat-free chicken broth
- 2 tablespoons fresh lemon juice
- ¼ teaspoon hot sauce
- Chopped green onions

BRING first 4 ingredients to a boil in a medium saucepan; gradually whisk in grits. Reduce heat, and simmer, stirring occasionally, 10 minutes or until thickened. Add Cheddar cheese and next 4 ingredients. Keep warm.

COOK bacon in a large skillet until crisp; remove bacon, and drain on paper towels, reserving 1 tablespoon drippings in skillet. Crumble bacon; set aside.

SPRINKLE shrimp with black pepper and ⅛ teaspoon salt; dredge in flour.

SAUTÉ mushrooms in hot drippings in skillet 5 minutes or until tender. Add ½ cup green onions, and sauté 2 minutes. Add shrimp and garlic, and sauté 2 minutes or until shrimp are lightly browned. **STIR** in ½ cup chicken broth, lemon juice, and hot sauce, and cook 2 more minutes, stirring to loosen particles from bottom of skillet.

SERVE shrimp mixture over hot cheese grits. Top with crumbled bacon and chopped green onions. **MAKES** 4 servings.

CHEF BILL SMITH
CROOK'S CORNER
CHAPEL HILL, NORTH CAROLINA

GALATOIRE'S SHRIMP RÉMOULADE

chef recipe

Prep: 15 min., Chill: 8 hrs.

Galatoire's Shrimp Rémoulade is delicious as an appetizer or entrée. It's a favorite starter at the restaurant.

- **4 celery ribs, coarsely chopped**
- **4 green onions, coarsely chopped**
- **1 small onion, chopped (about ½ cup)**
- **¾ cup fresh Italian parsley**
- **½ cup red wine vinegar**
- **½ cup ketchup**
- **½ cup tomato puree**
- **½ cup Creole mustard**
- **1 tablespoon prepared horseradish**
- **1 teaspoon Worcestershire sauce**
- **1 cup plus 2 tablespoons vegetable oil**
- **2 teaspoons paprika (optional)**
- **2 pounds cooked large fresh shrimp, peeled and deveined**
- **Lettuce leaves**

PULSE first 4 ingredients in a food processor until finely chopped. Add vinegar and next 5 ingredients, and process until well blended and smooth, stopping to scrape down sides. With processor running, pour oil in a slow, steady stream, processing until blended. Stir in paprika, if desired.

COVER and chill 6 to 8 hours.
STIR chilled sauce; pour over shrimp, gently tossing to coat. Serve on lettuce leaves. **MAKES** 12 appetizer servings.

CHEF ROSS EIRICH
GALATOIRE'S
NEW ORLEANS, LOUISIANA

BUTTERMILK-LIME ICE CREAM

chef recipe

Prep: 15 min., Cook: 5 min., Chill: 25 min., Freeze: 8 hrs.

This Buttermilk-Lime Ice Cream from Texas cowboy chef Grady Spears refreshes and soothes at the same time.

- **1 cup water**
- **1 cup sugar**
- **2 cups buttermilk**
- **1 teaspoon grated lime rind**
- **2 tablespoons fresh lime juice**
- **1 tablespoon corn syrup**
- **Dash of salt**
- **Garnish: lime rind curls**

BRING 1 cup water and sugar to a boil in a saucepan over medium-high heat, stirring until sugar dissolves. Remove mixture from heat; cover and chill 25 minutes.

STIR together chilled sugar syrup mixture, 2 cups buttermilk, grated lime rind, and next 3 ingredients. Pour mixture into freezer container of a 2- or 4-quart ice-cream maker, and freeze according to manufacturer's instructions. Garnish, if desired. **MAKES** 6 cups.

ADAPTED FROM *THE TEXAS COWBOY KITCHEN*
TEN SPEED PRESS, 2003
CHEF GRADY SPEARS
FORT WORTH, TEXAS

A Must-Try Side Dish

This recipe confirms that not all corn casseroles are created equal. Pair two Southern cousins—green tomatoes and tomatillos—with fresh corn, and this beloved side is elevated to a whole new level. So take advantage of summer's bounty in a new way.

GREEN TOMATO-TOMATILLO-CORN PUDDING

Prep: 20 min.; Bake: 1 hr., 5 min.; Stand: 10 min.

- **6 tomatillos, husked**
- **4 green tomatoes, chopped**
- **1 red bell pepper, chopped**
- **1 sweet onion, chopped**
- **2 garlic cloves, pressed**
- **2 tablespoons olive oil**
- **6 egg yolks**
- **2 cups fresh corn kernels (4 ears)**
- **1 cup milk**
- **½ cup sour cream**
- **3 tablespoons self-rising cornmeal**
- **¼ to ½ teaspoon dried thyme**
- **1 teaspoon salt**
- **½ teaspoon pepper**
- **2 cups (8 ounces) shredded sharp Cheddar cheese**

TOSS together first 6 ingredients in an aluminum foil-lined jellyroll pan.
BAKE at 450° for 20 minutes or until tomatillos and tomatoes are tender. Remove from oven; reduce oven temperature to 375°.
STIR together egg yolks and next 7 ingredients in a large bowl; stir in tomatillo mixture and cheese. Pour into a lightly greased 11- x 7-inch baking dish.
BAKE at 375° for 40 to 45 minutes or until set and a wooden pick inserted in center comes out clean. Let stand 10 minutes before serving. **MAKES** 8 servings.

Can-Do Grilled Chicken

These tasty recipes begin with canned drinks.

Believe it or not, chicken grilled over a can of cola or beer is tender, moist, and full of flavor. It's incredibly easy too. These delicious recipes are adapted from Steven Raichlen's book *Beer-Can Chicken* (Workman Publishing Company, New York, 2002).

BASIC BEER-CAN CHICKEN

Prep: 10 min.; Grill: 1 hr., 15 min.; Stand: 5 min.

- **2 tablespoons All-Purpose Barbecue Rub, divided**
- **1 (3½- to 4-pound) whole chicken**
- **1 tablespoon vegetable oil**
- **1 (12-ounce) can beer**

SPRINKLE 1 teaspoon All-Purpose Barbecue Rub inside body cavity and ½ teaspoon inside neck cavity of chicken.
RUB oil over skin. Sprinkle with 1 tablespoon All-Purpose Barbecue Rub, and rub over skin.
POUR out half of beer (about ¾ cup), and reserve for another use, leaving remaining beer in can. Make 2 additional holes in top of beer can. Spoon remaining 1½ teaspoons rub into beer can. (Beer will start to foam.)
PLACE chicken upright onto the beer can, fitting can into cavity. Pull legs forward to form a tripod, allowing chicken to stand upright.
PREPARE a fire by piling charcoal on 1 side of grill, leaving other side empty. (For gas grills, light only 1 side.) Place a drip pan on unlit side, and place food grate on grill. Place chicken upright over drip pan. Grill, covered with grill lid, 1 hour and 15 minutes or until golden and a meat thermometer inserted in thigh registers 180°.
REMOVE chicken from grill, and let stand 5 minutes; carefully remove can.
MAKES 2 to 4 servings.

All-Purpose Barbecue Rub:
fast fixin's
Prep: 5 min.

- **¼ cup coarse salt**
- **¼ cup firmly packed dark brown sugar**
- **¼ cup sweet paprika**
- **2 tablespoons pepper**

COMBINE all ingredients. Store mixture in an airtight jar, away from heat, up to 6 months. **MAKES** about 1 cup.

COLA-CAN CHICKEN

family favorite
Prep: 20 min.; Grill: 1 hr., 15 min.; Stand: 5 min.

- **2 tablespoons Barbecue Rub, divided**
- **1 (3½- to 4-pound) whole chicken**
- **3 tablespoons vegetable oil**
- **1 (12-ounce) can cola**
- **Cola Barbecue Sauce**

SPRINKLE 1 teaspoon Barbecue Rub inside body cavity and ½ teaspoon inside neck cavity of chicken.
RUB oil over skin. Sprinkle with 1 tablespoon Barbecue Rub, and rub over skin.
POUR out half of cola (about ¾ cup), and reserve for Cola Barbecue Sauce, leaving remaining cola in can. Make 2 additional holes in top of can. Spoon remaining 1½ teaspoons rub into cola can. (Cola will start to foam.)
PLACE chicken upright onto the cola can, fitting can into cavity. Pull legs forward to form a tripod, allowing chicken to stand upright.
PREPARE a fire by piling charcoal on 1 side of grill, leaving other side empty. (For gas grills, light only 1 side.) Place a drip pan on unlit side, and place food grate on grill. Place chicken upright over drip pan. Grill, covered with grill lid, 1 hour and 15 minutes or until golden and a meat thermometer inserted in thigh registers 180°.
REMOVE chicken from grill, and let stand 5 minutes; carefully remove can. Serve with Cola Barbecue Sauce.
MAKES 2 to 4 servings.

Barbecue Rub:
fast fixin's
Prep: 5 min.

- **1 tablespoon mild chili powder**
- **2 teaspoons salt**
- **2 teaspoons light brown sugar**
- **1 teaspoon black pepper**
- **1 teaspoon ground cumin**
- **½ teaspoon garlic powder**
- **¼ teaspoon ground red pepper**

COMBINE all ingredients. **MAKES** 3 tablespoons.

Cola Barbecue Sauce:
fast fixin's
Prep: 15 min., Cook: 8 min.

- **1 tablespoon butter**
- **½ small onion, minced**
- **1 tablespoon minced fresh ginger**
- **1 garlic clove, minced**
- **¾ cup reserved cola**
- **¾ cup ketchup**
- **½ teaspoon grated lemon rind**
- **2 tablespoons fresh lemon juice**
- **2 tablespoons Worcestershire sauce**
- **2 tablespoons steak sauce**
- **½ teaspoon liquid smoke**
- **½ teaspoon pepper**
- **Salt to taste**

MELT butter in a heavy saucepan over medium heat. Add onion, ginger, and garlic; sauté 3 minutes or until tender. **STIR** in reserved cola; bring to a boil. Stir in ketchup and remaining ingredients; bring to a boil. Reduce heat; simmer 5 minutes. **MAKES** about 1½ cups.

NOTE: For testing purposes only, we used A1 Steak Sauce.

Fresh Spin on Lettuce

Two lettuce combinations—romaine and spring mix salad blend—anchor these recipes. Romaine is a sturdy lettuce that holds up to creamy dressings, and the curls and texture of spring mix blends capture lightweight vinaigrette dressings beautifully. Both are available in ready-to-use bags. We wash ours, regardless of how they come. Be sure to spin the leaves dry in a salad spinner, or pat dry with paper towels. Otherwise, the dressing won't cling to wet leaves.

FRUITY SPRING MIX SALAD

fast fixin's • make ahead

Prep: 15 min.

The salad dressing and sugared almonds can be made several days ahead.

- 1 head Bibb lettuce, torn
- 10 ounces gourmet mixed salad greens*
- 2 cups chopped fresh pineapple (1-inch cubes)
- 2 kiwifruit, peeled and sliced
- 1 (11-ounce) can mandarin oranges, drained and chilled
- 16 green or red seedless grapes, cut in half lengthwise
- Sweet-Hot Vinaigrette
- Sugared Almonds

TOSS first 6 ingredients together in a large glass bowl. Drizzle evenly with Sweet-Hot Vinaigrette, and sprinkle with Sugared Almonds. **MAKES** 6 to 8 servings.

*Substitute 10 cups, loosely packed and torn, of your favorite salad greens, if desired.

Sweet-Hot Vinaigrette:
Prep: 5 min., Chill: 30 min.

- ¼ cup vegetable oil
- ¼ cup balsamic vinegar
- 2 tablespoons sugar
- ¼ teaspoon salt
- ¼ teaspoon pepper
- ¼ teaspoon hot sauce

WHISK together all ingredients. Cover and chill 30 minutes. **MAKES** ½ cup.

ANDREA DUCHARME
LAFAYETTE, LOUISIANA

Sugared Almonds:
Prep: 2 min., Cook: 10 min., Cool: 20 min.

- 1 cup slivered almonds
- ½ cup sugar

STIR together almonds and sugar in a heavy saucepan over medium heat; cook, stirring constantly, 10 minutes or until golden. Spread in a layer on lightly greased wax paper; cool 20 minutes. Break into pieces; store in an airtight container. **MAKES** 1 cup.

GRILLED ROMAINE SALAD WITH BUTTERMILK-CHIVE DRESSING

fast fixin's

Prep: 10 min., Grill: 11 min.

- 4 bunches romaine hearts
- 1 red onion
- 1 to 2 tablespoons olive oil
- Vegetable cooking spray or oil
- Buttermilk-Chive Dressing
- Kosher salt to taste
- Freshly ground pepper to taste
- ½ cup freshly shaved or shredded Parmesan cheese

CUT romaine hearts in half lengthwise, keeping leaves intact. Cut red onion crosswise into ½-inch slices, keeping rings intact; brush with olive oil, and set aside.

COAT food grate evenly with cooking spray, or brush lightly with vegetable oil. Place food grate on grill over medium heat (300° to 350°).

GRILL onion slices, covered with grill lid, 2 to 3 minutes on each side, or just until slices are tender. Set aside.

PLACE romaine halves, cut side down, on food grate. Grill, uncovered, 3 to 5 minutes or until just wilted. If desired, rotate halves once to get crisscross grill marks. Brush warm romaine halves with Buttermilk-Chive Dressing, coating lightly.

PLACE 2 romaine halves on each of 4 salad plates. Sprinkle with salt and pepper to taste. Top each evenly with onion slices and Parmesan cheese. Serve immediately with remaining Buttermilk-Chive Dressing. **MAKES** 4 servings.

Buttermilk-Chive Dressing:
Prep: 10 min.

- ¾ cup buttermilk
- ½ cup mayonnaise
- 2 tablespoons chopped fresh chives
- 1 tablespoon minced green onion
- 1 garlic clove, minced
- ½ teaspoon salt
- ¼ teaspoon freshly ground pepper

WHISK together all ingredients. Cover and chill until ready to use. **MAKES** 1¼ cups.

LAURA MARTIN
NEW ORLEANS, LOUISIANA

Best Drinks of the South

Here are a few creative twists on some old Southern favorite beverages. Mint Julep Martini combines Kentucky bourbon with vanilla vodka and crème de menthe, while Classic Cola Float offers old-fashioned flavor. Whatever your thirst demands, these Southern drinks are sure to wet your whistle.

MINT JULEP MARTINI

chef recipe • fast fixin's

Prep: 5 min.

The julep is considered the official drink of the Kentucky Derby. Kyle Tabler of The Red Lounge in Louisville adds a martini twist to this favorite sipper.

- **¼ cup bourbon**
- **¼ cup orange liqueur**
- **1 teaspoon vanilla vodka***
- **1 teaspoon clear crème de menthe**
- **6 ice cubes**
- **Garnishes: fresh mint sprig, orange rind curl**

COMBINE first 5 ingredients in a martini shaker. Cover with lid, and shake until thoroughly chilled. Remove lid, and strain into a chilled martini glass. Serve immediately. Garnish, if desired. **MAKES** 1 serving.

NOTE: This recipe can be easily doubled. Make desired amount of servings, and store in a pitcher. Serve chilled. For testing purposes only, we used Smirnoff Vanilla Twist for vanilla vodka and Grand Marnier for orange liqueur.

*Substitute ½ teaspoon vanilla extract, if desired .

KYLE TABLER
THE RED LOUNGE
LOUISVILLE, KENTUCKY

MIMOSA

fast fixin's

Prep: 5 min.

This drink is popular at the jazz brunch at Lulu White's Mahogany Hall in New Orleans.

POUR equal parts of chilled fresh orange juice and Champagne into a Champagne flute. Garnish with an orange slice and an orange blossom sprig, if desired. **MAKES** 1 serving.

SAZERAC

fast fixin's

Prep: 10 min., Cook: 5 min.

Said to be The Big Easy's first cocktail, it was originally served at the Sazerac Coffee House.

- **1 cup sugar**
- **1 cup water**
- **Ice cubes**
- **¼ cup rye whiskey or bourbon**
- **¼ teaspoon bitters**
- **¼ teaspoon anise liqueur**
- **Lemon rind twist**

COOK sugar and water in a saucepan over medium-high heat 5 minutes, stirring until sugar dissolves. Remove from heat; cool. **PACK** a 3½-ounce cocktail glass with ice cubes, and set glass aside. **COMBINE** whiskey, bitters, sugar syrup, and a few ice cubes in a cocktail shaker; stir to chill. **DISCARD** ice cubes in cocktail glass. Coat inside of glass with liqueur, shaking out excess liqueur. (For stronger licorice flavor, leave excess liqueur in glass.) Rub lemon rind over glass rim; discard rind. **STRAIN** whiskey mixture into glass. Serve immediately. **MAKES** 1 serving.

NOTE: For testing, we used Jim Beam Straight Rye Whiskey, Peychaud's Bitters, and Herbsaint anise liqueur. Rye whiskey is distilled from rye grain instead of wheat and barley, giving it a smooth, rich flavor similar to that of bourbon.

BLOODY MARY PUNCH

fast fixin's

Prep: 10 min.

Here's a spicy spin on this classic tomato cocktail.

- **1 (46-ounce) can vegetable juice, chilled**
- **¾ cup vodka, chilled**
- **1 tablespoon freshly ground pepper**
- **3 tablespoons lime juice**
- **1 to 2 tablespoons hot sauce**
- **2 tablespoons Worcestershire sauce**
- **1 teaspoon Old Bay seasoning**
- **Celery sticks (optional)**
- **Cooked shrimp (optional)**

COMBINE first 7 ingredients in a punch bowl or a pitcher. Serve over ice in glasses. Serve with celery and shrimp, if desired. **MAKES** about 1½ quarts.

AMOREENA SHENEFELT
ATLANTA, GEORGIA

WHISKEY SOUR SLUSHIES

Prep: 10 min., Steep: 10 min., Freeze: 2 hrs., Stand: 30 min.

We use brewed tea in this favorite Collins drink, also known as Tennessee Tea when paired with Jack Daniel's whiskey. Instead of freezing, you can chill and serve over ice.

- **4 regular-size tea bags**
- **2 cups boiling water**
- **2 cups sugar**
- **7 cups water**
- **1 (12-ounce) can frozen orange juice concentrate, thawed**
- **1 (12-ounce) can frozen lemonade concentrate, thawed**
- **2 cups whiskey**
- **Lemon-lime soft drink**

COMBINE tea bags and 2 cups boiling water; steep 10 minutes. Remove tea bags. **BRING** tea, sugar, 7 cups water, orange juice concentrate, and lemonade concentrate to a boil in a Dutch oven over medium heat, stirring until sugar dissolves. Remove from heat, and stir in whiskey; cool.

FREEZE in zip-top freezer bags or plastic containers at least 2 hours. Remove from freezer, and let stand at room temperature 30 minutes. Break up with fork. **SCOOP** ½ cup mixture into a cocktail glass. Fill glass with lemon-lime soft drink. Serve immediately. **MAKES** about 15 cups.

NOTE: For testing purposes only, we used Jack Daniel's whiskey.

WHISKEY SOUR: Chill instead of freezing. Pour ½ cup mixture into a cocktail glass with ice. Fill glass with lemon-lime soft drink.

ROBIN LEHMAN
EPHRATA, PENNSYLVANIA

STRAWBERRY MARGARITA

fast fixin's

Prep: 10 min.

This Southwestern staple uses sweet strawberries and sugar to smooth the tartness.

- **1 (8-ounce) package frozen strawberries, partially thawed**
- **5 cups ice**
- **¾ cup tequila**
- **½ cup thawed limeade concentrate**
- **⅓ cup powdered sugar**
- **3 tablespoons orange liqueur**
- **Lime juice**
- **Red sugar crystals**
- **Garnishes: lime slices, fresh strawberries**

PROCESS first 6 ingredients in a blender until smooth.
DIP margarita glass rims in lime juice; dip rims in red sugar crystals, coating well. Pour margarita mixture into glasses. Serve immediately. Garnish, if desired. **MAKES** about 5½ cups.

NOTE: For testing purposes only, we used Grand Marnier for orange liqueur.

MELISSA QUINONES
EUSTIS, FLORIDA

CLASSIC COLA FLOAT

fast fixin's

Prep: 5 min.

Add cherry syrup or flavored soda to this kid-friendly quencher. It's even better topped with a maraschino cherry with a stem.

SCOOP vanilla ice cream into a tall glass, filling half full. Top with your favorite cola soft drink, and gently stir in ¼ teaspoon vanilla extract. Serve immediately. **MAKES** 1 serving.

MELODY LEE
DOTHAN, ALABAMA

SOUTHERN SWEET TEA

fast fixin's

Prep: 15 min.

POUR 6 cups boiling water over 4 family-size tea bags; cover and steep 5 minutes. Stir in 1 to 1½ cups sugar. Pour into a 1-gallon pitcher, and add enough water to fill pitcher. Serve over ice in glasses. Add a lemon slice or mint sprig to each serving, if desired. **MAKES** 1 gallon.

Cheese Appetizers

When it comes to appetizers, nothing satisfies like cheese. Choices such as Cheddar and Parmesan offer loads of mellow flavor.

QUICK ARTICHOKE DIP

Prep: 5 min., Chill: 1 hr.

- **½ cup reduced-fat mayonnaise**
- **½ cup reduced-fat sour cream**
- **1 (0.6-ounce) envelope Italian dressing mix**
- **1 (16-ounce) can quartered artichoke hearts, drained**
- **¼ cup shredded Parmesan cheese**

PROCESS first 3 ingredients in a food processor until blended, stopping to scrape down sides. Add artichokes and cheese, pulsing 5 to 7 times or just until artichokes are coarsely chopped.
SPOON mixture into a serving bowl; cover and chill 1 hour. **MAKES** 2 cups.

JOSIE FLYNN
VIENNA, VIRGINIA

CHEESE PUFFS

Prep: 15 min., Cook: 5 min., Bake: 12 min.

- **1 (16-ounce) loaf French bread**
- **½ cup butter or margarine**
- **1 cup (4 ounces) shredded sharp Cheddar cheese**
- **1 (3-ounce) package cream cheese**
- **2 egg whites**

TRIM crust from bread; discard crust. Cut bread into 2-inch cubes; place in a large bowl, and set aside.
MELT butter and cheeses in a saucepan over low heat; stir occasionally.
BEAT egg whites at high speed with an electric mixer until stiff peaks form; fold one-fourth of egg white into cheese mixture. Fold into remaining egg white. Pour over bread cubes, tossing to coat. Place bread cubes in a single layer on an ungreased baking sheet.
BAKE at 400° for 12 minutes or until golden. **MAKES** 2 dozen.

CLARISSA MCCONNELL
ORLANDO, FLORIDA

Flavor Lamb With Fresh Herbs

Lamb is delicious for any springtime feast and is best served medium rare (150°) to medium (160°) for full, tender flavor. All these recipes use fresh herbs to bring out the terrific taste of the lamb. If you're looking for something really easy, try Creamy Dijon Lamb Chops or simply grill chops with salt, pepper, olive oil, and your favorite fresh herb.

ROSEMARY-CRUSTED LAMB WITH TZATZIKI SAUCE

Prep: 10 min., Bake: 45 min., Stand: 10 min.

- ¼ cup chopped fresh rosemary
- 3 garlic cloves
- 3 tablespoons fresh lemon juice
- 3 tablespoons olive oil
- 1 teaspoon salt
- 1 teaspoon pepper
- 1 (6-pound) leg of lamb, boned and trimmed
- Tzatziki Sauce
- Garnish: fresh rosemary sprigs

PROCESS first 6 ingredients in a food processor until smooth. Spread rosemary mixture evenly on lamb. Place on a lightly greased rack in a roasting pan.

BAKE at 450° for 45 minutes or until a meat thermometer inserted into thickest portion registers 160°.

LET stand 10 minutes before slicing. Serve with Tzatziki Sauce. Garnish, if desired. **MAKES** 4 servings.

Tzatziki Sauce:
fast fixin's

Prep: 20 min.

This Greek sauce can also be served as a dip or a spread for sandwiches or thinned out with good olive oil for a salad dressing.

- 1 (16-ounce) container plain yogurt
- 1 large cucumber, peeled, seeded, and diced
- 1 tablespoon chopped fresh dill
- 1 tablespoon chopped fresh mint
- 1 teaspoon salt
- 1 teaspoon grated lemon rind
- 1 garlic clove, pressed

STIR together all ingredients in a large bowl. Cover and chill until ready to serve. **MAKES** 2½ cups.

MATTHEW THOMAS ROCCHIO
HOUSTON, TEXAS

LAMB SOUP WITH SPRING VEGETABLES

Prep: 20 min.; Cook: 2 hrs., 40 min.

This soup is delicious with lots of hot bread. The Citrus-Mint Gremolata brightens up the whole dish, so you may want to make a double batch and serve some on the side for guests to use as they please.

- 3 pounds boneless lamb shoulder, cubed
- 1 teaspoon salt
- 1 teaspoon pepper
- 2 tablespoons all-purpose flour
- 1 tablespoon olive oil
- 5 garlic cloves, chopped
- 1½ cups dry white wine
- 2 cups beef broth
- ½ cup orange juice
- 2 tablespoons chopped fresh rosemary
- 2 tablespoons chopped fresh thyme
- 1 pound baby carrots
- 1 (16-ounce) bag frozen whole pearl onions, unthawed
- ½ pound fresh green beans, trimmed
- Citrus-Mint Gremolata

SPRINKLE lamb evenly with salt, pepper, and flour. Cook lamb in hot oil in a large Dutch oven, stirring constantly, over medium-high heat 5 to 7 minutes or until browned. Add garlic, and sauté 2 minutes.

ADD wine, and cook, stirring occasionally, 5 minutes. Stir in beef broth and next 3 ingredients, and bring to a boil. Reduce heat to low, cover, and simmer, stirring occasionally, 2 hours.

STIR in baby carrots and pearl onions; cook, uncovered, 10 minutes. Add green beans, and cook 15 minutes. Serve hot with Citrus-Mint Gremolata. **MAKES** 6 servings.

Citrus-Mint Gremolata:
fast fixin's

Prep: 10 min.

Gremolata is an aromatic Italian garnish of parsley, lemon rind, and garlic usually used to sprinkle over veal shanks or other meat and pasta dishes. Here, we've replaced the garlic and parsley with mint and toasted pine nuts for a fresh update.

- 2 tablespoons pine nuts, toasted
- 2 tablespoons chopped fresh mint
- 1 tablespoon grated lemon rind

COMBINE all ingredients in a small bowl. **MAKES** about ¼ cup.

CREAMY DIJON LAMB CHOPS

Prep: 15 min., Cook: 13 min., Bake: 15 min., Stand: 5 min.

- 8 (2-inch-thick) lamb chops, trimmed
- ½ teaspoon salt
- ¼ teaspoon freshly ground pepper
- 1 tablespoon olive oil
- 2 garlic cloves, pressed
- ½ cup whipping cream
- ⅓ cup Dijon mustard
- 2 tablespoons chopped fresh thyme
- 1 to 2 tablespoons chopped fresh rosemary

SPRINKLE lamb chops evenly with salt and pepper.

BROWN chops in hot oil in a large heavy skillet over medium-high heat 2 minutes on each side; place chops in a 13- x 9-inch baking dish, reserving drippings in skillet.

BAKE at 400° for 15 minutes or until a meat thermometer inserted into thickest portion registers 150° (medium rare). Let stand 5 minutes before serving.

SAUTÉ garlic in reserved drippings over medium heat 3 minutes or until lightly browned.

STIR together cream and next 3 ingredients in a small bowl. Add mixture to skillet, and bring to a boil over medium heat, stirring occasionally. Reduce heat, and simmer 5 minutes. Serve with chops. **MAKES** 4 servings.

Bake Dinner in a Tart

These tarts will become instant family favorites—and they're fancy enough for company. Take a shortcut to making your own tart shell by using a refrigerated piecrust as we did for Leek-Goat Cheese Tart. Simply unfold the piecrust, roll into a 12-inch circle, fold over the outer 2 inches of dough, and crimp. Be sure to lightly brown the crust in the oven for a firm shell. Then add your filling, and bake until golden.

SOUTHWESTERN TART

family favorite

Prep: 25 min., Chill: 15 min., Bake: 35 min., Cool: 10 min.

This irresistible pie tastes as good as it looks.

- 1 cup all-purpose flour
- ½ cup grated Parmesan cheese
- 2 tablespoons chopped fresh cilantro, divided
- ½ teaspoon salt, divided
- ⅓ cup shortening
- ¼ cup water
- 1 (8-ounce) package cream cheese, softened
- 2 large eggs
- 2 green onions, chopped
- ½ teaspoon ground cumin
- 1 large ripe avocado, chopped
- 1 to 2 tablespoons fresh lime juice
- ½ cup sour cream
- ½ cup (2 ounces) shredded Cheddar cheese
- 1 tomato, chopped
- Salsa (optional)

COMBINE flour, Parmesan cheese, 1 tablespoon cilantro, and ¼ teaspoon salt; cut in shortening with a pastry blender or fork until crumbly. Add ¼ cup water, 1 tablespoon at a time, and stir with a fork until dry ingredients are moistened.

SHAPE dough into a ball, and press into a 4-inch circle over heavy-duty plastic wrap. Cover with more plastic wrap, and chill 15 minutes.

ROLL dough, covered with plastic wrap, into an 11-inch circle. Remove plastic wrap, and fit dough into a 9-inch tart pan with removable bottom. Line pastry with aluminum foil, and fill with pie weights or dried beans.

BAKE at 450° for 10 minutes. Remove weights and foil; bake 4 to 5 more minutes or until lightly browned. Cool on a wire rack.

BEAT cream cheese at medium speed with an electric mixer until smooth. Add eggs, green onions, cumin, and remaining 1 tablespoon cilantro and ¼ teaspoon salt, beating until blended. Spread evenly over crust.

BAKE at 400° for 20 minutes. Cool on a wire rack 10 minutes.

TOSS together avocado and lime juice. Spread pie with ½ cup sour cream, and sprinkle with Cheddar cheese, avocado, and tomato. Serve with salsa, if desired. **MAKES** 4 to 6 servings.

LEEK-GOAT CHEESE TART

family favorite

Prep: 20 min., Cook: 15 min., Bake: 30 min.

- ½ (15-ounce) package refrigerated piecrusts
- 4 or 5 medium leeks
- 2 tablespoons olive oil
- 3 tablespoons whipping cream
- ½ teaspoon salt
- ¼ teaspoon ground white pepper
- 1½ tablespoons chopped fresh tarragon
- 3 ounces (¾ cup) crumbled goat cheese

UNFOLD piecrust, and roll into a 12-inch circle on a lightly greased baking sheet. Fold outer 2 inches of dough over, and crimp. Prick bottom of crust with a fork.

BAKE at 425° for 8 to 10 minutes or until lightly browned.

REMOVE root, tough outer leaves, and tops from leeks, leaving 2 inches of dark leaves. Thinly slice leeks; rinse well, and drain.

SAUTÉ leeks in hot oil in a skillet over medium heat 8 to 10 minutes or until tender. (Do not brown.) Stir in cream, salt, and pepper; cook, stirring constantly, 4 to 5 minutes or until slightly thickened. Stir in tarragon.

SPRINKLE 2 ounces (½ cup) goat cheese on crust; top with leek mixture. Sprinkle with remaining cheese.

BAKE at 375° for 18 to 20 minutes or until golden and bubbly. **MAKES** 4 servings.

Sweet on Lemon Pie

Greet the season with the fresh taste of citrus. Our selections mix and match two divine fillings to make three great desserts.

Pucker up—it's time to indulge in a refreshing slice of lemon pie. Test Kitchens' professionals Rebecca Kracke Gordon and Pam Lolley created two fillings for three citrus pies that are as beautiful as they are scrumptious. In the process, our staff squeezed lots of fresh lemons, but they also found that fresh frozen lemon juice (the kind in the yellow plastic bottle) worked equally well. So grab a fork—bliss is only a bite away.

LEMON MERINGUE PIE

family favorite

Prep: 25 min., Freeze: 10 min., Bake: 50 min.

Sealing meringue to the outer edge of crust over a hot filling ensures that the meringue topping will cook completely without shrinking.
(pictured on page 116)

 1 (15-ounce) package refrigerated
   piecrusts
 Lemon Meringue Pie Filling (see
   following recipe)
 6 egg whites
 ½ teaspoon vanilla extract
 6 tablespoons sugar

UNFOLD and stack piecrusts on a lightly floured surface. Roll into 1 (12-inch) circle. Fit piecrust into a 9-inch pieplate (about 1 inch deep); fold edges under, and crimp. Prick bottom and sides of piecrust with a fork. Freeze piecrust 10 minutes.

LINE piecrust with parchment paper; fill with pie weights or dried beans.

BAKE at 425° for 10 minutes. Remove weights and parchment paper; bake 12 to 15 more minutes or until crust is lightly browned. (Shield edges with aluminum foil if they brown too quickly.)

PREPARE Lemon Meringue Pie Filling; pour into piecrust. Cover with plastic wrap, placing directly on filling. (Proceed immediately with next step to ensure that the meringue is spread over the pie filling while it's still warm.)

BEAT egg whites and vanilla at high speed with an electric mixer until foamy. Add sugar, 1 tablespoon at a time, and beat 2 to 4 minutes or until stiff peaks form and sugar dissolves.

REMOVE plastic wrap from pie, and spread meringue evenly over warm Lemon Meringue Pie Filling, sealing edges.

BAKE at 325° for 25 minutes or until golden brown. Cool pie completely on a wire rack. Store leftovers in the refrigerator. **MAKES** 8 to 10 servings.

LEMON MERINGUE PIE FILLING

family favorite • fast fixin's

Prep: 10 min., Cook: 10 min.

 1 cup sugar
 ¼ cup cornstarch
 ⅛ teaspoon salt
 4 large egg yolks
 2 cups milk
 ⅓ cup fresh lemon juice
 3 tablespoons butter or margarine
 1 teaspoon grated lemon rind
 ½ teaspoon vanilla extract

WHISK together first 3 ingredients in a heavy nonaluminum medium saucepan. Whisk together egg yolks, milk, and lemon juice in a bowl; whisk into sugar mixture in pan over medium heat. Bring to a boil, and boil, whisking constantly, 1 minute. Remove pan from heat; stir in butter, lemon rind, and vanilla until smooth. **MAKES** enough for 1 (9-inch) pie.

> ## Cook's Notes
>
> Test Kitchens' Professional **Rebecca Kracke Gordon** shares these tips for a "perfect crust every time" when using a refrigerated piecrust to ensure top quality.
>
> ■ Use the crust by the expiration date on the box.
> ■ Pinch the same amount of dough each time you crimp the edges to promote even browning.
> ■ To keep the crust from sliding down the pieplate during baking, anchor the crust in four spots by attaching small dough scraps from the crust to a spot underneath the lip of the pieplate. Remove after crust is baked.
> ■ Shield the outer edges of the crust with aluminum foil to prevent excessive browning.

TANGY LEMON TART

family favorite

Prep: 25 min., Freeze: 10 min., Bake: 25 min., Chill: 4 hrs.

Look for parchment paper in kitchen stores or on the bags-and-wraps aisle of the supermarket. If you can't find parchment, coat aluminum foil with vegetable cooking spray; then press the coated side against the piecrust.

- **1 (15-ounce) package refrigerated piecrusts**
- **1 tablespoon coarse sparkling sugar**
- **2 recipes Tangy Lemon Tart Filling (see following recipe)**

UNFOLD and stack piecrusts on a lightly floured surface. Roll into 1 (12-inch) circle. Fit piecrust into the bottom and up sides of a 9-inch deep-dish tart or quiche pan (about 1½ to 1¾ inches deep). Prick bottom of crust with a fork. Freeze 10 minutes.
LINE piecrust with parchment paper; fill with pie weights or dried beans.
BAKE at 425° for 10 minutes. Remove weights and parchment paper; sprinkle crust with sugar, and bake 12 to 15 more minutes or until lightly browned.
POUR Tangy Lemon Tart Filling into crust; cover and chill 4 hours or until set.
MAKES 8 to 10 servings.

TANGY LEMON TART FILLING

family favorite

Prep: 10 min., Cook: 12 min., Stand: 10 min.

- **1 cup sugar**
- **3 tablespoons cornstarch**
- **½ cup fresh lemon juice (about 4 large lemons)***
- **4 large eggs, lightly beaten**
- **¼ cup butter, melted**
- **2 drops liquid yellow food coloring**

WHISK together sugar and cornstarch in a heavy nonaluminum medium saucepan; gradually whisk in lemon juice, eggs, and butter. Cook mixture, whisking constantly, over medium-low heat 8 to 12 minutes or until thick and bubbly. Remove from heat, add food coloring, and let stand 10 minutes. **MAKES** 1 cup.

NOTE: You can double this recipe and cook it in one saucepan if you need two recipes of the filling. For testing purposes only, we used Minute Maid 100% Pure Lemon Juice From Concentrate. It can be found with the other frozen juices and lemonades at your grocery store.

*Substitute ½ cup thawed lemon juice, if desired.

DOUBLE-DECKER LEMON TART

family favorite

Prep: 40 min., Freeze: 10 min., Bake: 25 min., Chill: 4 hrs.

Double-Decker Lemon Tart is refreshing and pretty. Thin lemon slices brighten dollops of sweetened whipped cream.

- **1 (15-ounce) package refrigerated piecrusts**
- **Tangy Lemon Tart Filling (see previous recipe)**
- **Lemon Meringue Pie Filling (recipe on facing page)**
- **1 cup whipping cream**
- **¼ cup sugar**
- **Garnish: lemon slices**

UNFOLD and stack piecrusts on a lightly floured surface. Roll into 1 (12-inch) circle. Fit piecrust into bottom and up sides of a 9-inch deep-dish tart or quiche pan (about 1½ to 1¾ inches deep). Prick bottom and sides of piecrust with a fork. Freeze 10 minutes.
LINE piecrust with parchment paper; fill with pie weights or dried beans.
BAKE at 425° for 10 minutes. Remove weights and parchment paper; bake 12 to 15 more minutes or until crust is lightly browned.
POUR Tangy Lemon Tart Filling into piecrust; top with Lemon Meringue Pie

Mastering Meringue

A perfect meringue is easy when you follow these instructions.

Let egg whites stand at room temperature 30 minutes before beating. Use a copper, stainless steel, or glass bowl for best results. Beat egg whites and vanilla until foamy (as shown). Gradually add sugar, 1 tablespoon at a time.

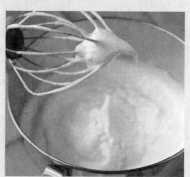

Beat egg whites and vanilla until stiff peaks form and sugar dissolves—about 2 to 4 minutes. A high-powered mixer will do the job more quickly than a handheld mixer.

Filling. Cover with plastic wrap, placing directly on Lemon Meringue Pie Filling. Chill at least 4 hours.
BEAT cream and sugar at medium speed with an electric mixer until soft peaks form. Remove plastic wrap from tart. Dollop whipped cream on tart. Garnish, if desired. **MAKES** 8 to 10 servings.

You'll Love This Easy-Does-It Cake

This cake is simple, quick, and good—but what about that name? Our Foods staff felt better when they understood that this dessert is called a Pig Pickin' Cake because its citrus lift is the perfect ending to a summer barbecue or pig pickin'.

While no one is sure of the cake's origin, Elaine Harvell, former director of the North Carolina Pork Producers Council, says her hunch is that the cake may have been made frequently at hog-killing time and then migrated to become a favorite at barbecue gatherings.

No matter where the cake started, you can track it through community cookbooks from Tennessee, North Carolina, and more. This version from Test Kitchens' professional Pam Lolley's mother-in-law captured our taste buds. Try it, and if you have information on where the cake came from, send us a note.

PIG PICKIN' CAKE

Prep: 15 min., Bake: 30 min., Chill: 4 hrs.

- **1 (18.25-ounce) package yellow cake mix**
- **⅓ cup water**
- **⅓ cup vegetable oil**
- **3 large eggs**
- **1 (11-ounce) can mandarin oranges, drained**
- **1 (15-ounce) can crushed pineapple, undrained**
- **1 (3.4-ounce) package vanilla instant pudding mix**
- **1 (12-ounce) container frozen whipped topping, thawed**
- **½ cup chopped pecans**
- **Garnish: chopped pecans**

BEAT first 4 ingredients in a large bowl at medium speed with an electric mixer until blended. Stir in oranges. Pour batter into 3 greased and floured 8-inch round cake pans. (Layers will be thin.)

BAKE at 350° for 25 to 30 minutes or until a wooden pick inserted in center comes out clean. Cool layers in pans on wire racks 10 minutes; remove layers from pans, and let cool completely on wire racks.

STIR together crushed pineapple and next 3 ingredients. Spread pineapple mixture evenly between layers and on top of cake. Chill cake 3 to 4 hours. Garnish, if desired. Store cake in refrigerator. **MAKES** 12 servings.

RUTH LOLLEY
WINNSBORO, LOUISIANA

Snacks to Go

When it's time again for the annual family summer vacation, whether you're heading down to the beach or driving cross-country, these goodies will help tide you over between stops.

CRISPY CARAMEL CORN

family favorite

Prep: 10 min., Bake: 1 hr.

- **1 cup sugar**
- **½ cup butter or margarine**
- **½ cup light corn syrup**
- **½ teaspoon salt**
- **1 teaspoon vanilla extract**
- **½ teaspoon baking soda**
- **2 (3-ounce) packages microwave popcorn, popped (16 cups)**
- **1 cup mixed nuts (optional)**

STIR together first 5 ingredients in a saucepan; bring to a boil over medium heat, stirring constantly. Remove mixture from heat, and stir in baking soda.

PLACE half of popcorn and, if desired, nuts in each of 2 lightly greased shallow roasting pans. Pour sugar mixture evenly over popcorn; stir well with a lightly greased spatula.

BAKE at 250° for 1 hour, stirring every 15 minutes. Spread on wax paper to cool, breaking apart large clumps as mixture cools. Store in airtight containers. **MAKES** 4 quarts.

KAREN WALKUP
FALLBROOK, CALIFORNIA

PUMPKIN MUFFINS

family favorite

Prep: 10 min., Bake: 20 min.

- **3 cups self-rising flour**
- **2 cups sugar**
- **2 teaspoons pumpkin pie spice**
- **4 large eggs**
- **½ cup vegetable oil**
- **1 (15-ounce) can pumpkin**
- **2 cups chopped dates**
- **1 cup chopped pecans, toasted**
- **Vegetable cooking spray**
- **Brown sugar**

STIR together first 3 ingredients in a large bowl, and make a well in center of mixture.

STIR together eggs, oil, and pumpkin; add to dry ingredients, stirring just until moistened. Stir in dates and pecans.

PLACE paper baking cups in muffin pans, and coat with cooking spray; spoon batter into cups, filling two-thirds full. Sprinkle with brown sugar.

BAKE at 400° for 18 to 20 minutes. Remove from pans immediately, and cool on wire racks. **MAKES** 2 dozen.

Fried Catfish, Best Barbecue Coleslaw, Potato Salad With Roasted Red Peppers, page 100

Crook's Corner Shrimp
and Grits, page 102

Spicy Grilled Pork Tenderloin page 96; Fruit Salad With Blackberry-Basil Vinaigrette, page 97; Twice-Baked Mashed Potatoes, page 97

Lemon Meringue Pie,
page 110

May

Texas-Style Celebration

With this tasty Southwestern menu and a mountain of make-ahead tips, your next gathering is sure to be a crowd-pleaser.

Celebration Menu

Serves 8 to 10

This make-ahead menu is designed to accommodate any guest list. We doubled—and even tripled—some of these recipes to serve a party of 30.

Longhorn cheese, grilled smoked sausage, and crackers

Beer-Can Chicken

Marinated Flank Steak

Creamy Lime Sauce

Warm flour tortillas

Chipotle Caesar Salad

Spicy Black Beans

Radish-Cucumber Salsa

Tomatillo Sauce

Pecan-Peach Cobbler

Vanilla ice cream

Texas beer and wine

A rustic setting, simple decorations, and a feast the size of Texas are just what Test Kitchens' Specialist Vanessa McNeil had in mind for her parents' 40th anniversary party. Houston residents Vance and Georgana McNeil chose their ranch in Weimar, Texas, as the gathering place for 30 of their closest friends and family.

Arriving guests are immediately enticed by the scrumptious aroma of Marinated Flank Steak and Beer-Can Chicken on the McNeils' colossal outdoor grill. Hungry partygoers gravitate toward a tempting appetizer table of cheese, smoked sausage, and wines from the nearby Hill Country.

Finally, the table is set and guests are invited to dig in. Flickering candles and casual flower arrangements decorate a bountiful buffet of grilled meats, Spicy Black Beans, Chipotle Caesar Salad, warm tortillas, and homemade salsas. Pecan-Peach Cobbler and ice cream create the perfect ending to a Texas-style celebration.

BEER-CAN CHICKEN

Prep: 20 min.; Chill: 8 hrs.;
Grill: 1 hr., 20 min.; Stand 10 min.

If you need more time to set up your serving table, keep the chicken warm in the oven at about 200° while you finish up.

**3 (2- to 3-pound) whole chickens
4 (12-ounce) cans beer, divided
1 (8-ounce) bottle Italian dressing
¼ to ⅓ cup fajita seasoning**

PLACE each chicken in a large zip-top freezer bag.

COMBINE 1 can beer, Italian dressing, and fajita seasoning; pour evenly over chickens. Seal bags, and chill 8 hours, turning occasionally.

REMOVE chicken from marinade, discarding marinade.

OPEN remaining 3 cans beer. Place each chicken upright onto a beer can, fitting into cavity. Pull legs forward to form a tripod, allowing chickens to stand upright.

PREPARE a hot fire by piling charcoal on 1 side of grill, leaving other side empty. (For gas grills, only light 1 side.) Place food grate on grill. Place chickens upright on unlit side of grill. Grill, covered with grill lid, 1 hour and 20 minutes or until golden and a meat thermometer inserted in thigh reaches 180°. Carefully remove cans, and cut chickens into quarters. **MAKES** 12 servings.

MARINATED FLANK STEAK: Omit 3 cans beer. Substitute 3 (2-pound) flank steaks for chicken, and marinate as directed. Remove steak from marinade, discarding marinade. Place steak on lit side of grill. Grill, covered with grill lid, over medium-high heat (350° to 400°) about 20 minutes or to desired degree of doneness. Let steak stand 10 minutes before slicing.

NOTE: For testing purposes only, we used Bolner's Fiesta Brand Extra Fancy Fajita Seasoning, which is available at discount supercenters and most supermarkets.

CREAMY LIME SAUCE

Prep: 10 min., Chill: 1 hr.

Dip grilled chicken or flank steak with tortillas in this tangy sauce.

- ¾ cup sour cream
- ⅓ cup whipping cream
- ⅓ cup mayonnaise
- ¼ cup fresh lime juice
- 1 garlic clove, pressed
- ½ teaspoon salt

WHISK together all ingredients. Cover and chill at least 1 hour. **MAKES** 1½ cups.

CHIPOTLE CAESAR SALAD

fast fixin's

Prep: 20 min.

- 1 large jícama
- 2 heads romaine lettuce, torn
- 1 large red bell pepper, thinly sliced
- Chipotle Caesar Dressing

CUT jícama into thin slices. Cut each slice into a star using a 1½-inch star-shaped cookie cutter (about 15 stars). **TOSS** together lettuce, bell pepper, and desired amount of dressing in a large bowl. Top with stars. **MAKES** 8 servings.

Chipotle Caesar Dressing:

fast fixin's • make ahead

Prep: 10 min.

- 2 garlic cloves
- 1 to 2 canned chipotle peppers
- ½ teaspoon salt
- ⅓ cup fresh lemon juice
- ⅓ cup egg substitute
- ¼ cup shredded Parmesan cheese
- ½ cup olive oil

PULSE first 3 ingredients in a food processor 3 or 4 times or until garlic is minced. Add lemon juice, egg substitute, and Parmesan cheese. With processor running, pour oil through food chute in a slow, steady stream; process until smooth. Cover and chill until ready to serve. **MAKES** 1¼ cups.

Small Details, Big Impact

Here's how to keep the decorations and color scheme simple yet eye-catching.

- Drape a gingham or other patterned fabric over a complementary, solid tablecloth to add depth and interest to the buffet.
- Display soft white daisies or other flowers in clay pots and galvanized buckets for inexpensive centerpieces.
- Place tall candles in clear, oversized vases. Anchor the candles with colored glass pebbles for more sparkle.
- Add ambience with mounted candlesticks and hanging lanterns.

SPICY BLACK BEANS

make ahead

Prep: 25 min., Soak: 8 hrs., Cook: 3½ hrs.

These spicy beans can be prepared a day ahead. Just reheat on the stove.

- 2 pounds dried black beans
- 2 pounds beef short ribs
- 3 medium-size sweet onions, chopped
- 4 garlic cloves, minced
- 12 cups water
- 2 tablespoons ground chipotle chile pepper
- 1 teaspoon salt
- 1½ teaspoons ground cumin
- Salt to taste

SOAK dried beans in water to cover 8 hours. Drain.
BROWN ribs in a large Dutch oven over medium-high heat. Add onions and garlic, and sauté until onions are tender. Add beans, 12 cups water, and next 3 ingredients. Bring to a boil; reduce heat, cover, and simmer, stirring occasionally, 2 to 3 hours or until beans are tender. Salt to taste. **MAKES** 8 to 10 servings.

NOTE: For testing purposes only, we used McCormick Gourmet Collection Chipotle Chile Pepper.

QUICK-SOAK METHOD: Place beans in a Dutch oven; add water 2 inches above beans. Bring to a boil. Boil 1 minute; cover, remove from heat, and let stand 1 hour. Drain. Proceed with recipe.

RADISH-CUCUMBER SALSA

make ahead

Prep: 25 min., Chill: 1 hr.

- 3 large tomatoes, chopped
- 2 medium cucumbers, chopped
- 4 large radishes, chopped
- 1 bunch green onions, chopped
- ½ teaspoon salt
- ¼ cup fresh lime juice
- 1 garlic clove, pressed

COMBINE all ingredients. Cover and chill at least 1 hour. Serve with grilled meats or fish. **MAKES** 2 cups.

TOMATILLO SAUCE

make ahead

Prep: 20 min., Cook: 6 min., Stand: 20 min.

For a milder sauce, remove the seeds from the jalapeño. Serve with chicken or flank steak.

- 10 fresh tomatillos, husks removed
- 1 small onion
- ½ cup water
- ⅓ cup packed fresh cilantro
- 1 small jalapeño, halved
- ½ teaspoon salt

COMBINE tomatillos, onion, and water to cover in a saucepan. Bring to a boil; cook 5 minutes. Turn off heat; let stand 20 minutes or until tomatillos are tender. Drain. **PROCESS** tomatillo mixture, ½ cup water, and remaining ingredients in a blender until smooth. Cover and chill until ready to serve. **MAKES** 1¼ cups.

PECAN-PEACH COBBLER

freezeable • make ahead

Prep: 35 min., Stand: 10 min.,
Cook: 15 min., Bake: 43 min.

12 to 15 fresh peaches, peeled and
  sliced (about 16 cups)*
3 cups sugar
⅓ cup all-purpose flour
½ teaspoon ground nutmeg
1½ teaspoons vanilla extract
⅔ cup butter
2 (15-ounce) packages refrigerated
  piecrusts
½ cup chopped pecans, toasted
¼ cup sugar
Vanilla ice cream

COMBINE first 4 ingredients in a Dutch oven, and let stand 10 minutes or until sugar dissolves. Bring peach mixture to a boil; reduce heat to low, and simmer 10 minutes or until tender. Remove from heat; add vanilla and butter, stirring until butter melts.

UNFOLD 2 piecrusts. Sprinkle ¼ cup pecans and 2 tablespoons sugar evenly over 1 piecrust; top with other piecrust. Roll into a 12-inch circle, gently pressing pecans into pastry. Cut into 1½-inch strips. Repeat with remaining 2 piecrusts, ¼ cup pecans, and 2 tablespoons sugar.

SPOON half of peach mixture into a lightly greased 13- x 9-inch baking dish. Arrange half of pastry strips in a lattice design over peach mixture.

BAKE at 475° for 20 to 25 minutes or until lightly browned. Spoon remaining peach mixture over baked pastry. Top with remaining pastry strips in a lattice design. Bake 15 to 18 more minutes. Serve warm or cold with vanilla ice cream. **MAKES** 8 to 10 servings.

NOTE: To make ahead, bake cobbler and cool; cover and freeze up to 1 month. Thaw in refrigerator overnight. Uncover and reheat in the oven at 250° for 45 minutes.

*Substitute 2 (20-ounce) packages frozen peaches, if desired. Reduce sugar to 2 cups, flour to 3 tablespoons, and nutmeg to ¼ teaspoon. Proceed as directed.

Make-Ahead Timeline

Throwing a party doesn't always have to be such a hectic event if your timing is right. Take the fuss out of feeding a crowd with this easy-to-follow schedule.

Up to 1 month ahead:
■ Prepare and bake Pecan-Peach Cobbler. Let cool. Cover and freeze.

Up to 2 days ahead:
■ Prepare Radish-Cucumber Salsa, Creamy Lime Sauce, and Tomatillo Sauce. Store in zip-top plastic bags or airtight containers in refrigerator.

The day before:
■ Remove Pecan-Peach Cobbler from freezer in the morning, and let thaw in refrigerator.
■ Soak black beans in water overnight. Or use the quick-soak method, and prepare entire recipe; reheat just before serving.
■ Marinate chicken and/or flank steak in refrigerator.
■ Prepare and chill salad dressing. Slice jícama, and refrigerate in a bowl of water to prevent browning. Prepare lettuce and bell pepper, and place in a bowl. Chill until ready to assemble.

That morning:
■ Ice down beer and wine.
■ Plan buffet arrangement and serving areas. Place decorations throughout the setting.

About 3 hours before guests arrive:
■ Preheat grill.
■ If you haven't done so already, prepare Spicy Black Beans, and simmer until supper's ready.

About 2 hours before guests arrive:
■ Place chicken on beer cans, and place on grill.

About 30 minutes before guests arrive:
■ Brown some smoked sausage on grill to serve with cheese and wine for a hearty appetizer, if desired.
■ Add flank steak to grill.

Just before supper is served:
■ Cut chicken into quarters, and slice flank steak.
■ Heat tortillas according to package directions. Cover with warm, damp kitchen towels to keep soft.
■ Drizzle lettuce and bell pepper with dressing. Garnish with jícama slices.
■ Reheat thawed cobbler as directed while guests enjoy the meal.

Note: If you run out of refrigerator room, ask a neighbor to help store some of your make-ahead items.

Straighten Up & Fry Right

Celebrate the South's favorite way to cook.

If our region's famous for one cooking method, it's frying. Southerners are all about attaching emotion to their food. Nothing stirs feelings of comfort and nostalgia like frying. There's just something to be said about the crispy, golden-brown crust of a fried catfish fillet or the tender inside of an apple fritter. Is your mouth watering yet?

What's the Difference?

The recipes for this story use one of two basic frying methods—pan-frying or deep-frying.

■ **Pan-Fry:** Items are usually breaded (a dry mixture) or battered (a combination of liquid and flour or starch), and cooked in enough oil—about ½ inch deep—to create a layer of fat between the items being cooked and the pan (example: chicken-fried steak, fried pork chops). Foods should be turned only once.

■ **Deep-Fry:** Items are usually breaded or battered and cooked in enough oil to completely submerge the item (such as hush puppies or beignets). Items are allowed to float to the surface and may be gently turned once for even browning.

DELTA-STYLE FRIED CATFISH

family favorite

Prep: 20 min., Chill: 8 hrs., Stand: 10 min.,
Fry: 4 min. per batch (pictured on page 150)

> 1½ cups milk
> 2 or 3 drops hot sauce
> 6 (4- to 6-ounce) catfish fillets
> ¾ cup yellow cornmeal
> ¼ cup all-purpose flour
> 2 teaspoons salt
> 1 teaspoon ground black pepper
> 1 teaspoon ground red pepper
> ¼ teaspoon garlic powder
> Vegetable oil
> Garnish: lemon wedges

WHISK together milk and hot sauce. Place fillets in a single layer in a 13- x 9-inch baking dish; cover with milk mixture. Cover; chill 8 hours, turning once.

COMBINE cornmeal and next 5 ingredients in a shallow dish, and set aside.

LET fillets stand at room temperature in milk mixture in baking dish 10 minutes. Remove from milk mixture; allow excess to drip off. Discard milk mixture.

DREDGE catfish fillets in cornmeal mixture, shaking off excess.

POUR oil to a depth of 1½ inches into a large deep cast-iron or heavy-duty skillet; heat to 360°. Fry fillets, in batches, 2 minutes on each side or until golden brown. Remove to a wire rack on a paper towel-lined jellyroll pan. Keep warm in a 225° oven until ready to serve. **MAKES** 4 servings.

JACK PERKINS
ISOLA, MISSISSIPPI

CHICKEN-AND-MASHED POTATO FRITTERS WITH LIME-CAYENNE MAYONNAISE

family favorite

Prep: 20 min., Cook: 20 min., Chill: 1 hr.,
Fry: 2 min. per batch (pictured on page 150)

> 1 pound russet or Idaho potatoes, peeled and cut into 2-inch pieces
> 2 teaspoons salt, divided
> 1½ cups chopped cooked chicken
> ½ cup shredded Parmesan cheese
> 1 large egg, lightly beaten
> ¼ cup sour cream
> ½ teaspoon dried thyme
> ½ teaspoon garlic powder
> ½ teaspoon pepper
> ¼ teaspoon grated lemon rind
> ⅔ cup fine, dry breadcrumbs
> Vegetable oil
> Lime-Cayenne Mayonnaise

BRING potatoes, 1 teaspoon salt, and water to cover to a boil in a small saucepan. Cook 20 minutes or until tender; drain and mash potatoes.

STIR together mashed potatoes, remaining 1 teaspoon salt, chicken, and next 7 ingredients. Cover and chill mixture 1 hour. Shape into 1¾-inch balls.

PLACE dry breadcrumbs in a shallow dish. Roll balls in breadcrumbs, coating evenly.

POUR oil to a depth of 4 inches into a Dutch oven; heat to 370°. Fry fritters, in batches, 2 minutes or until golden brown. Drain on wire racks over paper towels, and serve immediately. Serve with Lime-Cayenne Mayonnaise. **MAKES** about 8 appetizer servings.

BUDDY WEST
CUMMING, GEORGIA

Lime-Cayenne Mayonnaise:
fast fixin's
Prep: 5 min.

> ½ cup mayonnaise
> ½ teaspoon grated lime rind
> ¼ teaspoon ground red pepper
> 2 tablespoons fresh lime juice

STIR together all ingredients; cover and chill until ready to serve. **MAKES** ½ cup.

FRENCH FRIES

family favorite

Prep: 30 min., Fry: 7 min. per batch

Potatoes cut into strips are the crispiest of the potato shapes.

4 pounds russet or Idaho potatoes, peeled
Vegetable oil
Salt to taste

CUT potatoes into ¼-inch-wide strips.
POUR vegetable oil to a depth of 4 inches into a Dutch oven; heat to 325°.
FRY potato strips, in batches, until lightly golden, but not brown, 4 to 5 minutes per batch. Drain strips on paper towels.
HEAT oil to 375°. Fry strips, in small batches, until golden brown and crisp, 1 to 2 minutes per batch. Drain on clean paper towels. Sprinkle with salt. Serve immediately. **MAKES** 4 to 6 servings.

NOTE: For testing purposes only, we used Wesson vegetable oil.

CRINKLE-CUT FRIES: Cut potatoes into ½-inch-wide strips with a waffle cutter. Fry as directed.

WAFFLE CHIPS: Cut potatoes into ¼-inch-thick slices with a waffle cutter. Fry as directed.

Perfect French Fries Every Time

Choose low-moisture, high-starch potatoes such as russet or Idaho. For crisp fries, wash the cut, uncooked strips in several batches of cold water until the water is clear. However, for the crispiest fries, we found the double-fry method hard to beat. Frying strips twice in the same oil at different temperatures gives you fries like no others. This recipe, using the double-fry method, received our highest rating.

Successful Frying

■ The secret is using the right oil. Smoke point is the temperature at which fats and oils begin to smoke, indicating they've begun to break down. The higher the smoke point, the better the oil is for frying. Lard and some vegetable oils such as corn, canola, safflower, and peanut are good choices. Shortening is not suitable for high-temperature frying.

■ Moisture and food particles break down oil, so don't reuse it more than twice. If you see smoke, discard the oil and start over.

■ Achieving and maintaining proper oil temperature is a must. If it's not hot enough (often caused by overcrowding), the food soaks up oil, leaving it greasy. Too hot, and the outside burns before the inside cooks, creating food that's soggy.

■ Use heavy-duty aluminum, stainless steel, or cast-iron cookware for even heat distribution and the retention of high temperatures. Iron speeds up the breakdown of oil, so when using cast-iron cookware, it's best to use the oil only once.

■ Choose cookware that's large enough to leave at least 3 inches between the surface of the oil and the top of the skillet or Dutch oven.

■ Always allow the oil to return to its proper temperature between batches. We like to use a candy thermometer, which can handle high temperatures and be attached to the side of a large skillet or Dutch oven for instant temperature readings.

■ Make sure food is dry. Adding moist food to hot oil will cause spattering and popping.

■ Food soaks up only a small amount of oil when fried at the proper temperature.

CRACKER-BREADED FRIED SHRIMP

family favorite

Prep: 30 min., Fry: 2 min. per batch

We found that coarsely crushed crackers work best for this recipe. Place crackers in a zip-top plastic bag, and crush with a rolling pin.

2 pounds unpeeled, large fresh shrimp
1½ cups crushed buttery round crackers (about 26 crackers)
½ cup all-purpose flour
¾ teaspoon pepper, divided
½ teaspoon salt
½ cup buttermilk
2 or 3 drops hot sauce
1 large egg
Vegetable oil

PEEL shrimp, leaving tails intact, and devein, if desired.
COMBINE crushed crackers, flour, ½ teaspoon pepper, and salt in a shallow dish. Stir together buttermilk, hot sauce, egg, and remaining ¼ teaspoon pepper in a bowl until blended. Dip shrimp in buttermilk mixture; dredge in cracker mixture.
POUR oil to a depth of 2½ inches into a large deep cast-iron or heavy-duty skillet; heat to 375°. Fry shrimp, in batches, 1 to 2 minutes or until golden; drain on wire racks over paper towels. **MAKES** 6 servings.

JULIANNE POLAHA
TALUCA LAKE, CALIFORNIA

Tempura Dill Pickles

Prep: 15 min., Fry: 2½ min. per batch

This recipe blends an Asian-inspired batter—tempura—with fried dill pickles, a classic fish fry side in the Lower South. You'll find that these delicious pickles have a delicate, crunchy crust that surrounds tart slices of kosher dills. *(pictured on page 150)*

- 1 (24-ounce) jar sliced kosher dill pickles
- Vegetable oil
- 1 cup all-purpose flour
- 1 teaspoon garlic powder
- 1 teaspoon ground red pepper
- ¼ teaspoon salt
- 1 cup club soda, chilled

DRAIN pickles, reserving 2 tablespoons pickle juice. Press pickles between layers of paper towels. Set aside.

POUR oil to a depth of 3 inches into a Dutch oven; heat to 370°.

COMBINE flour and next 3 ingredients in a bowl. Stir in club soda and reserved 2 tablespoons pickle juice, stirring just until combined. (Batter will be lumpy.) Dip pickles into batter, letting excess drip off.

FRY pickles, in batches, 2½ minutes or until golden brown. Drain on wire racks over paper towels, and serve immediately. **MAKES** 6 servings.

JONATHAN CALVANO
BIRMINGHAM, ALABAMA

Quick & Easy
Meals From the Grill

Take advantage of this month's great weather to cook outdoors by pairing flavorful grilled meats with fresh, crisp salads.

What makes these recipes so special is that portions of the marinades are reserved to use as the dressing on the accompanying slaw or salad. There's less cleanup that way too.

Grilled Chicken With Sweet Soy Slaw and Dipping Sauce

Prep: 5 min., Cook: 10 min., Stand: 10 min., Grill: 16 min.

The dipping sauce will keep in the refrigerator, covered, for several weeks. Warm sauce over medium-low heat on cooktop before serving. Use as a marinade for steaks and shrimp too.

- 2 cups soy sauce
- 2 tablespoons canola oil
- 8 pieces crystallized ginger
- 2 garlic cloves, minced
- 3 cups sugar
- 6 skinned and boned chicken breasts
- 2 (12-ounce) packages broccoli slaw
- ¼ cup green onions, chopped
- 1 tablespoon sesame seeds, toasted
- Salt and pepper to taste

COMBINE first 4 ingredients in a small saucepan over medium heat. Stir in sugar. Cook 10 minutes or until sugar dissolves, stirring occasionally. Remove from heat. (Mixture will thicken.) Reserve 1½ cups soy mixture, and set aside.

BRUSH both sides of chicken evenly with remaining soy mixture; cover and let stand 10 minutes.

GRILL, covered with grill lid, over medium-high heat (350° to 400°) 6 to 8 minutes on each side or until done.

TOSS together broccoli slaw, green onions, sesame seeds, and ½ cup reserved soy mixture; top with grilled chicken. Season with salt and pepper to taste. Serve with remaining reserved 1 cup soy mixture for dipping. **MAKES** 6 servings.

GRILLED SALMON WITH SWEET SOY SLAW AND DIPPING SAUCE: Substitute 6 (4-ounce) salmon fillets for chicken, and grill 4 to 6 minutes on each side or just until fish flakes with a fork.

KRISTEN WILLIAMSON
CAPE CORAL, FLORIDA

Grilled Pork Cosmopolitan Salad

Prep: 15 min., Cook: 5 min., Chill: 15 min., Grill: 20 min., Stand: 10 min.

Reader Janice Elder based this tasty recipe on the ever cool, colorful Cosmopolitan cocktail.

- ¼ cup jellied cranberry sauce
- ¼ cup orange marmalade
- ⅓ cup orange juice
- ¼ cup fresh lime juice (about 3 limes)
- ¼ cup peanut oil
- 2¼ teaspoons salt, divided
- 2 tablespoons vodka
- 1 tablespoon minced or grated fresh ginger
- 2 (1-pound) pork tenderloins
- 2 teaspoons lemon pepper
- ½ teaspoon ground red pepper
- 2 (10-ounce) packages European blend salad greens
- ½ cup dried cranberries
- 1 (8-ounce) can mandarin oranges, drained

WHISK together cranberry sauce and marmalade in a small saucepan over low heat until melted. Remove from heat. Whisk in orange juice, lime juice, and oil. Reserve ½ cup cranberry mixture, add ¼ teaspoon salt to reserved mixture, and set aside.

POUR remaining cranberry mixture into a shallow dish or zip-top freezer bag; add vodka, ginger, and pork, turning to coat all sides. Cover or seal, and chill 15 minutes, turning occasionally. Remove pork from marinade, discarding marinade.

STIR together lemon pepper, red pepper, and remaining 2 teaspoons salt; sprinkle evenly over pork.

GRILL, covered with grill lid, over medium-high heat (350° to 400°) 10 minutes on each side or until a meat thermometer inserted into thickest portion registers 155°. Remove from grill, and cover with aluminum foil. Let stand 10 minutes until temperature reaches 160°. Cut pork diagonally into ¼-inch-thick slices.

TOSS together salad greens, cranberries, and oranges with reserved ½ cup cranberry mixture; top with pork. **MAKES** 6 to 8 servings.

JANICE ELDER
CHARLOTTE, NORTH CAROLINA

Chocolate-Lover's Cookies

No one can resist sweet treats made with this ingredient.

If you check your pantry, you'll likely find you have most of the ingredients on hand to make these cookies. That's good news because, with recipes this yummy, you'll want to bake a batch right away.

To have fresh cookies for guests, you can freeze the dough for Chocolate Chunk-Peanut Cookies in an airtight container up to one month. They'll love the "scrumdidlyumptious" combination of peanut butter, peanuts, and chocolate chunks.

CHOCO-NUT DAINTIES

freezeable • make ahead

Prep: 35 min., Bake: 15 min. per batch

These family-pleasing goodies can be stored in the freezer for up to 1 month.

- ¾ cup butter or margarine, softened
- ¾ cup sugar
- 1 large egg
- 1½ teaspoons vanilla extract
- 2¼ cups all-purpose flour
- ½ teaspoon salt
- 1 cup semisweet chocolate mini-morsels
- 1 (12-ounce) package semisweet chocolate morsels
- 2 cups finely chopped walnuts

BEAT butter and sugar at medium speed with an electric mixer until mixture is light and fluffy. Add egg and vanilla, beating until blended. Add flour and salt, and beat well. Stir in mini-morsels.

TURN dough out onto a lightly floured surface. Shape dough into 2- x ½-inch logs (about 1 heaping teaspoon each). Place each of the logs on ungreased baking sheets.

BAKE at 350° for 12 to 15 minutes or until lightly browned; remove to wire racks to cool.

MICROWAVE chocolate morsels at HIGH 4 minutes or until melted, stirring once.

DIP ends of cookies into melted chocolate. Roll ends in walnuts. Place on wax paper until set. Freeze up to 1 month, if desired. **MAKES** 4½ dozen.

PATTY VANN
BIRMINGHAM, ALABAMA

CHOCOLATE SNACK BARS

family favorite

Prep: 20 min., Bake: 30 min.

- 1⅓ cups all-purpose flour
- 1¼ cups sugar
- ½ cup unsweetened cocoa
- 1 teaspoon baking powder
- ½ teaspoon salt
- 4 large eggs
- ¾ cup butter or margarine, melted
- 1 cup semisweet chocolate morsels
- ½ cup milk chocolate morsels
- ½ cup white chocolate morsels
- 3 (2.07-ounce) chocolate-coated caramel-peanut nougat bars, cut into ¼-inch pieces

COMBINE first 5 ingredients in a large bowl. Add eggs and butter, stirring well. Stir in morsels. Spoon mixture into a lightly greased 13- x 9-inch pan.

BAKE at 350° for 30 minutes or until a wooden pick inserted in center comes out clean. Sprinkle immediately with candy pieces. Cool completely before cutting into bars. **MAKES** 16 bars.

NOTE: For testing purposes only, we used Snickers candy bars.

KIM MORTON
BIRMINGHAM, ALABAMA

66 Cook's Notes 99

Associate Foods Editor **Cynthia Briscoe** shares her best chocolate cookie secrets.

■ Fudgy and dense **Chocolate Snack Bars** have a brownie base topped with bits of caramel-peanut nougat candy bar. After baking and cooling, freeze for about 10 minutes for cleaner slices.

■ Don't throw away the end pieces after slicing bar cookies. Instead, use them for a trifle dessert or enjoy them with a glass of milk.

■ When making **Choco-Nut Dainties**, soften the butter for half an hour at room temperature before mixing the batter.

■ When cookie recipes call for baking soda and baking powder, check the expiration dates of these products before you begin. Old products yield flat cookies.

CHOCOLATE CHUNK-PEANUT COOKIES

freezeable • make ahead

Prep: 20 min., Bake: 15 min. per batch

A hint of cinnamon gives these cookies a delicious, subtly different flavor. *(pictured on page 151)*

- ½ cup butter, softened
- ½ cup shortening
- 1 cup chunky peanut butter
- 1 cup granulated sugar
- 1 cup firmly packed brown sugar
- 2 large eggs
- 2½ cups all-purpose flour
- 1½ teaspoons baking soda
- 1 teaspoon baking powder
- ½ teaspoon salt
- 1 teaspoon ground cinnamon
- 1 cup unsalted dry-roasted peanuts
- 1 (11.5-ounce) package chocolate chunks

BEAT butter and shortening at medium speed with an electric mixer until creamy; add peanut butter and sugars, beating well. Add eggs, beating until blended.

COMBINE flour and next 4 ingredients. Add to butter mixture, beating well.

STIR in peanuts and chocolate chunks.

SHAPE dough into 2-inch balls (about 2 tablespoons for each cookie). Flatten slightly, and place on ungreased baking sheets.

BAKE at 375° for 12 to 15 minutes or until lightly browned. Cool on pan 1 to 2 minutes; remove to a wire rack to cool completely. **MAKES** 28 cookies.

DOUBLE CHOCOLATE CHUNK-PEANUT COOKIES: Reduce flour to 2 cups; add ⅓ cup unsweetened cocoa, sifted. Proceed as directed.

MARSHA JOHNSON
MONTGOMERY, ALABAMA

Make a Meal With Leftover Rice

Supper's ready in about 30 minutes with this Southern-style fried rice.

Wondering what to do with last night's cooked rice? We found a tasty solution: a quick-and-easy fried rice with juicy ham, sautéed vegetables, and a spicy kick. If you don't have enough leftover rice, you can substitute quick-cooking rice instead—simply prepare and stir-fry other ingredients while the rice bags boil. We bet you won't have any leftovers this time.

HAM FRIED RICE

family favorite

Prep: 15 min., Cook: 20 min.

You can also use chicken or shrimp in this flavorful dish or any combination you may have on hand.

- 3 bacon slices
- 1½ cups chopped cooked ham
- 1 red or green bell pepper, chopped
- ½ cup sliced fresh mushrooms
- 3 green onions, chopped
- 1 celery rib, chopped
- 1 large garlic clove, minced
- ½ teaspoon dried crushed red pepper
- 3½ cups cooked rice*
- 2 large eggs, lightly beaten
- ¼ cup soy sauce

COOK bacon slices in a large skillet or wok at medium-high heat until crisp. Remove bacon slices, and drain on paper towels, reserving drippings in skillet. Crumble bacon, and set aside.

ADD chopped ham to hot drippings in skillet, and stir-fry 3 minutes or until ham is lightly browned. Add bell pepper and next 5 ingredients, and stir-fry 5 minutes. Add rice, and stir-fry 3 minutes or until thoroughly heated.

PUSH rice mixture to sides of skillet, forming a well in center. Pour eggs into well, and cook, stirring occasionally, until eggs are set. Stir rice mixture into eggs; stir in soy sauce and crumbled bacon. Spoon into individual serving bowls. **MAKES** 4 to 6 servings.

*Substitute 2 (3.5-ounce) bags quick-cooking long-grain rice, cooked, for leftover rice, if desired.

VICKI LONG
ORLANDO, FLORIDA

Squash Casserole

Try one of these recipes the next time you serve this beloved Southern side.

If Associate Foods Editor Kate Nicholson had a nickel for every squash casserole that has graced a Southern dinner table, she would, no doubt, be in the money. Whether at a church social, a holiday gathering, or a family dinner, this old favorite has been the workhorse of side dishes for decades. Squash casserole is the just-right accompaniment with everything from fried chicken at a summertime Sunday lunch to roast turkey at Thanksgiving.

The main ingredient is typically yellow squash, but some recipes call for other summer squash such as pattypan and zucchini. Most recipes usually include chopped onion, as well. Once you get past those two core ingredients, however, the differences begin.

If that certain ingredient that defines your memory of this dish is not represented here, we humbly apologize. Still, we're betting that after you try our versions, one will become your *other* favorite squash casserole.

SQUASH CASSEROLE

family favorite

Prep: 20 min., Cook: 20 min., Bake: 35 min.

- 3 pounds yellow squash, sliced
- 5 tablespoons butter or margarine, divided
- 1 small onion, chopped (about ½ cup)
- 1 cup (4 ounces) shredded sharp Cheddar cheese
- 2 large eggs, lightly beaten
- ¼ cup mayonnaise
- 2 teaspoons sugar
- 1 teaspoon salt
- 20 round buttery crackers, crushed (about ¾ cup)

COOK squash in boiling water to cover in a large skillet 8 to 10 minutes or just until tender. Drain well; gently press between paper towels.

MELT 4 tablespoons butter in skillet over medium-high heat; add onion, and sauté 5 minutes or until tender. Remove skillet from heat; stir in squash, cheese, and next 4 ingredients. Spoon mixture into a lightly greased 11- x 7-inch baking dish.

MELT remaining 1 tablespoon butter. Stir together melted butter and crushed crackers; sprinkle evenly over casserole.

BAKE at 350° for 30 to 35 minutes or until set. **MAKES** 8 servings.

NOTE: To lighten, reduce butter to 3 tablespoons, using 2 tablespoons to sauté onion. Substitute ½ cup egg substitute for eggs and low-fat versions of mayonnaise, cheese, and crackers. Proceed as directed.

TWO-CHEESE SQUASH CASSEROLE

family favorite

Prep: 30 min., Cook: 20 min., Bake: 40 min.

The combination of Parmesan and Cheddar cheeses gives this casserole a delicious taste all its own.

- 4 pounds yellow squash, sliced
- 4 tablespoons butter or margarine, divided
- 1 large sweet onion, finely chopped
- 2 garlic cloves, minced
- 2½ cups soft breadcrumbs, divided
- 1¼ cups shredded Parmesan cheese, divided
- 1 cup (4 ounces) shredded Cheddar cheese
- ½ cup chopped fresh chives
- ½ cup minced fresh parsley
- 1 (8-ounce) container sour cream
- 1 teaspoon salt
- 1 teaspoon freshly ground pepper
- 2 large eggs, lightly beaten
- ¼ teaspoon garlic salt

COOK squash in boiling water to cover in a large skillet 8 to 10 minutes or just until tender. Drain well; gently press between paper towels.

MELT 2 tablespoons butter in skillet over medium-high heat; add onion and garlic, and sauté 5 to 6 minutes or until tender. Remove skillet from heat; stir in squash, 1 cup breadcrumbs, ¾ cup Parmesan cheese, and next 7 ingredients. Spoon into a lightly greased 13- x 9-inch baking dish.

MELT remaining 2 tablespoons butter. Stir together melted butter, remaining 1½ cups soft breadcrumbs, ½ cup Parmesan cheese, and garlic salt. Sprinkle mixture evenly over casserole.

BAKE at 350° for 35 to 40 minutes or until set. **MAKES** 8 to 10 servings.

Burgers and Fries

Forget eating out—these homemade versions are grilled and seasoned to perfection.

> ## Try This Combo
> *Serves 6*
>
> Stuffed Border Burgers
>
> Seasoned Steak Fries
>
> Turtle Dessert

When it's burger and fries night at your house, steer away from the drive-through and head home. In five minutes these fries can be ready for the oven, where they'll crisp without any complicated frying. While they bake, make the burgers. If you prefer them cheese-topped rather than stuffed, shape the ground beef mixture into six (6-inch) patties. Grill according to directions, and top with the cheese slices during the last minute of grilling. To learn more about making great burgers, turn to "From Our Kitchen" on page 130.

STUFFED BORDER BURGERS

family favorite • fast fixin's

Prep: 20 min., Grill: 10 min.

- 1½ pounds lean ground beef
- ½ cup finely chopped onion
- 1 (4.25-ounce) can chopped ripe olives, drained
- 2 tablespoons ketchup
- 1 teaspoon chili powder
- 1 teaspoon fajita seasoning
- 6 (1-ounce) slices Monterey Jack cheese with peppers
- 6 onion rolls, split and toasted
- Tex-Mex Secret Sauce
- Toppings: shredded lettuce, sliced tomatoes, guacamole

COMBINE first 6 ingredients. Shape mixture into 12 (4-inch) patties. Fold cheese slices into quarters; place cheese on each of 6 patties. Top with remaining 6 patties, pressing to seal edges.

GRILL, covered with grill lid, over medium-high heat (350° to 400°) 4 to 5 minutes on each side or until done. Serve on rolls with Tex-Mex Secret Sauce and desired toppings. **MAKES** 6 servings.

NOTE: For testing purposes only, we used McCormick Fajita Seasoning and Sargento Monterey Jack Cheese With Peppers.

Tex-Mex Secret Sauce:

Prep: 5 min.

- ½ cup sour cream
- ⅓ cup ketchup
- 1 (4.5-ounce) can chopped green chiles
- 1 tablespoon minced fresh cilantro

STIR together all ingredients. Cover and chill until ready to serve. **MAKES** 1 cup.

PAM TRAYLOR
BRENHAM, TEXAS

SEASONED STEAK FRIES

family favorite

Prep: 5 min., Bake: 45 min.

OPEN 1 (28-ounce) bag frozen steak fries. Add 1 tablespoon olive oil and 1 to 2 teaspoons fajita seasoning to potatoes in the bag. Close bag, and shake to evenly coat potatoes.

SPREAD potatoes evenly on an aluminum foil-lined jellyroll pan. Bake at 375° for 45 minutes, stirring once. **MAKES** 6 servings.

TURTLE DESSERT

family favorite • make ahead

Prep: 10 min., Freeze: 1 hr., Stand: 5 min.

- 16 ice-cream sandwiches
- 1 (12-ounce) jar caramel sauce
- 1¼ cups chopped pecans, toasted
- 1 (12-ounce) container frozen whipped topping, thawed
- Hot fudge sauce, heated

PLACE 8 ice-cream sandwiches in a 13- x 9-inch baking dish. Spread caramel sauce evenly over sandwiches. Sprinkle evenly with 1 cup pecans. Top with remaining ice-cream sandwiches. Spread whipped topping evenly over sandwiches. Sprinkle with remaining ¼ cup pecans. Cover and freeze at least 1 hour. Let stand 5 minutes before serving; cut into squares. Drizzle with warm hot fudge sauce. **MAKES** 10 servings.

GLENDA ADAMS
MONTGOMERY, ALABAMA

Fresh Pasta Dinners, Fast

Pasta from your supermarket's refrigerated section tastes homemade and takes on a delicious personality in each of these recipes.

It's easy to please everyone with pasta, which often means a quick and easy supper. Buy it refrigerated, and you'll have speed plus homemade taste. Fresh pasta, unlike the dried varieties stashed in your pantry, has a high moisture content that makes it fast cooking, wonderfully tender, and ready for wholesome ingredients. Feel free to interchange equal-size packages of refrigerated varieties in any shape you like. If you can't find the fresh stuff, 1 (8-ounce) package of dried pasta takes the place of 1 (9-ounce) package refrigerated pasta.

Look in the dairy aisle or refrigerated deli section of your supermarket for various shapes, flavors, and filled pastas. If you're crunched, create a quick supper with a package of tortellini (little), tortelloni (big), or ravioli dressed with your favorite jar of pasta sauce. Just choose the type with lots of chunky veggies instead of sugar.

LINGUINE WITH GREEN BEANS AND WALNUT SAUCE

family favorite

Prep: 20 min., Cook: 12 min.

- 1 pound green beans, trimmed and cut into 2-inch pieces
- 1 (9-ounce) package refrigerated linguine
- 1 tablespoon butter
- 1 tablespoon olive oil
- 2 tablespoons chopped walnuts
- 1 garlic clove, minced
- ¼ cup chopped fresh Italian parsley
- 2 teaspoons grated lemon rind
- 2 tablespoons fresh lemon juice
- ¾ teaspoon salt

COOK green beans in a Dutch oven in boiling water to cover 1 minute or until crisp-tender. Add pasta, and cook 4 more minutes. Drain and rinse with cold water. Set aside.

MELT butter with oil in a large skillet over medium heat; add walnuts, and cook, stirring occasionally, 5 minutes or until golden. Add garlic, and sauté 1 minute. Add parsley and next 3 ingredients, stirring until thoroughly heated.

POUR sauce over linguine mixture, tossing to coat. Serve immediately. **MAKES** 6 servings.

Per serving: Calories 203 (30% from fat); Fat 6.9g (sat 1.8g, mono 2.7g, poly 1.9g); Protein 6.3g; Carb 29g; Fiber 4.8g; Chol 36mg; Iron 2mg; Sodium 323mg; Calc 52mg

ASIAN SHRIMP WITH PASTA

family favorite

Prep: 25 min., Cook: 8 min.

It may seem like a lot of ingredients, but you'll make this often, so keep these items on hand.

- 1 pound unpeeled, medium-size fresh shrimp
- 1 (9-ounce) package refrigerated angel hair pasta
- ¼ cup lite soy sauce
- ¼ cup seasoned rice wine vinegar
- 2 teaspoons sesame oil
- 6 green onions, chopped
- 1 cup frozen sweet green peas, thawed
- ¾ cup shredded carrots
- 1 (8-ounce) can sliced water chestnuts, drained
- ¼ cup chopped fresh cilantro
- 2 tablespoons minced fresh ginger
- 2 garlic cloves, minced
- 1 teaspoon vegetable oil
- 2 tablespoons fresh lime juice
- ½ teaspoon freshly ground pepper
- 2 tablespoons chopped unsalted dry-roasted peanuts

PEEL shrimp, and devein, if desired. Set shrimp aside.

PREPARE pasta according to package directions, omitting salt and fat. Drain and place in a large bowl or on a platter.

STIR together soy sauce, vinegar, and sesame oil. Drizzle over pasta. Add green onions and next 4 ingredients to pasta; toss.

SAUTÉ ginger and garlic in hot vegetable oil 1 to 2 minutes. (Do not brown.) Add shrimp, lime juice, and pepper; cook 3 to 5 minutes or just until shrimp turn pink. Add shrimp mixture to pasta mixture, and toss. Sprinkle with peanuts. Serve immediately. **MAKES** 6 servings.

CYNTHIA GRIPPALDI
HINSDALE, MASSACHUSETTS

Per serving: Calories 292 (19% from fat); Fat 6.2g (sat 0.9g, mono 2.1g, poly 2.3g); Protein 24g; Carb 36g; Fiber 4.7g; Chol 146mg; Iron 4.5mg; Sodium 517mg; Calc 81mg

CHICKEN PASTA WITH ARTICHOKES AND CAPERS

family favorite

Prep: 15 min., Cook: 20 min.

- 4 skinned and boned chicken breasts, cut into thin strips
- ½ teaspoon salt, divided
- ¼ teaspoon pepper
- Vegetable cooking spray
- 1 (10¾-ounce) can fat-free cream of chicken soup, undiluted
- ½ cup dry white wine
- ½ cup fat-free reduced-sodium chicken broth
- 2 tablespoons fresh lemon juice
- 1 (14-ounce) can quartered artichoke hearts, drained and coarsely chopped
- 1 tablespoon drained capers
- 1 (9-ounce) package refrigerated spinach fettuccine
- 2 bacon slices, cooked and crumbled

SPRINKLE chicken evenly with ¼ teaspoon salt and pepper.

SAUTÉ chicken in a large nonstick skillet coated with cooking spray over medium-high heat 5 to 7 minutes or until done.

WHISK together soup, next 3 ingredients, and remaining ¼ teaspoon salt. Pour mixture over chicken in skillet. Stir in artichoke hearts and capers. Bring mixture to a boil; reduce heat, and simmer 10 minutes.

PREPARE pasta according to package directions, omitting salt and fat. Drain pasta, and place in a large bowl. Pour chicken mixture over pasta, tossing to coat. Sprinkle evenly with bacon. Serve immediately. **MAKES** 6 servings.

DONNA STREET
DICKSON, TENNESSEE

Per serving: Calories 280 (13% from fat); Fat 4.1g (sat 1.1g, mono 0.8g, poly 0.8g); Protein 27g; Carb 33g; Fiber 4.3g; Chol 83mg; Iron 2.8mg; Sodium 797mg; Calc 48mg

WON TON SPINACH LASAGNA

family favorite • vegetarian

Prep: 25 min., Bake: 45 min., Stand: 10 min.

Drain spinach thoroughly and neatly by placing thawed spinach in a clean kitchen towel. Roll up towel over spinach, and twist ends, allowing liquid to drain into sink.

- 2 cups (8 ounces) shredded part-skim mozzarella cheese, divided
- 1½ teaspoons dried basil, divided
- ¾ teaspoon ground red pepper, divided
- 1 (15-ounce) container fat-free ricotta cheese
- 1 (10-ounce) package frozen chopped spinach, thawed
- 1 cup shredded carrots
- ½ cup shredded Parmesan cheese
- ¼ cup egg substitute
- ½ teaspoon garlic powder
- 1 (26-ounce) jar pasta sauce
- Vegetable cooking spray
- ½ (16-ounce) package won ton wrappers

STIR together 1 cup mozzarella cheese, 1 teaspoon basil, ¼ teaspoon red pepper, ricotta, and next 5 ingredients in a large bowl.

STIR together pasta sauce and remaining ½ teaspoon each of basil and red pepper. Spread ½ cup sauce mixture in a 13- x 9-inch baking dish coated with cooking spray.

ARRANGE 1 layer won ton wrappers over sauce, slightly overlapping wrappers. Top with one-third cheese mixture. Spoon one-third remaining sauce mixture over cheese mixture. Repeat layers twice, ending with sauce mixture. Sprinkle with remaining 1 cup mozzarella cheese.

BAKE at 350° for 45 minutes or until bubbly and cheese melts. Let stand 10 minutes before serving. **MAKES** 8 servings.

MELISSA NICHOLS
SCOTTSBORO, ALABAMA

Per serving: Calories 272 (24% from fat); Fat 7.1g (sat 3.9g, mono 1.9g, poly 0.5g); Protein 21g; Carb 31g; Fiber 3.6g; Chol 27mg; Iron 2.9mg; Sodium 757mg; Calc 535mg

CHICKEN-AND-VEGGIE SPAGHETTI SALAD

family favorite • fast fixin's

Prep: 20 min.

- ¾ cup seasoned rice wine vinegar
- ½ cup sugar
- 2 tablespoons vegetable oil
- 1 tablespoon lemon juice
- 1 tablespoon lite soy sauce
- 2 garlic cloves, minced
- 2 teaspoons dry mustard
- ½ to 1 teaspoon ground black pepper
- ½ teaspoon ground ginger
- 2 teaspoons sesame oil
- 1 (9-ounce) package refrigerated angel hair pasta
- 2 cups chopped cooked chicken breasts
- 1 red or green bell pepper, cut into thin strips
- 1 small zucchini, cut into thin strips
- ½ (8-ounce) package shredded carrots
- ¼ teaspoon ground red pepper
- ½ cup chopped green onions
- 2 tablespoons sesame seeds, toasted

WHISK together first 10 ingredients in a large bowl until sugar dissolves.

PREPARE pasta according to package directions, omitting salt and fat. Drain pasta.

ADD pasta, chicken, and next 4 ingredients to dressing in bowl; toss to coat. Sprinkle with green onions and sesame seeds. **MAKES** 6 servings.

KATHLEEN GIBSON
ENUMCLAW, WASHINGTON

Per serving: Calories 378 (31% from fat); Fat 13g (sat 2g, mono 5.5g, poly 4.2g); Protein 20.3g; Carb 44.4g; Fiber 4g; Chol 73mg; Iron 3.5mg; Sodium 756mg; Calc 78mg

from our kitchen

Cookie Secrets

Follow our Test Kitchens' tips for great results.
- Avoid using tub butter or margarine products labeled spread, reduced-calorie, liquid, or soft-style; they contain less fat than regular butter or margarine and do not make satisfactory substitutions.
- Prevent stiff cookie dough from straining handheld portable mixers by stirring in the last additions of flour by hand.
- Keep the mixing of cookie dough to a minimum; stir just until the flour disappears. Overmixing toughens the dough.
- Lightly grease baking sheets only if the recipe specifies, and use only vegetable cooking spray or solid shortening. Butter or margarine encourages burning.
- Drop cookies 2 inches apart on shiny heavy aluminum baking sheets. Dark sheets can absorb heat, causing cookies to brown too much on the bottom; nonstick baking sheets work well if not too dark. Insulated baking sheets will require a slightly longer baking time.
- Use 1 teaspoon (not measuring spoon) to pick up drop cookie dough and another to push the dough onto the baking sheet.
- Bake one batch at a time on the middle oven rack; if you have to bake more than one at the same time in the same oven, rotate the sheets from the top to the bottom rack halfway through baking time.
- Check cookies for doneness at the minimum baking time to promote even browning.

- Transfer baked cookies to a wire rack immediately after baking unless otherwise directed.
- Allow baking sheets to cool before reusing between baking; wipe surface with a paper towel or scrape off crumbs with a metal turner.
- If you're short on wire racks, place a sheet of wax paper on the counter and sprinkle with granulated sugar. Transfer cookies from baking sheet to sugared paper; cookies will cool without getting soggy.
- When baking many batches of cookies, save time by spooning out the dough onto sheets of parchment paper, assembly-line fashion. Then slide each batch onto a baking sheet when ready to bake. Parchment eliminates the need to grease baking sheets.

Ground Beef: Building the Best Burger

After testing the top-rated Stuffed Border Burgers for this month's "What's for Supper?" menu on page 127, the Foods staff had a lively discussion about the makings of a perfect hamburger. We all agree that you definitely want to start with fresh, good-quality ground beef—but what about that lean-to-fat ratio? And is it really worth it to pay more for an expensive cut of ground beef? There were lots of different opinions, so we headed for the local supermarket to do a little research.

Prices will vary according to store and weekly specials, but the minimum percentage of lean meat found in the different types of ground beef is set by government standards. We weighed the ground beef before and after cooking, shaping four burgers from each pound of meat.

Extra-lean ground beef ($4.19 per pound) and **ground sirloin** ($3.99 per pound) were both labeled 92% lean, but we found the sirloin had a much better flavor and was not quite as dry. **Ground round** ($3.29 per pound and 85% lean) proved to be the group's favorite. Juicy and flavorful, it tasted considerably less greasy than **ground chuck** ($2.79 per pound and 80% lean). Whether pan-fried or grilled, they all yielded a cooked weight of about 12 ounces, which let us know that there was still a good bit of fat hanging around in some of those burgers. **Ground beef** ($1.69 per pound and 73% lean) yielded a cooked weight of 10½ ounces and left an alarming amount of grease in the skillet. Where cost is concerned it's a bargain, but if a recipe doesn't allow for a good bit of fat to be drained off after browning (such as meat loaf or stuffed peppers), then opt for a leaner cut.

June

Big Fun, Great Food

The McCoys share good times and scrumptious recipes with friends and family on the water.

Summer Cookout

Serves 10

Hot 'n' Spicy Chicken Wings

Ribs McCoy

Grilled Marinated Vegetables

Dianne's Southwestern Cornbread Salad

Pink Lemonade-Lime Dip with sugar cookies and fruit

A houseboat may not have everything your home offers, but it can certainly qualify as a terrific second residence. And the well-equipped houseboat owned by Melvyn and Dianne McCoy of Monroe, Louisiana, is no exception. As owners of Melvyn's restaurant, a local favorite, Dianne and Melvyn are known as great cooks and hosts at work as well as on their houseboat. So Associate Foods Editor Kate Nicholson was thrilled to step onboard the *Real McCoy* and head into the air-conditioned cabin for yummy food, great tunes, and a relaxing cruise on the water.

Less than a mile from the McCoy family's land residence, the *Real McCoy* is docked on Bayou DeSaird, which feeds into the Ouachita River about 50 yards away. These recipes are some of their favorites for parties on the houseboat, but whether you serve them on land or water, they're perfect for any kind of warm-weather entertaining.

MELVYN'S SEASONING MIX

fast fixin's • make ahead

Prep: 5 min.

- **⅓ cup Creole seasoning**
- **⅓ cup garlic powder**
- **⅓ cup pepper**
- **1½ tablespoons Greek seasoning**

STIR together all ingredients. Store seasoning mix in an airtight container. **MAKES** about 1¼ cups.

NOTE: For testing purposes only, we used Tony Chachere's Original Creole Seasoning and Cavender's All Purpose Greek Seasoning.

HOT 'N' SPICY CHICKEN WINGS

Prep: 20 min., Chill: 3 hrs., Grill: 30 min.

Not surprisingly, Melvyn's choice for sauce is Red & White Louisiana Hot Sauce.

- **4 to 5 pounds chicken wings***
- **⅓ cup Melvyn's Seasoning Mix (see previous recipe)**
- **1 cup hot sauce**

CUT off wing tips, and discard; cut wings in half at joint, if desired.

STIR together Melvyn's Seasoning Mix and hot sauce.

PLACE wings in a large shallow dish or large zip-top freezer bag. Pour half of hot sauce mixture over wings. Cover or seal; chill for 3 hours, turning occasionally. Cover and chill remaining hot sauce mixture.

REMOVE wings from marinade, discarding marinade.

GRILL chicken, covered with grill lid, over medium-high heat (350° to 400°) 15 minutes on each side or until done, basting occasionally with reserved hot sauce mixture. **MAKES** 10 appetizer servings.

*Substitute 1 (4-pound) package frozen party-style chicken wings, thawed, if desired.

RIBS McCOY

family favorite

Prep: 20 min.; Grill: 3 hrs., 30 min.

Perfectly seasoned Ribs McCoy continues to be one of Melvyn's most requested items.

- **⅓ cup Melvyn's Seasoning Mix (recipe at left)**
- **5 pounds spareribs**
- **1 (32-ounce) bottle barbecue sauce**

PREPARE a hot fire by piling charcoal on 1 side of grill, leaving other side empty. (For gas grills, light only 1 side to high heat [400° to 500°]).

RUB Melvyn's Seasoning Mix on all sides of ribs. Arrange ribs on food grate over unlit side.

GRILL, covered with grill lid, 3 to 3½ hours, turning once and basting with barbecue sauce during last 30 minutes. Serve with additional barbecue sauce, if desired. **MAKES** 10 to 12 servings.

GRILLED MARINATED VEGETABLES

make ahead

Prep: 30 min., Chill: 30 min., Grill: 10 min.

These veggies are delicious warm off the grill or chilled and served later. *(pictured on page 152)*

8 large fresh mushrooms
4 yellow squash
4 zucchini
2 red bell peppers
2 yellow bell peppers
1 medium-size red onion
½ cup olive oil
¼ cup lite soy sauce
¼ cup lemon juice
2 garlic cloves, pressed
¼ teaspoon pepper
Salt to taste

REMOVE mushroom stems, and discard; cut mushrooms in half. Diagonally slice squash and zucchini; cut bell peppers and onion into 1-inch strips. Place vegetables in a large zip-top freezer bag.

WHISK together oil and next 5 ingredients until blended. Pour over vegetables. Chill at least 30 minutes. Remove vegetables from marinade, reserving marinade. **GRILL** vegetables in a grill wok or metal basket, covered with grill lid, over medium-high heat (350° to 400°) 10 minutes, stirring occasionally and basting with reserved marinade. **MAKES** 10 servings.

DIANNE'S SOUTHWESTERN CORNBREAD SALAD

family favorite • make ahead

Prep: 30 min., Bake: 15 min., Chill: 2 hrs. *(pictured on page 153)*

1 (6-ounce) package Mexican cornbread mix
1 (1-ounce) envelope buttermilk Ranch-style dressing mix
1 small head romaine lettuce, shredded
2 large tomatoes, chopped
1 (15-ounce) can black beans, rinsed and drained
1 (15-ounce) can whole kernel corn with red and green peppers, drained
1 (8-ounce) package shredded Mexican four-cheese blend
6 bacon slices, cooked and crumbled
5 green onions, chopped

PREPARE cornbread according to package directions; cool and crumble. Set aside. **PREPARE** salad dressing according to package directions.
LAYER a large bowl with half each of cornbread, lettuce, and next 6 ingredients; spoon half of dressing evenly over top. Repeat layers with remaining ingredients and dressing. Cover and chill at least 2 hours. **MAKES** 10 to 12 servings.

PINK LEMONADE-LIME DIP

make ahead

Prep: 10 min., Chill: 2 hrs.

Serve this tasty tart dip with fresh fruit for a healthy snack or with sugar cookies for an easy dessert.

1 (14-ounce) can sweetened condensed milk
1 (6-ounce) can frozen pink lemonade concentrate, thawed
1 teaspoon grated lime rind

STIR together all ingredients in a small bowl until blended. Cover and chill at least 2 hours. **MAKES** about 1¾ cups.

Outdoor Party Tips

■ The *Real McCoy* has a small refrigerator—consequently, storage space is at a premium. Melvyn solves this problem with large coolers and lots of ice, which he says are musts for entertaining onboard or outdoors.
■ Dianne finds zip-top freezer bags especially helpful for marinated meats and chopped fruits and vegetables. She suggests chopping and marinating foods ahead, then storing items in sealed bags in the cooler.
■ You can cook a variety of veggies in Grilled Marinated Vegetables. Dianne recommends a trip to the local farmers market to find your favorites.

Cook With Bold Flavor

Explore new ingredients and freshen up humdrum fare with tempting recipes.

Steven Raichlen's *Big Flavor Cookbook* (Black Dog & Leventhal Publishers, Inc., 2003) had Associate Foods Editor Joy Zacharia's mouth watering by the first page. Steven's formula is pretty simple: Buy fresh, seasonal ingredients, infuse them with interesting herbs and condiments, cook them perfectly, and then enjoy dishes from around the world or around the corner.

SATÉ MIXED GRILL WITH SPICY PEANUT SAUCE

Prep: 30 min., Chill: 30 min., Grill: 6 min.

- **8 ounces skinned and boned chicken breasts**
- **8 ounces lean pork loin**
- **8 ounces lean beef sirloin**
- **8 ounces unpeeled, medium-size fresh shrimp**
- **⅓ cup lite soy sauce**
- **⅓ cup fresh lime juice**
- **1 tablespoon honey**
- **4 garlic cloves, minced**
- **2 teaspoons ground coriander**
- **2 teaspoons ground turmeric**
- **40 (6-inch) wooden skewers**
- **Spicy Peanut Sauce**

CUT chicken and pork into 3- x ½-inch strips. Cut beef sirloin into thin long strips. Peel shrimp, and devein, if desired. Place chicken, pork, beef, and shrimp in separate bowls.
WHISK together soy sauce and next 5 ingredients. Drizzle evenly over bowls of meat and shrimp; toss to coat. Cover and chill 30 minutes. Soak skewers in cold water to prevent burning.
THREAD chicken, pork, beef, and shrimp evenly onto skewers (10 skewers of each ingredient).
GRILL, covered with grill lid, over medium-high heat (350° to 400°) 1 to 3 minutes on each side.
ARRANGE skewers on a platter, and serve with Spicy Peanut Sauce. **MAKES** 40 appetizer servings.

Spicy Peanut Sauce:
Prep: 10 min., Cook: 5 min.

This sauce tastes salty, tangy, and sweet.

- **⅔ cup chicken broth**
- **⅓ cup chunky peanut butter**
- **3 tablespoons lite soy sauce**
- **3 tablespoons fresh lime juice**
- **1 tablespoon honey**
- **1 tomato, peeled, seeded, and chopped**
- **4 green onions, minced**
- **2 garlic cloves, minced**
- **1 tablespoon minced fresh ginger**
- **1 jalapeño pepper, seeded and minced**
- **¼ cup chopped fresh cilantro**
- **Garnish: chopped fresh cilantro**

BRING first 11 ingredients to a boil in a small saucepan over medium-high heat. Reduce heat, and simmer, whisking constantly, 2 minutes or until thick and creamy. Garnish, if desired. **MAKES** 1⅓ cups.

Per serving: Calories 50 (35% from fat); Fat 2g (sat 0.5g, mono 0.8g, poly 0.4g); Protein 5.6g; Carb 2.6g; Fiber 0.4g; Chol 18mg; Iron 0.5mg; Sodium 162mg; Calc 9mg

GRILLED CORN IN THE STYLE OF OAXACA

fast fixin's
Prep: 10 min., Grill: 10 min.

It may seem unusual to spread sour cream and mayonnaise over corn, but trust us, it's really good. Sweet corn combined with the creamy mixture, salty cheese, and spicy chili powder is an irresistible union of flavors. *(pictured on page 151)*

- **6 ears fresh corn with husks**
- **2 tablespoons reduced-fat mayonnaise**
- **2 tablespoons fat-free sour cream**
- **3 tablespoons finely grated Parmesan cheese**
- **1 to 2 tablespoons chili powder**
- **2 limes, cut into wedges**
- **Vegetable cooking spray**
- **1½ teaspoons salt**
- **1 teaspoon pepper**

PREPARE a hot fire by piling charcoal on 1 side of grill, leaving other side empty. (For gas grills, light only 1 side of grill.)
REMOVE heavy outer husks from corn; pull back inner husks. Remove and discard silks. Tie inner husks together with string.
STIR together mayonnaise and sour cream in a small bowl, and set aside. Place Parmesan cheese, chili powder, and lime wedges in small serving bowls, and set aside.
COAT each corn cob lightly with cooking spray. Sprinkle corn evenly with salt and pepper. Position corn on food grate so that tied husks lie on unlit side to prevent burning husks.
GRILL corn, covered with grill lid, over medium-high heat (350° to 400°) 10 minutes or until golden brown, turning occasionally. Place grilled corncobs on a platter.
SPREAD corn evenly with mayonnaise mixture, and sprinkle evenly with cheese and chili powder. Squeeze lime wedges over corn. **MAKES** 6 servings.

Per serving: Calories 128 (26% from fat); Fat 3.7g (sat 1g, mono 0.6g, poly 0.6g); Protein 4.2g; Carb 24g; Fiber 3.2g; Chol 4mg; Iron 0.9mg; Sodium 698mg; Calc 56mg

Steven's Principles for Tastier, Healthier Cooking

- Use intense flavorings such as fresh herbs, spices, and condiments (mustards, hot sauce, horseradish) instead of oil or butter to make foods taste good.
- Put the fat where you can taste it. Brush or spray it on the surface of the dish. It'll be the first thing you taste without having the fat throughout the recipe.
- Oven fry. Give chicken, fish, or eggplant a crunchy coating by dipping in egg white, and then dredging in breadcrumbs.
- Use chicken or vegetable broth instead of oil, butter, or cream in salad dressings, soups, stews, and casseroles.
- Slow down. Enjoy more leisurely meals with your family, even if you have to plan them.

Fresh, Fabulous Pasta Dishes

These pasta sauces take 35 to 40 minutes from first chop to first bite, but each has a fresh, summery flavor that you can't beat—or buy off your grocer's shelf. Choosing the right type of noodle really enhances the dish, so in each one we recommend a pasta that best catches and matches the sauce.

EMPANADAS

Prep: 30 min., Cook: 5 min., Chill: 30 min., Bake: 12 min.

These little Latin turnovers (em-pah-NAH-dahs) are irresistible right out of the oven.

- 8 ounces skinned and boned chicken breasts, cut into ½-inch pieces
- ½ small onion, minced (about ¼ cup)
- ½ green bell pepper, minced
- ½ tomato, seeded and coarsely chopped
- 4 pimiento-stuffed green olives, coarsely chopped
- 2 tablespoons raisins
- 2 tablespoons chicken broth
- 1 tablespoon tomato paste
- 1 teaspoon minced fresh cilantro or parsley
- 1 garlic clove, minced
- ½ teaspoon salt
- ½ teaspoon ground cumin
- ½ teaspoon pepper
- Vegetable cooking spray
- 1 tablespoon fine, dry breadcrumbs (optional)
- 36 (3-inch) square won ton wrappers
- Salt to taste

COOK first 13 ingredients in a large skillet coated with cooking spray over medium heat 5 minutes or until chicken is done, stirring often.

PROCESS chicken mixture in a food processor until coarsely chopped. (Mixture should be fairly dry. Add 1 tablespoon breadcrumbs if mixture is wet.) Cover and chill 30 minutes.

ARRANGE 1 won ton wrapper on a clean, flat surface. Lightly brush edges of wrapper with water. Place 1 heaping teaspoon of chicken mixture in center of wrapper. Fold dough over filling, pressing edges with a fork to seal. Repeat with remaining wrappers and chicken mixture. Arrange empanadas on a baking sheet coated with cooking spray. Lightly coat empanadas with cooking spray.

BAKE at 400° for 12 minutes or until golden brown, turning after 6 minutes. Sprinkle with salt to taste. **MAKES** 36 servings.

Per serving: Calories 36 (8% from fat); Fat 0.3g (sat 0g, mono 0.1g, poly 0.1g); Protein 2.4g; Carb 5.8g; Fiber 0.3g; Chol 4.4mg; Iron 0.4mg; Sodium 98mg; Calc 7mg

FETTUCCINE WITH PORTOBELLO-ALFREDO SAUCE

family favorite

Prep: 15 min., Cook: 20 min.

- 1 (12-ounce) package fettuccine
- 1 (6-ounce) package portobello mushrooms
- ½ cup butter
- 3 garlic cloves, minced
- 1 cup whipping cream
- 1 cup milk
- 1 cup (4 ounces) shredded Parmesan cheese
- 1 teaspoon coarsely ground pepper
- ½ teaspoon salt
- 2 tablespoons chopped fresh Italian parsley

PREPARE pasta according to package directions; drain.

REMOVE brown gills from undersides of mushroom caps using a spoon, and discard gills. Chop mushrooms.

MELT butter in a large saucepan over medium heat; add mushrooms and garlic, and sauté 5 to 6 minutes or until tender. Stir in cream and milk. Bring to a boil over medium-high heat; reduce heat, and simmer, whisking constantly, 10 minutes. Stir in cheese, pepper, and salt; stir constantly until cheese melts and mixture thickens. Stir in 2 tablespoons parsley. Serve over hot cooked pasta. **MAKES** 6 to 8 servings.

LINDA KING
DUNWOODY, GEORGIA

GRILLED PEPPER-PESTO LINGUINE

Prep: 10 min., Grill: 20 min., Stand: 10 min.

- **1 (16-ounce) package linguine**
- **1 large yellow bell pepper, seeded and cut into 6 pieces**
- **1 large red bell pepper, seeded and cut into 6 pieces**
- **6 large mushrooms**
- **5 garlic cloves**
- **2 tablespoons capers, drained**
- **1½ cups loosely packed cilantro leaves (about 1 bunch, stems removed)**
- **2 tablespoons lemon juice, divided**
- **⅓ cup olive oil**
- **1 teaspoon salt**
- **½ teaspoon ground cumin**
- **½ teaspoon pepper**
- **Shredded Parmesan cheese (optional)**

PREPARE pasta according to package directions; drain.

PLACE bell peppers, mushrooms, and garlic cloves on a 24- x 12-inch piece of nonstick aluminum foil or lightly greased heavy-duty aluminum foil. Sprinkle bell pepper mixture with capers, cilantro, and 1 tablespoon lemon juice. Fold aluminum foil to seal, leaving an opening in top for steam to escape.

GRILL, covered with grill lid, over high heat (400° to 500°) 20 minutes or until peppers are almost blackened, and mushrooms are tender. Remove foil packet from grill. Seal foil, and let stand 10 minutes to loosen skin on peppers. Peel peppers, and discard skin.

PROCESS roasted peppers, remaining items in aluminum foil packet, olive oil, next 3 ingredients, and remaining 1 tablespoon lemon juice in a food processor or blender until smooth, stopping to scrape down sides. Serve sauce over hot cooked pasta. Sprinkle with cheese, if desired. **MAKES** 6 servings.

MARY RITZ
TROY, VIRGINIA

Take the Cake

Dressed up or right in the pan, these sweet treats are made to travel.

When we asked fellow Foods editors what the quintessential sheet cake is, chocolate was one emphatic response. Others swooned over the idea of coconut with lots of frosting. All this only reinforced what we already knew: Everyone loves a sheet cake. They're perfect for casual gatherings because they truly are quick, simple, and easy to transport. Here we offer some basic recipes, including a classic Mississippi Mud Cake.

MISSISSIPPI MUD CAKE

family favorite • freezeable

Prep: 20 min., Bake: 30 min.

The women of Huffman United Methodist Church in Birmingham used this classic cake recipe for the church's 125th anniversary celebration. Of the 100 cakes made, there wasn't any leftover. *(pictured on page 156)*

- **1 cup butter, melted**
- **2 cups sugar**
- **½ cup unsweetened cocoa**
- **⅛ teaspoon salt**
- **4 large eggs, lightly beaten**
- **1 teaspoon vanilla extract**
- **1½ cups all-purpose flour**
- **1½ cups coarsely chopped pecans, toasted**
- **1 (10.5-ounce) bag miniature marshmallows**
- **Chocolate Frosting**

WHISK together first 6 ingredients in a large bowl. Stir in flour and chopped pecans. Pour batter into a greased and floured 15- x 10-inch jellyroll pan.

BAKE at 350° for 20 to 25 minutes or until a wooden pick inserted in center comes out clean. Remove from oven;

top warm cake evenly with marshmallows. Return to oven, and bake 5 minutes. Drizzle Chocolate Frosting over warm cake. Cool completely. **MAKES** 15 servings.

NOTE: Substitute 2 (19.5-ounce) packages brownie mix prepared according to package directions for first 7 ingredients. Stir in chopped pecans. Bake at 350° for 30 minutes. Proceed with marshmallows and frosting as directed.

Chocolate Frosting:
fast fixin's

Prep: 10 min.

- **1 (16-ounce) package powdered sugar, sifted**
- **½ cup milk**
- **¼ cup butter, softened**
- **⅓ cup unsweetened cocoa**

BEAT all ingredients at medium speed with an electric mixer until smooth. **MAKES** 2 cups.

COCONUT SHEET CAKE

freezeable

Prep: 15 min., Bake: 45 min., Freeze: 30 min.

- **3 large eggs**
- **1 (8-ounce) container sour cream**
- **⅓ cup water**
- **1 (8.5-ounce) can cream of coconut**
- **½ teaspoon vanilla extract**
- **1 (18.25-ounce) package white cake mix**
- **Coconut-Cream Cheese Frosting**

BEAT eggs at high speed with an electric mixer 2 minutes. Add sour cream, ⅓ cup water, cream of coconut, and vanilla, beating well after each addition. Add cake mix, beating at low speed just until blended. Beat at high speed 2 minutes. Pour batter into a greased and floured 13- x 9-inch pan.

BAKE at 325° for 40 to 45 minutes or until a wooden pick inserted in center comes out clean. Cool cake in pan on a wire rack. Cover pan with plastic wrap, and freeze cake 30 minutes. Remove from freezer.

SPREAD Coconut-Cream Cheese Frosting on chilled cake. Cover and store in refrigerator. **MAKES** 12 servings.

NOTE: If desired, cake can be baked in a greased and floured 15- x 10-inch jellyroll pan for 30 to 32 minutes or until a wooden pick inserted in center comes out clean. **MAKES** 15 servings.

Coconut-Cream Cheese Frosting:
fast fixin's

Prep: 10 min.

This frosting is very thick.

- 1 (8-ounce) package cream cheese, softened
- ½ cup butter or margarine, softened
- 3 tablespoons milk
- 1 teaspoon vanilla extract
- 1 (16-ounce) package powdered sugar, sifted
- 1 (7-ounce) package sweetened flaked coconut

BEAT cream cheese and butter at medium speed with an electric mixer until creamy; add milk and vanilla, beating well. Gradually add sugar, beating until smooth. Stir in coconut. **MAKES** 4 cups.

JULIE STEIN
BIRMINGHAM, ALABAMA

STRAWBERRY-LEMON SHEET CAKE
freezeable

Prep: 25 min., Bake: 30 min.

Angie Beachy's divine cake layers inspired us to bake in a jellyroll pan, and then stack the halves with a simple strawberry-lemon filling.

- 2 cups cake flour
- 1½ cups sugar
- 2 teaspoons baking powder
- ½ teaspoon salt
- 3 large eggs
- ¾ cup whole milk
- ½ cup vegetable oil
- ¼ cup butter, melted and cooled
- 1 tablespoon grated lemon rind
- 1 tablespoon fresh lemon juice
- Strawberry-Lemon Filling
- 1½ cups whipping cream
- 6 tablespoons sugar

LINE a lightly greased 15- x 10-inch jellyroll pan with parchment paper; lightly grease parchment paper.

COMBINE cake flour and next 3 ingredients in a large bowl.

WHISK together eggs and next 5 ingredients in a medium bowl until mixture is blended; whisk into dry ingredients just until blended. Pour batter into prepared pan.

BAKE at 350° for 30 minutes or until a wooden pick inserted in center comes out clean. Cool in pan on a wire rack 10 minutes. Invert cake onto wire rack, and remove parchment paper; let cake cool completely. Transfer cake to a large cutting board.

CUT sheet cake in half to make 2 rectangles. Place 1 cake layer on a serving plate; spread top with half of Strawberry-Lemon Filling. Top with remaining cake layer. Spread remaining filling over top.

BEAT whipping cream and 6 tablespoons sugar at high speed with an electric mixer until stiff peaks form; spoon into a 1-gallon zip-top freezer bag. Press whipped cream into 1 corner of bag removing excess air, and snip a ¼-inch hole in corner of bag. Pipe whipped cream vertically onto cake sides. **MAKES** 15 servings.

ANGIE BEACHY
LUSBY, MARYLAND

Strawberry-Lemon Filling:
make ahead

Prep: 5 min., Cook: 15 min., Chill: 2 hrs.

Make up to three days ahead, if desired.

- 1 (16-ounce) package whole frozen strawberries
- 6 tablespoons sugar, divided
- ¼ cup fresh lemon juice
- ¼ cup all-purpose flour

BRING strawberries, 4 tablespoons sugar, and lemon juice to a boil in a medium saucepan, and cook 5 minutes.

WHISK together remaining 2 tablespoons sugar and flour in a saucepan. Whisk in strawberry mixture; cook over medium heat 5 minutes or until thickened and bubbling around edges. Pour into a glass bowl; cover surface with plastic wrap. Chill at least 2 hours. **MAKES** 1⅔ cups.

Test Kitchens Notes

■ For the smoothest frosting, freeze cake for at least 30 minutes; then frost. Freeze layers on a wire rack or on a baking sheet. If you're not using frozen layers right away, wrap them well in plastic wrap.

■ Cream of coconut can be found in the ethnic food or drink mixers section of supermarkets.

■ Mix homemade batter by hand for a more tender and moist cake.

Pork Tenderloin

This no-waste cut is a smart buy

for weeknight meals.

**Family Dinner
on the Patio**

Serves 6

Grilled Pork Tenderloin With Gingered Jezebel Sauce

Grilled Yellow Squash Halves

Fresh Tomato Biscuits

Candy Wrap Cookies

Grilled pork tenderloin makes a great supper at the end of a busy day; just be sure not to overcook the meat. The concerns of the past aren't the concerns of today, according to the National Pork Board. A light blush of pink in the center of the cooked tenderloin is a sign it will be juicy and flavorful.

GRILLED PORK TENDERLOIN WITH GINGERED JEZEBEL SAUCE

family favorite

Prep: 10 min., Chill: 20 min., Grill: 25 min., Stand: 10 min. *(pictured on page 152)*

- **½ cup lite soy sauce**
- **2 tablespoons dark brown sugar**
- **2 green onions, chopped**
- **2 tablespoons sherry (optional)**
- **3 pounds pork tenderloins**
- **Gingered Jezebel Sauce**
- **Garnish: fresh rosemary**

COMBINE first 3 ingredients and, if desired, sherry in a shallow dish or large zip-top freezer bag; add pork. Cover or seal, and chill 20 minutes.

REMOVE pork from marinade; discard marinade. Grill pork, covered with grill lid, over medium-high heat (350° to 400°) 25 minutes or until a meat thermometer inserted in thickest portion registers 155°, turning once and basting with ½ cup Gingered Jezebel Sauce the last 5 to 10 minutes. Let pork stand 10 minutes or until thermometer registers 160°. Slice and serve with remaining sauce. Garnish, if desired. **MAKES** 6 servings.

Gingered Jezebel Sauce:
Prep: 5 min.

Ginger replaces dry mustard in this version of jezebel sauce.

- **⅔ cup pineapple preserves**
- **⅓ cup apple jelly**
- **2 tablespoons prepared horseradish**
- **1 tablespoon grated fresh ginger**

MICROWAVE pineapple preserves and apple jelly in a glass bowl at HIGH 2 minutes or until melted. Stir in horseradish and ginger. **MAKES** 1¼ cups.

MARY FIERLE
ASHEVILLE, NORTH CAROLINA

GRILLED YELLOW SQUASH HALVES

family favorite • fast fixin's

Prep: 5 min., Chill: 20 min., Grill: 2 min. *(pictured on page 152)*

CUT 6 yellow squash in half lengthwise. Place squash in a zip-top freezer bag; add ½ cup Italian dressing. Seal and chill 20 minutes.

REMOVE squash from marinade, discarding marinade. Grill, covered with grill lid, over medium-high heat (350° to 400°) 2 minutes or until tender. **MAKES** 6 servings.

FRESH TOMATO BISCUITS

family favorite • fast fixin's

Prep: 10 min., Bake: 12 min.

- **¼ cup mayonnaise**
- **¼ teaspoon salt**
- **¼ teaspoon coarsely ground pepper**
- **¼ cup shredded fresh basil**
- **1 (16.3-ounce) can refrigerated flaky biscuits**
- **2 medium tomatoes, thinly sliced**

COMBINE first 4 ingredients. Set aside.
PRESS each biscuit into a 4-inch circle. Place biscuit circles on a lightly greased baking sheet.
BAKE at 400° for 6 minutes. Spread each biscuit evenly with about 2 teaspoons mayonnaise mixture. Top evenly with tomato slices. Bake 6 more minutes or until mayonnaise mixture is bubbly. Serve immediately. **MAKES** 10 biscuits.

NOTE: For testing purposes only, we used Pillsbury Golden Layers Buttermilk Biscuits.

CANDY WRAP COOKIES

family favorite • fast fixin's

Prep: 10 min., Bake: 15 min., Cool: 1 min.

CUT 1 (18-ounce) package refrigerated sugar cookie dough into ¼-inch slices. Wrap each slice around 1 miniature chocolate-coated caramel-and-creamy nougat bar. Place on ungreased baking sheets. Bake at 350° for 13 to 15 minutes. Cool 1 minute; remove to a wire rack. Dust with unsweetened cocoa, if desired. **MAKES** about 2 dozen.

NOTE: For testing purposes only, we used 1 (8-ounce) package Milky Way Miniatures.

Sauce Makes the Meal

A bottle of your favorite barbecue sauce can be used for a whole lot more than basting. These recipes prove that this reliable partner has other dimensions. So think outside the box next time you make pizza, potatoes, or other recipes: Barbecue sauce can make such a difference.

BARBECUE SCALLOPED POTATOES

family favorite

Prep: 15 min., Cook: 40 min., Bake: 45 min.

- **3 large baking potatoes (about 2½ pounds)**
- **1½ teaspoons salt, divided**
- **1 (10-ounce) can cream of mushroom soup, undiluted**
- **1 (5-ounce) can evaporated milk**
- **¼ cup spicy barbecue sauce**
- **¼ teaspoon onion salt**
- **2 cups (8 ounces) shredded sharp Cheddar cheese**
- **⅛ teaspoon paprika**

COOK potatoes with 1 teaspoon salt in boiling water to cover 30 to 40 minutes or just until tender. Let cool slightly; peel and slice. Set aside.

STIR together remaining ½ teaspoon salt, soup, and next 3 ingredients until blended.

LAYER half each of potato slices, barbecue sauce mixture, and cheese in a lightly greased 2-quart round baking dish. Repeat layers; sprinkle evenly with paprika.

BAKE at 350° for 45 minutes or until golden. **MAKES** 6 servings.

CAROLYN NOWICKI
BIRMINGHAM, ALABAMA

BARBECUE-BATTERED CHICKEN FINGERS

family favorite

Prep: 20 min., Fry: 7 min. per batch

- **3 pounds skinned and boned chicken breasts**
- **3 cups all-purpose flour**
- **1½ teaspoons seasoned salt**
- **1½ teaspoons pepper**
- **¾ teaspoon garlic powder**
- **2 cups buttermilk**
- **¾ cup honey smoke barbecue sauce**
- **2 large eggs**
- **Vegetable oil**
- **Honey smoke barbecue sauce**

CUT each chicken breast into 3- x 1-inch strips, and set aside.

COMBINE flour and next 3 ingredients in a large shallow dish.

WHISK together buttermilk, ¾ cup barbecue sauce, and eggs in a bowl. Dredge chicken pieces in flour mixture; dip in buttermilk mixture, and dredge again in flour mixture. (If flour gets gummy, just press into chicken pieces.)

POUR oil to a depth of 1½ inches in a deep skillet or Dutch oven; heat to 360°.

FRY chicken, in batches, 5 to 7 minutes or until golden. Drain on wire racks over paper towels. Serve chicken with extra barbecue sauce. **MAKES** 6 to 8 servings or 16 appetizer servings.

MARGE GOODACRE
SHREVEPORT, LOUISIANA

BARBECUE-BATTERED PORK CHOPS: Substitute 3 pounds boneless breakfast pork chops for chicken, and proceed as directed. For a delicious serving idea, serve cooked chops in biscuits.

QUICK 'N' EASY CHICKEN BARBECUE PIZZA

family favorite

Prep: 10 min., Cook: 10 min., Bake: 24 min.

For even more flavor, sprinkle pizza with chopped cooked bacon and chopped fresh cilantro before adding the cheese.

- **1 small onion, chopped**
- **½ red bell pepper, chopped**
- **½ teaspoon salt**
- **¼ teaspoon pepper**
- **1 teaspoon olive oil**
- **1 (10-ounce) can refrigerated pizza crust**
- **½ cup hickory smoke barbecue sauce**
- **2 (6-ounce) packages grilled boneless, skinless chicken breast strips**
- **2 cups (8 ounces) shredded Monterey Jack cheese with peppers**
- **Garnish: chopped fresh parsley**
- **Hickory smoke barbecue sauce**

SAUTÉ first 4 ingredients in hot oil in a large skillet over medium-high heat 8 to 10 minutes or until vegetables are tender. Drain well.

UNROLL pizza crust; press or pat into a lightly greased 13- x 9-inch pan.

BAKE crust at 400° for 12 to 14 minutes. Spread ½ cup barbecue sauce evenly over pizza crust. Arrange chicken strips evenly over barbecue sauce, top with onion mixture, and sprinkle evenly with cheese.

BAKE at 400° for 8 to 10 minutes or until cheese melts. Garnish, if desired. Serve with extra sauce for dipping. **MAKES** 6 servings.

No-Fuss Nibbles

Fresh veggies and super-sweet fruit inspire these quick, mouthwatering lunches and snacks.

When it's hot and humid outside, you probably aren't up for spending time heating up the kitchen. But you gotta eat, right? Luckily, these easy recipes offer fresh flavors without the toil.

MARINATED TOMATOES WITH BASIL AND BALSAMIC VINEGAR

make ahead

Prep: 20 min., Stand: 30 min., Chill: 30 min.

Soaking onion slices in ice water before assembling a dish makes them milder. It's a great trick to use for onions that are added to tuna, egg, or chicken salad. *(pictured on page 154)*

- 1 small red onion, thinly sliced
- 4 cups ice water
- ¾ cup balsamic vinegar
- ¼ cup olive oil
- 2 tablespoons water
- 2 teaspoons sugar
- ½ teaspoon salt
- ½ teaspoon pepper
- 2 garlic cloves, minced
- ½ to 1 cup chopped fresh basil
- 6 tomatoes, thinly sliced
- Parmesan cheese curls (optional)
- French bread (optional)

COMBINE onion and 4 cups ice water in a large bowl; let stand 30 minutes. Drain and pat dry with paper towels.
WHISK together vinegar, olive oil, 2 tablespoons water, and next 4 ingredients. Stir in basil.
LAYER half of tomato slices in a shallow dish. Top with half of onion slices. Drizzle with half of dressing. Repeat with remaining tomato slices, onion slices, and dressing. Cover and chill 30 minutes.

SPRINKLE with Parmesan cheese curls, if desired, and serve with bread, if desired. Serve at room temperature. **MAKES** 12 servings.

NOTE: Recipe can be prepared up to 3 hours ahead.

VICKI ARMSTRONG
FLORENCE, ALABAMA

Per serving: Calories 88 (51% from fat); Fat 5g (sat 0.7g, mono 3.6g, poly 0.6g); Protein 0.9g; Carb 11g; Fiber 1.2g; Chol 0mg; Iron 0.6mg; Sodium 108mg; Calc 12mg

Per serving (with bread and Parmesan): Calories 203 (36% from fat); Carb 28g; Fiber 2.2; Fat 7.8g; Sodium 414mg

---

Need a Serving Idea?

Try **Marinated Tomatoes With Basil and Balsamic Vinegar** in a variety of other delicious ways.
- Sprinkle with feta cheese for a zesty kick.
- Layer tomato and onion with fresh mozzarella.
- Chop the tomatoes and onion, and stir them into pasta for a quick side dish. They're also delicious served with dressing over grilled salmon, tuna, or grouper.
- Serve over mixed salad greens, and top with grilled chicken strips or shrimp for a light and healthy dinner.

BROCCOLI, CAULIFLOWER, AND CARROT SALAD

fast fixin's

Prep: 10 min.

- ½ cup light mayonnaise
- 1 tablespoon sugar
- 2 tablespoons rice wine vinegar
- 1 teaspoon salt
- ½ teaspoon ground ginger
- 1 (12-ounce) package pre-washed broccoli and cauliflower florets blend, coarsely chopped
- ½ (10-ounce) package shredded carrots
- ¼ cup roasted peanuts, chopped

WHISK together first 5 ingredients in a large bowl. Add broccoli mixture and carrots, tossing to coat. Sprinkle evenly with nuts. **MAKES** 6 servings.

Per serving: Calories 138 (64% from fat); Fat 9.8g (sat 1.5g, mono 1.5g, poly 1.1g); Protein 3.2g; Carb 11.2g; Fiber 2.8g; Chol 7mg; Iron 0.7mg; Sodium 572mg; Calc 31mg

TOMATO, SWISS, AND BACON SANDWICHES

family favorite • fast fixin's

Prep: 10 min., Cook: 6 min.

For a lower sodium option, choose reduced-sodium Canadian bacon and omit added salt. To decrease calories, prepare sandwiches with low-calorie whole wheat bread.

- 8 Canadian bacon slices
- Vegetable cooking spray
- 3 tablespoons light mayonnaise
- ½ teaspoon fresh dill
- 8 multigrain sandwich bread slices
- 1 large tomato, cut into 8 slices
- ¼ teaspoon salt
- ½ teaspoon freshly ground pepper
- 4 (⅔-ounce) slices reduced-fat Swiss cheese
- 4 iceberg lettuce leaves

COOK bacon in a skillet coated with cooking spray over medium heat 3 minutes per side or until browned. Drain on paper towels.
COMBINE mayonnaise and dill; spread mayonnaise evenly on 1 side of 4 bread slices. Top evenly with bacon slices and

tomato slices; sprinkle with salt and pepper. Top evenly with cheese and lettuce. Cover with remaining bread slices. **MAKES** 4 sandwiches.

NOTE: Canadian bacon is similar to lean ham. It has less fat and cholesterol than bacon.

Per serving (regular bread): Calories 330 (38% from fat); Fat 14g (sat 5g, mono 2.6g, poly 0.9g); Protein 23g; Carb 29.3g; Fiber 4.1g; Chol 46mg; Iron 2.5mg; Sodium 1,316mg; Calc 228mg

With low-calorie bread: Calories 291; Fat 13g; Carb 25g; Fiber 6.3g

Spicy Fruit and Veggies With Lime

fast fixin's

Prep: 20 min.

Jícama is a crunchy, mild-tasting root vegetable. Peel its thin skin before cutting into strips. Jícama is usually enjoyed uncooked, but some folks like it in stir-fried dishes.

- **½ small jícama, peeled and cut into spears**
- **½ pineapple, cored and cut into thick spears**
- **1 mango, peeled and cut into spears**
- **1 large cucumber, peeled and cut into spears**
- **1½ tablespoons fresh lime juice (about 2 limes)**
- **1 teaspoon salt**
- **¼ teaspoon ground red pepper or pequín chile powder**
- **Lime wedges**

PLACE first 4 ingredients in a shallow bowl or platter, dividing them in clusters. Drizzle with lime juice, and sprinkle with salt and red pepper. Serve immediately with lime wedges. **MAKES** 4 servings.

ELISA LEVY
TALLAHASSEE, FLORIDA

Per serving: Calories 99 (6% from fat); Fat 0.6 g (sat 0g, mono 0.1g, poly 0.2g); Protein 1.5 g; Carb 26g; Fiber 5.2g; Chol 0mg; Iron 0.9mg; Sodium 587mg; Calc 36mg

Cool, All-Natural Treats

As you enjoy a summer of outdoor activities, cool off with these recipes. From frozen pops to smoothies, these deliciously light treats made with vitamin-rich fruit will give you and your little ones a hydrating boost.

Strawberry Pops

family favorite • freezeable

Prep: 20 min., Cook: 5 min., Freeze: 4 hrs.

- **1 cup water**
- **½ cup sugar**
- **1 pint fresh strawberries**
- **2 tablespoons lemon juice**
- **2 tablespoons orange juice**

BRING 1 cup water and sugar to a boil in a saucepan, stirring until sugar dissolves. Remove from heat, and cool. **PROCESS** cooled sugar mixture, strawberries, and juices in a blender until mixture is smooth, stopping to scrape down sides. Pour into 12 (¼-cup) plastic pop molds. Insert plastic pop sticks, and freeze 4 hours or until firm. **MAKES** 12 servings.

STRAWBERRY FREEZE: Prepare sugar mixture, and cool. Process strawberries and juices in a blender until smooth. Stir together cooled sugar mixture and strawberry mixture in a freezer-safe container; freeze at least 3 hours. Spoon into bowls.

EILEEN LEDONNE
EVERETT, MASSACHUSETTS

Per serving: Calories 41 (2% from fat); Fat 0.1g (sat 0g, mono 0g, poly 0g); Protein 0.2g; Carb 10.5g; Fiber 0.1g; Chol 0mg; Iron 0.1mg; Sodium 1mg; Calc 4.3mg

Peach Pops

family favorite • freezeable

Prep: 5 min., Chill: 10 min., Freeze: 4 hrs.

- **2 cups fresh peach slices***
- **¼ cup sugar**
- **1⅓ cups unsweetened pineapple juice**
- **1 tablespoon lemon juice**

TOSS together peaches and sugar in a small bowl. Cover and chill 10 minutes. **PROCESS** peach mixture and juices in a blender until smooth. Pour into 14 (¼-cup) plastic pop molds. Insert plastic pop sticks; freeze at least 4 hours. **MAKES** 14 servings.

*Substitute frozen peaches, partially thawed, if desired.

PEACH SLUSH: Add 3 cups ice cubes to blender with peach mixture and juices. Process until ice is finely ground. Serve immediately, or freeze for later use.

CAROL S. NOBLE
BURGAW, NORTH CAROLINA

Per serving: Calories 38 (1% from fat); Fat .04g (sat 0g, mono 0.01g, poly 0.02g); Protein 0.25g; Carb 9.6g; Fiber 0.5g; Chol 0mg; Iron 0.09mg; Sodium 0.3mg; Calc 5.3mg

Blackberry Smoothies

fast fixin's

Prep: 5 min.

Sandi originally used strawberries instead of blackberries in this simple smoothie—you can use any of your favorite berries, or mix it up with a combination of fruit.

- **1 cup fat-free milk**
- **1 pint low-fat frozen vanilla yogurt, softened**
- **1 medium banana, coarsely chopped**
- **½ cup fresh blackberries**

PROCESS all ingredients in a blender until smooth, stopping to scrape down sides. Serve smoothie immediately. **MAKES** 4 servings.

SANDI PICHON
SLIDELL, LOUISIANA

Per 1-cup serving: Calories 163 (9% from fat); Fat 1.7g (sat 1.0g, mono 0.4g, poly 0.1g); Protein 7.3g; Carb 31g; Fiber 1.6g; Chol 6.3mg; Iron 0.3mg; Sodium 95.6mg; Calc 249mg

Starlight Picnic

Evening is the perfect time for an outdoor meal.

Starlight Supper

Serves 6

Stuffed Focaccia With Roasted Pepper Vinaigrette

Green Bean-Potato Salad

Amaretto-Walnut Brownies

Iced tea or lemonade

STUFFED FOCACCIA WITH ROASTED PEPPER VINAIGRETTE

family favorite • fast fixin's

Prep: 10 min., Bake: 8 min.

A serrated or bread knife slices this sandwich into clean pieces. Wrap the sandwich slices in brown parchment paper, and tie with colored raffia for a festive presentation.

- **1 (9-inch) round loaf focaccia bread**
- **Roasted Pepper Vinaigrette, divided**
- **1 (3-ounce) log goat cheese, crumbled**
- **¼ cup pine nuts or slivered almonds**
- **1 deli-roasted chicken**
- **3 cups mixed baby lettuces**
- **½ pint grape or cherry tomatoes, halved**

CUT bread in half horizontally, using a serrated knife; place cut sides up on a baking sheet. Drizzle evenly with 1 cup Roasted Pepper Vinaigrette. Sprinkle evenly with goat cheese and pine nuts.
BAKE at 400° for 6 to 8 minutes or until lightly browned.
REMOVE meat from chicken, and coarsely chop. Sprinkle chicken over bottom bread half. Top with lettuce and tomatoes; cover with top bread half. Cut into 6 wedges. Serve immediately with remaining ½ cup Roasted Pepper Vinaigrette. **MAKES** 6 servings.

NOTE: We used focaccia topped with peppers, onions, mushrooms, and cheese from a local bakery.

Roasted Pepper Vinaigrette:
Prep: 5 min.

- **1 cup oil-and-vinegar dressing**
- **1 (5.2-ounce) jar roasted red bell peppers, drained**

PROCESS dressing and roasted peppers in a blender or food processor until smooth. **MAKES** 1½ cups.

NOTE: For testing purposes only, we used Newman's Own Olive Oil & Vinegar dressing.

GREEN BEAN-POTATO SALAD

family favorite • make ahead

Prep: 20 min., Cook: 20 min., Chill: 2 hrs.

Preparing this dish a day ahead allows the flavors to mellow and blend.

- **2 pounds red potatoes**
- **1 pound fresh green beans, trimmed**
- **¼ cup red wine vinegar**
- **4 green onions, sliced**
- **2 tablespoons chopped fresh tarragon**
- **2 tablespoons Dijon mustard**
- **2 tablespoons olive oil**
- **2 teaspoons salt**
- **1 teaspoon pepper**

PLACE potatoes and water to cover in a large saucepan; bring to a boil over medium heat, and cook 13 minutes. Add green beans, and cook 7 minutes or until potatoes are tender; drain. Rinse with cold water. Cut each potato into 8 wedges.
WHISK together vinegar and next 6 ingredients in a large bowl; add potatoes and green beans, gently tossing to coat. Cover and chill at least 2 hours.
MAKES 6 to 8 servings.

AMARETTO-WALNUT BROWNIES

family favorite

Prep: 15 min., Soak: 6 hrs., Bake: 45 min.

If desired, sift powdered sugar over brownie squares before serving.

- **1 cup coarsely chopped walnuts, toasted**
- **½ cup almond liqueur**
- **1 cup butter**
- **8 (1-ounce) unsweetened chocolate squares**
- **5 large eggs**
- **3⅓ cups sugar**
- **¼ cup Swiss mocha instant coffee mix**
- **1 tablespoon vanilla extract**
- **1⅔ cups all-purpose flour**
- **⅛ teaspoon salt**

SOAK chopped walnuts in liqueur 4 to 6 hours. Drain, discarding liqueur. Set walnuts aside.

MELT butter and chocolate in a heavy saucepan over low heat.

BEAT eggs, sugar, and coffee mix at medium-high speed with an electric mixer 8 minutes. Gradually add chocolate mixture, beating at low speed until blended. Gradually add vanilla, flour, and salt, beating until blended. Stir in walnuts. Pour into a lightly greased aluminum foil-lined 13- x 9-inch pan.

BAKE at 350° for 35 to 45 minutes. Cool completely on a wire rack. Cut into squares. **MAKES** 15 brownies.

NOTE: For testing purposes only, we used International Coffees Suisse Mocha for coffee mix.

Cook's Notes

Take a stroll in the park with this gourmet feast. Associate Foods Editor **Cynthia Briscoe** offers both pretty and practical ideas.

■ To prevent **Stuffed Focaccia With Roasted Pepper Vinaigrette** from becoming soggy, make it the last thing you assemble before heading outdoors.

■ You don't need to make a fashion statement packing up the goodies, but delivery is an important part of the package. Make sure the carrier is ample enough to hold everything. Picnic baskets, colorful laundry baskets, or expandable totes are ideal.

■ If the group is small and your schedule allows, assemble individual box meals for your guests.

■ Visit a party store for a selection of textured boxes, containers, disposable flatware, and serving pieces.

■ Lastly, no picnic should be without handy disposable moistened towelettes; you can never have enough of these.

Sipping Summer

Drinking a tall glass of iced tea after cutting the grass on a summer day is like diving into a sparkling swimming pool after sunbathing. That all-the-way-down coolness makes you shut your eyes and sigh with contentment. So refresh your body with these tea-based drinks everyone is sure to enjoy. We've also included a favorite adult sipper that's perfect for entertaining.

ICED RED TEA

fast fixin's

Prep: 15 min., Steep: 5 min.

- 4 cups boiling water
- 8 regular-size red tea or red zinger tea bags
- 2 cups cold water
- ½ cup sugar*

POUR 4 cups boiling water over tea bags; cover and steep 5 minutes. Remove tea bags from water, squeezing gently. Add 2 cups cold water and ½ cup sugar, stirring until sugar dissolves. Serve over ice. **MAKES** 6 cups.

*Substitute ½ cup Splenda Granular to make a sugar-free beverage, if desired.

NOTE: For testing purposes only, we used Kalahari Red Tea.

FRUITY MINT TEA

fast fixin's

Prep: 5 min., Cook: 5 min., Steep: 5 min.

- 1 quart water
- 1 cup loosely packed fresh mint leaves
- 8 regular-size tea bags
- 1 (6-ounce) can frozen lemonade concentrate, thawed
- 1 (6-ounce) can frozen orange juice concentrate, thawed
- 2 cups cold water

HEAT 1 quart water and 1 cup mint leaves in a small saucepan just until water begins to boil. Remove from heat; add tea bags. Cover and steep 5 minutes. **REMOVE** tea bags, squeezing gently. Pour mixture through a fine wire-mesh strainer into a pitcher. Add concentrates and 2 cups cold water, stirring until concentrates dissolve. Cover and chill until ready to serve. Serve over ice. **MAKES** about 2 quarts.

PINEAPPLE-GRAPEFRUIT SPRITZER

Prep: 5 min., Chill: 1 hr.

For an alcohol-free, equally refreshing drink, use ginger ale instead of wine.

- 2 cups pineapple juice
- 1 cup pink grapefruit juice
- 2 tablespoons honey
- 1 tablespoon minced fresh ginger
- 1 (750-milliliter) bottle sparkling white wine, chilled
- Garnish: pink grapefruit slices

STIR together first 4 ingredients in a large container; cover and chill at least 1 hour. Pour mixture through a fine wire-mesh strainer into a pitcher, discarding ginger. Add wine just before serving. Serve over ice. Garnish, if desired. **MAKES** about 7 cups.

Fried Green Tomatoes With a Twist

This favorite side dish gets an update with new flavors and combinations.

While less-than-vine-ripened tomatoes are cause for despair on a salad, still-green tomatoes find redemption breaded and baptized in a skillet of bubbling oil. The most basic fried green tomatoes—in which flour, cornmeal, breadcrumbs, or wet batter encase the lemony flesh—are simply wonderful. But if you want a more creative approach, try one of these recipes. Stuffed Fried Green Tomato Casserole, for example, offers a regional twist on eggplant parmigiana. And Roasted Red Pepper Rémoulade and goat cheese provide tasty toppings for the crusty fried tomato slices.

FRIED GREEN TOMATOES WITH ROASTED RED PEPPER RÉMOULADE AND GOAT CHEESE

family favorite

Prep: 20 min., Fry: 4 min. per batch

Look for Japanese breadcrumbs, called "panko," on the ethnic food aisle of your supermarket or in Asian specialty markets.

- 1 cup all-purpose flour
- ½ teaspoon salt
- ¼ teaspoon pepper
- Seasoned batter mix
- 2 cups Japanese breadcrumbs
- 3 green tomatoes, cut into
  ¼-inch-thick slices
- Salt and pepper to taste
- Vegetable oil
- Roasted Red Pepper Rémoulade
- 3 ounces goat cheese, crumbled
- ¼ cup chopped fresh parsley

COMBINE first 3 ingredients in a shallow dish or pan; set aside.

PREPARE 1 cup seasoned batter according to package directions, and set aside.

PLACE Japanese breadcrumbs in a shallow dish.

SPRINKLE tomatoes evenly with salt and pepper to taste. Dredge tomato slices in flour mixture, dip in batter, and dredge in breadcrumbs.

POUR oil to a depth of 2 inches in a large nonstick skillet; heat over medium-high heat to 360°; fry tomatoes, in batches, 2 minutes on each side or until golden. Drain on a wire rack over paper towels.

PLACE fried green tomatoes on individual serving plates; drizzle evenly with ½ cup Roasted Red Pepper Rémoulade, and sprinkle with goat cheese and parsley. Serve immediately with remaining rémoulade. **MAKES** 4 servings.

NOTE: For testing purposes only, we used Old Bay Better Batter Seasoned Batter Mix.

Roasted Red Pepper Rémoulade:
fast fixin's • make ahead
Prep: 10 min.

- ¼ cup egg substitute
- ½ cup vegetable oil
- ½ (12-ounce) jar roasted red bell
  peppers, drained
- ¼ cup minced onions
- 1 tablespoon Creole mustard
- 1 teaspoon dry mustard
- 1 teaspoon lemon juice
- 1 garlic clove, minced
- ½ teaspoon sugar
- ½ teaspoon salt
- ½ teaspoon ground cumin
- ¼ teaspoon ground red pepper

PLACE egg substitute in food processor. With processor running, pour vegetable oil through food chute in a slow, steady stream; process until thickened, stopping to scrape down sides. Pour mixture into a small bowl.

PROCESS roasted peppers and next 9 ingredients in food processor, pulsing until smooth. Fold roasted pepper mixture into egg mixture. Cover and chill until ready to serve. **MAKES** 1 cup.

KAREN A. FELIX
PERRY, GEORGIA

STUFFED FRIED GREEN TOMATO CASSEROLE

family favorite

Prep: 10 min., Fry: 4 min. per batch,
Bake: 40 min., Stand: 10 min.

Prepare Basic Tomato Sauce first so the fried green tomatoes don't cool and get soggy while you're waiting for it to cook.

- **2 large eggs**
- **¾ cup milk**
- **1 cup grated Parmesan cheese**
- **2 cups fine, dry breadcrumbs**
- **6 medium-size green tomatoes, cut into ¼-inch-thick slices**
- **1½ cups all-purpose baking mix**
- **1¼ cups olive oil**
- **Salt and pepper to taste**
- **Basic Tomato Sauce**
- **1 (8-ounce) bag shredded mozzarella cheese**

COMBINE eggs and milk in a shallow bowl or pan. Set aside.

COMBINE Parmesan cheese and breadcrumbs in a shallow dish or pan.

DREDGE tomato slices in baking mix; dip in egg mixture, and dredge in breadcrumb mixture, reserving remaining breadcrumb mixture.

FRY tomatoes, in batches, in hot oil in a large nonstick skillet over medium-high heat 2 minutes on each side or until golden. Drain on a wire rack over paper towels. Sprinkle hot tomatoes evenly with salt and pepper to taste.

PLACE half of tomatoes in a single layer in a lightly greased 13- x 9-inch baking dish; spoon 1½ cups Basic Tomato Sauce over fried green tomatoes, and sprinkle evenly with mozzarella cheese.

LAYER remaining fried tomatoes evenly over mozzarella cheese. Spoon remaining sauce around tomatoes, being careful not to pour sauce on tops of tomatoes. Sprinkle reserved breadcrumb mixture over casserole.

BAKE at 350° for 40 minutes. Let stand 10 minutes before serving. **MAKES** 6 servings.

NOTE: For testing purposes only, we used Bisquick All-Purpose Baking Mix.

Basic Tomato Sauce:
fast fixin's
Prep: 5 min., Cook: 15 min.

- **1 (14.5-ounce) can diced tomatoes, crushed**
- **1 (8-ounce) can tomato sauce**
- **1 (6-ounce) can tomato paste**
- **½ cup dry red wine**
- **2 tablespoons sugar**
- **1 teaspoon dried basil**
- **1 teaspoon dried oregano**
- **¾ teaspoon salt**
- **½ teaspoon pepper**
- **2 garlic cloves, minced**

STIR together all ingredients in a heavy saucepan over medium heat. Bring to a boil; reduce heat to low, and cook, stirring occasionally, 15 minutes. **MAKES** 2½ cups.

KERRY KASPER
ORLAND PARK, ILLINOIS

FRIED GREEN TOMATO SANDWICHES

family favorite

Prep: 20 min., Cook: 4 min. per batch

- **1 cup fine, dry breadcrumbs**
- **2 tablespoons grated Parmesan cheese**
- **½ teaspoon salt**
- **Dash ground red pepper**
- **4 large green tomatoes, cut into ¼-inch-thick slices**
- **2 large eggs, lightly beaten**
- **¼ cup butter or margarine**
- **8 lettuce leaves**
- **1 large sweet onion, thinly sliced**
- **1 (16-ounce) package bacon, cooked**
- **8 sandwich rolls, split**
- **⅓ cup Ranch-style dressing**

STIR together first 4 ingredients in a shallow bowl.

DIP tomato slices in egg, and dredge in breadcrumb mixture.

MELT butter in a large skillet over medium heat. Cook tomatoes, in batches, 2 minutes on each side or until golden. Drain on a wire rack over paper towels.

LAYER lettuce, onion, fried green tomatoes, and bacon evenly on bottom half of each roll. Drizzle evenly with dressing. Cover with tops of rolls. Serve immediately. **MAKES** 8 servings.

NOTE: For testing purposes only, we used Pepperidge Farm Sandwich Rolls.

DEBORAH ALFORD
ALEXANDRIA, KENTUCKY

Cook's Notes

"You may think it's hard to improve on slices of crisp fried green tomatoes, but these recipes take them from humble to hip," says Senior Writer **Donna Florio.** She suggests serving **Stuffed Fried Green Tomato Casserole** in place of Eggplant Parmesan, or wowing your guests with a first course of **Fried Green Tomatoes With Roasted Red Pepper Rémoulade.** If you can't wait for the first tomato sandwich of summer, enjoy **Fried Green Tomato Sandwiches** until the real thing comes along.

Easy Appetizers

These can be put together fast, and the results are scrumptious.

Tasty snacks are even better when they're easy to make and call for short prep times. You might as well make copies of these distinctly delicious recipes; your friends will be asking for them.

QUICK PARTY SALSA

fast fixin's

Prep: 10 min.

Canned tomatoes shorten chopping time and allow you to enjoy great flavor when juicy, fresh tomatoes aren't in season.

- **1 (28-ounce) can diced tomatoes with roasted garlic**
- **1 small red onion, chopped**
- **1 large jalapeño pepper, seeded and chopped**
- **1 cup chopped fresh cilantro**
- **2 tablespoons lemon juice**
- **2 tablespoons lime juice**
- **1 teaspoon ground cumin**
- **1 teaspoon chili powder**
- **¼ teaspoon salt**
- **2 teaspoons sugar (optional)**
- **Tortilla chips**

COMBINE first 9 ingredients and, if desired, sugar in a large bowl. Cover and chill until ready to serve. Serve with tortilla chips. **MAKES** 4 cups.

CREAMY CHICKPEA SPREAD

fast fixin's

Prep: 15 min.

This Middle Eastern dip also known as hummus contains tahini, a paste made of ground toasted sesame seeds. Look for it on the condiment aisle or in the ethnic food section of most supermarkets.

- **1 (16-ounce) can chickpeas, rinsed and drained**
- **2 tablespoons lemon juice**
- **1 large garlic clove, minced**
- **1 tablespoon olive oil**
- **1 tablespoon plain yogurt**
- **1 to 2 tablespoons water**
- **1 teaspoon tahini**
- **½ teaspoon cumin seeds, toasted and ground***
- **½ teaspoon ground black pepper**
- **⅛ teaspoon ground red pepper**
- **¼ teaspoon salt**
- **Extra-virgin olive oil (optional)**
- **Pita bread triangles, pita chips, or assorted fresh vegetables**

PROCESS first 11 ingredients in a food processor until smooth, stopping to scrape down sides. Drizzle with olive oil, if desired. Serve with pita bread, pita chips, or vegetables. **MAKES** 1¼ cups.

*Substitute ¼ teaspoon ground cumin, if desired.

CITRUSY PECANS

make ahead

Prep: 15 min., Bake: 25 min.

These sweet, crunchy nuts are great by the handful, or you can also chop them and add to chicken or tuna salads. The pecans may become a bit sticky if not stored in a sealed container or zip-top freezer bag.

- **1 egg white**
- **2 cups pecan halves**
- **½ cup firmly packed light brown sugar**
- **2 teaspoons grated orange rind**
- **2 tablespoons fresh orange juice**
- **½ teaspoon salt**
- **¼ teaspoon ground cinnamon**

WHISK egg white in a medium bowl until frothy; toss with pecans.
STIR together light brown sugar and next 4 ingredients in a large bowl. Add pecans, and toss. Drain well. Place pecans in a single layer on a lightly greased aluminum foil-lined baking sheet.
BAKE at 325°, stirring occasionally, for 20 to 25 minutes. Let cool completely. Store in an airtight container. **MAKES** 2 cups.

CHICKEN-BACON NUGGETS

family favorite

Prep: 15 min., Chill: 2 hrs., Bake: 20 min.

If you're trying to cut back on sodium, use reduced-sodium bacon and lite soy sauce.

- **2 large skinned and boned chicken breasts**
- **8 bacon slices, cut into thirds**
- **½ cup orange marmalade**
- **¼ cup soy sauce**
- **2 tablespoons sesame oil**
- **1 teaspoon ground ginger**
- **1 garlic clove, minced**
- **Vegetable cooking spray**

CUT chicken breasts into 24 (1-inch) cubes. Wrap each chicken cube with bacon, and secure with a wooden pick.

STIR together orange marmalade, soy sauce, sesame oil, ground ginger, and minced garlic in a shallow dish or large zip-top freezer bag; add chicken nuggets. Cover or seal, and chill 2 hours, turning occasionally.

PLACE chicken nuggets on a lightly greased rack in broiler pan.

BAKE at 450° for 10 minutes; turn chicken, and bake 10 more minutes.

MAKES 6 servings.

DENISE GIEGER
WOODSTOCK, GEORGIA

Quick & Easy

Shrimp in a Hurry

People of all ages rave about Assistant Foods Editor Vicki Poellnitz's mother's boiled shrimp with her fabulous, not-too-spicy sauce—even kids like it.

Her mother never made the Shrimp Salad when she was younger; there was never enough boiled shrimp left. The salad recipe came later, when she was grown up. Now Vicki plans ahead and boils extra shrimp to make the salad with the leftovers. You can purchase a pound of cooked shrimp if you want only the salad.

SHRIMP SAUCE

fast fixin's

Prep: 10 min.

- **2 cups mayonnaise**
- **6 tablespoons ketchup**
- **4 teaspoons mustard**
- **4 teaspoons lemon juice**
- **2 teaspoons Worcestershire sauce**
- **1 teaspoon garlic powder**

WHISK together all ingredients. **MAKES** about 2½ cups.

BOOTS ABERCROMBIE
HOOVER, ALABAMA

Frozen Cooked Shrimp Trick

We decided to try a few bags of the frozen cooked shrimp that are already peeled and deveined as a substitute in these recipes. Such a convenience product is a great idea for last-minute appetizers or salads, but regardless of the brand we chose or how closely we followed the package directions, the shrimp always tasted slightly rubbery or undercooked.

Our Test Kitchens solved the problem by putting the frozen shrimp in a large strainer or colander, lowering it into boiling water for 2 to 3 minutes, and then immediately plunging it into a large bowl of ice water to stop the cooking process. Once the shrimp were cold, we simply lifted the strainer, allowing the water to drain back in the bowl. This process afforded the convenience of peeled and deveined frozen cooked shrimp with a texture like fresh. For extra flavor, add your favorite seasoning blend to the water before bringing it to a boil.

BOILED SHRIMP

Prep: 5 min., Cook: 5 min., Stand: 10 min.

Save 1 pound of these shrimp to make the salad. Enjoy the rest with Shrimp Sauce for dipping.

- **4 quarts water**
- **2 (3-ounce) packages boil-in-bag shrimp-and-crab boil**
- **1 large lemon, halved**
- **1 small onion**
- **3 tablespoons salt**
- **4 pounds unpeeled, large fresh shrimp**

BRING first 5 ingredients to a boil in a large Dutch oven over high heat. Cover and boil 3 to 4 minutes. Add shrimp; remove from heat. Cover and let stand 10 minutes. (Shrimp will turn pink, and shells will loosen slightly.) Drain, discarding lemon, onion, and boil bags. **MAKES** 6 to 8 servings.

NOTE: For testing purposes only, we used Zatarain's Shrimp & Crab Boil.

BOOTS ABERCROMBIE
HOOVER, ALABAMA

SHRIMP SALAD

Prep: 20 min.

- **1 pound Boiled Shrimp**
- **¼ cup minced celery**
- **2 tablespoons minced onion**
- **1¼ cups Shrimp Sauce**
- **1 head iceberg lettuce, shredded**
- **3 to 4 tomatoes, cut into wedges**
- **Garnish: chopped fresh chives**

PEEL shrimp, and devein, if desired. Coarsely chop shrimp, and place in a bowl.

STIR together celery, onion, and Shrimp Sauce. Add shrimp, and toss. Serve over iceberg lettuce with tomato wedges. Garnish, if desired. **MAKES** about 2½ cups.

BOOTS ABERCROMBIE
HOOVER, ALABAMA

from our kitchen

If you've ever known the pleasure of walking barefoot across dew-tinseled grass and gathering a handful of fresh blueberries, you'll want to consider growing your own. Although blueberries are available in stores almost year-round, they're never as deliciously sweet as the homegrown ones we find in the South during the summer months.

Whether you stock up at the local farmers market or corner grocery store, choose firm, plump berries with smooth, dark blue skins and a silvery sheen. Check the underside of the container for signs of mold or leakage; juice stains indicate the blueberries are overripe or bruised. Refrigerate them in the original plastic package or in a storage container, and wait to wash them until just before using.

Freeze unwashed blueberries in a zip-top freezer bag. The dry berries will freeze individually, allowing you to remove them as needed. Rinse quickly under cold running water, and add to your favorite recipes while still frozen.

For information on the incredible health benefits of blueberries, visit **www.ushbc.org.**

The Cakepan Lady

Throw away the masking tape and pack up that fuchsia nail polish because we've discovered the end all and be all in personalized cakepans. These high-quality Nordic Ware pans come with colorful snap-on lids for easy storage and delivery. Both the lid and bottom of each cakepan are personalized with an engraved name. Choose from dozens of different designs ($27-$29 plus shipping). For more information you can call toll free 1-866-892-7267, or you can visit **www.thecakepanlady.com.**

Pancake Pointers

We always look forward to pancakes in the Test Kitchens, especially when someone shows up on a summer morning with a basket of fresh-picked blueberries or peaches. The secret to light and fluffy pancakes is in the batter—stir just enough to moisten the dry ingredients.

Having the griddle at the right temperature before adding the batter is also important. Preheat the griddle or skillet, and then sprinkle with a few drops of water. If the water bounces and spatters across the surface, start spooning on the batter. (Water that sits and simmers indicates the temperature is too low; if the water vanishes, the temperature is too high.) When adding fruit, do so as soon as the batter is spooned onto the griddle.

Pancakes are ready to turn after 2 to 3 minutes, when bubbles appear on the surface and the edges begin to look dry. The second side will take only about half as long to cook as the first. Keep cooked pancakes warm in a 200° oven.

LEMON-BLUEBERRY PANCAKES: Add 1 to 2 teaspoons grated lemon rind to your favorite pancake batter. As soon as batter is spooned onto the griddle, sprinkle with blueberries. Serve with bacon, if desired. Garnish with fresh mint sprigs, lemon slices, and fresh blueberries, if desired.

Watermelon-Lemonade
Cooler, page 172

clockwise from top: Tempura Dill Pickles, page 123; Delta-Style Fried Catfish, page 121; Chicken-and-Mashed Potato Fritters With Lime-Cayenne Mayonnaise, page 121

Chocolate Chunk-Peanut
Cookies, page 125

Grilled Corn in the Style of
Oaxaca, page 134

Grilled Pork Tenderloin
With Gingered Jezebel
Sauce, page 138; Grilled
Yellow Squash Halves,
page 138

Grilled Marinated Vegetables,
page 133

Dianne's Southwestern Cornbread Salad, page 133

Fried Okra Salad,
page 167

Marinated Tomatoes With Basil
and Balsamic Vinegar, page 140

Peppery Texas Pickles, page 161

Mississippi Mud Cake, page 136

Fresh Food and Family Fun

Every meal is an adventure for this young chef and his kids. They've turned their vegetable garden—and kitchen—into the ultimate playroom.

In a sun-drenched garden in Maryville, Tennessee, Jackson Fleer heads over to monitor the progress of his lima beans. His father, John, renowned chef at Blackberry Farm, smiles at Jackson's enthusiasm. "Getting children involved in the garden automatically creates an interest in the end product," says John, who understands the relationship between garden and kitchen. Since 1992, he's been serving up his unique brand of Foothills Cuisine, combining the bounty of the Great Smoky Mountains with the flavors of his Southern upbringing.

In an age when many children are more interested in the latest video games, the Fleer boys, Jackson, 11, Daniel, 5, and Justin, 2, are learning where beans and tomatoes actually come from—and loving it. Using their backyard as a land of discovery, John and his wife, Katy, encourage their kids to explore the almost limitless world of colors, shapes, and sizes awaiting them in the garden. But the fun doesn't stop there. The family then heads inside where they combine the fresh ingredients with simple cooking techniques to create dishes bursting with flavor. "When we cook together, everyone gets to participate; no one is a spectator," John says.

Back in the garden, Daniel skillfully selects a handful of tiny tomatoes. Aware that he's being watched, Daniel turns and confidently says, "Me and daddy are good cookers." Of course, when asked for his favorite thing to prepare, without hesitation he replies, "Chocolate chip cookies." Some things never change.

YELLOW TOMATO GAZPACHO

make ahead

Prep: 30 min., Chill: 4 hrs.

Tender, just-ripe peaches and a sweet Vidalia onion slap a Southern stamp on this chilled summertime soup.

- **3 medium-size yellow tomatoes, seeded and chopped (about 2 pounds)**
- **1 yellow bell pepper, seeded and chopped**
- **1 medium cucumber, peeled, seeded, and chopped**
- **1 garlic clove, chopped**
- **3 fresh peaches, peeled and chopped**
- **1 small Vidalia onion, chopped**
- **¼ cup lime juice**
- **2 tablespoons rice wine vinegar**
- **1 tablespoon Worcestershire sauce**
- **½ teaspoon hot sauce**
- **1½ teaspoons salt**
- **½ teaspoon pepper**
- **Garnish: fresh peach slices**

PROCESS first 6 ingredients in a food processor or blender until smooth, stopping to scrape down sides.
STIR together vegetable puree, lime juice, and next 5 ingredients. Cover and chill at least 4 hours. Garnish, if desired. **MAKES** about 2 quarts.

GRANDMA'S PEPPER RELISH

family favorite • make ahead

Prep: 35 min., Cook: 10 min.

For the Fleers, this relish serves as everything from a sandwich spread to a topping for fresh peas and succotash. John uses his grandmother's grinder, but you can chop the peppers and onions as directed.

- **¾ cup sugar**
- **½ cup cider vinegar**
- **½ cup malt vinegar**
- **1 teaspoon mustard seed**
- **1 teaspoon celery seed**
- **¾ teaspoon salt**
- **⅛ teaspoon turmeric**
- **3 medium-size red bell peppers, seeded and diced**
- **3 medium-size green bell peppers, seeded and diced**
- **2 medium Vidalia onions, diced**

COMBINE first 7 ingredients in a saucepan, and bring to a boil over medium-high heat. Stir in peppers and onions; reduce heat, and simmer 5 minutes. Remove from heat, and let cool. Cover and chill up to 2 weeks. **MAKES** 6 servings (about 4½ cups).

BLACKBERRY ICED TEA

family favorite • make ahead

Prep: 10 min.; Stand: 1 hr., 3 min.

For the garnish, cut desired amount of wooden skewers into 5-inch lengths; then place fresh blackberries onto skewers.

- **3 cups fresh or frozen blackberries, thawed**
- **1¼ cups sugar**
- **1 tablespoon chopped fresh mint**
- **Pinch of baking soda**
- **4 cups boiling water**
- **2 family-size tea bags**
- **2½ cups cold water**
- **Garnishes: fresh blackberries, fresh mint sprigs**

COMBINE blackberries and sugar in a large container. Crush blackberries with a wooden spoon. Add mint and baking soda. Set aside.

POUR 4 cups boiling water over tea bags; cover and let stand 3 minutes. Discard tea bags.

POUR tea over blackberry mixture; let stand at room temperature 1 hour. Pour tea through a wire-mesh strainer into a large pitcher, discarding solids. Add 2½ cups cold water, stirring until sugar dissolves. Cover and chill until ready to serve. Garnish, if desired. **MAKES** about 7½ cups.

OLIVATA

fast fixin's

Prep: 10 min., Cook: 3 min.

John spreads this rich olive paste on grilled or toasted French baguette slices and serves them alongside Yellow Tomato Gazpacho.

- 1 tablespoon water
- 1 tablespoon balsamic vinegar
- 1 tablespoon red wine vinegar
- ¼ cup dried tomatoes
- ½ cup pitted kalamata olives
- 1 tablespoon chopped fresh basil
- 1 tablespoon olive oil
- ½ teaspoon chopped garlic
- ¼ teaspoon pepper
- ⅛ teaspoon salt
- French baguette slices

COMBINE first 4 ingredients in a small saucepan. Bring to a boil over medium-high heat; reduce heat, and simmer, stirring occasionally, 1 to 2 minutes or until liquid is absorbed and tomatoes are plump.

PROCESS tomato mixture, olives, and next 5 ingredients in a food processor or blender until smooth, stopping to scrape down sides. Serve with French baguette slices. **MAKES** about 1 cup.

SUMMER PUDDING

family favorite

Prep: 15 min., Stand: 2 hrs., Bake: 15 min.

- 2 cups fresh raspberries
- 1 cup fresh blackberries
- 1 cup quartered fresh strawberries
- ½ cup sugar
- 1 tablespoon grated lemon rind
- 2 tablespoons fresh lemon juice
- ½ teaspoon vanilla extract
- ⅛ teaspoon salt
- 2 tablespoons raspberry or blackberry liqueur (optional)
- 1 lemon verbena sprig (optional)
- ½ teaspoon crushed green peppercorns (optional)
- 2 cups day-old white bread slices, cut into ½-inch cubes
- Garnishes: fresh blackberries, fresh blueberries, fresh strawberries

COMBINE first 8 ingredients and, if desired, liqueur, lemon verbena, and peppercorns in a large nonaluminum bowl. Cover and let stand at room temperature at least 1½ hours.

SPREAD bread cubes evenly on a baking sheet; bake at 350° for 10 to 15 minutes or until toasted. Cool.

STIR bread into berry mixture, and let stand for 30 minutes. Discard lemon verbena.

SPOON pudding mixture into 4 (8-ounce) individual serving dishes. Garnish, if desired. **MAKES** 4 servings.

NOTE: For testing purposes only, we used Sara Lee Honey White Bakery Bread.

Tips for Tots

John Fleer shares his secrets for getting kids interested in food and cooking.

- Allow your kids to taste, smell, and touch every single ingredient.
- Avoid creating a sense of fear in the kitchen; heat and knives require caution and respect, not fear.
- Recipes are great tools for teaching young children to count and measure. Older kids can use recipes to build reading skills and hone their ability to follow directions.
- Encourage experimentation. Cooking is creative, just like the arts.
- Soft fruits, such as strawberries and ripe peaches, are perfect for teaching basic knife skills. Scrambling eggs teaches kids how to use a pan on the stove, and cookies make a terrific introduction to baking.
- Encourage kids to sample the fruits of their labor. Even if it's only small tastes of things from the garden, that's okay. A leaf or two of lettuce here or a small bite of tomato there fills their minds with all sorts of invaluable sensory data.
- Graters, salad spinners, peelers, and other small kitchen tools are smart preludes to knives. These gadgets are simple to use, have a direct effect on the food, and kids can easily learn the right way to use each of them.

GARDEN SUCCOTASH

family favorite

Prep: 25 min., Cook: 40 min.

- ¾ cup fresh lima or butter beans
- 1¼ cups fresh corn kernels (2 small ears)
- 1 cup chopped shiitake mushrooms
- 1 red bell pepper, seeded and diced
- 1 green bell pepper, seeded and diced
- ¾ teaspoon salt
- ¼ teaspoon pepper
- 2 tablespoons olive oil
- ½ teaspoon chopped garlic
- ¼ cup dry white wine
- ¾ cup whipping cream
- 2 tablespoons butter
- 1 medium tomato, peeled, seeded, and chopped
- 1 tablespoon chopped fresh parsley
- 1 tablespoon chopped fresh chives

PLACE beans in boiling water to cover in a small saucepan; simmer 3 minutes or until crisp-tender. Drain; rinse with cold water, and drain.

SAUTÉ corn kernels, chopped mushrooms, bell peppers, salt, and pepper in hot oil in a medium skillet over medium-high heat 5 minutes or until corn is crisp-tender. Add chopped garlic, and sauté 30 seconds. Stir in wine; cook 1 minute. Add whipping cream and beans; reduce heat to medium low, and simmer, covered, 25 to 30 minutes or until beans are tender. Remove from heat, and stir in butter. Add chopped tomato, parsley, and chives, and stir just until combined. **MAKES** 6 servings.

New-Fashioned Pickles

Let the fridge and freezer do the work—these are the most hassle free you can make.

When pickles come to mind, Executive Editor Susan Dosier thinks of summers in North Carolina, standing beside her mother and grandmother at the steamy canning area in their basement. While it would be fun to revisit the conversations and family secrets shared over hot jars and bubbling brines, she confesses that today she cringes at the thought of how much work it would take to make those pickles—especially with her 6- and 7-year-old daughters at her side.

That's why she's abandoning traditional canning methods and embracing the recipes here. Savvy cooks have munched on refrigerator or freezer pickles for years, but this particular batch of recipes is tailored for every busy Southern cook. The Test Kitchens' Staff updated the flavors with spicy peppers, aromatic garlic, and fresh dill. And the amounts aren't overwhelming. You can enjoy these small-batch pickles for a few days and have some to spare for the cookout this weekend. Be sure to use pickling cucumbers, which are short and stubby and mainly available in the summer. The results are terrific, and only you will know how easy they really are.

HOT-AND-SWEET FREEZER PICKLES

freezeable • make ahead

Prep: 30 min., Cook: 6 min., Chill: 48 hrs., Freeze: 8 hrs.

- 3½ cups thinly sliced pickling cucumbers (about 1 pound)
- 1 medium onion, sliced and separated into rings
- 2 jalapeño peppers, seeded and sliced
- 3 large garlic cloves, pressed
- 1 tablespoon salt
- 1 cup sugar
- 1 cup white vinegar (5% acidity)
- 2 tablespoons water

COMBINE first 5 ingredients in a large bowl.

COOK sugar, vinegar, and 2 tablespoons water in a saucepan over medium heat, stirring until sugar dissolves. Pour mixture over cucumber mixture. Cover and chill 48 hours.

SPOON evenly into 6 half-pint or 3 pint canning jars or freezer containers, leaving ½ inch of room at the top; seal, label, and freeze pickles 8 hours or up to 6 months. Thaw in refrigerator before serving; use thawed pickles within 1 week. **MAKES** about 3 pints.

PICKLED ASPARAGUS

make ahead

Prep: 15 min., Cook: 6 min., Chill: 8 hrs.

See page 174 for how-to photos and tips.

- 4 cups white vinegar (5% acidity)
- 3 cups water
- ½ cup sugar
- ¼ cup canning-and-pickling salt
- 1 tablespoon dried crushed red pepper
- 1 tablespoon pickling spices
- 3 pounds fresh asparagus spears (about 3 bunches)
- 6 fresh dill sprigs
- 3 garlic cloves

COOK first 6 ingredients in a medium saucepan over medium-high heat about 4 to 6 minutes or until sugar is dissolved. Remove saucepan from heat, and cool mixture completely.

SNAP off tough ends of asparagus.

PACK 1 bunch asparagus, 2 dill sprigs, and 1 garlic clove into 1 (1-quart) canning jar; repeat process with 2 remaining jars, asparagus, dill sprigs, and garlic.

POUR vinegar mixture evenly into jars; seal jars. Chill at least 8 hours; store in refrigerator up to 1 week. **MAKES** 3 quarts.

GEORGIE O'NEILL-MASSA
WELAKA, FLORIDA

PEPPERY TEXAS PICKLES

freezeable • make ahead

Prep: 15 min., Chill: 48 hrs., Freeze: 8 hrs.
(pictured on page 155)

- 2 pounds pickling cucumbers, sliced
- 1 cup chopped fresh cilantro
- 6 small dried red chile peppers
- 4 garlic cloves, thinly sliced
- 1 large sweet onion, sliced
- 3 cups white vinegar (5% acidity)
- 1 cup water
- ⅓ cup sugar
- 2 tablespoons canning-and-pickling salt
- 1 tablespoon pickling spices

PLACE first 5 ingredients in a large plastic bowl (do not use glass).

COMBINE vinegar, 1 cup water, and next 3 ingredients in a 4-cup glass measuring cup. Microwave at HIGH 3 minutes; remove from microwave, and stir until sugar dissolves. Pour hot mixture evenly over cucumber mixture. Cover and chill 48 hours.

SPOON evenly into quart canning jars or freezer containers, leaving ½ inch of room at the top; seal, label, and freeze pickles 8 hours or up to 6 months. Thaw in refrigerator before serving; use thawed pickles within 1 week. **MAKES** 3 quarts.

GEORGANA MCNEIL
HOUSTON, TEXAS

Pack a Pickle With Style

Here are some of our favorite ways to enjoy these delicacies.

■ Turn Pickled Asparagus into stirrers for Bloody Marys.

■ Peppery Texas Pickles and Hot-and-Sweet Freezer Pickles invite your basic burger to pucker up. Offer these choices at your next burger bash.

■ Liven up your deviled eggs by adding chopped pickles. Be sure to pat the pickles dry with paper towels before chopping and folding them in.

■ Add pickles to savory chicken salad. Or garnish your salad luncheon plate with a skewer of deviled eggs and pickles.

Summer Living.

As the weather heats up, we give you lots of suggestions for cooling down. From perfectly fried catfish to a fresh-and-creamy peach dessert to a no-cook wine-and-cheese party, there's something for every occasion. So whether you're hosting a casual summer supper or a pool party for the kids (and kids at heart), we invite you to try our mouthwatering recipes and fabulous ideas for entertaining.

Chillin' With the Children

Backyard Pool Party

Serves 8 to 10

Buried Treasure Snack Mix

Creamy Pineapple-and-Ham Rollups

Chicken-and-Bean Slaw Wraps

Lemonade Cupcakes

Emerald Sea Punch

Turn on the water and the fun for a cool backyard pool party. At least once this summer, give in to everyone's desire to run through a sprinkler by setting up a mini water park in your yard. Or create great outdoor memories with miniature swimming pools and slippery water slides. Invite your children's best pals and their parents, and whip up our super-easy menu of treats. Best of all, most of these crowd-pleasing recipes can be prepared in 30 minutes or less. That gives you more time to splash around in all the fun that the season has to offer. So go ahead—take the plunge into a day of play.

BURIED TREASURE SNACK MIX

family favorite • fast fixin's

Prep: 15 min.

- 1 (12.5-ounce) package Cheddar-flavored fish-shaped crackers
- 1 (13.5-ounce) package cinnamon corn-and-rice cereal
- 1 (10-ounce) package honey-flavored bear-shaped graham crackers
- 1 (15-ounce) package mini-twist pretzels
- 1 (21.3-ounce) bag candy-coated chocolate pieces
- 1 (11.5-ounce) package giant-size Cheddar-flavored fish-shaped crackers

LAYER half of ingredients in order listed in a large glass bowl; repeat layers once. **MAKES** 28 cups.

NOTE: For testing purposes only, we used Pepperidge Farm Goldfish, Kellogg's Cinnamon Crispix, Nabisco Teddy Grahams, and M&M's.

CREAMY PINEAPPLE-AND-HAM ROLLUPS

family favorite • fast fixin's

Prep: 15 min.

- 10 thin white bread slices, crusts removed
- 1 (8-ounce) container soft pineapple cream cheese
- 1 to 1½ cups shredded carrots
- 10 ounces thinly sliced deli ham or smoked turkey

ROLL bread slices with a rolling pin to ⅛-inch thickness. Spread 1 side of each slice evenly with cream cheese; sprinkle evenly with carrots. Top evenly with ham slices. Roll up slices, jellyroll fashion. Cut each roll into 3 (1½-inch-thick) slices. **MAKES** 10 servings.

CHICKEN-AND-BEAN SLAW WRAPS

fast fixin's

Prep: 10 min., Bake: 5 min.

Grilling chicken breasts for supper? Throw three or four extra on the grill; then chop and freeze to use when you're ready to make these sandwiches instead of using packaged cooked chicken.

- 2 (6-ounce) packages fully cooked chicken strips, chopped
- 1½ cups coleslaw mix with carrots
- 1 (15-ounce) can chili powder-seasoned pinto beans, drained
- ⅓ cup Ranch-style dressing
- ½ cup chopped green onions
- 8 (8-inch) flour tortillas
- 1 cup (4 ounces) shredded Cheddar cheese
- ¼ cup barbecue sauce

COMBINE first 5 ingredients; set aside.
PLACE tortillas on baking sheets, and sprinkle each tortilla evenly with Cheddar cheese.
BAKE at 350° for 3 to 5 minutes or until cheese is melted.

TOP evenly with chicken mixture. Drizzle evenly with barbecue sauce. Roll up, jellyroll fashion, and wrap in parchment paper, twisting ends of paper and tying with raffia to seal. Cut in half. Serve immediately. **MAKES** 8 servings.

NOTE: For testing purposes only, we used Ranch Style Beans for chili powder-seasoned pinto beans.

MARY KAY
NEW LLANO, LOUISIANA

LEMONADE CUPCAKES

family favorite

Prep: 15 min., Bake: 22 min.

- 1 (6-ounce) can frozen lemonade concentrate, thawed
- 1 (18.25-ounce) package white cake mix
- 1 (8-ounce) carton sour cream
- 1 (3-ounce) package cream cheese, softened
- 3 large eggs
- 1 (12-ounce) can cream cheese frosting
- Garnishes: chewy candies, colored sugar, and candy sprinkles

REMOVE 2 tablespoons lemonade concentrate from can, and reserve for another use.
COMBINE remaining concentrate, cake mix, and next 3 ingredients in a mixing bowl. Beat at low speed with an electric mixer until moistened. Beat at high speed 3 minutes, stopping to scrape down sides. Spoon batter into 30 paper-lined muffin cups, filling each three-fourths full.
BAKE at 350° for 22 minutes or until a wooden pick inserted in center comes out clean. Cool in pans on a wire rack 5 minutes. Remove cupcakes from pans; cool completely on wire rack. Spread evenly with frosting. Garnish, if desired. **MAKES** 30 cupcakes.

JANICE M. FRANCE
DEPAUW, INDIANA

EMERALD SEA PUNCH

family favorite • fast fixin's

Prep: 10 min.

- 3 (0.22-ounce) envelopes unsweetened blue raspberry lemonade mix
- 2 cups sugar
- 6 cups water, chilled
- 3 cups pineapple juice, chilled
- 1 (6-ounce) can frozen orange juice concentrate, thawed
- ¼ cup fresh lemon juice
- 1 quart ginger ale, chilled

COMBINE first 6 ingredients. Stir in ginger ale just before serving. **MAKES** 20 cups.

NOTE: For testing purposes only, we used Kool-Aid Island Twists Ice Blue Raspberry Lemonade Unsweetened Soft Drink Mix.

NORA HENSHAW
OKEMAH, OKLAHOMA

Safe Fun in the Sun

Here are a few tips to help keep everyone safe.
- **No-trip trick:** The hose leading from a faucet to a sprinkler can be a tripping hazard. Position your hose out of pathways, and drape bags of play sand across it to weigh it down.
- **Watering hole:** The best beverage for keeping the kids hydrated is water. Serve punch, juice, or soft drinks only once (okay, maybe twice) during the party.
- **Sunblock:** Have extra tubes of lip and body sunscreens with an SPF of 15 or higher on hand, along with hats and T-shirts.
- **Indoor breaks:** Lay a pathway of inexpensive rubber-backed rugs from the door to the bathroom to catch drips and prevent slipping on uncarpeted floors.

Lakeside Catfish Fry

Kick off your shoes and join this Mississippi family for a delicious down-home meal.

Delta-Style Dinner

Serves 6

Lela's Hush Puppies

Jack's Fried Catfish

Grilled Andouille Grits

Tomato-and-Crabmeat Cream Gravy

Ice cream

It's another gorgeous day on Lake Washington, near Glen Allan, Mississippi. The bream and crappie are biting (which is a lot better than the mosquitoes), and a light breeze tempers the warm summer air. At a nearby dock house, Jack and Lela Perkins—known throughout the area for their entertaining prowess—welcome family and friends for a Delta-style catfish fry.

When it comes to entertaining, Jack likes to have fun with his recipes, although he's famous for never making the same thing twice. Luckily, we were able to sneak a few of Jack's favorite recipes from his culinary bag of tricks.

LELA'S HUSH PUPPIES

family favorite

Prep: 10 min., Stand: 30 min.,
Fry: 4 min. per batch

A basket full of these tasty treats makes a delicious appetizer. If you were raised on hush puppies made with a mix of all-purpose flour and cornmeal, you'll be pleasantly surprised by the light texture and bold flavors of this all-cornmeal version.

**2¼ cups self-rising white
    cornmeal mix**
**½ cup chopped green bell
    pepper**
½ medium onion, chopped
1 teaspoon salt
½ teaspoon ground black pepper
¼ teaspoon ground red pepper
1 cup buttermilk
2 large eggs
Vegetable oil

COMBINE first 6 ingredients in a bowl; make a well in center of mixture.
WHISK together buttermilk and eggs; add to dry ingredients, stirring just until moistened. Let mixture stand 30 minutes.
POUR oil to a depth of 2 inches into a Dutch oven; heat to 375°.
DROP batter by heaping teaspoonfuls into hot oil. Fry in batches 2 minutes on each side or until golden. Drain on wire racks over paper towels; serve hot.
MAKES 6 to 8 servings.

JACK'S FRIED CATFISH

family favorite

Prep: 10 min., Chill: 1 hr., Stand: 10 min.,
Fry: 8 min. per batch

Jack says the catfish are done when "most of the bubbling stops and the fillets begin to float." The 4- to 6-ounce catfish fillets fry up crispy, slightly curled, and picture-perfect.

6 (4- to 6-ounce) catfish fillets
2 cups milk
2 cups yellow cornmeal
1 tablespoon seasoned salt
2 teaspoons pepper
½ teaspoon onion powder
½ teaspoon garlic powder
1 teaspoon salt
Vegetable oil

PLACE catfish fillets in a single layer in a shallow dish; cover with milk. Cover and chill 1 hour.
COMBINE cornmeal and next 4 ingredients in a shallow dish.
REMOVE catfish fillets from refrigerator, and let stand at room temperature 10 minutes. Remove from milk, allowing excess to drip off; discard milk. Sprinkle catfish fillets evenly with 1 teaspoon salt.
DREDGE catfish fillets in cornmeal mixture, shaking off excess. Pour oil to a depth of 1½ inches into a large skillet; heat to 350°. Fry fillets, in batches, about 3 to 4 minutes on each side or until golden brown. Drain on wire racks over paper towels. **MAKES** 6 servings.

GRILLED ANDOUILLE GRITS

family favorite

Prep: 5 min., Cook: 15 min., Chill: 8 hrs., Grill: 8 min.

Once chilled, the sturdy wedges of grits will hold their shape; just make sure the grill is good and hot to keep them from sticking.

- ½ **large Vidalia onion, chopped**
- ½ **cup chopped andouille or spicy smoked sausage**
- 2 **tablespoons vegetable oil**
- 1 **(14½-ounce) can chicken broth**
- ¾ **cup half-and-half**
- 1 **cup uncooked quick-cooking grits**
- ½ **teaspoon salt**
- 2 **tablespoons butter or margarine, melted**

SAUTÉ onion and sausage in hot oil in a 3-quart saucepan over medium-high heat until tender. Add chicken broth and half-and-half; bring to a boil. Gradually stir in grits and salt. Cover, reduce heat, and simmer, stirring occasionally, 10 minutes or until thickened.

POUR grits onto a lightly greased baking sheet into a 10½-inch circle (should be about ⅓ inch thick); cover and chill 8 hours.

INVERT grits circle onto a flat surface; cut into 6 wedges. Brush top and bottom of each wedge with melted butter.

GRILL, uncovered, over medium heat (300° to 350°) 3 to 4 minutes on each side. Remove and keep warm. **MAKES** 6 servings.

NOTE: Grits can be broiled, if desired. Prepare as directed, and arrange buttered wedges on a baking sheet. Broil 6 inches from heat 2 minutes on each side or until golden.

TOMATO-AND-CRABMEAT CREAM GRAVY

family favorite • fast fixin's

Prep: 10 min., Cook: 15 min.

- 4 **tablespoons butter**
- ¼ **cup diced onion**
- 3 **tablespoons all-purpose flour**
- 1½ **cups low-sodium chicken broth**
- 1 **cup whipping cream**
- ½ **teaspoon salt**
- ½ **teaspoon ground red pepper**
- 1 **pint fresh lump crabmeat, drained***
- 2 **tomatoes, diced**

MELT butter in a saucepan over medium heat; add onion, and sauté 1 minute. Whisk in flour, and cook, stirring constantly, 1 to 2 minutes or until smooth. (Do not brown.) Gradually add chicken broth and cream, whisking until smooth. Stir in salt and red pepper. Bring to a boil; reduce heat, and simmer until thickened. Stir in crabmeat and tomatoes; cook just until thoroughly heated. **MAKES** 6 servings.

*Substitute 1 pound unpeeled, large fresh shrimp, cooked and peeled, if desired.

Taste of the Islands

Perk up ordinary meals with easy-to-find ingredients. Unsweetened coconut milk creates a rich, creamy sauce for skillet chicken, while honey sweetens Spicy Tropical Fruit. Both recipes offer good, inexpensive ways to introduce new food combinations to your family.

ISLAND CHICKEN AND RICE

family favorite

Prep: 15 min.; Cook: 1 hr., 5 min.; Stand: 5 min.

This is our version of Ellen Burr's tasty dish.

- 4½ **pounds chicken pieces**
- 1½ **teaspoons salt, divided**
- ¾ **teaspoon pepper, divided**
- 1 **tablespoon vegetable oil**
- 1 **tablespoon butter or margarine**
- 1 **small onion, chopped**
- 1 **cup uncooked long-grain rice**
- 2 **garlic cloves, pressed**
- 1 **(14-ounce) can chicken broth**
- 1 **(13.5-ounce) can coconut milk**
- ¾ **cup unsweetened pineapple juice**
- ¼ **teaspoon dried crushed red pepper**
- 4 **green onions, chopped**
- 1 **(3.5-ounce) jar macadamia nuts, toasted and chopped**
- **Garnishes: fresh pineapple, green onion**

SPRINKLE chicken pieces evenly with 1 teaspoon salt and ½ teaspoon pepper. **BROWN** chicken in hot oil in a large skillet over medium-high heat 8 to 10 minutes on each side. Remove chicken from skillet, and drain, reserving 1 tablespoon drippings in skillet.

ADD butter to skillet, and melt, stirring to loosen particles from bottom of skillet; add 1 chopped onion, and sauté 4 minutes. Add rice, and sauté 4 minutes; add garlic, and sauté 1 minute. Stir in chicken broth and next 3 ingredients; return chicken to skillet. Sprinkle with remaining ½ teaspoon salt and ¼ teaspoon pepper; bring to a boil. Cover, reduce heat to low, and simmer 35 minutes or until rice is tender.

UNCOVER, fluff rice with a fork, and let stand 5 minutes before serving. Sprinkle with chopped green onions and nuts. Garnish, if desired. **MAKES** 6 servings.

NOTE: We used pick-of-the-chick (3 thighs, 3 breasts, 3 legs) for chicken pieces.

ELLEN BURR
TRURO, MASSACHUSETTS

SPICY TROPICAL FRUIT

family favorite • make ahead

Prep: 10 min., Chill: 2 hrs.

- **1 (8-ounce) container light sour cream**
- **1 (8-ounce) container plain yogurt**
- **¼ cup honey**
- **2 tablespoons chopped crystallized ginger**
- **¼ teaspoon ground allspice**
- **¼ teaspoon salt**
- **⅛ to ¼ teaspoon ground red pepper (optional)**
- **3 ripe mangoes, peeled, seeded, and diced**
- **3 bananas, peeled and diced**
- **1 (15.25-ounce) can pineapple tidbits, drained**
- **Garnish: ¼ cup pistachios, toasted and chopped**

STIR together first 6 ingredients, and, if desired, red pepper in a medium bowl. Fold in mangoes, bananas, and pineapple. Cover and chill at least 2 hours. Garnish, if desired. **MAKES** 7 cups.

ELLEN BURR
TRURO, MASSACHUSETTS

An Easy Party You Can Do

Looking to entertain in a casual, laid-back style this summer? Consider a wine-and-cheese party. No prior wine-or cheese-buying experience is necessary. This type of entertaining is really tailor-made for warm-weather gatherings.

When selecting cheeses, remember that soft ones tend to be either mild or tart, while hard cheeses are often salty and more assertive in flavor. Use this guide when selecting wines. Young, fresh, and creamy cheeses are best with light, acidic whites. Apply the same thought to most aged, full-bodied cheeses and red wine.

If you're new to wine, don't worry. The market is loaded with terrific, great-tasting wines for less than $12. Look for consistent producers such as Gallo of Sonoma, Columbia Crest, Woodbridge by Robert Mondavi, Beringer Founders' Estate, Wolf Blass, Lindemans, Rosemount Estate, and Santa Rita. For special occasions, Clos du Bois, William Hill, Clos du Val, and Morgan all make splurge-worthy wines.

The South also produces a wide array of outstanding reds and whites. Because of distribution regulations, however, many are tough to find. If luck is on your side, you can give a decidedly regional twist to your wine-and-cheese party with Southern favorites such as Château Élan, Biltmore Estate, Linden, Valhalla Vineyards, Stone Hill Winery, Shelton Vineyards, Becker Vineyards, and Llano Estacado.

Presentation can run from a simple two- or three-cheese selection with a couple of wines to a more elaborate sampling of multiple cheeses paired with individual wines. The event can be as loose or as formal as you prefer. Either way, stick with our pairing tips and serving suggestions, and you'll look like a pro.

Supporting Cast

Wine and cheese are best served with simple accompaniments such as these.

- Crusty bread and crackers: French baguette, Italian bread, plain crackers (all wrapped in a clean cloth to keep them from drying out)
- Fresh fruit: grapes, melons, pears, apples, berries, figs
- Nuts: pecans, almonds, walnuts, macadamias
- Assorted olives, pickled vegetables, or cured meats such as sliced country ham and sausage

Wine-and-Cheese Pairings

RED
Cabernet Sauvignon—sharp Cheddar, Swiss, Asiago, aged dry Jack
Merlot—sharp Cheddar, Monterey Jack, Gouda

WHITE
Chardonnay—mild Cheddar, smoked mozzarella
Sauvignon Blanc—blue (Gorgonzola and Roquefort), goat, Comte, Gruyère
Riesling—Brie, Camembert, Gruyère
Champagne or sparkling wine—Brie, Camembert, fontina

Box Wine Is Back

Not only are the new generation of box wines good, they're a terrific value. A three-liter box, or cask, holds four (750ml) bottles of wine and costs from $10 to $25. The wine is exposed to very little air, so it stays fresh in the refrigerator for up to six weeks. Look for producers such as Banrock Station, Sonoma Hill Winery, and Hardys.

Flavor Makeover

Turn this season's bounty into some of the best-tasting dishes you've ever put in your mouth.

Finding it a challenge to create new, great-tasting vegetable dishes? If so, we have just the recipes to inspire you to rush to your grocery store or farmers market. Each of these simple Southern favorites received an A+ at our tasting table. After sampling them yourself, we think you'll concur.

VIDALIA ONION SOUFFLÉ

Prep: 30 min., Cook: 20 min., Bake: 25 min.

- 2 tablespoons butter or margarine
- 5 medium Vidalia or sweet onions, chopped (about 4 cups)
- 2 cups fresh bread cubes (about 10 slices, crusts removed)
- 1 (12-ounce) can fat-free evaporated milk
- 3 large eggs, lightly beaten
- 1¼ cups (5 ounces) shredded Parmesan cheese
- 1 teaspoon salt

MELT butter in a large skillet over medium heat; add chopped onion, and sauté 10 to 15 minutes or until tender.
PLACE onion and bread cubes in a large bowl. Stir in milk, eggs, 1 cup cheese, and salt. Pour into a lightly greased 1½-quart soufflé or baking dish. Sprinkle with remaining ¼ cup cheese.
BAKE at 350° for 25 minutes or until set.
MAKES 8 servings.

FRIED OKRA SALAD

fast fixin's

Prep: 20 min., Fry: 2 min. per batch

Fried Okra Salad drizzled with tangy Lemon Dressing will transform even the fussiest eaters into okra lovers. *(pictured on page 154)*

- 1½ cups self-rising yellow cornmeal
- 1 teaspoon salt
- 1 pound fresh okra
- 1½ cups buttermilk
- Peanut oil
- 1 head Bibb lettuce
- 1 large tomato, chopped (about 1 cup)
- 1 medium-size sweet onion, thinly sliced (about ¾ cup)
- 1 medium-size green bell pepper, chopped
- Lemon Dressing
- 3 bacon slices, cooked and crumbled

COMBINE cornmeal and salt. Dip okra in buttermilk; dredge in cornmeal mixture.
POUR peanut oil to a depth of 2 inches into a Dutch oven or deep cast-iron skillet; heat to 375°. Fry okra, in batches, 2 minutes or until golden, turning once. Drain on a wire rack over paper towels.
ARRANGE lettuce leaves on a serving platter; top with tomato, onion slices, and bell pepper. Add Lemon Dressing, tossing to coat. Top with fried okra, and sprinkle with crumbled bacon. Serve immediately. **MAKES** 6 servings.

Lemon Dressing:
fast fixin's
Prep: 5 min.

This also makes a tangy dipping sauce for steamed artichokes or asparagus.

- ¼ cup fresh lemon juice
- 3 tablespoons chopped fresh basil
- 1 teaspoon salt
- 1 teaspoon paprika
- ½ teaspoon pepper
- ¼ cup olive oil

COMBINE first 5 ingredients in a bowl. Add oil, whisking until combined.
MAKES ¾ cup.

SMOKY SPECKLED BUTTERBEANS

Prep: 10 min., Cook: 3½ hrs.

You'll know when this dish is ready—the pork shreds easily, and the beans are creamy on the inside.

- 3 quarts water
- 1 pound smoked pork shoulder
- 2 pounds fresh or frozen speckled butterbeans
- 2 teaspoons salt
- 1 teaspoon pepper
- 1 jalapeño pepper, sliced
- Hot cooked rice (optional)
- Toppings: chopped sweet onion, hot sauce, or chowchow (optional)

BRING first 6 ingredients to a boil in a Dutch oven. Reduce heat to medium. Cover and simmer 3 hours or until beans are tender, stirring occasionally. Remove pork, and shred. Return to Dutch oven. Serve with rice and toppings, if desired.
MAKES 6 servings.

SHARON BRADBERRY
TALLAHASSEE, FLORIDA

Gather in the Bluegrass

Enjoy this flavorful seasonal menu.

A Sensational Summer Menu

Serves 6

Enjoy leftovers—if there are any—as part of a light Sunday lunch with omelets and salad.

Tomato-and-Goat Cheese Crostini

Fruit Salsa

Bourbon-Marinated
Pork Tenderloin

Stuffed Red Peppers With
Cheesy Polenta and Green Chiles

Green Bean Salad With Feta

Georgia Peach Trifle

When it comes to hosting outdoor gatherings, Jamie and Kevin Estes of Louisville rank with the best.

"We like to go outside, set up lawn chairs, listen to music, and play croquet," Jamie says. She and Kevin have a clear division of duties, allowing everything to be done efficiently and well. "Kevin is the organizer," she says. "I'm the cook, but he does the grilling. Wines and cocktails are my responsibility, but Kevin makes a wonderful bartender when the guests arrive."

Jamie shares some of her favorite summer recipes here, but you'll have to find your own grill cook and bartender. Kevin will be too busy getting ready for their next party.

TOMATO-AND-GOAT CHEESE CROSTINI

fast fixin's

Prep: 15 min., Grill: 4 min.

Heat leftover crostini in the toaster oven for tomorrow's lunch.

2 large tomatoes, seeded and diced
⅛ teaspoon salt
1 teaspoon olive oil
2 (3-ounce) logs herb-flavored goat cheese, crumbled
2 tablespoons chopped fresh basil
¼ teaspoon pepper
1 (12-ounce) French baguette
2 tablespoons olive oil
2 garlic cloves, halved
2 teaspoons chopped fresh parsley

STIR together tomatoes, salt, and 1 teaspoon oil in a bowl; set aside.
COMBINE cheese, basil, and pepper in a bowl; stir and set aside.
CUT bread loaf diagonally into 20 (½-inch-thick) slices. Brush both sides of slices evenly with 2 tablespoons olive oil. Grill over medium heat (300° to 350°) 2 minutes on each side or until golden. Remove from grill.
RUB cut sides of garlic over bread slices; spread about ½ tablespoon cheese mixture evenly over each bread slice. Top evenly with tomato mixture, and sprinkle evenly with parsley. **MAKES** 20 appetizer servings.

FRUIT SALSA

family favorite

Prep: 20 min., Chill: 1 hr.

1 cup diced cantaloupe
1 cup diced watermelon
1 cup peeled, seeded, and diced cucumber
4 large tomatoes, seeded and diced (about 2½ cups)
½ cup chopped red onion
¼ cup fresh lime juice
3 tablespoons chopped fresh cilantro
1 jalapeño pepper, minced (about 2 tablespoons)
1 to 1½ teaspoons salt
¼ teaspoon ground black pepper
Tortilla chips

STIR together first 10 ingredients in a bowl; cover and chill 1 hour. Serve with tortilla chips. **MAKES** 8 to 10 servings.

BOURBON-MARINATED PORK TENDERLOIN

family favorite

Prep: 5 min., Chill: 12 hrs., Grill: 30 min., Stand: 10 min.

2½ pounds pork tenderloins
¾ cup soy sauce
½ cup bourbon
¼ cup Worcestershire sauce
¼ cup water
¼ cup canola oil
4 garlic cloves, minced
3 tablespoons brown sugar
2 tablespoons ground black pepper
1 teaspoon white pepper
½ teaspoon ground ginger
1 teaspoon salt
Garnish: fresh parsley sprigs

RINSE tenderloins, and pat dry.
COMBINE soy sauce and next 9 ingredients in a large zip-top freezer bag or shallow dish; seal or cover, and chill at least 12 hours. Remove pork from

marinade, discarding marinade. Sprinkle evenly with salt.

GRILL, covered with grill lid, over high heat (400° to 500°) 30 minutes or until a meat thermometer inserted into thickest portion registers 155°, turning occasionally. Remove from heat; cover with aluminum foil, and let stand 10 minutes or until thermometer registers 160°. Garnish, if desired. **MAKES** 6 servings.

NOTE: For testing purposes only, we used Maker's Mark Kentucky Straight Bourbon Whisky.

Stuffed Red Peppers With Cheesy Polenta and Green Chiles

Prep: 25 min., Cook: 15 min., Bake: 30 min.

Bright red peppers make a colorful container for this tasty polenta filling.

- 3 medium-size red bell peppers
- ¾ cup polenta or yellow cornmeal
- 3 garlic cloves, minced
- 2 cups water
- 1 teaspoon salt
- ½ teaspoon garlic salt
- ¼ teaspoon freshly ground pepper
- ½ cup whipping cream
- 1 (7-ounce) can whole green chiles, drained and chopped
- ⅔ cup chopped cilantro
- 2 cups (8 ounces) shredded Monterey Jack cheese
- ½ cup (2 ounces) freshly grated Parmesan cheese
- Garnish: fresh cilantro sprigs

CUT bell peppers in half; remove and discard seeds and membranes. Place bell pepper cups in a lightly greased 13- x 9-inch baking dish.

WHISK together polenta and next 5 ingredients in a large saucepan over medium heat; bring to a boil. Cook, whisking constantly, 5 to 7 minutes or until polenta thickens. Stir in cream and next 4 ingredients, blending well.

SPOON mixture into pepper cups.

BAKE at 400°for 25 to 30 minutes or until peppers are tender. Garnish, if desired. **MAKES** 6 servings.

Green Bean Salad With Feta

family favorite

Prep: 5 min., Cook: 8 min., Chill: 2 hrs.

- 1½ pounds green beans, trimmed
- 1 small red onion, chopped (about ½ cup)
- ½ cup Lemon Vinaigrette
- 2 ounces crumbled feta cheese
- ½ cup walnuts, toasted and coarsely chopped
- Garnish: lemon slices

COOK green beans in boiling salted water to cover 8 minutes or until crisp-tender. Drain and plunge into ice water to stop the cooking process; drain and pat dry. Place in a serving bowl; cover and chill at least 2 hours.

ADD chopped onion and Lemon Vinaigrette to beans, tossing to coat. Sprinkle with feta and walnuts. Garnish, if desired. **MAKES** 6 to 8 servings.

Lemon Vinaigrette:

fast fixin's

Prep: 5 min.

Use leftover vinaigrette to marinate artichoke hearts or chicken breasts, or serve over salade niçoise.

- 3 tablespoons fresh lemon juice
- 3 tablespoons white wine vinegar
- 1 tablespoon Dijon mustard
- ½ teaspoon sugar
- ¼ teaspoon salt
- ⅛ teaspoon freshly ground pepper
- ½ cup vegetable oil

WHISK together first 6 ingredients in a small bowl; gradually whisk in oil until blended. **MAKES** about 1 cup.

Georgia Peach Trifle

family favorite

Prep: 15 min.; Chill: 2 hrs., 5 min.

Jamie's friend Daniel Maye shared this recipe for his favorite summer dessert.

- 1 (3½-ounce) package vanilla instant pudding mix
- 2 cups milk
- 6 large fresh peaches, peeled and sliced
- 3 tablespoons granulated sugar
- ½ (20-ounce) package pound cake
- ⅓ cup bourbon
- 1 cup whipping cream
- 2 tablespoons powdered sugar
- ½ cup sliced almonds, toasted

PREPARE pudding mix according to package directions, using 2 cups milk. Cover and chill 5 minutes.

TOSS sliced peaches with granulated sugar.

CUT pound cake into ½-inch slices. Place half of cake slices on bottom of a trifle dish or deep bowl; drizzle evenly with half of bourbon. Spoon half of peach mixture evenly over cake slices. Spread half of pudding over peaches. Repeat with remaining cake slices, bourbon, peach mixture, and pudding. Cover and chill at least 2 hours.

BEAT whipping cream at medium speed with an electric mixer until foamy; gradually add powdered sugar, beating until soft peaks form. Spread whipped cream over trifle; sprinkle with almonds. **MAKES** 8 servings.

DANIEL MAYE
LOUISVILLE, KENTUCKY

Open-Faced Sandwiches

All of these recipes, brimming with flavor, will get you out of the kitchen fast.

Sandwiches aren't just for lunch—grab your knives and forks to enjoy them for dinner. Piled high with a variety of toppings, we offer a not-too-spicy, cool guacamole over a ham-and-melted-cheese po'boy; a meatball sandwich; and a fried egg crowning a BLT sandwich made with sourdough bread.

GUACAMOLE-TOPPED HAM PO'BOYS

fast fixin's

Prep: 20 min., Broil: 1 min.

- **2 medium avocados, halved**
- **½ cup diced tomatoes and green chiles**
- **¼ cup sour cream**
- **2 teaspoons lemon juice**
- **2 green onions, chopped**
- **1 garlic glove, minced**
- **1 teaspoon salt**
- **¼ teaspoon pepper**
- **¼ cup mayonnaise**
- **¼ cup Cajun-style mustard**
- **6 French rolls, split**
- **2 pounds deli-sliced ham**
- **12 Monterey Jack cheese slices**
- **Shredded lettuce**
- **2 medium tomatoes, sliced**

SCOOP avocado pulp into bowl; mash with a fork or potato masher just until chunky. Stir in diced tomatoes and green chiles and next 6 ingredients. Set guacamole aside.

SPREAD mayonnaise and mustard evenly over cut sides of rolls; layer each half evenly with ham and cheese. Place on a baking sheet.

BROIL 2 inches from heat 1 minute or until cheese melts.

TOP evenly with lettuce, tomato slices, and guacamole. **MAKES** 6 servings.

NOTE: Substitute 1 cup prepared guacamole for avocado mixture, if desired.

KAREN SHELBY
FLIPPIN, ARKANSAS

MEATBALL SANDWICHES

family favorite

Prep: 10 min., Cook: 35 min.

- **1 small sweet onion, diced**
- **1 small green bell pepper, diced**
- **1 garlic clove, pressed**
- **1 tablespoon olive oil**
- **1 (26-ounce) jar five-cheese spaghetti sauce**
- **1 tablespoon chopped fresh basil**
- **1 (32-ounce) package frozen cooked Italian-style meatballs**
- **6 slices garlic butter Texas toast**
- **1 cup (4 ounces) shredded Parmesan cheese**
- **2 cups (8 ounces) shredded mozzarella cheese**
- **Toppings: shredded lettuce, chopped tomatoes, chopped bell peppers, black olives (optional)**

SAUTÉ onion, bell pepper, and garlic in hot oil in a large skillet over medium-high heat 3 minutes.

STIR in sauce, basil, and frozen meatballs; cook 30 minutes or until thoroughly heated, stirring often.

PREPARE Texas toast according to package directions.

SPOON meatball mixture over toast; top evenly with cheeses and, if desired, toppings. **MAKES** 6 servings.

NOTE: For testing purposes only, we used Bertolli Five Cheese tomato sauce and Rosina Italian Style Meatballs.

CAROL S. NOBLE
BURGAW, NORTH CAROLINA

BLT Breakfast Sandwiches

family favorite • fast fixin's

Prep: 10 min., Cook: 6 min.

Friends and family alike will appreciate this satisfying sandwich at any meal—breakfast, brunch, lunch, or supper. Check the hollandaise sauce package for the fresh ingredients needed to prepare it.

1 (0.9-ounce) envelope hollandaise
    sauce mix
6 bacon slices, cooked and
    crumbled
2 (3-ounce) packages cream cheese,
    softened
2 tablespoons chopped fresh chives
¾ teaspoon seasoned pepper,
    divided
4 sourdough bread slices, toasted
1 tablespoon butter or margarine
4 large eggs
4 lettuce leaves
2 small tomatoes, sliced

PREPARE hollandaise sauce according to package directions; keep warm.
STIR together bacon, cream cheese, chives, and ¼ teaspoon seasoned pepper; spread evenly on 1 side of each toasted bread slice.
MELT butter in a large nonstick skillet over medium heat. Gently break eggs into hot skillet, and sprinkle evenly with ¼ teaspoon seasoned pepper. Cook 2 to 3 minutes on each side or until done.
PLACE lettuce leaves and tomatoes on top of bread slices, and top with fried eggs. Drizzle hollandaise sauce evenly over top, and sprinkle evenly with remaining ¼ teaspoon seasoned pepper. Serve immediately. **MAKES** 4 servings.

Chill Out With Watermelon

Try some refreshing takes on this favorite fruit.

The season for watermelon is upon us. About all you need to enjoy a ruby-tinged slice are a good grip, a spot to deposit the seeds, and a napkin (or shirtsleeve) to wipe your chin. Add a salt shaker if you prefer a touch of salt to draw out even more of the melon's sweetness.

Still, try as we may to eat the entire thing in one sitting, there's usually a hunk or two left over. Not to worry. These creative recipes are easy to make and allow you to savor every last morsel. Each of the three beverages has its own unique appeal, and all are just right on a hot day. Be sure to try our Watermelon-Prosciutto Salad, a perfect combination of salty and sweet tastes.

Hint: When looking for the perfect melon, choose one with no bruises, cuts, or dents; it should feel heavy for its size. If you don't have room in your refrigerator for a whole melon, cut it in halves or quarters, cover tightly with plastic wrap, and chill for up to one week. For more tips and information, visit the National Watermelon Promotion Board's Web site at **www.watermelon.org**.

Watermelon Granita

family favorite • make ahead

Prep: 20 min., Freeze: 8 hrs., Stand: 15 min.

8 cups seeded and cubed
    watermelon
1 (6-ounce) can frozen orange juice
    concentrate, thawed
1½ cups lemon lime soft drink

PROCESS watermelon in a blender or food processor until smooth.
STIR together watermelon puree and remaining ingredients. Pour mixture into a 2-quart glass bowl. Cover and freeze 8 hours, stirring occasionally.
REMOVE from freezer 15 minutes before serving. Stir with a fork, and spoon into glasses. Serve immediately. **MAKES** 7 cups.

NOTE: For testing purposes only, we used 7 UP soft drink.

Watermelon-Prosciutto Salad

family favorite

Prep: 30 min., Cook: 5 min.

¼ pound prosciutto, cut into thin
    strips
1 tablespoon chopped fresh basil
3 tablespoons white balsamic
    vinegar
2 teaspoons honey
⅛ teaspoon paprika
⅓ cup olive oil
3 cups seeded and cubed
    watermelon
2 bunches watercress
½ teaspoon freshly ground pepper
Garnish: watermelon wedges

BROWN prosciutto in a small nonstick skillet over medium heat 5 minutes. Remove prosciutto, and set aside.
WHISK together basil and next 3 ingredients; gradually whisk in oil until blended.
ARRANGE watermelon cubes over watercress. Sprinkle with prosciutto and pepper, and drizzle with vinaigrette. Garnish, if desired. Serve immediately. **MAKES** 4 servings.

WATERMELON DAIQUIRI

Prep: 20 min., Freeze: 8 hrs.

- **4 cups seeded and cubed watermelon**
- **⅓ cup light rum**
- **¼ to ½ cup orange juice**
- **2 tablespoons orange liqueur**
- **4 teaspoons powdered sugar**
- **2 teaspoons fresh lime juice**

PLACE watermelon in a zip-top freezer bag. Seal bag; freeze 8 hours.

PROCESS watermelon, rum, and remaining ingredients in a blender or food processor until smooth, stopping to scrape down sides. Serve immediately. **MAKES** 3 cups.

NOTE: For testing purposes only, we used Cointreau for orange liqueur.

KATIE ROBINSON
BIRMINGHAM, ALABAMA

WATERMELON-LEMONADE COOLER

family favorite • make ahead

Prep: 25 min., Cook: 10 min., Chill: 8 hrs.

This is the perfect pick-me-up for a thirsty crowd. *(pictured on page 149)*

- **15 cups seeded and cubed watermelon**
- **2 (12-ounce) cans frozen lemonade concentrate, thawed**
- **2 mint sprigs**
- **Ice**
- **Garnishes: watermelon wedges, mint sprigs**

PROCESS watermelon, in batches, in a blender or food processor until smooth. **COMBINE** concentrate and 2 mint sprigs, and cook in a saucepan over medium-high heat 10 minutes. Stir together watermelon puree and lemonade mixture; cover and chill 8 hours. Remove and discard mint. Stir and serve over ice. Garnish, if desired. **MAKES** 14 cups.

MICHAEL ROCCHIO
BIRMINGHAM, ALABAMA

Top-Rated Menu

Enjoy Dinner Outside

Slow the pace of the day, and settle onto a breezy porch.

Weekend Supper

Serves 6

Grilled Maple Chipotle Pork Chops on Smoked Gouda Grits

Steamed broccoli

Dinner rolls

Mocha-Chocolate Shortbread with vanilla or coffee ice cream

Make supper with your family or friends an escape from the norm. Set up the table in an unexpected place—the front porch, if you have one, or in the backyard. These recipes offer familiar foods with a dash of style, certain to spoil diners "vacationing" at your house for the evening.

GRILLED MAPLE CHIPOTLE PORK CHOPS ON SMOKED GOUDA GRITS

family favorite • fast fixin's

Prep: 10 min., Grill: 20 min.

We adapted this recipe from one of the finalists in our 2002 Cook-Off recipe contest.

- **½ cup barbecue sauce**
- **½ cup maple syrup**
- **2 chipotle peppers in adobo sauce, seeded and minced**
- **1 teaspoon adobo sauce from can**
- **6 (1¼-inch-thick) bone-in pork loin chops**
- **1 teaspoon salt**
- **1 teaspoon pepper**
- **Smoked Gouda Grits**

WHISK together first 4 ingredients, and set aside.

SPRINKLE pork chops evenly with salt and pepper.

GRILL, covered with grill lid, over medium-high heat (350° to 400°) 20 minutes or until a meat thermometer inserted into thickest portion registers 155°, turning once. Baste with half of barbecue sauce mixture the last 5 minutes of cooking or when meat thermometer registers 145°.

SPOON Smoked Gouda Grits evenly onto 6 serving plates; top each with a pork chop, and drizzle evenly with remaining barbecue sauce mixture. **MAKES** 6 servings.

Smoked Gouda Grits:
fast fixin's
Prep: 5 min., Cook: 10 min.

Buy a 7-ounce wheel of smoked Gouda cheese to get the right amount.

- **6 cups low-sodium chicken broth or water**
- **2 cups milk**
- **1 teaspoon salt**
- **½ teaspoon ground white pepper**
- **2 cups uncooked quick-cooking grits**
- **1⅔ cups shredded smoked Gouda cheese**
- **3 tablespoons unsalted butter**

BRING first 4 ingredients to a boil in a medium saucepan; gradually whisk in grits. Cover, reduce heat, and simmer, stirring occasionally, 5 minutes or until thickened. Add cheese and butter to mixture, stirring until melted. **MAKES** 6 to 8 servings.

BOB GADSBY
GREAT FALLS, MONTANA

Cook's Notes

- Associate Foods Editor **Shirley Harrington** loves to plan menus—especially those that are unique, yet simple for the season. This screened porch supper serves up a hefty cut of meat with a sauce she uses year-round, a Southern side of grits, and her favorite vegetable—steamed broccoli. The plan is colorful, with varied textures and that fancy-restaurant appeal you want for special guests.

- Thick-cut pork chops are a favorite of Shirley's to grill. She says that great grill marks are a sign of patience, so put the meat on the grill, and step aside. Any prodding or wiggling of the meat even slightly will smear the lines you long for! Don't overcook pork, she explains with passion. Today's pork is leaner and cooks faster than in years past. Her "insurance" plan to great results includes having an instant read thermometer and checking the temperature the first time shortly after turning. Pork looks pretty and is at top quality with just a hint of pink in the center.

- Shirley thinks Smoked Gouda Grits are an awesome alternative to baked potatoes with simple grilled meats. Grits too thick at serving time? Simply thin them with additional milk. Buy about 7 ounces of Gouda cheese to get the 1⅔ cups shredded cheese called for in the recipe. For easy shredding, Shirley recommends freezing the cheese 10 minutes.

- If you have salted, rather than unsalted, butter on hand when making the grits, leave out the 1 teaspoon salt until all other ingredients are stirred together. Then add salt to taste, she adds.

- It's fun to serve mini-portions of our dessert idea, allowing your guests the pleasure of asking for more. Demitasse cup and saucer sets, and spoons are the perfect size. (Juice glasses, champagne flutes, or martini glasses are good alternatives. Offer iced tea spoons with deep, narrow glasses.) Place a 1 to 2 tablespoon-size scoop of coffee and vanilla ice creams into each cup. When ready to serve, push the tip of 1 Mocha-Chocolate Shortbread cookie into the top scoop, and lay another on the saucer.

MOCHA-CHOCOLATE SHORTBREAD

family favorite
Prep: 15 min., Bake: 20 min., Cool: 30 min.

- **1¼ cups all-purpose flour**
- **½ cup powdered sugar**
- **2 teaspoons instant coffee granules**
- **⅔ cup butter or margarine, softened**
- **½ teaspoon vanilla extract**
- **2 cups (12-ounce package) semi-sweet chocolate morsels, divided**
- **Vanilla or coffee ice cream (optional)**

COMBINE first 3 ingredients in a medium bowl; add butter and vanilla, and beat at low speed with an electric mixer until blended. Stir in 1 cup chocolate morsels.

PRESS dough into an ungreased 9-inch square pan; prick dough with a fork.

BAKE at 325° for 20 minutes or until lightly browned. Sprinkle remaining 1 cup morsels over top, and spread to cover. Cut shortbread into 25 (about 1¾-inch) squares; cut each square into 2 triangles. Let cool 30 minutes in pan before removing. Serve with ice cream, if desired. **MAKES** 50 triangles.

JEAN BRISCOE
LOUISVILLE, KENTUCKY

from our kitchen

Cool Tomato Comforts

Whether served as a salad with grilled meats or sidled-up to fried corn and field peas on a vegetable plate, the sharp-sweet taste of ice-cold cucumbers and red onion, dripping with Sugar-and-Vinegar Dressing, is powerful enough to make you shiver. For a light and refreshing supper, drizzle that same dressing over a handful of crisp, leafy salad greens layered with slices of fresh mozzarella cheese and vine-ripened tomatoes.
Sugar-and-Vinegar Dressing: Process ⅓ cup raspberry or red wine vinegar, ¼ cup sugar, 2 teaspoons Dijon mustard, 1 garlic clove, ½ teaspoon freshly ground pepper, and ½ teaspoon salt in a blender or food processor until smooth. With blender or processor running, add ½ cup vegetable oil in a slow, steady stream; process until smooth. Stir in 2 tablespoons chopped fresh basil. Makes about ¾ cup.

Fresh Mozzarella

Fresh mozzarella is a soft white cheese with a mild flavor that's perfect for summer salads and sandwiches. It's naturally low in sodium and has a limited shelf life, so use within several days after opening. Once made from the milk of water buffalo rather than cows and quite expensive, fresh mozzarella is now more reasonable ($3.29 for an 8-ounce package). For more information visit **www.belgioioso.com**.

Summer Suppers

Fire up the grill, and pull some extra patio chairs up to the picnic table because this month we're headed outdoors to cook. Visit **southernliving.com** (AOL Keyword: Southern Living), click on the Foods icon, and use the KitchenAssistant tool to search for some of our favorite recipes.

Pickled Asparagus—Easy as 1-2-3

To make our Pickled Asparagus on page 161, just follow these simple steps.
1. Rinse fresh asparagus well, and drain. Cut out any bruised or soft spots. Gather all your ingredients, and measure.
2. Snap off tough ends of asparagus. For this recipe, we used asparagus about the size of your pinkie finger. This size allows the pickling liquid to adequately penetrate and flavor it; large asparagus won't be as flavorful. The smallest size asparagus goes limp in this mixture. A (1-pound) bunch fills a quart jar.

3. Pack asparagus, 2 fresh dill sprigs, and 1 garlic clove into each jar. We used jars made for canning and food preservation with the appropriate size jar-lid rings. You can re-use jars and rings, but you'll need new lids. You can find these at supermarkets, hardware stores, and discount centers.
4. Heat the pickling liquid (a simple combination of vinegar, water, salt, sugar, and pickling spices) on the cooktop. (You can buy pickling spices in the food preservation or spice center at the supermarket.) Cool liquid completely before pouring over the asparagus in the jars. Seal jars with the lid and ring. Chill at least 8 hours, or store in the refrigerator up to 1 week.

Cool Down With Hot Sauce

Appetizers, sides, and main dishes burst with lively flavor thanks to this spicy condiment.

Here's refreshing news about hot sauce. This chile-containing condiment temporarily speeds up your metabolism and cools you off. Capsaicin (the heat-causing chemical in chile peppers) causes you to perspire, especially on the head and face. As moisture evaporates, heat pulls away from the body, producing a cooling sensation. That's why so many dishes in hot climates are spicy.

But let's face it: The real reason we use hot sauce is because we love its taste and the rush we feel while eating fiery foods. One bite of these tongue-tingling recipes and you'll experience new heights in zestful flavor. Check out "Healthy & Light" on page 183 for more recipes flavored with hot sauce.

Add a Dash

Here's what else is good with a bit of heat tossed in.
- pimiento cheese
- popcorn
- fresh pineapple, cucumber, and jícama
- creamy and broth-based soups
- steamed veggies
- tuna, potato, pasta, or egg salad
- deviled eggs
- gumbo
- smoked brisket

SPICY SHRIMP AND GRITS

Prep: 15 min., Cook: 30 min.

- 1½ cups quick-cooking grits
- ¼ cup (1 ounce) shredded sharp Cheddar cheese
- 1½ tablespoons butter
- 4 tablespoons hot sauce, divided
- 1 pound unpeeled, medium-size fresh shrimp
- ¼ teaspoon salt
- 2 bacon slices
- ½ cup chopped green onions
- 1 tablespoon fresh lemon juice
- 1 tablespoon chopped fresh flat-leaf parsley
- Hot sauce (optional)

COOK grits according to package directions. Remove from heat, and stir in cheese, butter, and 3 tablespoons hot sauce until melted and blended. Cover; set aside.
PEEL shrimp, and devein, if desired. Toss with salt and remaining 1 tablespoon hot sauce.
COOK bacon in a large skillet over medium-high heat 5 to 7 minutes or until crisp; remove bacon, reserving drippings in skillet. Crumble bacon. Add shrimp and green onions to skillet, and sauté 3 minutes or just until shrimp turn pink. Stir in lemon juice.
SPOON grits onto a serving platter; top evenly with shrimp mixture, and sprinkle with parsley and bacon. Serve with additional hot sauce, if desired. **MAKES** 4 servings.

NOTE: For testing purposes only, we used Frank's Original Hot Sauce.

TE OBEIDAT
MARIETTA, GEORGIA

NO-COOK SWEET-AND-SPICY PICKLES

fast fixin's • make ahead

Prep: 5 min.

Store pickles in refrigerator up to four weeks. (We doubt they'll last that long.)

- 1 (46-ounce) jar hamburger dill chips
- ½ cup sugar
- 2 large garlic cloves, thinly sliced
- 2 tablespoons hot sauce

DRAIN liquid from jar; remove pickles from jar. Rinse pickles with water, and drain.
LAYER half each of pickles, sugar, garlic, and hot sauce in jar. Press down gently. Repeat layers. Twist on lid to seal; invert jar, and shake 2 or 3 times to combine ingredients. Chill. **MAKES** about 4 cups.

NOTE: For testing purposes only, we used Tabasco Pepper Sauce.

ANN WILSON
BOWDON, GEORGIA

SWEET-AND-SPICY CHIPOTLE CHICKEN WINGS

family favorite

Prep: 10 min., Cook: 10 min.,
Fry: 8 min. per batch, Stand: 5 min.

- 1 (15-ounce) can tomato sauce
- 2 tablespoons butter
- ½ cup honey
- ¼ cup chipotle-flavored hot sauce
- 1 tablespoon grated lime rind (about 3 limes)
- 3 tablespoons fresh lime juice
- ¼ teaspoon ground red pepper
- 4 to 5 pounds chicken wings
- 1 tablespoon salt
- 1 teaspoon pepper
- 1 cup all-purpose flour
- Peanut or vegetable oil

HEAT tomato sauce and butter in a small saucepan over medium heat, stirring until butter melts. Stir in honey and next 4 ingredients, and bring to a boil.

Reduce heat, and simmer, stirring often, 5 minutes. Set tomato sauce mixture aside. **CUT** off wingtips, and discard. Cut wings in half at joint, if desired.

SPRINKLE wings evenly with salt and pepper; dredge lightly in flour, shaking off excess.

POUR oil to a depth of 1½ inches into a large deep skillet or Dutch oven; heat oil to 375°.

FRY wings, in 3 batches, 8 minutes per batch or until golden and crispy. Remove wings from oil using a slotted spoon; drain on layers of paper towels. (Allow oil to return to 375° before adding next batch of wings.)

PLACE wings in a large bowl. Drizzle with tomato sauce mixture, tossing well to coat. Let stand 5 minutes before serving. **MAKES** 4 to 6 servings.

FIERY CHEESE-AND-CHUTNEY APPETIZER

Prep: 30 min., Chill: 2 hrs.

Reader Tom Davis uses Tack Sauce, his favorite habanero hot sauce, when he makes this recipe. If you can't find Tack Sauce, use any habanero hot sauce.

> 1 (8-ounce) package cream cheese, softened
> 1 (3½-ounce) package Roquefort cheese, softened
> ⅓ cup mango chutney, chopped
> 1 tablespoon habanero pepper hot sauce
> ½ cup finely chopped honey-roasted peanuts
> 1 tablespoon chopped fresh cilantro
> Assorted crackers

STIR together first 4 ingredients in a small bowl until blended. Cover and chill 2 hours or until mixture is firm enough to be shaped. Shape mixture into a ball; roll in peanuts and cilantro. Serve with assorted crackers. **MAKES** 8 servings.

NOTE: For testing purposes only, we used Crosse & Blackwell Genuine Major Grey's Chutney and Habanero in Your Head for hot sauce.

TOM DAVIS
WAYNESBORO, MISSISSIPPI

SPICY CHICKEN SALAD WITH VEGGIES

Prep: 20 min., Chill: 1 hr.

> 3 tablespoons fresh lemon juice, divided
> ¼ cup plain yogurt
> ⅓ cup light mayonnaise
> 1 teaspoon salt
> ¼ to ½ teaspoon ground cumin
> 2 teaspoons hot sauce
> 4 cups chopped cooked chicken breasts
> ½ cup thin carrot strips
> ¼ cup finely chopped red bell pepper
> 4 green onions, finely chopped
> 1 tablespoon chopped fresh cilantro
> 2 avocados
> Red leaf lettuce leaves

STIR together 2 tablespoons lemon juice, yogurt, and next 4 ingredients in a medium bowl until blended. Stir in chicken and next 4 ingredients. Cover and chill 1 hour.

PEEL and thinly slice avocados. Spoon salad over lettuce leaves. Toss avocado slices in remaining 1 tablespoon lemon juice, and arrange slices around chicken salad. **MAKES** 4 to 6 servings.

NOTE: For testing purposes only, we used Tabasco Pepper Sauce for hot sauce.

BETH RHODES
SAN ANTONIO, TEXAS

High on Heat

Associate Foods Editor Joy Zacharia sampled many of these hot sauces straight out of the bottle. As she wrote with a glistening forehead and ruddy cheeks, here's her take on some. (Did she mention antacids make terrific palate cleansers?) After taking an informal coffeepot survey, she learned that Crystal, Tabasco (all flavors), and Louisiana Hot Sauce are tops with our staff.

■ **Bruce's Original Louisiana Hot Sauce:** super fiery—gotta love high heat.

■ **Buffalo Chipotle Mexican Hot Sauce:** smoky and not too hot; great in mashed potatoes, macaroni and cheese, or on grilled corn on the cob.

■ **Cajun Sunshine:** tangy flavor, not too hot.

■ **Cholula Hot Sauce:** smooth, tangy, and very flavorful; great on wings, quesadillas, omelets, French fries, and in cheese dip.

■ **Crystal Hot Sauce:** perfect blend of heat, tang, salt, and chile flavor. Joy's absolute favorite; she can't eat pizza without it.

■ **Hot Wachula's Cranberry:** subtle cranberry flavor and very tasty; great for marinating meats or as a vinaigrette base.

■ **Jump Up and Kiss Me Spicy Passion Fruit Sauce:** sweet, hot, and contains no salt; great for sodium-restricted diets. Try it in vinaigrette-type dressings.

■ **Mango Tango Sauce:** subtle mango taste and very spicy; great over black beans and rice or in creamy coleslaw.

■ **Tabasco Green Pepper Sauce:** milder than the original with a tangy, lemonlike flavor; great over scrambled eggs, chicken chili, and quesadillas.

■ **Texas Pete:** not too hot and lots of flavor. Good and salty, and tastes great on wings, tater tots, and fried fish. The company has a wing sauce, too.

■ **Tiger Sauce:** sweet, spicy, and loaded with flavor; try with grilled lamb chops or pork soft tacos.

It's Grilling Time

These days, folks are putting food items on grills they'd have never imagined years ago. Still, there's nothing like a good old-fashioned burger or an ear of fresh corn hot off the grill, as this menu will show.

Cookout Menu

Serves 10

Barbara's Big Juicy Burgers

Sweet-Hot Ketchup

Grilled Corn With Jalapeño-Lime Butter

Grilled Tomatoes

Homemade ice cream
(recipes on opposite page)

BARBARA'S BIG JUICY BURGERS

family favorite

Prep: 20 min., Grill: 18 min.

Shape into 12 patties for quarter-pound burgers.

- **2 (6-ounce) cans 100% vegetable juice**
- **3 white sandwich bread slices, torn into pieces**
- **3 pounds ground chuck or ground round**
- **1 large egg**
- **1½ teaspoons salt**
- **1 teaspoon pepper**
- **10 hamburger buns**
- **Vegetable cooking spray**
- **Garnish: dill pickle spears**

MICROWAVE vegetable juice in glass bowl at HIGH 1 minute; add sandwich bread pieces, and let cool. Combine with hands.
COMBINE vegetable juice mixture, ground chuck, and next 3 ingredients. Shape into 10 patties.

GRILL patties, covered with grill lid, over medium-high heat (350° to 400°) 6 to 8 minutes on each side or until beef is no longer pink.
SPRAY cut sides of buns with cooking spray; place buns, cut sides down, on grill rack, and grill 1 to 2 minutes or until lightly browned. Serve hamburgers on buns. Garnish, if desired. **MAKES** 10 servings.

NOTE: For testing purposes only, we used V-8 for vegetable juice.

BARBARA MANNING
BIRMINGHAM, ALABAMA

SWEET-HOT KETCHUP

Prep: 10 min., Chill: 2 hrs.

STIR together 1 cup ketchup, 3 tablespoons lime juice, 2 tablespoons honey, 1 teaspoon grated lime rind, and 1 teaspoon chipotle chile pepper seasoning until blended.
COVER and chill 2 hours. **MAKES** 1⅓ cups.

GRILLED CORN WITH JALAPEÑO-LIME BUTTER

Prep: 25 min., Chill: 1 hr., Grill: 20 min.

To make the butter a bit more kid-friendly, make a second batch, omitting the jalapeño peppers.

- **¾ cup butter, softened**
- **2 large jalapeño peppers, seeded and minced**
- **2 tablespoons grated lime rind**
- **1 teaspoon fresh lime juice**
- **10 ears fresh corn, husks removed**
- **2 tablespoons olive oil**
- **1 tablespoon kosher salt**
- **1 teaspoon freshly ground pepper**

COMBINE first 4 ingredients, and shape into a 6-inch log; wrap in wax paper or plastic wrap, and chill 1 hour.
RUB corn with olive oil; sprinkle evenly with salt and pepper.
GRILL, covered with grill lid, over high heat (400° to 500°), turning often, 15 to 20 minutes or until tender. Serve with flavored butter. **MAKES** 10 servings.

GRILLED TOMATOES

fast fixin's

Prep: 5 min., Grill: 4 min.

- **2 garlic cloves, minced**
- **2 tablespoons olive oil**
- **5 large tomatoes, cut in half crosswise**
- **½ teaspoon salt**
- **½ teaspoon pepper**
- **½ cup chopped fresh basil**

STIR together garlic and oil. Brush cut sides of tomato halves evenly with garlic mixture; sprinkle evenly with salt and pepper.
GRILL tomato halves, covered with grill lid, over medium-high heat (350° to 400°) about 2 minutes on each side. Sprinkle evenly with basil. **MAKES** 10 servings.

No-Cook Homemade Ice Cream

If your fondest memories of homemade ice cream are those of sitting on the ice-cream freezer while grandpa churned it, then you're just like Executive Editor Susan Dosier. But she's come to realize that her children have never even *seen* her make homemade ice cream. While this flaw in Southern parenting is alarming, it's fixable. The No-Cook Vanilla Ice Cream and variations here are her ticket to family reunion memories for years to come.

Several years ago, concerns about egg safety prompted us to cook any ice-cream base that used fresh eggs. Not to worry; this recipe doesn't use eggs. Instead, the mixture gets incredible richness from sweetened condensed milk. Use our basic vanilla ice cream as a base, and try every delicious flavor.

No-Cook Vanilla Ice Cream

Prep: 5 min.; Chill: 30 min.;
Freeze: 2 hrs., 5 min.

Lera Townley of Roanoke, Alabama, shared this recipe through her daughter, Wanda Stephens, our office manager at *Southern Living*. Mr. Townley wouldn't eat ice cream with eggs in it, and the result is this recipe.

- **1 (14-ounce) can sweetened condensed milk**
- **1 (5-ounce) can evaporated milk**
- **2 tablespoons sugar**
- **2 teaspoons vanilla extract**
- **2 cups whole milk**

WHISK all ingredients in a 2-quart pitcher or large bowl until blended. Cover and chill 30 minutes.

POUR milk mixture into freezer container of a 1-quart electric ice-cream maker, and freeze according to manufacturer's instructions. (Instructions and times will vary.)

REMOVE container with ice cream from ice-cream maker, and place in freezer 15 minutes. Transfer to an airtight container; freeze until firm, about 1 to 1½ hours. **MAKES** 1 quart.

NOTE: For testing purposes only, we used a Rival 4-quart Durable Plastic Bucket Ice Cream Maker and a Cuisinart Automatic Frozen Yogurt-Ice Cream & Sorbet Maker.

LERA TOWNLEY
ROANOKE, ALABAMA

NO-COOK CHOCOLATE ICE CREAM: Omit sugar, vanilla, and whole milk. Add 2 cups whole chocolate milk and ⅔ cup chocolate syrup. Proceed as directed. **MAKES** 1 quart.

NO-COOK CHOCOLATE-ALMOND ICE CREAM: Prepare No-Cook Chocolate Ice Cream as directed. Remove container with ice cream from ice-cream maker, and place in freezer. Freeze 15 minutes. Stir ¾ cup toasted sliced almonds into prepared ice cream. Place in an airtight container; freeze until firm. **MAKES** 1¼ quarts.

NO-COOK TURTLE ICE CREAM: Prepare No-Cook Vanilla Ice Cream as directed. Stir ¼ cup caramel sauce into prepared ice cream. Remove container with ice cream from ice-cream maker, and place in freezer. Freeze 15 minutes. Microwave ½ cup semisweet chocolate morsels and 1 teaspoon shortening in a microwave-safe glass bowl at HIGH 1 minute. Stir chocolate mixture until smooth. Place ¾ cup toasted chopped pecans on a parchment paper-lined baking sheet. Drizzle pecans with melted chocolate. Freeze 5 minutes. Break into bite-size pieces. Stir chocolate-and-pecan pieces into ice cream. Place in an airtight container; freeze until firm. **MAKES** 1½ quarts.

NO-COOK FIG-MINT ICE CREAM: *(pictured on page 192)* Prepare No-Cook Vanilla Ice Cream as directed. Remove container with prepared ice cream from ice-cream maker, and place in freezer. Freeze 15 minutes. Stir together 2 cups chopped peeled fresh figs, ¼ cup fresh lemon juice, 2 tablespoons sugar, and 2 teaspoons chopped fresh mint. Stir mixture into prepared ice-cream mixture. Place in an airtight container; freeze until firm. **MAKES** 1½ quarts.

NOTE: We used Black Mission Figs; any fresh figs in season should work in this recipe, including green figs.

NO-COOK PEACH ICE CREAM: Omit sugar and vanilla, and reduce whole milk to 1¼ cups. Process 4 peeled, sliced medium-size fresh ripe peaches or 1 (15.25-ounce) can peaches in light syrup, drained, with 2 tablespoons sugar; ¼ cup fresh lemon juice; and ¼ teaspoon salt in a blender or food processor until smooth. Stir into milk mixture with ¾ cup peach nectar. Proceed as directed. **MAKES** 1½ quarts.

NO-COOK STRAWBERRY ICE CREAM: Omit vanilla, and reduce whole milk to 1½ cups. Process 1 (16-ounce) container fresh strawberries or 1 (16-ounce) package thawed frozen strawberries, 2 tablespoons lemon juice, and ¼ teaspoon salt in a blender or food processor until smooth. Stir into milk mixture. Proceed as directed. **MAKES** 1½ quarts.

NO-COOK COCONUT ICE CREAM: Omit sugar and vanilla, and reduce whole milk to ½ cup. Whisk 1 (13.5-ounce) can coconut milk, 2 tablespoons fresh lemon juice, and ¼ teaspoon salt into milk mixture. Proceed as directed. Serve ice cream with toasted coconut, shaved chocolate, or chopped macadamia nuts. **MAKES** 1 quart.

TROPICAL SUNDAE: Top coconut ice cream with banana slices, mango slices, and pineapple chunks.

"Cook's Notes"

Here are a few tricks for getting the best ice-cream results:
- Chill the liquid ice-cream mixture 30 minutes before churning to ensure a smoother texture.
- To facilitate speedy freezing, place the freshly churned ice cream (in the freezing container from your ice-cream maker) directly into the freezer. Freeze 15 minutes, add any stir-ins, and then transfer to an airtight container; refreeze.
- Freeze ice cream 8 hours or longer for the best texture. Allow to stand at room temperature 30 minutes to 1 hour before serving.
- Customize with stir-ins: Add 1 cup chopped toasted nuts, chocolate chips, crushed cream-filled chocolate sandwich cookies, or toasted coconut to your favorite variation.

Supper Made Simple

These stand-alone suppers prepared on the cooktop offer effortless meals.

Easy Skillet Tacos

family favorite

Prep: 10 min., Cook: 25 min., Stand: 5 min.

These tacos get their flavor from cumin and chili powder without the additional sodium often found in packaged seasoning mixes.

- **1 pound ground beef**
- **1 small onion, chopped**
- **1 teaspoon olive oil**
- **1 tablespoon chili powder**
- **1½ teaspoons ground cumin**
- **1 teaspoon salt**
- **1 (15-ounce) can pinto beans, rinsed and drained**
- **1 (8-ounce) can tomato sauce**
- **¾ cup water**
- **½ cup salsa**
- **1½ cups (6 ounces) shredded Cheddar cheese**
- **1 tablespoon chopped fresh cilantro**
- **Taco shells or flour tortillas, warmed**
- **Toppings: shredded lettuce, diced tomatoes, salsa, sour cream**

COOK ground beef in a large skillet over medium-high heat, stirring until beef crumbles and is no longer pink. Drain well. Remove beef; wipe skillet with a paper towel.

SAUTÉ onion in hot oil in same skillet over medium-high heat. Add chili powder, cumin, salt, and beef. Cook 5 to 7 minutes, stirring occasionally. Stir in beans, tomato sauce, ¾ cup water, and salsa. Mash pinto beans in skillet with a fork, leaving some beans whole. Bring to a boil; reduce heat, and simmer, uncovered, 8 to 10 minutes or until liquid is reduced.

TOP evenly with cheese and cilantro. Cover, turn off heat, and let stand 5 minutes or until cheese melts. Serve with taco shells or tortillas and desired toppings. **MAKES** 4 to 6 servings.

DEBBIE SHEPARD
LYNCHBURG, VIRGINIA

Vermicelli With Chunky Vegetable Sauce

family favorite

Prep: 20 min., Cook: 30 min.

You can stir in 1 pound cooked ground beef or 2 cups chopped cooked chicken when adding the tomatoes.

- **1 red bell pepper, diced**
- **1 medium onion, diced**
- **1 (8-ounce) package sliced fresh mushrooms**
- **1 tablespoon olive oil**
- **2 small zucchini, diced**
- **4 garlic cloves, minced**
- **1 teaspoon salt, divided**
- **½ teaspoon freshly ground pepper, divided**
- **2 (28-ounce) cans diced tomatoes, undrained**
- **1 (6-ounce) can tomato paste**
- **1 tablespoon sugar**
- **1 tablespoon fresh lemon juice**
- **1½ teaspoons dried Italian seasoning**
- **1 (16-ounce) package vermicelli**
- **Freshly grated Parmesan cheese (optional)**

SAUTÉ bell pepper, onion, and mushrooms in hot oil in a large nonstick skillet over medium-high heat 8 minutes; stir in zucchini, garlic, ¼ teaspoon salt, and ¼ teaspoon pepper. Cook, stirring occasionally, 4 minutes or until zucchini is tender.

STIR in tomatoes, next 4 ingredients, remaining ¾ teaspoon salt, and remaining ¼ teaspoon pepper; bring to a boil, stirring occasionally. Reduce heat; cover and simmer 10 to 15 minutes.

PREPARE pasta according to package directions; drain. Serve sauce over pasta. Sprinkle with Parmesan cheese, if desired. **MAKES** 6 servings.

KAREN C. GREENLEE
LAWRENCEVILLE, GEORGIA

Smothered Chicken With Lemon Mashed Potatoes

family favorite

Prep: 20 min., Cook: 40 min.

Peel the garlic cloves, and crush them with the heel of your hand on a cutting board. A longer cooking time is needed to soften the larger pieces and mellow the flavor. Grate the lemon rind for the potatoes before you squeeze the fresh juice for the chicken.

- **4 skinned and boned chicken breasts**
- **¾ teaspoon salt, divided**
- **½ teaspoon pepper, divided**
- **½ cup Italian-seasoned breadcrumbs**
- **1 (8-ounce) package sliced fresh mushrooms**
- **1 teaspoon olive oil**
- **18 to 20 garlic cloves, crushed**
- **2 tablespoons olive oil, divided**
- **Lemon Mashed Potatoes**
- **2 tablespoons butter or margarine, divided**
- **1 (14-ounce) can chicken broth**
- **1 tablespoon fresh lemon juice**
- **½ teaspoon dried basil**
- **¼ teaspoon dried oregano**
- **3 tablespoons all-purpose flour**
- **¼ cup water**

PLACE chicken between 2 sheets of heavy-duty plastic wrap; flatten to ¼-inch thickness, using a meat mallet or rolling pin. Sprinkle both sides of chicken evenly with ½ teaspoon salt and ¼ teaspoon pepper. Dredge in breadcrumbs. Set aside.

SAUTÉ mushrooms in 1 teaspoon hot oil in a large nonstick skillet over medium-high heat 8 minutes or until edges are browned. Remove from skillet. Sprinkle with remaining ¼ teaspoon salt and ¼ teaspoon pepper; set aside.

SAUTÉ garlic in 1 tablespoon hot oil over medium heat 5 to 10 minutes or until lightly browned and soft. Remove from skillet, and mash lightly with a fork or potato masher; set aside.

PREPARE Lemon Mashed Potatoes, and keep warm.

MELT 1 tablespoon butter with ½ tablespoon oil in skillet over medium heat; add 2 chicken breasts, and cook

4 minutes on each side or until done. Remove to a wire rack in a jellyroll pan. Keep warm in oven at 225°. Repeat with remaining 1 tablespoon butter, ½ tablespoon oil, and 2 chicken breasts.

STIR broth and next 3 ingredients into skillet, and cook 2 minutes, stirring to loosen particles from bottom of skillet. Stir in sautéed mushrooms and garlic.

STIR together 3 tablespoons flour and ¼ cup water; whisk into broth mixture over medium-high heat. Cook 3 minutes, whisking constantly, or until thickened. Serve with chicken and Lemon Mashed Potatoes. **MAKES** 4 servings.

Lemon Mashed Potatoes:

Prep: 5 min., Cook: 12 min.

PREPARE 1 (22-ounce) bag frozen mashed potatoes according to package directions. Stir in ¼ cup butter or margarine, 1 teaspoon grated lemon rind, ¾ teaspoon salt, and ¼ to ½ teaspoon freshly ground black pepper. **MAKES** 4 servings.

TOMATO-RED ONION SALAD

fast fixin's

Prep: 15 min., Stand: 10 min.

Create other versions of this salad by adding crumbled feta or goat cheese, kalamata olives, or sliced cucumbers.

- 4 medium tomatoes, cut into ¼-inch-thick slices
- ¼ small red onion, thinly sliced
- 2 tablespoons chopped fresh oregano
- 2 tablespoons olive oil
- 1 tablespoon red wine vinegar
- ¼ teaspoon salt
- ⅛ teaspoon pepper

LAYER tomato and onion slices on a serving platter. Sprinkle evenly with chopped fresh oregano.

WHISK together oil, vinegar, salt, and pepper. Drizzle evenly over tomato and onion slices. Let stand 10 minutes before serving. **MAKES** 4 servings.

NORA HENSHAW
OKEMAH, OKLAHOMA

PORK IN GARLIC SAUCE

Prep: 25 min., Stand: 15 min., Cook: 9 min.

Add a simple green salad to complete this meal.

- 4 teaspoons cornstarch, divided
- 5½ tablespoons soy sauce, divided
- 1 pound lean, boneless pork chops, cut into thin strips
- 1 cup uncooked long-grain rice
- ¼ cup water
- 4 teaspoons hoisin sauce
- 1 teaspoon sesame oil
- 1 tablespoon peanut oil
- ½ (8-ounce) package sliced fresh mushrooms
- 4 green onions, sliced
- 1 (8-ounce) can sliced water chestnuts, drained
- 3 garlic cloves, minced
- 2 teaspoons minced fresh ginger
- ½ teaspoon dried crushed red pepper
- 2 tablespoons fresh orange juice
- Garnishes: chopped green onions, orange slices

STIR together 2 teaspoons cornstarch and 1½ tablespoons soy sauce in a medium bowl until smooth. Add pork, tossing to coat. Let stand 15 minutes.

PREPARE rice according to package directions. Keep warm.

STIR together remaining 2 teaspoons cornstarch, remaining 4 tablespoons soy sauce, ¼ cup water, and 4 teaspoons hoisin sauce.

HEAT oils in a large skillet or wok over medium-high heat 2 minutes. Add pork mixture, and stir-fry 3 to 4 minutes or until pork is browned. Add mushrooms and next 5 ingredients; stir-fry 2 minutes. Stir in hoisin sauce mixture, and stir-fry 1 minute or until thickened. Stir in orange juice. Serve over warm rice. Garnish, if desired. **MAKES** 4 servings.

Stress-Free Sides

When it comes to rounding out weeknight suppers, you need recipes you can pull together easily. All of these have a prep time of 10 minutes or less without sacrificing a lick of flavor—and they require minimal hands-on cooking. The most you'll have to do is some sautéing for the Zucchini With Citrus-Herb Dressing. Once you quickly cook the beans for the Roasted Green Beans With Mushrooms, simply assemble the dish, and pop it in the oven for about 25 minutes. The Apple-Bacon Coleslaw, which requires no cooking at all, uses precooked bacon and a bag of coleslaw mix to make it extra-simple to prepare.

APPLE-BACON COLESLAW

family favorite

Prep: 10 min., Chill: 30 min.

- 3 tablespoons olive oil
- 2 tablespoons mayonnaise
- 1 tablespoon Dijon mustard
- 1 tablespoon lemon juice
- ½ teaspoon hot sauce
- ¼ teaspoon salt
- 1 (16-ounce) package shredded coleslaw mix
- 1 large Gala apple, peeled and finely diced
- Freshly ground pepper to taste
- 4 precooked bacon slices, crumbled

WHISK together first 6 ingredients in a large bowl. Add coleslaw mix, apple, and ground pepper, tossing well to coat. Cover and chill 30 minutes. Sprinkle with bacon just before serving. **MAKES** 4 cups.

NOTE: For testing purposes only, we used Oscar Mayer Ready-to-Serve Bacon for precooked bacon slices.

JULIE DEMATTEO
CLEMENTON, NEW JERSEY

ROASTED GREEN BEANS WITH MUSHROOMS

family favorite • fast fixin's

Prep: 5 min., Cook: 1 min., Bake: 25 min.

- **1 pound fresh green beans, trimmed**
- **1 (8-ounce) package fresh button, shiitake, or cremini mushrooms**
- **4 garlic cloves, thinly sliced**
- **2 tablespoons minced fresh ginger**
- **2 tablespoons sesame oil**
- **4 teaspoons soy sauce**
- **½ teaspoon red chili flakes**
- **⅛ teaspoon salt**

COOK green beans in boiling water to cover 1 minute; drain. Plunge into ice water to stop the cooking process; drain and spread evenly in a 13- x 9-inch baking dish.

COMBINE mushrooms and next 6 ingredients in a medium bowl. Pour over green beans.

BAKE at 450° for 20 to 25 minutes or until beans are tender, stirring occasionally. **MAKES** 4 servings.

CAROLINE KENNEDY
LIGHTHOUSE POINT, FLORIDA

ZUCCHINI WITH CITRUS-HERB DRESSING

fast fixin's

Prep: 5 min., Cook: 12 min.

For extra flavor, top this dish with long Parmesan cheese curls created by using a vegetable peeler. *(pictured on page 191)*

- **1½ pounds medium zucchini**
- **½ teaspoon salt**
- **1 garlic clove, minced**
- **2 tablespoons olive oil**
- **Citrus-Herb Dressing**
- **Garnish: lemon slices**

CUT zucchini lengthwise in half, and cut into ¼-inch-thick wedges about 1½ inches long. Sprinkle wedges with salt.
SAUTÉ minced garlic in hot oil in a skillet over medium-high heat until lightly browned. Add zucchini; cook, stirring occasionally, 8 to 10 minutes or until tender.

POUR Citrus-Herb Dressing over zucchini, tossing to coat. Garnish, if desired. Serve immediately. **MAKES** 4 servings.

Citrus-Herb Dressing:

fast fixin's

Prep: 5 min.

- **3 tablespoons chopped fresh basil**
- **1 tablespoon chopped fresh thyme**
- **3 tablespoons fresh orange juice**
- **2 tablespoons fresh lemon juice**
- **1 teaspoon Dijon mustard**
- **¼ teaspoon salt**
- **¼ teaspoon pepper**

WHISK together all ingredients in a medium bowl. **MAKES** ½ cup.

SHIRL CIEUTAT
NEW ORLEANS, LOUISIANA

What's for Supper?

Make-Ahead Chicken Casserole

School Night Supper

Serves 4 to 6

Chicken Casserole D'Iberville

Tossed salad

Caramel-Apple Grahams

Stock your freezer with this A+ chicken-and-rice casserole, and you have dinners ready to bake. For a family, divide mixture into three 8-inch square baking dishes. (To keep a big casserole on hand for potluck suppers, place the mixture in a 4-quart dish.) If you're short on baking dishes, use foil pans, which also allow for easy cleanup.

CHICKEN CASSEROLE D'IBERVILLE

freezeable • make ahead

Prep: 30 min.; Cook: 1 hr., 40 min.;
Bake: 40 min.

This recipe, from Charlotte Skelton's book *Absolutely a la Carte* (Wimmer, 1999), is named after a community north of Biloxi. When pressed for time, try the Kitchen Express method on the opposite page.

- **2 (3-pound) whole chickens**
- **1 cup water**
- **1 cup dry sherry**
- **2 celery ribs**
- **1 onion, quartered**
- **1½ teaspoons salt**
- **½ teaspoon curry powder**
- **¼ teaspoon pepper**
- **¼ teaspoon poultry seasoning**
- **2 (6-ounce) packages long-grain and wild rice mix**
- **½ cup butter or margarine**
- **2 (8-ounce) packages sliced fresh mushrooms**
- **1 bunch green onions, chopped (about 1 cup)**
- **1 (8-ounce) container sour cream**
- **1 (10¾-ounce) can cream of mushroom soup**
- **1 sleeve round buttery crackers, crushed (about 1½ cups)**
- **1 (6-ounce) can French fried onion rings, crushed**
- **¼ cup butter or margarine, melted**
- **¼ teaspoon paprika**
- **⅛ teaspoon garlic powder**

BRING first 9 ingredients to a boil in a large Dutch oven; reduce heat, cover, and simmer 1 hour or until chicken is done. (Chicken will cook in this amount of liquid.) Remove chicken, reserving broth in Dutch oven. Let chicken cool. Pour broth through a fine wire mesh strainer into an 8-cup liquid measuring cup; discard solids.
COOK rice according to package directions, substituting 4¼ cups reserved chicken broth for water and omitting butter. (Add water to broth to equal 4¼ cups, if necessary.)
SKIN, bone, and coarsely chop or shred chicken.
MELT ½ cup butter in a large Dutch oven over medium heat; add mushrooms and

green onions, and sauté 10 minutes or until tender. Stir in rice, chicken, sour cream, and soup. Spoon mixture into lightly greased 8 (2-cup) casserole dishes, 8 (5½- x 3½-inch) mini-loaf pans, 3 (8-inch or 9-inch) square baking dishes, or 1 (4-quart or 15- x 10-inch) casserole dish.

STIR together crushed crackers and fried onions. Stir in ¼ cup melted butter, paprika, and garlic powder. Sprinkle casserole with cracker mixture.

BAKE, covered, at 350° for 20 to 30 minutes. Uncover and bake 5 to 10 more minutes or until bubbly. **MAKES** 12 to 16 servings.

CHARLOTTE SKELTON
CLEVELAND, MISSISSIPPI

TO MAKE AHEAD: Cover casseroles tightly with foil, and freeze unbaked up to 1 month. Thaw overnight in refrigerator. Bake as directed. (Casserole may also be baked frozen. Plan to double the baking times.)

TO MICROWAVE ONE FROZEN, UNBAKED 8-INCH SQUARE CASSEROLE: Casserole must be in a microwave-safe dish. Cover dish with wax paper. Microwave at HIGH 15 to 16 minutes or until bubbly, giving dish a half-turn once.

TO MICROWAVE ONE THAWED, UNBAKED 8-INCH SQUARE CASSEROLE: Follow directions to microwave a frozen, unbaked casserole, reducing microwave time to 7 to 8 minutes.

KITCHEN EXPRESS: Use 2 deli-roasted chickens (about 2 pounds each) in place of boiled chickens. Use 1 cup dry sherry and 3¼ cups (26 ounces) canned chicken broth to cook rice.

CARAMEL-APPLE GRAHAMS

Prep: 5 min.

BREAK 2 whole graham crackers in half.
TOP each half with 1 caramel, and microwave each at HIGH 20 seconds or until caramel starts to melt.
REMOVE from microwave, and top each cracker with 3 Granny Smith apple slices. **MAKES** 4 servings.

Peanut Butter-Apple Grahams:
SPREAD each graham cracker half with 1 tablespoon peanut butter, and microwave at HIGH 10 seconds.
REMOVE from microwave, and top each with 3 apple slices.

Healthy & Light

Turn Up the Flavor

A generous splash of hot sauce gives these dishes a little something extra. For more recipes using this spicy favorite, turn to page 176.

MANGO-PINEAPPLE HOT SAUCE

make ahead

Prep: 10 min., Cook: 35 min., Stand: 1 hr.

Always handle habaneros with kitchen gloves. We used 2 habaneros for this recipe; use 1 for a milder finish. For a quick appetizer, pour some of the sauce over a block of cream cheese and serve with assorted crackers.

- **1 cup mango nectar**
- **1 cup pineapple juice**
- **¼ cup plus 1 tablespoon cider vinegar**
- **4 garlic cloves, minced**
- **1 to 2 habanero peppers, seeded and chopped**
- **1¼ teaspoons salt**
- **1 teaspoon ground turmeric**

STIR together all ingredients in a 1-quart saucepan over medium-high heat; bring to a boil, stirring often. Cover, reduce heat to low, and simmer 30 minutes. Remove from heat; let stand at room temperature 1 hour or until completely cool. Store leftover sauce in refrigerator up to 2 months. **MAKES** 1⅔ cups.

Per 1 tablespoon sauce: Calories 12 (2% from fat); Fat .03g (sat .01g, mono .01g, poly .01g); Protein .09g; Carb 3.2g; Fiber 0.1g; Chol 0mg; Iron .09mg; Sodium 112mg; Calc 3.4mg

BREAKFAST SAUSAGE QUESADILLAS

family favorite

Prep: 10 min., Cook: 34 min.

- **1 (12-ounce) package 97% fat-free ground pork sausage**
- **Vegetable cooking spray**
- **1 to 2 teaspoons hot sauce**
- **1 (15-ounce) container Southwestern-flavored egg substitute**
- **1½ cups (6 ounces) shredded reduced-fat Mexican cheese blend**
- **6 (10-inch) whole-wheat or white flour tortillas**
- **½ cup nonfat sour cream**
- **3 green onions, chopped**
- **Salsa (optional)**

COOK sausage in a large nonstick skillet coated with cooking spray over medium-high heat 10 minutes or until sausage crumbles and is no longer pink. Drain sausage, and pat dry with paper towels. Return to skillet; stir in hot sauce. Set aside.

COOK egg substitute in a large skillet coated with vegetable cooking spray over medium-high heat without stirring 1 to 2 minutes or until it begins to set on bottom.

DRAW a spatula across bottom of skillet to form large curds. Cook 3 to 4 minutes or until thickened and moist. (Do not stir constantly.) Remove skillet from heat.

SPOON sausage, egg substitute, and cheese evenly over half of each tortilla. Fold in half, pressing gently to seal. Lightly coat both sides of tortillas with cooking spray.

COOK in a large skillet coated with cooking spray over medium-high heat, in 3 batches, 3 minutes on each side or until lightly browned and cheese is melted. Top quesadillas evenly with sour cream, green onions, and, if desired, salsa. Serve immediately. **MAKES** 6 servings.

NOTE: For testing purposes only, we used Jimmy Dean 97% fat-free sausage and EggBeaters Southwestern.

Per serving: Calories 288 (28% from fat); Fat 9g (sat 4.1g, mono 0.7g, poly 1.3g); Protein 28g; Carb 25g; Fiber 2.2g; Chol 36.4mg; Iron 2.9mg; Sodium 828mg; Calc 289mg

SWEET PORK TENDERLOIN WITH LIME AND CHIPOTLE

family favorite

Prep: 20 min., Chill: 2 hrs., Grill: 18 min., Stand: 10 min., Cook: 5 min.

Aromatic and juicy, Sweet Pork Tenderloin With Lime and Chipotle makes a spectacular main dish.

- **1 cup honey-Dijon mustard**
- **⅔ cup chopped fresh cilantro**
- **½ cup fresh lime juice**
- **2 to 3 tablespoons canned chipotle peppers in adobo sauce, minced**
- **4 garlic cloves, minced**
- **1 teaspoon ground cumin**
- **¾ teaspoon salt**
- **¾ teaspoon ground cinnamon**
- **2 (¾-pound) pork tenderloins**
- **¼ cup water**
- **¼ cup chopped honey-roasted peanuts**
- **Garnish: chopped fresh cilantro**

STIR together first 8 ingredients; reserve 1 cup honey-Dijon mustard mixture.

PLACE pork in a large shallow dish or zip-top freezer bag; pour remaining honey-Dijon mustard mixture over pork. Cover or seal, and chill, turning occasionally, 2 hours.

REMOVE pork from marinade, discarding marinade.

GRILL pork, covered with grill lid, over medium-high heat (350° to 400°) 8 to 9 minutes on each side or until a meat thermometer inserted into thickest portion registers 150°. Remove from grill, and let stand 10 minutes. Cut pork into slices.

BRING reserved mustard mixture and ¼ cup water to a boil in a saucepan; reduce heat, and simmer 2 minutes. Sprinkle peanuts over pork, and serve with sauce. Garnish, if desired. **MAKES** 8 servings.

Per serving: Calories 229 (32% from fat); Fat 8.2g (sat 1.9g, mono 1.6g, poly 0.5g); Protein 22g; Carb 20g; Fiber 1.8g; Chol 57mg; Iron 1.7mg; Sodium 579mg; Calc 30mg

BUFFALO CHICKEN TWICE-BAKED POTATOES

Prep: 20 min., Bake: 51 min., Cook: 8 min.

To check potatoes for doneness, partially unwrap the largest potato, and pierce center with a fork (avoid piercing fork directly into aluminum foil). If the fork glides in easily, potatoes are done.

- **4 (6-ounce) russet baking potatoes**
- **¾ cup (3 ounces) 2% reduced-fat shredded Cheddar cheese, divided**
- **½ cup nonfat sour cream**
- **1 teaspoon Buffalo-style hot sauce**
- **1 pound skinned and boned chicken breasts, cut into thin strips**
- **¼ teaspoon salt**
- **¼ teaspoon chili powder**
- **1 tablespoon vegetable oil**
- **2 tablespoons white vinegar**
- **2 tablespoons Buffalo-style hot sauce**
- **2 tablespoons light margarine**
- **Toppings: nonfat sour cream, chopped green onions**

WRAP each potato in a piece of aluminum foil; place potatoes on a baking sheet.

BAKE at 425° for 45 minutes or until potatoes are tender.

CUT potatoes in half lengthwise; carefully scoop out pulp into a large bowl, leaving shells intact. Stir together potato pulp, ½ cup shredded Cheddar cheese, ½ cup sour cream, and 1 teaspoon hot sauce.

SPOON potato mixture evenly into shells; sprinkle tops evenly with remaining ¼ cup shredded Cheddar cheese. Return potatoes to baking sheet, and bake at 425° for 5 to 6 minutes or until cheese melts.

SPRINKLE chicken with salt and chili powder; cook in hot vegetable oil in a large nonstick skillet over medium-high heat 7 minutes or until chicken is browned, stirring often. Stir in vinegar, 2 tablespoons hot sauce, and margarine; stir until sauce is blended and chicken is coated. Cook 1 minute; remove skillet from heat.

SPOON chicken mixture evenly over baked potatoes. Serve with desired toppings. **MAKES** 8 servings.

Per serving: Calories 216 (27% from fat); Fat 6.4g (sat 2.3g, mono 1.5g, poly 1.4g); Protein 18g; Carb 21g; Fiber 1.7g; Chol 42mg; Iron 1.4mg; Sodium 376mg; Calc 112mg

SWEET-AND-HOT BEAN-AND-VEGGIE SALAD

Prep: 15 min., Chill: 3 hrs.

For milder chopped onions, soak them in cold water for 30 minutes; drain and pat dry. Proceed with recipe as directed.

- **1 tablespoon no-calorie sweetener**
- **3 tablespoons fresh lemon juice**
- **2 teaspoons olive oil**
- **1 teaspoon salt**
- **1 teaspoon ground cumin**
- **1 to 2 teaspoons hot sauce**
- **1 garlic clove, minced**
- **1 (15-ounce) can black beans, rinsed and drained**
- **1 (10-ounce) can diced tomatoes and green chiles, drained**
- **1 cup fresh or frozen corn kernels, thawed**
- **1 red or green bell pepper, chopped**
- **2 celery ribs, chopped**
- **½ medium-size red onion, chopped**

WHISK together first 7 ingredients in a large bowl. Stir in beans and remaining ingredients, tossing to coat. Cover and chill 3 hours. **MAKES** 8 servings.

NOTE: For testing purposes only, we used Splenda Granular for no-calorie sweetener.

Per serving: Calories 71 (18% from fat); Fat 1.4g (sat 0.2g, mono 1g, poly 0.2g); Protein 2.7g; Carb 14g; Fiber 3.4g; Chol 0mg; Iron 0.9mg; Sodium 534mg; Calc 29mg

September

Casual Outdoor Gathering

Surrounded by friends and family, the Mondavis toast the season. Try their scrumptious menu paired with the perfect wine.

Fall Gathering for Friends

Serves 4 to 6

Goat Cheese Torta With Garden Pesto

Saffron Butternut Squash Soup

Barbecued Pork Quesadillas

Kettle Corn

"This is my favorite time of the year in the South," offers Rob Mondavi as he adds a handful of wet hickory chips to his smoker. "There's a crispness in the air, which is perfect for outdoor entertaining. I mean, I can't think of a better time to barbecue." Neither can his friends and family, all of whom will clamor later this afternoon for his downright irresistible Barbecued Pork Quesadillas.

Not bad for a guy born and raised in California wine country. Of course, you'd expect the grandson of legendary winemaker Robert Mondavi—the man who many folks consider to have put American wines on the world stage—to know a thing or two about entertaining.

A few steps away, Rob's new bride, Lydia, a Southern woman through and through, ices down a few of their favorite white wines in anticipation of arriving guests. "Rob loves everything about the South, including the humidity," she says with a big smile. "He even loves vegetables that have been cooked all afternoon," playfully adds Anita Wilbanks, Lydia's mom. Anita's home in Canton, Georgia, which just oozes regional charm, serves as the backdrop for many get-togethers, including those hosted by Rob and Lydia.

Though the couple experienced very different childhoods, both see striking similarities between their Southern and Italian-American families. "Food, cooking, and being around the table have always been important in our lives," says Rob. Both intend to carry on the tradition. Meantime, we're happy to pass along a few of their favorite recipes.

GOAT CHEESE TORTA

make ahead

Prep: 10 min., Chill: 8 hrs.

- 1 (10.5-ounce) package goat cheese
- 1 (8-ounce) package cream cheese, softened
- 4 garlic cloves, minced
- ½ teaspoon salt
- ¼ teaspoon pepper
- ½ to ¾ cup Garden Pesto
- Garnishes: fresh basil sprigs, pecans, pine nuts
- French baguette slices

PROCESS first 5 ingredients in a blender or food processor until smooth, stopping to scrape down sides. Line a 2- or 3-cup glass bowl with plastic wrap, allowing 3 inches to hang over sides.

SPREAD half of cheese mixture into bowl; top with ½ to ¾ cup Garden Pesto. Top with remaining cheese mixture. Cover and chill 8 hours. Invert chilled torta onto a serving platter; remove plastic wrap. Garnish, if desired. Serve with baguette slices. **MAKES** 6 to 8 servings.

Garden Pesto:

freezeable • make ahead

Prep: 10 min., Bake: 15 min., Cool: 5 min.

- ¼ cup chopped pecans
- ¼ cup pine nuts
- 2½ cups firmly packed fresh basil leaves
- ½ cup chopped fresh parsley
- 2 garlic cloves, chopped
- ⅔ cup olive oil, divided
- ¾ cup shredded Parmesan cheese

BAKE pecans and pine nuts in a shallow pan at 350° for 12 to 15 minutes or until toasted, stirring once. Let cool 5 minutes.
PROCESS basil, parsley, garlic, and ⅓ cup olive oil in a food processor until coarse paste forms. Add nuts and cheese, and process until blended, stopping to scrape down sides. With processor running, pour remaining ⅓ cup oil through food chute in a slow, steady stream; process until smooth. Cover and chill up to 5 days, or freeze up to 1 month, if desired. **MAKES** 1½ cups.

ANITA WILBANKS
CANTON, GEORGIA

SAFFRON BUTTERNUT SQUASH SOUP

Prep: 25 min., Cook: 45 min.

Only a small amount of saffron is needed to add a distinctive robust flavor and vibrant orange-red color to soups and sauces. If it isn't available, you'll still get great results.

- 1 large leek
- 4 tablespoons butter
- 1 pinch saffron threads
- 1 cup dry white wine
- 3 pounds butternut squash, peeled, seeded, and chopped
- 2 carrots, diced
- 1 (32-ounce) container chicken broth
- ⅛ teaspoon ground cinnamon
- ⅛ teaspoon ground nutmeg
- ⅛ teaspoon ground red pepper
- ¼ cup whipping cream
- ½ teaspoon salt
- ¼ teaspoon ground black pepper
- Garnish: crushed almond biscotti

CUT and discard green top from leek; cut white portion into slices.

MELT butter in a Dutch oven over medium heat; add leek slices and saffron, and sauté 5 minutes or until leek slices are tender. Add white wine, and cook 1 to 2 minutes. Add squash and next 5 ingredients, and bring to a boil. Reduce heat, and simmer, uncovered, 20 minutes or until squash and carrots are tender. Remove from heat, and let cool slightly.

PROCESS squash mixture, in batches, in a blender or food processor until smooth, stopping to scrape down sides. (A handheld immersion blender can also be used.)

RETURN squash mixture to Dutch oven. Add cream, salt, and pepper; simmer 10 to 15 minutes or until thickened. Garnish, if desired. MAKES 4 to 6 servings.

ROB MONDAVI
CANTON, GEORGIA

BARBECUED PORK QUESADILLAS

Prep: 20 min., Cook: 20 min.

For this recipe, use leftovers or pick up pork from your favorite barbecue joint. Be sure to ask for the sauce on the side.

- ½ pound shredded barbecued pork
- ½ cup barbecue sauce
- ¼ cup chopped fresh cilantro
- 5 green onions, minced
- 8 (6-inch) flour tortillas
- 1 cup shredded Mexican four-cheese blend
- 2 tablespoons butter or margarine, softened
- Toppings: sour cream, sliced green onions, barbecue sauce
- Garnish: fresh cilantro sprig

STIR together first 4 ingredients.

SPOON pork mixture evenly on half of each tortilla; sprinkle with cheese. Fold tortillas in half, pressing gently to seal. Spread butter on both sides of quesadillas.

HEAT a large nonstick or cast-iron skillet over medium heat, and cook quesadillas 2 to 3 minutes on each side or until browned. Cut each quesadilla in half for main-dish servings or in quarters for appetizer servings. Serve with desired toppings. Garnish, if desired. MAKES 4 to 6 main-dish or 8 to 12 appetizer servings.

ROB MONDAVI
CANTON, GEORGIA

KETTLE CORN

fast fixin's

Prep: 5 min., Cook: 3 min.

Rob and Lydia use a hand-cranked popper for this homemade version of the sweet-and-salty treat. If a hand-cranked popper isn't available, look for pre-packed Kettle Corn popcorn at your local grocery store.

- 1½ tablespoons vegetable oil
- ½ cup unpopped popcorn kernels
- ¼ cup sugar
- ½ teaspoon kosher salt

PLACE first 3 ingredients in a hand-cranked popcorn popper.

COOK popcorn kernel mixture over medium-high heat, rapidly turning hand crank. Once kernels begin to pop, reduce heat to low, and continue cranking until popping stops.

PLACE popcorn in a large bowl, and sprinkle with salt. MAKES 12 cups.

NOTE: For testing purposes only, we used a Whirley-Pop Popcorn Popper.

LYDIA MONDAVI
CANTON, GEORGIA

Smart Wine Pairings

"When it comes to wine, the only rule is to drink what you enjoy with the foods you enjoy," says Rob Mondavi. Here, he offers the following pairings ranging from budget friendly to those worth the splurge. All are widely available throughout the South. (Prices may vary.)

- **Goat Cheese Torta:** Danzante, Pinot Grigio ($10); Robert Mondavi Winery, Fumé Blanc ($18)
- **Saffron Butternut Squash Soup:** Woodbridge, Select Vineyard Series, Chardonnay ($10); Frescobaldi, Castello di Pomino, Benefizio ($27)
- **Barbecued Pork Quesadillas:** Danzante, Pinot Grigio ($10); Woodbridge, Select Vineyard Series, Zinfandel ($10); Robert Mondavi Winery, Zinfandel ($20)

Meat Loaf Sandwiches

Make a variety of meals from one dynamite recipe.

ALABAMA MEAT LOAF

freezeable • make ahead

Prep: 25 min., Bake: 1 hr., Stand: 10 min.

The hot sauce plays against the brown sugar, making this neither too hot nor too sweet. Smoked deli ham and ground pork add dimension to ground beef.

- 2 pounds lean ground beef
- 1 pound ground pork
- 1 large green bell pepper, minced (about ½ cup)
- 1 small onion, minced (about ½ cup)
- 2 large eggs, lightly beaten
- 4 cups soft breadcrumbs
- ¾ cup finely chopped smoked ham
- ⅓ cup ketchup
- ¼ cup firmly packed brown sugar
- ¼ cup maple syrup
- 3 tablespoons Worcestershire sauce
- 2 tablespoons hot sauce
- 1 (15-ounce) can tomato sauce
- 4 bacon slices

STIR together first 12 ingredients in a large bowl just until combined. Shape mixture into 2 (9- x 4-inch) loaves; place in an aluminum foil-lined broiler pan.
POUR half of tomato sauce evenly over each loaf, and arrange 2 bacon slices over each loaf.
BAKE at 350° for 1 hour. Let meat loaf stand 10 minutes before serving. **MAKES** 10 to 12 servings.

BELINDA SELF
HIGH POINT, NORTH CAROLINA

MINI ALABAMA MEAT LOAVES: Shape mixture into 12 (2- x 4-inch) loaves, and arrange on a rack in a foil-lined broiler pan. Bake 40 to 45 minutes.

TO MAKE AHEAD: Omit tomato sauce and bacon. Wrap unbaked meat loaf in plastic wrap and foil. Freeze up to 1 month. Thaw in refrigerator overnight, unwrap, and proceed as directed.

GRILLED CHEESE MEAT LOAF SANDWICHES

family favorite • fast fixin's

Prep: 10 min., Cook: 10 min.

- ¼ cup butter, melted
- 8 hearty white bread slices
- 12 American cheese slices
- 8 (½-inch-thick) cold meat loaf slices
- Garnish: sweet gherkin pickles

HEAT electric griddle to 350° or a nonstick skillet over medium-high heat.
BRUSH butter evenly on 1 side of each bread slice. Place 4 bread slices on griddle or in skillet, buttered side down. Top each with 1½ slices cheese, 2 meat loaf slices, and an additional 1½ slices cheese (total of 3 cheese slices on each sandwich). Top with remaining bread slices, buttered side up.
COOK 4 to 5 minutes on each side or until golden. Serve immediately. Garnish, if desired. **MAKES** 4 servings.

BARBECUE MEAT LOAF SANDWICHES

family favorite

Prep: 30 min., Cook: 10 min.

This hearty sandwich is almost a meal in itself. Cook extra onion rings to serve on the side.

- 1 (9.5-ounce) box frozen five-cheese Texas toast
- 1 (8-ounce) box frozen onion rings
- Vegetable cooking spray
- 6 (1-inch-thick) cold meat loaf slices
- ½ cup barbecue sauce
- 1 cup prepared coleslaw

PREPARE Texas toast according to package directions.
PREPARE onion rings according to package directions.
SPRAY a large nonstick skillet with cooking spray, and heat over medium-high heat. Add meat loaf slices, and cook 5 minutes. Turn, brush evenly with barbecue sauce, and cook 5 more minutes or until thoroughly heated.
TOP each slice of toast evenly with meat loaf slices, coleslaw, and onion rings. Serve sandwiches immediately. **MAKES** 6 sandwiches.

NOTE: For testing purposes only, we used Pepperidge Farm Five Cheese Texas Toast and Ore-Ida Vidalia O's.

Make It Great

- Mince (very finely chop) the bell pepper and onion. Large pieces cause the meat loaf to break apart.
- Don't take a shortcut and substitute dry breadcrumbs for soft, or the loaf will be dry. To make soft breadcrumbs, pulse about 8 slices of white sandwich bread in a food processor until finely crumbled (yields 4 cups).
- For the least shrinkage and nice slices, we tested with lean ground beef that was specifically labeled 93% lean and 7% fat.

Apricot-Almond Coffee Cake, page 193

Turkey Scaloppine, page 321

Zucchini With Citrus-Herb
Dressing, page 182

Broiled Parmesan
Tomatoes, page 322

191

No-Cook Fig-Mint Ice Cream, page 179

192

Easiest Coffee Cakes

Use a pound cake mix to stir together these breakfast treats in minutes.

Celebrate a leisurely Sunday morning or a day playing hooky with a luscious, uncomplicated coffee cake. You can bake one and still have plenty of time to enjoy the day. So sit, relax, and savor every last crumb of the easiest coffee cakes ever.

APRICOT-ALMOND COFFEE CAKE

Prep: 25 min., Bake: 28 min., Cool: 20 min.

A swirl of tart apricot preserves and a sprinkle of almonds add flavor and crunch to this delicious coffee cake. *(pictured on page 189)*

- **4 ounces cream cheese, softened**
- **½ cup apricot preserves**
- **1 (16-ounce) package pound cake mix, divided**
- **Pinch of orange food coloring powder (optional)**
- **1 (8-ounce) container sour cream**
- **½ cup milk**
- **2 large eggs**
- **½ teaspoon almond extract**
- **½ cup sliced almonds**
- **Glaze**

BEAT cream cheese, preserves, 1 tablespoon cake mix, and, if desired, food coloring powder just until blended; set mixture aside.
BEAT sour cream, milk, eggs, almond extract, and remaining cake mix at low speed with an electric mixer 30 seconds or until blended. Increase speed to medium, and beat 3 more minutes.
POUR into a lightly greased 13- x 9-inch pan. Drop cream cheese mixture by rounded teaspoonfuls evenly over batter.

Swirl batter gently with a knife. Sprinkle almonds evenly over top.
BAKE at 350° for 25 to 28 minutes or until golden.
COOL on a wire rack 20 minutes. Drizzle Glaze over slightly warm cake or individual pieces. **MAKES** 15 servings.

NOTE: For testing purposes only, we used Candy-n-Cake Powdered Food Color #5531 Orange.

Glaze:
fast fixin's
Prep: 5 min.

- **1 cup powdered sugar**
- **½ teaspoon vanilla extract**
- **1 to 2 tablespoons milk**

STIR together powdered sugar, vanilla, and 1 tablespoon milk until smooth. Add additional milk, if needed. **MAKES** ⅓ cup.

HEAVEN CAKE

Prep: 20 min., Bake: 35 min., Broil: 1 min.

- **1 (16-ounce) package pound cake mix**
- **1 cup whipping cream**
- **2 large eggs**
- **2 cups sliced almonds**
- **½ cup cold butter, cut into 1-inch pieces and softened**
- **1 cup sugar**
- **5 tablespoons all-purpose flour**
- **6 tablespoons whipping cream**

BEAT first 3 ingredients at low speed with an electric mixer 30 seconds. Increase speed to medium, and beat 3 more minutes. Pour into a lightly greased 13- x 9-inch pan.
BAKE at 350° for 25 minutes.
PROCESS almonds and next 4 ingredients in a food processor until almonds are finely chopped and mixture is creamy, stopping to scrape down sides.
REMOVE cake from oven. Drop almond mixture by rounded teaspoonfuls evenly over warm cake.
BAKE 10 more minutes or until almond mixture is bubbly. Remove from oven; spread almond mixture evenly over cake.
BROIL cake 4 inches from heat 1 minute or until top is lightly browned (edges of cake may get dark). Cool on a wire rack. **MAKES** 15 servings.

BEATE RUFFIN
ALEXANDRIA, VIRGINIA

" Cook's Notes "

"When I was in Germany last fall, I tasted a wonderful cake—not too sweet, with a dense texture and crunchy topping. It was absolutely yummy with a cup of hot tea on a chilly day. I asked around and found that it was called, appropriately enough, Himmelkuchen or Heaven Cake. After more digging, I found a reader with a recipe. With her permission, we transformed it into one that uses a pound cake mix, with terrific results—it received our highest rating."

Donna Florio
Senior Writer

CHOCOLATE CHIP COFFEE CAKE

Prep: 25 min., Bake: 25 min.

- 1 cup semisweet chocolate
  morsels
- 1 (16-ounce) package pound cake
  mix, divided
- 1 (8-ounce) container sour cream
- ½ cup milk
- 2 large eggs
- Streusel Topping

STIR together chocolate morsels and 1 tablespoon cake mix; set aside.

BEAT sour cream, milk, eggs, and remaining cake mix at low speed with an electric mixer 30 seconds or until blended. Increase speed to medium, and beat 3 more minutes.

SPOON half of batter into a lightly greased 13- x 9-inch pan; sprinkle morsel mixture evenly over batter. Spread remaining batter on top. Sprinkle Streusel Topping evenly over batter.

BAKE at 350° for 25 minutes or until a wooden pick inserted in center of cake comes out clean. Cool on a wire rack.

MAKES 15 servings.

Streusel Topping:

fast fixin's

Prep: 10 min.

- ½ cup firmly packed brown sugar
- 2 tablespoons all-purpose flour
- 1½ teaspoons ground cinnamon
- 1 cup chopped pecans, toasted
- 2 tablespoons melted butter or
  margarine

COMBINE first 3 ingredients; stir in pecans and butter until crumbly. **MAKES** 1½ cups.

BANANA-SOUR CREAM COFFEE CAKE: Prepare batter as directed, reducing sour cream to ½ cup and adding 1 cup mashed ripe banana. Sprinkle 1 cup toffee bits evenly over top of batter; sprinkle with Streusel Topping, and bake 30 minutes. Prep: 25 min., Bake: 30 min.

Let's Do Italian

With a few time-saving convenience products, this menu is a cinch.

Festive Italian Menu

Serves 6

Tapenade

Spicy Vegetables With Penne Pasta

Mixed gourmet greens with vinaigrette

Italian bread

Tiramisù Toffee Trifle Pie

Merlot

No doubt about it—folks are crazy for the hearty flavors of Italian food. So, if you're looking for a meal high on taste and low on difficulty, then look no further than these recipes. An assortment of fresh vegetables makes Spicy Vegetables With Penne Pasta a truly flavorful dish; a purchased pasta sauce cuts prep time to 30 minutes. End with Tiramisù Toffee Trifle Pie to complete your own taste of Italy at home.

TAPENADE

fast fixin's

Prep: 10 min.

Garnish this classic spread with lemon slices and chopped parsley. It's also great with grilled fish.

- 1 (6-ounce) jar pitted kalamata
  olives, drained
- 1 anchovy fillet, rinsed
- 2 garlic cloves, chopped
- 1 small shallot, chopped
- 1 teaspoon capers, drained
- 1 tablespoon olive oil
- 1 tablespoon lemon juice
- 1 tablespoon chopped fresh parsley
- Assorted crackers (optional)
- Fresh raw vegetables (optional)

PULSE first 5 ingredients in a food processor 4 or 5 times or until finely chopped. Stir in olive oil and lemon juice until blended; stir in parsley. Serve with crackers and vegetables, if desired.

MAKES 1 cup.

Spicy Vegetables With Penne Pasta

Prep: 30 min., Stand: 30 min., Cook: 15 min.

Pasta sauce from a jar adds a bit of heat to this dish. Tone it down by choosing a less spicy sauce.

- ½ cup dried tomatoes
- ½ cup boiling water
- 12 ounces uncooked penne pasta
- 2 medium-size sweet onions, chopped
- 2 small zucchini, chopped
- 1 medium-size green bell pepper, chopped
- 1 medium-size red bell pepper, chopped
- 1 cup sliced fresh mushrooms
- 2 garlic cloves, minced
- 2 tablespoons olive oil
- 1 (26-ounce) jar hot-and-spicy pasta sauce
- ½ cup chopped fresh basil
- ½ teaspoon salt

STIR together dried tomatoes and ½ cup boiling water in a bowl; let stand 30 minutes. Drain, chop, and set aside.

PREPARE pasta according to package directions; drain and set aside.

SAUTÉ onions and next 5 ingredients in hot olive oil in a large skillet over medium-high heat 6 to 8 minutes or until vegetables are tender. Stir in chopped tomatoes.

STIR in pasta sauce, and bring to a boil. Reduce heat to medium; stir in basil and salt, and simmer, stirring occasionally, 5 minutes. Serve over hot cooked pasta. **MAKES** 6 servings.

NOTE: For testing purposes only, we used Newman's Own Fra Diavolo Sauce for hot-and-spicy pasta sauce.

Tiramisù Toffee Trifle Pie

make ahead

Prep: 30 min., Chill: 8 hrs.

- 1½ tablespoons instant coffee granules
- ¾ cup warm water
- 1 (10.75-ounce) frozen pound cake, thawed
- 1 (8-ounce) package cream cheese or mascarpone, softened
- ½ cup powdered sugar
- ½ cup chocolate syrup
- 1 (12-ounce) container frozen whipped topping, thawed and divided
- 2 (1.4-ounce) English toffee candy bars, coarsely chopped

STIR together coffee granules and ¾ cup warm water until granules are dissolved. Cool.

CUT pound cake into 14 slices. Cut each cake slice in half diagonally. Place triangles on bottom and up sides of a 9-inch deep-dish pieplate. Drizzle coffee over cake.

BEAT cream cheese, sugar, and chocolate syrup at medium speed with an electric mixer until smooth. Add 2½ cups whipped topping, and beat until light and fluffy.

SPREAD cheese mixture evenly over cake. Dollop remaining whipped topping around edges of pie. Sprinkle with chopped candy. Chill 8 hours. **MAKES** 8 to 10 servings.

NOTE: Tiramisù Toffee Trifle Pie can be made the day before serving. Store in the refrigerator.

LINDA MORTEN
KATY, TEXAS

Fast Chicken and Rice

Chicken and rice always makes a warm and inviting meal. These recipes are terrific with plain rice, but even better when paired with seasoned rice mixes (see "From Our Kitchen" on page 204).

Maple-Balsamic Chicken

family favorite

Prep: 10 min., Cook: 25 min.

Serve with Saffron Rice Pilaf (see recipe on page 204).

- 8 skinned and boned chicken thighs
- ¾ teaspoon salt
- ¾ teaspoon paprika
- ¾ teaspoon dried thyme
- 1 tablespoon olive oil
- 1 (14½-ounce) can chicken broth
- ⅓ cup maple syrup
- ⅓ cup balsamic vinegar
- ½ teaspoon freshly ground black pepper
- ¼ teaspoon ground red pepper
- 3 tablespoons chunky peanut butter

SPRINKLE chicken evenly with salt, paprika, and thyme.

COOK chicken in hot oil in a large nonstick skillet over medium-high heat 2 minutes on each side or until golden brown. Stir in chicken broth and next 4 ingredients, and bring to a boil. Cover, reduce heat to low, and simmer 15 minutes. Remove chicken to a serving platter, and keep warm. Reserve liquid in skillet.

WHISK peanut butter into reserved liquid, and boil over medium-high heat, uncovered, 5 minutes or until sauce is thickened; spoon sauce evenly over chicken. **MAKES** 4 servings.

JIM PLEASANTS
WILLIAMSBURG, VIRGINIA

GRILLED SOUTHWESTERN CHICKEN WITH PINEAPPLE SALSA

family favorite • fast fixin's

Prep: 10 min., Grill: 8 min.

Serve with yellow rice garnished with chopped fresh cilantro. This dish is ready for the table in less than 20 minutes.

- **4 skinned and boned chicken breasts**
- **2 tablespoons olive oil**
- **1 tablespoon chili powder**
- **2 teaspoons garlic salt**
- **2 teaspoons paprika**
- **Pineapple Salsa**
- **Garnish: lime slices**

PLACE chicken between 2 sheets of heavy-duty plastic wrap; flatten to ½-inch thickness using a meat mallet or rolling pin.
RUB chicken evenly with olive oil, and sprinkle evenly with chili powder, garlic salt, and paprika.
GRILL chicken, covered with grill lid, over medium-high heat (350° to 400°) 4 minutes on each side or until done. Serve with Pineapple Salsa. Garnish, if desired. **MAKES** 4 servings.

Pineapple Salsa:

fast fixin's

Prep: 10 min., Cook: 4 min.

- **¼ cup diced red bell pepper**
- **3 tablespoons light brown sugar**
- **2 tablespoons chopped fresh cilantro**
- **2 tablespoons orange juice**
- **2 tablespoons fresh lime juice**
- **1 tablespoon chopped chipotle pepper in adobo sauce**
- **1 tablespoon butter or margarine**
- **1 (15-ounce) can sliced pineapple, drained**

STIR together first 6 ingredients.
MELT butter in a large nonstick skillet over medium-high heat; add pineapple slices, and cook 2 minutes on each side or until golden brown. Coarsely chop pineapple, and combine with red bell pepper mixture. **MAKES** 2 cups.

ROBIN ANDREWS
MORRISTOWN, TENNESSEE

CHICKEN DIJON

family favorite • fast fixin's

Prep: 5 min., Cook: 25 min.

Serve with Cranberry-Almond Wild Rice (see recipe on page 204).

- **3 tablespoons butter**
- **6 skinned and boned chicken breasts**
- **1 (14½-ounce) can chicken broth**
- **1 medium-size sweet onion, diced**
- **3 tablespoons all-purpose flour**
- **3 tablespoons Dijon mustard**

MELT butter in a large skillet over medium-high heat; add chicken, and cook 2 minutes on each side or until golden brown. Whisk together broth and remaining 3 ingredients; pour over chicken. Cover, reduce heat to low, and simmer 20 minutes. **MAKES** 6 servings.

FRANCES MATTHEWS
BIRMINGHAM, ALABAMA

Quick & Easy
Snacks Start a Party

Wow everybody at a moment's notice with easy, portable appetizers. Spicy Pistachios and Caribbean Cashews are a good snack for those counting their carbs, and your guests will like having a choice of sandwiches.

CARIBBEAN CASHEWS

fast fixin's • make ahead

Prep: 5 min., Bake: 23 min.

- **1½ teaspoons butter or margarine**
- **2 cups lightly salted whole cashews**
- **2 teaspoons grated orange rind**
- **2 teaspoons Caribbean Jerk Seasoning**

PREHEAT oven to 350°. Heat butter in an 8-inch cakepan in oven for 2 to 3 minutes or until melted; stir in nuts and remaining ingredients, tossing to coat.
BAKE at 350° for 20 minutes, stirring occasionally.
ARRANGE cashews in a single layer on wax paper, and let cool. Store in an airtight container. **MAKES** 2 cups.

BACON-OLIVE PARTY SANDWICHES

fast fixin's • make ahead

Prep: 10 min.

One basic recipe makes both these sandwiches.

- **16 white bread slices**
- **Bacon-Olive Cream Cheese**

REMOVE and discard crusts from bread; toast bread.
SPREAD 1 side of 8 bread slices evenly with Bacon-Olive Cream Cheese, and top with remaining 8 bread slices; cut evenly into 3 strips. **MAKES** 2 dozen.

MINI MUFFULETTA BACON-OLIVE PARTY SANDWICHES: Layer bottom of 24 split cocktail bun or dinner roll halves evenly with Bacon-Olive Cream Cheese and 48 pepperoni slices; cover with bun halves. **MAKES** 12 appetizer servings. Prep: 15 min.

Bacon-Olive Cream Cheese:

fast fixin's

Prep: 15 min.

- **1 (8-ounce) package cream cheese, softened**
- **8 bacon slices, cooked and crumbled**
- **24 pimiento-stuffed olives, chopped**
- **4 tablespoons chopped fresh chives**
- **¼ teaspoon pepper**

COMBINE all ingredients. **MAKES** about 1½ cups.

TO MAKE AHEAD: Cover and chill up to 3 days. For easier spreading, let stand 30 minutes or until softened.

QUICK PARTY NUTS

make ahead

Prep: 10 min., Stand: 10 min., Bake: 35 min.

- **2 cups pecan halves**
- **2 cups whole almonds**
- **1½ cups sugar, divided**
- **4 cups warm water**
- **¼ cup butter or margarine, melted**
- **2 tablespoons chili powder**
- **2 teaspoons grated lime rind**
- **½ teaspoon salt**
- **½ teaspoon ground cumin**
- **½ teaspoon ground red pepper**

PLACE pecans and almonds in a large bowl; stir in 1 cup sugar and 4 cups warm water. Let stand 10 minutes. Drain well; return to bowl. Pour butter over nuts, stirring to coat.

STIR together remaining ½ cup sugar, chili powder, and next 4 ingredients; pour over nut mixture, tossing to coat. Spread mixture in a single layer on a 15- x 10-inch jellyroll pan.

BAKE at 350° for 30 to 35 minutes, stirring occasionally. Arrange in a single layer on wax paper, and let cool. Store in an airtight container. **MAKES** 4 cups.

SUGAR-AND-SPICE PEANUTS

make ahead

Prep: 5 min., Cook: 12 min., Bake: 30 min.

- **¾ cup sugar**
- **½ cup water**
- **2 cups shelled raw peanuts**
- **1 teaspoon pumpkin pie spice**

COOK sugar and ½ cup water in a small saucepan over medium heat, stirring occasionally, until sugar dissolves. Stir in peanuts, and cook 10 minutes or until sugar starts to crystallize on peanuts. Sprinkle pumpkin pie spice evenly over peanuts, stirring to coat. Spread in a single layer on a lightly greased baking sheet.

BAKE at 300° for 30 minutes, stirring every 10 minutes. Cool on baking sheet. Store in an airtight container. **MAKES** 2 cups.

LISA U. SMITH
RICHMOND, VIRGINIA

SPICY PISTACHIOS

fast fixin's • make ahead

Prep: 5 min., Bake: 25 min.

This snack is a homemade version of the spicy pistachios available in pricey food catalogs.

- **¼ cup Worcestershire sauce**
- **3 tablespoons butter or margarine, melted**
- **1 teaspoon ground chipotle chile pepper**
- **½ teaspoon garlic powder**
- **½ teaspoon ground cinnamon**
- **4 cups shelled dry-roasted pistachios (about 8 cups unshelled)**

STIR together first 5 ingredients; add pistachios, tossing to coat. Arrange pistachios in a single layer on a lightly greased 15- x 10-inch jellyroll pan.

BAKE at 350° for 20 to 25 minutes, stirring after 10 minutes. Arrange in a single layer on wax paper; let cool. Store in an airtight container. **MAKES** 4 cups.

NOTE: For testing purposes only, we used McCormick Gourmet Collection Chipotle Chile Pepper.

DEBORAH STONE
PALM HARBOR, FLORIDA

Terrific Tailgate Food

These recipes are great recruits for your menu. "If you want wider eyes and bigger smiles from fellow fans, include easy-to-fix homemade foods," says Nina Swan-Kohler, a native Missourian and a pro at football food. Thanks to Nina and reader Kate Blood (she sent us the recipe for deviled eggs), you'll have a powerful team of winning recipes. Nina's selections come from her book, *Tailgates to Touchdowns: Fabulous Football Food,* (Willing Vessel Books, 2003), available at **www.footballfood.net.**

HONEY BARBECUE CHICKEN

family favorite

Prep: 5 min.; Grill: 1 hr., 10 min.

The delicious Honey Barbecue Sauce can be made up to a week in advance.

- **Vegetable cooking spray**
- **6 bone-in chicken breasts**
- **8 chicken drumsticks**
- **Honey Barbecue Sauce**

COAT food grate with cooking spray; place on grill over medium-high heat (350° to 400°). Place chicken on grate, and grill, covered with grill lid, 5 to 10 minutes on each side. Reduce heat to low (under 300°); grill, covered, 40 to 50 minutes for breasts and 30 to 40 minutes or until done for drumsticks. Brush with 1 cup Honey Barbecue Sauce during last 10 minutes of grilling. Serve chicken with remaining 1 cup sauce. **MAKES** 8 to 10 servings.

Honey Barbecue Sauce:

fast fixin's • make ahead

Prep: 15 min., Cook: 12 min.

- **¼ cup butter or margarine**
- **1 medium onion, diced (about 1 cup)**
- **1 cup ketchup**
- **⅓ cup water**
- **¼ cup honey**
- **2 tablespoons lemon juice**
- **1 tablespoon Worcestershire sauce**
- **¼ teaspoon ground black pepper**

MELT butter in a small saucepan over medium heat; add onion, and sauté 4 to 5 minutes or until tender. Stir in ketchup and remaining ingredients; bring to a boil. Reduce heat, and simmer, uncovered, 5 minutes. Store leftover sauce in refrigerator up to 1 week. **MAKES** about 2 cups.

SPICY-SWEET DEVILED EGGS

fast fixin's • make ahead

Prep: 30 min.

    1 dozen hard-cooked eggs, peeled
    ½ cup mayonnaise
    3 tablespoons mango chutney
    ⅛ teaspoon ground red pepper
    Kosher salt to taste
    Garnish: sliced fresh chives

CUT eggs in half lengthwise; carefully remove yolks. Mash yolks; stir in mayonnaise, chutney, and red pepper until blended. Spoon yolk mixture evenly into egg white halves. Sprinkle with desired amount of salt. Garnish, if desired. Chill eggs until ready to serve. **MAKES** 10 to 12 servings.

KATE BLOOD
SAN JOSE, CALIFORNIA

CREAMY DIJON MUSTARD SAUCE

fast fixin's

Prep: 5 min.

It's so simple yet so great with take-out fried chicken strips, hamburgers, grilled bratwurst sandwiches, or fresh vegetable dippers.

STIR together ½ cup mayonnaise, ½ cup sour cream, 4 teaspoons Dijon mustard, and 3 tablespoons finely chopped green onions. Cover and chill. Garnish with finely chopped green onions, if desired. **MAKES** about 1 cup.

Easy, Fun Hot Dog Bar

Plan an inexpensive party with our update on an old-fashioned wienie roast.

Tasty Tailgate

Serves 8

Marrow's Famous Dogs

Hot Dog Chili

Sweet-and-Tangy Slaw

Southern-Style Potato Salad

Purchased cookies and brownies

Test Kitchens Professional Rebecca Kracke Gordon and her husband, Marrow, enjoy gathering with friends, especially during football season. One of their favorite things to do is to create a build-your-own grilled hot dog bar with budget-friendly, make-ahead recipes. Grilling is the secret to these sought-after hot dogs. The Gordons throw on a package of franks every time they fire up the grill. (Simply reheat leftovers in the microwave at HIGH for 30 seconds to 1 minute per dog.) By keeping the menu simple and filling in with store-bought chips and dessert, the Gordons can relax with friends and catch all of the game too.

MARROW'S FAMOUS DOGS

fast fixin's

Prep: 5 min., Grill: 10 min.

    2 (16-ounce) packages bun-length
        hot dogs
    2 tablespoons Worcestershire sauce
    ¼ teaspoon Creole seasoning
    Hot dog buns

DRIZZLE hot dogs with Worcestershire sauce; sprinkle with Cajun seasoning.
GRILL, covered with grill lid, over medium-high heat (350° to 400°) 3 to 5 minutes per side. Serve in buns.
MAKES 10 to 12 servings.

NOTE: For testing purposes only, we used Oscar Mayer Bun-Length Wieners and Tony Chachere's Original Creole Seasoning.

MARROW GORDON
HOMEWOOD, ALABAMA

Hot Dog Chili

Prep: 10 min., Cook: 1 hr.

- **2 pounds lean ground beef**
- **1 small onion, finely chopped**
- **1 teaspoon vegetable oil**
- **1 teaspoon salt**
- **4 teaspoons chili powder**
- **2¼ cups water**
- **1 cup ketchup**
- **4 teaspoons Worcestershire sauce**
- **1 teaspoon white vinegar**
- **½ teaspoon dry mustard**
- **¼ to ½ teaspoon pepper**

COOK ground beef in a Dutch oven over medium-high heat, stirring until beef crumbles and is no longer pink; drain well. Wipe Dutch oven clean with a paper towel.

SAUTÉ onion in hot oil in Dutch oven 5 minutes. Add salt, chili powder, and beef, and cook 3 to 5 minutes. Stir in 2¼ cups water and next 5 ingredients. Bring to a boil; reduce heat to low, and simmer, stirring occasionally, 45 minutes or until most of the liquid evaporates. **MAKES** 5 cups.

CARRIE TREICHEL
JOHNSON CITY, INDIANA

Sweet-and-Tangy Slaw

fast fixin's • make ahead

Prep: 5 min., Chill: 20 min.

This slaw is terrific as a side dish or on a hot dog. It makes a great addition to your hot dog bar because you can whip it up in a matter of minutes—and make it ahead.

- **1 cup mayonnaise**
- **2 tablespoons brown sugar**
- **2 tablespoons lemon juice**
- **2 tablespoons white vinegar**
- **1 tablespoon light corn syrup**
- **½ teaspoon red wine vinegar**
- **¼ teaspoon salt**
- **¼ teaspoon pepper**
- **2 (16-ounce) packages coleslaw mix**
- **Freshly ground black pepper (optional)**

WHISK together first 8 ingredients in a large bowl. Add coleslaw mix, tossing to coat. Sprinkle coleslaw with pepper, if desired. Cover coleslaw and chill 20 minutes or until ready to serve. **MAKES** 8 servings.

JULIETTE BENDER
TAMPA, FLORIDA

Southern-Style Potato Salad

make ahead

Prep: 25 min., Cook: 40 min.

You can substitute light mayonnaise and sour cream with good results.

- **4 pounds potatoes (about 4 large)**
- **3 hard-cooked eggs, grated**
- **1 cup mayonnaise**
- **½ cup sour cream**
- **¼ cup finely chopped celery**
- **2 tablespoons finely chopped onion**
- **2 tablespoons sweet pickle relish**
- **1 tablespoon mustard**
- **1 teaspoon salt**
- **½ teaspoon freshly ground pepper**
- **½ pound bacon, cooked and crumbled**
- **Garnishes: chopped fresh parsley, grape tomato halves**

COOK potatoes in boiling water to cover 40 minutes or until tender; drain and cool. Peel potatoes, and cut into 1-inch cubes.

STIR together potatoes and eggs.

STIR together mayonnaise and next 7 ingredients; gently stir into potato mixture. Cover and chill. Sprinkle with bacon just before serving. Garnish, if desired. **MAKES** 8 servings.

MARCIA WALKER
TOCCOA, GEORGIA

Taste-Testing Hot Dogs

After our staff tasted many hot dog brands, they offer these tips.

■ Some brands were considerably juicier than others due to extra fat. Use nutritional information on the package to guide you.

■ Cheaper is cheaper. Although we found it wasn't necessary to buy the most expensive brand, hot dogs are affordable compared to other grilling meats, so go ahead and spend an extra 50 cents per package.

■ Our top dogs were the Oscar Mayer Bun-Length Wieners (made with pork and turkey).

Muffin-Crust Cobblers

Cook up a sweet Southern favorite everyone will love.

September brings an abundance of fruit for cobbler. In keeping with the cooler days ahead, we've replaced the thinly rolled piecrust of more conventional cobblers with rich stir-and-bake muffin batters.

The secret to these cakelike cobblers is in the timing: Spooning the muffin batter over a piping-hot filling ensures the underside of the crust cooks as quickly and evenly as the top. To speed this procedure, measure the ingredients for the muffin batter before preparing the fruit filling. It will take only a minute to stir it together before the filling cools.

While fresh is best, we've also come up with options using frozen fruit and canned pie filling. After each cobbler recipe, you'll find the reader's original directions for baking their top-rated muffins.

NECTARINE COBBLER WITH BLUEBERRY MUFFIN CRUST

family favorite

Prep: 30 min., Cook: 5 min., Bake: 25 min.

- **4 pounds nectarines, peeled and sliced***
- **¾ cup sugar**
- **2 tablespoons all-purpose flour**
- **¼ cup butter**
- **Blueberry Muffin Batter**
- **Vanilla ice cream**

TOSS together first 3 ingredients in a large bowl.
MELT butter in a large skillet over medium-high heat. Add nectarine mixture to skillet; bring to a boil, and cook, stirring often, 5 minutes. Spoon hot nectarine mixture into a lightly greased 13- x 9-inch baking dish. Spoon Blueberry Muffin Batter evenly over hot nectarine mixture.
BAKE at 400° for 25 minutes or until crust is golden brown. Serve with vanilla ice cream. **MAKES** 8 servings.

*Substitute 3 (21-ounce) cans peach pie filling for nectarines, if desired. Omit sugar and flour. Melt butter in a large skillet over medium-high heat. Add peach pie filling, and bring to a boil; remove from heat. Proceed with recipe as directed.

Blueberry Muffin Batter:

fast fixin's

Prep: 10 min.

- **2 cups all-purpose flour**
- **¼ cup sugar**
- **1 tablespoon baking powder**
- **½ teaspoon salt**
- **1 cup milk**
- **¼ cup vegetable oil**
- **1 large egg, lightly beaten**
- **1 cup fresh or frozen blueberries**

COMBINE first 4 ingredients in a large bowl; make a well in center. Stir together milk, vegetable oil, and egg; add to dry ingredients, and stir just until moistened. Gently fold in blueberries. **MAKES** about 4 cups.

BLUEBERRY MUFFINS: Spoon Blueberry Muffin Batter evenly into lightly greased muffin pans, filling two-thirds full. Bake at 400° for 20 to 25 minutes. **MAKES** 12 muffins.

BETH CRAWFORD
KNOXVILLE, TENNESSEE

APPLE-PECAN PIE COBBLER

family favorite

Prep: 20 min., Cook: 10 min., Bake: 20 min.

This recipe also can be baked for the same amount of time in a shallow 2-quart baking dish.

- **6 large Granny Smith apples, peeled and sliced (about 3 pounds)***
- **½ cup firmly packed light brown sugar**
- **2 tablespoons all-purpose flour**
- **¼ cup butter**
- **½ cup dark corn syrup**
- **Pecan Pie Muffin Batter**

TOSS together first 3 ingredients in a large bowl.
MELT butter in a large skillet over medium-high heat. Add apple mixture and corn syrup to skillet; bring to a boil, and cook, stirring often, 10 minutes.
SPOON hot apple mixture evenly into 6 lightly greased 6-ounce ovenproof ramekins or custard cups. Spoon Pecan Pie Muffin Batter evenly over hot apple mixture.
BAKE at 425° for 15 to 20 minutes or until golden brown. **MAKES** 6 servings.

*Substitute 3 (12-ounce) packages frozen, cooked apples, thawed (such as Stouffer's Harvest Apples), for Granny Smith apples, if desired. Proceed with recipe as directed.

Pecan Pie Muffin Batter:

fast fixin's

Prep: 10 min.

- **1 cup firmly packed light brown sugar**
- **1 cup chopped pecans**
- **½ cup all-purpose flour**
- **½ teaspoon baking powder**
- **¼ teaspoon salt**
- **½ cup butter, melted**
- **2 large eggs, lightly beaten**
- **1 teaspoon vanilla extract**

COMBINE first 5 ingredients in a large bowl; make a well in center of mixture. Stir together butter, eggs, and vanilla; add to dry ingredients, and stir just until moistened. **MAKES** about 2 cups.

PECAN PIE MUFFINS: Spoon Pecan Pie Muffin Batter evenly into lightly greased miniature muffin pans, filling three-fourths full. Bake at 425° for 8 to 10 minutes. **MAKES** 24 muffins.

PATTI EASON
MEMPHIS, TENNESSEE

PLUM COBBLER WITH SPICED PLUM MUFFIN CRUST

family favorite

Prep: 30 min., Cook: 5 min., Bake: 25 min.

- **3 pounds plums, sliced**
- **¾ cup sugar**
- **2 tablespoons all-purpose flour**
- **¼ cup butter**
- **Spiced Plum Muffin Batter**

TOSS together first 3 ingredients.
MELT butter in a large skillet over medium-high heat. Add plum mixture to skillet; bring to a boil, and cook, stirring often, 5 minutes. Spoon hot plum mixture into a lightly greased, shallow 2-quart baking dish. Spoon Spiced Plum Muffin Batter evenly over hot plum mixture.
BAKE at 400° for 25 minutes or until golden brown. **MAKES** 8 servings.

Spiced Plum Muffin Batter:

fast fixin's

Prep: 10 min.

- **1 cup self-rising flour**
- **1 cup sugar**
- **½ cup chopped pecans, toasted**
- **½ teaspoon ground allspice**
- **½ cup vegetable oil**
- **2 large eggs, lightly beaten**
- **1 (3.5-ounce) container plum baby food**

COMBINE first 4 ingredients in a large bowl; make a well in center of mixture. Stir together oil, eggs, and baby food; add to dry ingredients, and stir just until moistened. **MAKES** about 3 cups.

SPICED PLUM MUFFINS: Spoon Spiced Plum Muffin Batter evenly into lightly greased muffin pans, filling two-thirds full. Bake at 400° for 15 to 20 minutes. **MAKES** 12 muffins.

MARQUITA MATHIS
IUKA, MISSISSIPPI

CARAMEL APPLE-PEAR COBBLER WITH OATMEAL MUFFIN CRUST

family favorite

Prep: 30 min., Cook: 15 min., Bake: 25 min.

- **3 large Granny Smith apples, peeled and sliced (about 1½ pounds)***
- **1 cup firmly packed light brown sugar**
- **2 tablespoons all-purpose flour**
- **¼ cup butter**
- **3 large pears, peeled and sliced (about 1½ pounds)**
- **Oatmeal Muffin Batter**
- **Garnish: toasted pecan halves**

COMBINE first 3 ingredients in a large bowl, stirring to coat apples.
MELT butter in a large skillet over medium-high heat. Add apple mixture; bring to a boil, and cook, stirring often, 10 minutes. Add pears to skillet, and cook, stirring often, 5 minutes. Spoon hot fruit mixture into a lightly greased 10-inch (8-cup) deep-dish pieplate or shallow 2-quart baking dish. Spoon Oatmeal Muffin Batter evenly over fruit mixture.
BAKE at 425° for 20 to 25 minutes or until crust is golden brown. Garnish, if desired. **MAKES** 6 to 8 servings.

*****Substitute 2 (21-ounce) cans apple pie filling for apples and pears, if desired.

Omit brown sugar and flour. Melt butter in a large skillet over medium-high heat. Add pie filling, and bring to a boil; remove from heat. Proceed with recipe as directed.

Oatmeal Muffin Batter:

fast fixin's

Prep: 10 min.

- **¾ cup all-purpose flour**
- **1 cup uncooked regular oats**
- **½ cup chopped dates**
- **¼ cup sugar**
- **1 tablespoon baking powder**
- **½ teaspoon salt**
- **¾ cup milk**
- **3 tablespoons butter, melted**
- **1 large egg, lightly beaten**

COMBINE first 6 ingredients in a large bowl; make a well in center of mixture. Stir together milk, melted butter, and beaten egg; add to dry ingredients, and stir just until moistened. **MAKES** about 2½ cups.

OATMEAL MUFFINS: Spoon Oatmeal Muffin Batter evenly into lightly greased muffin pans, filling two-thirds full. Bake at 425° for 15 minutes. **MAKES** 10 muffins.

KATRINA ROSS
MINT HILL, NORTH CAROLINA

❝ Cook's Notes ❞

- Use a wooden spoon or whisk, not an electric mixer, to prepare the muffin batter. Once you've combined the liquid and dry ingredients, stir just until blended—a few lumps are fine. Overmixing the batter results in a tough, rubbery crust.
- Choose apples and pears that remain flavorful and firm when cooked. McIntosh apples arrive early in September and, like Granny Smith and Rome apples, have a slightly tart flavor. If you prefer a sweeter taste, try Gala or Golden Delicious apples. Bartlett pears are sweeter than Bosc, but both will make a delicious cobbler.
- For the best flavor and texture, don't thaw frozen berries before cooking or adding to muffin batter.

Mary Allen Perry
Associate Foods Editor

Rich Without the Fat

Savor great-tasting, satisfying meals as you welcome the cool autumn weather.

Don't you miss the days when you sat down to dinner without a care about calories? In a way, you still can. After the last bite of these recipes, you'll leave the table gratified with no need to nibble in the evening.

BRAISED TUSCAN PORK LOIN

family favorite

Prep: 20 min., Stand: 25 min., Bake: 2 hrs.

- **1¼ teaspoons salt**
- **2 teaspoons pepper**
- **1 (4- to 5-pound) bone-in pork loin roast**
- **Vegetable cooking spray**
- **1 large sweet onion, coarsely chopped**
- **1 (28-ounce) can crushed tomatoes**
- **½ cup ketchup**
- **¼ cup balsamic vinegar**
- **2 tablespoons brown sugar**
- **2 (9-ounce) cans cannellini beans, rinsed and drained**

RUB salt and pepper evenly over roast; let stand at room temperature 15 minutes.
BROWN roast in an ovenproof Dutch oven coated with cooking spray over medium heat until browned on all sides. Remove roast, and set aside.
ADD onion to Dutch oven, and sauté 3 to 5 minutes. Return roast to Dutch oven. Stir together tomatoes, ketchup, vinegar, and brown sugar. Pour tomato mixture over roast.

BAKE, covered, at 350° for 1 hour. Stir in beans, and bake, covered, 45 more minutes. Stir beans and sauce; bake, uncovered, 15 more minutes or until a meat thermometer inserted into thickest portion of roast registers 160°. Remove from oven, and let stand 5 to 10 minutes before slicing. Slice roast evenly into 8 chops, and serve with beans and sauce. **MAKES** 8 servings.

MARY ANN LEE
NAPLES, FLORIDA

Per serving: Calories 347 (25% from fat); Fat 9.6g (sat 3.2g, mono 4.1g, poly 1.3g); Protein 38g; Carb 26g; Fiber 5g; Chol 94mg; Iron 3.7mg; Sodium 862mg; Calc 95.2mg

SWEET GLAZED CHICKEN THIGHS

fast fixin's • family favorite

Prep: 15 min., Cook: 15 min.

Serve this sweet-and-tangy dish with crisp-tender green beans, broccoli, or sugar snap peas, and chewy brown rice.

- **1 cup pineapple juice**
- **2 tablespoons brown sugar**
- **1 tablespoon lite soy sauce**
- **1 teaspoon cornstarch**
- **¾ teaspoon salt**
- **½ teaspoon pepper**
- **2 pounds skinned and boned chicken thighs**
- **3 tablespoons all-purpose flour**
- **1 tablespoon butter or margarine**
- **Vegetable cooking spray**

WHISK together first 4 ingredients until smooth; set aside.
SPRINKLE salt and pepper evenly over chicken. Dust evenly with flour.
MELT butter in a large nonstick skillet coated with cooking spray over medium-high heat. Cook chicken 5 to 6 minutes on each side. Remove chicken from pan, and keep warm. Add pineapple juice mixture to skillet, and cook, whisking constantly, 1 minute or until thickened and bubbly. Pour over chicken. **MAKES** 8 servings.

CHARLES EVERSON
CLERMONT, KENTUCKY

Per serving: Calories182 (29% from fat); Fat 5.9g (sat 2g, mono 1.8g, poly 1.1g); Protein 22.8g; Carb 7.9g; Fiber 0.2g; Chol 98mg; Iron 1.4mg; Sodium 407mg; Calc 18mg

CREAMY LAMB CURRY

family favorite

Prep: 20 min.; Cook: 1 hr., 15 min.

Serve this aromatic, full-flavored dish over basmati rice, a nutty-tasting long-grain variety. Look for garam masala, a fragrant spice mixture, in Indian markets or in the spice or ethnic sections of supermarkets. It's available in the McCormick Gourmet Collection, or you can find it online at **www.ethnicgrocer.com.** The wonderful flavor of this dish makes it worth the search.

- **2 pounds lean boneless lamb, cut into 2-inch pieces**
- **½ teaspoon salt**
- **Vegetable cooking spray**
- **1 medium onion, chopped (1 cup)**
- **1 (1-inch) piece fresh ginger, peeled and minced**
- **2 garlic cloves, minced**
- **2 teaspoons ground coriander**
- **1 teaspoon ground cumin**
- **⅛ teaspoon ground cloves**
- **2 bay leaves**
- **1 (1-inch) cinnamon stick**
- **2 cups fat-free reduced-sodium chicken broth**
- **1 (14.5-ounce) can diced tomatoes, undrained**
- **½ cup plain nonfat yogurt**
- **1 tablespoon garam masala**
- **8 fresh mint leaves, chopped**

SPRINKLE lamb pieces with salt.

COOK lamb, in batches, in a Dutch oven coated with cooking spray over medium-high heat 5 minutes, stirring often, or until lamb is lightly browned. Remove from pan, and set aside.

SAUTÉ onion and ginger in Dutch oven coated with cooking spray over medium-high heat 1 to 2 minutes. Add garlic; cook 1 minute. Stir in coriander and next 4 ingredients. Add cooked lamb, broth, and tomatoes; bring to a boil. Cover, reduce heat, and simmer 1 hour or until lamb is tender. Remove from heat; discard bay leaves. Add yogurt and garam masala, stirring until blended. Sprinkle with mint. **MAKES** 6 servings.

MARIET VAN DEN MUNCKOF-VEDDER
DUBLIN, GEORGIA

Per serving: Calories 257 (38% from fat); Fat 11g (sat 4.5g, mono 4g, poly 0.5g); Protein 29.6g; Carb 9.2g; Fiber 1.3g; Chol 100.5mg; Iron 2.4mg; Sodium 512mg; Calc 109mg

WILD MUSHROOM SOUP

Prep: 25 min., Cook: 50 min., Stand: 30 min.

Look for dried wild mushrooms in the produce section of large supermarkets. Fresh mushrooms shouldn't be substituted; they'll make the soup watery.

2 vegetable bouillon cubes
2 cups boiling water
¾ cup Madeira wine
4 cups fat-free reduced-sodium chicken broth, divided
1 (½-ounce) package dried porcini mushrooms, chopped
1 (½-ounce) package dried morel mushrooms, chopped
1 (½-ounce) package dried chanterelle mushrooms, chopped
2 tablespoons butter or margarine
6 green onions, sliced
1 medium onion, diced
3 tablespoons all-purpose flour
1 pound fresh white mushrooms, quartered
¼ teaspoon freshly ground pepper
Toppings: fat-free sour cream, chopped green onions
Garnish: green onions

DISSOLVE bouillon cubes in 2 cups boiling water. Set aside.

BRING wine, ½ cup chicken broth, and dried mushrooms to a boil in a small saucepan. Remove from heat, and let stand 30 minutes.

MELT butter in a Dutch oven over medium-high heat; add sliced green onions and diced onion. Sauté until tender.

STIR in flour, and cook, stirring constantly, 1 minute. Gradually stir in vegetable broth and remaining 3½ cups chicken broth. Stir in wild mushroom mixture, white mushrooms, and pepper. Bring to a boil, stirring occasionally; reduce heat, and simmer, stirring occasionally, 30 minutes. Cool slightly.

PROCESS mixture, in batches, in a blender or food processor (or use an immersion blender) until smooth, stopping to scrape down sides. Return to Dutch oven.

COOK over low heat, stirring occasionally, 5 minutes or until thoroughly heated. Serve with desired toppings. Garnish, if desired. **MAKES** 8 (1-cup) servings.

NOTE: For testing purposes only, we used Melissa's dried mushrooms.

Per serving: Calories 107 (32% from fat); Fat 3.8g (sat 2g, mono 1g, poly 0.2g); Protein 5.1g; Carb 10.8g; Fiber 1.7g; Chol 7.8mg; Iron 1.5mg; Sodium 689mg; Calc 17 mg

Strike a Healthy Balance

Confused about what to eat? Mom's nutrition advice still applies.

■ **Eat your vegetables.** There are no bad vegetables, but some are less caloric than others. So fill your dish with low-cal, low-starch veggies such as green beans, cabbage, broccoli, yellow squash, zucchini, snap peas, tomatoes, bell peppers, and spinach. Take smaller portions of higher calorie, starchy vegetables such as corn, potatoes, and peas. Choose sweet potatoes—they're a great source of fiber and cancer-fighting antioxidants.

■ **Choose your protein.** Protein-rich foods keep us satisfied longer, but not all are created equal. Choose lean meats: pork loin, lean sirloin, any fish/shellfish, and skinless chicken/turkey. Dried beans are also an awesome source of protein and supply plenty of cholesterol-lowering soluble fiber. Nuts are a terrific choice, too, but at about 170 calories per ounce, you'll want to stick to a single serving.

■ **Go for hardworking carbs.** Highly processed starches (snack crackers, bagels, muffins, and instant cereals) are a breeze for your body to break down. That means you'll be snacking soon after you eat. Enjoy whole-grain bread, cereal, and pasta to keep hunger pangs at bay.

■ **Fruit is still your friend.** Your best bet for getting the nutrients of fruit is to grab whole fresh or dried (unsweetened) fruit instead of juices, which are high in calories (about 120 per cup) and contain virtually no fiber. So don't count on them for staying with you through the morning or afternoon. Oranges, peaches, pears, cantaloupes, and apples are delicious, versatile, and pack plenty of fiber.

from our kitchen

Cooking for a Crowd

Kick off a party weekend of fun and football with a big bowl of Chicken-and-Smoked Sausage Pilau. This winning one-pot rice dish from South Carolina's Lowcountry is a Test Kitchen's favorite for entertaining.

CHICKEN-AND-SMOKED SAUSAGE PILAU

Prep: 15 min.; Cook: 1 hr., 25 min.; Stand: 15 min.

- 1 (5-pound) whole chicken
- 3 celery ribs, cut in half
- 2 carrots, cut in half
- 2 large sweet onions, chopped
- 8 cups water
- 1 bay leaf
- 1½ tablespoons seasoned salt
- 1½ tablespoons seasoned pepper
- 1 pound hot or mild smoked pork sausage links, cut into ¼-inch slices
- 4 cups uncooked long-grain rice

BRING first 8 ingredients to a boil in a large Dutch oven or stockpot over medium-high heat. Reduce heat to low, cover, and simmer 1 hour or until chicken is tender. Remove from heat, and let stand 15 minutes.

REMOVE and discard celery, carrots, and bay leaf from broth, reserving broth in Dutch oven. Remove chicken, and cool slightly; remove skin and bones, and coarsely chop chicken.

SAUTÉ sausage in a large skillet over medium-high heat 5 minutes or until browned; drain.

ADD chicken and sausage to reserved broth in Dutch oven, and bring to a boil over medium-high heat; stir in rice, and return to boil. Cover, reduce heat to low, and cook 20 minutes or until broth is absorbed and rice is tender. **MAKES** 8 to 10 servings.

Signature Sides

Supermarket shelves are loaded with festive rice mixes that include all the seasonings for a sensational side dish. Get creative—mix-and-match cooked packages of similar flavors such as wild rice and brown rice. Add a sprinkling of fresh herbs or a handful of dried fruit and toasted nuts. The flavor only gets better. Here are a few combinations we enjoy.

SAFFRON RICE PILAF: Prepare 1 (5-ounce) package saffron yellow rice mix according to package directions. Stir in ½ red bell pepper, diced; ½ cup currants; and 1 tablespoon fresh thyme. **MAKES** 4 servings. Prep: 5 min., Cook: 20 min.

NOTE: Jim Pleasants of Williamsburg, Virginia, serves this with his Maple-Balsamic Chicken on page 195.

CRANBERRY-ALMOND WILD RICE: Prepare 1 (6-ounce) package long-grain and wild rice according to package directions. Stir in 1 (3.5-ounce) bag quick-cooking brown rice prepared according to package directions, ¾ cup sweetened dried cranberries, and ⅓ cup toasted slivered almonds. **MAKES** 4 to 6 servings. Prep: 5 min., Cook: 20 min.

PECAN RICE: Prepare 1 (7-ounce) package pecan rice according to package directions. Stir in ¾ cup toasted chopped pecans. **MAKES** 4 servings. Prep: 5 min., Cook: 20 min.

NOTE: Konriko Wild Pecan Aromatic Rice from Louisiana is one of our Test Kitchens favorites. Look for the rice in your local supermarket, or order directly from **www.konriko.com.**

Tips and Tidbits

- Uncle Ben's now has five varieties of great-tasting ready-to-eat rice that can be stored in the pantry—just heat for 90 seconds in the microwave, and serve ($1.69 for an 8.8-ounce package).
- When you don't have time to marinate before grilling, transfer hot, cooked boneless chicken breasts to a shallow dish, pour in your favorite vinaigrette, and let stand 2 to 4 minutes; drain before serving.
- A meat-and-poultry pounder (about $7 at kitchen stores) makes fast work of flattening and tenderizing boneless chicken breasts for quick cooking. For easy cleanup, slip the chicken inside a zip-top plastic bag before pounding.

October

Comfort Food Texas Style

When this cowboy-turned-chef entertains, the food and the mood are casual and easygoing.

Southwestern Supper

Serves 6 to 8

Taquitos With Pork Picadillo

Gonzales Meat Loaf

Mac and Texas Cheeses With Roasted Chiles

José Falcón's Slaw

Spoonbread With Simple Chorizo

Rancher's Buttermilk Pie

"The heat of a pepper is contained in its seeds and ribs. We want just a touch of heat, so I'm scraping out the seeds this time," says Grady Spears as he cleans a roasted poblano chile for his soul-warming Mac and Texas Cheeses With Roasted Chiles. "Eating this is about as good as getting a big hug from your grandma—it makes you feel all happy inside." There's no doubt this Texan's talent in the kitchen is exceeded only by his gentle manner and boyish enthusiasm. He puts even the most intimidated cook at ease.

Grady was kind enough to share a few of his favorite recipes from his latest cookbook, *The Texas Cowboy Kitchen* (Ten Speed Press, 2003). When asked why he has such a connection to humble comfort food, Grady simply answers, "It makes people feel good from the inside out. It's simple, real, and honest, like cowboys." Amen.

TAQUITOS WITH PORK PICADILLO

Prep: 15 min., Cook: 12 min.,
Fry: 2 min. per batch

Taquitos are small, meat-filled tacos that are rolled and deep-fried. Serve with José Falcón's Slaw (recipe on facing page) for a cool contrast.

12 (5½-inch) corn tortillas
1 pound chopped cooked pork*
2 tablespoons vegetable oil, divided
1 medium onion, chopped
4 garlic cloves, minced
3 jalapeño peppers, seeded and chopped
¼ cup tomato paste
¼ cup red wine vinegar
1 teaspoon pepper
½ teaspoon salt
¼ cup chopped fresh cilantro
1 cup (4 ounces) shredded Monterey Jack cheese
Vegetable oil

HEAT corn tortillas according to package directions. Cut tortillas into circles with a 3-inch cutter. Put tortilla circles on a plate, and cover with a towel; set aside.

COOK pork in a large nonstick skillet in 1 tablespoon hot vegetable oil over medium heat 5 minutes or until lightly browned, stirring constantly. Remove pork from pan, and drain on paper towels. Wipe skillet clean.

SAUTÉ onion, garlic, and peppers in remaining 1 tablespoon hot oil over medium-high heat 3 to 4 minutes or until onion is tender. Stir in pork, tomato paste, vinegar, pepper, and salt; cook, stirring occasionally, 2 to 3 minutes. Remove from heat, and stir in cilantro.

SPOON 2 tablespoons pork mixture evenly down center of each tortilla circle; top evenly with cheese. Roll up, and secure with a wooden pick.

POUR vegetable oil to a depth of 1½ inches into a large heavy skillet. Fry taquitos, in batches, in hot oil (350°) over medium-high heat 1 to 2 minutes or until golden brown. Remove wooden picks, and serve immediately. **MAKES** 6 to 8 servings.

*You can substitute 1 pound chopped or shredded pork (without sauce) from your favorite barbecue restaurant.

GONZALES MEAT LOAF

family favorite

Prep: 15 min., Bake: 1 hr., Stand: 10 min.

For a spicier meat loaf, add more hot sauce.

2 pounds ground sirloin
3 large eggs, lightly beaten
1 cup fine, dry breadcrumbs
4 garlic cloves, minced
1 medium-size red onion, chopped
2 plum tomatoes, seeded and chopped
1½ cups (6 ounces) shredded Monterey Jack cheese
¼ to ½ cup firmly packed brown sugar
½ cup chopped fresh cilantro
¼ cup Worcestershire sauce
2 tablespoons hot sauce
2 teaspoons salt
1 teaspoon pepper

COMBINE all ingredients. Shape into a 9- x 5-inch loaf, and place on a lightly greased wire rack in a pan.

BAKE at 350° for 45 minutes; increase heat to 425°, and bake 15 more minutes or until done. Let meat loaf stand 10 minutes before serving. **MAKES** 6 to 8 servings.

MAC AND TEXAS CHEESES WITH ROASTED CHILES

Prep: 15 min., Broil: 15 min., Stand: 10 min., Cook: 7 min., Bake: 40 min.

- 4 poblano chile peppers
- 1 pound uncooked elbow macaroni
- ½ cup butter
- ½ cup all-purpose flour
- 2 cups whipping cream
- 1 cup milk
- 3 cups (12 ounces) shredded Monterey Jack cheese, divided
- 1 (4-ounce) package goat cheese, crumbled
- 1 teaspoon salt
- ¼ cup Italian-seasoned breadcrumbs
- ½ cup (2 ounces) shredded Parmesan cheese

BROIL chile peppers on an aluminum foil-lined baking sheet 5 inches from heat about 5 minutes on each side or until chiles look blistered.

PLACE chiles in a zip-top plastic bag; seal and let stand 10 minutes to loosen skins. Peel chiles; remove and discard seeds, and cut chiles into strips. Set aside.

PREPARE macaroni according to package directions; drain and set aside.

MELT butter in a Dutch oven over low heat; whisk in flour until smooth. Cook 1 minute, whisking constantly. Gradually whisk in cream and milk; cook over medium heat, whisking constantly, 5 minutes or until mixture is thickened and bubbly.

STIR in 2¾ cups Monterey Jack cheese, crumbled goat cheese, and salt until smooth. Stir in roasted chiles and macaroni.

SPOON into a lightly greased 13- x 9-inch baking dish. Top with breadcrumbs and Parmesan cheese.

BAKE at 375° for 40 minutes. Remove from oven, and sprinkle evenly with remaining ¼ cup Monterey Jack cheese.

BROIL 5 inches from heat about 3 to 5 minutes or until cheese is golden and bubbly. **MAKES** 8 servings.

JOSÉ FALCÓN'S SLAW

make ahead • chef recipe

Prep: 15 min., Chill: 1 hr.

This recipe was inspired by one of Grady's favorite chefs in Boquillas, Mexico, who's said to make the best tacos around.

- ¼ cup mayonnaise
- 3 tablespoons malt or cider vinegar
- 2 teaspoons sugar
- 2 cups finely shredded red cabbage*
- 1 cup finely shredded green cabbage*
- 1 red bell pepper, thinly sliced
- 1 cup chopped fresh cilantro
- ¼ teaspoon salt

STIR together first 3 ingredients in a large bowl.

ADD red cabbage and remaining ingredients, tossing to coat. Cover and chill at least 1 hour. **MAKES** 6 to 8 servings.

*Substitute 1 (16-ounce) package shredded coleslaw mix for shredded red and green cabbages, if desired.

SPOONBREAD WITH SIMPLE CHORIZO

Prep: 20 min., Cook: 5 min., Stand: 20 min., Bake: 30 min.

This hearty Texas twist on a classic Southern side features chorizo, a spicy Mexican sausage. Chorizo is also terrific in scrambled eggs and tacos.

- Simple Chorizo
- 2 cups cornmeal
- 4 cups milk
- 2 garlic cloves, minced
- ¼ cup butter
- 1½ teaspoons salt
- 4 large eggs, separated
- 2 teaspoons baking powder
- 1½ cups (6 ounces) shredded Monterey Jack cheese

COOK Simple Chorizo in a large skillet over medium-high heat, stirring until it crumbles and is no longer pink; drain well. Set aside.

PLACE cornmeal in a large bowl.

HEAT milk and garlic in a heavy-duty saucepan over medium-high heat (do not boil). Pour hot milk mixture over cornmeal, stirring until smooth. Add butter and salt, stirring until well blended; let stand 20 minutes.

LIGHTLY beat egg yolks. Add yolks, baking powder, cheese, and Simple Chorizo to cornmeal mixture, stirring until blended.

BEAT egg whites at high speed with an electric mixer until stiff peaks form. Fold egg whites gently into cornmeal mixture. Pour into a lightly greased 13- x 9-inch baking dish.

BAKE at 375° for 25 to 30 minutes or until spoonbread is lightly browned. **MAKES** 8 servings.

Simple Chorizo:
freezeable • make ahead

Prep: 5 min.

- 1 pound ground pork
- 1 garlic clove, minced
- 2 teaspoons dried crushed red pepper
- 1½ teaspoons ground cinnamon
- 1¼ teaspoons salt
- 1 teaspoon ground coriander
- 1 teaspoon dried oregano

COMBINE all ingredients, stirring to combine. Store in refrigerator up to 3 days, or freeze up to 1 month. **MAKES** 1 pound.

RANCHER'S BUTTERMILK PIE

make ahead

Prep: 15 min., Bake: 45 min.

- ½ (15-ounce) package refrigerated piecrusts
- 2 cups sugar
- 2 tablespoons cornmeal
- 5 large eggs, lightly beaten
- ⅔ cup buttermilk
- ½ cup crushed pineapple, drained
- ½ cup sweetened flaked coconut
- ¼ cup butter, melted
- 2 teaspoons grated lemon rind
- 2 teaspoons fresh lemon juice
- 1 teaspoon vanilla extract

FIT piecrust into a 9-inch pieplate according to package directions; fold edges under, and crimp.
COMBINE sugar and cornmeal in a large bowl. Stir in eggs and buttermilk until combined. Stir in pineapple and next 5 ingredients. Pour filling into piecrust.
BAKE at 350° for 45 minutes or until pie is set and top is lightly brown. Serve warm, at room temperature, or cover pie and chill until ready to serve. **MAKES** 8 servings.

Food and Hospitality

Easy Home-Baked Bread

Most of these top-rated recipes can be ready to bake in the time it takes your oven to preheat. Baking soda gives rise to terrific flavor in Whole Wheat Date-Nut Bread. A few simple techniques and a handful of everyday ingredients are all that are needed to create an endless number of recipes. A quick roll of the dough turns Italian Bread into pizza crust or focaccia, and breakfast biscuits become a tasty base for appetizers. See "From Our Kitchen" on page 224 for some great baking tips.

ITALIAN BREAD

family favorite

Prep: 15 min., Stand: 15 min., Rise: 30 min., Bake: 16 min.

A heavy-duty electric stand mixer with a dough hook makes this yeast bread extra easy. If you don't have a heavy-duty mixer, just mix the dough by hand, and knead on a lightly floured surface for 8 to 10 minutes.

- 1 (¼-ounce) envelope active dry yeast
- 1 teaspoon sugar
- 1 cup warm water (100° to 110°)
- 2 to 3 cups bread flour
- 2 tablespoons olive oil
- 1 teaspoon salt

COMBINE yeast, sugar, and 1 cup warm water in bowl of a heavy-duty electric stand mixer; let stand 5 minutes. Add 2 cups flour, oil, and salt to bowl, and beat at low speed, using dough hook attachment, 1 minute. Gradually add additional flour until dough begins to leave the sides of the bowl and pull together. (**NOTE:** The dough will take on a "shaggy" appearance as the flour is being added. When enough flour has been added, the dough will look soft and smooth, not wet and sticky or overly dry with a rough surface.)
INCREASE speed to medium, and beat 5 minutes. Cover bowl of dough with plastic wrap, and let stand in a warm place (85°), free from drafts, 30 minutes or until doubled in bulk. Punch dough down, and let stand 10 minutes.
TURN dough out onto a lightly floured surface; shape dough into a 12-inch loaf, and place on a lightly greased baking sheet. Cut 3 (¼-inch-deep) slits across top of dough with a sharp paring knife. (The slits release interior steam and prevent the loaf from blowing apart at the side.)
BAKE at 400° for 16 minutes or until golden brown. Cool on a wire rack. **MAKES** 1 loaf.

HERBED FOCACCIA: Proceed with recipe as directed, shaping dough into a ball instead of a loaf. Roll dough into an 11- x 14-inch rectangle on a lightly greased baking sheet. Press handle of a wooden spoon into dough to make indentations at 1-inch intervals. Drizzle

dough evenly with 1 tablespoon olive oil; sprinkle evenly with 1 teaspoon dried Italian seasoning. Bake at 475° for 12 to 15 minutes or until golden brown.

PIZZA CRUST: Proceed with recipe as directed, shaping dough into a ball instead of a loaf. Roll dough into an 11- x 14-inch rectangle on a lightly greased baking sheet. Drizzle with olive oil, or spread with pesto or pizza sauce; sprinkle with desired toppings. Bake at 475° for 20 to 25 minutes.

GAYE GROOVER CHRISTMUS
COLUMBIA, SOUTH CAROLINA

WHOLE WHEAT DATE-NUT BREAD

Prep: 15 min.; Bake: 1 hr., 15 min.

Don't be surprised by the heavy weight when you remove this hearty bread from the pan. Even though the batter has no egg or oil, it still produces a moist and tender loaf. *(pictured on page 226)*

- 2 cups whole wheat flour
- 1 cup all-purpose flour
- 1 cup chopped pecans, toasted
- ¾ cup chopped dates
- ½ cup sugar
- 1 teaspoon salt
- 1 teaspoon baking soda
- 1½ cups milk
- ½ cup molasses

COMBINE first 6 ingredients in a large bowl; make a well in center of mixture.
DISSOLVE baking soda in milk; stir in molasses. Add to flour mixture, stirring just until dry ingredients are moistened. Spoon into a greased and floured 9- x 5-inch loafpan.
BAKE at 325° for 1 hour to 1 hour and 15 minutes or until a wooden pick inserted in center comes out clean. Remove from pan, and cool on a wire rack. **MAKES** 1 (9-inch) loaf.

WHOLE WHEAT RAISIN-NUT BREAD: Substitute ¾ cup raisins for ¾ cup chopped dates; proceed as directed.

WHOLE WHEAT NUT BREAD: Omit chopped dates; proceed as directed.

DIANE E. ONACHILA
HENDERSONVILLE, NORTH CAROLINA

Homemade Biscuits

family favorite • fast fixin's

Prep: 10 min., Bake: 12 min.

Self-rising flour contains salt and baking powder, which can leave a bitter taste, so be sure to sprinkle all-purpose flour on the surface when rolling and shaping biscuits. The biscuits and both variations received our highest rating.

- ¼ cup shortening
- 2 cups self-rising flour
- ⅔ cup milk

CUT shortening into flour with a pastry blender or fork until crumbly. Add milk, stirring just until dry ingredients are moistened.
TURN dough out onto a lightly floured surface, and knead lightly 3 or 4 times. Pat or roll dough to ½-inch thickness; cut with a 2-inch round cutter, and place on a lightly greased baking sheet.
BAKE at 475° for 10 to 12 minutes or until golden brown. **MAKES** 14 (2-inch) biscuits.

DOTTIE B. MILLER
JONESBOROUGH, TENNESSEE

SOUR CREAM BISCUITS: Substitute 1 (8-ounce) container sour cream for ⅔ cup milk. Proceed as directed.

HAM-AND-SWISS CHEESE BISCUITS: Stir ⅔ cup finely chopped ham and ⅔ cup finely chopped Swiss cheese into the flour and shortening mixture; add milk, and proceed as directed.

Parmesan Cheese Muffins

family favorite • fast fixin's

Prep: 10 min., Bake: 18 min. (pictured on page 227)

- 2 cups self-rising flour
- ¾ cup shredded Parmesan
  cheese
- 2 tablespoons sugar
- 1 cup milk
- ¼ cup vegetable oil
- 2 large eggs

COMBINE first 3 ingredients in a large bowl; make a well in center of mixture.

WHISK together milk, oil, and eggs until well blended. Add to flour mixture; stir just until dry ingredients are moistened.
SPOON mixture into lightly greased muffin pans, filling two-thirds full. Bake at 400° for 15 to 18 minutes or until golden brown. **MAKES** 1 dozen.

TELIA JOHNSON
BIRMINGHAM, ALABAMA

BREAKFAST MUFFINS: Add 1 cup cooked and crumbled ground pork sausage to flour mixture. Proceed with recipe as directed.

BLUEBERRY MUFFINS: Omit Parmesan. Increase sugar to ½ cup; proceed with recipe as directed, folding 1 cup fresh or frozen blueberries into prepared batter.

CRANBERRY-ORANGE MUFFINS: Increase sugar to ½ cup. Omit Parmesan, and add ¾ cup sweetened dried cranberries and 1 tablespoon grated orange rind to flour mixture. Proceed with recipe as directed.

Lemon Tea Bread

Prep: 15 min., Bake: 1 hr. (pictured on page 226)

- ½ cup butter, softened
- 1 cup granulated sugar
- 2 large eggs
- 1½ cups all-purpose flour
- 1 teaspoon baking powder
- ½ teaspoon salt
- ½ cup milk
- 2 tablespoons grated lemon rind,
  divided
- 1 cup powdered sugar
- 2 tablespoons fresh lemon juice
- 1 tablespoon granulated sugar

BEAT softened butter at medium speed with an electric mixer until creamy. Gradually add 1 cup granulated sugar, beating until light and fluffy. Add eggs, 1 at a time, beating just until blended after each addition.
STIR together flour, baking powder, and salt; add to butter mixture alternately with milk, beating at low speed just until blended, beginning and ending with flour mixture. Stir in 1 tablespoon lemon rind. Spoon batter into a greased and floured 8- x 4-inch loafpan.

BAKE at 350° for 1 hour or until a wooden pick inserted in center of bread comes out clean. Let cool in pan 10 minutes. Remove bread from pan, and cool completely on a wire rack.
STIR together powdered sugar and lemon juice until smooth; spoon evenly over top of bread, letting excess drip down sides. Stir together remaining 1 tablespoon lemon rind and 1 tablespoon granulated sugar; sprinkle on top of bread. **MAKES** 1 (8-inch) loaf.

DORSELLA UTTER
LOUISVILLE, KENTUCKY

LEMON-ALMOND TEA BREAD: Stir ½ teaspoon almond extract into batter. Proceed as directed.

Rich, Warm Chocolate

Wrap your taste buds in these heavenly brews for cold nights.

Hot Chocolate Mix

fast fixin's • make ahead

Prep: 5 min.

- 1 (9.6-ounce) package nonfat dry milk
- 4 cups miniature marshmallows
- 1½ cups powdered sugar
- 1 cup unsweetened cocoa

STIR together nonfat dry milk, miniature marshmallows, powdered sugar, and unsweetened cocoa in a large bowl. Store chocolate mixture in an airtight container at room temperature. **MAKES** 14 servings.

Hot Chocolate:

Prep: 5 min.

STIR ½ cup Hot Chocolate Mix into 1 cup hot milk. Serve Hot Chocolate immediately. **MAKES** 1 serving.

KIM CUMMINS
BIRMINGHAM, ALABAMA

White Chocolate Latte

fast fixin's

Prep: 5 min., Cook: 5 min. *(pictured on page 228)*

- **2 cups milk**
- **1 cup half-and-half**
- **⅔ cup white chocolate morsels**
- **2 tablespoons instant coffee granules**
- **1 teaspoon vanilla extract**
- **¼ teaspoon almond extract**
- **Whipped cream (optional)**
- **Garnish: cinnamon sticks**

STIR together first 4 ingredients in a small saucepan over low heat until white chocolate morsels are melted. Stir in vanilla and almond extracts; pour evenly into 4 mugs. Top with whipped cream, if desired. Garnish, if desired, and serve immediately. **MAKES** 4 cups.

KARYN DARDAR
MONTEGUT, LOUISIANA

Mexican Hot Chocolate

fast fixin's

Prep: 5 min., Cook: 10 min.

Mexican chocolate is flavored with cinnamon, almonds, and vanilla. Purchase it at ethnic grocery stores.

- **2 cups milk**
- **4 ounces Mexican chocolate, chopped**
- **1 teaspoon vanilla extract**
- **Whipped cream (optional)**
- **Cinnamon sticks (optional)**

STIR together 2 cups milk, chopped Mexican chocolate, and vanilla extract in a saucepan over low heat until chocolate melts and mixture is smooth. Cook, whisking constantly, just until mixture is thoroughly heated. Remove from heat, and whisk mixture until foamy. (An immersion blender also works well.) Pour evenly into 2 mugs; top with whipped cream, and add a cinnamon stick, if desired. **MAKES** 2 servings.

J. CARLOS MARTINEZ
ATLANTA, GEORGIA

Fun Candy Treats

Turn leftover Halloween goodies into irresistible desserts.

Editor John Alex Floyd, Jr., remembers that when *Southern Living* published a luscious three-layer Milky Way Cake in *Our Best Recipes, Volume Three,* the recipe caused a run on the candy bar at grocery stores 'round the South. More than a quarter of a century has passed, so it's about time to offer the recipe to you again. This time we transformed it into Heavenly Candy Bar Cupcakes (layer cake directions are provided as well) and developed an easy frosting. We've also included two other recipes using popular candies and cookies. Grocery store owners, get ready.

Heavenly Candy Bar Cupcakes

family favorite

Prep: 20 min., Cook: 5 min., Bake: 18 min.

- **9 fun-size or 21 mini chocolate-coated caramel and creamy nougat bars**
- **½ cup butter or margarine**
- **2 cups sugar**
- **1 cup shortening**
- **3 large eggs**
- **2½ cups all-purpose flour**
- **1 teaspoon salt**
- **1½ cups buttermilk**
- **½ teaspoon baking soda**
- **1 teaspoon vanilla extract**
- **Chocolate-Marshmallow Frosting**
- **Garnishes: chopped frozen fun-size chocolate-coated caramel and creamy nougat bars, candy corn**

MELT candy bars and butter in a heavy saucepan over low heat about 5 minutes, stirring until smooth. Set aside.

BEAT sugar and shortening at medium speed with an electric mixer about 3 minutes or until well blended. Add eggs, 1 at a time, beating just until blended after each addition.

COMBINE flour and salt. Stir together buttermilk and baking soda. Gradually add flour mixture to sugar mixture, alternately with buttermilk mixture, beginning and ending with flour mixture. Beat at low speed just until blended after each addition. Stir in melted candy bar mixture and vanilla. Place 36 paper baking cups in muffin pans; spoon batter evenly into paper baking cups, filling two-thirds full. **BAKE** at 350° for 18 minutes or until a wooden pick inserted in center comes out clean. Remove cupcakes from pan, and let cool completely on wire racks. Spread cupcakes evenly with Chocolate-Marshmallow Frosting. Garnish, if desired. **MAKES** 36 cupcakes.

NOTE: For testing purposes only, we used Milky Way Bars.

Chocolate-Marshmallow Frosting:
fast fixin's

Prep: 15 min., Cook: 5 min.

- **3 cups miniature marshmallows**
- **¾ cup butter or margarine, cut up**
- **¾ cup evaporated milk**
- **6 ounces unsweetened chocolate, chopped**
- **6 cups powdered sugar**
- **1 tablespoon vanilla extract**

MELT first 4 ingredients in a 2-quart saucepan over medium-low heat, stirring 5 minutes or until mixture is smooth.

TRANSFER chocolate mixture to a large bowl. Place the bowl into a larger bowl filled with ice and water. Gradually add powdered sugar, beating at low speed with an electric mixer. Increase speed to medium-high, and beat 5 minutes or until frosting is cool, thick, and spreadable. Stir in 1 tablespoon vanilla. **MAKES** 4½ cups.

Heavenly Candy Bar Cake:

Prep: 15 min., Cook 5 min., Bake: 30 min.

SPOON batter into 3 greased and floured 9-inch cakepans. Bake at 350° for 30 minutes or until a wooden pick comes out clean. Cool in pans on a wire rack 10 minutes; remove cakes from pans, and let cool completely on wire rack. Spread half of Chocolate-Marshmallow Frosting evenly between cake layers. Spread remaining frosting evenly over top and sides of cake. Garnish, if desired. **MAKES** 12 servings.

CHOCOLATE MINT SNOWBALLS

fast fixin's • make ahead

Prep: 20 min.

- 1 (18-ounce) package cream-filled chocolate sandwich cookies
- 1 (8-ounce) package 1/3-less-fat cream cheese
- 1 (12.5-ounce) package chocolate-covered creamy mints
- 2 (12-ounce) packages semisweet chocolate morsels
- 1 tablespoon shortening

PULSE half of cookies in a food processor 3 or 4 times or until crumb consistency. Add remaining cookies to crumbs in food processor, and pulse until crumb consistency. Cut cream cheese into 4 pieces; add to food processor, 1 piece at a time, processing well after each addition.

ROLL cream cheese mixture into 1-inch balls. Push 1 chocolate-covered mint into the center of each ball; roll each ball smooth.

MICROWAVE chocolate morsels and shortening in a glass bowl at HIGH for 90 seconds or until melted, stirring every 30 seconds.

DIP balls in melted chocolate mixture; place on wax paper to harden. Store in refrigerator. **MAKES** about 5 dozen.

NOTE: For testing purposes only, we used Oreo Sandwich Cookies and Junior Mints.

SHAWN MOORE
KENTON, OHIO

FUDGY PEANUT BUTTER CUP PIE

freezeable • make ahead

Prep: 15 min.; Stand 20 min.; Freeze 2 hrs., 10 min.

- 1 (1.75-quart) container vanilla ice cream with peanut butter cups swirled with fudge
- 1/3 cup creamy or chunky peanut butter
- 1 (6-ounce) ready-made chocolate crumb piecrust
- 6 (0.6-ounce) peanut butter cup candies, halved
- Chocolate-peanut butter shell coating

ALLOW container of ice cream to stand at room temperature 20 minutes to soften.

SPREAD peanut butter over crust; freeze 10 minutes.

SPREAD ice cream evenly over peanut butter in crust. Arrange peanut butter cup candy halves, cut sides down, around edges of crust. Drizzle chocolate-peanut butter shell coating evenly over ice cream.

FREEZE at least 2 hours. Cut frozen pie with a warm knife to serve. **MAKES** 10 to 12 servings.

NOTE: For testing purposes only, we used Mayfield's Moose Tracks Ice Cream, Reese's Peanut Butter Cups, and Reese's Shell topping.

HEIDI VAN LIERE
SPRINGFIELD, VIRGINIA

Add Flavor With Root Beer

For most folks, enjoying the distinctive flavor of root beer means sipping it from a frosty mug. It's time to discover that our old friend makes a great ingredient in some unexpected places.

ROOT BEER FLOAT

fast fixin's

Prep: 5 min.

SCOOP vanilla ice cream into a tall glass, filling half full. Top with root beer, and gently stir. Serve immediately. **MAKES** 1 serving.

ROOT BEER FLOAT CAKE

Prep: 15 min., Bake: 30 min., Cool: 10 min.

This sweet treat is sure to make you want to stock up on root beer for both drinking and cooking.

- 1 (18.25-ounce) package German chocolate cake mix
- 1 1/4 cups root beer (not diet)
- 1/4 cup vegetable oil
- 2 large eggs
- Root Beer Frosting

COMBINE first 4 ingredients in a mixing bowl. Beat mixture at low speed with an electric mixer until dry ingredients are moistened. Pour batter into a greased and floured 13- x 9-inch pan.

BAKE at 350° for 30 minutes or until a wooden pick inserted in center comes out clean. Cool cake 10 minutes. Spread Root Beer Frosting evenly over warm cake. **MAKES** 12 servings.

Root Beer Frosting:

fast fixin's

Prep: 10 min., Cook: 5 min.

- 1/2 cup butter or margarine
- 7 tablespoons root beer (not diet)
- 3 tablespoons unsweetened cocoa
- 1 (16-ounce) package powdered sugar
- 1 teaspoon vanilla extract

BRING first 3 ingredients to a boil in a large saucepan over medium heat, stirring until butter melts. Remove from heat; whisk in powdered sugar and vanilla until smooth. **MAKES** 2 1/4 cups.

ROOT BEER BAKED BEANS

family favorite

Prep: 5 min., Cook: 12 min., Bake: 55 min.

You don't taste the root beer in this recipe—it's just used for sweetening instead of the traditional brown sugar.

- 3 bacon slices
- 1 small onion, diced
- 2 (16-ounce) cans pork and beans
- ½ cup root beer (not diet)
- ¼ cup hickory-smoked barbecue sauce
- ½ teaspoon dry mustard
- ⅛ teaspoon hot sauce

COOK bacon in a skillet over medium heat until crisp; remove and drain on paper towels, reserving 2 tablespoons drippings in skillet. Crumble bacon.

SAUTÉ diced onion in hot bacon drippings in skillet over high heat 5 minutes or until tender. Stir together onion, crumbled bacon, beans, and remaining ingredients in a lightly greased 1-quart baking dish.

BAKE beans, uncovered, at 400° for 55 minutes or until sauce is thickened. **MAKES** 4 servings.

ROOT BEER POT ROAST

family favorite

Prep: 10 min., Cook: 10 min., Bake: 3 hrs.

Serve this juicy and tender roast with mashed potatoes or rice.

- 1 (4-pound) eye of round roast
- 1½ teaspoons salt, divided
- 1 teaspoon pepper, divided
- 1 tablespoon vegetable oil
- 1 large onion, thinly sliced
- 1 (12-ounce) bottle root beer (not diet)
- 1 (12-ounce) bottle chili sauce
- 1 garlic clove, minced

SPRINKLE roast evenly with 1 teaspoon salt and ½ teaspoon pepper.

BROWN roast on all sides in hot oil in a large ovenproof Dutch oven over medium-high heat. Add onion. Remove Dutch oven from heat.

STIR together remaining ½ teaspoon salt, remaining ½ teaspoon pepper, root beer, chili sauce, and garlic until blended. Pour root beer mixture over roast mixture in Dutch oven.

BAKE, covered, at 300° for 3 hours or until tender. **MAKES** 8 to 10 servings.

PATSY GRIFFIN
SHREVEPORT, LOUISIANA

Try Turnips

When cooking turnip greens, don't throw away the roots. Greens bought by the bunch have the pale purple and white bottoms still attached, and those are key to these recipes. If you don't want greens, you can just buy turnips by the pound.

SWEET SKILLET TURNIPS

Prep: 20 min., Cook: 25 min.

- 1 tablespoon butter or margarine
- 1 small onion, finely chopped
- 1 pound turnips, peeled and shredded
- ½ cup chicken broth
- 1 tablespoon sugar
- ½ teaspoon salt
- ¼ teaspoon pepper

MELT butter in a large skillet over medium heat; add onion, and sauté 3 to 5 minutes or until tender.

STIR in turnips and remaining ingredients. Cook, stirring often, 20 minutes or until turnips are tender. (Turnips will turn a light brown-caramel color as they cook.) **MAKES** 2 to 3 servings.

CHARLOTTE BRYANT
GREENSBURG, KENTUCKY

TURNIP TURNOVERS

Prep: 20 min., Bake: 17 min.

- 1 small turnip, peeled and grated
- ½ small onion, finely chopped
- ¼ teaspoon salt
- ¼ teaspoon pepper
- 1 (15-ounce) package refrigerated piecrusts
- 2 tablespoons butter, melted

COMBINE turnip and onion in a small bowl. Toss with salt and pepper.

UNFOLD piecrusts, and press out fold lines. Cut out 30 rounds with a 2-inch round cutter.

PLACE 1 teaspoon turnip mixture on half of each round, and fold the other half over. Press edges together with a fork to

---

Make Your Own Root Beer

Stir together 1 liter chilled seltzer water or sparkling water, 8 heaping tablespoons sugar (or no-calorie sweetener adjusted to taste), and ½ tablespoon root beer extract in a large pitcher until blended. Serve immediately in a frosty mug or over ice. **MAKES** about 5 cups.

Note: For testing purposes only, we used Zatarain's Root Beer Extract. It can be ordered from **www.thecajunconnection.com.** The recipe can be found on the back of the bottle.

seal. Place on an ungreased baking sheet; brush tops with melted butter. **BAKE** at 375° for 15 to 17 minutes or until edges are lightly browned. **MAKES** about 30 turnovers.

JERRY JENNINGS
OKLAHOMA CITY, OKLAHOMA

TURNIP-BACON TURNOVERS: Add 4 to 5 pieces finely chopped, cooked bacon to filling mixture. Proceed as directed.

TURNIP CASSEROLE

family favorite

Prep: 15 min., Cook: 25 min., Bake: 30 min.

If you like potato casserole, you'll enjoy this sweeter-tasting turnip version.

- **2 pounds turnips, peeled and chopped**
- **¼ cup butter or margarine, divided**
- **1 small onion, finely chopped**
- **½ cup milk**
- **1½ cups (6 ounces) grated white Cheddar cheese, divided**
- **½ teaspoon salt**
- **½ teaspoon pepper**
- **⅓ cup Italian-seasoned breadcrumbs**

COMBINE turnips and water to cover in a saucepan. Bring to a boil; cook 20 minutes or until tender. Drain well; transfer to a large bowl, and mash with a potato masher.

MELT 1 tablespoon butter in a skillet over medium heat; add onion, and sauté 3 minutes or until tender.

ADD onion, milk, 1 cup Cheddar cheese, salt, pepper, and remaining 3 tablespoons butter to mashed turnips, stirring to combine. Spoon into a lightly greased 11- x 7-inch baking dish. Sprinkle evenly with breadcrumbs and remaining ½ cup Cheddar cheese.

BAKE at 350° for 30 minutes or until lightly browned. **MAKES** 4 servings.

CAROL DAVIS
EMERALD ISLE, NORTH CAROLINA

Taste of the South

Classic Gumbo

Gumbo is one of the crowning glories of Louisiana cuisine. This flavorful stew is named for the West African word for okra, *"gombo."* It can feature any number of main ingredients, most commonly shrimp, crab, chicken, duck, and sausage. A well-made gumbo offers a savory combination of tastes and textures that's unlike any other dish. Our recipe, a chicken-and-sausage version, came from the late *Southern Living* Food and Travel Editor Dana Adkins Campbell.

All gumbos start with a roux, but after the initial browning of fat and flour, other decisions are left to the cook's discretion and what ingredients are on hand. Most gumbos are seasoned with garlic and what Louisianans call the "holy trinity"— bell pepper, onion, and celery. Some cooks add okra, but an equal number don't. Other possible ingredients include tomatoes, bay leaves, and filé powder (crushed sassafras leaves).

There're a few things to consider before you make gumbo. It'll take a lot of time, some of it spent stirring the roux, but most of the time is basically hands free. You'll just need to stir the pot occasionally to prevent sticking.

White rice is the most traditional accompaniment, but for a truly authentic Cajun touch, serve potato salad on the side.

CHICKEN-AND-SAUSAGE GUMBO

family favorite

Prep: 55 min., Cook: 3 hrs. *(pictured on page 225)*

- **1 pound andouille sausage, cut into ¼-inch-thick slices**
- **4 skinned bone-in chicken breasts**
- **Vegetable oil**
- **¾ cup all-purpose flour**
- **1 medium onion, chopped**
- **½ green bell pepper, chopped**
- **2 celery ribs, sliced**
- **2 quarts hot water**
- **3 garlic cloves, minced**
- **2 bay leaves**
- **1 tablespoon Worcestershire sauce**
- **2 teaspoons Creole seasoning**
- **½ teaspoon dried thyme**
- **½ to 1 teaspoon hot sauce**
- **4 green onions, sliced**
- **Filé powder (optional)**
- **Hot cooked rice**
- **Garnish: chopped green onions**

COOK sausage in a Dutch oven over medium heat, stirring constantly, 5 minutes or until browned. Drain on paper towels, reserving drippings in Dutch oven. Set sausage aside.

COOK chicken breasts in reserved drippings in Dutch oven over medium heat 5 minutes or until browned. Remove to paper towels, reserving drippings in Dutch oven. Set chicken aside.

ADD enough oil to drippings in Dutch oven to measure ½ cup. Add flour, and cook over medium heat, stirring constantly, 20 to 25 minutes, or until roux is chocolate colored.

STIR in onion, bell pepper, and celery; cook, stirring often, 8 minutes or until tender. Gradually add 2 quarts hot water, and bring mixture to a boil; add chicken, garlic, and next 5 ingredients. Reduce heat to low, and simmer, stirring occasionally, 1 hour. Remove chicken; let cool.

ADD sausage to gumbo; cook 30 minutes. Stir in sliced green onions; cook 30 more minutes.

BONE chicken, and cut meat into strips; return chicken to gumbo, and simmer 5 minutes. Remove and discard bay leaves.

REMOVE gumbo from heat. Sprinkle with filé powder, if desired. Serve over hot cooked rice. Garnish, if desired. **MAKES** 4 to 6 servings.

Pick a Potato

Take convenience products to the max with recipes starring refrigerated, ready-to-put-in-the-pan potatoes available at your local grocery store. All of these reader recipes originally started with whole potatoes that had to be washed and prepared. We've trimmed away time using pre-packaged products.

GOLDEN GARLIC-AND-POTATO SOUP

fast fixin's • family favorite

Prep: 5 min., Cook: 25 min.

This soup is ready to serve in 30 minutes.

- ½ cup diced sweet onion
- 4 garlic cloves, minced
- 1 tablespoon olive oil
- ½ cup white wine
- 2 (14-ounce) cans chicken broth
- 2 (1-pound, 4-ounce) packages refrigerated mashed potatoes
- ½ cup half-and-half
- ¼ cup diced red bell pepper
- Salt to taste
- ¼ cup chopped fresh chives

SAUTÉ onion and garlic in hot oil in a Dutch oven over medium-high heat 5 minutes. Stir in wine; cook 5 minutes. Whisk in broth and potatoes until smooth. Bring to a boil, reduce heat to medium, and simmer 10 minutes; stir in half-and-half and bell pepper, and cook 5 more minutes or until thoroughly heated. Add salt to taste. Top with chives. **MAKES** 8 servings.

NOTE: For testing purposes only, we used Simply Potatoes Mashed Potatoes for refrigerated mashed potatoes.

HELEN WOLT
COLORADO SPRINGS, COLORADO

TANGY OLIVE POTATOES

family favorite

Prep: 10 min., Cook: 35 min.

- 1 (1-pound, 4-ounce) package refrigerated diced potatoes*
- 2 tablespoons butter or margarine
- 4 ounces Canadian bacon, finely chopped
- 1 medium-size onion, chopped
- ½ teaspoon dried thyme
- 1 cup whipping cream
- 1½ teaspoons salt
- ½ teaspoon pepper
- 3 tablespoons sliced pimiento-stuffed olives

ARRANGE potatoes in a steamer basket over boiling water. Cover and steam 20 minutes or until tender.
MELT butter in a large skillet over medium heat; add bacon, onion, and thyme, and sauté 10 minutes. Stir in potatoes, whipping cream, salt, and pepper. Cook 5 minutes or until thoroughly heated; stir in sliced olives. Serve immediately. **MAKES** 4 servings.

NOTE: For testing purposes only, we used Simply Potatoes Diced Potatoes.

*Substitute 1 pound, 4 ounces potatoes, peeled and diced, if desired.

JEANNE STEADMAN
MADISON, ALABAMA

BLUE CHEESE POTATOES

family favorite

Prep: 10 min., Bake: 25 min.

If you prefer other taste pairings, use your favorite salad dressing and cheese combination to create your own new recipe.

- 1 (1-pound, 4-ounce) package refrigerated new potato wedges*
- 1 tablespoon olive oil
- ½ cup refrigerated blue cheese dressing
- ¼ teaspoon freshly ground black pepper
- ¼ cup crumbled blue cheese

DRIZZLE potatoes with oil, tossing to coat. Place potatoes evenly in a 13- x 9-inch baking dish.
BAKE at 450° for 25 minutes.
TRANSFER potatoes to a serving bowl. Toss with dressing and pepper. Sprinkle with cheese. **MAKES** 4 servings.

NOTE: For testing purposes only, we used Simply Potatoes New Potato Wedges and Naturally Fresh Bleu Cheese Dressing.

*Substitute 1 pound, 4 ounces potatoes, peeled and cut into wedges, if desired.

SUSI EDWARDS
MEMPHIS, TENNESSEE

FETA CHEESE POTATOES: Substitute Ranch dressing for blue cheese dressing and crumbled feta cheese for crumbled blue cheese.

Chopped Cooked Chicken

It's easy to have chopped cooked chicken on hand for a casserole or salad. Cook fresh chicken; then chop and freeze in ready-to-use portions. See page 221 for a delicious Chicken Tetrazzini recipe that uses chopped cooked chicken.

GRILLED CHICKEN BREASTS

freezeable • make ahead

Prep: 10 min., Grill: 20 min., Cool: 10 min.

- 6 skinned and boned chicken breasts (about 2½ pounds)
- 1 teaspoon salt
- ½ teaspoon pepper

SPRINKLE chicken evenly with salt and pepper or desired seasoning.

GRILL, covered with grill lid, over medium-high heat (350° to 400°) about 8 to 10 minutes on each side or until done. Cool chicken slightly; chop meat, and store in airtight containers in freezer up to 3 months. **MAKES** about 6 cups.

BASIC BAKED CHICKEN BREASTS

freezeable • make ahead

Prep: 15 min.; Bake: 1hr., 30 min.; Cool: 10 min.

The chicken breasts we purchased for testing were on the large side—six breasts totaled 4.78 pounds. Lower cooking time and the pan size for smaller pieces.

- **4 celery ribs with tops, cut into 4-inch pieces**
- **2 carrots, sliced**
- **2 medium onions, sliced**
- **6 bone-in chicken breasts (about 4 pounds)**
- **½ teaspoon salt**
- **¼ teaspoon pepper**

ARRANGE celery, carrots, and onions in a lightly greased 15- x 12-inch roasting pan. Top with chicken; sprinkle with salt and pepper.

BAKE, covered, at 350° for 1 to 1½ hours or until chicken is done. Cool chicken slightly; remove and discard skin and bones. Chop meat, and store in airtight containers in freezer up to 3 months. **MAKES** about 8 cups.

BOILED CHICKEN BREASTS

freezeable • make ahead

Prep: 20 min., Cook: 40 min., Cool: 10 min.

- **6 bone-in chicken breasts (about 4 pounds)**
- **2 quarts water**
- **1 small onion, quartered**
- **2 celery ribs with tops, quartered**
- **2 carrots, quartered**
- **1 garlic clove**
- **1 bay leaf**
- **2 teaspoons salt**
- **1 teaspoon pepper**

BRING all ingredients to a boil in a Dutch oven. Cover, reduce heat, and simmer 30 to 40 minutes or until done. Cool chicken slightly; remove and discard skin and bones. Chop meat, and store in airtight containers in freezer up to 3 months. Strain and reserve broth to use fresh, or freeze, if desired. Broth may be frozen in airtight containers. **MAKES** about 8 cups chicken and 8 cups broth.

Other Chicken Options

- Remove meat from a deli-roasted chicken, and chop. They cost around $4.99 each and yield about 3 cups meat.
- Packaged, oven-roasted chicken breast cuts from the meat case yield 2 cups of chopped chicken for about $9.87.
- Grill frozen skinned and boned chicken breasts, covered with grill lid, over medium-high heat (350° to 400°) about 12 minutes on each side or until done. (Do not refreeze chicken.)

Cook's Corner

Take advantage of these informative brochures from Maytag Appliances, the National Country Ham Association, and Gold Medal Flour.

Stain Removal Guide

If you've ever struggled to remove wax from an heirloom tablecloth or nail polish from your daughter's pillow sham, this handy guide is a great resource. You'll be able to get rid of every type of stain, from beverages to water-based paint. The procedures listed apply to washable items only; they are not intended for fabrics that should be dry-cleaned. This handy guide is available only through the Maytag Web site. Print it directly from **www.maytag.com/sl.**

Country Ham Recipes and Tips

October is National Country Ham month, and the National Country Ham Association has a brochure just for you. For more than 200 years, Americans have been curing and eating country ham. The brochure contains tips, historical information, recipes from chefs, and a list of country ham suppliers. For a free copy, call the National Country Ham Association at 1-800-820-4426, or send a self-addressed, stamped, business-size envelope to: National Country Ham Association, P.O. Box 948, Conover, NC 28616. Visit **www.countryham.org** for a variety of recipes, storage tips, and facts.

Cookbooks for Little Chefs

Gold Medal Flour is offering two great cookbooks kids will love—*The Rainbow Bakery: A Color-Full Adventure Children's Cookbook* and the *Alpha-Bakery Children's Cookbook.* Designed for kids of all ages, they feature delightful color illustrations, easy-to-read text, and graphics of measuring cups and spoons to indicate quantities. Simple tips, safety concerns, and directions will help get youthful food lovers off to a great start in the kitchen.

The books are $2.50 each; educators may purchase 20 or more at a discounted price. Visit **www.bettycrocker.com/products/GM_cookbooksforkids_order.asp,** or call 1-800-345-2443. You can also find order forms on 5-pound bags of Gold Medal All-Purpose Flour.

Get a Kick Out of Yogurt

We used this breakfast staple to create a fresh and lively appetizer and zesty main dishes.

Yogurt is like your mother-in-law—you either love it or tolerate it. You'll learn to love calcium- and protein-rich yogurt when you try amazing-tasting recipes complemented with this cool-creamy food.

GRILLED PORK TENDERLOIN WITH YOGURT AND LIME

family favorite

Prep: 20 min., Chill: 2 hrs., Grill: 20 min., Stand: 10 min.

- **2 (1-pound) pork tenderloins**
- **1 teaspoon salt**
- **1 teaspoon pepper**
- **3 cups plain yogurt**
- **3 garlic cloves, minced**
- **½ cup chopped fresh mint**
- **2 teaspoons ground coriander**
- **1 teaspoon grated lime rind**
- **2 tablespoons fresh lime juice**
- **2 teaspoons olive oil**

SPRINKLE pork evenly with salt and pepper. Place in a baking dish or large zip-top freezer bag.
STIR together yogurt and next 6 ingredients. Reserve 1 cup yogurt mixture; cover and chill.
SPOON remaining yogurt mixture over pork, rubbing evenly over pork. Cover or seal, and chill 2 hours. Remove pork from marinade, discarding marinade.
GRILL, covered with grill lid, over medium-high heat (350° to 400°), 20 minutes, turning once, or until a meat thermometer inserted into thickest portion registers 155°. Remove from heat; let stand 10 minutes or until temperature registers 160°. Cut into ½-inch slices; serve with reserved 1 cup yogurt mixture. **MAKES** 8 servings.

Per serving: Calories 298 (36% from fat); Fat 11.8g (sat 4.3g, mono 5.1g, poly 1g); Protein 39g; Carb 7.3g; Fiber 0.4g; Chol 112mg; Iron 1.8mg; Sodium 423mg; Calc 172.4mg

SHRIMP WITH YOGURT-CUCUMBER SAUCE

Prep: 10 min., Chill: 20 min., Cook: 20 min.

This high-calcium, high-fiber dish makes a satisfying and colorful entrée. The Yogurt-Cucumber Sauce is also called tzatziki. Try it on burgers, beef strips, or chicken.

- **2 pounds unpeeled, medium-size fresh shrimp**
- **½ cup dry white wine**
- **2 teaspoons grated lemon rind**
- **2 tablespoons fresh lemon juice**
- **2 garlic cloves, minced**
- **1 teaspoon dried oregano**
- **1 teaspoon salt, divided**
- **1 teaspoon pepper, divided**
- **2 teaspoons olive oil, divided**
- **1 large onion, cut into thin strips**
- **1 large red bell pepper, cut into thin strips**
- **2 cups grape or cherry tomatoes, halved**
- **Yogurt-Cucumber Sauce**

PEEL shrimp, and devein, if desired.
COMBINE wine, next 4 ingredients, ½ teaspoon salt, and ½ teaspoon pepper in a shallow dish or zip-top freezer bag; add shrimp. Cover or seal, and chill 15 to 20 minutes. Remove shrimp from marinade, discarding marinade.
COOK marinated shrimp in 1 teaspoon hot olive oil in a large nonstick skillet over medium-high heat 3 minutes or just until shrimp turn pink. Remove shrimp from skillet; cover and keep warm.
SAUTÉ onion, bell pepper strips, remaining ½ teaspoon salt, and remaining ½ teaspoon pepper in remaining 1 teaspoon hot oil in skillet over medium-high heat 15 minutes or until onion is tender. Add tomato halves; cook 1 minute or until thoroughly heated. Spoon onion mixture over shrimp, and serve with Yogurt-Cucumber Sauce. **MAKES** 8 servings.

Per serving: Calories (including Yogurt-Cucumber Sauce): 163 (26% from fat); Fat 4.7g (sat 1.7g, mono 1.7g, poly 0.8g); Protein 20g; Carb 9g; Fiber 1.5g; Chol 137mg; Iron 2.5mg; Sodium 593mg; Calc 129mg

Yogurt-Cucumber Sauce:
make ahead

Prep: 5 min., Chill: 3 hrs.

- **2 cups regular or low-fat plain yogurt**
- **1 small cucumber, peeled, seeded, and chopped**
- **1 garlic clove, minced**
- **1 teaspoon grated lemon rind**
- **½ teaspoon salt**
- **Garnishes: lemon wedges, cherry tomato half**

LINE a fine wire-mesh strainer with 3 layers of cheesecloth or 1 coffee filter. Place strainer over a bowl. Spoon yogurt into strainer. Cover yogurt with plastic wrap, and chill 2 hours.
SPOON yogurt into a bowl, discarding strained liquid. (Yogurt will be thick.) Stir in chopped cucumber and next 3 ingredients. Cover and chill at least 1 hour. Garnish, if desired. **MAKES** 2½ cups.

Lowdown on Yogurt

We used either low-fat or regular plain yogurt in our recipes because it has a smoother and creamier consistency than fat-free yogurt.

- **Regular:** Made from whole milk with at least 3.25% milk fat.
- **Low-fat:** Made with low-fat or part-skim milk. It varies from 0.5% to 2% milk fat.
- **Fat-free:** Made from skim or fat-free milk and contains less than 0.5% milk fat. Many brands add gelatin for thickness. We tried nonfat yogurt in our recipes but weren't pleased with the results.

YOGURT CHEESE APPETIZER

fast fixin's

Prep: 15 min.

Make the Yogurt Cheese the night before because it needs 24 hours to chill. We tried it with fat-free yogurt, which didn't work well, so stick with plain yogurt.

- **Yogurt Cheese (see recipe below)**
- **1 teaspoon salt**
- **½ teaspoon sesame seeds**
- **¼ teaspoon dried thyme**
- **¼ teaspoon dried marjoram**
- **2 teaspoons olive oil**
- **1 cup kalamata olives**
- **1 cucumber, peeled and sliced**
- **4 (6-inch) whole wheat pita rounds, warmed and cut into wedges**

SPOON Yogurt Cheese into a serving bowl, pressing lightly to flatten. Sprinkle cheese with salt, sesame seeds, thyme, and marjoram; drizzle with olive oil. Serve with kalamata olives, cucumber slices, and warm whole wheat pita wedges. **MAKES** 10 appetizer servings.

Per serving: Calories 150 (29% from fat); Fat 4.9g (sat 1.2g, mono 2.6g, poly 0.6g); Protein 6.8g; Carb 21g; Fiber 2.2g; Chol 8mg; Iron 1.2mg; Sodium 540mg; Calc 131mg

Yogurt Cheese:

Prep: 5 min., Chill: 24 hrs.

LINE a fine wire-mesh strainer with 3 layers of cheesecloth or 1 coffee filter. Place strainer over a bowl. Spoon 3 (8-ounce) containers plain yogurt into strainer. Cover with plastic wrap, and chill 24 hours. Remove yogurt cheese, discarding strained liquid.

VEGETABLE CURRY

Prep: 30 min., Cook: 35 min.

- **4 large garlic cloves**
- **1 (2-inch) piece fresh ginger, peeled**
- **½ teaspoon ground cumin**
- **½ teaspoon ground cloves**
- **¼ teaspoon ground allspice**
- **¼ teaspoon ground cinnamon**
- **1 bay leaf**
- **2 teaspoons vegetable oil**
- **1 medium onion, chopped**
- **2 teaspoons curry powder**
- **1 jalapeño pepper, seeded and minced**
- **½ cup canned diced tomatoes, undrained**
- **½ cup plain yogurt**
- **1 (14-ounce) can vegetable or chicken broth**
- **6 small red potatoes, quartered**
- **2 cups cauliflower florets**
- **½ pound fresh green beans, trimmed and cut into 1-inch pieces**
- **1 cup canned chickpeas, rinsed and drained**
- **1 teaspoon salt**
- **Hot cooked basmati or long-grain rice**
- **Mango chutney (optional)**

PULSE garlic and ginger in a small food processor until the consistency of paste, or mince using a sharp knife. Set aside. **SAUTÉ** cumin and next 4 ingredients in hot oil in a Dutch oven over medium-high heat 30 seconds or until fragrant. Add onion; cook 3 minutes or until lightly browned.

STIR in garlic mixture, curry powder, and jalapeño. Cook, stirring constantly, 1 minute. Stir in tomatoes and yogurt; cook, stirring constantly, 5 minutes. Add broth and potatoes; bring to a boil. Cover, reduce heat, and simmer 10 minutes or just until potatoes are tender. Add cauliflower, green beans, and chickpeas. Cook, uncovered, 10 minutes or until vegetables are tender and mixture is thickened.

DISCARD bay leaf; add salt. Serve over rice, and top with chutney, if desired. **MAKES** 6 servings.

NOTE: Mango chutney may be found in the condiment aisle of supermarkets.

Per serving with ½ cup cooked rice: Calories 282 (11% from fat); Fat 3.6g (sat 0.7g, mono 1.3g, poly 0.9g); Protein 9g; Carb 55g; Fiber 6.7g; Chol 3mg; Iron 3.1mg; Sodium 712mg; Calc 109mg

Yogurt Uses

- Try strained yogurt instead of mayonnaise in potato, tuna, or chicken salad.
- Cool off a fiery dish by serving with a dollop of yogurt.
- Swirl honey or maple syrup into plain nonfat yogurt, and top with sliced pears and toasted pecans.
- Top baked russet or sweet potatoes with yogurt instead of sour cream.
- Enjoy a breakfast of plain or vanilla yogurt blended with fresh fruit.

Fall Porch Party

Take the party outside, and relax
with this casual gathering.

Dinner on the Deck

Serves 4

Steak-and-Vegetable Kebabs
over mixed salad greens

Orphan's Rice

Apple-Gingerbread Cobbler

It's not too late to fire up the grill and enjoy the crisp air. Show off this easy harvest menu to family and friends. Serve fork-tender Steak-and-Vegetable Kebabs over a bed of mixed salad greens. Put the greens on the serving platter early in the day, cover with damp paper towels, and refrigerate until ready to serve. A package of yellow rice lets you jump-start your side dish, while a gingerbread mix and canned pie filling make Apple-Gingerbread Cobbler easy to prepare.

STEAK-AND-VEGETABLE KEBABS

family favorite

Prep: 20 min.; Chill: 2 hrs., 20 min.;
Grill: 12 min.

If you use wooden skewers instead of metal, soak them in cold water 30 minutes before grilling.

> ½ cup dry sherry
> ½ cup olive oil
> 2 tablespoons grated orange rind
> ½ cup fresh orange juice
> ¼ cup soy sauce
> 4 garlic cloves, minced
> 2 tablespoons minced fresh ginger
> ½ teaspoon dried crushed red pepper (optional)
> 1½ pounds rib-eye steak, cut into 1-inch cubes
> 1 small red onion, cut into 1½-inch pieces
> 1 medium-size yellow bell pepper, cut into ½- to ¾-inch pieces
> 2 small zucchini, cut into 8 slices
> Mixed salad greens

WHISK together first 7 ingredients, and, if desired, crushed red pepper. Remove and reserve ¾ cup marinade. Pour remaining marinade into a shallow dish or large zip-top freezer bag; add steak. Cover or seal, and chill 2 hours. Add onion, bell pepper, and zucchini; toss to coat, cover or seal, and chill 20 minutes.

REMOVE steak and vegetables from marinade, discarding marinade. Thread steak and vegetables, separately, onto 6 to 8 (12-inch) metal skewers.

GRILL, covered with grill lid, over medium-high heat (350° to 400°) 10 to 12 minutes or until done. Serve over mixed salad greens with reserved ¾ cup marinade. **MAKES** 4 servings.

ORPHAN'S RICE

family favorite

Prep: 10 min., Cook: 30 min., Stand: 10 min.

> 1 tablespoon butter
> ¾ cup pecan halves
> ½ cup slivered almonds
> ⅓ cup pine nuts
> ½ small onion, minced
> 1 garlic clove, minced
> 2 tablespoons vegetable oil
> 1 (10-ounce) package yellow rice
> 3 cups low-sodium chicken broth
> 2 bacon slices, cooked and crumbled
> ¼ cup finely chopped cooked ham
> 1 tablespoon minced fresh parsley

MELT butter in a skillet over medium heat. Add ¾ cup pecan halves, ½ cup slivered almonds, and ⅓ cup pine nuts, and cook, stirring often, 3 minutes or until almonds are light golden brown. Set aside.

SAUTÉ minced onion and garlic in hot vegetable oil in a saucepan over medium-high heat 5 minutes or until onion is tender. Add yellow rice, and sauté, stirring constantly, 1 minute. Add chicken broth; cover and cook 18 minutes. Remove saucepan from heat.

STIR in nuts, crumbled bacon, chopped ham, and fresh parsley. Cover and let stand 10 minutes. Serve immediately. **MAKES** 6 to 8 servings.

APPLE-GINGERBREAD COBBLER

family favorite

Prep: 15 min., Cook: 5 min., Bake: 35 min.

- ı (14-ounce) package gingerbread mix, divided
- ¾ cup water
- ¼ cup firmly packed light brown sugar
- ½ cup butter, divided
- ½ cup chopped pecans
- 2 (21-ounce) cans apple pie filling
- Vanilla ice cream

STIR together 2 cups gingerbread mix and ¾ cup water until smooth; set mixture aside.

STIR together remaining gingerbread mix and brown sugar; cut in ¼ cup butter until mixture is crumbly. Stir in chopped pecans; set pecan mixture aside.

COMBINE apple pie filling and remaining ¼ cup butter in a large saucepan, and cook, stirring often, over medium heat 5 minutes or until thoroughly heated. Spoon hot apple pie filling mixture evenly into a lightly greased 11- x 7-inch baking dish. Spoon gingerbread mixture evenly over hot apple pie filling mixture; sprinkle evenly with pecan-and-brown sugar mixture.

BAKE at 375° for 30 to 35 minutes or until set. Serve cobbler with vanilla ice cream. **MAKES** 8 servings.

Pastas for Fall Entertaining

What is it about pasta that makes the pickiest of eaters suddenly swoon? Whether it be penne, fettuccine, or good old spaghetti, it seems that everyone has a noodle of choice.

Kids as well as adults will love these recipes, which offer a variety of pasta shapes and sauces to choose from. Try a simple baked lasagna using egg noodles, delicious for a weeknight meal or a romantic dinner for two. A hearty wild mushroom ragù over cheese tortellini is perfect for fall entertaining. Try pasta in a whole new way in the Honeyed Orzo-Pecan Pie, which is delicious served with a sweet dessert wine such as *Vin Santo* or a late-harvest Riesling.

HONEYED ORZO-PECAN PIE

family favorite

Prep: 10 min., Cook: 5 min., Bake: 45 min.

Orzo, a tiny rice-shaped pasta, cooks quickly and is good in both savory and sweet dishes.

- ½ (15-ounce) package refrigerated piecrusts
- 1 cup uncooked orzo
- 2 large eggs
- 1 cup fat-free evaporated milk
- ½ cup firmly packed light brown sugar
- ½ cup honey
- ½ cup chopped pecans, toasted
- ½ cup chopped dates
- Whipped cream (optional)
- Chopped toasted pecans (optional)

FIT piecrust into a 9-inch pieplate according to package directions; fold edges under, and crimp.

COOK orzo according to package directions; drain well.

WHISK together eggs and next 3 ingredients in a medium bowl. Add in orzo, ½ cup chopped pecans, and dates, stirring well. Spoon orzo mixture into piecrust.

BAKE at 350° for 40 to 45 minutes or until set; cool on a wire rack. Serve warm with whipped cream and additional chopped pecans, if desired. **MAKES** 1 (9-inch) pie.

JANICE ELDER
CHARLOTTE, NORTH CAROLINA

EGG-NOODLE LASAGNA

family favorite

Prep: 20 min., Cook: 30 min., Bake: 30 min., Stand: 10 min.

Mascarpone, a delicately flavored triple cream cheese essential in tiramisù, offers a creamier texture than ricotta.

- 1 (8-ounce) package wide egg noodles
- 1 pound lean ground beef
- 6 green onions, sliced
- 2 large garlic cloves, minced
- ¾ teaspoon salt, divided
- 1 (26-ounce) jar tomato-basil pasta sauce
- ⅛ teaspoon pepper
- 1 (8-ounce) package fresh mascarpone cheese*
- 1 cup sour cream
- ¼ cup shredded Parmesan cheese

PREPARE egg noodles according to package directions. Drain noodles, and set aside.

COOK ground beef, green onions, garlic, and ½ teaspoon salt in a large nonstick skillet over medium-high heat, stirring 10 minutes or until beef crumbles and is no longer pink. Drain well.

STIR in tomato-basil pasta sauce and pepper. Cover, reduce heat, and simmer 20 minutes.

STIR together egg noodles, mascarpone cheese, 1 cup sour cream, and remaining ¼ teaspoon salt until blended.

LAYER half each of egg noodle mixture and ground beef mixture in a lightly greased 2-quart baking dish. Repeat layers.

BAKE at 350° for 25 minutes. Remove from oven; sprinkle evenly with Parmesan cheese, and bake 5 more minutes.

LET stand 10 minutes before serving. **MAKES** 6 servings.

*Substitute 1 (8-ounce) package cream cheese for fresh mascarpone cheese, if desired.

NORMA F. BONE
TALLAHASSEE, FLORIDA

WILD MUSHROOM RAGÙ WITH TORTELLINI

Prep: 10 min., Cook: 35 min.

Pasta is best served in warmed bowls. Heat ovenproof bowls in a low-temperature oven.

- **1 pound refrigerated cheese-filled tortellini**
- **2 cups whipping cream**
- **1 teaspoon salt, divided**
- **1 pinch fresh ground nutmeg**
- **4 tablespoons unsalted butter**
- **¼ cup shallots, minced**
- **2 large garlic cloves, minced**
- **½ pound cremini mushroom caps, sliced***
- **½ pound shiitake mushrooms, sliced***
- **½ pound oyster mushrooms, sliced***
- **1 large portobello mushroom cap, minced**
- **1 cup freshly grated Parmigiano-Reggiano cheese, divided**
- **½ teaspoon freshly ground pepper**
- **Garnishes: fresh parsley, freshly shaved Parmigiano-Reggiano cheese**

COOK tortellini according to package directions. Drain and set aside.

STIR together cream, ½ teaspoon salt, and nutmeg in a saucepan over medium heat; bring to a boil, reduce heat, and cook 15 minutes or until cream has thickened and will coat back of spoon. Remove from heat, and set aside.

MELT butter in a large skillet over medium heat. Add shallots and garlic; cook, covered, 2 to 3 minutes, stirring occasionally. Increase heat to medium high; add mushrooms and remaining ½ teaspoon salt. Cover and cook 8 minutes. Uncover and cook until liquid evaporates.

ADD cream mixture, ⅓ cup grated Parmigiano-Reggiano cheese, and pepper to skillet; stir until blended.

TOSS pasta with mushroom sauce.

SPRINKLE with remaining ⅔ cup grated cheese. Serve pasta in warmed bowls. Garnish, if desired. **MAKES** 4 servings.

*Substitute equal amounts of fresh button mushrooms, sliced, if desired.

SUE-SUE HARTSTERN
LOUISVILLE, KENTUCKY

Fix-and-Freeze Favorites

Home-cooked convenience is this busy mom's specialty.

Almost everyone loves a good Chicken Tetrazzini, and Marta Hill makes one of the best. Owner of Marta's Bakery in Cahaba Heights, Alabama, she's as well known for her freezer-friendly casseroles as she is for her cakes and pies.

With a family of six, Marta takes a divide-and-conquer approach to stocking her freezer. She chops or cooks the ingredients for a casserole one evening, and then assembles it the next.

DOUBLE CHOCOLATE BROWNIES

freezeable • make ahead

Prep: 15 min., Bake: 40 min.

Both versions of this tasty treat are sure to satisfy your chocolate craving.

- **2 (1-ounce) squares unsweetened chocolate**
- **2 (1-ounce) squares semisweet chocolate**
- **1 cup butter, softened**
- **2 cups sugar**
- **4 large eggs**
- **1 cup all-purpose flour**
- **½ teaspoon salt**
- **1 teaspoon vanilla extract**
- **¾ cup chopped, toasted pecans**
- **¾ cup semisweet chocolate morsels**

MICROWAVE chocolate squares in a small microwave-safe bowl at MEDIUM (50% power) for 30-second intervals until chocolate is melted (about 1½ minutes total time). Stir chocolate until smooth.

BEAT butter and sugar at medium speed with an electric mixer until light and fluffy. Add eggs, 1 at a time, beating just until blended after each addition. Add melted chocolate, beating just until blended.

ADD flour and salt, beating at low speed just until blended. Stir in vanilla, ½ cup pecans, and ½ cup chocolate morsels. Spread batter into a greased and floured 13- x 9-inch pan. Sprinkle with remaining ¼ cup pecans and ¼ cup chocolate morsels.

BAKE at 350° for 40 minutes or until set. Cool completely on a wire rack. **MAKES** 32 brownies.

NOTE: Freeze brownies in an airtight container up to 1 month.

DOUBLE CHOCOLATE BROWNIES WITH CARAMEL FROSTING: Prepare Double Chocolate Brownies as directed. Melt ¾ cup butter in a large saucepan over low heat. Stir in 2 cups sugar, ½ cup buttermilk, 12 large marshmallows, 1 tablespoon light corn syrup, and ½ teaspoon baking soda. Cook over medium heat, stirring occasionally, 20 to 25 minutes or until a candy thermometer registers 234° (soft ball stage). Remove from heat, and pour mixture immediately into a large mixing bowl. Beat mixture at high speed with an electric mixer 5 minutes or until mixture thickens and begins to lose its gloss. Spread Caramel Frosting evenly over brownies.

CHICKEN TETRAZZINI

freezeable • make ahead

Prep: 20 min., Bake: 35 min.

This is Marta Hill's most requested casserole.

- **1 (16-ounce) package vermicelli**
- **½ cup chicken broth**
- **4 cups chopped cooked chicken breast (see recipes beginning on page 214)**
- **1 (10¾-ounce) can cream of mushroom soup**
- **1 (10¾-ounce) can cream of chicken soup**
- **1 (10¾-ounce) can cream of celery soup**
- **1 (8-ounce) container sour cream**
- **1 (6-ounce) jar sliced mushrooms, drained**
- **½ cup (2 ounces) shredded Parmesan cheese**
- **1 teaspoon pepper**
- **½ teaspoon salt**
- **2 cups (8 ounces) shredded Cheddar cheese**

COOK vermicelli according to package directions; drain. Return to pot, and toss with chicken broth.

STIR together chicken and next 8 ingredients in a large bowl; add vermicelli, and toss well. Spoon chicken mixture into 2 lightly greased 11- x 7-inch baking dishes. Sprinkle evenly with Cheddar cheese.

BAKE, covered, at 350° for 30 minutes; uncover and bake 5 more minutes or until cheese is melted and bubbly. **MAKES** 12 servings.

NOTE: Freeze unbaked casserole up to 1 month, if desired. Thaw casserole overnight in refrigerator. Let stand 30 minutes at room temperature, and bake as directed.

Low Price, Big Flavor

A large boneless pork loin offers lots of options for quick and easy meals. Often on sale, this cut of meat is a thrifty way to have dozens of different entrées literally at your fingertips. Freeze extra portions in zip-top freezer bags for up to 3 months.

The secret to serving moist and tender pork is simple. Have the skillet or grill hot enough to sear the meat and seal in the juices. Be careful not to overcook the meat—a little pink on the inside is fine.

PORK SCALOPPINE

family favorite

Prep: 25 min., Cook: 10 min.

- **1½ pounds pork loin**
- **4 large eggs**
- **¼ cup milk**
- **½ cup freshly grated Romano cheese**
- **1½ teaspoons garlic powder**
- **½ teaspoon salt**
- **½ cup all-purpose flour**
- **¼ cup butter or margarine**
- **¼ cup olive oil**
- **2 lemons, quartered**

CUT pork loin into ½-inch-thick slices. Place pork between 2 sheets of heavy-duty plastic wrap; flatten to ¼-inch thickness using a meat mallet or rolling pin. **WHISK** together eggs and next 4 ingredients. Dredge pork in flour, shake to remove excess, and dip in egg mixture. **MELT** butter with olive oil in a large skillet over medium-high heat. Cook pork, in batches, 1 minute on each side or until browned. Serve with lemon quarters. **MAKES** 4 servings.

JO BRICE
MELBOURNE, FLORIDA

PORK FILLETS WITH DARK CHERRY SAUCE

family favorite

Prep: 10 min., Cook: 25 min.

We tied a piece of kitchen string around extra-thick slices of pork loin to retain the round shape during cooking. Just use a pair of scissors to cut away the string before serving.

- **2 pounds pork loin**
- **½ teaspoon salt**
- **½ teaspoon freshly ground pepper**
- **2 tablespoons olive oil**
- **½ cup beef broth**
- **¼ cup bourbon**
- **1 (17-ounce) can pitted dark sweet cherries**
- **1 tablespoon cornstarch**
- **2 teaspoons grated lemon rind**
- **2 tablespoons fresh lemon juice**
- **1½ teaspoons chopped fresh rosemary**
- **½ teaspoon whole cloves**
- **½ cup chopped pecans, toasted**
- **Garnish: fresh watercress**

CUT pork loin into 4 (1½-inch-thick) fillets; sprinkle evenly with salt and pepper. Securely tie a 12-inch piece of kitchen string around each fillet, if desired. **COOK** fillets in hot oil in a skillet over medium-high heat 2 to 3 minutes on each side or until golden brown. Stir together beef broth and bourbon; add to skillet, stirring to loosen particles from bottom of skillet. Reduce heat to low; cover and simmer 10 to 15 minutes or until pork is done. Remove fillets to a serving platter, reserving pan juices, and keep warm. Remove and discard kitchen string. **DRAIN** cherries, reserving syrup in a small bowl. **WHISK** together cherry syrup, cornstarch, and next 4 ingredients; add to skillet with reserved pan juices. Bring to a boil over medium heat, and cook, stirring constantly, 1 minute or until thickened. Remove from heat; remove cloves, and stir in cherries and chopped toasted pecans. Spoon mixture evenly over warm pork fillets. Garnish, if desired, and serve immediately. **MAKES** 4 servings.

KAREN SHELBY
FLIPPIN, ARKANSAS

Foil-Packet Dinners

These meal-in-one packets will please everyone.

Make tonight's supper a "wrap party." Line up ingredients for one of these recipes on the kitchen counter, and let each family member make his or her own personalized foil packet. The result? A tasty dinner with minimal cleanup.

BARBECUED CHICKEN IN FOIL

family favorite

Prep: 15 min., Bake: 40 min.

- 8 chicken legs
- 4 small ears frozen corn, thawed
- 1 teaspoon salt
- ½ teaspoon pepper
- 2 tablespoons butter, melted
- ½ cup barbecue sauce
- 1 (15-ounce) can pinto beans, rinsed and drained
- Toppings: barbecue sauce, shredded Cheddar cheese, chopped green onions

TEAR off 4 (18- x 12-inch) sheets of aluminum foil; lightly grease 1 side of each sheet.

PLACE 2 chicken legs and 1 ear of corn in center on greased side of each foil sheet. Sprinkle evenly with salt and pepper; drizzle corn evenly with butter. Spoon barbecue sauce evenly over chicken; top evenly with beans.

BRING together 2 sides of each foil sheet over ingredients, and double fold with about 1-inch-wide folds. Double fold each end to form a packet, leaving room for heat circulation inside packet. Place packets on a baking sheet.

BAKE at 450° for 40 minutes. Carefully open packets to prevent burns from hot steam. Serve with desired toppings. **MAKES** 4 servings.

ITALIAN MEATBALL PACKETS

family favorite

Prep: 15 min., Bake: 30 min.

- 32 Italian-style frozen meatballs
- ½ medium-size sweet onion, cut into thin strips
- ½ medium-size green bell pepper, cut into thin strips
- ½ medium-size red bell pepper, cut into thin strips
- 1 cup marinara or spaghetti sauce
- 4 tablespoons grated Parmesan cheese

TEAR off 4 (18- x 12-inch) sheets of aluminum foil; lightly grease 1 side of each sheet.

PLACE 8 meatballs in center on greased side of each foil sheet. Top meatballs evenly with onion and bell peppers. Top each with ¼ cup marinara sauce.

BRING together 2 sides of each foil sheet over ingredients, and double fold with about 1-inch-wide folds. Double fold each end to form a packet, leaving room for heat circulation inside packet. Place packets on a baking sheet.

BAKE at 450° for 30 minutes. Carefully open packets to prevent burns from hot steam. Sprinkle each serving with 1 tablespoon cheese before serving. **MAKES** 4 servings.

CHICKEN OLÉ FOIL SUPPER

family favorite

Prep: 15 min., Bake: 20 min.

- 4 skinned and boned chicken breasts
- 2 teaspoons vegetable oil
- ½ teaspoon salt
- ¼ teaspoon pepper
- ¾ cup salsa
- 1 (15-ounce) can black beans, rinsed and drained
- 1 (11-ounce) can whole kernel corn, drained (optional)
- 1 cup (4 ounces) shredded Mexican cheese blend, Cheddar, or Monterey Jack cheese
- Toppings: chopped fresh cilantro, sliced black olives, sour cream, guacamole

TEAR off 4 (18- x 12-inch) sheets of aluminum foil; lightly grease 1 side of each sheet.

PLACE 1 chicken breast in center on greased side of each foil sheet. Brush both sides of chicken evenly with oil; sprinkle evenly with salt and pepper. Spoon salsa evenly over chicken. Top evenly with black beans and, if desired, corn.

BRING together 2 sides of each foil sheet over ingredients, and double fold with about 1-inch-wide folds. Double fold each end to form a packet, leaving room for heat circulation inside packet. Place packets on a baking sheet.

BAKE at 450° for 20 minutes. Carefully open foil packets to prevent burns from hot steam. Sprinkle evenly with cheese before serving. Serve chicken with desired toppings. **MAKES** 4 servings.

KATHLEEN JENNINGS
AUSTIN, TEXAS

To Open Packets

Cut a slit in the top (through the folds) to allow the first burst of steam to escape. (Step back, but take in the aroma.) Carefully pull open the packet as you would a microwave popcorn bag.

Winning Recipes

These player favorites are guaranteed to keep
your next dinner on course.

When the players of the Ladies Professional Golf Association are between tournaments, their cooking concerns are much like our own. They want recipes that are quick and easy—and tasty!

SNICKERDOODLES

family favorite

Prep: 10 min., Bake: 10 min. per batch
(pictured on page 228)

> 2 tablespoons sugar
> 2 teaspoons ground cinnamon
> ½ cup stick margarine, softened
> 1½ cups sugar
> 2 large eggs
> 2¾ cups all-purpose flour
> 2 teaspoons cream of tartar
> 1 teaspoon baking soda
> ¼ teaspoon salt

STIR together 2 tablespoons sugar and cinnamon, and set aside.

BEAT margarine and 1½ cups sugar at medium speed with an electric mixer until creamy; add eggs, 1 at a time, beating just until blended after each addition.

COMBINE flour and next 3 ingredients; gradually add to margarine mixture, beating until blended.

SHAPE dough into 1-inch balls; roll in cinnamon-sugar mixture. Place 2 inches apart on an aluminum foil-lined baking sheet.

BAKE at 350° 8 to 10 minutes or until lightly browned. Transfer to wire racks to cool. **MAKES** 3½ dozen.

DONNA ANDREWS
PINEHURST, NORTH CAROLINA

ANGEL HAIR PASTA WITH VEAL AND SHRIMP

family favorite

Prep: 12 min., Cook: 24 min.

> 8 ounces angel hair pasta
> ½ pound (¼-inch-thick) veal cutlets
> ¼ teaspoon salt
> ⅛ teaspoon pepper
> 2 teaspoons olive oil
> 2 garlic cloves, minced
> ⅓ cup sundried tomato pesto
> 1 (14½-ounce) can diced tomatoes
>   with basil, oregano, and garlic,
>   undrained
> ½ cup dry red wine
> ½ pound cooked, peeled shrimp

PREPARE pasta according to package directions; drain and set aside.

SPRINKLE veal cutlets evenly with salt and pepper.

COOK veal in hot olive oil, in batches, in a large nonstick skillet over medium-high heat 1 minute on each side or until lightly browned. Remove veal cutlets from pan, and keep warm.

ADD garlic to skillet, and cook over medium heat 1 minute. Stir in sundried tomato pesto, tomatoes, and wine. Add veal; cook over medium heat 5 to 7 minutes or until tender. Stir in shrimp; cook 1 minute or until thoroughly heated. Serve over hot cooked pasta. **MAKES** 4 servings.

NOTE: For testing purposes only, we used Melissa's Sun Dried Tomato Pesto.

JEN HANNA
GREENVILLE, SOUTH CAROLINA

SUGARED GREEN BEANS

family favorite

Prep: 10 min., Cook: 25 min.

> 1 pound green beans, trimmed
> ½ teaspoon salt
> ½ small onion, finely chopped
> 1½ tablespoons olive oil, divided
> 1 teaspoon sugar
> 3 garlic cloves, chopped
> ½ teaspoon pepper

SPRINKLE green beans with salt, and arrange in a steamer basket over boiling water; cover and steam 10 minutes or until crisp-tender.

SAUTÉ onion in 1 tablespoon hot oil in a skillet over medium heat until tender; add 1 teaspoon sugar, and cook over low heat 5 to 7 minutes until golden. Add chopped garlic, and sauté 1 minute. Add pepper and green beans, tossing to coat. Drizzle evenly with remaining ½ tablespoon olive oil. **MAKES** 4 servings.

ROSIE JONES
ATLANTA, GEORGIA

SUMMER PASTA

family favorite • fast fixin's

Prep: 15 min.

Stir in a few more tablespoons of olive oil if this dish tastes too dry.

> 12 ounces penne pasta
> 2 pints grape tomatoes, cut in
>   half
> 3 garlic cloves, minced
> ⅓ cup fresh basil,
>   chopped
> ¼ cup olive oil
> ¾ teaspoon salt
> ¼ teaspoon pepper
> Freshly grated Parmesan cheese

PREPARE pasta according to package directions; drain.

STIR together grape tomato halves, minced garlic, basil, olive oil, salt, and pepper. Toss with pasta; sprinkle with cheese. **MAKES** 4 servings.

KRIS TSCHETTER
WARRENTON, VIRGINIA

from our kitchen

The type of flour used in a recipe affects both the flavor and texture. Here's what you need to know to produce great baked goods every time.

Type of Flour	Source	Use
All-purpose flour	Blend of hard and soft wheat	All baking
Self-rising flour	A combination of all-purpose flour, baking powder, and salt	In recipes calling for self-rising flour
Bread flour	Milled from hard wheat; has a high-protein content that produces strong gluten, which gives yeast breads the structure they need to rise	Yeast breads
Cake flour	Milled from soft wheat; has a low-protein content, which gives cakes a tender, fine-grained texture. Substitute cake flour for all-purpose by increasing the amount of flour by 2 tablespoons per cup.	Cakes
Southern flours	Soft wheat (such as White Lily) and soft wheat blends (such as Martha White)	Biscuits, cakes, quick breads, piecrusts

Measuring Up

Successful baking depends on adding just the right amount of ingredients. Glass measuring cups with a pouring spout are best for liquids. Place on a flat surface, and read at eye level, filling exactly to the line indicated. If you use a liquid measuring cup like this for flour, you'll end up with at least an extra tablespoon per cup. It may not sound like much, but it can make a big difference in the moistness of your baked goods.

Nested metal or plastic cups are best for measuring dry ingredients. Flour settles during storage, so always stir before spooning into a dry measuring cup. Fill to the top, and level with the straight edge of a knife or metal spatula.

On the Rise

Yeast is actually a living organism that remains dormant until it comes in contact with moisture. The best way to activate yeast is to mix it with warm water (100° to 115°) and a small amount of sugar. It's important that the water be the right temperature—too hot, and it will kill the yeast; too cold, and the yeast will remain dormant.

Sugar provides food for the yeast. As it grows, yeast creates gas bubbles that cause the dough to rise. Salt controls the growth of yeast, strengthening the gluten and preventing the dough from rising too quickly. Direct contact with salt will kill the dissolved yeast, so always combine the salt with flour before adding.

To let yeast breads rise, cover the bowl of dough with plastic wrap or a towel, and set in a draft-free location with a temperature between 80° and 85°.

Quick-Bread Techniques

Several different methods are used when mixing the batters for muffins and quick breads, and each produces a unique texture. Beating softened butter and sugar together until light and fluffy helps to create the delicate cakelike crumb of Lemon Tea Bread (see recipe on page 209).

Whole Wheat Date-Nut Bread and Parmesan Cheese Muffins (see recipes on pages 208 to 209) have a coarser, more breadlike texture. In this method, the liquid and dry ingredients are first stirred together in separate bowls. Making a well in the center of the dry ingredients creates a space so that when the liquid ingredients are added, the two can be quickly and easily combined without overmixing.

A pastry blender makes fast work of cutting butter or shortening into small pieces and combining them with flour for light, high-rising Homemade Biscuits (see recipe on page 209). When the dough is baked in a hot oven, the butter melts, creating tender, flaky layers.

Chicken-and-Sausage
Gumbo, page 213

Lemon Tea Bread, page 209

Whole Wheat Date-Nut
Bread, page 208

Parmesan Cheese Muffins,
page 209

Snickerdoodles, page 223

White Chocolate Latte,
page 210

Thanksgiving on the Farm

Update your menu with luscious dishes.

Farmhouse Feast

Serves 10

Pecan-Cornmeal Shortbreads

Roast Turkey With Sage and Thyme
with Muscadine Sauce

Caramelized Onion Macaroni and Cheese

Turnip greens with Miss Kitty's Chili Sauce

Bakery rolls with Honey-Lemon Butter

Sweet Potato-Apple Cobbler

Wish you could serve something new and scrumptious this Thanksgiving? Kitty and Walter Forbes of Fort Valley, Georgia, shared some favorite family recipes with us, and we think you'll absolutely love their dressed-up yet doable selections. We added a fun touch by including nuts from Savage Creek Farms, the family pecan farm, in several of these dishes.

From melt-in-your-mouth savory shortbreads (terrific with a glass of Chardonnay or sweet seedless grapes) to a rich Sweet Potato-Apple Cobbler (irresistible with vanilla ice cream), each recipe is worth raving over. Just when you think mac and cheese couldn't be improved, this family managed to do so by adding sweet caramelized onions and, of course, pecans.

PECAN-CORNMEAL SHORTBREADS

family favorite • make ahead

Prep: 15 min., Chill: 2 hrs., Bake: 25 min.

Serve these nutty, mildly spiced bites alongside cheese and fresh fruit for a light appetizer.

- ¾ cup butter, softened
- 1½ cups all-purpose flour
- ½ cup cornmeal
- 2 tablespoons sugar
- ½ teaspoon salt
- ¼ teaspoon ground red pepper
- 1 large egg, lightly beaten
- ½ cup chopped pecans
- 30 pecan halves

BEAT butter at medium speed with an electric mixer until creamy. Add flour and next 5 ingredients, beating at low speed until blended. Stir in chopped pecans. Wrap dough with plastic wrap; chill 1 hour.
SHAPE dough into 2 (9-inch-long) logs. Wrap in plastic wrap, and chill 1 hour.
CUT dough into ½-inch-thick slices. Place rounds on lightly greased baking sheets; top each round with a pecan half.

BAKE at 350° for 25 minutes or until lightly browned; remove to wire racks, and let cool completely. **MAKES** 2½ dozen.

ROAST TURKEY WITH SAGE AND THYME

family favorite

Prep: 30 min.; Bake: 3 hrs., 30 min.; Stand: 20 min.

- 1 (14-pound) frozen whole turkey, thawed*
- ¼ cup butter or margarine, softened and divided
- ½ teaspoon salt
- ½ teaspoon pepper
- ¼ cup fresh sage leaves
- 4 fresh thyme sprigs
- 1 pear or apple, halved
- 2 celery ribs, halved
- 1 large onion, halved
- 2 garlic cloves, peeled
- Garnishes: flat-leaf parsley, pecans, Seckel pears, muscadines, fresh sage leaves, fresh thyme sprigs

REMOVE and discard giblets and neck from turkey. Rinse turkey with cold water; pat dry with paper towels.
LOOSEN skin from turkey breast without totally detaching skin. Stir together 2 tablespoons butter, salt, and pepper. Rub butter mixture evenly over turkey breast under skin. Carefully place sage leaves and thyme sprigs evenly on each side of breast under skin. Replace skin.
PLACE pear halves, celery, onion, and garlic inside cavity. Place turkey, breast side up, on a lightly greased wire rack in an aluminum foil-lined shallow roasting pan. Rub entire turkey evenly with remaining 2 tablespoons butter.
BAKE at 325° for 2 hours and 45 minutes to 3 hours and 30 minutes or until a meat thermometer inserted into thigh registers 180°, basting turkey every 30 minutes with pan drippings. (Prevent overcooking turkey by checking for doneness after 2 hours.) Remove turkey from roasting pan, and let stand 20 minutes before slicing. Garnish, if desired.
MAKES 12 servings.

*Substitute 1 (14-pound) whole fresh turkey, if desired.

MUSCADINE SAUCE

make ahead

Prep: 45 min.; Cook: 2 hrs., 50 min.; Process: 20 min.

Jennie Hart Robinson uses muscadines from the farm. "This is a sauce, not a jelly. It will have some run to it," Jennie says. "Don't overcook it, or it won't come out of the jar." This sauce pairs perfectly with poultry.

- **5 pounds muscadine grapes, halved***
- **9 cups sugar**
- **2 cups cider vinegar**
- **1 tablespoon ground cinnamon**
- **1 tablespoon ground allspice**
- **1 teaspoon ground cloves**

SQUEEZE pulp from grape halves into a bowl, reserving skins.

BRING skins to a boil in a large sauce-pan over medium-high heat. Cover, reduce heat to medium, and cook, stirring occasionally, 15 minutes or until tender.

BRING pulp to a boil(do not add water) in a saucepan; reduce heat to medium, and cook 20 minutes or until seeds separate from pulp. Pour mixture through a wire-mesh strainer into saucepan containing skins, discarding solids. Add sugar, and cook, stirring occasionally, over medium heat, 2 hours or until thickened. Stir in vinegar and next 3 ingredients. Cook 10 to 15 minutes or until a candy thermometer registers 225° to 230°.

LADLE hot mixture into hot, sterilized pint-size jars, filling to ½ inch from top. Remove air bubbles; wipe jar rims. Cover at once with metal lids, and screw on bands.

PROCESS in boiling water bath 20 minutes. Serve with turkey, biscuits, or toast. **MAKES** 5 (1-pint) jars.

*Substitute 5 pounds seedless red grapes, if desired. Crush whole grapes slightly. Bring to a boil; reduce heat, and simmer 20 minutes. Strain mixture into a saucepan, discarding solids. Stir in sugar, and proceed as directed.

JENNIE HART ROBINSON
FORT VALLEY, GEORGIA

CARAMELIZED ONION MACARONI AND CHEESE

family favorite

Prep: 30 min., Cook: 20 min., Bake: 1 hr., Stand: 10 min.

Feel free to omit the pecans in this recipe. It'll still taste fantastic.

- **1 (8-ounce) package large elbow macaroni**
- **2 tablespoons butter**
- **2 large onions, halved and thinly sliced**
- **1 teaspoon sugar**
- **1 (16-ounce) block white Cheddar cheese, shredded**
- **1 cup (4 ounces) shredded Parmesan cheese**
- **32 saltine crackers, finely crushed and divided**
- **6 large eggs**
- **4 cups milk**
- **1 teaspoon salt**
- **½ teaspoon pepper**
- **2 tablespoons butter, melted**
- **½ cup chopped pecans (optional)**

PREPARE macaroni according to pack-age directions; drain and set aside.

MELT 2 tablespoons butter in a large skil-let over medium-high heat. Add sliced onions and sugar. Cook, stirring often, 15 to 20 minutes or until onions are caramel colored.

LAYER half each of cooked macaroni, onions, cheeses, and cracker crumbs in a lightly greased 13- x 9-inch baking dish. Layer with remaining macaroni, onions, and cheeses.

WHISK together eggs and next 3 ingredi-ents; pour over macaroni mixture.

STIR together remaining half of cracker crumbs, 2 tablespoons melted butter, and, if desired, pecans. Sprinkle evenly over macaroni mixture.

BAKE at 350° for 1 hour or until golden brown and set. Let stand 10 minutes before serving. **MAKES** 8 to 10 servings.

KITTY FORBES
FORT VALLEY, GEORGIA

MISS KITTY'S CHILI SAUCE

make ahead

Prep: 45 min., Cook: 3 hrs., Process: 20 min.

- **3 jalapeño peppers**
- **12 bell peppers, halved and seeded**
- **12 yellow onions, peeled and quartered**
- **1 quart cider vinegar**
- **8 (28-ounce) cans crushed tomatoes**
- **2 (16-ounce) packages brown sugar**
- **½ cup salt**
- **1 tablespoon black pepper**
- **1 tablespoon ground allspice**
- **1 teaspoon ground cloves**
- **½ to 1 teaspoon ground red pepper**

CUT jalapeño peppers in half; remove and discard seeds, if desired. Process peppers and next 3 ingredients, in batches, in a food processor or blender until smooth, stopping to scrape down sides.

COOK pepper mixture, crushed tomatoes, and next 5 ingredients in a large stockpot or 2 large Dutch ovens over medium-low heat, stirring occasionally, 3 hours or until thickened. Stir in red pepper.

PACK hot mixture into hot, sterilized pint-size jars, filling to ½ inch from top. Remove air bubbles; wipe jar rims.

COVER at once with metal lids, and screw on bands. Process in boiling water bath 20 minutes. **MAKES** 12 (1-pint) jars.

KITTY FORBES
FORT VALLEY, GEORGIA

HONEY-LEMON BUTTER

family favorite • make ahead

Prep: 15 min., Chill: 1 hr.

Serve this sweet, nutty butter with warm rolls or breakfast waffles or pancakes.

- **½ cup butter, softened**
- **2 tablespoons honey**
- **1 teaspoon grated lemon rind**
- **½ cup chopped pecans, toasted**

STIR together first 3 ingredients. Roll mixture on wax paper, forming a 6-inch-long log. Roll log in chopped pecans. Wrap in wax paper; chill 1 hour or until firm. **MAKES** about ¾ cup.

SWEET POTATO-APPLE COBBLER

family favorite

Prep: 20 min.; Bake: 1 hr., 45 min.

This fall-friendly recipe makes a scrumptious finale to a fine meal.

- 4 medium-size sweet potatoes
- 2 Granny Smith apples, peeled and thinly sliced
- 1½ cups orange juice
- ½ cup granulated sugar
- ¼ cup firmly packed dark brown sugar
- 3 tablespoons all-purpose flour
- ½ teaspoon ground cinnamon
- ¼ teaspoon ground nutmeg
- ¼ teaspoon salt
- ½ cup butter or margarine, divided
- 1 cup chopped pecans, toasted
- 1 (15-ounce) package refrigerated piecrusts
- 2 teaspoons granulated sugar
- Bourbon Whipped Cream (optional)

PIERCE sweet potatoes several times with a fork, and place on an aluminum foil-lined baking sheet.

BAKE at 400° for 1 hour or until done; cool slightly. Peel and cut crosswise into ¼-inch-thick slices.

PLACE apple slices in an even layer in a lightly greased 13- x- 9-inch baking dish; top with sweet potato slices.

STIR together 1½ cups orange juice and next 6 ingredients. Pour over sweet potato mixture. Dot with 6 tablespoons butter.

SPRINKLE ½ cup chopped pecans on a cutting board. Unroll 1 piecrust, and place on pecans; gently roll piecrust dough into pecans. Cut with a leaf-shaped cookie cutter; place leaves over sweet potato mixture. Repeat procedure with remaining ½ cup chopped pecans and piecrust.

MICROWAVE remaining 2 tablespoons butter in a 1-cup glass measuring cup at HIGH 20 to 30 seconds or until melted. Brush butter over crust, and sprinkle with 2 teaspoons granulated sugar.

BAKE at 400° for 45 minutes or until golden. Serve warm with Bourbon Whipped Cream, if desired. **MAKES** 12 servings.

Bourbon Whipped Cream:
fast fixin's

Prep: 5 min.

- 1 cup whipping cream
- 2 tablespoons granulated sugar
- 1 tablespoon bourbon

BEAT whipping cream and sugar at medium speed with an electric mixer until stiff peaks form; stir in bourbon. **MAKES** about 2 cups.

KITTY FORBES
FORT VALLEY, GEORGIA

Quick & Easy

Turkey Day Leftovers

Once you've enjoyed your fill of sandwiches from your inexhaustible supply of Thanksgiving turkey, transform the rest of the bird into delicious dishes. You can also use chicken in any of the recipes and enjoy them all year long.

HOLIDAY LEFTOVERS CASSEROLE

family favorite

Prep: 30 min., Cook: 7 min., Bake: 15 min.

- 1 (7-ounce) package spaghetti, broken into 2-inch pieces
- 2 cups chopped cooked turkey or chicken
- ¾ cup diced ham
- 1 (2-ounce) jar diced pimiento, drained*
- ¼ cup minced green bell pepper
- ¼ small onion, grated
- 1 (10¾-ounce) can cream of mushroom soup
- ½ cup chicken or turkey broth
- ⅛ teaspoon celery salt
- ⅛ teaspoon pepper
- 1½ cups (6 ounces) shredded Cheddar cheese

COOK spaghetti according to package directions in a large Dutch oven. Drain well, and return spaghetti to pot. Stir in turkey and next 8 ingredients; cook 7 minutes or until heated through. Remove from heat, and stir in 1 cup cheese. Pour into a lightly greased 8-inch square baking dish. Sprinkle evenly with remaining ½ cup cheese. **BAKE** at 350° for 15 minutes or until cheese melts. **MAKES** 4 to 6 servings.

*Substitute 1 jarred roasted red bell pepper, diced, if desired.

JEANNE WOOD
NEW ORLEANS, LOUISIANA

TURKEY À LA KING

family favorite • fast fixin's

Prep: 15 min., Cook: 16 min.

- 1 tablespoon butter or margarine
- 1 bunch green onions, chopped
- 1 (10¾-ounce) can cream of celery soup
- 1 (10¾-ounce) can cream of chicken soup
- 1 cup milk
- ½ teaspoon chicken bouillon granules
- ¼ teaspoon seasoned pepper
- ⅛ teaspoon white pepper
- 3 cups chopped cooked turkey or chicken
- Split biscuits or toast points

MELT butter in a medium saucepan over medium heat; add green onions, and sauté 8 minutes or until tender. Whisk in cream of celery soup and next 5 ingredients until smooth; cook 5 minutes. Stir in turkey; cook 2 to 3 minutes or until thoroughly heated. Serve over split biscuits or toast points. **MAKES** 4 to 6 servings.

JUDY GRIMES
BRANDON, MISSISSIPPI

Fiesta Turkey Soup With Green Chile Biscuits

Prep: 15 min., Cook: 30 min.

- 1 medium onion, diced
- 1 teaspoon vegetable oil
- 1 garlic clove, minced
- 3 cups chopped cooked turkey or chicken
- 1 (15-ounce) can chili beans
- 3½ cups chicken or turkey broth
- 1 (11-ounce) can whole kernel corn with red and green peppers, drained
- 1 (10-ounce) can diced tomatoes and green chiles
- ½ teaspoon chili powder
- ½ teaspoon ground cumin
- ⅛ teaspoon salt
- ⅛ teaspoon pepper
- Toppings: sour cream, shredded Mexican four-cheese blend
- Green Chile Biscuits

SAUTÉ onion in hot oil in a large Dutch oven over medium heat 7 minutes or until tender. Add garlic, and sauté 1 minute. Stir in turkey and next 8 ingredients. Bring to a boil, stirring occasionally; reduce heat, and simmer 15 minutes. Serve with desired toppings and Green Chile Biscuits. **MAKES** 8 servings.

Green Chile Biscuits:
Prep: 5 min., Bake: 12 min.

- 2 cups all-purpose baking mix
- 1 cup (4 ounces) shredded Mexican four-cheese blend
- 1 (4.5-ounce) can chopped green chiles, drained
- ⅔ cup milk

STIR together all ingredients until a soft dough forms. Turn onto a lightly floured surface; knead 3 or 4 times.
PAT or roll dough to ½-inch thickness; cut with a 2½-inch round cutter, and place on an ungreased baking sheet.
BAKE at 450° for 10 to 12 minutes or until biscuits are golden brown. **MAKES** 1 dozen.

NOTE: For testing purposes only, we used Bisquick all-purpose baking mix.

JACQUELYN W. BOYLES
MEMPHIS, TENNESSEE

Taste of the South
Ambrosia

Often nestled among a host of traditional Christmas dishes on the Southern sideboard is a big crystal bowl of ambrosia. This "food of the gods" in its purest form is simplicity itself—fresh oranges layered with flakes of coconut.

"People who add grapefruit, pineapple, grapes, and bananas, and Lord knows what else to ambrosia simply don't understand ambrosia," proclaims Martha Pearl Villas in *My Mother's Southern Desserts* (Morrow Cookbooks, 1998) written by her son, James. Her recipe has just four ingredients: oranges, coconut, sugar, and orange juice.

In our Test Kitchens, the purist-orange-coconut coalition looked on in disbelief at the pro-pineapple-ites and the grapefruit groupies. Finally, we were all content with this one and the shortcut version. The be-all and end-all of ambrosia is that it is what *you* want it to be. Personalizing it with whipped cream, pistachios, marshmallows, dried cranberries, or bright red maraschino cherries doesn't make it wrong—it makes it *yours.*

AMBROSIA

family favorite • make ahead

Prep: 30 min., Chill: 2 hrs. *(pictured on page 264)*

- 12 navel oranges, peeled and sectioned
- 1 fresh pineapple, peeled, cored, and cut into cubes
- 2 tablespoons powdered sugar
- 1 cup freshly grated coconut
- Garnish: orange rind curls

TOSS together oranges, pineapple, and powdered sugar in a large bowl.
PLACE one-third of fruit mixture in a serving bowl. Top with one-third coconut. Repeat layers twice. Cover and chill 2 hours. Garnish, if desired. **MAKES** 8 to 10 servings.

NOTE: Three red grapefruit, peeled and sectioned, can be added to fruit mixture, if desired.

KITCHEN EXPRESS AMBROSIA

Prep: 30 min., Chill: 2 hrs.

TOSS together 2 tablespoons lemon juice, 1 (24-ounce) jar drained mandarin orange segments, and 1 (24-ounce) jar drained pineapple chunks. Place one-third of fruit mixture in a serving bowl. Top with ¼ cup frozen grated coconut, thawed. Repeat layers twice. Cover and chill 1 hour. **MAKES** 6 servings.

NOTE: For testing purposes only, we used Del Monte SunFresh jarred fruits, located in the produce section of the grocery store.

Freshly Grated Coconut

Try our heat-and-crack method for getting the meat out of the shell.
Step 1: Pierce soft areas at the top of coconut (the eyes) with an ice pick or clean screwdriver. Drain the milk.
Step 2: Bake coconut at 400° for 15 minutes. Using oven mitts, wrap hot coconut with a kitchen towel, bringing 4 corners together and twisting to form a handle. Hold the handle in one hand as you hit wrapped coconut with a hammer. Remove meat from shell with a knife. **Note:** Heating helps separate the meat from the thick, outer shell. A thin, brown skin will still cover the meat.
Step 3: Remove brown skin with a vegetable peeler or paring knife. Grate coconut—you'll have 2½ to 3 cups of coconut. Test Kitchens professional Rebecca Kracke Gordon recommends using a Y-shaped peeler and hand grating with a Microplane grater (available at most kitchen shops) or the fine side of a box grater.

Toffee Everything

In no time at all, you can have delicious homemade candy and cookies.

All the components for confectionary perfection are in this treat: freshly toasted pecans, a buttery crunch, and rich dark chocolate. Although one bite would make you think toffee's hard to make, it's anything but. It makes delicious holiday desserts and treats—and great gifts.

MICROWAVE PEANUT TOFFEE

fast fixin's • make ahead

Prep: 20 min.

- ¾ cup finely chopped unsalted peanuts, divided
- ½ cup butter or margarine
- 1 cup sugar
- ¼ cup water
- 1 cup peanut butter-and-milk chocolate morsels

SPREAD ½ cup chopped peanuts into a 9-inch circle on a lightly greased baking sheet.

COAT top 2 inches of a 2½-quart glass bowl with butter; place remaining butter in bowl. Add sugar and ¼ cup water. (Do not stir.) Microwave at HIGH 8 minutes or just until mixture begins to turn light brown; pour over peanuts on baking sheet.

SPRINKLE with chocolate morsels; let stand 1 minute. Spread melted morsels evenly over peanut mixture, and sprinkle with remaining ¼ cup chopped peanuts. Chill until firm. Break into bite-size pieces. Store in an airtight container. **MAKES** 1 pound.

NOTE: We used an 1100-watt microwave oven.

TOFFEE-COFFEE ICE-CREAM TORTE

freezeable • make ahead

Prep: 30 min., Freeze: 8 hrs., Cook: 5 min.

This torte is made in two loafpans so you can serve one and keep one frozen for later.

- 6 tablespoons coffee liqueur, divided
- 1 tablespoon instant coffee granules
- 1 quart chocolate ice cream, softened
- 1 (12-ounce) bag chocolate-covered toffee candy bars, finely chopped
- ½ gallon coffee ice cream, softened
- 1 (3-ounce) package ladyfingers
- 1 cup strong-brewed coffee or espresso
- ½ cup sugar
- 1½ tablespoons cornstarch
- Garnishes: whipped topping, chopped toffee

LINE 2 (9- x 5-inch) loafpans with plastic wrap, allowing excess to hang over sides.

STIR together 1 tablespoon coffee liqueur and instant coffee granules until dissolved. Combine coffee mixture, chocolate ice cream, and half of the chopped toffee in a large bowl. In a separate bowl, combine ½ gallon coffee ice cream and remaining chopped toffee. Spread half of chocolate ice-cream mixture evenly into 1 prepared loafpan; top with half of coffee ice-cream mixture. Repeat layers in remaining loafpan.

BRUSH ladyfingers with 3 tablespoons coffee liqueur; place ladyfingers, brushed sides down, evenly over ice cream in loafpans. Fold plastic wrap over to seal; freeze at least 8 hours.

STIR together brewed coffee, sugar, and cornstarch in a heavy saucepan over medium-high heat; cook, stirring constantly, until mixture starts to boil. Reduce heat to low, and cook 2 to 3 minutes or until thickened and clear. Remove from heat; cool. Stir in remaining 2 tablespoons liqueur; cover and chill coffee sauce until ready to serve.

INVERT tortes onto serving plates; remove and discard plastic wrap. Garnish, if desired. Serve with chilled coffee sauce. **MAKES** 12 servings.

NOTE: For testing purposes only, we used Hershey's Heath Snack Bars.

MARCIA WHITNEY
HOUSTON, TEXAS

OATMEAL-TOFFEE COOKIES

make ahead

Prep: 15 min., Bake: 10 min. per batch

- ½ cup butter or margarine, softened
- ½ cup firmly packed brown sugar
- 2 large eggs
- 1 teaspoon vanilla extract
- 1½ cups uncooked regular oats
- 1 cup all-purpose flour
- ½ teaspoon baking soda
- ¼ teaspoon salt
- ½ cup chopped pecans
- 1 (10-ounce) package almond toffee bits

BEAT butter at medium speed with an electric mixer 2 to 3 minutes or until light and fluffy. Add sugar, beating well. Add eggs and vanilla, beating until blended.

COMBINE oats and next 3 ingredients; add to butter mixture, beating just until blended. Stir in chopped pecans and toffee bits.

DROP dough by heaping tablespoonfuls onto lightly greased baking sheets.

BAKE at 375° for 10 minutes. Cool on wire racks. **MAKES** 4 dozen.

NOTE: For testing purposes only, we used Hershey's Heath Bits O' Brickle Almond Toffee Bits.

PAGE SOSTEK
WENHAM, MASSACHUSETTS

Mildred's Toffee 101

- Simmer sugar mixture over medium heat until sugar and butter melt.
- Cook until sugar mixture reaches 290° to 310° on a candy thermometer. The color will change to a deep golden brown, and the mixture will get slightly thicker.
- Carefully pour sugar mixture over nuts that have been spread into a 9-inch circle on a baking sheet lightly greased with vegetable cooking spray.
- Sprinkle morsels evenly on top, and let stand for 30 seconds or until they are totally melted. Spread melted morsels over surface.
- Sprinkle chopped toasted nuts over chocolate, and chill until firm.
- Break toffee into small pieces before storing in airtight containers.

MILDRED'S TOFFEE

make ahead

Prep: 10 min., Cook: 20 min., Chill: 1 hr.

> 1½ cups chopped toasted pecans, divided
> 1 cup sugar
> 1 cup butter
> 1 tablespoon light corn syrup
> ¼ cup water
> 1 cup semisweet chocolate morsels

SPREAD 1 cup pecans into a 9-inch circle on a lightly greased baking sheet.

BRING sugar and next 3 ingredients to a boil in a heavy saucepan over medium heat, stirring constantly. Cook until mixture is golden brown and a candy thermometer registers 290° to 310° (about 15 minutes). Pour sugar mixture over pecans on baking sheet.

SPRINKLE with morsels; let stand 30 seconds. Spread melted morsels over top; sprinkle with remaining ½ cup chopped pecans. Chill 1 hour. Break into bite-size pieces. Store in an airtight container. **MAKES** about 1½ pounds.

MILDRED HAYWARD
KENOSHA, WISCONSIN

ALMOND TOFFEE: Substitute 1 cup chopped toasted slivered almonds for 1 cup chopped pecans to sprinkle on baking sheet. Substitute ½ cup toasted sliced almonds for ½ cup chopped pecans to sprinkle over chocolate. Proceed as directed.

BOURBON-PECAN TOFFEE: Substitute ¼ cup bourbon for ¼ cup water. Proceed as directed.

HAWAIIAN TOFFEE: Substitute 1 cup chopped toasted macadamia nuts for 1 cup chopped pecans to sprinkle on baking sheet. Substitute ½ cup toasted sweetened flaked coconut for ½ cup chopped pecans to sprinkle over chocolate. Proceed as directed.

Bananas Foster Bread Pudding

Chef Don Boyd of Café Reconcile in New Orleans combines the classic flavors of rum and brown sugar, distinctive in the original Brennan's Restaurant recipe for Bananas Foster, to create this delicious bread pudding.

BANANAS FOSTER BREAD PUDDING

chef recipe

Prep: 15 min., Cook: 10 min., Bake: 55 min., Stand: 30 min. *(pictured on page 266)*

> 3 large eggs
> 1 cup granulated sugar
> 1 cup firmly packed brown sugar
> ½ cup whipping cream
> ¼ cup rum
> 1 tablespoon banana extract
> 4 cups milk
> ¼ cup butter
> 1 (16-ounce) stale French bread loaf, cut into 1-inch cubes
> Bread Pudding Sauce

STIR together first 6 ingredients in a large bowl.

HEAT milk and butter in a large saucepan over medium-high heat until melted, stirring constantly. (Do not boil.)

STIR about one-fourth of hot milk mixture gradually into egg mixture; add to remaining hot milk mixture, stirring constantly.

PLACE bread cubes in a lightly greased 13- x 9-inch baking dish. Pour egg mixture evenly over bread. Press bread to absorb mixture.

BAKE at 325° for 45 to 55 minutes. Remove from oven, and let stand 30 minutes before serving.

SERVE with Bread Pudding Sauce.
MAKES 10 to 12 servings.

Bread Pudding Sauce:

fast fixin's

Prep: 5 min., Cook: 5 min.

> ½ cup butter
> ½ cup firmly packed brown sugar
> ¼ cup dark rum
> ½ teaspoon banana extract
> 2 bananas, sliced

COMBINE all ingredients in a saucepan over medium-high heat, and cook, stirring occasionally, 5 minutes. (Do not boil.) Remove sauce from heat. **MAKES** 1¼ cups.

DON BOYD
CAFÉ RECONCILE
NEW ORLEANS, LOUISIANA

Pork Roast Menu

Learn to cook a lean and luscious roast with side dishes that round out its orange-rosemary essence.

Light Pork Roast Dinner

Serves 6 to 8

Orange-Glazed Pork Roast

Onion Rice Pilaf

Asparagus With Ginger

Apple-Cranberry Compote

Strawberry-Lemon Cheesecake

Just because you've decided to make healthy food choices a priority doesn't mean dinner can't taste to-die-for good.

Reader Rena Marshall of Rex, Georgia, agrees. She shared some of her favorite seasonal recipes with flavors that complement each other so well, their nutritious virtues are just bonus. Fresh herbs as well as citrus and other fruits boost the flavor of simple ingredients to make a truly luscious-tasting meal. And you won't be missing out on dessert either. Reader Deborah Smith's Strawberry-Lemon Cheesecake is a must-try. Serve this spread in lieu of your usual Thanksgiving menu for a fresh take on the season.

ORANGE-GLAZED PORK ROAST

family favorite

Prep: 10 min., Bake: 1 hr., Stand: 10 min., Cook: 6 min. *(pictured on page 265)*

1 (3-pound) boneless pork loin roast
Vegetable cooking spray
1½ teaspoons coarsely ground pepper
½ teaspoon salt
1 cup orange marmalade
2 tablespoons Creole mustard
2 teaspoons fresh or dried rosemary
2 tablespoons all-purpose flour
1 (14½-ounce) can fat-free reduced-sodium chicken broth
Garnish: fresh rosemary sprigs

PLACE roast on a rack coated with cooking spray in an aluminum foil-lined shallow roasting pan.

RUB roast with pepper and salt.

HEAT marmalade in a microwave-safe bowl at HIGH 10 seconds or until melted. Add mustard and 2 teaspoons rosemary, stirring until blended. Brush over roast.

BAKE at 375° for 1 hour or until a meat thermometer inserted into thickest portion registers 155°. Cover with foil; let stand 10 minutes or until a thermometer registers 160°. Remove roast from pan, and cut into slices; cover and keep warm.

SPRINKLE roasting pan with flour; place on cooktop, and cook over medium heat, 1 minute, whisking constantly. Add broth, and cook 5 more minutes, whisking constantly or until mixture thickens. Serve with sliced pork. Garnish, if desired. **MAKES** 16 servings.

RENA MARSHALL
REX, GEORGIA

Per serving: Calories 185 (29% from fat); Fat 6g (sat 2.2g, mono 2.6g, poly 0.5g); Protein 18g; Carb 15g; Fiber 0.5g; Chol 49mg; Iron 0.8mg; Sodium 163mg; Calc 24mg

ONION RICE PILAF

family favorite

Prep: 10 min., Cook: 7 min., Bake: 25 min., Stand: 5 min.

Basmati rice—a fluffy, long-grain variety—gives off a nutty, popcornlike fragrance while it's cooking. *(pictured on page 265)*

½ medium-size sweet onion, chopped
2 teaspoons olive oil
2 garlic cloves, minced
1½ cups uncooked basmati rice
2 ounces uncooked vermicelli, broken into ½-inch pieces
2 (14½-ounce) cans fat-free reduced-sodium chicken broth
¼ teaspoon salt
¼ teaspoon pepper
¼ cup chopped fresh parsley

SAUTÉ onion in hot oil in an ovenproof saucepan 5 minutes. Add minced garlic, rice, and vermicelli; sauté 2 minutes, stirring constantly. Stir in broth, salt, and pepper.

BAKE, covered, at 350° for 25 minutes or until liquid is absorbed. Let stand 5 minutes. Stir in parsley. **MAKES** 8 servings.

RENA MARSHALL
REX, GEORGIA

Per serving: Calories 197 (10% from fat); Fat 2.2g (sat 0.6g, mono 0.9g, poly 0.2g); Protein 5g; Carb 42g; Fiber 1.7g; Chol 2.1mg; Iron 1.5mg; Sodium 134mg; Calc 18mg

ASPARAGUS WITH GINGER

fast fixin's

Prep: 5 min., Cook: 9 min.

Try this recipe with broccoli or green beans.

1½ pounds fresh asparagus,
    trimmed
2 teaspoons vegetable oil
2 teaspoons minced fresh ginger
½ teaspoon sugar
¼ teaspoon salt
¼ teaspoon pepper
1 teaspoon sesame oil

SAUTÉ asparagus in 2 teaspoons hot oil over medium-high heat in a large nonstick skillet 7 minutes. Add ginger, and sauté 1 minute. Stir in sugar and remaining ingredients, and cook 1 minute. **MAKES** 6 servings.

RENA MARSHALL
REX, GEORGIA

Per serving: Calories 53 (40% from fat); Fat 2.3g (sat 0.3g, mono 1g, poly 1g); Protein 2.5g; Carb 5.4g; Fiber 2.5g; Chol 0mg; Iron 0.5mg; Sodium 97mg; Calc 25mg

APPLE-CRANBERRY COMPOTE

family favorite

Prep: 20 min., Cook: 5 min., Bake: 50 min.

Look for cranberry-orange sauce near the applesauce in the canned fruit aisle of your supermarket. If you can't find it, 1 (16-ounce) can whole-berry cranberry sauce also will work.

1 (12-ounce) container whole
    cranberry-orange sauce
2 tablespoons brown sugar
2 tablespoons fresh lemon juice
2 teaspoons grated fresh
    ginger
¼ teaspoon salt
6 Granny Smith apples, peeled,
    cored, and quartered
Vegetable cooking spray
¼ cup chopped pecans
Garnishes: orange rind strips, fresh
    rosemary sprigs

BRING first 5 ingredients to a boil in a medium saucepan over medium-high heat, stirring constantly. Remove from heat.

ARRANGE apple quarters in a round baking dish coated with cooking spray; pour cranberry mixture over apples.
BAKE at 350° for 45 minutes or until apples are tender. Sprinkle evenly with chopped pecans. Bake 5 more minutes. Garnish, if desired. **MAKES** 16 servings.

RENA MARSHALL
REX, GEORGIA

Per serving: Calories 86 (14% from fat); Fat 1.3g (sat 0.1g, mono 0g, poly 0g); Protein 0.3g; Carb 20g; Fiber 2g; Chol 0mg; Iron 0.2mg; Sodium 44mg; Calc 3.5mg

STRAWBERRY-LEMON CHEESECAKE

make ahead

Prep: 20 min., Bake: 40 min., Stand: 1 hr., Cool: 4 hrs., Chill: 8 hrs., Cook: 5 min.

You will never miss the sugar in this rich, lemony dessert. It's even delicious for breakfast with a cup of tea or coffee.

1 cup graham cracker crumbs
3 tablespoons light butter,
    melted
1 tablespoon no-calorie sweetener
Vegetable cooking spray
1 (16-ounce) container fat-free
    ricotta cheese
2 (8-ounce) packages ⅓-less-fat
    cream cheese, softened
1 (8-ounce) container fat-free
    sour cream
¾ cup no-calorie sweetener
¼ cup all-purpose flour
3½ tablespoons fresh lemon juice,
    divided
1 teaspoon vanilla extract
3 large eggs
½ cup water
1 tablespoon no-calorie sweetener
2 teaspoons cornstarch
2 tablespoons strawberry extract
½ teaspoon red food coloring
1 pint fresh strawberries, sliced

COMBINE graham cracker crumbs, melted butter, and 1 tablespoon sweetener; press on bottom and up sides of a 10-inch springform pan coated with cooking spray.
BAKE at 350° for 10 minutes. Remove from oven. Wrap outside of pan with heavy-duty aluminum foil.

BEAT ricotta cheese, cream cheese, and sour cream at medium speed with an electric mixer until smooth. Add ¾ cup sweetener, flour, 2½ tablespoons lemon juice, and vanilla, beating until blended. Add eggs, 1 at a time, beating until blended after each addition. Pour batter into prepared pan. Pour water to a depth of 1 inch in a broiler pan. Place springform pan in water pan.
BAKE at 350° for 25 to 30 minutes. Turn oven off. Let cheesecake stand in oven 1 hour. (Do not open oven door.) Remove springform pan from water pan; remove foil from springform pan. Cool cheesecake in pan at room temperature 4 hours. Cover and chill 8 hours.
COMBINE ½ cup water, next 4 ingredients, and remaining 1 tablespoon lemon juice in a small saucepan; bring to a boil, whisking constantly. Boil 1 minute or until thickened, whisking constantly. Remove pan from heat, and cool completely. Stir in strawberries. Serve over cheesecake slices. **MAKES** 12 servings.

NOTE: For testing purposes only, we used Splenda Granular for no-calorie sweetener and Land O Lakes Light Butter for light butter.

DEBORAH A. SMITH
BOCA RATON, FLORIDA

Per serving: Calories 196 (50% from fat); Fat 11g (sat 2.2g, mono 1.6g, poly 0.7g); Protein 8.8g; Carb 13g; Fiber 0.6g; Chol 70mg; Iron 0.6mg; Sodium 108mg; Calc 126mg

---

❝ Cook's Notes ❞

■ Don't be tempted to substitute dried or ground ginger for fresh in the **Asparagus With Ginger** recipe. The fresh imparts a more fragrant, slightly spicy flavor.
■ Try **Apple-Cranberry Compote** over low-fat vanilla yogurt for a high calcium, great-tasting breakfast.
■ If you have leftover **Onion Rice Pilaf**, add a little water, cover loosely with plastic wrap, and microwave until heated. The added moisture makes rice taste freshly made.

Joy Zacharia
Associate Foods Editor

Goodies to Give

These flavorful, make-ahead food gifts
will liven up any holiday get-together.

GARLIC-AND-DILL FETA CHEESE SPREAD

freezeable • make ahead

Prep: 15 min., Chill: 8 hrs.

- **1 (8-ounce) package cream cheese, softened**
- **1 (4-ounce) package crumbled feta cheese**
- **¼ cup mayonnaise**
- **1 garlic clove, minced**
- **1 tablespoon chopped fresh dill or ½ teaspoon dried dillweed**
- **½ teaspoon seasoned pepper**
- **¼ teaspoon salt**
- **Cucumber slices (optional)**

PROCESS first 7 ingredients in a food processor until smooth, stopping to scrape down sides. Cover and chill 8 hours. Serve with cucumber slices, if desired. **MAKES** about 1 cup.

NOTE: Spread can be frozen in an airtight container up to 1 month. Thaw in refrigerator at least 24 hours. Stir before serving.

CHEESE MARINADE

fast fixin's • make ahead

Prep: 5 min.

Give the marinade alone in decorative bottles or include the cheese, olives, and peppers for an appetizer-in-a-jar.

- **1½ cups olive oil**
- **1 cup white balsamic vinegar**
- **¼ cup fresh thyme leaves**
- **2 tablespoons chopped fresh rosemary**
- **1 teaspoon salt**
- **½ teaspoon pepper**

WHISK together all ingredients. Pour mixture into an airtight jar or decorative container. Store in refrigerator up to 1 week. **MAKES** about 3 cups.

MARINATED CHEESE, OLIVES, AND PEPPERS: Combine 1½ pounds cubed firm cheeses (such as Cheddar, Gouda, Havarti, or Monterey Jack); 2 cups olives; and 1 (7-ounce) jar roasted red bell peppers, drained, in a large zip-top freezer bag or decorative airtight container. Pour Cheese Marinade over mixture, and chill 1 hour or up to 2 days. **MAKES** 6 to 8 appetizer servings. Prep: 15 min., Chill: 1 hr.

RALEIGH MCDONALD HUSSING
BRENTWOOD, TENNESSEE

CREAM CHEESE-AND-OLIVE BISCUITS WITH OLIVE-PARSLEY SPREAD

freezeable • make ahead

Prep: 30 min., Bake: 10 min.

- **2¼ cups all-purpose baking mix**
- **1 (3-ounce) package cream cheese, softened**
- **½ cup green olives, chopped**
- **⅓ cup buttermilk**
- **1 (6-ounce) jar pitted kalamata olives**
- **1 tablespoon capers, drained**
- **1 garlic clove, pressed**
- **1 tablespoon chopped fresh parsley**
- **2 tablespoons balsamic vinegar**
- **2 tablespoons olive oil**
- **¼ teaspoon black pepper**
- **1 (3-ounce) log goat cheese or package cream cheese, softened**

PULSE first 4 ingredients in a food processor 3 or 4 times or until combined.
TURN dough out onto a lightly floured surface. Pat dough to a ½-inch thickness; cut with a 2-inch fluted cutter. Place on ungreased baking sheets.
BAKE biscuits at 425° for 10 minutes or until golden.
PULSE kalamata olives and next 6 ingredients in a food processor until combined.
SPLIT biscuits in half, and spread cut sides evenly with goat cheese; top with olive mixture. **MAKES** 30 appetizer servings.

NOTE: To make ahead, bake biscuits as directed. Cool completely on baking sheets on wire racks. Cover and freeze until firm. Place biscuits in zip-top freezer bags; freeze up to 2 weeks. Remove from freezer; place on baking sheets, and let stand 30 minutes. Bake at 325° for 7 to 10 minutes. Prepare olive-parsley mixture as directed. Place in an airtight container; freeze up to 2 weeks. Thaw in refrigerator 24 hours. Stir before serving.

NOTE: For testing purposes only, we used Bisquick all-purpose baking mix.

Make It Personal

- Purchase an assortment of airtight jars from craft, grocery, and discount stores for the marinade and spreads. Wash and thoroughly dry containers before filling.
- Create recipe cards with your computer and printer using card stock in a variety of designs. Include freezing or storage information and instructions for reheating. Punch a hole in the corner of the card, and attach it to the container with a pretty ribbon or raffia.
- Convenient three-dimensional scrapbook die cuts found in crafts stores can be used to decorate everything. Stick them to recipe cards, gift tags, airtight plastic containers, paper bags, and jars.

Wine Club 101

This D.C.-area retailer takes the mystery out of enjoying wine.

"I'd been selling wine for almost 20 years before it finally hit me, like a ton of bricks, that very few of my female friends knew anything about wine," remembers Cecile Giannangeli. This owner of finewine.com shops in Gaithersburg, Maryland, and McLean, Virginia, decided it was time for a change. The solution? Create a forum for women from all walks of life to "realize they are smart enough, savvy enough, and educated enough to learn about wine," says Cecile. In 2002, the Women's Wine Tasting Club was born. (Sorry, no men are allowed.)

A successful businesswoman and active mother of two, Cecile structures meetings—during the day and in the evening—at each of her shops to fit the schedules of both on-the-go moms and corporate executives. "Our club tries to dispel all the wine myths and make folks feel comfortable," she explains in her easy-going style.

Tierney Banks agrees. She's been a club member for more than a year. "It's given me a much better understanding of what I'm looking for in wine and how to describe what I enjoy," says the mortgage loan underwriter from Silver Spring, Maryland. "For example, Cecile encourages you to describe a wine's aroma and taste in terms you understand, and that can mean everything from 'tangy' to 'juicy.' The more you understand what you like, the more confidence you'll have in wine stores and restaurants," Tierney adds.

For those outside the Washington, D.C., area, there's a free Internet-based monthly newsletter available from **www.finewine.com** that includes Cecile's food and wine pairing suggestions and tips on starting your own wine-tasting group. Also, a wine-club subscription is available that delivers three new wines to your door each month.

Cecile's Best Bets for Holiday Wines

"When it comes to Thanksgiving, I'm a fan of American-made Pinot Noir. It's a red that goes with a wide variety of foods," says Cecile. If you prefer white wine, she recommends Pinot Gris or Riesling. Here are a few of her favorites for less than $15 (prices may vary).

Red:
- Holloran Stafford Hill, Pinot Noir, Oregon
- Lemelson Vineyards, Six Vineyards, Pinot Noir, Oregon
- Domaine Sainte Eugénie, Cabernet Sauvignon Merlot, France
- Savannah-Chanelle Vineyards, Pierre's Ghost Red, California

White:
- Martin Schaetzel, Tokay-Pinot Gris Cuvée Réserve, France

Wine-Tasting Guide

Use this handy guide to host your own wine tasting. Whether you're new to wine or looking to expand your knowledge, these recommendations offer both great taste and quality for the price.

Beginner:
This selection gives you an introduction to four of the most popular wine-producing grapes in the world. (Taste in the order listed.)
White:
1. Allan Scott, Sauvignon Blanc, New Zealand (medium-bodied)
2. Columbia Crest, Chardonnay, Washington (full-bodied)
Red:
3. Meridian, Merlot, California (medium-bodied)
4. Woodbridge, Select Vineyard Series, Red Dirt Ridge Cabernet Sauvignon, California (full-bodied)

Intermediate:
This selection offers familiar grapes in distinctive regional styles. (Taste in the order listed.)
White:
1. Hogue, Johannisberg Riesling, Washington (light-bodied)
2. Red Bicyclette, Chardonnay, France (full-bodied)
Red:
3. Guigal, Côtes-du-Rhône, Vin Rouge, France (medium-bodied)
4. Excelsior, Cabernet Sauvignon, South Africa (full-bodied)

Top-Rated Menu

Quail and Cheese Grits

Set aside a quiet evening to savor these recipes.

Game Night

Serves 6

Lemon-Rum Slush

Chipotle-Marinated Quail

Chile-Blue Cheese Grits

Mixed green salad

Almond-Orange Flan

The rustic flavors of this menu are perfect for a cozy dinner. Don't overlook pan roasting the spices for the quail. This step gives the dish an intense flavor and aroma that makes it spectacular.

LEMON-RUM SLUSH

freezeable • make ahead

Prep: 5 min., Freeze: 6 hrs.

- ¼ cup sugar
- 2 (6-ounce) cans frozen lemonade concentrate
- 2 cups water
- 1½ cups pineapple juice
- 2 cups rum

COMBINE all ingredients, and freeze 6 hours, stirring occasionally. Remove lemonade mixture from freezer, and stir until slushy. **MAKES** 7 cups.

CHIPOTLE-MARINATED QUAIL

Prep: 25 min., Chill: 3 hrs., Cook: 50 min.

If fresh quail are unavailable, look for frozen ones at your supermarket, or order them from Haute @ Home (1-888-466-3992 or **www.hauteathome.com**).

- 2 teaspoons black peppercorns
- 2 teaspoons coarse sea salt
- 1 teaspoon coriander seeds
- 10 whole allspice
- 1 (7-ounce) can chipotle peppers in adobo sauce, undrained
- ½ cup white wine
- ½ cup frozen orange juice concentrate, thawed and undiluted
- ⅓ cup white wine vinegar
- ¼ cup minced onion
- 4 garlic cloves, minced
- 12 (3.5-ounce) semiboneless quail
- ½ teaspoon salt
- 2 to 4 tablespoons olive oil

COOK first 4 ingredients in a large skillet over medium heat, stirring occasionally, 4 to 5 minutes or until toasted; cool.

Process toasted spices in a blender until finely ground.

PROCESS chipotle peppers in a blender until smooth. Measure 2 tablespoons puree, reserving remainder for another use. Stir together 2 tablespoons chipotle puree, spice mixture, wine, and next 4 ingredients.

POUR chipotle puree mixture into a large zip-top freezer bag; add quail. Seal and chill 3 hours, turning every 30 minutes.

REMOVE quail from marinade, reserving marinade. Sprinkle quail with ½ teaspoon salt.

BROWN quail, in batches, in hot oil in a large heavy-duty skillet over medium-high heat about 6 minutes on each side, adding more oil, if necessary. Drain on paper towels.

BRING quail and reserved marinade to a boil in skillet. Reduce heat; cover and simmer 25 minutes or until done. **MAKES** 6 servings.

CHILE-BLUE CHEESE GRITS

Prep: 20 min., Cook: 10 min., Bake: 1 hr.

Saga blue is a soft, mellow-flavored blue cheese that has a white, edible rind.

- 3 cups milk
- 1 garlic clove, minced
- 1¼ teaspoons salt, divided
- 1 cup quick-cooking grits
- ½ cup crumbled Saga blue cheese
- ⅓ cup butter or margarine, cubed
- ½ cup whipping cream
- 2 large eggs, lightly beaten
- 2 egg whites, lightly beaten
- 1 (4-ounce) can whole green chiles, drained and chopped
- 2 tablespoons freshly grated Parmesan cheese
- 2 teaspoons chopped fresh basil
- 1 teaspoon chopped fresh thyme
- ¼ teaspoon pepper

BRING milk, minced garlic, and 1 teaspoon salt to a boil in a medium saucepan; gradually stir in grits. Cover, reduce heat, and simmer, stirring occasionally, 10 minutes.

WHISK in blue cheese and butter until melted. Whisk in remaining ¼ teaspoon salt, cream, and remaining ingredients;

pour into a lightly greased 1½-quart soufflé dish.

BAKE at 325° for 1 hour. (Center may be slightly soft.) **MAKES** 6 servings.

ALMOND-ORANGE FLAN

make ahead

Prep: 25 min., Bake: 1 hr., Stand: 30 min., Chill: 8 hrs.

This recipe requires 1¼ cans of sweetened condensed milk. Stir leftover milk into coffee.

- ½ cup sugar
- 1⅔ cups sweetened condensed milk
- 1 cup milk
- 3 large eggs
- 3 egg yolks
- 2 tablespoons grated orange rind
- 1 teaspoon fresh orange juice
- 1 (2.25-ounce) package slivered almonds
- 4 oranges, sectioned

SPRINKLE sugar in an 8-inch round cakepan. Place over medium heat, and cook, tilting pan or stirring until sugar melts and turns a light golden brown. Remove from heat. (Mixture may crack slightly as it cools.)

PROCESS condensed milk and next 6 ingredients in a blender 15 seconds; pour over caramelized sugar. Cover pan with aluminum foil, and place in a 13- x 9-inch pan. Pour hot water into larger pan to a depth of 1 inch.

BAKE at 350° for 1 hour or until set. Remove pan from water; uncover and cool in pan on a wire rack at least 30 minutes. Cover and chill 8 hours. Loosen edges with a thin knife. Invert flan onto serving plate; arrange orange sections on top. **MAKES** 6 servings.

Simply Delicious Shrimp

These easy-to-prepare dishes offer something for everyone and every occasion. Test Kitchens Director Lyda Jones raves about the Italian-inspired Shrimp Palermo. "It's perfect for both laid-back entertaining or spur-of-the-moment company," she says.

These recipes are just the ticket for a special dinner. If fresh shrimp aren't available in your area, frozen will do just fine.

SHRIMP PALERMO

family favorite

Prep: 25 min., Cook: 10 min., Broil: 3 min.
(pictured on page 261)

- 5 plum tomatoes, cut into ¼-inch slices
- 1 (12-ounce) jar roasted red bell peppers, drained and chopped
- ½ cup Italian vinaigrette dressing
- 1¼ pounds unpeeled, large fresh shrimp
- ½ cup all-purpose baking mix
- 1 tablespoon salt-free Cajun seasoning
- 3 tablespoons butter, divided
- 2 cups (8 ounces) shredded provolone cheese
- Garnish: fresh parsley

COMBINE first 3 ingredients; spoon evenly into 4 (1½-cup) lightly greased individual baking dishes. Set aside.

PEEL shrimp, and devein, if desired.

COMBINE baking mix and Cajun seasoning. Dredge shrimp in mixture.

MELT 1½ tablespoons butter in a large nonstick skillet over medium heat; add half of shrimp, and cook, stirring constantly, 3 to 5 minutes or just until shrimp turn pink. Repeat with remaining 1½ tablespoons butter and shrimp. Spoon shrimp evenly over tomato mixture. Sprinkle evenly with cheese.

BROIL 5 inches from heat 3 minutes or until cheese is melted and lightly browned. Garnish, if desired. **MAKES** 4 servings.

NOTE: Recipe can also be prepared in a lightly greased 11- x 7-inch baking dish. Reduce dressing to ¼ cup and cheese to 1½ cups. Bake at 425° for 5 to 8 minutes or until cheese is melted and lightly browned. For testing purposes only, we used Bisquick all-purpose baking mix and McCormick's Cajun seasoning.

GILDA LESTER
WILMINGTON, NORTH CAROLINA

SAUTÉED SHRIMP WITH COUNTRY HAM AND CAPERS

family favorite

Prep: 25 min., Cook: 6 min.

Serve with lots of French bread to sop up every last drop of the savory sauce.

- 3 pounds unpeeled, extra-large fresh shrimp
- ⅓ cup butter
- ⅓ cup olive oil
- 1 cup (4 ounces) thinly sliced country ham, prosciutto, or baked ham
- ¼ cup vermouth or dry white wine
- 2 to 3 tablespoons fresh lemon juice
- 2 tablespoons capers
- 1 teaspoon salt-free Cajun seasoning
- 2 tablespoons minced fresh parsley
- French bread

PEEL shrimp, and devein, if desired.

MELT butter with olive oil in a large, deep skillet over medium-high heat. Increase heat to high, and add shrimp and ham; cook, stirring constantly, 3 to 5 minutes or until shrimp turn pink. Reduce heat to medium high, add vermouth and next 3 ingredients; bring to a boil. Pour into a large, deep serving platter or individual bowls. Sprinkle with parsley, and serve immediately. Serve with French bread. **MAKES** 8 servings.

NOTE: For testing purposes only, we used McCormick's Cajun seasoning.

HELEN CONWELL
FAIRHOPE, ALABAMA

Stack Up Your Chili

Quick Chili Supper

Serves 4

Chili-Corn Chip Stack-Up Salad

Quick Apple Bundles

The frozen chili left over from last week's supper can be a springboard for quick meals or an impromptu party.

CHILI-CORN CHIP STACK-UP SALAD

fast fixin's

Prep: 15 min., Cook: 15 min.

To serve, arrange salad ingredients on the kitchen counter or sideboard in the order listed below. Have each person spoon rice on a plate first to anchor the stack-up and prevent sliding. Add items your family likes such as corn, chopped bell pepper, and sliced fresh jalapeño peppers.

- 1 (3.5-ounce) package boil-in-bag rice
- 1 tablespoon chopped fresh cilantro (optional)
- 1 (15-ounce) bag corn chips
- 5 to 6 cups Big-Batch Chili, thawed and reheated (recipe at right)
- ½ head iceberg lettuce, shredded, or 1 (10-ounce) package shredded iceberg lettuce
- 1 (8-ounce) package shredded Cheddar-Jack cheese
- 3 plum tomatoes, chopped
- 4 green onions, chopped
- Sour cream
- 1 (2.25-ounce) can sliced ripe black olives, drained (optional)
- 1 (12-ounce) jar pickled jalapeño peppers (optional)

PREPARE rice according to package directions. Stir in cilantro, if desired.
LAYER rice mixture, chips, chili, next 5 ingredients and, if desired, black olives and jalapeño peppers in individual serving bowls. **MAKES** 4 to 6 servings.

BIG-BATCH CHILI

freezeable • make ahead

Prep: 20 min., Cook: 6 hrs.

- 4 pounds ground chuck
- 2 medium onions, chopped
- 1 green pepper, chopped
- 2 garlic cloves, minced
- 3 (14½-ounce) cans diced tomatoes, undrained
- 4 (8-ounce) cans tomato sauce
- 1 (6-ounce) can tomato paste
- ¼ cup chili powder
- 1 tablespoon sugar
- 1 teaspoon salt
- 1 teaspoon pepper
- ½ teaspoon paprika
- ½ teaspoon ground red pepper
- 1 bay leaf
- 2 (16-ounce) cans light red kidney beans, rinsed and drained (optional)
- Toppings: sour cream, shredded Cheddar cheese, chopped green onions, sliced ripe black olives

COOK ground chuck, in batches, in a large skillet over medium-high heat about 5 minutes, stirring until meat crumbles and is no longer pink; drain. Place meat in a 6-quart slow cooker; stir in onions, next 12 ingredients, and, if desired, beans. Cook, covered, at HIGH 5 to 6 hours or at LOW 6 to 8 hours. Remove and discard bay leaf. Serve with desired toppings. **MAKES** 15 to 18 cups.

COOKTOP PREPARATION: Cook ground chuck, in batches, in a large Dutch oven. Drain beef; return to Dutch oven. Add onions, next 12 ingredients, and, if desired, beans. Bring to a boil over medium-high heat; reduce heat, cover, and simmer 4 to 6 hours. Remove and discard bay leaf.

TO FREEZE: Let chili stand 30 minutes. Evenly divide chili mixture into 3 (1-gallon) zip-top freezer bags; seal and lay each bag flat. Stack bags of chili in freezer. Freeze up to 1 month. Thaw frozen chili overnight in refrigerator or defrost in microwave. Pour thawed chili into a 9-inch square baking dish. Cover tightly with heavy-duty plastic wrap, and fold back a corner to allow steam to escape. Microwave at HIGH 6 to 7 minutes or until bubbly, stirring after 3½ minutes.

ELAINE AND BERNIE MARTIN
ALEXANDRIA, VIRGINIA

QUICK APPLE BUNDLES

fast fixin's

Prep: 10 min., Bake: 20 min.

Refrigerated piecrust and frozen apples let you get this dessert ready for the oven in 10 minutes.

- ½ (15-ounce) package refrigerated piecrusts
- 1 (12-ounce) package frozen spiced apples, thawed
- 1 egg white, lightly beaten
- Sugar
- 1 (12-ounce) jar butterscotch topping, warmed

UNROLL piecrust according to package directions. Cut into fourths. Place apples evenly in center of each fourth. Pull corners over apples, pinching to seal. Place on a baking sheet; brush evenly with egg white, and sprinkle with sugar.
BAKE at 425° for 18 to 20 minutes or until golden. Serve warm with butterscotch topping. **MAKES** 4 servings.

NOTE: For testing purposes only, we used Stouffer's Harvest Apples.

Onion Soups

Around-the-world flavors warm you on a chilly day.

Nothing goes better with sweater season than a bowl of soup—the heartier the better. These luscious smells floating in the air will lead you into the kitchen.

MEXICAN ONION SOUP

family favorite

Prep: 20 min.; Cook: 1 hr., 10 min.

- 5 medium-size yellow onions, thinly sliced (about 3 pounds)
- 4 (14½-ounce) cans chicken broth, divided
- 2 garlic cloves, minced
- 1 teaspoon ground cumin
- ½ teaspoon ground coriander
- ½ teaspoon dried oregano
- 2 (14½-ounce) cans beef broth
- 1 (10-ounce) can diced tomatoes and green chiles, undrained
- 2 tablespoons ground chipotle pepper
- 1¼ cups (5 ounces) shredded Monterey Jack cheese with peppers
- Tortilla Strips
- ⅓ cup chopped fresh cilantro

COMBINE onions, 1 cup chicken broth, minced garlic, and next 3 ingredients in a Dutch oven over medium heat; cook, stirring occasionally, 25 to 30 minutes or until most of the liquid evaporates. Increase heat to medium high, and cook, stirring often to loosen particles from bottom of Dutch oven, 15 to 20 minutes or until onions are caramel colored.

STIR in beef broth, tomatoes and green chiles, chipotle pepper, and remaining chicken broth. Bring to a boil over high heat; reduce heat, and cook, stirring often, 15 to 20 minutes. Ladle soup into 6 bowls; sprinkle evenly with cheese, Tortilla Strips, and chopped cilantro. **MAKES** 6 servings.

Tortilla Strips:
fast fixin's
Prep: 5 min., Bake: 10 min.

To cut the tortillas into strips quickly, use a pizza cutter.

- 6 (6-inch) corn tortillas
- Vegetable cooking spray
- Salt to taste

CUT 6 corn tortillas into 1½-inch strips. Coat with cooking spray; place on a baking sheet.
BAKE at 400° for 5 minutes. Stir and bake 5 more minutes or until crisp. Sprinkle lightly with salt. **MAKES** 6 servings.

SUSIE BRENNAN
DALLAS, TEXAS

TOMATO-ONION SOUP

family favorite

Prep: 20 min., Cook: 50 min., Broil: 3 min.

This soup has an herby tomato flavor that gives it an Italian accent.

- 2 (14½-ounce) cans Italian-style stewed tomatoes, undrained
- ¼ cup butter
- 4 large white onions, chopped (about 2½ pounds)
- 4 (10½-ounce) cans beef consommé, undiluted
- ½ cup dry sherry
- ½ teaspoon dried rosemary
- ½ teaspoon dried oregano
- 8 (¾-inch-thick) French or sourdough bread slices
- 3 cups (12 ounces) shredded Italian three-cheese blend
- ½ cup freshly grated Parmesan-Romano cheese

PROCESS tomatoes in a blender or food processor until smooth, stopping to scrape down sides.
MELT ¼ cup butter in a Dutch oven over medium-high heat; add onions, and cook, stirring often, 30 to 40 minutes or until golden brown. Stir in pureed tomatoes, beef consommé, and next 3 ingredients; bring mixture to a boil. Reduce heat; simmer, stirring occasionally, 10 minutes.
LADLE soup into 8 ovenproof bowls; top with bread slices, and sprinkle evenly with cheeses.
BROIL 5½ inches from heat 3 minutes or until cheese is browned and bubbly. **MAKES** 8 servings.

PETER HALFERTY
CORPUS CHRISTI, TEXAS

FRENCH ONION SOUP

family favorite

Prep: 20 min., Cook: 1 hr., Broil: 3 min.

- ¼ cup butter
- 5 medium-size white onions, thinly sliced (about 3 pounds)
- 1 (32-ounce) container chicken broth
- 2 (10½-ounce) cans beef consommé, undiluted
- ¼ cup dry white wine
- 3 sprigs fresh thyme
- 2 sprigs fresh parsley
- Salt and freshly ground pepper to taste
- 6 (¾-inch-thick) French baguette slices
- 6 (1-ounce) Swiss cheese slices

MELT butter in a Dutch oven over medium-high heat; add onions, and cook, stirring often, 30 to 40 minutes or until golden brown.
ADD chicken broth and next 4 ingredients; bring to a boil. Reduce heat, and simmer, stirring occasionally, 20 minutes. Remove and discard herbs. Add salt and pepper to taste.
LADLE into 6 ovenproof bowls; top with bread and cheese slices. Broil 5½ inches from heat 3 minutes or until cheese is browned and bubbly. **MAKES** 6 servings.

HOLIDAY DINNERS.

Join us as we create lasting memories
and traditions around the table with family and friends.

From Home to Home

On one night in December, two supper club groups in the community of Glen Laurel, North Carolina came together to feast on extraordinary food and to savor friendships. The phrase "From the icy North to the sunny South" became the theme for the evening. Here they share their recipes and planning tips for a successful progressive dinner.

ENDIVE WITH HERBED GOAT CHEESE

fast fixin's • make ahead

Prep: 25 min.

The goat cheese mixture can be made a day in advance. Assemble the appetizer on a platter, cover, and chill up to 4 hours ahead of the party.

14 ounces goat cheese
2 tablespoons olive oil
2 teaspoons grated lemon rind
1 tablespoon fresh lemon juice
3 tablespoons chopped fresh cilantro
3 tablespoons chopped fresh chives
¼ teaspoon salt
¼ teaspoon freshly ground pepper
60 Belgian endive leaves (about 8 heads)
6 grape or cherry tomatoes, thinly sliced
Garnish: fresh cilantro leaves

PROCESS first 4 ingredients in a food processor until smooth. Spoon into a small bowl; stir in cilantro and next 3 ingredients.

PIPE or spoon about 1½ teaspoons cheese mixture onto each tip of endive leaf; top with 1 tomato slice. Garnish, if desired. Serve immediately, or cover and chill up to 4 hours. **MAKES** about 60 appetizers.

JANE GLASS
CLAYTON, NORTH CAROLINA

BEGGAR'S PURSES WITH SMOKED SALMON

fast fixin's • make ahead

Prep: 20 min., Cook: 5 min.

For a simpler presentation, spoon cream cheese mixture in miniature phyllo cups, top with caviar, and sprinkle with sliced green onion tops or chives.

1 (8-ounce) package cream cheese, softened
¼ cup sour cream
1 tablespoon dried chives
¼ teaspoon salt
¼ teaspoon freshly ground black pepper
8 green onions
Basic Crêpes
1 (2-ounce) jar red or black caviar
1 pound smoked salmon
Garnish: fresh parsley

BEAT cream cheese and sour cream at medium speed with an electric mixer until smooth. Stir in chives, salt, and pepper.
CUT off white portion from green onions, reserving for another use. Separate tops into individual pieces. (You'll need 24 strips.) Cook green onion tops in boiling water 1 minute or until bright green and tender; drain. Plunge into ice water to stop the cooking process; drain and press between paper towels to dry.
SPOON about 2 tablespoons cream cheese mixture in center of each crêpe; top with 1 teaspoon caviar. Bring edges of crêpe up around filling to form a sack; tie with 1 green onion top. Arrange bundles around smoked salmon to serve. Garnish, if desired. **MAKES** about 24 appetizers.

Basic Crêpes:
freezeable • make ahead
Prep: 10 min.; Chill: 1 hr.;
Cook: 2 min., 30 sec. each

- 4 large eggs
- 1 cup all-purpose flour
- ½ cup milk
- ½ cup water
- 3 tablespoons butter, melted
- 1 tablespoon sugar
- ½ teaspoon salt

WHISK together all ingredients in a large bowl. Cover and chill 1 hour.
PLACE a lightly greased 8-inch nonstick skillet over medium heat until skillet is hot.
POUR 2 tablespoons batter into skillet; quickly tilt in all directions so that batter covers bottom of skillet.
COOK 2 minutes or until crêpe can be shaken loose from skillet. Turn crêpe, and cook about 30 seconds. Repeat with remaining batter. Stack crêpes between sheets of wax paper until ready to fill. **MAKES** about 24 crêpes.

TO MAKE AHEAD: Place crêpes, stacked with wax paper between each, in a zip-top freezer bag. Freeze crêpes up to 1 month. Thaw overnight before using; reheating is not necessary.

SHARYL AGNEW
CLAYTON, NORTH CAROLINA

WINTER WALDORF SALAD

make ahead

Prep: 25 min., Chill: 1 hr.

Serve in martini glasses, and add a crunchy breadstick to garnish.

- ¾ cup mayonnaise
- ¾ cup sour cream
- ⅓ cup honey
- 1 tablespoon grated lemon rind
- 1½ tablespoons fresh lemon juice
- ¾ teaspoon ground ginger
- 3 large Granny Smith apples, chopped
- 3 large Red Delicious apples, chopped
- 3 large Golden Delicious apples, chopped
- 1½ cups diced celery
- 1½ cups seedless red grapes, halved
- ½ cup raisins*
- 1 to 1¼ cups chopped walnuts, toasted
- Garnishes: pomegranate seeds, breadsticks

WHISK together first 6 ingredients in a large bowl. Stir in Granny Smith apples and next 5 ingredients. Cover and chill 1 hour.
STIR IN walnuts just before serving. Garnish, if desired. **MAKES** 12 servings.

*Substitute ½ cup dried cranberries for raisins, if desired.

SHARYL AGNEW
CLAYTON, NORTH CAROLINA

Progressive Party Tips

- Host homes should be within walking distance or a short drive.
- Allow an hour to eat and mingle at each home. Give extra time for the main-course stop.
- Host couples should plan to slip out halfway through the course served prior to theirs.

JOHNSTON COUNTY CROWN PORK ROAST WITH CRANBERRY STUFFING

family favorite

Prep: 10 min.; Bake: 3 hrs., 30 min.;
Stand: 15 min.; Cook: 7 min.

- 3 teaspoons coarse-grained salt, divided
- 1 tablespoon pepper
- 1 (16-rib) crown pork roast, trimmed and tied (about 10¼ pounds)
- 2 cups reserved unbaked Cranberry Stuffing (recipe on following page)
- 2 tablespoons all-purpose flour
- ¾ cup water
- Garnishes: fresh cranberries, fresh rosemary and thyme sprigs, fresh sage leaves

RUB 2 teaspoons salt and 1 tablespoon pepper evenly over all sides of pork roast. Place roast, rib ends down, in a 1-quart round soufflé or casserole dish. Place soufflé dish in an aluminum foil-lined roasting pan.
BAKE at 325° for 2½ hours. Remove from oven. Remove dish from pan; remove roast from dish, and invert. Place rib ends up on aluminum foil in roasting pan. Pour drippings from dish into roasting pan. Spoon 2 cups reserved unbaked Cranberry Stuffing into center of roast; cover with a 12-inch square of heavy-duty aluminum foil, and fold foil over tips of roast.
BAKE roast 45 minutes to 1 hour more or until meat thermometer registers 155°. Remove foil, and let stand 15 minutes or until thermometer registers 160° before slicing.
POUR pan drippings into a skillet, and cook over medium-high heat until mixture comes to a boil.
STIR together 2 tablespoons flour, remaining 1 teaspoon salt, and ¾ cup water. Whisk into pan drippings; cook, whisking constantly, 5 minutes or until thickened. Serve with roast. Garnish, if desired. **MAKES** 12 servings.

Cranberry Stuffing:

Prep: 15 min., Cook: 5 min., Bake: 35 min.

The cranberry sauce and pecans add texture and flavor to this stuffing. Use it in the Johnston County Crown Pork Roast on the previous page.

- ¼ cup butter or margarine
- 1 cup chopped celery
- 1 cup chopped onion
- 1 (16-ounce) package herb-seasoned cornbread stuffing mix
- 2 cups chicken broth
- 1 (16-ounce) can whole-berry cranberry sauce
- 1 cup chopped pecans

MELT ¼ cup butter in a large Dutch oven over medium heat; add celery and onion, and sauté 5 minutes or until tender.

STIR in stuffing mix and remaining ingredients, stirring just until moistened. Remove 2 cups unbaked stuffing; reserve to stuff in pork roast. Spoon remainder into a lightly greased 11- x 7-inch baking dish.

BAKE, covered, at 325° for 30 to 35 minutes or until thoroughly heated. Serve stuffing with pork roast. **MAKES** 10 to 12 servings.

NOTE: For testing purposes only, we used Pepperidge Farm Corn Bread Stuffing.

JANE GLASS
CLAYTON, NORTH CAROLINA

Bourbon-Sweet Potato Stacks

family favorite

Prep: 20 min., Cook: 45 min., Bake: 25 min.

(pictured on page 1)

- 6 medium-size sweet potatoes
- ½ cup chopped pecans
- 6 tablespoons butter, melted
- ½ cup firmly packed brown sugar
- ½ cup orange juice
- ½ cup bourbon
- ½ teaspoon ground cinnamon
- ¼ teaspoon ground cloves
- ¼ teaspoon ground nutmeg
- Garnish: pecan halves

BRING sweet potatoes and water to cover to a boil in a large Dutch oven over high heat. Reduce heat, and cook 30 to 45 minutes or just until potatoes are tender. Drain and let cool to touch; peel. Cut ends off, and discard. Cut remaining potato into 1-inch-thick rounds. Arrange slices evenly into 12 stacks in a lightly greased 13- x 9-inch baking dish. Sprinkle evenly with chopped pecans.

COMBINE butter and next 6 ingredients; pour evenly over potatoes.

BAKE at 350° for 25 minutes or until thoroughly heated. Garnish, if desired. **MAKES** 12 servings.

SARAH BROOKS
CLAYTON, NORTH CAROLINA

Garlic-Tarragon Green Beans

family favorite

Prep: 20 min., Cook: 15 min.

(pictured on page 1)

- 2 quarts water
- 2 tablespoons salt
- 2 pounds thin fresh green beans
- 2 garlic cloves, minced
- ½ teaspoon dried tarragon leaves
- 2 tablespoons olive oil
- ½ teaspoon salt
- ½ teaspoon pepper

BRING 2 quarts water and 2 tablespoons salt to a boil in a Dutch oven; add beans. Cook 6 minutes or until crisp-tender; drain. Plunge into ice water to stop the cooking process; drain.

SAUTÉ garlic and tarragon in hot oil in Dutch oven over medium heat 2 to 3 minutes or until garlic is tender. (Do not brown garlic.) Add beans, ½ teaspoon salt, and pepper, and cook, stirring constantly, 2 minutes or until thoroughly heated. **MAKES** 12 servings.

JANE GLASS
CLAYTON, NORTH CAROLINA

Piña Colada Crème Brûlée

Prep: 10 min., Bake: 55 min., Cool: 45 min., Chill: 8 hrs., Broil: 7 min., Stand: 5 min.

(pictured on page 264)

- 1 (8-ounce) can crushed pineapple
- 1 cup whipping cream
- 1 cup coconut milk
- 8 egg yolks
- ⅓ cup sugar
- ¼ cup coconut rum*
- 1 teaspoon vanilla extract
- 6 teaspoons sugar
- ½ cup sweetened flaked coconut, toasted

DRAIN pineapple, and pat dry with paper towels.

STIR together pineapple, whipping cream, and next 5 ingredients. Pour mixture evenly into 6 (6-ounce or ¾ cup) ramekins; place ramekins in a large roasting pan. Add hot water to pan to a depth of ½ inch.

BAKE at 300° for 50 to 55 minutes or until almost set. Cool 30 to 45 minutes in water in pan on a wire rack. Remove ramekins from pan; cover and chill at least 8 hours.

SPRINKLE 1 teaspoon sugar evenly over each custard, and place ramekins in roasting pan.

BROIL 5½ inches from heat 7 minutes or until sugar melts. Let custard stand 5 minutes to allow sugar to harden. Sprinkle coconut evenly over each custard. **MAKES** 6 servings.

NOTE: Make a second batch (rather than double the recipe) for a larger crowd. Sugar may be browned with a professional culinary torch available from specialty kitchen shops.

*Substitute 1 teaspoon coconut extract for coconut rum, if desired.

LESLIE BARRANCO
CLAYTON, NORTH CAROLINA

GRILLED PINEAPPLE SKEWERS WITH RUM SAUCE

Prep: 20 min., Soak: 30 min.,
Cook: 10 min., Grill: 8 min.

12 (6-inch) wooden skewers
1 cup firmly packed brown sugar
½ cup butter
⅓ cup dark rum
½ teaspoon ground cinnamon
¼ teaspoon ground nutmeg
3 fresh pineapples
Vegetable cooking spray

SOAK skewers in water 30 minutes.
STIR together brown sugar and next 4 ingredients in a small saucepan over medium heat, stirring constantly, until blended. Cook over low heat, without stirring, 10 minutes or until sauce begins to thicken. Remove from heat; keep warm.
CUT pineapples lengthwise into fourths, leaving crown ends on. Remove hard core from each quarter; cut pineapple pulp away from shell in one wedge-shaped piece, keeping the crown and shell intact. Set pineapple shell aside. Cut pineapple wedge into 8 equal crosswise slices, and thread onto wooden skewers. Repeat procedure with remaining wedges.
SPRAY food grate with cooking spray, and place on grill. Place pineapple on food grate. Grill, covered with grill lid, over medium-high heat (350° to 400°) 4 minutes on each side or until thoroughly heated.
ARRANGE skewers in reserved pineapple shells, and drizzle with warm rum mixture. **MAKES** 12 servings.

LESLIE BARRANCO
CLAYTON, NORTH CAROLINA

Busy Mom's Do-Ahead Menu

Melanie Appell Dillenberg, a busy working mother, enjoys this casual holiday feast to celebrate the eight-day Festival of Lights.

Hanukkah Celebration

Serves 8

Spicy Apricot Brisket

Quick Potato-Chive Pancakes

Green Beans With Shallots

Chunky Chocolate Brownies

SPICY APRICOT BRISKET

freezeable • make ahead

Prep: 20 min.; Bake: 3 hrs., 30 min.; Stand: 20 min.

If you love barbecue, put this entrée on your list. Melanie Appell Dillenberg's friend, Rosalyn Bloomston, shared this recipe with her. Melanie freezes it in portions for fast weeknight meals.

1 (5½-pound) beef brisket, trimmed
2 teaspoons garlic salt
¼ teaspoon pepper
2 (10-ounce) cans shredded sauerkraut, drained
2 (10-ounce) jars apricot preserves
2 (12-ounce) bottles chili sauce

PLACE brisket, fat side up, in a roasting pan. Sprinkle with garlic salt and pepper. Stir together sauerkraut, preserves, and chili sauce; pour over beef. Bake, covered, at 350° for 3½ hours or until tender.
REMOVE brisket from pan, reserving sauce mixture in pan; let stand 20 minutes. Cut brisket across the grain into thin slices using a sharp knife.
POUR sauce mixture from roasting pan through a wire-mesh strainer into a bowl; reserve, if desired. Serve strained sauce and, if desired, sauerkraut with sliced brisket. **MAKES** 8 servings.

TO MAKE AHEAD: Prepare and bake as directed. Remove brisket from pan, reserving sauce mixture in pan; let stand 1 hour. Cut brisket across the grain into thin slices using a sharp knife. Place brisket slices in a 13- x 9-inch baking dish. Pour sauce mixture through a wire-mesh strainer into a bowl, reserving sauerkraut mixture, if desired. Pour strained sauce over brisket slices; cover and chill up to 24 hours. Reheat as directed.

TO FREEZE UP TO 3 MONTHS: Place brisket slices and strained sauce evenly into large zip-top freezer bags; freeze. Thaw in refrigerator overnight. Place brisket and sauce in a 13- x 9-inch baking dish. Reheat as directed.

TO REHEAT: Let stand at room temperature 30 minutes. Bake, covered, at 325° for 45 minutes or until hot.

MELANIE APPELL DILLENBERG
BIRMINGHAM, ALABAMA

Celebrating Hanukkah

Known as the Festival of Lights, Hanukkah usually occurs in December. Pot roast, applesauce, latkes, homemade fried doughnuts, and sugar cookies are traditional Hanukkah foods. During each night of the celebration, a candle is lit to symbolize the miracle that occurred when the eternal flame in the temple in Jerusalem burned for eight days on a single day's supply of oil 21 centuries ago. This is why Hanukkah is celebrated for eight nights.

QUICK POTATO-CHIVE PANCAKES

family favorite

Prep: 10 min., Stand: 20 min., Cook: 30 min.

PREPARE 1 (6-ounce) package potato pancake mix according to package directions for batter. Stir 2 tablespoons chopped fresh chives into batter. Let batter stand 20 minutes. Fry pancakes according to package directions using heaping tablespoonfuls of batter. If desired, top with applesauce or sour cream and chopped fresh chives. **MAKES** 6 to 8 servings.

QUICK SWEET POTATO-CHIVE PAN-CAKES: Substitute 1 (6-ounce) package sweet potato pancake mix for regular; proceed as directed.

TO KEEP WARM: Place fried pancakes on a wire rack on an aluminum foil-lined baking sheet. Keep warm in a 200° oven up to 30 minutes.

NOTE: For testing purposes only, we used Manischewitz Potato Pancake Mixes.

GREEN BEANS WITH SHALLOTS

make ahead

Prep: 25 min., Cook: 15 min.

The first step is a cooking technique called blanching. You cook the green beans just a little, and then stop the cooking process by plunging vegetables in ice water.

- **2 pounds fresh green beans, trimmed**
- **2 medium shallots, diced**
- **1 tablespoon olive oil**
- **1½ teaspoons herb-vegetable seasoning blend**
- **Freshly ground pepper to taste**

COOK green beans in boiling salted water to cover 8 minutes or until crisp-tender; drain. Plunge into ice water to stop the cooking process; drain.

SAUTÉ shallots in hot oil in a large skillet over medium heat 3 minutes or until lightly browned. Add green beans, seasoning blend, and pepper; sauté until thoroughly heated. Serve immediately. **MAKES** 8 servings.

NOTE: For testing purposes only, we used Spike's Seasoning.

TO MAKE AHEAD: Wrap blanched green beans in a dry paper towel, and place in a large zip-top plastic bag. Chill up to 24 hours. Proceed with recipe as directed.

MELANIE APPELL DILLENBERG
BIRMINGHAM, ALABAMA

CHUNKY CHOCOLATE BROWNIES

freezeable • make ahead

Prep: 20 min., Cook: 5 min., Cool: 5 min.,
Bake: 28 min.

Chocolate chunks make these brownies fudgy; decrease baking time to 23 minutes to make them extra gooey.

- **2 tablespoons water**
- **¾ cup granulated sugar**
- **⅓ cup butter**
- **1 (11.5-ounce) package semisweet chocolate chunks, divided**
- **2 large eggs**
- **1 teaspoon vanilla extract**
- **¾ cup all-purpose flour**
- **¼ teaspoon salt**
- **½ cup chopped hazelnuts or pecans, toasted**
- **Powdered sugar**

COMBINE first 3 ingredients in a 3½-quart saucepan. Bring to a boil over medium heat, stirring constantly. Remove from heat, and stir in 1 cup chocolate chunks until smooth. Let cool 5 minutes. Add eggs, 1 at a time, stirring just until blended. Stir in vanilla.
COMBINE flour and salt; stir in remaining chocolate chunks and hazelnuts. Stir flour mixture into chocolate mixture in saucepan. Spread into a lightly greased 9-inch square pan.

BAKE at 325° for 23 to 28 minutes. Cool in pan on a wire rack. Dust with powdered sugar. Cut into squares. **MAKES** 9 brownies.

TO FREEZE UP TO 3 MONTHS: Wrap baked brownies in aluminum foil, and place in a large zip-top freezer bag. To thaw, remove brownies from bag, and let stand at room temperature for 3 hours; unwrap and serve.

MELANIE APPELL DILLENBERG
BIRMINGHAM, ALABAMA

Bed-and-Breakfast Recipes

Owners of the historic Queen Anne-style Byrn-Roberts Inn in Murfreesboro, Tennessee, share their favorite recipes. For more information about the inn, visit **www.byrn-roberts-inn.com,** or call 1-888-877-4919.

CANADIAN BACON-AND-BRIE QUICHE

Prep: 10 min., Bake: 35 min., Stand: 5 min.

Inn Owner Julie Becker says the surprise crust in this recipe makes it "the quiche that men will eat."

- **16 Canadian bacon slices**
- **1 (8-ounce) round Brie cheese**
- **8 large eggs, lightly beaten**
- **½ cup mayonnaise**
- **½ teaspoon white pepper**
- **½ teaspoon grated Parmesan cheese**
- **½ teaspoon dried Italian seasoning**
- **Garnishes: edible flowers, fresh rosemary sprigs**

ARRANGE bacon slices on bottom and up sides of a lightly greased 9-inch pieplate, slightly overlapping slices.

REMOVE rind from Brie, and cut into cubes.

STIR together eggs, cubed Brie, mayonnaise, and next 3 ingredients in a bowl. Pour mixture into prepared pieplate.

BAKE at 375° for 30 to 35 minutes or until a knife inserted in center comes out clean. Let quiche stand 5 minutes before serving. Garnish, if desired. **MAKES** 8 servings.

BAKED APPLE PANCAKES WITH CARAMEL SAUCE

Prep: 20 min., Bake: 29 min.

Julie calls this recipe her version of breakfast apple pie. "And apple pie always calls for ice cream!" she says. Look for oval baking dishes in cook shops or kitchen sections of department stores.

- **8 large eggs**
- **1 cup all-purpose flour**
- **3 tablespoons granulated sugar**
- **½ teaspoon salt**
- **½ teaspoon ground cinnamon**
- **1½ cups buttermilk**
- **1 teaspoon vanilla extract**
- **Vegetable cooking spray**
- **½ cup butter or margarine**
- **3 Granny Smith apples, peeled and thinly sliced**
- **½ cup firmly packed brown sugar**
- **½ cup chopped pecans**
- **Powdered sugar**
- **Vanilla ice cream**
- **Caramel Sauce**
- **Chopped, toasted pecans**

WHISK together first 5 ingredients. (Mixture will be lumpy.) Add buttermilk and vanilla, whisking until batter is blended.

COAT 8 (7- x 4- x 1½-inch) oval baking dishes with cooking spray. Place 1 tablespoon butter in each dish.

BAKE at 425° for 3 to 4 minutes or until butter melts. Place apple slices evenly into dishes; bake 5 more minutes. Spoon about ½ cup batter into each dish. Sprinkle batter evenly with brown sugar and ½ cup chopped pecans. Bake 20 more minutes.

SPRINKLE pancakes with powdered sugar, and top with a scoop of vanilla ice cream; drizzle with Caramel Sauce, and sprinkle with chopped, toasted pecans. **MAKES** 8 servings.

Caramel Sauce:
fast fixin's

Prep: 5 min., Cook: 5 min., Cool: 5 min.

- **1 cup firmly packed brown sugar**
- **½ cup whipping cream**
- **2 tablespoons butter or margarine**
- **1 teaspoon vanilla extract**

COMBINE brown sugar and whipping cream in a heavy saucepan; cook over medium-low heat, stirring constantly, 3 minutes or until bubbly. (Mixture may look curdled.) Cook, stirring constantly, 2 more minutes. Remove from heat; add butter and vanilla, stirring until blended. Cool 3 to 5 minutes. **MAKES** 1 cup.

ALMOND-VANILLA BREAKFAST RING

Prep: 10 min.; Stand: 3 hrs., 10 min.; Bake: 30 min.

For a flavor variation of this easy coffee cake, use butterscotch pudding mix instead of vanilla.

- **1 cup firmly packed brown sugar**
- **½ cup butter or margarine**
- **½ teaspoon almond extract**
- **24 frozen unbaked yeast dinner rolls**
- **2 tablespoons vanilla-flavored cook-and-serve pudding mix**
- **½ cup sliced almonds**

HEAT first 3 ingredients in a glass microwave-safe bowl at HIGH 1 minute. Stir until blended; microwave 1 more minute or until bubbly.

ARRANGE frozen rolls in a lightly greased 10-cup Bundt pan. Drizzle sugar mixture evenly over rolls; sprinkle with pudding mix and almonds. Cover and let stand at room temperature 3 hours.

BAKE, uncovered, on lower oven rack at 350° for 30 minutes or until golden brown. Remove from oven, and let stand 10 minutes. Invert pan onto a lightly greased plate. Serve warm. **MAKES** 8 to 10 servings.

NOTE: For testing purposes only, we used Jell-O Cook & Serve Vanilla Pudding and Pie Filling and Bridgford Parkerhouse Style Rolls made with fresh yeast.

CITRUS-STRAWBERRY SALAD

make ahead

Prep: 20 min., Chill: 1 hr.

Arrange grapefruit shells filled with this refreshing salad on a tray for an attractive presentation.

- **2 pink grapefruit**
- **2 tangerines**
- **3 cups strawberries, coarsely chopped**
- **4 kiwifruit, peeled and cubed**
- **3 tablespoons powdered sugar**
- **1 teaspoon orange flower water (optional)***
- **Garnish: fresh mint sprigs**

CUT grapefruit in half. Carefully remove grapefruit segments with a paring knife, leaving shells intact. Remove and discard seeds and bitter pith from segments. Cut segments into bite-size pieces; place in a bowl. Peel tangerines with a paring knife, removing membranes between segments; cut segments into bite-size pieces, and add to bowl.

ADD strawberries, kiwifruit, powdered sugar, and, if desired, orange flower water to bowl, stirring gently. Cover and chill 1 hour. Spoon mixture evenly into grapefruit shells; garnish, if desired. **MAKES** 8 servings.

NOTE: Orange flower water can be found in some ethnic markets such as Asian, Mediterranean, or Italian.

*Substitute ½ teaspoon grated orange rind for 1 teaspoon orange flower water, if desired.

Fabulous Entrées

Three choices for your holiday dinner.

Do you ever find yourself buried in a stack of open cookbooks trying to plan a special menu, only to be baffled by the number of choices? We're with you—it can be overwhelming. So Test Kitchens professional (and busy mom) Vanessa McNeil developed these three selections to help narrow the field. Each entrée has a menu designed around it, using recipes from our other "Holiday Dinners" stories in this issue. Here's to your fabulous, festive occasion.

Small Dinner Party

Serves 6

Cheddar cheese and fruit appetizer tray

Apple-Sage Stuffed Pork Chops (recipe at right)

Steamed baby carrots and pearl onions

Fruited Rice Pilaf, page 271

Mocha Mousse Torte, page 260

Family Gathering

Serves 8 to 10

Peach Holiday Ham (on facing page)

Bell's Sweet Potato Casserole, page 271

Winter Waldorf Salad, page 245

Garlic-Tarragon Green Beans, page 246

Rudolph's Chocolate Truffle Cake, page 253

Pecan Squares, page 271

Supper Club Menu

Serves 6

Goat Cheese-Olive Sandwiches, page 272

— or —

Endive With Herbed Goat Cheese, page 244
(prepare half of recipe)

Citrus-Strawberry Salad, page 249

Cranberry-Glazed Pork Loin (recipe on facing page)

Couscous with toasted pecans

Steamed broccoli

Piña Colada Crème Brûlée, page 246

APPLE-SAGE STUFFED PORK CHOPS

family favorite

Prep: 30 min., Cook: 22 min., Stand: 25 min., Bake: 40 min.

3 tablespoons butter
½ cup finely chopped yellow onion
½ cup finely chopped celery
½ cup finely chopped Granny Smith apple
½ cup finely chopped fresh mushrooms
1½ cups herb stuffing mix
1 (14.5-ounce) can chicken broth
5 fresh sage leaves, finely chopped*
6 tablespoons finely chopped fresh flat-leaf parsley, divided
1 teaspoon salt, divided
1 teaspoon ground black pepper, divided
¼ teaspoon ground red pepper
6 (2-inch-thick) bone-in center-cut pork chops
¼ cup olive oil, divided
1 cup water
Garnishes: steamed baby carrots, pearl onions, flat-leaf parsley

MELT butter in a large skillet over medium-high heat; add onion and next 3 ingredients; sauté 10 minutes or until vegetables are tender and liquid evaporates. Remove from heat. Add stuffing mix and broth; stir until liquid is absorbed. Stir in sage, 2 tablespoons chopped parsley, ½ teaspoon salt, ½ teaspoon black pepper, and ground red pepper. Let stand 20 minutes.

TRIM excess fat from each pork chop, and cut a slit in 1 side of each chop to form a pocket. Spoon stuffing mixture evenly into each pocket.

COMBINE remaining 4 tablespoons parsley, ½ teaspoon salt, and ½ teaspoon black pepper. Rub both sides of stuffed pork chops evenly with 2 tablespoons oil, and spread parsley mixture evenly over chops.

COOK chops in remaining 2 tablespoons hot oil in a large nonstick skillet over medium-high heat, in batches, 2 minutes on each side or until browned. Place on a lightly greased rack in a broiler pan. Add 1 cup water to broiler pan.

BAKE at 375° for 30 to 40 minutes. Let stand 5 minutes before serving. Garnish, if desired. **MAKES** 6 servings.

NOTE: For testing purposes only, we used Pepperidge Farm Herb Stuffing Mix.

*Substitute ½ teaspoon rubbed sage, if desired.

PEACH HOLIDAY HAM

family favorite

Prep: 25 min.; Bake: 1 hr., 30 min.; Stand: 10 min.

See "From Our Kitchen" on page 276 for sensational garnish ideas perfect for this main dish.

- 1 (8-pound) smoked, fully cooked ham
- 1 cup peach preserves
- 1 cup peach nectar
- 3 tablespoons coarse-grained mustard
- ¼ teaspoon ground cloves

REMOVE skin and excess fat from ham. Score fat on ham in a diamond pattern. Place the ham, fat side up, in a heavy-duty aluminum foil-lined roasting pan.

STIR together peach preserves and next 3 ingredients; pour mixture over ham.

BAKE at 325° for 1½ hours or until a meat thermometer inserted into thickest portion registers 140°, basting every 20 minutes. Shield with aluminum foil after 30 minutes to prevent excess browning. Let stand 10 minutes before slicing. **MAKES** 8 to 10 servings.

CRANBERRY-GLAZED PORK LOIN

family favorite

Prep: 20 min., Cook: 7 min., Bake: 45 min., Stand: 10 min. *(pictured on page 1)*

- 1 (8.5-ounce) jar cranberry chutney
- 1 cup apple jelly
- 1 tablespoon Creole mustard
- 1 cup chicken broth
- 2 garlic cloves, pressed
- 2 tablespoons fresh or 2 teaspoons dried thyme leaves
- 1 teaspoon salt
- 1 teaspoon pepper
- 1 (4½-pound) center-cut boneless pork loin roast
- Garnishes: Granny Smith apple slices, fresh thyme sprigs

STIR together first 6 ingredients in a medium saucepan; bring to a boil over medium heat. Reduce heat, and simmer 5 minutes.

SPRINKLE salt and pepper evenly on pork roast; place roast in an aluminum foil-lined roasting pan. Pour chutney mixture evenly over pork.

BAKE at 425° for 45 minutes or until a meat thermometer inserted into thickest portion registers 160°, basting every 20 minutes. Let stand 10 minutes before slicing. Garnish, if desired. **MAKES** 8 to 10 servings.

NOTE: For testing purposes only, we used Crosse & Blackwell Cranberry Chutney.

Holiday Hotlines

Here's the insider's list of toll-free telephone numbers for quick answers to last-minute questions about roasting turkey, baking, and food safety issues.

USDA Meat and Poultry Hotline: 1-800-535-4555
USDA Center for Food Safety: 1-888-723-3366
Butterball Turkey Talk-Line: 1-800-288-8372
Reynolds Kitchen Tips Line: 1-800-745-4000
Land O'Lakes Bakeline: 1-800-782-9606
Fleischmann's Yeast Help Line: 1-800-777-4959
Nestlé Bakeline: 1-800-637-8537, or visit **www.verybestbaking.com**
Ocean Spray Consumer Help Line: 1-800-662-3263

Food, Fun, and a Theme

Reindeer set the stage for this luncheon and ornament exchange.

Ladies Reindeer Luncheon

Serves 8

Blitzen's Baked Salmon With Caribbean Fruit Salsa

Dasher's Dill Mini-Muffins

Cupid's Creamy Peppermint Punch

Rudolph's Chocolate Truffle Cake with Chocolate Truffle Filling

Chocolate Rudolph Reindeer

Vixen's vices (coffee and store-bought chocolate)

As the Christmas season gears up, friends in and around Dunwoody, Georgia, eagerly await an invitation to the luncheon and ornament exchange hosted by Ann Nickerson and Shelley Ford. The invitation, you see, reveals the theme for their famous party. It was Santa's reindeer, particularly the one with the red nose, that ruled their 13th annual soiree. Even the recipes, such as Blitzen's Baked Salmon With Caribbean Fruit Salsa and Rudolph's Chocolate Truffle Cake, reflected the theme. And good friend Bonnie Davis contributed adorable chocolate reindeer. We've included easy step-by-step instructions. So check out all the ideas, and be inspired to start your own holiday-themed party.

BLITZEN'S BAKED SALMON WITH CARIBBEAN FRUIT SALSA

Prep: 5 min., Chill: 2 hrs., Bake: 25 min.

A whole salmon fillet is perfect for serving. If necessary, ask the butcher at your grocery store to remove the skin.

- 1 (3-pound) whole skinless salmon fillet
- 1 tablespoon Caribbean jerk seasoning*
- 1½ tablespoons olive oil
- Caribbean Fruit Salsa
- Garnish: lime wedges

PLACE salmon fillet in a roasting pan; sprinkle evenly on 1 side with jerk seasoning. Drizzle with oil. Cover and chill 2 hours.
BAKE salmon at 350° for 20 to 25 minutes or until fish flakes with a fork.

Serve with Caribbean Fruit Salsa. Garnish, if desired. **MAKES** 8 to 10 servings.

*Substitute Jamaican jerk seasoning, if desired. Caribbean jerk seasoning has a hint of sweetness.

Caribbean Fruit Salsa:
make ahead

Prep: 20 min., Chill: 2 hrs.

This is also great as an appetizer served with tortilla chips.

- 1 mango (about ½ pound), peeled and diced*
- 1 papaya (about ½ pound), peeled and diced*
- 1 medium-size red bell pepper, diced
- 1 medium-size green bell pepper, diced
- 1 cup diced fresh pineapple
- 1 small red onion, diced
- 3 tablespoons chopped fresh cilantro
- 2 tablespoons fresh lime juice
- 1 tablespoon olive oil

STIR together all ingredients. Cover and chill at least 2 hours. **MAKES** 5 cups.

*Substitute 1 cup each diced, refrigerated jarred mango and papaya, if desired.

ANN NICKERSON
DUNWOODY, GEORGIA

DASHER'S DILL MINI-MUFFINS

freezeable • make ahead

Prep: 10 min., Bake: 25 min.

Baked muffins can be frozen in an airtight container up to 1 month.

- 1 cup butter, softened
- 1 (8-ounce) container sour cream
- 2 cups self-rising flour
- 1 tablespoon dill seed
- 2 tablespoons dried parsley flakes
- ¼ teaspoon onion powder

BEAT softened butter at medium speed with an electric mixer until creamy; add sour cream, and beat at low speed until blended.

COMBINE flour and next 3 ingredients. Stir flour mixture into butter mixture until blended. Spoon dough into greased miniature muffin pans, filling three-fourths full.

BAKE at 375° for 22 to 25 minutes or until golden. **MAKES** about 3 dozen.

ANN NICKERSON
DUNWOODY, GEORGIA

CUPID'S CREAMY PEPPERMINT PUNCH

fast fixin's • make ahead

Prep: 10 min.

If you serve this dreamy drink in a large punch bowl, hang peppermint candy canes on the rim of the bowl.

- **1 quart eggnog**
- **1 (1-liter) bottle club soda, chilled**
- **½ gallon peppermint ice cream, softened**
- **Hard peppermint candies, crushed**

STIR together first 3 ingredients in a punch bowl or large bowl; sprinkle with peppermint candies, and serve immediately. **MAKES** about 1 gallon.

NOTE: Punch can be made ahead, without crushed peppermint candies, and chilled 2 hours. Stir well, and sprinkle with candies just before serving.

SHELLEY FORD
DUNWOODY, GEORGIA

RUDOLPH'S CHOCOLATE TRUFFLE CAKE

family favorite

Prep: 30 min., Cook: 10 min., Bake: 30 min., Chill: 30 min.

This cake is so decadent you might think it's Rudolph's revenge. It pairs perfectly with Vixen's vices (coffee and store-bought chocolates). You'll need 3 (8-ounce) packages semisweet chocolate squares to make the cake. This magnificent cake garnered our highest rating.

- **8 (1-ounce) semisweet chocolate squares**
- **2½ cups milk**
- **1 cup butter, softened**
- **3 large eggs**
- **2 teaspoons vanilla extract**
- **2⅔ cups all-purpose flour**
- **2 cups sugar**
- **1¼ teaspoons baking soda**
- **½ teaspoon salt**
- **Chocolate Truffle Filling, divided**
- **10 (1-ounce) semisweet chocolate squares, coarsely chopped**
- **½ cup plus 2 tablespoons whipping cream**
- **1 to 2 (1-ounce) semisweet chocolate squares, finely grated**

STIR together first 3 ingredients in a large heavy saucepan over low heat, and cook, stirring constantly, 8 to 10 minutes or until chocolate melts and mixture is smooth. Remove from heat, and let mixture cool slightly (about 10 minutes).

WHISK together eggs and vanilla in a large bowl. Gradually whisk in melted chocolate mixture until blended and smooth.

COMBINE flour and next 3 ingredients; whisk into chocolate mixture until blended and smooth.

POUR batter into 3 greased and floured 9-inch round cakepans.

BAKE at 325° for 25 to 30 minutes or until a wooden pick inserted in center comes out clean. Cool cake layers in pans on wire racks 10 minutes. Remove from pans, and let cool completely on wire racks.

SPREAD ½ cup plus 2 tablespoons Chocolate Truffle Filling evenly on top of 1 cake layer. Top with 1 cake layer; spread ½ cup plus 2 tablespoons Chocolate Truffle Filling evenly on top, reserving remaining ½ cup Chocolate Truffle Filling. Top with remaining cake layer.

MICROWAVE coarsely chopped semisweet chocolate squares and cream in a 2-quart microwave-safe bowl at HIGH 1½ to 2 minutes, stirring after 1 minute and then every 30 seconds until chocolate melts and mixture is smooth and slightly thickened. Let cool slightly (about 15 minutes).

SPREAD warm semisweet chocolate mixture over top and sides of cake. Chill cake 30 minutes or until chocolate glaze is firm. Pipe border using a rosette tip around bottom of cake with remaining ½ cup Chocolate Truffle Filling. Sprinkle finely grated semisweet chocolate evenly over top of cake. **MAKES** 12 servings.

Chocolate Truffle Filling:
fast fixin's

Prep: 10 min.

- **4 (1-ounce) semisweet chocolate squares**
- **6 tablespoons butter**
- **¼ to ½ cup whipping cream, divided**
- **2½ cups powdered sugar, sifted**

MICROWAVE chocolate squares and butter in a large microwave-safe bowl at HIGH 1½ to 2 minutes or until melted and smooth, stirring every 30 seconds. Stir in ¼ cup whipping cream. Stir in 2½ cups powdered sugar, adding remaining ¼ cup whipping cream, 1 tablespoon at a time, if necessary, until mixture is smooth and creamy. Let mixture cool completely. **MAKES** 1¾ cups.

ANN NICKERSON
DUNWOODY, GEORGIA

CHOCOLATE RUDOLPH REINDEER

freezeable • make ahead

Prep: 30 min., Freeze: 30 min. per batch,
Stand: 15 min.

- 12 (2-ounce) chocolate bark coating
    squares, divided
- 4 plastic deer candy molds
    (2 deer shapes per mold; deer
    are about 5½ inches tall)
- 8 mini-pretzel twists
- 1 (2-ounce) white vanilla bark
    coating square
- 8 red cinnamon candies
- Thin red satin ribbon

MICROWAVE 6 (2-ounce) chocolate bark coating squares in a 4-cup glass measuring cup at HIGH 1½ minutes, stirring at 30-second intervals. Stir until smooth. Pour melted chocolate evenly into 4 deer shapes (in 2 candy molds), filling each just over top (photo 1).

LEVEL chocolate with a small spatula, scraping excess back into measuring cup (photo 2). Gently tap candy molds on kitchen counter 2 or 3 times to remove air bubbles, if necessary. Freeze 20 minutes or until firm. Repeat procedure with remaining 6 (2-ounce) chocolate bark coating squares and 2 candy molds.

BREAK curved sides away from the center of each pretzel twist to form antlers. Dip antler tops into remaining melted chocolate bark in measuring cup, and place on a wax paper-lined baking sheet; freeze 10 minutes or until firm.

INVERT chocolate deer from molds onto wax paper; carefully trim any rough edges around bottom flat sides with a paring knife, if necessary.

MICROWAVE vanilla bark coating square in a small glass measuring cup at HIGH 1 minute, stirring after 30 seconds. Stir until smooth. Dip a small wooden pick into melted vanilla bark; dot eyes onto reindeer.

REHEAT chocolate in measuring cup in microwave at HIGH in 15-second intervals, stirring until smooth, if necessary. Dip a small wooden pick into melted chocolate. Dot melted chocolate onto head of 1 deer; attach 1 red cinnamon candy for nose, holding candy in place until adhered. Repeat procedure with remaining candies and remaining deer. Dip bottom of 1 set of antlers into melted chocolate bark, and attach to forehead of 1 deer, holding in place until adhered (photo 3). Repeat procedure with remaining antlers.

LET reindeer stand 15 minutes on wax paper before handling. Tie ribbon around neck of each reindeer. **MAKES** 8 reindeer.

BONNIE DAVIS
ATLANTA, GEORGIA

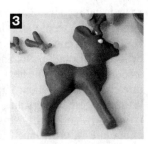

Tips and Ideas for Chocolate Reindeer

- Try to hold the reindeer by the outside edges using just a few fingers to prevent getting prints on the decorative side.
- To stand the reindeer, lean the flat side against a cake plate or decorative item.
- Wrap individually in cellophane, and give as party favors.

Note: We ordered our deer candy molds (#90-4509) from Cake Art in Stone Mountain, Georgia. Each mold, sold separately, is a bargain at $2. To order, visit **www.cakeart77.com,** or call (404) 294-5005.

Cooking With Love

When Sandy Kizlik and her son, Stephen, spend time together in the kitchen, they fill the room with good-natured teasing and heavenly aromas. This Boca Raton, Florida, pair turns out some seriously good food, much of it based on Sandy's Italian heritage. Sandy and Stephen offer three recipes that are perfect for casual family meals.

KEY LIME PIE

fast fixin's • make ahead

Prep: 5 min., Bake: 15 min.

Stephen sold his Key Lime Pies to a nearby restaurant when he lived outside New York City.

- 3 large egg yolks
- ½ cup Key lime juice
- 1 (14-ounce) can sweetened
    condensed milk
- ¼ teaspoon vanilla extract
- Pinch of salt
- 1 (9-inch) graham cracker crust
- Garnishes: whipped cream, lime
    slices

WHISK egg yolks until blended; whisk in Key lime juice. Add condensed milk, vanilla, and salt, whisking until blended. Pour mixture into crust. Bake at 350° for 15 minutes.

REMOVE from oven; cool completely on a wire rack. Chill until ready to serve. Garnish, if desired. **MAKES** 8 servings.

NOTE: For pies with more filling, triple the filling ingredients, and divide evenly between 2 graham cracker crusts.

STEPHEN KIZLIK
DELRAY BEACH, FLORIDA

CHICKEN WITH MUSHROOM SAUCE

family favorite

Prep: 25 min., Cook: 35 min.

This breaded chicken tastes great with spaghetti topped with tomato pasta sauce.

- 4 skinned and boned chicken breasts
- 1½ teaspoons salt, divided
- ¼ cup all-purpose flour
- ¼ teaspoon pepper
- ½ cup milk
- 1 cup Italian-seasoned breadcrumbs
- Olive oil
- 1 garlic clove, minced
- 12 fresh mushrooms, sliced
- 4 green onions, chopped
- 3 tablespoons chopped fresh parsley
- 2 tablespoons capers
- ½ cup chicken broth or water
- ½ cup Marsala or white wine
- 2 tablespoons lemon juice
- 2 lemons, sliced
- Hot cooked spaghetti (optional)
- Tomato pasta sauce (optional)

PLACE chicken breasts between 2 sheets of heavy-duty plastic wrap; flatten to ½-inch thickness, using a meat mallet or rolling pin. Sprinkle chicken evenly with ½ teaspoon salt.

COMBINE ¼ cup flour, ½ teaspoon salt, and ¼ teaspoon pepper in a shallow dish; dredge chicken in flour mixture, shaking off excess. Dip chicken in milk; dredge in breadcrumbs.

POUR oil to a depth of ¼ inch in a large skillet. Fry chicken, in batches, in hot oil over medium-high heat 5 to 6 minutes on each side. Remove chicken from skillet, and drain on paper towels, reserving 2 tablespoons drippings in pan.

SAUTÉ garlic in hot drippings 20 seconds; add mushrooms, and sauté 3 minutes or until lightly browned. Add green onions, parsley, and capers; sauté 1 minute. Stir in chicken broth, next 3 ingredients, and remaining ½ teaspoon salt. Bring mixture to a boil over medium-high heat, and cook, stirring

constantly, 2 minutes or until slightly thickened. Serve mushroom sauce over chicken. Serve chicken with spaghetti topped with tomato pasta sauce, if desired. **MAKES** 4 servings.

SANDY KIZLIK
BOCA RATON, FLORIDA

HERBED SEAFOOD PASTA

family favorite • fast fixin's

Prep: 15 min., Cook: 7 min.

Herb-Pesto Butter provides a grand base for sautéing the seafood and for tossing with the pasta.

- 1 (16-ounce) package fettuccine
- ½ pound unpeeled, medium-size shrimp
- 2 tablespoons olive oil
- 5½ tablespoons Herb-Pesto Butter, divided
- ½ pound large sea scallops
- 6 green onions, cut into 2-inch strips
- 1 cup freshly grated Parmesan cheese, divided

PREPARE pasta according to package directions; drain and set aside. Keep warm.

PEEL shrimp, and devein, if desired.

HEAT olive oil and 2 tablespoons Herb-Pesto Butter in a large skillet over medium-high heat. Add shrimp, scallops, and green onions; cook, stirring often, 3 to 5 minutes or just until shrimp turn pink. Stir in 2 more tablespoons Herb-Pesto Butter. Remove seafood mixture from skillet, and keep warm.

MELT remaining 1½ tablespoons Herb-Pesto Butter in skillet; remove from heat. Add warm pasta and ½ cup Parmesan cheese, tossing to coat. Divide pasta mixture evenly between 4 pasta bowls; top evenly with seafood mixture and remaining ½ cup cheese. Serve immediately. **MAKES** 4 servings.

Herb-Pesto Butter:

fast fixin's

Prep: 10 min.

Serve remaining Herb-Pesto Butter on bread, warm pasta, grilled vegetables, steak, or chicken breasts.

- 1½ cups fresh basil leaves
- ½ cup chopped fresh parsley
- ¼ cup pine nuts
- 3 tablespoons Marsala or white wine
- 2 tablespoons chopped fresh oregano leaves
- 8 garlic cloves, chopped
- 1 cup butter, softened
- 1 to 2 tablespoons olive oil

PROCESS first 6 ingredients in a food processor until smooth, stopping to scrape down sides. Add butter and 1 tablespoon olive oil, and process until combined; add remaining 1 tablespoon oil, if necessary, to achieve desired consistency. **MAKES** 2 cups.

SANDY KIZLIK
BOCA RATON, FLORIDA

A Fabulous Open House

A couple throws their first party.

Sharon and Jeff Humphrey of Irving, Texas, planned their first party carefully. Sharon had a vision of a grown-up get-together—open-house style and classy yet comfortable. This couple's creativity, attention to detail, and splurge-and-save shopping skills (which we share with you on the opposite page) can help you pull off your first holiday gathering.

Add a Little Flavor Tonight

Serves 24

Grilled Parsleyed Shrimp and Vegetables

Lemon-Vinaigrette Marinated Antipasto

Hummus with pita bread rounds

Pork Tenderloin on Cornmeal Biscuits

Wine: Georges Duboeuf Beaujolais Nouveau, France; Goats do Roam White or Red, South Africa

Beer and water

Gingerbread Bites With Orange-Cream Cheese Frosting

Sparkling white wines and liqueur sampling

Note: At most open house parties, you offer guests heavy nibbles. So don't worry if you run out of a dish; simply remove the platter.

GRILLED PARSLEYED SHRIMP AND VEGETABLES

make ahead

Prep: 15 min., Grill: 20 min., Chill: 8 hrs.

We estimated 7 or 8 shrimp per person and tripled this recipe for 24 guests. The lemon halves placed in the bottom of the serving bowl add color and act as a strainer. The shrimp and veggies sit on top, while the marinade settles to the bottom of the bowl. *(pictured on pages 262-263)*

- **3 pounds unpeeled, jumbo fresh shrimp (16 to 20 count per pound)**
- **2 lemons, halved**
- **2 large yellow bell peppers**
- **2 large green bell peppers**
- **2 large red onions**
- **1 cup chopped fresh flat-leaf parsley**
- **1 clove garlic, pressed**
- **1 (16-ounce) bottle olive oil-and-vinegar dressing**
- **Garnish: fresh flat-leaf parsley sprigs**

PEEL shrimp, leaving tails on; devein, if desired.
SQUEEZE lemon juice from lemon halves to measure ¼ cup; set juice aside. Reserve and chill lemon halves for later use.
GRILL shrimp, covered with grill lid, over medium-high heat (350° to 400°) 2 to 3 minutes on each side or until shrimp turn pink. Place in a large bowl.
CUT each pepper into 4 large pieces; cut each onion horizontally into 3 large slices.

GRILL vegetables, covered with a grill lid, over medium-high heat (350° to 400°) 5 to 7 minutes on each side or until bell peppers look blistered and onions are crisp-tender; cut into 2-inch pieces. Add grilled vegetables, chopped parsley, and garlic to shrimp in bowl. Pour vinaigrette and lemon juice over mixture, and stir to coat and combine. Cover and chill 8 hours or overnight.
ARRANGE reserved lemon halves in a deep serving bowl. Spoon marinated shrimp and vegetable mixture over top of lemon halves. Garnish, if desired.
MAKES 6 to 8 appetizer servings.

NOTE: For testing purposes only, we used Newman's Own Olive Oil & Vinegar dressing.

LEMON-VINAIGRETTE MARINATED ANTIPASTO

make ahead

Prep: 25 min., Cook: 5 min., Chill: 2 hrs.

The Humphreys made two recipes of this dish for their party. *(pictured on pages 262-263)*

- **1 pound fresh green beans, trimmed**
- **1 (8-ounce) package feta cheese, cubed**
- **1 (8-ounce) jar pitted kalamata olives, rinsed and drained**
- **1 (6-ounce) jar pitted large Spanish olives, rinsed and drained**
- **1 (16-ounce) jar pickled okra, drained**
- **1 (12-ounce) jar roasted red bell peppers, drained and cut into thin strips**
- **1 (10.5-ounce) log goat cheese**
- **1½ cups olive oil-and-vinegar dressing**
- **1 teaspoon sugar**
- **¼ teaspoon grated lemon rind**
- **¼ cup fresh lemon juice**
- **1 (5-ounce) package sliced hard salami (optional)**
- **Toasted French bread slices or large crackers**
- **Garnish: lemon wedges**

COOK green beans in boiling salted water to cover 5 minutes or until crisp-tender; drain. Plunge into ice water to stop cooking process; drain.

ARRANGE green beans, feta cheese, and next 5 ingredients in a 13- x 9-inch dish, keeping each ingredient separate from others.

WHISK together dressing and next 3 ingredients. Drizzle evenly over ingredients. Cover and chill 2 hours.

TRANSFER marinated ingredients to a large serving platter. Add salami, if desired. Serve with toasted French bread slices or large crackers. Garnish, if desired. **MAKES** 12 to 14 appetizer servings.

NOTE: For testing purposes only, we used Newman's Own Olive Oil & Vinegar dressing.

PORK TENDERLOIN ON CORNMEAL BISCUITS

Prep: 5 min., Broil: 5 min., Bake: 20 min., Stand: 15 min.

One recipe was just right for 24 guests. Running out of time to assemble sandwiches? Let guests make their own—serve sliced pork on a platter with chutney and biscuits on the side. *(pictured on pages 262-263)*

> 4 (¾- to 1-pound) pork tenderloins
> 2 teaspoons salt
> 2 teaspoons ground black pepper
> 2 tablespoons olive oil
> Cornmeal Biscuits, halved
> Texas Cranberry Chutney
> Garnish: sliced green onions

PLACE pork in a lightly greased 15- x 10-inch jellyroll pan; sprinkle with salt and pepper. Rub evenly with oil.

BROIL 5½ inches from heat 5 minutes; reduce oven temperature to 450°, and bake 20 minutes or until a meat thermometer inserted into thickest portion registers 160°. Let stand 15 minutes before slicing. Cut into ¼-inch-thick slices (about 18 slices each).

PLACE pork slices over Cornmeal Biscuit halves; top with Texas Cranberry Chutney. Garnish, if desired. **MAKES** 24 servings.

Cornmeal Biscuits:
Prep: 20 min., Bake: 15 min.

This is an easy recipe, but have some patience. The butter needs to be cut into the flour evenly and finely, almost until you can't see any bits of butter. Large pieces of butter will melt and leak out of the biscuits.

> 4 cups self-rising flour
> ½ cup yellow cornmeal*
> 1 cup butter, cut up
> 2 cups buttermilk
> ¼ cup milk

COMBINE flour and cornmeal in a large bowl; cut in butter with a pastry blender or fork until mixture is crumbly. Add buttermilk, stirring just until dry ingredients are moistened.

TURN dough out onto a lightly floured surface; knead 2 or 3 times.

PAT or roll dough to a ½-inch thickness, and cut with a 2-inch round cutter. Place on lightly greased baking sheets. Reroll remaining dough, and repeat procedure. Brush tops with milk.

BAKE at 425° for 13 to 15 minutes or until golden. **MAKES** about 3 dozen.

NOTE: For testing purposes only, we used Pillsbury Self-Rising Flour.

*White cornmeal can be substituted.

Texas Cranberry Chutney:
fast fixin's
Prep: 5 min., Cook: 10 min.

> 2 (8-ounce) cans crushed pineapple
> 1 (16-ounce) can whole-berry cranberry sauce
> ¼ cup firmly packed brown sugar
> ½ teaspoon ground ginger
> ¼ teaspoon salt
> 1 to 2 jalapeño peppers, seeded and minced
> 3 green onions, chopped

DRAIN pineapple well; pat dry with paper towels.

STIR together pineapple and next 4 ingredients in a small saucepan over medium heat, and bring to a boil. Reduce heat to low, and simmer, stirring often, 5 minutes or until thickened. Remove from heat, and stir in jalapeño and green onions. Cover and chill until ready to serve. **MAKES** 3 cups.

GINGERBREAD BITES WITH ORANGE-CREAM CHEESE FROSTING

freezeable • make ahead

Prep: 30 min., Bake: 15 min. per batch

One recipe made three treats for each guest at this party. Use a vegetable peeler to peel carrots and ginger and to make the garnish. Peel a thin layer of rind from 1 orange, and cut into thin strips using a knife. Unfrosted gingerbread muffins may be frozen in zip-top freezer bags up to 1 week. Frost and garnish in the morning, and refrigerate until serving time. *(pictured on page 262)*

- 1¾ cups sugar
- 1½ cups vegetable oil
- 4 large eggs
- 2 large carrots, finely grated (about 1 cup)
- 1 cup minced fresh ginger (about ½ pound)
- 2 cups all-purpose flour
- 2 teaspoons baking powder
- 1½ teaspoons baking soda
- 1½ teaspoons ground cinnamon
- ¾ teaspoon salt
- ½ teaspoon ground allspice
- ¼ teaspoon ground cloves
- 1½ cups chopped pecans, toasted
- Orange-Cream Cheese Frosting
- Garnishes: small pecan halves, crystallized ginger, orange rind strips

BEAT sugar and vegetable oil at medium speed with an electric mixer 3 minutes or until smooth. Add eggs, 1 at a time, beating well after each addition. Beat in carrots and ginger.

COMBINE all-purpose flour and next 6 ingredients; gradually add to egg mixture, beating at low speed until moistened. Stir in 1½ cups chopped toasted pecans.

POUR batter into lightly greased miniature muffin tins, filling two-thirds full.

BAKE at 350° for 12 to 15 minutes or until a wooden pick inserted in center comes out clean. Cool in pan on a wire rack 5 minutes. Remove from pan, and cool completely on wire racks. Spread tops evenly with Orange-Cream Cheese Frosting. Garnish, if desired. **MAKES** about 6 dozen.

MARIE A. DAVIS
CHARLOTTE, NORTH CAROLINA

Orange-Cream Cheese Frosting:
fast fixin's

Prep: 5 min.

- 2 (8-ounce) packages cream cheese, softened
- 2 tablespoons orange liqueur*
- ½ cup powdered sugar

BEAT softened cream cheese and orange liqueur at medium speed with an electric mixer until blended. Gradually add powdered sugar, beating until light and fluffy. **MAKES** 2 cups.

*Substitute 2 tablespoons orange juice for liqueur, if desired.

Three-Step Centerpiece

Senior Photo Stylist Buffy Hargett taught Sharon how to make a stunning centerpiece.

1. Buy two or three amaryllis in colors that go with your decor—Sharon chose coral and a burnished red. Cream amaryllis is beautiful in any home.

2. Wrap the pot in loosely woven mesh or sheer fabric. Secure with florist pins pushed through the fabric into the soil. Tie with ribbon or a strip of the fabric around the base of the plant.

3. Push florist picks into lime halves, and insert them into the pot so the pretty cut side of the fruit shows. Tuck in a few small ornaments.

Christmas Tea in the Delta

Christmas Tea

Serves 8

Olive-Nut Spread Sandwiches

Shrimp Butter on Crostini

Chicken-Mandarin Orange Spread Sandwiches

Banana-Nut Bread with Lemon Curd

Assorted hot teas

While relaxing on a *Southern Living at Sea* cruise, Lynn Brandon told Assistant Test Kitchens Director James Schend the story of the birth of her mother's Christmas tradition now celebrated in Kilbourne, Louisiana. Captivated by her English high tea experience at The Ritz in London, Barbara Brandon wanted to re-create that special moment for her friends and family back home. From her first party eight years ago, it was clear the event was a huge success.

The first cup of Darjeeling tea is served promptly at 3 in the afternoon. It's soon followed by Earl Grey, English breakfast, and assorted flavored teas along with Barbara's delicious goodies. "The Shrimp Butter on Crostini and Olive-Nut Spread Sandwiches are always a hit, and both are very easy to prepare," she says. The sandwich fillings can be made ahead and spread on the bread an hour before guests arrive.

Because all of her guests won't fit around her dining room table, Barbara sets up a number of small tables in her living and dining rooms. They need only a few roses in a tea cup to make them festive. Guests decide where they are going to sit by choosing the place setting with their favorite tea cup. Individual lap trays make space for a few more lucky guests.

OLIVE-NUT SPREAD SANDWICHES

fast fixin's • make ahead

Prep: 10 min.

- **1 (8-ounce) package cream cheese, softened**
- **½ cup chopped pimiento-stuffed green olives**
- **1 cup chopped pecans, toasted**
- **1 to 2 tablespoons mayonnaise**
- **Thin pumpernickel bread slices**
- **Garnish: toasted pecan halves**

STIR together first 4 ingredients in a large bowl. Cover and chill mixture until ready to serve. Cut crusts from bread slices; cut each slice into 4 squares. Serve spread on bread slices. Garnish, if desired. **MAKES** 2 cups spread.

SHRIMP BUTTER ON CROSTINI

fast fixin's • make ahead

Prep: 10 min., Bake: 5 min.

- **1 (16-ounce) French bread loaf, cut into 40 slices**
- **2 (8-ounce) packages cream cheese, softened**
- **½ pound butter, softened**
- **1 pound peeled cooked shrimp, finely chopped**
- **1 small onion, grated**
- **2 tablespoons lemon juice**
- **1 tablespoon mayonnaise**
- **¼ teaspoon garlic salt**
- **¼ teaspoon pepper**
- **Garnishes: peeled cooked shrimp, chopped chives**

PLACE bread slices on a baking sheet; bake at 350° for 5 minutes or until lightly toasted.
BEAT cream cheese and butter at medium speed with an electric mixer until fluffy. Stir in chopped shrimp and next 5 ingredients; spread mixture evenly on toasted bread slices. Garnish, if desired. **MAKES** 40 appetizers.

CHICKEN-MANDARIN ORANGE SPREAD SANDWICHES

fast fixin's

Prep: 15 min., Bake: 5 min.

- **12 raisin bread slices**
- **1 (8-ounce) package cream cheese, softened**
- **1½ cups chopped cooked chicken breast**
- **½ cup chopped pecans, toasted**
- **1 to 2 tablespoons mayonnaise**
- **¼ teaspoon dried thyme**
- **¼ teaspoon salt**
- **¼ teaspoon pepper**
- **½ cup mandarin orange segments**

CUT crusts from bread slices. Cut bread slices into 4 triangles, and place on a baking sheet. Bake at 400° for 5 minutes or until toasted.
COMBINE cream cheese and next 6 ingredients in a large bowl until blended. Cover and chill until ready to serve. Spoon 1 tablespoon cream cheese mixture on each raisin bread triangle; top each with a mandarin orange segment. **MAKES** 3 cups spread or 6 to 8 appetizer servings.

BANANA-NUT BREAD

Prep: 10 min., Bake: 1 hr.

Use bananas that have turned dark brown. *(pictured on page 267)*

- **1 cup sugar**
- **½ cup butter or margarine, softened**
- **3 very ripe bananas, mashed**
- **2 large eggs**
- **1 teaspoon vanilla extract**
- **2 cups self-rising flour**
- **½ teaspoon baking soda**
- **½ cup chopped pecans, toasted**
- **Lemon Curd (optional; recipe at right)**

BEAT 1 cup sugar and butter at medium speed with an electric mixer until creamy. Add mashed bananas, eggs, and vanilla, beating well.

COMBINE flour and baking soda; add to banana mixture, beating until just combined. Stir in chopped pecans.
POUR into a greased and floured 8- x 4-inch loafpan.
BAKE at 350° for 1 hour or until a wooden pick inserted in center comes out clean. Cool in pan on a wire rack 10 minutes; remove from pan, and cool completely on wire rack. Serve with Lemon Curd, if desired. **MAKES** 1 loaf.

LEMON CURD

fast fixin's • make ahead

Prep: 10 min., Cook: 20 min.

Lemon Curd adds a nice citrus flavor when served alongside Banana-Nut Bread. Or pour into a decorative jar for a great holiday gift. *(pictured on page 267)*

- **2 cups sugar**
- **½ cup butter, coarsely chopped**
- **¼ cup grated lemon rind**
- **1 cup fresh lemon juice (about 6 lemons)**
- **4 large eggs, lightly beaten**

STIR together sugar, butter, lemon rind, and juice in a large saucepan over medium heat, and cook, stirring constantly, until sugar dissolves and butter melts.
WHISK about one-fourth hot sugar mixture gradually into eggs; add egg mixture to remaining hot sugar mixture, whisking constantly.
COOK over medium-low heat, stirring constantly, 15 minutes or until mixture thickens and coats a spoon. Remove from heat; cool. Cover and chill up to 2 weeks. **MAKES** 2 cups.

Legally Grand Desserts

From legal tort to dessert torte, this lawyer knows his way around a courtroom and a kitchen.

Lawyers are known for their attention to detail. What a bonus for Kent Massie's wife, Ann, and their friends that this corporate attorney from Lexington, Virginia, has taken that attribute with him into the kitchen. We've featured two of his desserts that were a highlight at a recent party.

MOCHA MOUSSE TORTE

make ahead

Prep: 15 min., Cook: 5 min., Cool: 15 min., Bake: 50 min., Chill: 6 hrs.

- 1½ cups butter
- 1 (12-ounce) package semisweet chocolate morsels
- 1 (4-ounce) bittersweet chocolate bar
- 1 cup sugar
- 1 cup strong-brewed coffee
- 7 large eggs, lightly beaten
- Mocha Ganache
- Garnishes: whole strawberries, kiwifruit slices, raspberries
- Melted red currant jelly (optional)

COOK first 5 ingredients in a large saucepan over low heat, whisking constantly until smooth; remove from heat, and cool 15 minutes.
WHISK together chocolate mixture and beaten eggs; pour into a greased and floured 10-inch springform pan.
BAKE at 325° for 50 minutes or until set. Cool completely in pan on a wire rack;

remove sides of pan. Cover and chill at least 6 hours.
SPREAD Mocha Ganache on top and sides of torte. Garnish and glaze with melted jelly, if desired. **MAKES** 8 to 10 servings.

Mocha Ganache:
Prep: 10 min., Chill: 30 min.

- 1 cup whipping cream
- 1 (12-ounce) package semisweet chocolate morsels
- 1 tablespoon instant coffee granules

MICROWAVE cream in a glass bowl at HIGH 1 minute and 30 seconds or until hot, stirring once. Add chocolate morsels and coffee granules; stir until smooth. Cover and chill 30 minutes or until spreading consistency. **MAKES** about 2 cups.

Kent's Tips

- Before unmolding Raspberry Mousse, dip the mold in warm (not hot) water for a few seconds.
- Mocha Mousse Torte can be made two or three days before serving. Garnish with fresh fruit just before serving, and brush with melted jelly, if desired.
- If using strawberries, cut off stem ends to make the fruit level.

RASPBERRY MOUSSE

make ahead

Prep: 15 min.; Stand: 1 min.; Cook: 20 min.; Chill: 8 hrs., 30 min.

- 2 (6-ounce) packages fresh raspberries*
- 1 tablespoon lemon juice
- 1 tablespoon cold water
- 1 envelope unflavored gelatin
- ¾ cup granulated sugar
- 2 large eggs
- 2 egg yolks
- 1 tablespoon raspberry liqueur
- 1½ cups whipping cream
- ¼ cup powdered sugar

PROCESS raspberries in a blender or food processor until smooth. Pour through a wire-mesh strainer into a bowl, discarding seeds; set puree aside. (Pulp and liquid should equal about 1½ cups.)
STIR together lemon juice and 1 tablespoon cold water; sprinkle gelatin over lemon juice mixture. Stir and let stand 1 minute; set aside.
WHISK together 1 cup raspberry puree, granulated sugar, eggs, and egg yolks in top of a double boiler. Bring water to a slight boil in bottom pan; reduce heat to low, and cook, whisking constantly, 20 minutes or until mixture thickens and reaches 160°. Remove pan from heat.
WHISK gelatin mixture into raspberry puree mixture in pan, whisking constantly, 1 minute and 30 seconds or until blended.
WHISK in remaining ½ cup raspberry puree and raspberry liqueur; cover and chill 30 minutes or until consistency of unbeaten egg white.
BEAT whipping cream until foamy; gradually add powdered sugar, beating until soft peaks form. Fold in raspberry mixture. Pour into a lightly greased 6-cup mold; cover and chill 8 hours or until firm. Unmold onto a serving dish. **MAKES** 8 to 10 servings.

*Substitute 1 (10-ounce) package frozen raspberries, thawed, if desired.

Shrimp Palermo,
page 241

Gingerbread Bites With
Orange-Cream Cheese
Frosting, page 258

Grilled Parsleyed Shrimp
and Vegetables, page 256

Hummus with pita
bread rounds

Grilled Parsleyed Shrimp
and Vegetables, page 256

Lemon-Vinaigrette
Marinated Antipasto,
page 256

Pork Tenderloin on
Cornmeal Biscuits,
page 257

Piña Colada Crème
Brûlée, page 246

Ambrosia, page 233

Orange-Glazed Pork Roast,
page 236, and Onion Rice
Pilaf, page 236

Bananas Foster Bread
Pudding, page 235

Frozen pumpkin pie garnished with piecrust leaves and pecan acorns, page 276

Banana-Nut Bread and Lemon Curd, page 259

Pecan Squares, page 271

Perfecting Congealed Salad

Add a special touch to your holiday table with a colorful, easy-to-do salad.

A cool congealed salad is the perfect accompaniment with a holiday meal. Assistant Foods Editor Vicki Poellnitz remembers sampling a variety of these jelled concoctions at many a big meal as a child. They're not as popular now, though, and she wonders why—especially because cooks everywhere scramble to prepare as many feast-day dishes ahead as possible. A congealed salad was and is *the* do-ahead dish. Our tips will show you how to make it.

Congealed Salad Secrets

Follow these tips for perfectly shaped congealed salads.
- Lightly spray the inside of the mold with vegetable cooking spray before filling.
- Be sure gelatin is firm before unmolding. Gently press the top with your finger—it should spring back or jiggle.
- Before unmolding, gently run a small knife around the outer edge to break the seal.
- Dip bottom of mold in warm water for about 15 seconds before unmolding. Be careful not to get any water in the mold.
- If salad sticks to mold, return to warm water for 5 more seconds, and try again.
- You may also wrap the outside of the mold with a warm, damp tea towel. Wet the towel with hot water, and wring it out. Wrap the towel around the bottom and partially up the sides of mold. Let stand 1 to 2 minutes.
- To serve on a bed of crisp lettuce leaves, place the greens face down on the salad in the mold. Top with the platter, and turn over.
- When serving directly on a platter, moisten platter with a little water before inverting mold to help gelatin adhere to surface.
- Be sure to include the whipped cream or topping in the center of the ring, or serve on the side.
- To fix a small broken piece of congealed salad, put it back into place; then use a tiny bit of water to seal the edges of the seam.
- If you have a major mishap, cube the entire congealed salad, and serve in a large bowl.

PICKLED PEACH SALAD

make ahead

Prep: 10 min., Cook: 5 min., Chill: 8 hrs.

- 1 (25.5-ounce) jar spiced pickled peaches*
- 1 (3-ounce) package lemon-flavored gelatin
- ½ cup orange juice
- ½ cup water
- 1 (15-ounce) jar pitted Royal Ann cherries in light syrup
- 1 cup chopped pecans
- Bibb lettuce leaves (optional)
- 1 cup whipping cream
- 1 tablespoon mayonnaise
- Garnish: fresh cranberries

DRAIN pickled peaches, reserving 1 cup liquid in a saucepan. Coarsely chop peaches.

BRING reserved 1 cup liquid to a boil; remove from heat. Stir in gelatin, stirring 2 minutes or until gelatin dissolves. Stir in juice and ½ cup water. Stir in peaches, cherries, and pecans.

SPOON mixture into a lightly greased 4½-cup ring mold. Cover and chill 8 hours or until firm. Unmold salad onto Bibb lettuce leaves, if desired, or onto a platter or serving dish.

BEAT whipping cream at high speed with an electric mixer until soft peaks form; fold in mayonnaise. Serve salad with whipped cream mixture. Garnish, if desired. **MAKES** 6 to 8 servings.

NOTE: For testing purposes only, we used Oregon Fruit Products Pitted Light Sweet Royal Ann Cherries in light syrup.

*Substitute 2 (15-ounce) cans harvest spice sliced peaches for spiced pickled peaches, if desired. Proceed as directed, using a 5½-cup mold.

CAROLYN NOWICKI
MOUNTAIN BROOK, ALABAMA

A Cozy and Casual Celebration

Put on your hiking boots, and grab a walking stick. You have to get there early if you want a tour. Beebe and David Roberts begin their Thanksgiving celebration each year with a peaceful hike through the woods, where friends and relatives are greeted with inspiring messages as they stroll through David's homemade labyrinth—a meandering maze of stones and pebbles. After the hike, the group enjoys a smorgasbord of Thanksgiving favorites, including turkey, stuffing, sweet potato casserole, and fresh cranberry sauce along with dessert.

OLD-FASHIONED ROASTED TURKEY WITH GRAVY

family favorite

Prep: 30 min., Bake: 5 hrs., Cook: 1 hr.

Start cooking the giblets, neck, and vegetables the last 45 minutes of baking.

> 1 (14- to 16-pound) whole turkey
> 1½ teaspoons mixed-up salt, divided
> 1½ teaspoons garlic powder, divided
> 1½ teaspoons poultry seasoning, divided
> 1 teaspoon ground sage
> 1 teaspoon pepper
> 5 (14-ounce) cans chicken broth, divided
> ½ cup butter, melted
> 2 carrots, sliced
> 3 celery ribs, sliced
> 1 medium-size yellow onion, sliced
> ½ cup chopped fresh parsley
> ½ cup all-purpose flour
> ½ cup water
> Garnishes: fresh parsley sprigs, orange slices, fresh cranberries

REMOVE giblets and neck from turkey, and chill for gravy. Rinse turkey with cold water; pat dry with paper towels.

COMBINE 1 teaspoon each mixed-up salt, garlic powder, poultry seasoning, sage, and pepper; sprinkle cavity and outside of turkey evenly with mixture.

PLACE turkey, breast side up, in a large roasting pan, tucking wingtips under. Pour 2 cans chicken broth into roasting pan; drizzle melted butter over turkey.

BAKE, uncovered, at 450° for 1 hour. Reduce heat to 425°; shield with aluminum foil to prevent excessive browning. Bake 3½ to 4 hours or until a meat thermometer inserted in thigh registers 180°, basting every 45 minutes with pan drippings.

BRING remaining 3 cans broth, neck, giblets, carrots, and next 3 ingredients to a boil in a saucepan. Cover, reduce heat, and simmer 45 minutes or until vegetables are tender.

REMOVE turkey to a serving platter, reserving drippings in roasting pan.

Skim excess fat from drippings in pan, if desired.

POUR giblet mixture through a wire-mesh strainer into drippings in roasting pan, discarding solids. Bring to a boil in roasting pan over medium-high heat, stirring to loosen browned bits on bottom of pan.

STIR together flour and ½ cup water until smooth; add to giblet mixture, and cook over medium-high heat, stirring constantly, 10 minutes or until thickened. Stir in remaining ½ teaspoon each of mixed-up salt, garlic powder, and poultry seasoning. Serve with turkey. Garnish, if desired.

MAKES 12 to 15 servings.

NOTE: For testing purposes only, we used Jane's Krazy Original Mixed-Up Salt.

DAVID ROBERTS
BIRMINGHAM, ALABAMA

PIGLET'S STUFFING

freezeable • make ahead

Prep: 20 min., Bake: 45 min.

Affectionately known as "Piglet," David's mother, the late Cecil Roberts, created this recipe by adding vegetables, pecans, and seasonings to commercial stuffing mix.

> 1 (16-ounce) package herb-seasoned stuffing mix
> 1 (8-ounce) package cornbread stuffing mix
> 4 (14-ounce) cans low-fat chicken broth, divided
> 2 celery ribs, chopped
> ½ medium onion, chopped
> ½ green bell pepper, chopped
> ½ cup chopped fresh parsley
> ¼ cup chopped pecans, toasted
> ½ teaspoon poultry seasoning
> ½ teaspoon garlic powder

COMBINE stuffing mixes, 3 cans chicken broth, chopped celery, and next 6 ingredients. Spoon stuffing mixture evenly into a lightly greased 13- x 9-inch pan or baking dish.

POUR remaining 1 can broth evenly over stuffing in pan.

Holiday Dinners

BAKE at 350° for 40 to 45 minutes or until golden. **MAKES** 8 to 10 servings.

NOTE: For testing purposes only, we used Pepperidge Farm stuffing mix.

TO MAKE AHEAD: Spoon unbaked stuffing mixture into a lightly greased freezer-safe, disposable aluminum pan; cover and freeze up to 1 month. Thaw in refrigerator. Uncover and bake as directed.

BEEBE ROBERTS
BIRMINGHAM, ALABAMA

BELL'S SWEET POTATO CASSEROLE

Prep: 20 min., Cook: 40 min., Bake: 35 min.

- 8 medium-size sweet potatoes (6 pounds)
- 1 cup milk
- ¼ cup butter
- 3 tablespoons sugar
- 1 teaspoon vanilla extract
- 1 tablespoon orange juice
- ¼ teaspoon ground cinnamon
- ¼ teaspoon ground nutmeg
- ¼ teaspoon salt
- 1 (10.5-ounce) package miniature marshmallows

BRING sweet potatoes and water to cover to a boil, and cook 20 to 30 minutes or until tender; drain. Peel potatoes, and place in a mixing bowl.
HEAT milk and next 3 ingredients in a saucepan over medium heat, stirring until butter melts and sugar dissolves. (Do not boil.) Stir in orange juice, spices, and salt.
BEAT potatoes at medium speed with an electric mixer until mashed. Add milk mixture, beating until smooth. Spoon half of mashed sweet potatoes into a lightly greased 13- x 9-inch baking dish; top with half of marshmallows. Spread remaining mashed potatoes over marshmallows.
BAKE at 350° for 25 minutes. Top with remaining half of marshmallows; bake 8 to 10 more minutes or until marshmallows are golden. **MAKES** 8 to 10 servings.

BEEBE ROBERTS
BIRMINGHAM, ALABAMA

FRUITED RICE PILAF

family favorite

Prep: 15 min., Cook: 30 min.

This scrumptious dish is easily doubled.

- 1 tablespoon butter or margarine
- 1 tablespoon olive oil
- ½ small onion, diced
- 2 garlic cloves, minced
- ¼ cup pine nuts, toasted
- 1 cup golden raisins
- 1 cup uncooked long-grain rice
- 2¼ cups water
- ½ teaspoon salt
- 2 tablespoons chopped fresh parsley

MELT butter in olive oil in a large saucepan over medium heat; add onion, and sauté 4 to 5 minutes or until tender. Add garlic and next 3 ingredients; cook, stirring constantly, 3 to 4 minutes.
ADD 2¼ cups water and ½ teaspoon salt. Bring to a boil; reduce heat to low, cover, and simmer 17 to 20 minutes or until liquid is absorbed and rice is tender. Stir in chopped parsley. **MAKES** 6 to 8 servings.

CHARLES AND JUDY RUSSELL
BIRMINGHAM, ALABAMA

FRESH CRANBERRY SAUCE

make ahead

Prep: 20 min., Cook: 10 min., Chill: 1 hr.

Serve this sauce over turkey or consider serving it as an appetizer over cream cheese.

- 1 cup sugar
- 1 cup water
- 1 (12-ounce) package fresh cranberries
- 1 tablespoon grated orange rind
- 1 tablespoon orange liqueur
- ¼ cup chopped pecans or sliced almonds, toasted (optional)

BRING sugar and 1 cup water to a boil in a saucepan, stirring until sugar dissolves. Add cranberries, rind, and liqueur; return to a boil, reduce heat, and simmer 10 minutes. If desired, stir in toasted pecans. Cover and chill 1 hour or until firm. **MAKES** about 2 cups.

NOTE: For testing purposes only, we used Cointreau for orange liqueur.

BEEBE ROBERTS
BIRMINGHAM, ALABAMA

PECAN SQUARES

family favorite

Prep: 20 min., Cook: 5 min., Bake: 50 min.

Judy Russell always brings this recipe, adapted from *The Silver Palate Cookbook* (Workman, 1982). She uses salted butter and brings the filling to a rolling boil before pouring it over the crust. *(pictured on page 268)*

- 2 cups all-purpose flour
- ⅔ cup powdered sugar
- ¾ cup butter, softened
- ½ cup firmly packed brown sugar
- ½ cup honey
- ⅔ cup butter
- 3 tablespoons whipping cream
- 3½ cups coarsely chopped pecans

SIFT together 2 cups flour and ⅔ cup powdered sugar. Cut in ¾ cup softened butter using a pastry blender or fork just until mixture resembles coarse meal. Pat mixture on bottom and 1½ inches up sides of a lightly greased 13- x 9-inch baking dish.
BAKE at 350° for 20 minutes or until edges are lightly browned. Cool.
BRING brown sugar, honey, ⅔ cup butter, and whipping cream to a boil in a saucepan over medium-high heat. Stir in pecans, and pour hot filling into prepared crust.
BAKE at 350° for 25 to 30 minutes or until golden and bubbly. Cool completely before cutting into 2-inch squares. **MAKES** about 28 squares.

JUDY RUSSELL
BIRMINGHAM, ALABAMA

Holiday Social in North Cove

These neighbors share a very special evening to celebrate the season.

Appetizer Party

Serves 12

Hampton Place Beef Tenderloin with bakery rolls

Goat Cheese-Olive Sandwiches

Cranberry-Nut Triangles

Cupcake Cookies

Ground Pecan Torte

With an unmistakable clip-clop, a horse-drawn carriage weaves its way though the streets of North Cove subdivision, south of Atlanta, carrying area residents to their annual Christmas social. The only thing missing is snow, and judging by the chill in the air, that could happen at any moment.

The carriage pulls up to the home of Brent and Karen Wilkes, who are hosting the party. "This year we wanted something relaxed, so we decided to have an appetizer party," says Karen.

Each family contributes a dish or two, so everyone shares in the work. And even though the dress is formal, the mood is decidedly laid-back, allowing folks to mingle and catch up with one another. "Our event is more about celebrating the season and fellowshipping with our neighbors," says Brent.

HAMPTON PLACE BEEF TENDERLOIN

Prep: 10 min., Chill: 3 hrs., Bake: 45 min., Stand: 15 min.

1 cup lite soy sauce
⅓ cup blended sesame oil*
4 garlic cloves, minced
1 tablespoon minced fresh ginger
1 (5-pound) trimmed and tied beef tenderloin
1 tablespoon coarse sea salt
1 tablespoon pepper

STIR together first 4 ingredients in a large shallow dish or large zip-top freezer bag; add beef. Cover or seal, and chill 3 hours, turning occasionally.
REMOVE beef from marinade, discarding marinade. Sprinkle salt and pepper on all sides of beef, and place in a roasting pan.
BAKE, uncovered, at 500° for 15 minutes. Reduce heat to 325°, and bake 30 more minutes or to desired degree of doneness. Cover loosely with foil, and let stand 15 minutes before slicing. **MAKES** about 20 appetizer servings.

NOTE: Tying the tenderloin with butcher's twine allows for more even cooking. You can ask your butcher to tie it for you.

*Substitute 3 tablespoons sesame oil and 3 tablespoons canola oil, if desired.
KAREN WILKES
PEACHTREE CITY, GEORGIA

GOAT CHEESE-OLIVE SANDWICHES

make ahead

Prep: 25 min., Chill: 2 hrs.

When chilling, cover sandwiches with damp paper towels to keep bread moist. Though we liked very thin white bread slices in our Test Kitchens, Linda prefers sourdough.

1 (4.25-ounce) can chopped ripe black olives (about ¾ cup)
1 (4-ounce) package goat cheese, softened
1 green onion, finely chopped
1 small garlic clove, minced
¼ teaspoon hot sauce
26 slices very thin white bread
¼ cup chopped fresh parsley

STIR together first 5 ingredients in a small bowl until well blended. (The goat cheese mixture can be prepared up to 1 day ahead.)
CUT 2 rounds out of each bread slice using a 1½-inch round cutter. Spread olive mixture evenly on 1 side of half of bread rounds; top with remaining bread rounds. Roll sides in chopped parsley. Cover and chill 2 hours before serving. **MAKES** 26 appetizers.

NOTE: For testing purposes only, we used Pepperidge Farm Very Thin White Bread Slices.

LINDA KUBALIK
PEACHTREE CITY, GEORGIA

CRANBERRY-NUT TRIANGLES

family favorite

Prep: 15 min., Bake: 40 min., Cook: 5 min.

- ½ cup butter or margarine, softened
- ½ cup powdered sugar
- 1 large egg yolk
- 1½ cups all-purpose flour
- 1¼ cups chopped pecans
- ¾ cup dried cranberries
- 1 cup firmly packed brown sugar
- 5 tablespoons butter
- 3 tablespoons whipping cream
- 3 tablespoons light corn syrup
- 2 tablespoons maple syrup

BEAT ½ cup butter and powdered sugar at medium speed with an electric mixer until creamy. Add egg yolk, beating just until blended. Add flour, and beat at low speed just until mixture is crumbly.

PRESS flour mixture on bottom and slightly up sides of a lightly greased 13- x 9-inch baking dish.

BAKE at 350° for 20 to 25 minutes or until edges and surface are lightly browned. Remove from oven; sprinkle crust evenly with chopped pecans and cranberries, and let cool.

BRING brown sugar and next 4 ingredients to a boil, stirring constantly, in a saucepan over medium-high heat. Pour brown sugar mixture evenly over chopped pecans and cranberries in baking dish.

BAKE at 350° for 15 minutes or until golden. Remove from oven, and let cool completely. Cut into 15 squares; cut squares in half diagonally to form triangles. **MAKES** 2½ dozen.

LYNN AMOS
PEACHTREE CITY, GEORGIA

CUPCAKE COOKIES

family favorite

Prep: 15 min., Bake: 10 min. per batch

- 1 (14.4-ounce) package graham cracker crumbs*
- 1 cup firmly packed brown sugar
- 1 cup whipping cream
- ½ cup unsalted butter, melted
- 1 cup semisweet chocolate morsels
- 1 cup chopped pecans
- 1 cup chopped walnuts

STIR together first 4 ingredients until blended. Stir in chocolate morsels and nuts until blended.

SHAPE dough into 1-inch balls (about 1 tablespoon of dough). Place into miniature paper candy liners; place on a baking sheet.

BAKE at 375° for 10 minutes or until done. Let cool 1 minute on baking sheet; remove to wire racks to cool completely. **MAKES** about 5 dozen.

*Substitute 3½ cups finely crushed graham crackers (about 3 sleeves crackers, crushed), if desired.

JERRI BALL
PEACHTREE CITY, GEORGIA

GROUND PECAN TORTE

family favorite

Prep: 25 min., Bake: 30 min., Cool: 35 min.

- 1 cup butter or margarine, softened
- 1 cup sugar
- 3 large eggs
- 3 cups pecan meal (see note)
- 1 tablespoon grated lemon rind
- ⅓ cup cake flour
- Cream Cheese Filling
- ½ cup raspberry preserves

BEAT butter and sugar at medium speed with an electric mixer until creamy. Add eggs, 1 at a time, beating just until blended after each addition; add pecan meal and lemon rind, and beat at low speed until blended.

ADD flour, and beat at low speed just until blended. Spread into 2 greased and floured 9-inch round cakepans.

BAKE at 350° for 25 to 30 minutes or until a wooden pick inserted in center comes out clean. Cool in pans on wire racks 5 minutes; remove from pans, and cool 30 minutes.

SPREAD half of Cream Cheese Filling on top of 1 cake layer; top evenly with half of raspberry preserves. Top with remaining cake layer; repeat procedure with remaining Cream Cheese Filling and preserves. **MAKES** 10 to 12 servings.

NOTE: Commercially ground pecans have a very fine texture and are often sold as pecan meal. We found this to be more economical than grinding whole or halved pecans. To make your own pecan meal, place 2½ cups pecan halves in a food processor, and pulse about 45 seconds or until pecans are finely ground.

Cream Cheese Filling:

fast fixin's

Prep: 5 min.

- 1 (8-ounce) package cream cheese, softened
- ½ cup sugar
- 1 teaspoon vanilla extract

BEAT cream cheese at medium speed with an electric mixer until creamy; gradually add sugar and vanilla, beating well. **MAKES** 1⅓ cups.

DEEDEE HARVEY
PEACHTREE CITY, GEORGIA

Southwest Celebration

Ease into entertaining with this menu of no-fuss recipes.

Festive Fiesta

Serves 6

Fresh Salsa with colorful tortilla chips

Chicken-Sour Cream Enchiladas

Fiesta Coleslaw

Chocolate Wedding Cookies

Vanilla Ice Cream

Merry Margaritas

A simple cactus ornament discovered in a box of family holiday decorations serves as the springboard for Kathryn and Todd Hollifield's no-fuss party decor and menu. These native Texans call Alabama home these days, but you know, no matter where they live, Texans always consider themselves as such. And it shows.

Whether you're from the Lone Star State or just wish you were, you'll be able to step right into this easy-to-do, make-ahead menu just like your favorite pair of jeans.

FRESH SALSA

make ahead

Prep: 20 min., Chill: 1 hr.

Habaneros are among the hottest chiles. Removing the seeds and membranes lessens the heat. Be sure to wear gloves, and don't touch your eyes when handling hot peppers.

- **1 habanero chile pepper, seeded and minced***
- **1 medium cucumber, peeled and diced**
- **4 large plum tomatoes, chopped**
- **1 cup finely chopped fresh cilantro**
- **2 tablespoons white vinegar**
- **2 tablespoons olive oil**
- **1 teaspoon sugar**
- **1 teaspoon ground cumin**
- **½ teaspoon salt**
- **Garnish: whole jalapeño pepper**
- **Tortilla chips**

STIR together first 9 ingredients in a small bowl. Cover and chill at least 1 hour. Garnish, if desired. Serve with tortilla chips. **MAKES** 3½ cups.

*Substitute 1 jalapeño pepper, seeded and minced, if desired.

KATHRYN HOLLIFIELD
HOMEWOOD, ALABAMA

CHICKEN-SOUR CREAM ENCHILADAS

family favorite

Prep: 20 min., Cook: 5 min., Bake: 25 min.

- **1 medium onion, chopped**
- **1 tablespoon olive oil**
- **2 cups chopped cooked chicken**
- **1 (16-ounce) container sour cream, divided**
- **4 cups (16 ounces) shredded Monterey Jack cheese, divided**
- **12 (6-inch) flour tortillas**
- **3 (4.5-ounce) cans diced green chiles, divided**
- **1¼ cups milk**
- **2 tablespoons all-purpose flour**

SAUTÉ onion in hot oil over medium-high heat 5 minutes or until tender.

STIR together chicken, ¼ cup sour cream, and 1½ cups shredded Monterey Jack cheese. Stir in onion. Spoon chicken mixture evenly on 1 end of each tortilla, and roll up. Arrange seam side down in a lightly greased 13- x 9-inch baking dish.

WHISK together 2 cans green chiles, milk, and flour in a saucepan over medium heat; gradually add remaining 2½ cups cheese, stirring constantly, until cheese is melted and mixture is smooth. Pour sauce evenly over top of enchiladas. Spread remaining sour cream over sauce.

BAKE enchiladas at 400° for 20 to 25 minutes or until bubbly. Drain remaining can of green chiles; spread evenly on top of enchiladas. **MAKES** 6 servings.

KATHRYN HOLLIFIELD
HOMEWOOD, ALABAMA

FIESTA COLESLAW

family favorite

Prep: 30 min., Stand: 30 min.

This recipe is adapted from the *Santa Fe School of Cooking Cookbook* (Gibbs Smith, 1995). For maximum color and flavor, serve within 3 to 4 hours. This colorful slaw variation is more like a salad.

- ½ **pound green cabbage, shredded***
- ½ **pound red cabbage, shredded***
- 1 **medium cucumber, peeled, seeded, and diagonally sliced**
- 1 **medium-size red bell pepper, cut into thin strips**
- 1 **medium-size green bell pepper, cut into thin strips**
- 5 **green onions, sliced**
- 2 **celery ribs, diagonally sliced**
- 1 **large carrot, shredded**
- 1 **small white onion, thinly sliced**
- ¼ **cup fresh lime juice**
- 2 **tablespoons sugar**
- 2 **tablespoons sherry vinegar or cider vinegar**
- 1 **tablespoon pepper sauce (liquid from hot peppers in vinegar)**
- 1 **teaspoon salt**
- 2 **tablespoons olive oil**

COMBINE first 9 ingredients in a bowl. **STIR** together lime juice and next 4 ingredients in a small bowl until sugar is dissolved. Pour dressing over cabbage mixture, tossing to coat. Let stand 30 minutes, tossing often. Drizzle evenly with olive oil, tossing to coat, just before serving. **MAKES** 6 servings.

*Substitute 1 (16-ounce) package coleslaw mix for shredded green and red cabbage, if desired.

SUSAN CURTIS
THE SANTA FE SCHOOL OF COOKING COOKBOOK
SANTA FE, NEW MEXICO

CHOCOLATE WEDDING COOKIES

fast fixin's

Prep: 11 min., Bake: 10 min. per batch

These not-too-sweet cookies pair well with Vanilla Ice Cream.

- ½ **cup powdered sugar**
- 2 **tablespoons unsweetened cocoa**
- ½ **cup butter or margarine, softened**
- ¾ **cup all-purpose flour**
- ¼ **cup granulated sugar**
- ¼ **cup unsweetened cocoa**
- 1 **teaspoon vanilla extract**
- 1 **cup finely chopped pecans**

SIFT together powdered sugar and 2 tablespoons cocoa. Set aside.
BEAT butter at medium speed with an electric mixer until creamy. Add flour and next 3 ingredients, beating until blended. Stir in pecans. (Dough will be stiff.) Shape into 1-inch balls, and place on ungreased baking sheets.
BAKE at 400° for 10 minutes. Remove cookies to wire racks, and cool slightly. Roll warm cookies in powdered sugar mixture, and cool completely on wire racks. **MAKES** 2 dozen.

VANILLA ICE CREAM

make ahead • freezeable

Prep: 10 min., Cook: 24 min., Chill: 8 hrs., Freeze: according to manufacturer's instructions

Start this recipe a day ahead. You can serve it right out of the freezer container. To dress it up, secure a colorful towel around the container with raffia.

- 4 **cups milk**
- 2¼ **cups sugar**
- ¼ **cup all-purpose flour**
- ¼ **teaspoon salt**
- 6 **large eggs, lightly beaten**
- 4 **cups half-and-half**
- 1 **tablespoon vanilla extract**
- **Garnish: sifted unsweetened cocoa**

WHISK together first 4 ingredients in a Dutch oven over medium heat, stirring constantly, 15 to 20 minutes or until mixture thickens and coats a spoon. Do not boil.
STIR about one-fourth of hot milk mixture gradually into eggs; add egg mixture to remaining hot mixture, stirring constantly. Cook 4 minutes; remove from heat. Stir in half-and-half and vanilla, and cool completely. Cover and chill at least 8 hours.
POUR into freezer container of a 4-quart electric ice-cream maker. Freeze according to manufacturer's instructions. Serve immediately, and garnish, if desired, or remove container from ice-cream maker, and place in freezer 15 minutes. Transfer to an airtight container, and freeze 2 hours or until firm. Store leftover ice cream in an airtight container. **MAKES** ½ gallon.

KATHRYN HOLLIFIELD
HOMEWOOD, ALABAMA

MERRY MARGARITAS

fast fixin's

Prep: 5 min.

Dip the rims of glasses in lime juice and tinted sugar to dress up these yummy libations. Tinted decorating sugar, used to decorate cookies, is found in the baking aisle of the grocery store. Don't worry if you don't have enough matching stemware to serve a crowd. Mix several styles for a festive look.

- 1 **(10-ounce) can frozen margarita mix**
- ¾ **cup tequila**
- 3 **tablespoons thawed cranberry juice concentrate**
- 2 **tablespoons orange liqueur**
- 2 **tablespoons fresh lime juice**
- **Ice**

COMBINE first 5 ingredients in a blender. Fill blender with ice to 5-cup level, and process until smooth. Serve margaritas immediately. **MAKES** about 5 cups.

from our kitchen

Crowning Glories

Pastry leaves are one of our favorite fall garnishes, and we use them to decorate sweet and savory foods. Quick and easy to make using refrigerated piecrust, these colorful cookie-cutter leaves can turn a simple cake or a store-bought pie into a showstopping dessert.

Step 1: Unroll piecrusts on a lightly floured surface. Cut leaves from piecrust using leaf-shaped cutters. Mark leaf veins using the tip of a small paring knife. One (15-ounce) package of refrigerated piecrusts will make about 24 (2- to 3-inch) leaves.

Step 2: To make the tinted egg wash, whisk together 3 large eggs and 2 tablespoons water. Pour mixture evenly into small cups, tinting each with a few drops of liquid food coloring to create different colors. We painted our leaves using four colors of egg wash—red, yellow, orange, and green. For easy cleanup and to prevent the excess egg wash from burning on the baking sheet, paint leaves on pieces of parchment or wax paper (do not bake on wax paper). Brush leaves evenly with egg wash, beginning with lighter colors, and overlaying with areas of darker color. Use a small artist's brush to add bold accents with undiluted liquid food coloring.

Step 3: Crumple 2 (14-inch-long) pieces of aluminum foil into 1-inch-wide strips. Coat with vegetable cooking spray, and place on a baking sheet lined with parchment paper. Gently drape pastry leaves over strips of foil to give them a natural-looking shape; place several leaves on baking sheet. Bake at 400° for 6 to 8 minutes or until golden. Cool on baking sheet on a wire rack 10 minutes. Gently remove leaves; cool completely on wire rack. Repeat procedure with remaining leaves.

Candy acorns: Sandwich a thin layer of melted chocolate between the flat sides of two pecan halves. To create the textured caps, dip the upper third of each "acorn" into melted chocolate, and roll in finely chopped pecans. The leaves and acorns can be made up to one month ahead and frozen between layers of wax paper in an airtight container.

Sweet Sensations

An impressive dessert can actually start with a frozen pumpkin pie. Cut autumn leaf shapes from refrigerated piecrust, and brush with bright colors of egg wash before baking (see directions above).

Finely chopped nuts and melted chocolate transform toasted pecan halves into candy acorns (see photo at right and on pages 1 and 267).

Both garnishes can be made weeks ahead and added at the last minute to spruce up cakes, pastries, appetizers, and entrées. We also used the garnishes to add sparkle to a cheese tray and baked ham.

The Main Event

Wreathed in a colorful harvest of fall produce, baked ham makes a spectacular centerpiece. The same presentation is equally eye-catching with turkey or pork. Use a large serving tray or carving board, allowing space for a 4- to 6-inch decorative border around your entrée. All you'll need are a few items from your local supermarket produce and plant aisles.

Consider the curly-leafed kale for the border's base and then add miniature lady apples, pear-shaped gourds, and purple pansies, along with a handful of fresh kumquats and cranberries. You could also use miniature pumpkins and pomegranates, crab apples, and Seckel and Forelle pears, clusters of rosemary, or bundles of cinnamon sticks tied with raffia.

Fresh Starts

A bottle of wine and an artfully arranged plate of fruit and cheeses can turn the smallest of gatherings into a celebration. In France, cheeses are often served on trays of fresh leaves. Add a Southern twist with ivory-veined cabbage leaves or collard greens (flatten the leaves by removing the stem and midrib). Offer a variety of cheeses with different textures and flavors. Include a cheese ball, or scoop the seeds from a winter squash, and spoon in a favorite spread. Hollow out hearty bread loaves, leaving a 1-inch-thick shell, and fill with crackers and breadsticks.

CHRISTMAS ALL THROUGH THE HOUSE

Holiday Pound Cakes

Nothing beats the rich and buttery flavor of a really good homemade pound cake.

When we asked readers to share their special pound cake recipes, we received hundreds of replies.

Originally made with a pound each of butter, sugar, eggs, and flour, pound cakes have evolved over time. Creative cooks have come up with countless variations, such as replacing a portion of the butter with cream cheese or substituting sour cream and leavening for a few of the eggs. You're sure to find a new favorite here.

These pound cakes are all easy to prepare. You can bake them days ahead and store them in the pantry, or place them in large zip-top freezer bags and freeze up to two months. For tips on preparing the perfect pound cake, see "From Our Kitchen" on page 306.

BROWN SUGAR POUND CAKE

freezeable • make ahead

Prep: 20 min.; Bake: 1 hr., 45 min.

Don't preheat the oven for this scrumptious pound cake—it gets its start in a cold oven. To add a light dusting of powdered sugar, spoon a few tablespoons into a wire-mesh strainer and gently shake over the cake's surface.

- **1 cup butter, softened**
- **½ cup shortening**
- **2 cups firmly packed brown sugar**
- **1 cup granulated sugar**
- **6 large eggs**
- **3 cups cake flour**
- **1 teaspoon baking powder**
- **1 cup evaporated milk**
- **2 teaspoons vanilla extract**
- **2 cups chopped pecans, toasted**

BEAT butter and shortening at medium speed with an electric mixer until creamy. Gradually add sugars, beating until light and fluffy. Add eggs, 1 at a time, beating just until the yellow yolk disappears.

SIFT together flour and baking powder; add to butter mixture alternately with milk, beginning and ending with flour mixture. Beat batter at low speed just until blended after each addition. Stir in vanilla and pecans. Pour batter into a greased and floured 12-cup tube pan. Place pan in a cold oven; set oven temperature at 300°.

BAKE 1 hour and 30 minutes to 1 hour and 45 minutes or until a long wooden pick inserted in center of cake comes out clean. Cool in pan on a wire rack 10 to 15 minutes. Remove from pan; cool completely on wire rack. **MAKES** 10 to 12 servings.

RUTH RIPPETOE
GREENSBORO, NORTH CAROLINA

SULLIVAN'S LEMON-ALMOND POUND CAKE

freezeable • make ahead

Prep: 20 min.; Bake: 1 hr., 40 min.

- **1 cup butter, softened**
- **3 cups sugar**
- **6 large eggs**
- **2 teaspoons vanilla extract**
- **1 teaspoon lemon extract**
- **1 teaspoon almond extract**
- **3 cups all-purpose flour**
- **1 (8-ounce) container sour cream**

BEAT butter at medium speed with an electric mixer until creamy. Gradually add sugar, beating at medium speed until light and fluffy. Add eggs, 1 at a time, beating just until the yellow yolk disappears. Add extracts, beating just until blended.

ADD flour to butter mixture alternately with sour cream, beginning and ending with flour. Beat batter at low speed just until blended after each addition. Pour into a greased and floured 12-cup tube pan.

BAKE at 325° for 1 hour and 40 minutes or until a long wooden pick inserted in center of cake comes out clean. Cool in pan on a wire rack 10 to 15 minutes. Remove from pan; cool completely on wire rack. **MAKES** 10 to 12 servings.

KATHY ROBERTS
LITTLE ROCK, ARKANSAS

LEMON CURD POUND CAKE

freezeable • make ahead

Prep: 20 min.; Bake: 1 hr., 30 min.

Wait to prepare the Lemon Curd until the cake comes out of the oven so it will still be warm when spread over the cake. *(pictured on page 4)*

- **1 cup butter, softened**
- **½ cup shortening**
- **3 cups sugar**
- **6 large eggs**
- **3 cups all-purpose flour**
- **½ teaspoon baking powder**
- **⅛ teaspoon salt**
- **1 cup milk**
- **1 teaspoon vanilla extract**
- **1 teaspoon lemon extract**
- **Lemon Curd**
- **Garnishes: fresh rosemary, Sugared Cranberries (see box on facing page), lemon rind strips**

BEAT butter and shortening at medium speed with an electric mixer until creamy. Gradually add sugar, beating at medium speed until light and fluffy. Add eggs, 1 at a time, beating just until the yellow yolk disappears.

SIFT together flour, baking powder, and salt; add to butter mixture alternately with milk, beginning and ending with flour mixture. Beat batter at low speed just until blended after each addition. Stir in vanilla and lemon extracts. Pour batter into a greased and floured 12-cup tube pan.

BAKE at 325° for 1 hour and 30 minutes or until a long wooden pick inserted in center of cake comes out clean. Cool in pan on a wire rack 10 to 15 minutes. Remove from pan; carefully brush Lemon Curd over top and sides of cake. Cool completely on wire rack. Garnish, if desired. **MAKES** 10 to 12 servings.

Lemon Curd:
fast fixin's
Prep: 10 min., Cook: 12 min.

  ⅔ cup sugar
  1½ tablespoons butter, melted
  2 teaspoons grated lemon rind
  2 tablespoons fresh lemon juice
  1 large egg, lightly beaten

STIR together first 4 ingredients in a small heavy saucepan; add egg, stirring until blended.

COOK mixture, stirring constantly, over low heat, 10 to 12 minutes or until mixture thickens slightly (cooked mixture will have a thickness similar to unwhipped whipping cream) and begins to bubble around the edges. Remove from heat. (The curd should be brushed immediately over cake because mixture will continue to thicken as it cools.) **MAKES** about ¾ cup.

DEBBIE LEWIS
CLINTON, MISSISSIPPI

NOEL POUND CAKE LOAF

freezeable • make ahead
Prep: 20 min., Bake: 1 hr., Cool: 10 min.

  1 (6-ounce) jar red maraschino
    cherries
  1 (6-ounce) jar green maraschino
    cherries
  ½ cup butter, softened
  1⅓ cups sugar
  3 large eggs
  1½ cups all-purpose flour
  ½ teaspoon salt
  ⅛ teaspoon baking soda
  ½ cup sour cream
  ½ teaspoon vanilla extract

DRAIN cherries well, and finely chop. Press gently between paper towels to absorb excess moisture; set aside.

BEAT butter at medium speed with an electric mixer until creamy. Gradually add sugar, beating until light and fluffy. Add eggs, 1 at a time, beating just until the yellow yolk disappears.

SIFT together flour, salt, and baking soda; stir in chopped cherries. Add flour mixture to butter mixture alternately with sour cream, beginning and ending with flour mixture. Beat batter at low speed just until blended after each addition. Stir in vanilla. Pour batter into a greased and floured 9- x 5-inch loafpan.

BAKE at 325° for 1 hour or until a long wooden pick inserted in center of cake comes out clean. Cool in pan on a wire rack 10 minutes. Remove from pan; cool completely on wire rack. **MAKES** 6 to 8 servings.

B. A. LEWIS
BRUNSWICK, GEORGIA

Puttin' on the Glitz

Heaped high with a snowy drift of coconut, the Cream Cheese-Coconut-Pecan Pound Cake on our cover (recipe on following page) is made all the more merry when trimmed with a wreath of sugared rosemary. We chose rosemary not only because its needle-shaped leaves resemble those of a fir tree, but also because it's known as the herb of remembrance. We could think of nothing more fitting to honor the special memories that were sent along with your treasured family recipes.

Pound cakes are grand without any adornment, of course, but a festive presentation can add something extra special to your holiday table.

Any flavor of pound cake that pairs well with coconut can be decorated using these easy instructions.

■ Invert completely cooled pound cake onto a serving plate or cake stand; spoon Powdered Sugar Glaze (recipe below) evenly over cake.
■ Toss together ¾ cup each of coconut chips and sweetened flaked coconut; sprinkle evenly over cake. Sprinkle coconut mixture evenly with 2 tablespoons white cake sparkles.
■ Arrange Sugared Rosemary and Sugared Cranberries (recipes below) around bottom edge of cake and then add pecan halves.

NOTE: Coconut chips can be found in the produce section of many supermarkets or ordered online ($3.99 for 8 ounces) from **www.kalustyans.com.** White cake sparkles (edible glitter) can be found in stores that carry cake-decorating supplies or ordered online from **www.wilton.com.**

POWDERED SUGAR GLAZE: Stir together 2 cups powdered sugar, 3 tablespoons milk, and 1 teaspoon vanilla extract until smooth, adding another 1 tablespoon milk, if necessary, for desired consistency. Makes about 1 cup.
SUGARED ROSEMARY: Microwave ½ cup corn syrup at HIGH for 10 seconds or until warm. Brush 10 to 12 rosemary sprigs lightly with corn syrup; sprinkle evenly with granulated sugar. Arrange in a single layer on wax paper. Use immediately, or let stand at room temperature, uncovered, up to 24 hours.
SUGARED CRANBERRIES: Bring ½ cup granulated sugar, ½ cup water, and 1 cup fresh cranberries to a boil in a small saucepan, stirring often, over medium-high heat. (Do not overcook; cranberries should swell and just begin to pop.) Remove from heat, and drain, reserving liquid for another use. Toss cranberries with ¼ cup granulated sugar, and arrange in a single layer on wax paper. Use immediately, or let stand at room temperature, uncovered, up to 24 hours.

CREAM CHEESE-BOURBON-PECAN POUND CAKE

freezeable • make ahead

Prep: 20 min.; Bake: 1 hr., 35 min.

Bourbon gives this pound cake a wonderful aroma and flavor, but you can substitute an equal amount of milk, if desired.

- 1½ cups butter, softened
- 1 (8-ounce) package cream cheese, softened
- 3 cups sugar
- 6 large eggs
- 3 cups all-purpose flour
- ½ teaspoon salt
- ¼ cup bourbon
- 1½ teaspoons vanilla extract
- 1½ cups chopped pecans, toasted

BEAT butter and cream cheese at medium speed with an electric mixer until creamy. Gradually add sugar, beating at medium speed until light and fluffy. Add eggs, 1 at a time, beating just until the yellow yolk disappears.

SIFT together flour and salt; add to butter mixture alternately with bourbon, beginning and ending with flour mixture. Beat batter at low speed just until blended after each addition. Stir in vanilla and pecans. Pour batter into a greased and floured 12-cup tube pan.

BAKE at 325° for 1 hour and 30 minutes to 1 hour and 35 minutes or until a long wooden pick inserted in center of cake comes out clean. Cool in pan on a wire rack 10 to 15 minutes. Remove from pan; cool completely on wire rack. **MAKES** 10 to 12 servings.

DAPHNE HARRELL
BROWNWOOD, TEXAS

CREAM CHEESE-COCONUT-PECAN POUND CAKE: (*pictured on cover*) Substitute 1 cup chopped toasted pecans and ½ cup shredded coconut for 1½ cups chopped toasted pecans. Proceed with recipe as directed. Top with Powdered Sugar Glaze (recipe in box on previous page) and additional shredded coconut. Garnish platter with Sugared Rosemary and Sugared Cranberries (recipes in box on previous page) and pecan halves.

Brunch Favorites From Our Staff to You

These doable gems are guaranteed to add sparkle to your mid-morning gathering.

Looking for an easy but festive holiday party idea? Try brunch. It's more casual than supper and, with these flavor-packed recipes and simple decorations, you'll create a relaxed and joyful celebration worthy of the season.

Several folks from our *Southern Living* Foods staff—James Schend, Rebecca Kracke Gordon, and Angela Sellers of our Test Kitchens, along with Associate Foods Editor Mary Allen Perry—shared their favorite recipes as a gift to our readers.

Whether you're new to cooking or a seasoned pro, there's something for everyone. Make-ahead options and hands-off cooking and baking allow you to have more time to spend with family and friends.

BASIC BUTTERY BISCUITS

fast fixin's • freezeable

Prep: 10 min., Bake: 9 min.

Rebecca Kracke Gordon of our Test Kitchens keeps a dozen or two of these tasty gems in the freezer for drop-in company or a last-minute morning treat.

- 2¼ cups all-purpose baking mix
- ⅓ cup buttermilk
- 6 tablespoons unsalted butter, melted and divided

STIR together baking mix, buttermilk, and 5 tablespoons melted butter just until blended.

TURN dough out onto a lightly floured surface, and knead 1 or 2 times. Pat to a ½-inch thickness; cut with a 1½-inch round cutter, and place on lightly greased baking sheets.

BAKE at 450° for 7 to 9 minutes or until lightly browned. Brush tops evenly with remaining 1 tablespoon melted butter. **MAKES** about 2 dozen.

NOTE: For testing purposes only, we used Bisquick all-purpose baking mix.

TO MAKE AHEAD: Freeze unbaked biscuits on a lightly greased baking sheet 30 minutes or until frozen. Store in a zip-top freezer bag up to 3 months. Bake as directed 8 to 10 minutes or until lightly browned. Proceed with recipe as directed.

CRANBERRY-ORANGE-GLAZED BISCUITS: Decrease baking mix to 2 cups plus 2 tablespoons. Add ½ cup chopped dried cranberries to baking mix. Prepare dough, and bake as directed. Omit 1 tablespoon butter for brushing biscuits after baking. Stir together 6 tablespoons powdered sugar, 1 tablespoon orange juice, and ¼ teaspoon grated orange rind. Drizzle glaze evenly over warm biscuits.

BRUNCH PUNCH

make ahead

Prep: 5 min., Chill: 2 hrs.

Test Kitchens professional Angela Sellers recommends chilling the juices before stirring them together, eliminating the need for additional time in the refrigerator.

- **1 (46-ounce) can pineapple juice**
- **3 cups orange juice**
- **2 cups cranberry juice**
- **¾ cup powdered sugar**
- **¼ cup lime juice**
- **Garnishes: fresh mint leaves, lime slices, orange slices, cranberries**

STIR together first 5 ingredients. Cover and chill 2 hours. Stir before serving. Garnish, if desired. **MAKES** about 3 quarts.

BREAKFAST ENCHILADAS

make ahead

Prep: 20 min., Cook: 10 min., Bake: 30 min.

Associate Foods Editor Mary Allen Perry likes the make-ahead ease of this casserole. Prepare as directed, without baking, and refrigerate overnight. Let stand at room temperature 30 minutes, and bake as directed. Tip: Prepare the Cheese Sauce before scrambling the eggs so it will be ready to add at the proper time.

- **1 (1-pound) package hot ground pork sausage**
- **2 tablespoons butter or margarine**
- **4 green onions, thinly sliced**
- **2 tablespoons chopped fresh cilantro**
- **14 large eggs, beaten**
- **¾ teaspoon salt**
- **½ teaspoon pepper**
- **Cheese Sauce**
- **8 (8-inch) flour tortillas**
- **1 cup (4 ounces) shredded Monterey Jack cheese with jalapeños**
- **Toppings: halved grape tomatoes, sliced green onions, chopped fresh cilantro**

COOK sausage in a large nonstick skillet over medium-high heat, stirring until sausage crumbles and is no longer pink. Remove from pan; drain well, pressing between paper towels.

MELT butter in large nonstick skillet over medium heat. Add green onions and cilantro, and sauté 1 minute. Add eggs, salt, and pepper, and cook, without stirring, until eggs begin to set on bottom. Draw a spatula across bottom of pan to form large curds. Continue to cook until eggs are thickened but still moist; do not stir constantly. Remove from heat, and gently fold in 1½ cups Cheese Sauce and sausage.

SPOON about ⅓ cup egg mixture down the center of each tortilla; roll up. Place seam side down in a lightly greased 13-x- 9-inch baking dish. Pour remaining Cheese Sauce evenly over tortillas; sprinkle with Monterey Jack cheese.

BAKE at 350° for 30 minutes or until sauce is bubbly. Serve with desired toppings. **MAKES** 6 to 8 servings.

Cheese Sauce:

fast fixin's

Prep: 10 min., Cook: 8 min.

- **⅓ cup butter**
- **⅓ cup all-purpose flour**
- **3 cups milk**
- **2 cups (8 ounces) shredded Cheddar cheese**
- **1 (4.5-ounce) can chopped green chiles, undrained**
- **¾ teaspoon salt**

MELT butter in a heavy saucepan over medium-low heat; whisk in flour until smooth. Cook, whisking constantly, 1 minute. Gradually whisk in milk; cook over medium heat, whisking constantly, 5 minutes or until thickened. Remove from heat, and whisk in cheese and remaining ingredients. **MAKES** about 4 cups.

NUT BREAD

family favorite

Prep: 15 min.; Bake: 1 hr., 15 min.

Assistant Test Kitchens Director James Schend learned this recipe from his mom, who bakes her bread in coffee cans instead of a loafpan.

- **3 cups all-purpose flour**
- **1 cup sugar**
- **4 teaspoons baking powder**
- **2 teaspoons salt**
- **1½ cups milk**
- **1 large egg, lightly beaten**
- **¼ cup shortening, melted**
- **1 teaspoon vanilla extract**
- **1½ cups chopped walnuts or pecans**
- **½ cup sweetened dried cranberries (optional)**

SIFT first 4 ingredients into a large bowl, and stir to combine. Add milk and next 3 ingredients, stirring just until moistened. Stir in nuts, and, if desired, cranberries.

POUR into a greased and floured 9- x 5-inch loafpan, or divide batter between 2 greased (13-ounce) coffee cans.

BAKE at 350° for 1 hour and 10 minutes to 1 hour and 15 minutes or until a long wooden pick inserted in center comes out clean. Cool in pan on a wire rack 10 minutes; remove from pan, and cool completely on wire rack. **MAKES** 1 loaf.

NOTE: For testing purposes only, we used Ocean Spray Craisins for dried cranberries.

NOTE: To remove coffee odor from coffee cans, rinse cans well with soap and water, removing all coffee grounds. Sprinkle 1 to 2 tablespoons baking soda into each can; add 1 teaspoon water and mix, forming a paste. Scrub paste onto entire interior of coffee can; let stand 15 minutes. Rinse well and dry.

LINDA SCHEND
KENOSHA, WISCONSIN

New Take on Turkey Dinner

Juicy turkey slices with roasted peppers, pine nuts, and lemon anchor a Mediterranean menu sure to satisfy everyone at the dinner table.

How do you eat your turkey—carved from the whole bird at holiday meals or in skinny slices from the supermarket deli section? If those are your only two choices, it's time you tasted this version. It starts with a boneless turkey breast, making it easy to cook and serve. We cut the breast into slices, shortening cooking time to 15 minutes. The turkey is seasoned with fragrant herbs, then topped with sweet red peppers and tender white beans. The outcome is a luscious, colorful entrée. We served it over ultra-creamy Roasted Garlic-and-Cheese Risotto with a refreshing Grecian Tossed Salad. Feel good about serving this on weeknights as well as at your holiday table. It's a welcome change.

HERBED TURKEY STRIPS WITH ROASTED PEPPERS AND BEANS

family favorite

Prep: 20 min., Chill: 30 min., Cook: 15 min.

Be sure to grate the lemon rind before squeezing the juice needed for the recipe. Use the entire 2 tablespoons of lemon juice in the marinade if you like a tangier flavor.

1 (3-pound) boneless, skinless turkey breast, cut into 1/2- to 3/4-inch-thick slices
1 tablespoon dried Italian seasoning
1 1/2 tablespoons olive oil, divided
1 to 2 tablespoons fresh lemon juice
2 garlic cloves, minced
1 teaspoon salt
1/2 to 1 teaspoon freshly ground pepper
1 (19-ounce) can cannellini beans, rinsed and drained
1 (7-ounce) jar roasted red bell peppers, drained and chopped
2 tablespoons pine nuts, lightly toasted
1 teaspoon grated lemon rind
1/4 cup chopped fresh flat-leaf parsley

PIERCE turkey slices evenly with a fork.
STIR together Italian seasoning, 1/2 tablespoon oil, lemon juice, and next 3 ingredients. Coat turkey slices with oil mixture. Cover and chill 30 minutes.
COOK turkey slices, in batches, in remaining 1 tablespoon hot oil in a large nonstick skillet over medium heat 3 minutes on each side or until done. Remove turkey from skillet, cover, and keep warm. Add beans and peppers to skillet; cook over medium heat until thoroughly heated, stirring gently.
CUT turkey slices crosswise into 1/2-inch strips. Arrange on a serving platter. Top with bean mixture. Combine pine nuts, grated lemon rind, and parsley. Sprinkle over beans. Serve immediately. **MAKES** 8 servings.

LARRY ELDER
CHARLOTTE, NORTH CAROLINA

Per serving: Calories 269 (18% from fat); Fat 5.3g (sat 0.8g, mono 2.5g, poly 1.5g); Protein 43g; Carb 9g; Fiber 2.5g; Chol 112mg; Iron 3.3mg; Sodium 537mg; Calc 48mg

ROASTED SWEET ONIONS

family favorite

Prep: 10 min., Bake: 30 min., Stand: 10 min.

We used Vidalia onions in this recipe. If you can't find them, yellow or white onions will work fine; they just won't be as sweet.

Vegetable cooking spray
4 medium-size sweet onions
2 tablespoons olive oil
1 teaspoon salt
1/2 teaspoon dried thyme
1/4 cup balsamic vinegar
1/4 teaspoon pepper

LINE a 13 -x 9-inch pan with aluminum foil, allowing several inches to extend over sides; coat pan with cooking spray. Peel and cut each onion into 8 wedges. Place onions in pan, and drizzle with olive oil. Sprinkle evenly with salt and thyme.
BAKE at 450° for 15 minutes; gather up edges of foil and seal. Bake 15 more minutes. Let stand 10 minutes. Drizzle with vinegar, sprinkle with pepper, and toss. **MAKES** 8 servings.

NOTE: Fat percentage appears to be high because olive oil, a healthful fat, provides most of the calories in the recipe. Onions have very few calories.

JEANNE S. HOTALING
AUGUSTA, GEORGIA

Per serving: Calories 67 (47% from fat)*; Fat 3.5g (sat 0.5g, mono 2.7g, poly 0.3g); Protein 1g; Carb 8g; Fiber 1.6g; Chol 0mg; Iron 0.3mg; Sodium 295mg; Calc 24mg

ROASTED GARLIC-AND-CHEESE RISOTTO

family favorite

Prep: 15 min., Bake: 30 min., Cook: 50 min.

Arborio rice is a short-grain, starchy rice traditionally used for risotto. Long-grain rice will not work in this recipe. Serve with beef tenderloin, boneless pork chops, or as a main dish with crisp-tender veggies.

- 1 garlic bulb
- 7 shiitake mushrooms
- 1 teaspoon butter
- 1 teaspoon olive oil
- 1 medium onion, chopped
- 1½ cups uncooked Arborio rice
- ½ cup frozen corn kernels
- ½ cup dry white wine
- 7 to 8 cups fat-free reduced-sodium chicken broth, heated
- 1½ teaspoons minced fresh or ½ teaspoon dried thyme
- ½ teaspoon salt
- ½ teaspoon pepper
- ¼ teaspoon rubbed sage
- ½ (8-ounce) package ⅓-less-fat cream cheese, softened

CUT off pointed end of garlic; place garlic on a piece of foil. Fold foil to seal.

BAKE at 425° for 30 minutes; cool. Squeeze pulp from garlic cloves, and chop. Set aside.

REMOVE stems from mushrooms, and discard. Thinly slice mushroom caps.

MELT butter with olive oil in a 2-quart saucepan over medium-high heat. Add onion and mushrooms, and sauté 2 to 3 minutes. Add rice; sauté 1 minute. Stir in corn and wine; reduce heat to medium, and simmer, stirring constantly, until wine is reduced by half. Add ½ cup hot broth, and cook, stirring constantly, until liquid is absorbed. Repeat procedure with remaining hot broth, ½ cup at a time, until rice is tender. (Total cooking time is about 35 to 45 minutes.)

STIR in thyme and next 3 ingredients. Add cream cheese and chopped roasted garlic, stirring until blended. Serve immediately. **MAKES** 8 servings.

DAN HARDY
HIGH POINT, NORTH CAROLINA

Calories 243 (17% calories from fat); Fat 4.7g (sat 2.2g, mono 0.8g, poly 0.5g); Protein 9.5g; Carb 42g; Fiber 1.7g; Chol 10mg; Iron 0.4mg; Sodium 301mg; Calc 40mg

GRECIAN TOSSED SALAD

fast fixin's

Prep: 20 min.

Chicken broth smoothes out vinegar's tang so less oil is needed.

- ¼ cup red wine vinegar
- ¼ cup olive oil
- ¼ cup fat-free reduced-sodium chicken broth
- 2 teaspoons sugar
- ½ teaspoon salt
- 1½ teaspoons dried oregano
- ½ teaspoon pepper
- ½ head iceberg lettuce, torn
- 4 to 5 endive leaves, torn
- ½ cucumber, thinly sliced
- 1 tomato, cut into wedges
- ¼ cup chopped green bell pepper
- 3 green onions, chopped
- 4 radishes, sliced
- ¼ cup crumbled feta cheese
- 6 kalamata olives, chopped

WHISK together first 7 ingredients in a large bowl. Add lettuce and remaining ingredients, tossing to coat. **MAKES** 6 servings.

NOTE: Fat percentage appears to be high because fat (oil, cheese, and olives) provides most of the calories in the recipe. Salad vegetables have very few calories.

MARY PAPPAS
RICHMOND, VIRGINIA

Calories 140 (75% from fat); Fat 11.6g (sat 2.3g, mono 7.7g, poly 1g); Protein 2.2g; Carb 7.8g; Fiber 1.9g; Chol 5.7mg; Iron 0.8mg; Sodium 343mg; Calc 58mg

BLUEBERRY SHERBET

freezeable • make ahead

Prep: 15 min., Freeze: 8 hrs.

This easy and flavorful dessert calls for five ingredients, a pan, your freezer, and a blender.

- 2 cups fresh or frozen blueberries, thawed
- 1 cup fat-free buttermilk
- ½ cup sugar
- 1 tablespoon fresh lemon juice
- ½ teaspoon vanilla extract
- **Garnish: fresh mint sprig**

PROCESS first 5 ingredients in a blender until smooth. Pour into a 9-inch square pan; cover and freeze 4 hours or until firm.

PROCESS frozen mixture, in batches, in a blender until smooth. Cover and freeze 4 hours or until frozen. Garnish, if desired. **MAKES** 6 (½-cup) servings.

CYNTHIA GUNN
TALLAHASSEE, FLORIDA

Calories 110 (4% from fat); Fat 0.5g (sat 0.2g, mono 0.1g, poly 0.1g); Protein 1.7g; Carb 26g; Fiber 1.3g; Chol 1.4mg; Iron 0.1mg; Sodium 46mg; Calc 51mg

Welcome Home

This year, because we brought the wreath indoors, we decided to bring some flowers to the front door. Fruit, flowers, ribbons, and greenery all come together to create an elegant arrangement. Re-create the look with some of your own seasonal favorites.

Start with a block of water-soaked florist oasis cut to fit the wall basket. Line the container with plastic so that water will not drip from the arrangement. Because our basket featured an open weave, we also lined the inside with sheet moss to mask the oasis.

Inspired by the colors of the season, white roses, red tulips, and green kermit mums provide the focal point. Green hypericum berries, red holly, and aucuba highlight the arrangement while long pieces of ivy trail alongside red wired ribbon. Small green apples tucked into the oasis with florist picks are the final touch.

Favorite Holiday Cookies

As part of her Christmas Eve feast, Amy Westmoreland of Scottsboro, Alabama, serves a smorgasbord of favorite sweets. (See her complete buffet-style menu on page 286.) Amy likes to make her own colored sugar for the Spritz Cookies using a touch of food coloring gel, but you can decorate yours with store-bought crystals. For a fruity twist, top Spritz Cookies with chopped candied cherries instead.

PECAN CRESCENTS

family favorite

Prep: 40 min., Chill: 1 hr., Bake: 12 min. per batch

Be sure to sift the powdered sugar *after* measuring, and sift the flour *before* measuring.

- **1 cup pecan halves, toasted**
- **1 cup butter, softened**
- **¾ cup powdered sugar, sifted**
- **2 teaspoons vanilla extract**
- **2½ cups sifted all-purpose flour**
- **Powdered sugar**

PULSE pecans in a food processor until coarse like sand.

BEAT butter and ¾ cup powdered sugar at medium speed with an electric mixer until creamy. Stir in vanilla and ground pecans. Gradually add flour, beating until a soft dough forms. Beat at low speed just until combined. Cover and chill 1 hour.

DIVIDE dough into 5 portions; divide each portion into 12 pieces. Roll dough pieces into 2-inch logs, curving ends to form crescents. Place on ungreased baking sheets.

BAKE at 350° for 10 to 12 minutes or until lightly browned. Cool 5 minutes. Roll warm cookies in powdered sugar. Cool completely on wire racks. **MAKES** about 5 dozen.

SPRITZ COOKIES

family favorite

Prep: 1 hr., Chill: 10 min., Bake: 10 min. per batch

For this recipe, sift the flour *after* measuring it.

- **1 cup shortening**
- **¾ cup sugar**
- **1 large egg**
- **1 teaspoon vanilla extract**
- **2¼ cups all-purpose flour, sifted**
- **¼ teaspoon salt**
- **½ teaspoon baking powder**
- **⅓ cup sugar***
- **⅛ teaspoon red or green food coloring gel***
- **Chopped candied cherries (optional)**

BEAT shortening at medium speed with an electric mixer until creamy. Gradually add ¾ cup sugar, beating until light and fluffy. Add egg and vanilla, beating until blended.

COMBINE flour, salt, and baking powder; gradually add to shortening mixture, beating at low speed until blended. Cover and chill 10 minutes.

COMBINE ⅓ cup sugar and food coloring gel in a zip-top plastic bag, and seal; shake and squeeze bag to evenly distribute color. (Too much gel will make sugar wet.)

PRESS dough into desired shapes using a cookie press. Sprinkle cookies with colored sugar, or top with candied cherries, if desired. Place cookies on ungreased baking sheets.

BAKE at 400° for 8 to 10 minutes or until lightly browned. Cool completely on wire racks. **MAKES** about 6 dozen.

*Substitute red or green decorator sugar crystals for sugar and coloring gel, if desired.

Lamb Chops With Attitude

Combine this delicious lamb recipe with a three-ingredient horseradish sauce, and it's sure to be a holiday hit.

MAPLE-GLAZED LAMB CHOPS WITH ZESTY HORSERADISH SAUCE

Prep: 10 min., Chill: 8 hrs., Broil: 14 min., Stand: 5 min.

- **⅓ cup maple syrup**
- **¼ cup Dijon mustard**
- **2 tablespoons balsamic vinegar**
- **2 tablespoons olive oil**
- **1 shallot, minced**
- **¼ teaspoon dried crushed red pepper**
- **8 (½-inch-thick) lamb loin chops**
- **½ teaspoon salt**
- **½ teaspoon ground black pepper**
- **Zesty Horseradish Sauce**

COMBINE first 6 ingredients in a shallow dish or large zip-top freezer bag; add lamb chops. Cover or seal, and chill up to 8 hours, turning occasionally.

REMOVE lamb chops from marinade, discarding marinade. Sprinkle chops evenly with salt and pepper; place chops on a lightly greased rack in a broiler pan.

BROIL chops 3 inches from heat 5 to 7 minutes on each side or to desired degree of doneness. Cover with aluminum foil, and let stand 5 minutes. Serve with Zesty Horseradish Sauce. **MAKES** 4 main-dish or 8 appetizer servings.

ZESTY HORSERADISH SAUCE

make ahead

Prep: 5 min.

Store leftover sauce in the refrigerator up to a week—it's the ideal spread for roast beef sandwiches.

- **½ cup sour cream**
- **2 tablespoons prepared horseradish**
- **2 tablespoons roughly chopped mint leaves**

STIR together all ingredients. Cover and chill until ready to serve. **MAKES** about ½ cup.

GILDA LESTER
WILMINGTON, NORTH CAROLINA

Green and Good for You

You'll want to remember these heart-healthy dishes as you pass the produce section. All have short ingredient lists that deliver lots of flavor without a lot of saturated fat. Broccoli With Orange Sauce uses lemon yogurt for a creamy base, while Fresh Spinach Sauté is a simple toss of prepackaged greens, olive oil, seasonings, and a sprinkle of Parmesan cheese.

FRESH SPINACH SAUTÉ

fast fixin's

Prep: 10 min., Cook: 10 min.

This quick sauté is an excellent source of fiber and cancer-preventing antioxidants.

> **3 (10-ounce) packages fresh spinach, torn**
> **2 garlic cloves, pressed**
> **¼ teaspoon salt**
> **¼ teaspoon ground red pepper**
> **2 teaspoons olive oil**
> **1 tablespoon freshly grated Parmesan cheese, divided**

SAUTÉ first 4 ingredients in hot oil in a nonstick skillet over medium-high heat 5 to 10 minutes or until spinach wilts. Drain well. Sprinkle with cheese. **MAKES** 6 servings.

NOTE: For best results, cook spinach a handful at a time.

Calories 48 (42% from fat); Fat 2.2g (sat 0.4g, mono 1.2g, poly 0.3g); Protein 4.2g; Carb 5g; Fiber 3.6g; Chol 0.7mg; Iron 3.4mg; Sodium 217mg; Calc 138mg

Spinach-Feta Stuffed Tomatoes:

Prep: 25 min., Cook 10 min., Bake 20 min.

SCOOP pulp from 6 medium tomatoes, leaving shells intact. Sprinkle with ¼ teaspoon salt. Place in a lightly greased 11- x 7-inch baking dish. Prepare spinach mixture as directed, omitting Parmesan cheese. Stir in ½ cup crumbled feta cheese. Spoon mixture evenly into tomato shells. Top evenly with 1½ teaspoons Italian-seasoned breadcrumbs. Bake at 350° for 15 to 20 minutes or until thoroughly heated. Top evenly with 1 tablespoon toasted pine nuts.

Calories 113 (46% from fat); Fat 5.8g (sat 2.3g, mono 2g, poly 0.9g); Protein 7.1g; Carb 11.9g; Fiber 5g; Chol 11mg; Iron 4.2mg; Sodium 465mg; Calc 195mg

BROCCOLI WITH ORANGE SAUCE

fast fixin's

Prep: 20 min., Cook: 11 min.

These beautiful florets are a powerful source of vitamins A and C, important nutrients thought to reduce the risk of cancer.

> **2 oranges**
> **1½ pounds fresh broccoli, cut into florets**
> **1 teaspoon butter or margarine**
> **1 small onion, chopped**
> **2 teaspoons finely chopped crystallized ginger**
> **1 (8-ounce) container low-fat lemon yogurt**

GRATE 1 orange, reserving 1 teaspoon rind. Peel and section oranges, removing seeds; set sections aside.
PLACE broccoli florets in a steamer basket over boiling water, and cook 3 to 4 minutes or until crisp-tender.
MELT butter in a nonstick skillet over medium-high heat; add onion and ginger, and sauté until tender. Remove from heat.
TOSS together broccoli, onion mixture, reserved rind, and orange sections in a large bowl. Stir in yogurt. Serve immediately. **MAKES** 6 servings.

NORA HENSHAW
OKEMAH, OKLAHOMA

Calories 110 (12% from fat); Fat 1.5g (sat 0.8g, mono 0.3g, poly 0.2g); Protein 5.7g; Carb 22.8g; Fiber 5.8g; Chol 3.6mg; Iron 1.3mg; Sodium 161mg; Calc 147mg

LEMON-PECAN GREEN BEANS

Prep: 20 min., Cook: 15 min.

The percentage of fat in this low-calorie dish may appear high, but the olive oil and chopped pecans add the benefit of cholesterol-reducing monounsaturated fat.

> **1 pound fresh green beans, trimmed**
> **½ teaspoon salt, divided**
> **2 green onions, sliced (about ¼ cup)**
> **2 teaspoons chopped fresh rosemary**
> **1 teaspoon olive oil**
> **¼ cup chopped pecans, toasted**
> **2 teaspoons grated lemon rind**

SPRINKLE green beans with ¼ teaspoon salt, and place in a steamer basket over boiling water; cook 10 minutes or until crisp-tender. Plunge into ice water to stop the cooking process.
SAUTÉ green onions and rosemary in hot oil in a large nonstick skillet over medium-high heat 2 to 3 minutes or until tender. Add green beans, pecans, lemon rind, and remaining ¼ teaspoon salt, stirring until thoroughly heated. Serve immediately. **MAKES** 6 servings.

MARY PAPPAS
RICHMOND, VIRGINIA

Calories 69 (54% from fat); Fat 4.5g (sat 0.5g, mono 2.6g, poly 1.2g); Protein 1.9g; Carb 7g; Fiber 3g; Chol 0mg; Iron 1mg; Sodium 197mg; Calc 38mg

Did You Know?

Vegetables, particularly green ones, can help reduce blood pressure and lower the risk of heart disease as well as some cancers.

Overcooking vegetables can result in a loss of nutrients. Light cooking, such as steaming or sautéing, will minimize the loss and enhance your body's vitamin and mineral absorption.

You need at least three to five servings of vegetables every day. The more variety, the better.

Fancy Without the Fuss

Dress up this simple menu with your best serving pieces for a dazzling Christmas Eve buffet.

Holiday Gathering

Serves 12 to 15

Pork Tenderloin Sandwiches With
Cranberry-Coriander Conserve

Blue Cheese-Bacon Dip
with grapes and assorted crackers

Raspberry-Brie Tartlets

Pecan Crescents (page 284)

Spritz Cookies (page 284)

Entertaining family and friends is Amy Westmoreland's favorite part of the holidays—that and, of course, the food. "We love any tradition that has to do with eating," jokes Amy, a seventh-grade French teacher. For nearly 10 years, the Scottsboro, Alabama, hostess and her husband John have been cooking up a scrumptious Christmas Eve dinner, arguably the most anticipated party in town. "Usually, we all gather to enjoy a candlelight church service, and then we hotfoot it home for a big feast."

Her buffet-style menu includes everyone's favorites, from creamy Blue Cheese- Bacon Dip to hearty Pork Tenderloin Sandwiches With Cranberry-Coriander Conserve. All are elegantly displayed in an eclectic mix of silver, fine china, and sparkling crystal.

Naturally, Amy prefers to spend less time in the kitchen and more time with her loved ones, so she makes most of her menu items in advance. Her popular four-ingredient Raspberry-Brie Tartlets are the perfect make-ahead appetizer. "I just

freeze the bread shells up to a month ahead, thaw them, assemble the tartlets before church, and pop them in the oven when I return," she explains.

For dessert, Amy shares fudge and other goodies that she receives as gifts from students and friends throughout the season, though nothing compares to her homemade cookies. Flip to page 284 for more tempting treats, and help yourself to this bountiful buffet.

PORK TENDERLOIN SANDWICHES WITH CRANBERRY-CORIANDER CONSERVE

Prep: 20 min., Cook: 3 min., Bake: 45 min., Stand: 15 min.

- **3 (11-ounce) packages frozen dinner rolls**
- **8 teaspoons coriander seeds, divided***
- **¼ cup olive oil**
- **2 tablespoons kosher salt**
- **1 teaspoon freshly ground black pepper**
- **2 teaspoons dried crushed red pepper**
- **1 teaspoon ground cumin**
- **4 pounds small boneless pork tenderloins**
- **Melted butter**
- **Poppy or sesame seeds (optional)**
- **Cranberry-Coriander Conserve**

THAW dinner rolls according to package directions.

PREHEAT oven to 375°.

COOK coriander seeds in a hot skillet over medium-high heat, stirring constantly, 2 to 3 minutes or until seeds are toasted and fragrant.

PULSE seeds in an electric spice or coffee grinder until crushed. (If you don't have a grinder, use a mortar and pestle, or place coriander seeds in a zip-top plastic bag, seal, and pound seeds with a meat mallet or rolling pin until crushed.) Reserve 2 teaspoons crushed coriander for Cranberry-Coriander Conserve.

STIR together remaining crushed coriander, olive oil, and next 4 ingredients. Place pork on a lightly greased rack in a broiler pan. Rub all sides of pork with spice mixture.

PLACE pork in preheated oven. Increase heat to 450°, and bake 25 minutes or until a meat thermometer registers 150°. Remove pork from oven, and reduce heat to 350°. Cover pork loosely with foil, and let stand 15 minutes or until thermometer registers 160°.

BRUSH thawed dinner rolls with melted butter; sprinkle with poppy or sesame seeds, if desired.

BAKE rolls at 350° for 15 to 20 minutes or until golden.

CUT pork into ¼-inch slices; serve with dinner rolls and Cranberry-Coriander Conserve. **MAKES** 12 to 15 servings.

*Substitute 3 teaspoons store-bought ground coriander, if desired. Omit toasting and crushing steps. Reserve ¾ teaspoon to use for Cranberry-Coriander Conserve; use remaining as directed.

NOTE: For testing purposes only, we used Sister Schubert's Parker House Style frozen yeast rolls.

Cranberry-Coriander Conserve:
make ahead
Prep: 10 min., Cook: 30 min., Chill: 2 hrs.

Prepare this spiced mixture up to 1 week ahead, and store in the refrigerator.

- **3 cups fresh cranberries**
- **1½ cups orange juice**
- **⅔ cup apple cider**
- **½ cup granulated sugar**
- **⅓ cup firmly packed brown sugar**
- **2 tablespoons cider vinegar**
- **2 teaspoons reserved crushed or ¾ teaspoon ground coriander**
- **1 (3-inch) cinnamon stick**
- **6 fresh mint leaves**

COOK all ingredients in a heavy saucepan over medium heat 30 minutes or until mixture thickens. Cool. Remove cinnamon stick. Cover and chill at least 2 hours. **MAKES** 2 cups.

BLUE CHEESE-BACON DIP

Prep: 20 min., Bake: 15 min.

This rich, creamy dip goes a long way. It can be baked in individual cups or a 1-quart dish.

- **7 bacon slices, chopped**
- **2 garlic cloves, minced**
- **2 (8-ounce) packages cream cheese, softened**
- **⅓ cup half-and-half**
- **4 ounces crumbled blue cheese**
- **2 tablespoons chopped fresh chives**
- **3 tablespoons chopped walnuts, toasted**
- **Grape clusters**
- **Flatbread or assorted crackers**

COOK bacon in a skillet over medium-high heat 10 minutes or until crisp. Drain bacon, reserving drippings in skillet, and set bacon aside. Add garlic to skillet, and sauté 1 minute.
BEAT cream cheese at medium speed with an electric mixer until smooth. Add half-and-half, beating until combined. Stir in bacon, garlic, blue cheese, and chives. Spoon mixture evenly into 4 (1-cup) individual baking dishes.
BAKE at 350° for 15 minutes or until golden and bubbly. Sprinkle with chopped walnuts, and serve with grapes and flatbread or crackers. **MAKES** 12 to 15 servings.

RASPBERRY-BRIE TARTLETS

make ahead
Prep: 1 hr., Bake: 17 min.

According to Amy, not all of these deliciously gooey appetizers make it to the table. She says, "We can't resist sneaking a few right off the baking sheet!"

- **20 white bread slices**
- **Melted butter**
- **1 (8-ounce) wedge Brie, cut up**
- **1 (13-ounce) jar raspberry jam**

REMOVE crusts from bread with a serrated knife. Roll and flatten each bread slice with a rolling pin. Cut 3 circles out of each bread slice with a 1¾-inch fluted or round cookie cutter.
BRUSH mini muffin pans with melted butter. Press bread circles on bottom and up sides of muffin cups; brush bread cups with melted butter.
BAKE at 350° for 7 minutes or until lightly toasted.
REMOVE bread cups from muffin pans, and place on ungreased baking sheets. Fill cups evenly with cheese pieces; top each with ¼ teaspoon jam.
BAKE at 300° for 10 minutes or until cheese is melted. **MAKES** 5 dozen.

NOTE: To make ahead, freeze toasted bread shells up to 1 month in advance. Thaw at room temperature about 30 minutes. Assemble tartlets, and bake as directed.

Tricks of the Trade

Year after year the *Southern Living* photo stylists master the art of decorating for Christmas with ease. So, what's their secret? Here are some of their must-haves for getting through the busy season.
- A great pair of clippers and a spool of florist wire
- Ribbon and lots of it! Not just for packages under the tree, use it to drape from a chandelier or to create napkin rings.
- Holiday collectibles such as small ornaments or figurines: These staples can be a quick, easy centerpiece or added to any arrangement for an extra special touch.
- Don't forget your Christmas spirit—crank up the holiday tunes, and get the kids involved. You'll create more than just beautiful arrangements; you'll have memories that will last a lifetime.

Casual Holiday Entertaining

Take a break from traditional holiday fare, and add a touch of Louisiana to your weeknight meals. These streamlined versions of gumbo, jambalaya, and dirty rice are sure to please.

JAMBALAYA

family favorite

Prep: 20 min., Cook: 40 min.

- 1 pound smoked sausage, cut into ¼-inch diagonal slices
- 1 small onion, chopped
- 3 celery ribs, chopped
- 1 bell pepper, chopped
- 1 garlic clove, minced
- 1 (14-ounce) can beef broth
- ¼ cup water
- 1 cup uncooked rice
- 1½ cups chopped cooked ham or chicken
- 1 (14½-ounce) can diced tomatoes, drained

COOK sausage in a Dutch oven over medium-high heat, stirring constantly, 7 minutes or until sausage is browned; drain. Stir in onion and next 3 ingredients; cook, stirring occasionally, 2 to 3 minutes or until tender.
ADD beef broth, ¼ cup water, and rice; bring to a boil. Reduce heat to low, cover, and simmer 20 minutes. Add ham and tomatoes, and cook, uncovered, 5 to 10 more minutes, stirring occasionally. MAKES 8 servings.

NOTE: For testing purposes only, we used Conecuh Original Smoked Sausage for smoked sausage.

KAYE WILLIS
KINDER, LOUISIANA

GARLIC BREAD

family favorite

Prep: 10 min., Bake: 20 min., Stand: 3 min.

- ½ cup butter or margarine, softened
- 2½ teaspoons garlic powder
- ¾ teaspoon dried Italian seasoning
- ½ teaspoon dried oregano
- ¼ teaspoon pepper
- 1 cup (4 ounces) shredded Italian three-cheese blend
- 1 (16-ounce) loaf French bread, split

COMBINE first 5 ingredients and ⅓ cup cheese; spread mixture evenly on cut sides of bread. Sprinkle evenly with remaining ⅔ cup cheese. Place on a baking sheet.
BAKE at 375° for 15 to 20 minutes or until cheese is melted and golden. Let stand 2 to 3 minutes before serving. MAKES 8 servings.

ANDREA WHEELER
CORONA, CALIFORNIA

CHICKEN-SAUSAGE GUMBO

family favorite

Prep: 20 min., Cook: 25 min.

- ½ pound smoked sausage, cut into ½-inch slices
- 1 to 3 tablespoons oil
- 5 tablespoons all-purpose flour
- 1 cup coarsely chopped onion
- 1 cup chopped celery
- 2 large garlic cloves, pressed
- 1 medium bell pepper, chopped
- 2 cups chicken broth
- 1 (28-ounce) can diced tomatoes
- 1 to 2 teaspoons Creole seasoning
- 4 cups chopped cooked chicken
- Hot cooked rice

COOK sausage over high heat in a Dutch oven 5 minutes, stirring often. Remove sausage with a slotted spoon. Drain on paper towels.
ADD enough oil to drippings in Dutch oven to equal 3 tablespoons; whisk in flour, and cook over medium-high heat, whisking constantly, 5 minutes. Add onion and next 3 ingredients; cook 5 minutes, stirring often. Stir in broth, tomatoes, and Creole seasoning. Bring to a boil; cover, reduce heat, and simmer 5 minutes. Add sausage and chicken; simmer, covered, 5 minutes. Serve over rice. MAKES 4 to 6 servings.

NOTE: For testing purposes only, we used Conecuh Original Smoked Sausage for smoked sausage.

CLAIRIECE GILBERT HUMPHREY
CHARLOTTESVILLE, VIRGINIA

CAJUN DIRTY RICE

family favorite

Prep: 20 min., Cook: 35 min.

- 1 (14-ounce) box boil-in-bag quick-cooking rice
- 1 pound ground chuck
- 1 pound ground spicy pork sausage
- 1 onion, chopped
- 1 bell pepper, chopped
- 3 celery ribs, chopped
- 1 (10¾-ounce) can reduced-sodium cream of mushroom soup
- 1 (1.4-ounce) envelope dry onion soup mix
- ½ teaspoon dried crushed red pepper

PREPARE 3 bags rice according to package directions. (Reserve fourth bag for another use.)
COOK beef and sausage in a large skillet over medium-high heat, stirring until meat crumbles and is no longer pink. Remove beef and sausage, reserving 2 tablespoons drippings in skillet. Drain beef mixture, and return to skillet. Add onion, bell pepper, and celery; cook, covered, 5 minutes or until tender.
STIR together canned soup, soup mix, and crushed pepper in a large bowl. Stir into beef mixture. Stir in cooked rice, and cook over low heat 5 to 10 minutes or until thoroughly heated, stirring often, to prevent sticking. MAKES 6 (2-cup) main-dish servings.

MELISSA LANDRUM
OVETT, MISSISSIPPI

Suppertime Solutions

This on-the-go dad shares his favorite recipes.

As owner of the Crescent City Grill and Purple Parrot Cafe in Hattiesburg, Mississippi, Robert St. John keeps a busy schedule. For help in preparing supper for his wife, Jill, and their sons, Holleman, 7, and Harrison, 3, Robert turns to recipes in his cookbook, *A Southern Palate* (Different Drummer Press, 2002), and one of his favorites, Crescent City Grill Creole Sauce.

CRESCENT CITY GRILL CREOLE SAUCE

chef recipe

Prep: 15 min., Cook: 25 min.

Toss this with your favorite pasta, or use as a topping for grilled shrimp, chicken, or vegetables. For extra richness, add ¼ cup of whipping cream.

- **3 tablespoons butter or margarine**
- **1 medium onion, chopped**
- **1 green bell pepper, chopped (about 1 cup)**
- **3 celery ribs, chopped**
- **4 garlic cloves, minced**
- **1 bay leaf**
- **2 tablespoons Crescent City Grill Creole Seasoning (recipe at right)**
- **1 tablespoon paprika**
- **1 (28-ounce) can diced tomatoes, undrained**
- **2 cups vegetable juice**
- **2 tablespoons hot sauce**
- **1 tablespoon Worcestershire sauce**
- **2 tablespoons cornstarch**
- **3 tablespoons cold water**

MELT butter in a large skillet over medium heat; add onion, bell pepper, and celery, and sauté 5 minutes or until vegetables are tender. Stir in garlic and next 3 ingredients, and cook 2 minutes. Stir in tomatoes and next 3 ingredients; reduce heat, and simmer 10 minutes. **COMBINE** cornstarch and 3 tablespoons cold water, stirring until smooth. Stir into tomato mixture in skillet, and bring to a boil over medium heat, stirring constantly. Boil, stirring constantly, 1 minute. Remove from heat. **MAKES** 8 cups.

PASTA WITH CRESCENT CITY GRILL CREOLE SAUCE: Cook 1 (16-ounce) package linguine in a large Dutch oven according to package directions; drain. Return to Dutch oven. Stir in 3 cups Crescent City Grill Creole Sauce, and cook 2 minutes over medium heat or until thoroughly heated.

ROBERT ST. JOHN
CRESCENT CITY GRILL AND
PURPLE PARROT CAFE
HATTIESBURG, MISSISSIPPI

CRESCENT CITY GRILL CREOLE SEASONING

chef recipe • fast fixin's

Prep: 5 min.

Robert uses this as an all-purpose seasoning and rub for meats and vegetables as well.

- **½ cup seasoned salt**
- **2 tablespoons onion powder**
- **2 tablespoons paprika**
- **1 tablespoon plus 1 teaspoon garlic powder**
- **1 tablespoon white pepper**
- **1 tablespoon ground red pepper**
- **1 teaspoon dry mustard**
- **1 teaspoon dried oregano**
- **1 teaspoon dried thyme**

COMBINE all ingredients. Store in an airtight container up to 6 months. **MAKES** 1 cup.

CREOLE GRILLED CHICKEN: Rub 1 to 2 tablespoons Crescent City Grill Creole Seasoning over 6 skinned and boned chicken breasts. Grill, covered with grill lid, over medium-high heat (350° to 400°) 7 minutes on each side or until done.

ROBERT ST. JOHN
CRESCENT CITY GRILL AND
PURPLE PARROT CAFE
HATTIESBURG, MISSISSIPPI

PURPLE PARROT SENSATION SALAD

chef recipe • fast fixin's

Prep: 10 min.

- **4 cups mixed salad greens**
- **2 cups fresh baby spinach**
- **1 cup freshly grated Romano cheese**
- **¼ cup crumbled blue cheese**
- **3 to 4 tablespoons Purple Parrot Sensation Dressing**
- **Garnish: freshly grated Romano cheese**

PLACE salad greens and spinach in a large bowl. Sprinkle with 1 cup Romano cheese and blue cheese. Drizzle with Purple Parrot Sensation Dressing. Garnish, if desired. Serve immediately. **MAKES** 6 to 8 servings.

Purple Parrot Sensation Dressing:
fast fixin's • make ahead

Prep: 10 min.

- **½ cup white wine vinegar**
- **½ cup lemon juice**
- **4 to 6 garlic cloves**
- **1 teaspoon salt**
- **1 teaspoon pepper**
- **½ cup extra-virgin olive oil**
- **½ cup canola oil**

PROCESS first 5 ingredients in a blender or food processor until smooth, stopping to scrape down sides. With blender or processor running, gradually add oils in a slow, steady stream; process until smooth. **MAKES** 2 cups.

NOTE: Store remaining dressing in an airtight container in refrigerator up to 1 week.

ROBERT ST. JOHN
CRESCENT CITY GRILL AND
PURPLE PARROT CAFE
HATTIESBURG, MISSISSIPPI

Christmas All Through the House

Discover easy-going recipes and simple decorations.

Supper Club Celebration

Pull out all the stops for your supper club with these top-rated recipes. Follow our party planner on the opposite page for a doable make-ahead schedule that will get your dinner off to a festive start.

ORANGE THING

chef recipe • make ahead

Prep: 5 min.

This drink is the house specialty at Birmingham's Bottega Restaurant. Now you can serve it in your home as well.

> 2 cups ice cubes
> ¼ cup vodka
> 2 tablespoons orange liqueur
> ¼ cup fresh orange juice
> Garnish: orange slice

COMBINE first 4 ingredients in a martini shaker. Cover with lid, and shake until thoroughly chilled. Remove lid, and strain into a chilled martini glass. Serve immediately. Garnish, if desired. **MAKES** 1 serving.

WAYNE RUSSELL
BOTTEGA ITALIAN RESTAURANT
BIRMINGHAM, ALABAMA

BACON-STUFFED EGGS

make ahead

Prep: 15 min., Cook: 10 min., Stand: 15 min.

Reader Charles Hosch recommends adding a teaspoon of salt to the cooking water and chilling the hard-cooked eggs overnight to make them easier to peel. This recipe offers a twist on the perennial favorite, deviled eggs.

> 12 large eggs
> ⅓ cup mayonnaise
> 1 (3-ounce) package cream cheese, softened
> 2 teaspoons Worcestershire sauce
> ¼ teaspoon salt
> ½ teaspoon pepper
> 1 teaspoon prepared horseradish (optional)
> 4 bacon slices, cooked and crumbled
> Garnish: chopped chives

PLACE eggs in a large saucepan; add water to a depth of 3 inches. Bring to a boil; cover, remove from heat, and let stand 15 minutes.

DRAIN immediately, and fill saucepan with cold water and ice. Tap each egg firmly on the counter until cracks form all over the shell. Peel under cold running water.

SLICE eggs in half lengthwise, and carefully remove yolks. Mash yolks with mayonnaise. Add cream cheese, next 3 ingredients, and, if desired, horseradish to yolk mixture; stir well. Spoon yolk mixture into egg whites; sprinkle with bacon. Garnish, if desired. **MAKES** 6 to 8 servings.

CHARLES HOSCH
MARIETTA, GEORGIA

BAKED PIMIENTO CHEESE

make ahead

Prep: 15 min., Bake: 20 min.

What could be better than pimiento cheese? Gooey, warm Baked Pimiento Cheese dip. Serve this dip with crackers or your favorite crunchy vegetables.

- **1½ cups mayonnaise**
- **1 (4-ounce) jar diced pimiento, drained**
- **1 teaspoon Worcestershire sauce**
- **1 teaspoon finely grated onion**
- **¼ teaspoon ground red pepper**
- **1 (8-ounce) block extra-sharp Cheddar cheese, shredded**
- **1 (8-ounce) block sharp Cheddar cheese, shredded**
- **Garnish: chopped fresh parsley**

STIR together first 5 ingredients in a large bowl; stir in cheeses. Spoon mixture into a lightly greased 2-quart or 11- x 7-inch baking dish.

BAKE at 350° for 20 minutes or until golden and bubbly. Garnish, if desired. Serve with crackers or crunchy vegetables. **MAKES** 4 cups.

Party Planner

Use our timeline to make and serve this menu without a hitch.

Two days ahead
- Cook and peel hard-cooked eggs. Place in a zip-top plastic bag, and chill. Cook and crumble bacon. Chill.
- Set the table; cover with a clean sheet or spare tablecloth.
- Set up bar.

One day ahead
- Mix up Baked Pimiento Cheese, and place in baking dish; chill.
- Make Bacon-Stuffed Eggs without the garnish, and place on a serving dish; chill.
- Make Red Velvet Cheesecake; chill. Wash mint for garnish, wrap in paper towels, and place in a zip-top plastic bag.
- Assemble Crabmeat-and-Spinach Lasagna; chill.
- Squeeze orange juice and slice oranges for Orange Thing; chill.

Day of the party
- Place cheesecake on a serving plate, and garnish; chill.

1½ hours before dinner
- Bake lasagna; cover and keep warm.
- Bake okra; cover and keep warm. Toast walnuts.
- Bake pimiento cheese appetizer; cover and keep warm.
- Garnish eggs.
- Set out crackers or vegetables to go with Baked Pimiento Cheese.

30 minutes before dinner
- Bake breadsticks.
- Serve eggs, cheese dip, and Orange Thing.

Last minute
- Heat salad dressing, and assemble the salad.
- Garnish lasagna, and serve the meal.

OKRA-WALNUT SALAD

Prep: 15 min., Bake: 20 min.

Frozen breaded okra, red onion, and toasted walnuts drizzled with warm spinach salad dressing offer a variety of flavors and textures.

- **1 (24-ounce) package frozen breaded cut okra**
- **3 (5-ounce) packages salad greens**
- **1 large red onion, thinly sliced**
- **½ to 1 cup chopped walnuts, toasted**
- **1 (15-ounce) bottle spinach salad dressing**

BAKE okra at 425° in a single layer on a lightly greased baking sheet 20 minutes or until golden brown, or fry okra according to package directions.

TOSS together okra and next 3 ingredients in a large bowl.

HEAT dressing according to package directions. Serve warm with salad. **MAKES** 8 servings.

NOTE: For testing purposes only, we used T. Marzetti's Spinach Salad Dressing.

CRABMEAT-AND-SPINACH LASAGNA

make ahead

Prep: 25 min.; Bake: 1 hr., 5 min.; Cook: 5 min.; Stand: 10 min.

Press drained spinach between paper towels to absorb additional liquid.

- **9 uncooked lasagna noodles**
- **2 tablespoons butter or margarine**
- **½ cup finely chopped celery**
- **½ cup finely chopped onion**
- **1 red bell pepper, finely chopped**
- **3 garlic cloves, minced**
- **3 (8-ounce) containers sour cream**
- **¼ cup chopped fresh basil**
- **¼ teaspoon salt**
- **⅛ teaspoon ground white pepper**
- **⅛ teaspoon ground nutmeg**
- **2 (10-ounce) packages frozen chopped spinach, thawed and well drained**
- **1 pound fresh lump crabmeat, drained**
- **4 cups (16 ounces) shredded mozzarella and provolone cheese, divided**
- **Garnish: fresh basil leaves**

COOK noodles according to package directions; drain and set aside.

MELT butter in a large skillet over medium-high heat; add celery and next 3 ingredients. Sauté 4 to 5 minutes or until vegetables are tender.

COMBINE sour cream and next 4 ingredients in a large bowl; stir in vegetable mixture and spinach. Add crabmeat; toss.

ARRANGE 3 lasagna noodles in a lightly greased 13- x 9-inch baking dish; top with half of crabmeat mixture. Top with half of cheese. Repeat layers with 3 lasagna noodles and remaining crabmeat mixture. Top with remaining 3 lasagna noodles.

BAKE, covered, at 350° for 50 minutes or until thoroughly heated. Uncover and top evenly with remaining 2 cups cheese. Bake, uncovered, 15 minutes or until cheese is melted. Let stand 10 minutes before serving. Garnish, if desired. **MAKES** 8 servings.

NOTE: For testing purposes only, we used Sargento Chef Style Mozzarella & Provolone cheese blend.

RED VELVET CHEESECAKE

make ahead

Prep: 20 min.; Bake: 1 hr., 25 min.; Stand: 1 hr.; Chill: 8 hrs.

The cheesecake's deep red filling and snowy topping make it a wonderfully dramatic dessert.

- **1½ cups chocolate graham cracker crumbs**
- **¼ cup butter, melted**
- **1 tablespoon granulated sugar**
- **3 (8-ounce) packages cream cheese, softened**
- **1½ cups granulated sugar**
- **4 large eggs, lightly beaten**
- **3 tablespoons unsweetened cocoa**
- **1 cup sour cream**
- **½ cup whole buttermilk**
- **2 teaspoons vanilla extract**
- **1 teaspoon white vinegar**
- **2 (1-ounce) bottles red food coloring**
- **1 (3-ounce) package cream cheese, softened**
- **¼ cup butter, softened**
- **2 cups powdered sugar**
- **1 teaspoon vanilla extract**
- **Garnish: fresh mint sprigs**

STIR together graham cracker crumbs, melted butter and 1 tablespoon granulated sugar; press mixture into bottom of a 9-inch springform pan.

BEAT 3 (8-ounce) packages cream cheese and 1½ cups granulated sugar at medium-low speed with an electric mixer 1 minute. Add eggs and next 6 ingredients, mixing on low speed just until fully combined. Pour batter into prepared crust.

BAKE at 325° for 10 minutes; reduce heat to 300°, and bake 1 hour and 15 minutes or until center is firm. Run a knife along outer edge of cheesecake. Turn oven off. Let cheesecake stand in oven 30 minutes. Remove cheesecake from oven; cool in pan on a wire rack 30 minutes. Cover and chill 8 hours.

BEAT 1 (3-ounce) package cream cheese and ¼ cup butter at medium speed until smooth; gradually add powdered sugar and 1 teaspoon vanilla, beating until smooth. Spread evenly over top of cheesecake. Remove sides of springform pan. Garnish, if desired. **MAKES** 8 to 10 servings.

RHONDA Y. COKER
COLUMBIA, SOUTH CAROLINA

Wreaths That Say Welcome

Greet your holiday guests with a great-looking door decoration. And who says a wreath has to be round? Metal forms, available at crafts and floral stores, come in all shapes and sizes. Keep it simple using the same material to cover the form, or mix it up and blend a variety of greenery and berries. Grab some clippers, florist wire, and a bunch of greenery and make your own stylish wreath. Here's how.

Bundle four sprigs of greenery together, and secure with florist wire. Twenty-five bundles will cover a 12- x 14–inch form. Start by attaching a bundle in one corner, and work in a continuous clockwise motion. Cover the base of one bundle with the top of the next bunch. Repeat these steps until the form is completely covered.

(Tip: Don't ruin that fresh paint job; use suction cup hooks to hang holiday decorations to walls or windows. Available at most home-improvement stores, they come in a variety of sizes and can hold up to 25 pounds.)

Layered Appetizers

Hungry guests can't resist a hearty appetizer, especially one that looks as good as it tastes. These no-fuss starters are the perfect prelude to any party. We've kept the hands-on prep time less than 30 minutes, and all of these recipes can be made ahead.

SOUTHWEST CHEESECAKE

make ahead

Prep: 20 min., Bake: 52 min., Stand: 10 min., Chill: 3 hrs.

Your guests might think you spent all day making this spread—little do they know it can be easily prepared in advance. Colorful ingredients, such as the guacamole and chopped tomato that top this appetizer, will brighten your holiday buffet table.

- 1½ cups finely crushed tortilla chips
- ¼ cup butter or margarine, softened
- 2 (8-ounce) packages cream cheese, softened
- 2 cups (8 ounces) shredded Monterey Jack cheese
- ¼ teaspoon salt
- 3 (8-ounce) containers sour cream, divided
- 3 large eggs
- 1 cup thick and chunky salsa
- 1 (4-ounce) can chopped green chiles, drained
- 1 cup fresh or frozen guacamole, thawed
- 1 medium tomato, seeded and diced
- Tortilla chips or crackers (optional)

COMBINE 1½ cups crushed tortilla chips and butter, and press into bottom of a lightly greased 9-inch springform pan. BAKE at 350° for 12 minutes. Cool on a wire rack.

BEAT cream cheese, shredded cheese, and salt at medium speed with an electric mixer 3 minutes or until fluffy. Add 1 container sour cream, beating until blended. Add eggs, 1 at a time, beating well after each addition. Stir in salsa and chiles. Pour into prepared crust.

BAKE at 350° for 40 minutes or until center is almost set. Let stand 10 minutes on a wire rack. Gently run a knife around edge of pan to loosen sides. Remove sides of pan, and let cheesecake cool completely.

SPREAD remaining 2 containers sour cream evenly over top; cover and chill at least 3 hours. Spread with guacamole; sprinkle with tomatoes before serving. Serve with tortilla chips or crackers, if desired. **MAKES** 25 appetizer servings.

SHARLA SANDERSON
ABERDEEN, MISSISSIPPI

LASAGNA CUPS

make ahead

Prep: 15 min., Cook: 10 min., Bake: 20 min.

Luscious lasagna ingredients are layered inside these easy biscuit bites. Your guests won't be able to eat just one!

- ½ pound lean ground beef
- 1 small onion, chopped
- 2 garlic cloves, minced
- 1 cup thick pizza sauce
- 1 large egg, lightly beaten
- ½ cup ricotta cheese
- 1 (10-ounce) can refrigerated buttermilk biscuits
- ¾ cup (3 ounces) shredded mozzarella cheese

COOK first 3 ingredients in a large skillet over medium heat, stirring until beef crumbles and is no longer pink. Drain well. Return beef to skillet; stir in pizza sauce. Remove from heat.

STIR together egg and ricotta cheese.

SEPARATE biscuits, and split in half. Press each biscuit half on bottom and up sides of lightly greased muffin pans. Spoon meat mixture evenly into biscuit cups; top evenly with egg mixture, and sprinkle with shredded cheese.

BAKE at 375° for 18 to 20 minutes or until golden. Serve immediately. **MAKES** 20 appetizer servings.

TRICIA GROVER
JAMISON, PENNSYLVANIA

CREAM CHEESE-VEGETABLE SQUARES

make ahead

Prep: 10 min., Bake: 12 min., Chill: 2 hrs.

This favorite appetizer is given an update by using broccoli slaw mix rather than the traditional chopped veggies.

- 1 (8-ounce) package refrigerated crescent rolls
- 1 (8-ounce) package ⅓-less-fat cream cheese, softened
- ½ cup light mayonnaise
- 1 (1-ounce or 1.4-ounce) envelope Ranch salad dressing mix
- 1 cup broccoli slaw mix*
- 1 cup (4 ounces) finely shredded Cheddar cheese

PRESS crescent roll dough into a 13- x 9-inch pan; press perforations to seal.

BAKE at 350° for 12 minutes or until golden; cool.

STIR together cream cheese, mayonnaise, and dressing mix; spread over crust. Sprinkle with broccoli slaw, and top with cheese; gently press into cream cheese mixture. Cover and chill at least 2 hours. Cut into squares before serving. **MAKES** 20 squares.

*Substitute ⅓ cup each of finely chopped broccoli, cauliflower, and celery for broccoli slaw mix, if desired.

CARMEN CAMPBELL
PORTSMOUTH, VIRGINIA

ARTICHOKE-CHEESE SPREAD

Prep: 25 min., Chill: 2 hrs.

For a smaller crowd, halve the recipe, and use a 2-cup bowl.

- **2 (8-ounce) packages cream cheese, softened**
- **¼ cup finely chopped green onion tops**
- **1 (14-ounce) can artichoke hearts, drained and finely chopped**
- **1 cup freshly grated Parmesan cheese**
- **2 garlic cloves, pressed**
- **2 tablespoons olive oil**
- **1 tablespoon lemon juice**
- **½ teaspoon ground red pepper**
- **¾ cup bottled roasted red bell peppers, drained and chopped**
- **Assorted fresh lettuce**
- **Thin white or wheat bread slices, crusts removed and cut into triangles**
- **Red, yellow, and orange bell pepper strips**
- **Garnishes: bottled roasted red bell pepper strip, slivered; radish slices**

STIR together cream cheese and green onion tops, blending well; set aside.
STIR together artichoke hearts and next 5 ingredients.
SPREAD one-third of cream cheese mixture on bottom of a 4-cup glass bowl lined with plastic wrap. Layer with half of chopped roasted bell peppers, ¾ cup artichoke mixture, and one-third of cream cheese mixture. Repeat layers with remaining chopped roasted bell peppers, artichoke mixture, and cream cheese mixture. Cover and chill at least 2 hours.
INVERT onto a serving plate, and remove plastic wrap. Serve over lettuce with bread slices and bell pepper strips. Garnish, if desired. **MAKES** 8 to 10 appetizer servings.

DANIELLE MCINERNEY
TUSCALOOSA, ALABAMA

Catch-up Time

Take time out to savor a weeknight dinner with your family.

Post-Shopping Supper

Serves 6

Unforgettable Chicken Casserole

Orange-Ginger Peas

Toasted Herb Rice

Peppery Cheese Bread

Baked Lemon Pudding

A special weeknight meal with your family is a fine way to relax during the holidays. You can even plan a project, such as our Peppermint Tree (on facing page), as a weekend activity.

UNFORGETTABLE CHICKEN CASSEROLE

family favorite

Prep: 10 min., Bake: 45 min., Stand: 10 min.

- **3 cups chopped deli-roasted chicken**
- **2 cups finely chopped celery**
- **1 cup (4 ounces) shredded Cheddar cheese**
- **½ cup slivered almonds**
- **½ cup light sour cream**
- **½ cup light mayonnaise**
- **1 (10¾-ounce) can reduced-sodium cream of chicken soup**
- **1 (4-ounce) can water chestnuts, drained and chopped**
- **1½ cups French fried onion rings**

STIR together first 8 ingredients in a large bowl. Spoon into a lightly greased 11- x 7-inch baking dish.

BAKE at 350° for 40 minutes; sprinkle onion rings evenly over top. Bake 5 more minutes or until bubbly around edges. Let stand 10 minutes before serving. **MAKES** 6 to 8 servings.

KAY REGNIER
WINTERVILLE, NORTH CAROLINA

ORANGE-GINGER PEAS

family favorite • fast fixin's

Prep: 5 min., Cook: 7 min.

This dish is equally good without ginger, so if you don't have it or don't like it, leave it out.

- **1 (16-ounce) package frozen green peas**
- **1 cup water**
- **1 tablespoon grated orange rind**
- **2 tablespoons honey**
- **¼ to ½ teaspoon salt**
- **¼ teaspoon ground red pepper**
- **1 (1-inch) piece ginger, peeled (optional)**

COMBINE first 6 ingredients and ginger, if desired, in a large saucepan over medium-high heat. Bring to a boil; reduce heat, and simmer 3 minutes. Remove and discard ginger. Serve with a slotted spoon. **MAKES** 8 servings.

TOASTED HERB RICE

family favorite

Prep: 10 min., Bake: 55 min.

- 1 cup uncooked long-grain rice
- 2 tablespoons butter or margarine
- 1 (10-ounce) can condensed chicken broth, heated
- ¾ cup boiling water
- 4 green onions, chopped
- 1 teaspoon dried basil
- ¼ cup pine nuts, toasted

PLACE rice in an ovenproof Dutch oven; cover with lid.

BAKE at 325° for 20 to 25 minutes or until rice is golden brown. Add butter, and stir until melted. Carefully stir in broth and ¾ cup boiling water; cover. Bake 30 more minutes or until water is absorbed and rice is tender.

STIR in onions, basil, and pine nuts; serve immediately. **MAKES** 4 to 6 servings.

MILDRED BICKLEY
BRISTOL, VIRGINIA

PEPPERY CHEESE BREAD

family favorite

Prep: 15 min.; Bake: 50 min.;
Cool: 1 hr., 10 min.

Grease only the bottom of the pan so this bread will rise nicely. If the loaf sticks to the side, run a knife between the edge of the bread and the pan.

- 2½ cups all-purpose flour
- 1 tablespoon sugar
- 2 teaspoons cracked black pepper
- 1 teaspoon baking powder
- ¾ teaspoon salt
- ½ teaspoon baking soda
- 2 large eggs, lightly beaten
- 1 (8-ounce) container plain low-fat yogurt
- 1 cup (4 ounces) shredded Cheddar cheese
- ½ cup vegetable oil
- ¼ cup thinly sliced green onions
- ¼ cup milk
- 1 tablespoon spicy brown mustard

COMBINE first 6 ingredients in a large bowl; make a well in center of mixture. Stir together eggs and next 6 ingredients; add to dry ingredients, stirring just until moistened.

LIGHTLY grease bottom of a 9- x 5-inch loafpan; pour batter into loafpan.

BAKE at 350° for 45 to 50 minutes or until a wooden pick inserted in center comes out clean. Cool in pan on a wire rack 10 minutes; remove from pan, and let cool 1 hour on wire rack. **MAKES** 1 loaf.

BETTY RABE
PLANO, TEXAS

BAKED LEMON PUDDING

family favorite • make ahead

Prep: 10 min., Bake: 45 min., Chill: 1 hr.

- 3 large eggs, separated
- 2 teaspoons grated lemon rind
- 1½ cups milk
- ¼ cup fresh lemon juice
- 2 teaspoons butter or margarine, melted
- 1½ cups sugar, divided
- ½ cup all-purpose flour
- ½ teaspoon baking powder
- ¼ teaspoon salt
- Whipped cream
- Garnishes: grated lemon zest, fresh blueberries

BEAT egg yolks at medium speed with an electric mixer until thick and pale; add lemon rind and next 3 ingredients, beating well.

COMBINE 1 cup sugar and next 3 ingredients; add to lemon mixture, beating until smooth.

BEAT egg whites until soft peaks form; add remaining ½ cup sugar, and beat until blended. Fold into lemon mixture. Pour into a greased 2-quart baking dish. Place baking dish in a large shallow pan. Add hot water to pan to a depth of 1 inch.

BAKE at 350° for 45 minutes or just until center is set. Remove baking dish from water bath; cool completely on a wire rack. Cover and chill at least 1 hour. Top with whipped cream, and garnish, if desired. **MAKES** 8 to 10 servings.

GWEN KORKOLIS
WOODBRIDGE, VIRGINIA

Create a Peppermint Tree

Make your own sweet tree. It's a fun activity you can do with your kids, plus it makes a great centerpiece that lasts through the season.

Foam topiary forms are available at most crafts stores. Remove the plastic from each piece of candy, and apply unwrapped candy to the tree with a glue gun. Once the form is completely covered, apply a protective sealer. This prevents the candy from getting sticky; be sure to do this in a well-ventilated area. **NOTE:** Make sure children understand that the candies on the tree aren't edible. To keep your kids from pulling candies off the tree, fill the base with a supply of peppermints.

Use ribbon to fill in any holes left on the tree. Tie 3-inch-long pieces of ribbon in a knot, and secure them to the tree with a small amount of glue. Continue this process until all the holes are filled. Finish the arrangement with a small bow tied at the base.

Casual Holiday Gathering

This Christmas dinner is simple and crowd-pleasing.

Casual Christmas Menu

Serves 8

Bourbon-Glazed Ham

Out-of-This-World Scalloped Potatoes

Julienned Orange Carrots

Bing Cherry-and-Cranberry Salad

Pumpkin Roll

This make-ahead menu stands on its own, or you can add all those favorite family dishes your mom is sure to bring. Best of all, you can prepare most of the recipes early in the day on Christmas Eve, leaving time for evening festivities. It'll leave you time to visit and open gifts.

BOURBON-GLAZED HAM

family favorite

Prep: 20 min.; Bake: 2 hrs., 20 min.; Stand: 15 min.

It's best to bake the ham the day you plan to serve it. It takes only a moment to wrap the ham in foil and prepare for baking; then you have 2 hours of hands-off time.

- **1 (10-pound) fully cooked smoked ham**
- **¾ cup whole cloves**
- **¾ cup bourbon or apple juice**
- **2 cups firmly packed dark brown sugar**
- **1 tablespoon dry mustard**
- **2 navel oranges, sliced**

WRAP ham in aluminum foil, and place in a lightly greased 13- x 9-inch pan.
BAKE at 325° for 2 hours. Remove ham from oven, and increase temperature to 450°.
UNWRAP ham; discard foil. Remove skin and excess fat from ham. Make ¼-inch-deep cuts in a diamond design, and insert cloves at 1-inch intervals.
BRUSH ham evenly with ½ cup bourbon. Stir together remaining ¼ cup bourbon, sugar, and mustard in a small bowl. Pat sugar mixture evenly over ham; arrange orange slices over sugar mixture, and secure with wooden picks. Lightly baste with drippings; bake 15 to 20 minutes or until a meat thermometer inserted into thickest portion registers 140° and sugar has melted and formed a glaze. Let stand 15 minutes before slicing. **MAKES** 8 to 10 servings.

CLAIRIECE GILBERT HUMPHREY
CHARLOTTESVILLE, VIRGINIA

OUT-OF-THIS-WORLD SCALLOPED POTATOES

family favorite • make ahead

Prep: 30 min.; Bake: 2 hrs., 30 min.; Cook: 15 min.

- **¼ cup butter or margarine**
- **¼ cup all-purpose flour**
- **3 cups milk**
- **1 (10-ounce) block Cheddar cheese, shredded**
- **½ cup thinly sliced green onions**
- **1 teaspoon salt**
- **¼ teaspoon pepper**
- **4 pounds potatoes, thinly sliced**
- **1½ cups soft breadcrumbs**
- **¼ cup butter or margarine, melted**
- **¼ cup grated Parmesan cheese**
- **Garnish: sliced green onions**

MELT ¼ cup butter in a large saucepan over medium heat. Whisk in flour, and cook, whisking constantly, 2 to 3 minutes or until flour is lightly browned. Whisk milk into butter mixture; bring to a boil. Reduce heat, and simmer 6 minutes or until thickened. Stir in Cheddar cheese and next 3 ingredients, stirring until cheese melts.
SPREAD ¼ cup cheese sauce evenly in a lightly greased 13- x 9-inch baking dish. Layer half of potatoes over sauce; top with half of remaining cheese sauce. Repeat with remaining potatoes and cheese sauce.
BAKE, covered, at 325° for 1½ to 2 hours.
STIR together breadcrumbs, melted butter, and Parmesan cheese in a small bowl; spread evenly over potatoes. Bake, uncovered, 20 to 30 more minutes or until potatoes are tender. Garnish, if desired. **MAKES** 8 to 10 servings.

DELLA TAYLOR
JONESBOROUGH, TENNESSEE

JULIENNED ORANGE CARROTS

family favorite • fast fixin's

Prep: 5 min., Cook: 10 min.

    5 cups water
    2 (10-ounce) packages julienned
       carrots
    ¼ cup butter or margarine
    4 teaspoons fresh orange juice
    1 teaspoon grated orange rind
    1 teaspoon salt
    ¼ teaspoon ground red pepper

BRING 5 cups water to a boil in a 3-quart saucepan; add carrots, and cook 5 minutes or until tender; drain.
MELT butter in a large nonstick skillet over medium heat; add carrots, orange juice, and remaining ingredients, tossing to combine. Cook just until heated through. **MAKES** 8 servings.

MARLENE MCDONALD
SANFORD, NORTH CAROLINA

BING CHERRY-AND-CRANBERRY SALAD

family favorite • make ahead

Prep: 15 min., Cook: 5 min., Chill: 8 hrs.

This updated congealed salad adds rich color and sweet-tart flavor to the meal.

    2½ cups water
    3 (3-ounce) packages black cherry-
       flavored gelatin
    2 cups cola soft drink
    1 (16-ounce) can whole-berry
       cranberry sauce
    1 (15-ounce) can pitted Bing
       cherries, drained and quartered
    2 cups chopped pecans, toasted

BRING 2½ cups water to a boil in a large saucepan over high heat; remove from heat. Add gelatin, stirring 2 minutes or until gelatin dissolves.
STIR cola and next 3 ingredients into gelatin mixture; pour into a lightly greased 12-cup ring mold. Cover and chill 8 hours or until firm. Unmold onto a serving platter. **MAKES** 10 to 12 servings.

KAREN TORRES
AGUADELLA, PUERTO RICO

NOTE: For testing purposes only, we used Coca-Cola for cola soft drink.

PUMPKIN ROLL

make ahead • family favorite

Prep: 25 min., Bake: 15 min., Chill: 3 hrs.

    Vegetable cooking spray
    3 large eggs
    1 cup granulated sugar
    ¾ cup all-purpose flour
    2 teaspoons ground cinnamon
    1 teaspoon baking soda
    1 teaspoon baking powder
    1 teaspoon ground ginger
    ½ teaspoon salt
    ½ teaspoon ground nutmeg
    ⅔ cup canned unsweetened
       pumpkin
    ½ cup finely chopped pecans,
       toasted
    1 teaspoon lemon juice
    1½ cups powdered sugar, divided
    2 (3-ounce) packages cream cheese,
       softened
    ¼ cup butter or margarine, softened
    1 teaspoon vanilla extract
    1 teaspoon lemon juice
    Garnishes: powdered sugar,
       chocolate-coated pecan halves

COAT bottom and sides of a 15- x 10-inch jellyroll pan with cooking spray, and line with wax paper. Coat wax paper with cooking spray; set aside.
BEAT eggs at medium speed with an electric mixer 5 minutes or thick and lemon-colored; gradually add granulated sugar, beating until well combined. Combine flour and next 6 ingredients. Gradually add to egg mixture, beating well. Combine pumpkin, toasted pecans, and lemon juice, and gradually add to egg and flour mixture, beating well. Spread batter evenly in prepared pan.
BAKE at 375° for 15 minutes or until a wooden pick inserted in center comes out clean.
SIFT ½ cup powdered sugar in a 15- x 10-inch rectangle on a clean, dry dish towel. Run a knife around edges of pan to loosen cake, and turn cake out onto prepared towel. Peel off wax paper. Starting at narrow end, roll up cake and towel together; place seam side down on a wire rack to cool completely.
BEAT cream cheese and butter at medium speed until creamy; gradually add remaining 1 cup powdered sugar, beating until smooth. Stir in vanilla and lemon juice.
UNROLL cake; remove towel. Spread cream cheese mixture on cake, leaving a 1-inch border around edges. Roll up cake without towel, and place seam side down on a serving platter. Cover and chill at least 3 hours. Garnish, if desired. **MAKES** 8 servings.

ANGELA M. KOTOWICZ
ST. LOUIS, MISSOURI

Make-Ahead Tips

■ Prepare Bing Cherry-and-Cranberry Salad early the day before.
■ Assemble Out-of-This-World Scalloped Potatoes the day before; cover with foil, and refrigerate. Let stand at room temperature 30 minutes before baking as directed.
■ Make Pumpkin Roll the day before; garnish before serving.
■ Set the table several days ahead, and cover with a clean sheet or table-cloth. Add flowers or greenery the day before the meal.

Soup With Santa

A tree-decorating party with St. Nick adds
up to happy memories.

St. Nick Supper

Serves 8

Cheeseburger Soup with
Easy Breadsticks

BLT Wrap

Mexican Hot Chocolate and
Chocolate-Dipped Orange Cookies

Schedule a special party for your younger children and their friends—and invite Santa to help decorate the tree. An afternoon during the week is the perfect time to let youngsters work off after-school energy. When they're ready for a snack, offer kid-friendly fuel, such as these recipes. They're easy to whip up and pleasing to young taste buds, so partygoers will be nice instead of naughty.

Trimming the Outdoor Tree

An outdoor tree filled with lights simply glows at night but during the day, turn it into a delicious feast for the birds. Stringing popcorn is a fun activity the kids can do while waiting to visit with the jolly man in the red suit. Add dried apricots and cranberries for a burst of color—they're also yummy to snack on.

For bird-friendly ornaments, spread pinecones with peanut butter; then roll in birdseed. Hang on the tree with pieces of red raffia.

CHEESEBURGER SOUP

family favorite

Prep: 30 min., Cook: 40 min.

- ½ **pound lean ground beef**
- ½ **cup chopped onion**
- ¾ **cup shredded carrots**
- ¾ **cup chopped celery**
- 1 **teaspoon dried basil**
- 1 **teaspoon dried parsley**
- 6 **cups chicken broth**
- 2 **pounds potatoes, peeled and diced**
- 3 **tablespoons butter or margarine**
- ¼ **cup all-purpose flour**
- ¾ **pound processed reduced-fat American cheese, cubed**
- 1½ **cups milk**
- ¾ **teaspoon salt**
- ½ **teaspoon pepper**
- **Easy Breadsticks (optional)**

COOK ground beef in a large Dutch oven over medium-high heat about 3 minutes, stirring until it crumbles. Add onion and next 4 ingredients, and sauté 4 minutes or until beef is no longer pink. Drain well. Return beef mixture to Dutch oven.

STIR in chicken broth and potatoes. Bring to a boil; cover, reduce heat, and simmer 10 to 12 minutes or until tender.

MELT 3 tablespoons butter in a nonstick skillet over medium heat. Gradually stir in flour, and cook, stirring constantly, 2 to 3 minutes or until flour is lightly browned. Whisk flour mixture into simmering beef mixture; bring to a boil. Reduce heat, and simmer 6 minutes or until thickened.

WHISK in cheese and next 3 ingredients just until cheese melts. Serve with Easy Breadsticks, if desired. **MAKES** 12 cups.

TRACEY MAXWELL
WAKE FOREST, NORTH CAROLINA

Easy Breadsticks:

Prep: 5 min., Bake: 10 min.

SEPARATE 8 hot dog buns into halves; brush halves evenly with 4 tablespoons melted butter. Cut each piece in half lengthwise and then crosswise. Place buns, buttered sides down, on a lightly greased baking sheet. Bake at 400° for 5 to 10 minutes or until golden brown. Serve breadsticks immediately. **MAKES** 64 breadsticks.

BLT WRAP

family favorite • fast fixin's

Prep: 20 min.

- 1 **cup mayonnaise**
- ½ **cup dried tomatoes in oil, drained and chopped**
- 8 **(10-inch) flour tortillas**
- 1 **large head iceberg lettuce, chopped**
- 16 **bacon slices, cooked and crumbled**
- 1 **medium onion, thinly sliced (optional)**
- 1 **teaspoon salt**
- 1 **teaspoon pepper**

COMBINE mayonnaise and tomatoes in a small bowl. Spread evenly over 1 side of each tortilla, leaving a ½-inch border.

LAYER lettuce, bacon, and, if desired, onions over tortillas; sprinkle with salt and pepper. Roll up tortillas; secure with wooden picks, and cut in half diagonally. **MAKES** 8 servings.

Christmas All Through the House

MEXICAN HOT CHOCOLATE

family favorite • fast fixin's

Prep: 10 min., Cook: 5 min.

Triple this recipe to serve in the menu for 8 people.

- 1½ (1-ounce) unsweetened chocolate baking squares
- ¾ cup water
- ¼ cup sugar
- 1 teaspoon instant coffee granules
- ½ teaspoon ground cinnamon
- Dash of salt
- 2 cups milk
- Miniature marshmallows

STIR together first 6 ingredients in a 3½-quart saucepan over medium-low heat until chocolate is melted and mixture is smooth. Cook, stirring constantly, just until mixture comes to a boil. Reduce heat, and cook, stirring constantly, 4 minutes.
STIR in milk, and cook until thoroughly heated. Whisk mixture until foamy.
POUR into mugs; top with marshmallows. **MAKES** 3 servings.

LAURI HUSS
MT. PLEASANT, SOUTH CAROLINA

CHOCOLATE-DIPPED ORANGE COOKIES

family favorite

Prep: 45 min., Chill: 1 hr., Bake: 12 min. per batch, Cool: 3 min. per batch

- 1 cup butter, softened
- ½ cup powdered sugar
- 1 teaspoon grated orange rind
- 1 teaspoon orange extract
- 2 cups all-purpose flour
- 1 (6-ounce) package semisweet chocolate morsels, melted
- ¾ cup finely chopped almonds, toasted (optional)
- ¾ cup sweetened flaked coconut, toasted (optional)

BEAT butter at medium speed with an electric mixer until creamy; gradually add powdered sugar, beating well. Stir in orange rind and extract. Gradually add flour, beating well. Cover and chill 1 hour.
DIVIDE dough in half. Cover and chill 1 portion. Divide remaining portion into 24 pieces; shape each piece into a 2½- x ½-inch log on a lightly floured surface. Repeat procedure with reserved portion. Place cookies on baking sheets, about 2 inches apart.
BAKE at 350° for 12 minutes. Cool on baking sheets 3 minutes; remove to wire racks to cool completely.
DIP tips of cookies in melted chocolate, and, if desired, chopped nuts or coconut. Place on wire racks; let stand until firm.
MAKES 4 dozen.

Bake and Share

Baked goods are terrific gifts for friends and neighbors. What better way to show your affection than with a charmingly packaged treat that you baked and wrapped by hand? Both these recipes make two cakes, so you can make one to share and one to keep.

Take disposable foil containers to the next level with one of these easy but impressive wrapping ideas. Include a copy of the recipe with the gift—your friends will want to make more of these treats.

TRIPLE-CHOCOLATE COFFEE CAKE

Prep: 15 min., Bake: 30 min.

- 1 (18.25-ounce) package devil's food cake mix
- 1 (3.9-ounce) package chocolate instant pudding mix
- 2 cups sour cream
- 1 cup butter or margarine, softened
- 5 large eggs
- 1 teaspoon vanilla extract
- 3 cups semisweet chocolate morsels, divided
- 1 cup white chocolate morsels
- 1 cup chopped pecans, toasted

BEAT first 6 ingredients at low speed with an electric mixer 30 seconds or just until moistened; beat at medium speed 2 minutes. Stir in 2 cups semisweet chocolate morsels; pour batter evenly into 2 greased and floured 9-inch square cakepans.
BAKE at 350° for 25 to 30 minutes or until a wooden pick inserted in center comes out clean. Cool completely in pans on wire racks.
MICROWAVE white chocolate morsels in a small glass bowl at HIGH 30 to 60 seconds or until morsels melt, stirring at 30-second intervals until smooth. Drizzle evenly over cakes; repeat procedure with remaining 1 cup semisweet morsels. Sprinkle cakes evenly with pecans. **MAKES** 2 (9-inch) coffee cakes.

MARCIA WHITNEY
HOUSTON, TEXAS

Festive Packaging Ideas

- From our family to yours—create personalized stickers. Use your computer to print labels with a special message, and secure to the lid.
- Don't throw away those scraps of wrapping paper. Use them to create a band around the package. Fold the sides of the paper to form a clean crease on the outer edges, and secure the ends with double-sided tape.
- Give two gifts in one. Tie an inexpensive, colorful kitchen towel around the container. Tuck in a sprig of berries for the final touch.

ORANGE- POPPY SEED BREAD

Prep: 15 min., Bake: 1 hr.

3 cups all-purpose flour
2½ cups sugar
1½ cups milk
1½ cups vegetable oil
3 large eggs
1½ tablespoons poppy seeds
1 tablespoon grated orange rind
1½ teaspoons baking powder
1½ teaspoons salt
2 teaspoons vanilla extract

BEAT all ingredients at medium speed with an electric mixer until creamy. Pour into 2 greased and floured 8- x 4-inch loafpans. **BAKE** at 350° for 1 hour or until a long wooden pick inserted in center comes out clean. Cool on wire racks 10 minutes; remove loaves from pans, and cool completely on wire racks. **MAKES** 2 loaves.

Dressed-up Gingerbread

The rich flavor and aroma of gingerbread make it a perennial fall favorite as a casual dessert or snack. But if you want a version that will wow your guests, try one of these updated recipes. Spiced Ginger Cake With Candied Cream is exceptional, thanks to fresh ginger, walnuts, and ginger-flavored whipped cream. Gingerbread Soufflés take traditional flavors to new heights. As the soufflés rise, each sports an airy, tender crown. Sassy Lemon Cream lends them a tart counterpoint. Try these, and you'll never think of gingerbread as square, brown, and boring again.

SPICED GINGER CAKE WITH CANDIED CREAM

Prep: 20 min., Bake: 50 min.

1¾ cups sugar
1½ cups vegetable oil
4 large eggs
3 large carrots, finely grated
1 cup minced fresh ginger
**   (about ½ pound)**
2 cups all-purpose flour
2 teaspoons baking powder
1½ teaspoons baking soda
¾ teaspoon salt
2½ tablespoons ground ginger
2½ teaspoons ground cinnamon
1 teaspoon ground allspice
½ teaspoon ground cloves
1½ cups chopped walnuts or
**   pecans**
Candied Cream

BEAT sugar and oil at medium speed with an electric mixer 3 minutes or until smooth. Add eggs, 1 at a time, beating well after each addition. Beat in carrots and fresh ginger.
COMBINE flour and next 7 ingredients; gradually add to egg mixture, beating at low speed until moistened. Stir in nuts.
POUR batter into a lightly greased 13- x 9-inch baking dish.
BAKE at 350° for 45 to 50 minutes or until a wooden pick inserted in center comes out clean. Cool on a wire rack; serve with Candied Cream. **MAKES** 12 servings.

Candied Cream:
fast fixin's
Prep: 5 min.

1 cup whipping cream
2 tablespoons powdered sugar
1 teaspoon vanilla extract
⅓ cup chopped candied ginger

BEAT cream at high speed with an electric mixer until foamy; gradually add sugar and vanilla, beating mixture until stiff peaks form. Stir in candied ginger. **MAKES** 2¼ cups.

MARIE A. DAVIS
CHARLOTTE, NORTH CAROLINA

GINGERBREAD SOUFFLÉS WITH LEMON CREAM

Prep: 20 min., Cook: 10 min., Cool: 20 min., Bake: 20 min.

Butter or margarine
Sugar
¼ cup butter or margarine
¼ cup all-purpose flour
1¼ cups milk
⅔ cup sugar
¼ cup molasses
2 teaspoons ground ginger
1 teaspoon ground cinnamon
¼ teaspoon salt
1 teaspoon vanilla extract
5 large eggs, separated
Lemon Cream

GREASE bottom and sides of 8 (6-ounce) custard cups evenly with butter. Lightly coat bottom and sides evenly with sugar, shaking out excess. Place cups in a 13- x 9-inch pan. Set aside.
MELT ¼ cup butter in a large saucepan over medium heat; whisk in flour. Cook, whisking constantly, 1 minute. Gradually whisk in milk, whisking constantly until thickened. Remove from heat. Whisk in ⅔ cup sugar and next 5 ingredients.
WHISK egg yolks until thick and pale. Gradually stir about one-fourth of hot mixture into yolks; add to remaining hot mixture, stirring constantly. Cook over medium heat 1 minute. Cool 20 minutes.
BEAT egg whites at high speed with an electric mixer until soft peaks form. Gradually fold egg whites into custard. Spoon evenly into custard cups.
BAKE at 400° for 18 to 20 minutes or until puffed and set. Serve immediately with Lemon Cream. **MAKES** 8 servings.

Lemon Cream:
Prep: 5 min.

1 cup whipping cream
2 tablespoons sugar
1 tablespoon grated lemon rind
1 tablespoon fresh lemon juice

BEAT whipping cream until foamy; gradually add sugar, rind, and juice, beating until soft peaks form. **MAKES** 2 cups.

Grilled Shrimp, Orange, and Watermelon Salad With
Peppered Peanuts in a Zesty Citrus Dressing, page 308

Chimichurri Cheesesteaks,
page 312

Hushpuppy-Battered Catfish
Nuggets With Spicy Tartar
Sauce, page 313

Beef Burgers With Dill Pickle Rémoulade, page 310

X-Treme Chocolate Double Nut
Caramel Ladyfinger Torte, page 315

Holiday Sampler

Sweeten the season with rich and buttery cream cheese pastries.

Cream cheese pastries are irresistibly delicious. Cranberry-pecan crescents and miniature tarts are shaped using easy-to-make dough.

Keeping the dough as cold as possible before baking is the secret to the tender and flaky texture of these bite-size treats. If the chilled dough gets too firm and difficult to roll, let it stand at room temperature for a few minutes to soften. To avoid sticking, lightly flour your work surface and rolling pin, adding just enough flour to handle the dough without overworking.

After baking, place completely cooled pastries between layers of wax paper in a zip-top plastic freezer bag or airtight container; store up to 1 week or freeze up to 1 month.

CRANBERRY-PECAN RUGALACH

freezeable • make ahead

Prep: 45 min., Chill: 8 hrs., Bake: 20 min.

We sprinkled our rugalach with sparkling sugar, but granulated sugar will work equally well. Sparkling sugar is available at stores that carry cake-decorating supplies.

- 1 cup butter, softened
- 1 (8-ounce) package cream cheese, softened
- ½ cup granulated sugar
- 2¾ cups all-purpose flour
- ½ teaspoon salt
- Cranberry-Pecan Filling
- 1 large egg, lightly beaten
- ½ cup sparkling sugar

BEAT butter and cream cheese at medium speed with an electric mixer until creamy; gradually add granulated sugar, beating until fluffy. Stir in flour and salt until blended. Divide dough into 8 equal portions; flatten each portion into a disk, and wrap each disk separately in plastic wrap. Chill 8 hours.

ROLL 1 portion of dough at a time into an 8-inch circle on a lightly floured surface. Spread with 3 tablespoons Cranberry-Pecan Filling, leaving a ½-inch border around edge. Cut circle into 8 wedges; roll up wedges, starting at wide end, to form a crescent shape. Place point side down on a lightly greased baking sheet. Brush gently with egg, and sprinkle evenly with sparkling sugar. Repeat procedure with remaining dough and filling.

BAKE at 350° on a lightly greased baking sheet for 20 minutes or until golden brown. Remove to wire racks to cool completely. **MAKES** 64 pastries.

Cranberry-Pecan Filling:
fast fixin's
Prep: 10 min.

- ¾ cup sugar
- ⅔ cup chopped pecans, toasted
- ⅔ cup finely chopped sweetened dried cranberries*
- ½ cup butter, melted
- 1½ teaspoons ground cinnamon
- ¾ teaspoon ground allspice

STIR together all ingredients until blended. **MAKES** about 1½ cups.

*Substitute ⅔ cup finely chopped dried cherries or apricots, if desired.

ANN NACE
PERKASIE, PENNSYLVANIA

COCONUT-PECAN COOKIE TARTS

freezeable • make ahead

Prep: 45 min., Chill: 1 hr., Bake: 25 min.

These tarts are very similar to pecan tassies, but with a thicker, cookie-type crust.

- 1 cup butter, softened
- 2 (3-ounce) packages cream cheese, softened
- 1 cup sweetened flaked coconut
- 2 cups all-purpose flour
- Pecan Filling

BEAT butter and cream cheese at medium speed with an electric mixer until creamy; stir in coconut. Gradually add flour to butter mixture, beating at low speed after each addition. Shape dough into 36 balls; cover and chill 1 hour. Place dough balls in lightly greased miniature muffin pans, shaping each into a thick shell. Spoon Pecan Filling evenly into tart shells.

BAKE at 350° for 15 minutes; reduce heat to 250°, and bake 10 more minutes or until filling is set. Cool in pan on a wire rack 10 minutes. Remove from pan; cool completely on wire rack. **MAKES** 3 dozen.

Pecan Filling:
fast fixin's
Prep: 5 min.

- ¾ cup firmly packed brown sugar
- ½ cup chopped pecans, toasted
- 1 large egg, lightly beaten
- 1 tablespoon butter, melted
- ½ teaspoon vanilla extract
- ⅛ teaspoon salt

WHISK together all ingredients until well blended. **MAKES** about 1 cup.

RUTH DEVEY
CHURCH HILL, TENNESSEE

from our kitchen

Pound Cake Perfection

Pound cakes are always a favorite with our Foods staff, and we were delighted to receive so many wonderful recipes from our readers (see page 278). We ended up baking for weeks, and we ate ourselves silly—each cake tasted just as delicious as the one before. Here are some of our tips for turning out a perfect pound cake.

- Carefully read through the entire recipe, and prepare any special ingredients, such as chopped fruits or toasted nuts, before starting to mix the batter.
- Prepare the recipe as directed, and use name-brand ingredients. Store brands of sugar are often more finely ground than name brands, yielding more sugar per cup, which can cause the cake to fall. Store brands of butter may contain more liquid fat and flours more hard wheat, making the cake heavy.
- Measure accurately. Extra sugar or leavening causes a cake to fall; extra flour makes it dry.
- For maximum volume, have ingredients at room temperature. We like to premeasure our ingredients, and line them up in the order listed. That way, if interrupted, we're less likely to make a mistake.
- Beat softened butter (and cream cheese or vegetable shortening) at medium speed with an electric mixer until creamy. This can take from 1 to 7 minutes, depending on the power of your mixer. Gradually add sugar, continuing to beat until light and fluffy. These steps are important because they whip air into the batter so the cake will rise during baking.
- Add the eggs 1 at a time, beating just until the yellow yolk disappears. Over-beating the eggs can cause the batter to overflow the sides of the pan when baked, or create a fragile crust that crumbles and separates from the cake as it cools.
- To prevent the batter from curdling, always add the dry ingredients alternately with the liquid, beginning and ending with the dry ingredients. Mix just until blended after each addition.

Overmixing batter once the flour has been added creates a tough, rubbery cake.
- Be sure to use the correct type of cake pan. Pound cake recipes calling for a tube pan won't always fit in a Bundt pan. (Tube pans have straight, high sides, while Bundt pans are more shallow and fluted.) Although both may measure 10 inches in diameter, each holds a different amount of batter. We also found that some 10-inch tube pans hold 12 cups of batter while others hold 14 to 16 cups. The same pound cake recipe rises and bakes differently in each pan. Although all the cakes were light and tender, the 12-cup tube pan yielded a taller, more domed cake than the larger pans. When unsure of size, use a cup measure to fill the cakepan with water.
- Grease cakepans with solid vegetable shortening and always dust with flour—a slippery surface keeps the batter from rising to its full volume.
- Use an oven thermometer to check your oven's temperature for accuracy. Many home ovens bake hotter or cooler than the temperatures to which they're set.
- Place the cake pan in the center of the oven, and keep the door closed until the minimum baking time has elapsed. If the cake requires more baking, gently close the oven door as soon as possible after testing to prevent jarring and loss of heat—both can cause a cake to fall if it's not done.
- Test for doneness by inserting a long wooden pick into the center of the cake. It should come out clean, with no batter or wet crumbs clinging to it. Some cakes will have a crack in the center that appears wet, even when fully cooked, so try to avoid this area when testing.
- After removing the cake from the oven, place it right side up in the pan on a wire rack, away from drafts, and let cool for 10 minutes. This allows the cake to become firm enough to remove from the pan without breaking. Cooling too long in the pan will cause the cake to be damp and stick to the cakepan.

Softened Butter

Recipes often call for softened butter, but exactly how soft should it be to incorporate the maximum amount of air needed for a light and tender cake? Butter will usually soften at room temperature in about 30 minutes, but the time can vary depending on the warmth of your kitchen. Before beginning your recipe, test the butter by gently pressing the top of the stick with your index finger. If an indentation remains but the stick of butter still holds its shape (see the center stick in the photo below), it's perfectly softened. The butter on the left is still too firm, while the butter on the right has become too soft. Avoid softening butter in the microwave because it can melt too quickly and unevenly.

Mixing It Up

Stand mixers are usually sold with three different attachments, each with a unique function. The dough hook (below, left) makes quick work of mixing and kneading yeast breads. The wire whisk attachment (center) is terrific for whipping egg whites or cream, as well as emulsifying homemade mayonnaise and salad dressing. The flat paddle attachment is used for general mixing, including cake batter and cookie dough. This is the attachment you'll want to use when making a pound cake.

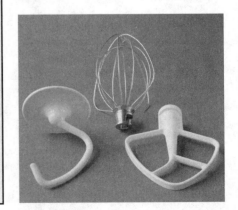

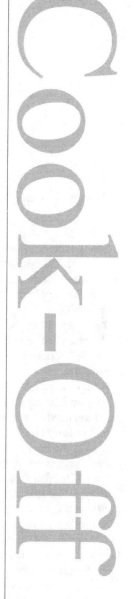

Cook-Off 2004 Winners

The third annual Cook-Off showcased winning recipes and Southern hospitality.

Finally, there were only 15 finalists and their 15 fabulous recipes. It was an unbelievable weekend of exciting competition and sincere comradery. Here's a "taste" of some of the memorable experiences.

Thursday: The finalists arrived in Birmingham and were driven to the offices of *Southern Living* magazine for a reception and tour.

Friday: This was "judging day." All 15 recipes were prepared by the finalists and tasted and rated by a panel of judges.

Saturday: The finalists enjoyed a brunch at the headquarters of *Southern Living*, then headed off to participate in the big show. This year welcomed a new contest host, Tyler Florence, one of TV Food Network's well-known and popular personalities. Finally, after each contestant prepared his or her dish with the assistance of a *Southern Living* food expert, the winners of each of the five categories were announced. Then, the moment everyone had waited for arrived. The 2004 Cook-Off winner was revealed and a very elated Linda Rohr of Westport, Connecticut, stepped forward to accept the grand prize of $100,000.

HEALTHY AND GOOD FOR YOU

GRAND PRIZE WINNER

HEALTHY AND GOOD FOR YOU
Category Winner

PAM® NO-STICK COOKING SPRAY
Brand Winner

GRILLED SHRIMP, ORANGE, AND WATERMELON SALAD WITH PEPPERED PEANUTS IN A ZESTY CITRUS DRESSING

Prep: 1 hr., Bake: 12 min., Cook: 2 min., Grill: 4 min.

If using wooden skewers, soak them in water at least 30 minutes to prevent them from burning on the grill. *(pictured on page 301)*

- ½ cup coarsely chopped dry-roasted peanuts
- ½ teaspoon CRISCO Pure Canola Oil
- ½ teaspoon sugar
- ½ teaspoon pepper
- ¼ teaspoon MORTON Salt
- 2 cups fully cooked, frozen, shelled edamame (green soybeans), thawed*
- 16 unpeeled, jumbo fresh shrimp
- 4 metal or wooden skewers
- 5 SUNKIST Oranges, divided
- ½ cup hoisin sauce
- ½ cup fresh lime juice
- 2 garlic cloves, minced
- 1 teaspoon minced fresh ginger
- PAM No-Stick Cooking Spray
- MORTON Salt to taste
- Pepper to taste
- 6 cups loosely packed torn red leaf lettuce (about 6 ounces)
- 2 (4-ounce) bags watercress, stems removed
- 2 pounds red seedless watermelon, peeled and cut into ½-inch cubes (about 4 cups cubes)
- 4 green onions, thinly sliced
- ¼ cup chopped fresh cilantro
- ¼ cup chopped fresh basil

Judges' Notes

"The grand prize winner, Grilled Shrimp, Orange, and Watermelon Salad With Peppered Peanuts in a Zesty Citrus Dressing, is a clear winner," stated *Southern Living* Foods Editor Scott Jones, chief judge for the Cook-Off. "The recipe is a perfect representation of the Healthy and Good for You category, each and every component working together to make it tops. Lots of color made for a beautiful visual while the combination of shrimp, endamame, watermelon, peanuts, and orange made for a wonderful texture. In fact, the flavor combination was out of this world—each ingredient joining up to make remarkable complements and contrasts."

TOSS together first 5 ingredients in a small bowl, and spread peanut mixture in a single layer on a baking sheet.
BAKE at 400° for 10 to 12 minutes, stirring once. Cool.
COOK edamame in boiling water to cover 2 minutes or until crisp-tender; drain. Plunge into ice water to stop the cooking process; drain and set aside.
PEEL shrimp, leaving tails on; devein, if desired. Thread 4 shrimp onto each skewer. Set aside.
PEEL 4 oranges, and cut each into 6 (½-inch-thick) slices; set slices aside.
GRATE remaining orange to equal ½ teaspoon grated rind in a small bowl; squeeze juice from orange into bowl. Add hoisin sauce and next 3 ingredients to bowl, and stir until blended. Remove 2 tablespoons citrus dressing, and brush evenly on shrimp. Reserve remaining dressing.
COAT cold cooking grate with cooking spray, and place on grill over medium-high heat (350° to 400°). Place shrimp skewers on grate, and grill 2 minutes on each side or just until done. Salt and pepper to taste.
ARRANGE lettuce and watercress on 4 serving plates, and top evenly with edamame, orange slices, watermelon, and green onions. Top each salad with 4 shrimp. Sprinkle each salad evenly with cilantro, basil, and peanut mixture; drizzle with reserved citrus dressing. **MAKES** 4 servings.

*Substitute 2 cups uncooked fresh green shelled soybeans for frozen, if desired. Boil soybeans in lightly salted water to cover 15 to 20 minutes or until crisp-tender; drain. Plunge into ice water to stop the cooking process; drain. Proceed with recipe as directed. Edamame may also be found fully cooked and ready to eat in the produce section of most supermarkets.

LINDA ROHR
WESTPORT, CONNECTICUT

Per serving: Calories 494 (34% from fat); Fat 19g (sat 4g, mono 0.8g, poly 1g); Protein 25.2g; Carb 64g; Fiber 9.4g; Chol 44mg; Iron 4.5mg; Sodium 871mg**; Calc 263mg

**Analysis does not include added salt to taste.

DOMINO® SUGAR *Brand Winner*

POLYNESIAN PORK TENDERLOIN WITH ORANGE-CURRY SAUCE AND COCONUT RICE

Prep: 30 min., Chill: 1 hr., Cook: 14 min., Cool: 10 min., Grill: 22 min., Stand: 10 min.

To reduce sodium, prepare recipe with lite soy sauce and reduced-sodium chicken broth.

- 1 (8-ounce) can pineapple slices in juice
- ½ cup soy sauce
- ¼ cup DOMINO Light Brown Sugar
- 2 tablespoons minced fresh ginger, divided
- 1½ tablespoons red curry paste, divided
- 2 (¾-pound) pork tenderloins, trimmed
- 2 SUNKIST Oranges
- PAM No-Stick Cooking Spray
- 1 tablespoon minced fresh garlic
- 1 bunch green onions (white bottoms and light green parts of tops only), minced and divided
- 1 cup SWANSON Chicken Broth
- ½ cup bottled roasted red bell peppers, chopped
- ¼ cup light chive and onion cream cheese
- 2 (3.5-ounce) bags SUCCESS White Rice
- Freshly ground pepper
- 1 SUNKIST Orange, cut into 8 wedges
- ½ cup sweetened flaked coconut
- MORTON Salt to taste

DRAIN pineapple, reserving juice. Set pineapple slices aside.
WHISK together reserved pineapple juice, soy sauce, brown sugar, and 1 tablespoon each of ginger and curry paste. Pour mixture into a large zip-top freezer bag; add pork. Seal and chill at least 1 hour and up to 3 hours.
GRATE 2 oranges to equal 2 teaspoons grated rind; set rind aside. Squeeze juice from both oranges to equal 1 cup; set aside.
COAT a medium saucepan with cooking spray; heat saucepan over medium-high

heat. Add garlic, half of green onions, and remaining 1 tablespoon ginger, and sauté 2 minutes. Stir in reserved orange juice, broth, bell peppers, and remaining ½ tablespoon curry paste until blended. Bring to a boil, and cook 12 minutes or until mixture is reduced by half. Cool 10 minutes.
PROCESS orange juice mixture in a blender or food processor until smooth, stopping to scrape down sides. Return orange juice mixture to saucepan, and whisk in cream cheese over low heat until smooth. Keep warm.
PREPARE rice according to package directions. Keep warm.
REMOVE pork from marinade, discarding marinade. Lightly season pork with pepper.
GRILL pork, covered with grill lid, over medium-high heat (350° to 400°) 15 to 18 minutes, turning once, or until a meat thermometer inserted into thickest portion registers 150°. Remove to a cutting board, and let pork stand 10 minutes or until meat thermometer registers 155°. Cut into ¼-inch slices.
GRILL pineapple slices and orange wedges 2 minutes on each side or until lightly browned. Chop pineapple.
STIR together cooked rice, chopped pineapple, grated orange rind, coconut, and remaining green onions. Add salt and pepper to taste.
SPOON rice mixture evenly onto 4 dinner plates; top with pork slices, and drizzle with sauce. Arrange grilled orange wedges on plates. Serve with remaining sauce. **MAKES** 4 to 6 servings.

NOTE: For testing purposes only, we used Thai Kitchen Red Curry Paste.

JAMIE MILLER
MAPLE GROVE, MINNESOTA

Per serving (4 large): Calories 633 (25% from fat); Fat 17.5g (sat 8.2g, mono 5g, poly 1.6g); Protein 46g; Carb 72g; Fiber 4.4g; Chol 125mg; Iron 3.9mg; Sodium 1297mg*; Calc 99mg

Per serving (6): Calories 422 (25% from fat); Fat 11.7g (sat 5.5g, mono 3.3g, poly 1g); Protein 31g; Carb 48g; Fiber 2.9g; Chol 83mg; Iron 2.6mg; Sodium 865mg*; Calc 66mg

*Analysis does not include added salt to taste.

CARIBBEAN CATFISH WITH SPICY ISLAND SWEET POTATOES

Prep: 30 min., Cook: 27 min., Broil: 8 min.

- **7 tablespoons fresh lime juice, divided**
- **6 tablespoons dark molasses**
- **2 tablespoons lite soy sauce**
- **2 tablespoons minced fresh ginger**
- **¼ teaspoon ground allspice**
- **⅛ teaspoon ground red pepper**
- **3 garlic cloves, minced**
- **2 pounds sweet potatoes, peeled and shredded (about 3 medium potatoes)**
- **1 teaspoon minced canned chipotle peppers in adobo sauce**
- **1 teaspoon adobo sauce from can**
- **1 teaspoon ground cumin**
- **½ teaspoon MORTON Salt**
- **Black pepper to taste**
- **1½ tablespoons CRISCO Pure Canola Oil**
- **½ cup minced green onions**
- **REYNOLDS WRAP Heavy Duty Foil**
- **6 U.S. FARM-RAISED CATFISH fillets (about 2¼ pounds)**
- **PAM No-Stick Cooking Spray**
- **MORTON Salt to season**
- **2½ tablespoons minced fresh cilantro**
- **Garnishes: tropical flowers, fresh cilantro sprigs**

BRING 6 tablespoons lime juice, molasses, and next 5 ingredients to a boil in a small heavy saucepan over medium heat. Reduce heat to medium low, and simmer, stirring occasionally, 15 minutes or until mixture is reduced to about ½ cup; cool.

SAUTÉ sweet potatoes, next 4 ingredients, and pepper to taste in a large non-stick skillet in hot oil 6 to 7 minutes or just until tender. (Do not brown.) Stir in green onions and remaining 1 tablespoon lime juice. Remove from heat; cover with foil to keep warm.

PLACE catfish fillets on a broiler pan coated with cooking spray; season fillets with salt.

BROIL 6 inches from heat 3 minutes; brush sauce evenly on fillets, and broil 3 to 5 minutes or just until fish flakes with a fork.

SPOON sweet potato mixture evenly onto 6 serving plates; top each with 1 catfish fillet. Sprinkle minced cilantro evenly over fillets. Garnish, if desired. **MAKES** 6 servings.

CAMILLA SAULSBURY
BLOOMINGTON, INDIANA

Per serving: Calories 314 (25% from fat); Fat 8.7g (sat 1.5g, mono 3.5g, poly 2.6g); Protein 30g; Carb 30g; Fiber 2.6g; Chol 99mg; Iron 3.8mg; Sodium 517mg*; Calc 156mg

*Analysis does not include added salt to taste.

KIDS LOVE IT!

KIDS LOVE IT!
Category Winner

JIMMY DEAN® PORK SAUSAGE
Brand Winner

BEEF BURGERS WITH DILL PICKLE RÉMOULADE

Prep: 15 min., Cook: 14 min.

Virginia Jones loves to make a traditional Rémoulade recipe. She developed this one that pairs nicely with burgers. *(pictured on page 303)*

- **1 pound Lean Ground U.S. BEEF**
- **½ pound JIMMY DEAN Pork Sausage**
- **⅓ cup grated carrot**
- **¼ cup finely chopped onion**
- **2 tablespoons chopped fresh parsley**
- **2 tablespoons dill pickle relish**
- **2 tablespoons Dijon mustard**
- **¼ teaspoon MORTON Salt**
- **¼ teaspoon pepper**
- **PAM No-Stick Cooking Spray**
- **Dill Pickle Rémoulade**
- **6 seeded hamburger buns, split and lightly toasted**
- **6 Swiss cheese slices**
- **6 cooked bacon slices**
- **Toppings: green leaf lettuce, sliced ripe tomatoes, thin Vidalia onion slices**

COMBINE first 9 ingredients in a large bowl. Shape into 6 patties.

COOK patties over medium heat in a large skillet or on a griddle coated with cooking spray 5 to 7 minutes on each side or until done.

SPREAD Dill Pickle Rémoulade on cut sides of each bun half; layer bottoms with hamburgers, cheese slices, bacon slices, and desired toppings. Top with top halves of buns. **MAKES** 6 servings.

Judges' Notes for Kids Love It!

"I, as well as the other judges, thought that the Beef Burgers With Dill Pickle Rémoulade were exceedingly moist even though they were done through and through," says Jo Ellen O'Hara, judge at the 2004 Cook-Off and Food Editor of the *Birmingham News*. "We attributed the moistness to the minced carrots and other vegetables that were included in the meat patties. Also, the Dill Pickle Rémoulade was very flavorful. Everything added up to just a real fine burger."

Dill Pickle Rémoulade:
Prep: 5 min.

- ½ cup HELLMANN'S Real Mayonnaise
- ¼ cup dill pickle relish, drained
- 1 tablespoon Dijon mustard
- ¼ teaspoon paprika

STIR together all ingredients until blended; cover and chill until ready to serve. **MAKES** ¾ cup.

VIRGINIA MOON
HARVEST, ALABAMA

HUNT'S® CANNED TOMATOES
Brand Winner

SWEET 'N' SOUR CHICKEN

Prep: 25 min., Cook: 30 min.,
Fry: 5 min. per batch

- 1 (8-ounce) can crushed pineapple
- 1½ cups DOMINO Granulated Sugar
- 1 (14½-ounce) can HUNT'S Petite Diced Tomatoes, undrained
- ½ cup white vinegar
- ½ cup finely chopped onion
- ½ cup finely chopped green bell pepper
- 1 tablespoon soy sauce
- ¼ teaspoon ground ginger
- 1 tablespoon cornstarch
- 2 cups all-purpose flour
- 2 cups cornstarch
- 4 teaspoons baking powder
- 4 teaspoons baking soda
- 4 teaspoons DOMINO Granulated Sugar
- 2⅔ cups cold water
- CRISCO Vegetable Oil
- 3 pounds skinned and boned chicken breasts, cut into 1-inch pieces
- Hot cooked SUCCESS Rice

DRAIN pineapple, reserving juice.
COMBINE drained pineapple, 1½ cups sugar, and next 6 ingredients in a medium saucepan, and bring to a boil over medium heat. Reduce heat, and simmer, stirring occasionally, 20 minutes.

STIR together 1 tablespoon cornstarch and reserved pineapple juice in a small bowl until smooth; add to tomato mixture in saucepan, and bring to a boil. Boil, stirring constantly, 2 minutes or until slightly thickened; remove from heat.
STIR together flour and next 5 ingredients in a large bowl until smooth.
ADD oil to a large frying pan or Dutch oven to a depth of 1½ inches; heat oil to 375°. Dip chicken pieces in batter, and drop into hot oil a few at a time. Fry 5 minutes or until golden brown and juices run clear. Serve immediately with sauce over hot rice. **MAKES** 8 to 10 servings.

HARRIET VALLEN
AMERICAN FORK, UTAH

U.S. FARM-RAISED CATFISH
Brand Winner

BAJA-STYLE FRIED CATFISH TACOS

Prep: 20 min., Fry: 6 min. per batch

- ¾ cup all-purpose flour
- ½ teaspoon MORTON Salt
- ¼ teaspoon pepper
- ¼ teaspoon garlic powder
- 24 ounces U.S. FARM-RAISED CATFISH fillets, cut into 4- x ½-inch strips
- CRISCO Canola Oil
- VIVA Paper Towels
- 12 MISSION Super Size Corn Tortillas, warmed
- ¼ head red cabbage, thinly sliced
- Pico de Gallo
- 3 limes, cut into wedges
- Creamy Jalapeño-Cilantro Dressing

COMBINE first 4 ingredients; dredge catfish in flour mixture.
POUR oil to a depth of ½ inch in a large skillet, and heat to 375°. Fry catfish in batches, in hot oil, 2 to 3 minutes on each side or until lightly browned. Drain on a wire rack over paper towels.

PLACE catfish on warmed tortillas; top with cabbage and Pico de Gallo. Squeeze lime juice over tacos, and drizzle with Creamy Jalapeño-Cilantro Dressing. **MAKES** 12 tacos.

Pico de Gallo:
Prep: 20 min.

- 1 large tomato, coarsely chopped
- ½ large red onion, coarsely chopped
- 1 cup loosely packed fresh cilantro leaves, coarsely chopped
- 1 jalapeño pepper, finely chopped
- ¼ teaspoon MORTON Salt
- ¼ teaspoon pepper

STIR together all ingredients. **MAKES** 2½ cups.

Creamy Jalapeño-Cilantro Dressing:
Prep: 10 min.

- 1 cup loosely packed fresh cilantro leaves
- 1 cup sour cream
- 1 large jalapeño pepper, seeded and cut into large pieces
- 2 tablespoons fresh lime juice
- 4 teaspoons powdered Ranch dressing mix
- ⅛ teaspoon MORTON Salt

PLACE all ingredients in blender; blend just until combined. (Dressing should be slightly chunky.) Cover and chill until ready to serve. **MAKES** 1¼ cups.

SUSAN RILEY
ALLEN, TEXAS

EASY ENTRÉES

EASY ENTRÉES
Category Winner

SARA LEE® BAKERY BREADS
Brand Winner

CHIMICHURRI CHEESESTEAKS

Prep: 20 min., Cook: 15 min., Grill: 24 min.

Julie Dematteo lives in "cheesesteak country," where she got the inspiration for this recipe. *(pictured on page 302)*

- **2 cups packed fresh flat-leaf parsley leaves (about 2 bunches)**
- **4 garlic cloves, chopped**
- **¼ cup lemon juice**
- **2 tablespoons extra-virgin olive oil**
- **1¾ teaspoons MORTON Salt, divided**
- **1¼ teaspoons pepper, divided**
- **4 cups thinly sliced sweet onion (about 2)**
- **2 tablespoons CRISCO Vegetable Oil**
- **1½ pounds U.S. BEEF Boneless Chuck-Eye Steaks (¾ to 1 inch thick)**
- **4 to 6 SARA LEE Center-Split Deli Rolls**
- **¼ pound thinly sliced provolone cheese**
- **REYNOLDS WRAP Heavy Duty Foil**

PULSE parsley and garlic in a blender or food processor just until finely chopped. (Do not puree.) Remove to a medium bowl, and stir in lemon juice, olive oil, ¾ teaspoon salt, and ¾ teaspoon pepper; set aside.

COOK onion and ½ teaspoon salt in hot vegetable oil over medium-high heat, stirring often, 15 minutes or until onions are golden brown and tender.

SPRINKLE steaks evenly with remaining ½ teaspoon salt and remaining ½ teaspoon pepper.

GRILL, covered with grill lid, over medium-high heat (350° to 400°) 7 to 10 minutes on each side or to desired degree of doneness.

GRILL cut sides of rolls during the last few minutes of cooking steaks. Remove steaks and rolls.

CUT steaks into thin slices. Spread parsley mixture evenly on cut sides of bread; place steak slices and onion evenly on bottom bread halves, and top each evenly with cheese and remaining bread halves. Wrap each sandwich in foil. Grill, covered with grill lid, 3 to 4 minutes or until cheese melts. **MAKES** 4 to 6 servings.

JULIE DEMATTEO
CLEMENTON, NEW JERSEY

EASY SPANISH PORK DIP SANDWICHES

Prep: 20 min., Cook: 6 hrs.

- **1 (4- to 5-pound) boneless pork butt roast**
- **3 tablespoons garlic pepper**
- **2 teaspoons MORTON Salt**
- **¼ cup CRISCO Vegetable Oil**
- **12 ounces mojo criollo Spanish marinating sauce**
- **2 (0.75-ounce) envelopes pork gravy mix**
- **2 cups water**
- **¼ cup white vinegar**
- **2 bay leaves**
- **1 medium-size sweet onion, thinly sliced**
- **1 fresh Cuban bread loaf**

RINSE roast, and cut in half. Sprinkle pepper and salt evenly on halves. Cook roast in hot oil in a large skillet 2 minutes on each side or until lightly browned. Place roast halves in a 6-quart slow cooker, fat sides up.

COMBINE Spanish marinating sauce and next 3 ingredients; pour over roast in slow cooker. Add bay leaves, and top with sliced onions.

COVER and cook on HIGH 1 hour. Reduce heat to LOW, and cook 4 to 5 hours or until meat is tender and shreds easily. Discard bay leaves.

REMOVE pork and onions to a large bowl, reserving liquid; shred meat. Add 1 cup reserved liquid to shredded pork to moisten.

SLICE bread into 8 equal portions; slice each portion in half lengthwise. Place shredded pork on bottom bread slices; top with remaining bread slices.

SPOON reserved liquid into individual bowls for dipping. **MAKES** 8 sandwiches.

NOTE: For testing purposes only, we used La Lechonera Mojo Criollo Spanish Marinating Sauce.

LAURA E. TAYLOR
BUFORD, GEORGIA

RALPH H. "SKIP" TOMPKINS
BUSHNELL, FLORIDA

Judges' Notes

Warm and juicy Chimichurri Cheesesteaks are reminiscent of that famous sandwich said to have originated in Philadelphia. The contestant used an inexpensive cut of steak but one would never know. It's grilled to perfection and paired with just the right ingredients, making this a hearty and delicious sandwich. It's perfect for a weeknight supper or an informal gathering. One thing's for sure, it's destined to become a big time favorite.

TASTE OF THE SOUTH

DEEP-FRIED WHOLE PORK TENDERLOIN WITH MINT SAUCE

Prep: 20 min., Cook: 35 min., Fry: 10 min., Stand: 5 min.

- 2 tablespoons **MORTON Salt**
- 2 tablespoons garlic salt
- 2 tablespoons seasoned salt
- 2 tablespoons dried Italian seasoning
- 2 tablespoons pepper
- 1 (10½-ounce) can condensed beef broth
- 1 (10-ounce) jar mint jelly
- 1 (1½ pounds) whole pork tenderloin, trimmed
- 2 large eggs, beaten
- 2 cups all-purpose flour
- **CRISCO Corn Oil**

COMBINE first 5 ingredients in a small bowl; set aside.

WHISK together broth and jelly in a small saucepan; bring to a simmer over medium-low heat, and cook 25 minutes or until liquid coats the back of a spoon. Remove from heat; set aside.

SPRINKLE tenderloin evenly with 1 to 2 tablespoons of the salt mixture, pressing mixture into meat. Reserve remaining salt mixture for other uses. Dip seasoned tenderloin in egg; dredge in flour, coating evenly.

POUR oil to a depth of 1½ inches in a deep frying pan; heat to 360°. Place tenderloin carefully in hot oil, and fry 8 to 10 minutes or until thermometer inserted into tenderloin reaches 155°. Drain on a wire rack over paper towels. Let stand 5 minutes or until thermometer registers 160°. Cut tenderloin diagonally into ½-inch-thick slices. Serve with sauce. **MAKES** 2 servings.

FUDGY BRABHAM
MOUNT PLEASANT, SOUTH CAROLINA

HUSHPUPPY-BATTERED CATFISH NUGGETS WITH SPICY TARTAR SAUCE

Prep: 30 min., Stand: 5 min., Fry: 8 min. per batch

Surprisingly, Christa Tomlin isn't a fish lover. That's why she chose this recipe—she wanted one everyone would love. (*pictured on page 302*)

- 1 (8-ounce) package hushpuppy mix
- ½ cup milk
- ½ cup water
- 1 large egg, beaten
- 1 tablespoon sliced pickled jalapeño peppers, minced
- 1 tablespoon hot sauce
- ½ teaspoon ground red pepper
- 2 cups **CRISCO Vegetable Oil**
- 1¼ pounds **U.S. FARM-RAISED CATFISH fillets** (about 4 fillets)
- **VIVA Paper Towels**
- 1 cup all-purpose flour
- **Spicy Tartar Sauce**

STIR together first 7 ingredients in a medium bowl; let stand 5 minutes.

POUR oil in a large deep skillet over medium heat (oil should be to a depth of ½ inch in skillet); heat oil to 350°.

PAT catfish fillets dry with paper towels, and cut into bite-size pieces. Dredge catfish pieces in flour, and then dip in hushpuppy batter mixture. Drop catfish pieces into hot oil, and fry in batches 3 to 4 minutes on each side or until golden. Serve with Spicy Tartar Sauce. **MAKES** 4 servings.

Spicy Tartar Sauce:
Prep: 5 min.

- 1 cup **HELLMANN'S Real Mayonnaise**
- 1 tablespoon sliced pickled jalapeño peppers, finely minced
- 1 tablespoon finely minced onion
- 1 garlic clove, finely minced
- 1 teaspoon hot sauce
- ½ teaspoon lemon juice
- ¼ teaspoon chili powder
- 1 pinch **MORTON Salt**

STIR together all ingredients in a medium bowl. Cover and chill until ready to serve. **MAKES** about 1 cup.

CHRISTA TOMLIN
WINDER, GEORGIA

Judges' Notes

Chris Hastings, another judge at the 2004 Cook-Off and an award-winning chef and owner of Hot and Hot Fish Club, states, "I chose the Hushpuppy-Battered Catfish Nuggets With Spicy Tartar Sauce because of the ease of preparation and the simplicity. The next thing that caught my eye was the quality of frying—the consistency of the batter was perfect. Finally, it was the flavor combination of the catfish, the batter, and the Spicy Tartar Sauce. I was impressed that such a simple dish had such a great flavor." Mary Allen Perry, judge and Associate Foods Editor states, "I thought this recipe was truly clever—great twists on Southern favorites. The nuggets were perfectly fried. This recipe is sure to be a hit with kids and adults alike."

GREEN TOMATO GUMBO

Prep: 45 min.; Cook: 1 hr., 20 min.

- **¾ cup CRISCO Vegetable Oil**
- **¾ cup all-purpose flour**
- **1 medium-size green bell pepper, finely chopped**
- **2 medium-size yellow onions, finely chopped**
- **2 celery ribs, finely chopped**
- **4 jalapeño peppers, finely chopped**
- **6 garlic cloves, minced**
- **1 tablespoon green hot sauce**
- **4 tablespoons fresh lime juice**
- **1 tablespoon Cajun seasoning**
- **3 (14-ounce) cans SWANSON Natural Goodness Chicken Broth**
- **4 pounds green tomatoes, cored and chopped**
- **1 pound New Orleans-style smoked sausage, cut in ¼-inch-thick slices**
- **2 bay leaves**
- **MORTON Kosher Salt to taste**
- **Freshly ground pepper to taste**
- **1 (16-ounce) package frozen cut okra**
- **2⅔ cups uncooked MAHATMA Extra Long Grain White Rice**
- **1 pound unpeeled, medium-size fresh shrimp**
- **1 cup fresh cilantro, coarsely chopped**
- **1 tablespoon filé powder**
- **8 precooked hickory-smoked bacon slices, crumbled**
- **Garnish: fresh cilantro sprigs**

HEAT oil in a large Dutch oven over high heat; gradually whisk in flour, and cook, whisking constantly, 5 minutes or until flour is the color of a copper penny. (Do not burn mixture.)

REDUCE heat to medium; stir in bell pepper and next 7 ingredients, and cook, stirring constantly, 3 minutes. Stir in chicken broth and next 3 ingredients. Increase heat to medium high, and bring to a boil. Reduce heat to low, and simmer, uncovered, stirring occasionally,

45 minutes. Remove and discard bay leaves. Skim off fat with a spoon. Season with salt and pepper. Stir in okra, and cook, stirring occasionally, 15 minutes.

PREPARE rice according to package directions; set aside.

PEEL shrimp, and devein, if desired.

STIR in shrimp, chopped cilantro, and filé powder; cook 5 minutes or until shrimp turn pink and are done.

SPOON ½ cup cooked rice in each of 16 serving bowls; spoon 1¼ cups gumbo over rice, and sprinkle evenly with bacon. Garnish, if desired. **MAKES** 16 servings.

NOTE: For testing purposes only, we used Johnsonville New Orleans Brand Andouille Recipe Spicy Smoked Sausage.

BARRY AND CATHY DELOZIER
BIRMINGHAM, ALABAMA

SOUTH BY SOUTHWEST CATFISH WITH GUACAMOLE AÏOLI

Prep: 20 min., Fry: 10 min. per batch

- **2 cups crushed MISSION Tortilla Chips**
- **2 large eggs**
- **1 tablespoon water**
- **⅛ teaspoon ground coriander**
- **6 U.S. FARM-RAISED CATFISH fillets (about 3 pounds)**
- **VIVA Paper Towels**
- **CRISCO Pure Canola Oil**
- **Guacamole Aïoli**
- **1 (10-ounce) can RO*TEL Original Diced Tomatoes & Green Chilies, drained**
- **Garnish: fresh cilantro sprigs**

PLACE crushed chips in a large shallow bowl. Whisk together eggs, 1 tablespoon water, and coriander in a large bowl. Pat catfish fillets dry with paper towels. Dip fillets in egg mixture, coating completely; dredge in crushed chips, coating evenly.

POUR oil to a depth of 1½ inches in a large skillet; heat to 350°. Fry catfish in hot oil, in batches, 5 minutes on each side. Drain on paper towels.

SPOON ¼ cup Guacamole Aïoli on each of 6 serving plates; top with catfish fillets. Drizzle evenly with remaining Guacamole Aïoli, and sprinkle with diced tomatoes and green chilies. Garnish, if desired. **MAKES** 6 servings.

Guacamole Aïoli:

Prep: 15 min.

- **2 large avocados**
- **⅓ cup fresh lime juice**
- **1 cup HELLMANN'S Real Mayonnaise**
- **1 (8-ounce) package PHILADELPHIA Cream Cheese, softened**
- **1 tablespoon minced garlic**
- **1 teaspoon freshly ground black pepper**
- **¼ teaspoon MORTON Salt**
- **⅓ cup chopped fresh cilantro**

CUT avocados in half. Scoop pulp into a medium bowl; mash into large chunks with a fork. Add lime juice and next 5 ingredients.

PROCESS avocado mixture with a hand-held immersion blender or mixer until smooth; stir in chopped cilantro. Cover and chill until ready to serve. **MAKES** about 3 cups.

JEANETTE SPALDING
SIMPSONVILLE, KENTUCKY

SIGNATURE DESSERTS

X-TREME CHOCOLATE DOUBLE NUT CARAMEL LADYFINGER TORTE

Prep: 30 min., Cool: 5 min., Cook: 5 min., Chill: 1 hr.

The inspiration for Kathy Specht's recipe came from a combination of her favorite flavors.
(pictured on page 304)

- 1½ cups **NESTLÉ TOLL HOUSE Semi-Sweet Chocolate Morsels**
- 2 (3-ounce) packages ladyfingers
- 1 (13-ounce) jar hazelnut spread
- 20 caramels
- 2⅓ cups whipping cream, divided
- 1½ cups chopped pecans
- ⅓ cup **DOMINO 10-X Confectioners Sugar**
- 1 (8-ounce) package **PHILADELPHIA Cream Cheese, softened**
- 2 tablespoons crème de cacao
- 3 (1-ounce) semisweet chocolate baking squares
- 2 tablespoons **DOMINO 10-X Confectioners Sugar**

MICROWAVE chocolate morsels at HIGH 90 seconds or until melted, stirring at 30-second intervals; cool 5 minutes, and set aside.

SPLIT ladyfingers, and stand halves around edge of a 9-inch springform pan, placing rounded sides against pan; line bottom of pan with remaining halves. Reserve remaining ladyfingers for other uses. Spread hazelnut spread evenly over ladyfingers on bottom of pan.

COOK caramels and ⅓ cup whipping cream in a medium saucepan over low heat, stirring constantly, just until melted. Stir in pecans until coated; spoon caramel mixture evenly over hazelnut spread.

BEAT ⅓ cup confectioners sugar and cream cheese in a medium bowl at medium speed with an electric mixer until fluffy. Add crème de cacao, and beat until blended. Beat in melted chocolate morsels until blended.

BEAT remaining 2 cups whipping cream in a medium bowl at medium speed with an electric mixer until stiff; fold into cream cheese mixture, and spoon evenly over caramel layer in pan.

SHAVE chocolate baking squares with a vegetable peeler evenly on top. Sprinkle evenly with 2 tablespoons confectioners sugar. Chill torte 1 hour. **MAKES** 12 servings.

NOTE: For testing purposes only, we used Nutella for hazelnut spread.

KATHY SPECHT
CAMBRIA, CALIFORNIA

SOUTH SEAS ICE CREAM WITH SWEET HEAT SALSA AND CINNAMON CRISPS

Prep: 30 min., Freeze: 8 hrs., Chill: 2 hrs., Bake: 10 min.

- ½ gallon vanilla ice cream, slightly softened
- 1 (15-ounce) can cream of coconut
- ¾ cup sweetened flaked coconut, lightly toasted
- ¾ cup chopped macadamia nuts
- 1 small lime
- 1½ cups chopped fresh mango
- 1½ cups chopped fresh pineapple
- 1 kiwifruit, peeled and diced
- ½ cup peeled, seeded, and chopped cucumber
- 2 tablespoons Asian sweet chili sauce
- ¼ teaspoon freshly ground black pepper
- 2 tablespoons mint leaves, chopped
- ¼ cup **DOMINO Granulated Sugar**
- 2 teaspoons ground cinnamon
- 4 (8-inch) **MISSION Soft Taco Size Flour Tortillas**
- 4 tablespoons butter, melted
- **REYNOLDS WRAP Heavy Duty Foil**

STIR together first 4 ingredients in a large bowl; freeze 8 hours or until firm.

GRATE lime rind in a large bowl; squeeze juice from lime, and combine with grated rind. Stir in mango and next 6 ingredients. Cover and chill 2 hours.

COMBINE sugar and cinnamon in a small bowl.

BRUSH 1 side of tortillas with melted butter; cut each into 8 wedges or decorative shapes using a cookie cutter. Arrange in a single layer on an aluminum foil-lined baking sheet, and sprinkle evenly with sugar mixture.

BAKE at 400° for 7 to 10 minutes or until lightly browned. Cool.

SPOON ice-cream mixture into 8 bowls; top evenly with salsa mixture, and serve with cinnamon crisps. Serve immediately. **MAKES** 8 servings.

NOTE: For testing purposes only, we used Yeo's Chili Sauce Sweet.

JANICE ELDER
CHARLOTTE, NORTH CAROLINA

Judges' Notes

X-Treme Chocolate Double Nut Caramel Ladyfinger Torte is truly a divine dessert experience. One bite of this confection and your every chocolate dream will be answered. Cream cheese, melted chocolate morsels, and whipped cream team up to make an incredibly smooth and creamy filling. And this layer makes the perfect partner to the hazelnut spread and caramel-pecan layers. Winner Kathy Specht created this fabulous recipe for the 2004 Cook-Off and knew she had a decadent chocolate creation that just had to be "signature."

PEANUT BUTTER TURTLE TORTE

Prep: 40 min.; Bake: 5 min.; Cook: 5 min.; Chill: 8 hrs., 35 min.

- **18 chocolate wafer cookies, finely crushed**
- **2 tablespoons butter, melted**
- **16 chocolate wafer cookies**
- **1½ cups NESTLÉ TOLL HOUSE Semi-Sweet Chocolate Morsels**
- **2 cups whipping cream, divided**
- **2 tablespoons butter**
- **1 cup pecan halves, toasted**
- **½ cup butterscotch-caramel topping**
- **1 (8-ounce) package PHILADELPHIA Cream Cheese, softened**
- **1 cup creamy peanut butter**
- **1¼ cups DOMINO 10-X Confectioners Sugar**

COMBINE crushed cookies and 2 tablespoons melted butter. Press mixture on bottom of a 9-inch springform pan. Stand 16 cookies around edge of pan, slightly overlapping and pressing into crumb mixture on bottom of pan. Bake cookie crust at 350° for 5 minutes; cool.

STIR together morsels, ½ cup whipping cream, and 2 tablespoons butter in a small saucepan over medium-low heat, and cook, stirring constantly, until chocolate melts and mixture is smooth. Remove 2 tablespoons chocolate mixture, and place in a small zip-top plastic bag. Pour remaining chocolate mixture evenly over cookie crust in pan, and chill 30 minutes or until chocolate layer is firm.

ARRANGE pecans in an even layer on chocolate layer in pan. Spread butterscotch-caramel topping evenly over pecans, starting from center, leaving a 1-inch border around sides of crust. Chill at least 5 minutes.

BEAT cream cheese, peanut butter, and confectioners sugar at medium-high speed with an electric mixer until well blended. Increase speed to high, and gradually add remaining 1½ cups cream, beating 1½ minutes or until mixture is thick and creamy.

SPREAD cream cheese mixture over caramel layer. Snip a tiny hole in 1 corner of chocolate-filled zip-top bag, and drizzle chocolate over mixture in pan. Cover and chill at least 8 hours or overnight.

REMOVE sides of pan just before serving; serve immediately. **MAKES** 12 to 16 servings.

NOTE: For testing purposes only, we used Nabisco Famous Chocolate Wafers and Mrs. Richardson's Butterscotch Caramel Topping.

LISA KEYS
MIDDLEBURY, CONNECTICUT

BRAND WINNERS

These recipes won recognition for best use of a sponsor's product.

MOSTACCIOLI CASSEROLE

Prep: 15 min., Cook: 23 min., Bake: 30 min.

- **3 cups uncooked BARILLA Mostaccioli or Penne Pasta**
- **1 pound JOHNSONVILLE Italian Sausage, casings removed**
- **1 (26-ounce) jar pasta sauce**
- **1 cup HUNT'S canned Diced Tomatoes, undrained**
- **1 garlic clove, crushed**
- **1 tablespoon dried parsley flakes**
- **1 tablespoon DOMINO Brownulated Sugar**
- **1 teaspoon dried Italian seasoning**
- **½ teaspoon dried oregano**
- **Fresh ground pepper to taste**
- **2 cups (8 ounces) shredded colby-Monterey Jack cheese blend**

PREPARE pasta according to package directions; drain, rinse, and set aside.

COOK sausage in a large skillet, stirring until it crumbles and is no longer pink. Drain well, and return to skillet. Add pasta sauce and next 7 ingredients.

BRING sausage mixture to a boil over high heat; reduce heat to medium low, and simmer 15 minutes. Stir in cooked pasta and 1¾ cups shredded cheese; pour into a 2-quart baking dish. Sprinkle casserole evenly with remaining ¼ cup cheese.

BAKE, covered, 20 minutes at 350°; uncover and bake 5 to 10 minutes or until cheese is melted and bubbly. **MAKES** 4 to 6 servings.

NOTE: For testing purposes only, we used Newman's Own Tomato, Peppers + Spices Sockarooni Pasta Sauce.

JANEL LANDON
CHICAGO, ILLINOIS

SOUTHERN SPINACH SALAD WITH CHEESE GRITS CROUTONS AND VIDALIA ONION-BALSAMIC VINAIGRETTE

Prep: 10 min., Cook: 10 min., Chill: 2 hrs., Fry: 20 min.

- **1 (14-ounce) can SWANSON Chicken Broth**
- **½ cup uncooked quick-cooking grits**
- **1 (3-ounce) package PHILADELPHIA Cream Cheese, cubed**
- **½ cup KRAFT 100% Grated Parmesan Cheese**
- **PAM No-Stick Cooking Spray**
- **½ cup all-purpose flour**
- **2 tablespoons butter, divided**
- **2 tablespoons olive oil, divided**
- **1 (6-ounce) bag prewashed baby spinach**
- **1 cup cherry or grape tomatoes, halved**
- **Vidalia Onion-Balsamic Vinaigrette**
- **6 bacon slices, cooked and crumbled**

BRING chicken broth to a boil over medium-high heat in a medium saucepan. Gradually stir in grits; reduce heat to low, and simmer, stirring constantly, 5 minutes or until thickened. Remove from heat. Stir in cream cheese and Parmesan cheese until melted.

POUR grits mixture into an 8-inch square pan coated with cooking spray; spread evenly. Chill 2 hours or until firm.

CUT grits into 1-inch cubes with a wet knife. Dredge cubes in flour.

MELT 1 tablespoon butter in a large skillet over medium heat; add 1 tablespoon oil. Fry half of cubes in hot oil and butter 10 minutes, turning once to lightly brown. Repeat procedure with remaining cubes, 1 tablespoon butter, and 1 tablespoon oil.

PLACE spinach in a large serving bowl; add tomatoes. Drizzle Vidalia Onion-Balsamic Vinaigrette evenly over salad; toss to coat. Add grits croutons, and sprinkle evenly with crumbled bacon. **MAKES** 4 servings.

Vidalia Onion-Balsamic Vinaigrette:
Prep: 10 min.

- 2 tablespoons balsamic vinegar
- 2 tablespoons honey
- 1 teaspoon Dijon mustard
- ½ teaspoon MORTON Salt
- ¼ teaspoon pepper
- 3 tablespoons finely chopped Vidalia onion
- 4 tablespoons olive oil

STIR together first 5 ingredients in a small bowl; stir in onion. Whisk in olive oil, 1 tablespoon at a time, until well blended. **MAKES** about 1 cup.

LAURIE PEARCE
NASHVILLE, TENNESSEE

SUNKIST® *Brand Winner*

AMBROSIA SORBET

Prep: 10 min., Cook: 5 min., Chill: 2 hrs., Freeze: 20 min.

- 11 to 12 SUNKIST Oranges
- 2 cups water
- 1 cup DOMINO Granulated Sugar
- 1 cup cream of coconut

GRATE orange rind in a small bowl to equal 2 teaspoons; set aside. Cut oranges in half, and squeeze halves to equal 3 cups juice; set aside.

BRING 2 cups water and sugar to a boil in a large saucepan over high heat. Cook, stirring constantly, 3 minutes or just until sugar dissolves; remove from heat, and cool.

STIR in cream of coconut, juice, and grated rind; cover and chill at least 2 hours.

POUR mixture into freezer container of a 4-quart electric ice-cream maker, and freeze according to manufacturer's instructions. (Instructions and times will vary.) **MAKES** about 2 quarts.

NOTE: For testing purposes only, we used a Rival 4-quart Durable Plastic Bucket Ice Cream Maker.

KEN STONE
MELBOURNE, FLORIDA

VIVA® TOWELS *Brand Winner*

THAI-RIFIC ORANGE SCALLOP SALAD

Prep: 10 min., Bake: 5 min., Cook: 10 min.

- 4 (3-inch) square won ton wrappers
- PAM No-Stick Cooking Spray
- 2 teaspoons sesame seeds
- ⅓ cup sliced shallots
- 4 teaspoons CRISCO Pure Canola Oil, divided
- VIVA Paper Towels
- 12 large sea scallops
- ¼ teaspoon MORTON Kosher Salt
- ¼ teaspoon pepper
- 2 (5-ounce) packages gourmet mixed salad greens
- 2 SUNKIST Oranges, peeled and sectioned
- ½ cup diced avocado
- Salad Dressing

SPRAY both sides of won ton wrappers lightly with cooking spray; cut into ½-inch strips. Place on a baking sheet, 1 inch apart; sprinkle tops with sesame seeds.

BAKE at 375° for 4 to 5 minutes or until golden; set aside.

SAUTÉ shallots in 2 teaspoons hot canola oil in a large nonstick skillet over

medium-high heat 2 minutes or until crispy; remove shallots with a slotted spoon, and let drain on paper towels. Set aside.

PAT scallops dry with paper towels; season with salt and pepper. Cook in remaining 2 teaspoons hot oil in skillet over medium-high heat 4 minutes on each side.

PLACE greens evenly on each of 4 plates; place orange sections and avocado evenly over greens. Top each salad with 3 scallops. Drizzle evenly with Salad Dressing; top with won ton strips and shallots. **MAKES** 4 servings.

Salad Dressing:
Prep: 5 min., Cook: 2 min., Cool: 5 min.

- 1 large SUNKIST Orange
- 1 tablespoon Thai fish sauce
- 2 teaspoons DOMINO Granulated Sugar
- 1 teaspoon minced garlic
- 1 teaspoon minced fresh ginger
- 1½ teaspoons toasted sesame oil
- 2 teaspoons Chinese hot mustard
- ¼ cup chopped fresh mint

GRATE orange rind in a small saucepan to equal 1 teaspoon grated rind. Cut orange in half, and squeeze juice into saucepan.

WHISK in fish sauce and next 4 ingredients, and cook, whisking constantly, over medium heat 2 minutes. Remove pan from heat; whisk in mustard and mint, and let cool 5 minutes or until slightly cool. **MAKES** about ⅓ cup.

MARGEE BERRY
WHITE SALMON, WASHINGTON

VEG·ALL® CANNED MIXED VEGETABLES *Brand Winner*

CHICKEN-HERB STRUDEL WITH WHITE WINE GRAVY

Prep: 25 min., Cook: 6 min., Bake: 25 min.

- **1 (17.3-ounce) package frozen puff pastry**
- **3 tablespoons butter**
- **3 tablespoons all-purpose flour**
- **½ teaspoon MORTON Salt**
- **⅛ teaspoon ground dried thyme**
- **⅛ teaspoon pepper**
- **1 (14-ounce) can SWANSON Chicken Broth**
- **½ cup dry white wine**
- **½ cup half-and-half**
- **3 cups chopped cooked boneless skinless chicken breast**
- **1 (15-ounce) can VEG·ALL Original Mixed Vegetables, drained**
- **PAM No-Stick Cooking Spray**

THAW puff pastry according to package directions.

MELT butter in a medium saucepan over medium heat; stir in flour and next 3 ingredients. Cook, stirring constantly, 1 minute or until smooth. Gradually add broth, wine, and half-and-half. Bring to a boil, and cook, stirring constantly, 3 to 5 minutes or until mixture is thickened.

REMOVE ½ cup gravy from pan. Keep remaining gravy in pan warm over low heat, stirring occasionally.

STIR together ½ cup gravy, chicken, and mixed vegetables in a large bowl; set aside.

COAT a baking sheet with cooking spray. Unfold 1 pastry sheet, and place on the right half of prepared baking sheet. Unfold remaining pastry sheet, and place on the left half of baking sheet, overlapping by ½ inch over pastry sheet on pan. Press overlapping portion to seal seam.

SPOON chicken mixture lengthwise in a 4-inch strip down center of pastry, leaving a 2-inch border at ends. Cut slits 1-inch apart on long sides of pastry, cutting to within ½ inch of chicken mixture. Fold and cross pastry strips over chicken mixture, alternating sides for a braided appearance. Fold 2-inch pastry border at each end over, and gently press to seal ends.

BAKE at 400° for 20 to 25 minutes or until golden brown. Serve with warm gravy. **MAKES** 6 servings.

BETSY DELL
FAIRPORT, NEW YORK

BUSH'S® BEANS *Brand Winner*

FAJITA CHICKEN PIZZA WITH MANGO PICO DE GALLO

Prep: 10 min., Bake: 10 to 13 min. per pizza

- **2 cups Mango Pico de Gallo, divided**
- **1 (15-ounce) can BUSH'S BEST Black Beans, drained**
- **2 teaspoons garlic salt**
- **1 teaspoon ground cumin**
- **2 (12-inch) prebaked pizza crusts**
- **4 cups (16 ounces) shredded Cheddar cheese***
- **1 skinned and boned chicken breast, cooked and cubed (about 1 cup)**

REMOVE 1 to 2 tablespoons liquid from Mango Pico de Gallo, and process with beans, garlic salt, and cumin in a blender or food processor until thickened. (Sauce should be chunky.)

PLACE crusts on aluminum foil-lined baking sheets or pizza pans. Spread half of bean mixture on 1 side of each crust.

Spread half of Mango Pico de Gallo evenly on top of bean mixture on each crust; sprinkle each with 2 cups cheese. Top each with half of cooked chicken.

BAKE pizzas according to package directions or until cheese is melted and bubbly. **MAKES** 2 (12-inch) pizzas.

Mango Pico de Gallo:
Prep: 10 min., Chill: 8 hrs.

- **2 small or 1 large mango, chopped**
- **3 plum tomatoes, seeded and diced**
- **1 small white onion, diced**
- **¾ cup chopped fresh cilantro**
- **1 jalapeño pepper, seeded and chopped**
- **Juice of 1 lime**
- **1 teaspoon salt**

STIR together all ingredients in a medium bowl; cover tightly, and chill 4 to 8 hours. **MAKES** 4 cups.

NOTE: For testing purposes only, we used 1 (24-ounce) package Mama Mary's Gourmet Pizza Crusts.

*Substitute Mexican cheese blend for Cheddar cheese, if desired.

NATHAN ALDERMAN
SAN ANTONIO, TEXAS

MORE BRAND-WINNING RECIPES

- **Pam® No-Stick Cooking Spray:** Grilled Shrimp, Orange, and Watermelon Salad With Peppered Peanuts in a Zesty Citrus Dressing, page 308

- **Domino® Sugar:** Polynesian Pork Tenderloin With Orange-Curry Sauce and Coconut Rice, page 309

- **Jimmy Dean® Pork Sausage:** Beef Burgers With Dill Pickle Rémoulade, page 310

- **Hunt's® Canned Tomatoes:** Sweet 'n' Sour Chicken, page 311

- **U.S. Farm-Raised Catfish:** Baja-Style Fried Catfish Tacos, page 311

- **Sara Lee® Bakery Breads:** Chimichurri Cheesesteaks, page 312

- **Crisco® Oils, Shortening, and Cooking Sprays:** Deep-Fried Whole Pork Tenderloin With Mint Sauce, page 313

- **Hellmann's® Real Mayonnaise:** Hushpuppy-Battered Catfish Nuggets With Spicy Tartar Sauce, page 313

- **Mahatma®/Success® Rice:** Green Tomato Gumbo, page 314

- **Ro*Tel® Diced Tomato Products:** South by Southwest Catfish With Guacamole Aïoli, page 314

- **Nestlé® Toll House® Morsels:** X-Treme Chocolate Double Nut Caramel Ladyfinger Torte, page 315

- **Philadelphia® Cream Cheese:** Peanut Butter Turtle Torte, page 316

Southern Living 2004

Cooking School

Invite family and friends to the table with these doable recipes from the *Southern Living* Cooking School. They're perfect for weeknight meals as well as casual gatherings.

Three Easygoing Get-togethers

Each month of fall invites a gathering, and these casual menus will help you host a party—or three—with ease. Sizzle in September with Dinner on the Grill; welcome November's chill with a cozy Fall Supper Club; and throw a fiesta in October with a Tex-Mex Sampler Party. You can even divvy up the cooking among party guests—they, too, will love making these simple recipes.

Dinner on the Grill

Serves 4

Grilled Salmon With
Tangy Dill Sauce
or
Lime-Grilled Chicken

Grilled vegetables

Rice-Cabbage Salad
With Honey-Dijon Vinaigrette

Lemon or raspberry sorbet

GRILLED SALMON WITH TANGY DILL SAUCE

fast fixin's

Prep: 5 min., Grill: 10 min.

Colorful, grilled vegetables are a great side dish. Slice vegetables such as squash and zucchini into ¼-inch-thick slices and red bell peppers into 1-inch-wide strips. Brush each side with mayonnaise, and sprinkle with salt and pepper. Grill 2 to 4 minutes or until crisp-tender, turning once.

- **4 (8-ounce) salmon fillets**
- **½ teaspoon salt**
- **½ teaspoon pepper**
- **2 tablespoons HELLMANN'S Real Mayonnaise**
- **1 tablespoon fresh lemon juice**
- **Garnish: lemon wedges**
- **Tangy Dill Sauce**

SPRINKLE fillets evenly with salt and pepper; lightly brush with mayonnaise. **GRILL,** covered with grill lid, over medium-high heat (350° to 400°) 10 minutes or just until salmon flakes with a fork. Sprinkle with lemon juice; garnish, if desired. Serve with Tangy Dill Sauce. **MAKES** 4 servings.

Tangy Dill Sauce:
make ahead
Prep: 10 min., Chill: 1 hr.

- **½ cup sour cream**
- **½ cup HELLMANN'S Real Mayonnaise**
- **2 tablespoons chopped fresh dill**
- **¼ teaspoon grated lemon rind**
- **1 tablespoon fresh lemon juice**
- **½ teaspoon ground red pepper**
- **Garnish: fresh dill sprig**

STIR together all ingredients. Cover and chill at least 1 hour. **MAKES** 1 cup.

LIME-GRILLED CHICKEN

family favorite

Prep: 10 min., Chill: 1 hr., Grill: 12 min.

- **⅓ cup lime juice**
- **1 tablespoon peanut oil**
- **1½ teaspoons soy sauce**
- **1 garlic clove, minced**
- **1 bay leaf**
- **4 PILGRIM'S PRIDE Skinless and Boneless Chicken Breasts**

COMBINE first 5 ingredients in a shallow dish or zip-top freezer bag; add chicken. Cover or seal, and chill 1 hour.

REMOVE chicken from marinade, discarding marinade.

GRILL, covered with grill lid, over medium-high heat (350° to 400°) 4 to 6 minutes on each side or until done. **MAKES** 4 servings.

RICE-CABBAGE SALAD WITH HONEY-DIJON VINAIGRETTE

fast fixin's • make ahead

Prep: 10 min.

- ½ cup uncooked **MAHATMA**
    Brown Rice
- ½ teaspoon salt
- 2 green onions, chopped
- 1 cup coleslaw mix
- 4 pecan halves, chopped and
    toasted
- Honey-Dijon Vinaigrette

PREPARE rice with salt according to package directions. Cool.

COMBINE rice, green onions, coleslaw mix, and pecans. Add 4 tablespoons Honey-Dijon Vinaigrette, tossing gently to coat. **MAKES** 4 servings.

NOTE: Recipe can be prepared one day in advance.

Honey-Dijon Vinaigrette:
fast fixin's • make ahead
Prep: 10 min.

Use remaining vinaigrette over salad greens or drizzled over fish.

- ⅓ cup olive oil
- 3 tablespoons fresh lemon juice
- 3 tablespoons rice wine vinegar
- 2 tablespoons honey
- 1 teaspoon Dijon mustard
- ½ teaspoon salt

PROCESS all ingredients in a blender until blended. Cover and chill until ready to serve. **MAKES** ¾ cup.

Fall Supper Club

Serves 6

Turkey Scaloppine
or
Smothered Swiss Steak
with mashed potatoes or rice

Broiled Parmesan Tomatoes

Mixed Greens With
Creamy Garlic Dressing

Bakery pecan pie à la mode

TURKEY SCALOPPINE

family favorite

Prep: 25 min., Cook: 45 min. *(pictured on page 190)*

- 1 (1.5- to 2-pound) package turkey
    tenderloins, thinly sliced
- ½ teaspoon salt, divided
- ½ cup all-purpose flour
- 2 tablespoons vegetable oil
- 2 (8-ounce) packages sliced
    mushrooms
- ¼ cup capers
- 4 garlic cloves, pressed
- 1½ cups whipping cream
- ¾ cup chicken broth
- 2 to 4 tablespoons fresh lemon juice
- 1 (1-pound) box **BARILLA** Linguine
    Pasta
- Garnishes: chopped fresh parsley,
    fresh parsley sprigs, lemon
    wedges

SPRINKLE turkey slices evenly with ¼ teaspoon salt; dredge in flour.

COOK turkey slices, in batches, in hot vegetable oil in a large nonstick skillet over medium-high heat 3 minutes on each side. Remove turkey from skillet. Add mushrooms to skillet, and sauté 7 to 9 minutes or until golden brown.

ADD capers, garlic, and remaining ¼ teaspoon salt to skillet; sauté 2 minutes. Stir in whipping cream and chicken broth; reduce heat to medium, and simmer 20 minutes or until slightly thickened. Stir in lemon juice.

COOK pasta according to package directions in a Dutch oven; drain and return to Dutch oven.

STIR turkey and mushroom-cream mixture into pasta in Dutch oven; cook until thoroughly heated. Garnish, if desired. **MAKES** 6 to 8 servings.

SMOTHERED SWISS STEAK

family favorite

Prep: 10 min.; Cook: 1 hr., 30 min.

These delicious steaks pair well with either mashed potatoes or rice.

- ½ teaspoon salt
- 6 (4-ounce) cube steaks
- ½ cup all-purpose flour
- 1 teaspoon seasoned pepper
- 4½ tablespoons vegetable oil
- 1 medium onion, diced
- 1 medium-size green bell pepper,
    diced
- 1 (14.5-ounce) can **HUNT'S** Petite
    Diced Tomatoes
- 1 (12-ounce) cola soft drink
- 1 tablespoon beef bouillon granules
- 2 tablespoons **HUNT'S** Tomato Paste

SPRINKLE salt evenly on both sides of cube steaks. Combine flour and pepper in a shallow dish. Dredge steaks in flour mixture.

BROWN 2 steaks in 1½ tablespoons hot oil in a large nonstick skillet over medium-high heat 3 minutes on each side; drain on paper towels. Repeat procedure with remaining steaks and oil. Drain drippings from skillet, reserving 1 tablespoon in skillet.

SAUTÉ onion and bell pepper in hot drippings 7 minutes or until tender.

ADD diced tomatoes and next 3 ingredients to skillet. Bring to a boil, and cook, stirring often, 5 minutes or until slightly thickened. Return steaks to skillet; cover and cook over low heat 55 to 60 minutes or until tender. **MAKES** 6 servings.

BROILED PARMESAN TOMATOES

fast fixin's

Prep: 10 min., Broil: 8 min. *(pictured on page 191)*

- ½ cup **KRAFT 100% Grated Parmesan Cheese**
- ¼ cup chopped fresh basil
- ¼ cup fine, dry breadcrumbs
- 3 bacon slices, cooked and crumbled
- 8 plum tomatoes, halved lengthwise
- ½ teaspoon salt
- ½ teaspoon freshly ground pepper
- Garnish: fresh basil sprigs

COMBINE Parmesan cheese, basil, bread-crumbs, and bacon in a small bowl.
SPRINKLE tomato halves with salt and pepper, and place on a lightly greased aluminum foil-lined baking sheet. Spoon cheese mixture evenly over tomato halves.
BROIL tomato halves 5 inches from heat 7 to 8 minutes or until topping is golden brown. Garnish, if desired. Serve tomatoes immediately. **MAKES** 8 servings.

MIXED GREENS WITH CREAMY GARLIC DRESSING

fast fixin's • make ahead

Prep: 10 min.

This zesty dressing is a great dip for hot chicken wings too—just omit the milk and salad greens.

- ½ cup **HELLMANN'S Real Mayonnaise**
- ¼ cup milk
- 3 garlic cloves, pressed
- ½ teaspoon salt
- 3 tablespoons lemon juice
- 3 tablespoons vegetable oil
- 1 tablespoon chopped fresh parsley
- 6 cups mixed salad greens

WHISK together first 7 ingredients, blending well. Cover and chill until ready to serve. Serve over mixed greens. **MAKES** 6 servings.

NOTE: Dressing can be made one day ahead. Garlic flavor intensifies as it chills.

Tex-Mex Sampler Party

Serves 6

Ranchero Catfish

Black Bean-Corn Salsa

Roasted Vegetable Quesadillas

Fiesta Chicken Soup

Margaritas

Store-bought pralines or brownies

RANCHERO CATFISH

Prep: 30 min., Bake: 12 min.

Cutting the fillets in half lengthwise shortens cooking time and yields especially tender, crisp results.

- 6 (3- to 5-ounce) **U.S. FARM-RAISED CATFISH fillets**
- 1 cup finely crushed tortilla chips
- 2 teaspoons chili powder
- ½ teaspoon salt
- ½ teaspoon pepper
- 3 tablespoons fresh lime juice
- 1 tablespoon vegetable oil
- 1 cup salsa, warmed
- Garnish: fresh cilantro sprig

RINSE catfish fillets, and pat dry with paper towels. Cut each fillet in half lengthwise; set aside.
COMBINE crushed tortilla chips and next 3 ingredients in a shallow dish. Stir together lime juice and oil in a separate shallow dish.
DIP fillets in lime juice mixture, and dredge in tortilla chip mixture, coating evenly. Place on a lightly greased rack in an aluminum foil-lined 15- x 10-inch jellyroll pan or broiler pan. Sprinkle evenly with any remaining tortilla chip crumb mixture.
BAKE at 450° for 10 to 12 minutes or until fillets are crisp, golden, and flake with a fork. Serve with warmed salsa, and garnish, if desired. **MAKES** 6 servings.

BLACK BEAN-CORN SALSA

make ahead

Prep: 10 min., Chill: 2 hrs.

- 1 (15-ounce) can **BUSH'S BEST Black Beans**, rinsed and drained
- 1 (11-ounce) can sweet whole kernel corn, drained
- 2 medium tomatoes, chopped
- 1 red bell pepper, chopped
- ⅓ cup chopped fresh cilantro
- ¼ cup diced red onion
- 1 tablespoon minced fresh jalapeño pepper
- 3 tablespoons fresh lime juice
- 1 teaspoon salt
- ½ teaspoon ground black pepper
- 1 avocado, chopped
- Tortilla chips

COMBINE first 10 ingredients in a bowl. Cover and chill at least 2 hours. Add avocado just before serving. Serve with tortilla chips. **MAKES** 3½ cups.

ROASTED VEGETABLE QUESADILLAS

Prep: 20 min., Bake: 35 min., Cook: 2 min. per batch

- **PAM Original No-Stick Cooking Spray**
- 2 medium-size sweet potatoes, peeled and cubed
- 1 medium-size red bell pepper, cut into ½-inch pieces
- 1 medium-size sweet onion, coarsely chopped
- 1 teaspoon salt
- 1 teaspoon ground cumin
- 6 (8-inch) flour tortillas
- 1 (8-ounce) block Monterey Jack cheese with peppers, shredded
- Garnishes: sour cream, fresh cilantro sprigs, lime wedges

COAT a 15- x 10-inch jellyroll pan with cooking spray.

PLACE potatoes, bell pepper, and onion in pan; sprinkle with salt and cumin, and toss until vegetables are coated with cooking spray.

BAKE at 450° for 30 to 35 minutes or until potatoes are tender.

SPOON vegetable mixture evenly on half of each tortilla; sprinkle evenly with cheese. Fold each tortilla over filling. Cook quesadillas, in batches, on a hot griddle or nonstick skillet coated with cooking spray 1 minute on each side or until lightly browned and cheese is melted. Garnish, if desired. Serve immediately. MAKES 6 servings.

FIESTA CHICKEN SOUP

Prep: 25 min., Bake: 15 min., Cook: 25 min.

- **6 corn tortillas**
- **1 small onion, chopped**
- **2 garlic cloves, minced**
- **1 tablespoon vegetable oil**
- **1 (31-ounce) can refried beans**
- **2 (14.5-ounce) cans HUNT'S Petite Diced Tomatoes**
- **1 (14.5-ounce) can HUNT'S Petite Diced Tomatoes with Mild Green Chilies**
- **1 (14½-ounce) can chicken broth**
- **4 cups chopped cooked chicken**
- **2 tablespoons chopped fresh cilantro (optional)**
- **1 (8-ounce) container sour cream**
- **2 cups (8 ounces) shredded Monterey Jack or Cheddar cheese**

CUT tortillas into thin strips, and arrange in a single layer on a lightly greased baking sheet.

BAKE tortillas at 350° for 15 minutes or until browned, stirring every 5 minutes. Cool.

SAUTÉ chopped onion and minced garlic in hot vegetable oil in a Dutch oven over medium-high heat 5 minutes or until tender. Add refried beans and next 4 ingredients, stirring until smooth; bring mixture to a boil. Reduce heat to medium, and simmer 15 minutes. Stir in chopped cilantro, if desired.

LADLE into individual soup bowls; dollop with sour cream, and top with cheese and baked tortilla strips. Serve immediately. MAKES about 14 cups.

Crowd-Pleasing Appetizers

Get your party going with these delicious starters. Any of our tasty recipes will stimulate appetites as a first course, or serve all six with a veggie tray for a spectacular buffet-style gathering.

THREE-LAYER CHEESE TORTA

make ahead

Prep: 20 min., Chill: 3 hrs.

- **3 (8-ounce) packages PHILADELPHIA Cream Cheese, softened and divided**
- **3 tablespoons chopped pimiento-stuffed green olives**
- **2 teaspoons olive juice**
- **1 tablespoon mayonnaise**
- **1 cup (4 ounces) shredded sharp Cheddar cheese**
- **1 (2-ounce) jar diced pimiento, drained**
- **1 teaspoon grated onion**
- **¼ cup butter or margarine, softened**
- **2 garlic cloves, pressed**
- **1 teaspoon dried Italian seasoning**
- **Garnish: parsley sprigs**
- **Assorted crackers and grapes**

BEAT 1 package cream cheese at medium speed with an electric mixer until creamy; stir in olives and olive juice. Spread olive mixture into bottom of a plastic wrap-lined 8- x 4-inch loafpan.

BEAT 1 package cream cheese at medium speed until creamy; add mayonnaise and Cheddar cheese, beating until blended. Stir in diced pimiento and grated onion; spread over olive mixture.

BEAT remaining package cream cheese and butter at medium speed until creamy; add garlic and Italian seasoning, beating until blended. Spread over pimiento mixture. Cover and chill at least 3 hours or until firm. Invert onto a serving platter; remove plastic wrap. Garnish, if desired. Serve Torta with assorted crackers and grapes. MAKES 18 appetizer servings.

HOT BEAN DIP

fast fixin's

Prep: 10 min., Bake: 20 min.

- **2 (16-ounce) cans pinto beans, rinsed and drained**
- **½ cup chicken broth**
- **1 (10-ounce) can RO*TEL Original Diced Tomatoes and Green Chilies, drained and divided**
- **½ teaspoon salt**
- **¼ teaspoon ground black pepper**
- **¼ teaspoon ground cumin**
- **⅛ teaspoon ground red pepper (optional)**
- **¾ cup (3 ounces) shredded sharp Cheddar cheese**
- **Tortilla chips**

PROCESS half of beans and ½ cup chicken broth in a food processor until smooth, stopping to scrape down sides. Stir in remaining beans, 1 cup diced tomatoes and green chilies, salt, black pepper, cumin, and, if desired, ground red pepper. Spoon mixture into a lightly greased 1½-quart baking dish. Top with cheese.

BAKE at 350° for 20 minutes or until golden and bubbly. Top with remaining tomatoes and green chilies. Serve with tortilla chips. MAKES 4 to 6 servings.

FISH TACO APPETIZERS

Prep: 20 min., Cook: 6 min. per batch

Set up a bar for these yummy tacos, and let guests make their own.

- ½ cup all-purpose flour
- 2 tablespoons chili powder
- 2 teaspoons ground cumin
- 2 teaspoons ground coriander
- 6 (3-ounce) U.S. FARM-RAISED CATFISH fillets
- 1 teaspoon salt
- ¼ teaspoon pepper
- ¼ cup vegetable or peanut oil
- Small corn or flour tortillas
- Zesty Shredded Salad
- Lime Sour Cream
- Toppings: salsa, sliced fresh mango, diced avocado

COMBINE first 4 ingredients in a bowl. **CUT** catfish into 1½-inch pieces. Sprinkle evenly with salt and pepper. Toss catfish in flour mixture, shaking off excess. **COOK** catfish, in batches, in hot oil in a large nonstick skillet over medium-high heat 2 to 3 minutes on each side or until done. Remove catfish to a platter; serve with tortillas, Zesty Shredded Salad, Lime Sour Cream, and desired toppings. **MAKES** 8 to 10 appetizer servings or 4 main-dish servings.

Zesty Shredded Salad:

fast fixin's

Prep: 20 min.

Remove the jalapeño seeds before mincing the pepper to reduce the heat.

- ½ teaspoon grated lime rind
- 1 tablespoon fresh lime juice
- 1 tablespoon honey
- 1 small jalapeño, minced
- ¼ teaspoon salt
- ¼ cup olive oil
- 4 cups shredded Napa cabbage
- ½ cup chopped fresh cilantro

STIR together first 5 ingredients in a large bowl; gradually whisk in oil until blended. Add cabbage and cilantro, tossing to coat. **MAKES** about 4 cups.

Lime Sour Cream:

fast fixin's • make ahead

Prep: 5 min.

- 1 cup sour cream
- 2 teaspoons grated lime rind
- 1 tablespoon lime juice
- ½ teaspoon salt

COMBINE all ingredients. Cover and chill until ready to serve. **MAKES** 1 cup.

CHICKEN SKEWERS WITH PEANUT SAUCE

Prep: 15 min., Chill: 2 hrs., Grill: 6 min.

If using wooden skewers instead of metal, soak them in cold water for 30 minutes before grilling.

- 1 pound PILGRIM'S PRIDE Skinless and Boneless Chicken Breasts
- 1 (14-ounce) can lite coconut milk
- 2 tablespoons sugar
- 1 tablespoon grated lemon rind
- 1 tablespoon curry powder
- 2 teaspoons grated lime rind
- 2 teaspoons ground coriander
- 1 teaspoon salt
- ½ teaspoon ground red pepper
- 1 tablespoon fish sauce (optional)
- 16 (8-inch) skewers
- Peanut Sauce

CUT chicken into ½-inch-wide strips. Place in a shallow dish or zip-top plastic freezer bag. Stir together coconut milk, next 7 ingredients, and, if desired, fish sauce; pour over chicken. Cover or seal, and chill 2 hours.
THREAD 2 or 3 chicken pieces onto each skewer.
GRILL, uncovered, over medium-high heat (350° to 400°) 2 to 3 minutes on each side or until done. Serve with Peanut Sauce. **MAKES** 8 appetizer servings.

NOTE: Fish sauce adds authentic Asian flavor to this recipe and can be found in the Asian section of larger grocery stores or at Asian markets. This recipe tastes great without it too.

Peanut Sauce:

Prep: 15 min., Cook: 20 min.

- ¾ cup lite coconut milk
- ⅓ cup crunchy peanut butter
- 2 tablespoons fresh lemon juice
- 1 tablespoon soy sauce
- 1 tablespoon brown sugar
- 1 garlic clove
- 1 teaspoon chopped fresh ginger
- ¼ teaspoon ground red pepper
- ¼ cup milk
- 1 teaspoon grated lemon rind

COOK first 8 ingredients in a small saucepan over medium heat, stirring often, 15 minutes or until thickened. Process mixture in a food processor or blender until smooth. Return to pan; whisk in milk and lemon rind until thoroughly heated. **MAKES** 1½ cups.

BACON-AND-CHEESE MELTS

fast fixin's

Prep: 15 min., Bake: 12 min.

You can also use this recipe to make 5 delicious sandwiches.

- 1 cup (4 ounces) shredded Swiss cheese
- 8 bacon slices, cooked and crumbled
- ¼ cup mayonnaise
- 1 tablespoon chopped fresh chives
- 1 tablespoon grated onion
- ½ teaspoon celery salt
- ⅛ teaspoon ground red pepper
- 10 slices SARA LEE Delightful White Bread, crusts removed

STIR together first 7 ingredients, and spread over bread slices. Cut each slice into 3 strips. Place on a lightly greased baking sheet.
BAKE on lowest oven rack at 325° for 12 minutes. **MAKES** 30 appetizer servings.

CHILE-PIMIENTO CHEESE

make ahead

Prep: 10 min., Chill: 8 hrs.

Use this cheesy spread for grilled party sandwiches too.

- **1 (8-ounce) package PHILADELPHIA Cream Cheese, softened**
- **½ cup mayonnaise**
- **2 garlic cloves, minced**
- **2 teaspoons sweet pickle relish, drained**
- **4 cups (16 ounces) shredded sharp Cheddar cheese**
- **2 (4-ounce) jars diced pimiento, drained**
- **1 (4-ounce) can chopped green chiles**
- **½ cup chopped pecans, toasted**
- **Pita chips, assorted crackers, or vegetables**

BEAT first 4 ingredients at medium speed with an electric mixer until smooth. Stir in Cheddar cheese and next 3 ingredients. Cover and chill up to 8 hours. Serve with pita chips, crackers, or vegetables. **MAKES** 4½ cups.

One-Dish Dinner Winners

Coming up with creative and easy dinner ideas can be a formidable task. That's why we've selected family-friendly ingredients your gang will love. Fix one dish with plenty of hearty ingredients, and all that will be left after the meal is quick cleanup and full bellies.

TURKEY-VEGETABLE-SAUSAGE COBBLER

family favorite

Prep: 15 min., Cook: 10 min., Bake: 20 min.

This grown-up version of a pot pie with its meaty filling will appeal to kids too.

- **2 tablespoons butter or margarine**
- **½ pound smoked sausage or kielbasa, diced**
- **2 tablespoons all-purpose flour**
- **2 cups milk**
- **1 (15-ounce) can VEG•ALL Original Mixed Vegetables, drained**
- **2 cups diced cooked turkey or chicken**
- **½ teaspoon salt**
- **½ teaspoon seasoned pepper**
- **½ (15-ounce) package refrigerated piecrusts**

MELT butter in a large saucepan over medium-high heat; add sausage, and sauté 5 minutes. Stir in flour. Whisk in milk; cook, whisking constantly, 5 minutes or until thickened.

REMOVE from heat; stir in canned vegetables and next 3 ingredients. Pour into a lightly greased 9-inch deep-dish pieplate.

UNFOLD 1 piecrust, and roll to press out fold lines; place piecrust over turkey mixture, trimming to fit. Crimp edges, and cut slits on top for steam to escape.

BAKE at 400° for 20 minutes or until crust is golden. **MAKES** 4 to 6 servings.

BEAN-AND-HAM SOUP

fast fixin's

Prep: 5 min, Cook: 25 min.

- **3 (15.8-ounce) cans BUSH'S BEST Great Northern Beans, divided**
- **1 (14-ounce) can chicken broth, divided**
- **2 tablespoons butter**
- **1 small onion, diced**
- **8 ounces cooked ham, cubed**
- **¼ teaspoon pepper**

RINSE and drain beans. Process one-third can of beans and half of chicken broth in a food processor until smooth. Set aside.

MELT butter in a Dutch oven over medium heat. Add onion, and sauté 5 minutes or until onion is tender. Add ham, and sauté 10 minutes or until lightly browned, stirring constantly.

ADD bean puree, remaining beans, and remaining chicken broth. Bring to a boil; reduce heat, and simmer 10 minutes. Stir in pepper. Serve immediately. **MAKES** 4 servings.

EASY CHICKEN CASSOULET

family favorite

Prep: 25 min., Cook: 15 min., Bake: 1 hr.

- **8 PILGRIM'S PRIDE Skinless and Boneless Chicken Thighs**
- **3 tablespoons olive oil**
- **2 cups sliced fresh mushrooms**
- **2 to 3 teaspoons finely chopped fresh or dried rosemary**
- **½ cup vermouth or dry white wine**
- **4 (15-ounce) cans navy beans, drained and divided**
- **1 cup shredded Parmesan cheese**
- **1 cup fine, dry breadcrumbs**
- **1 teaspoon salt**
- **½ teaspoon pepper**
- **1 (12-ounce) jar mushroom gravy**
- **2 tablespoons butter or margarine, cut up**

BROWN thighs on both sides in hot oil in a 12-inch cast-iron skillet over medium-high heat. Add mushrooms and rosemary; sauté 3 minutes.

STIR in vermouth; cook 5 minutes. Add 2 cans beans, pressing into skillet.

SPRINKLE with ½ cup Parmesan cheese, ½ cup breadcrumbs, salt, and pepper. Drizzle with gravy. Add remaining 2 cans beans. Sprinkle with remaining ½ cup Parmesan cheese and ½ cup breadcrumbs; dot with butter.

BAKE, covered with aluminum foil, at 350° for 40 minutes. Remove foil, and bake 20 more minutes or until golden brown. **MAKES** 8 to 10 servings.

CHICKEN-VEGETABLE CHOWDER

family favorite

Prep: 10 min., Cook: 30 min.

- **3 bacon slices, chopped**
- **1 small onion, diced**
- **3 tablespoons all-purpose flour**
- **2 (14-ounce) cans chicken broth**
- **2 (15-ounce) cans VEG•ALL Original Mixed Vegetables, drained**
- **2 cups chopped cooked chicken**
- **½ cup whipping cream**
- **¼ teaspoon pepper**

COOK bacon in a Dutch oven over medium-high heat 10 minutes or until crisp. Add onion, and sauté 5 minutes or until tender. Stir in flour; whisk in chicken broth until smooth. Bring mixture to a boil; reduce heat, and simmer 10 minutes or until thickened. Stir in canned vegetables and remaining ingredients; cook until thoroughly heated. Serve immediately. **MAKES** 4 servings.

GRILLED CATFISH OVER MIXED GREENS

Prep: 20 min., Chill: 30 min., Grill: 10 min.

Tarragon has a lovely fragrance, but a little goes a long way. Out of balsamic vinegar? Use apple cider vinegar with a pinch or two of sugar whisked in.

- **2 (6- to 7-ounce) U.S. FARM-RAISED CATFISH fillets**
- **½ cup olive oil**
- **3 tablespoons balsamic vinegar**
- **1 small shallot, diced**
- **1 tablespoon chopped fresh or 1 teaspoon dried tarragon**
- **¾ teaspoon freshly ground pepper, divided**
- **½ teaspoon salt, divided**
- **Vegetable cooking spray**
- **4 cups gourmet mixed salad greens**
- **¼ pound fresh button mushrooms, thinly sliced**

RINSE catfish fillets; pat dry with paper towels, and place in a large shallow dish.

WHISK together olive oil, next 3 ingredients, ½ teaspoon pepper, and ¼ teaspoon salt; pour ¼ cup marinade over fillets, turning to coat. Reserve remaining marinade. Cover and chill fillets 30 minutes.

REMOVE fillets from marinade, discarding marinade; sprinkle evenly with remaining ¼ teaspoon pepper and ¼ teaspoon salt.

COAT food grate with cooking spray; place over medium-high heat (350° to 400°). Place fillets on food grate; grill 5 minutes on each side or until fish flakes with a fork.

TOSS together salad greens, mushrooms, and reserved marinade; serve on individual plates, topped with grilled fillets. **MAKES** 2 servings.

LAYERED PASTA BAKE

family favorite

Prep: 20 min., Cook: 20 min, Bake: 30 min.

Pair this hearty casserole with a side dish of crisp-tender green beans or sugar snap peas tossed with a touch of olive oil, lemon juice, salt, and pepper.

- **½ (1-pound) box BARILLA Penne Pasta**
- **1 tablespoon olive oil**
- **1 pound ground beef**
- **1 medium onion, chopped**
- **1 garlic clove, pressed**
- **¼ cup dry red wine**
- **1 (15½-ounce) jar spaghetti sauce with mushrooms**
- **1 cup beef broth**
- **1 (6-ounce) can tomato paste**
- **1 teaspoon salt**
- **½ teaspoon pepper, divided**
- **1 (16-ounce) container small-curd cottage cheese**
- **1 cup grated Parmesan cheese**
- **1 cup (4 ounces) shredded mozzarella cheese**
- **2 large eggs, lightly beaten**
- **⅓ cup Italian-seasoned breadcrumbs**

COOK pasta according to package directions. Drain. Toss pasta with oil, and spoon into a lightly greased 13- x 9-inch baking dish. Set aside.

COOK ground beef, onion, and garlic in a skillet over medium-high heat 5 to 6 minutes, stirring until beef crumbles and is no longer pink. Drain and return to skillet.

ADD wine, spaghetti sauce, and next 3 ingredients to skillet; bring to a boil. Reduce heat, and simmer 10 minutes. Stir in ¼ teaspoon pepper.

COMBINE cottage cheese, ½ cup Parmesan cheese, ½ cup mozzarella cheese, remaining ¼ teaspoon pepper, and eggs; spoon over pasta. Spread with beef mixture. Sprinkle with remaining ½ cup Parmesan and ½ cup mozzarella cheeses; top with breadcrumbs.

BAKE, uncovered, at 350° for 30 minutes or until bubbly. **MAKES** 6 to 8 servings.

SKILLET PEPPER STEAK AND RICE

family favorite

Prep: 20 min., Cook: 20 min.

Don't be put off by the long list of ingredients. Most items are probably already in your pantry, spice cabinet, or fridge.

- **1 (3.5-ounce) bag SUCCESS White Rice**
- **1 (10½-ounce) can beef broth**
- **3 tablespoons cornstarch, divided**
- **2 tablespoons soy sauce**
- **1 teaspoon sugar**
- **2 teaspoons minced fresh or 1 teaspoon ground ginger**
- **½ teaspoon garlic-chili sauce (optional)**
- **½ teaspoon salt**
- **½ teaspoon pepper**
- **1 pound boneless top sirloin steak, cut into thin slices**
- **1 tablespoon vegetable oil**
- **2 teaspoons sesame oil**
- **1 green bell pepper, sliced**
- **1 medium-size red onion, sliced**
- **½ (8-ounce) container sliced fresh mushrooms**
- **1 garlic clove, pressed**

PREPARE rice according to package directions; set aside.

WHISK together beef broth, 1 tablespoon cornstarch, soy sauce, sugar, ginger, and, if desired, garlic-chili sauce; set aside.

COMBINE remaining 2 tablespoons cornstarch, salt, and pepper; dredge steak slices in mixture.

HEAT oils in a large skillet or wok over medium-high heat; add steak, and stir-fry 4 minutes or until browned. Add bell pepper, onion, and mushrooms; stir-fry 8 minutes or until tender. Add garlic; stir-fry 1 minute.

STIR in broth mixture. Bring to a boil; reduce heat, and simmer 3 to 5 minutes or until thickened. Remove from heat; stir in rice. MAKES 4 to 6 servings.

Serve a Simple Side

When you need supper on the table fast, let these speedy side dishes help. Most are prepared quickly on the cooktop, while others require no cooking at all. You can even turn some of these sides into hearty main dishes by simply adding chicken, beef, pork, or shrimp.

PARMESAN GREEN BEANS

family favorite • fast fixin's

Prep: 10 min., Cook: 8 min.

- 1½ pounds fresh green beans, trimmed
- ¼ cup KRAFT 100% Grated Parmesan Cheese
- ¼ cup olive oil
- 3 tablespoons chopped fresh basil
- 3 tablespoons cider vinegar
- 1 teaspoon sugar
- ½ teaspoon salt
- ¼ teaspoon pepper

COOK green beans in boiling salted water to cover 3 to 5 minutes or until crisp-tender.

PLUNGE green beans into ice water to stop the cooking process; drain and set aside.

PROCESS Parmesan cheese and next 6 ingredients in a food processor until smooth, stopping to scrape down sides.

TOSS together green beans and dressing. Cover and chill until ready to serve. MAKES 4 to 6 servings.

ITALIAN MACARONI AND CHEESE

family favorite

Prep: 20 min., Bake: 1 hr., Stand: 10 min.

This rich and creamy macaroni and cheese calls for just 20 minutes of hands-on work.

- 1 (8-ounce) package large elbow macaroni
- PAM Original No-Stick Cooking Spray
- ½ cup Italian-seasoned breadcrumbs, divided
- 1 (10-ounce) block white Cheddar cheese, shredded*
- 2 cups (8 ounces) shredded mozzarella cheese
- ¾ cup (3 ounces) shredded Parmesan cheese
- 6 large eggs, lightly beaten
- 4 cups milk
- 1 teaspoon salt
- 1 teaspoon seasoned pepper
- Tomato-Basil Topping

PREPARE macaroni according to package directions; drain and set aside.

COAT bottom and sides of a 13- x 9-inch baking dish with cooking spray. Sprinkle ¼ cup breadcrumbs evenly over bottom of baking dish; tilt dish to coat sides evenly with breadcrumbs.

LAYER one-third macaroni, one-third shredded cheeses, and one-third remaining ¼ cup breadcrumbs in baking dish. Repeat layers twice, ending with breadcrumbs.

WHISK together eggs and next 3 ingredients; pour evenly over layered mixture.

BAKE at 350° for 55 to 60 minutes or until golden and set. Let stand 10 minutes before serving. Sprinkle evenly with Tomato-Basil Topping. MAKES 8 to 10 servings.

*Substitute 1 (10-ounce) block sharp Cheddar cheese, shredded, if desired.

Tomato-Basil Topping:

fast fixin's

Prep: 10 min.

- 4 large plum tomatoes, seeded and diced
- ¼ cup (1 ounce) shredded Parmesan cheese
- 3 tablespoons chopped fresh basil

STIR together all ingredients. MAKES about 2 cups.

SPICY OKRA-TOMATO-CORN SAUTÉ

fast fixin's

Prep: 5 min., Cook: 15 min.

- ½ small onion, chopped
- ½ tablespoon vegetable oil
- 1 (16-ounce) package frozen whole okra, thawed
- 1 cup frozen corn, thawed
- 1 (10-ounce) can RO*TEL Original Diced Tomatoes and Green Chilies, undrained
- 1 teaspoon sugar
- ¾ teaspoon salt
- ¼ teaspoon pepper

SAUTÉ chopped onion in hot vegetable oil in a large nonstick skillet over medium-high heat 5 minutes or until tender. Add okra; cook, stirring occasionally, 5 minutes.

STIR in corn and remaining ingredients, and cook 5 minutes or until thoroughly heated. Serve immediately. MAKES 6 servings.

PENNE WITH SPINACH AND FETA

family favorite • fast fixin's

Prep: 15 min., Cook: 15 min.

- ½ (1-pound) box BARILLA Penne Pasta
- 5 large plum tomatoes, seeded and chopped
- 3 cups fresh spinach
- 2 tablespoons olive oil
- ½ teaspoon Greek seasoning
- ¼ teaspoon salt
- ¼ teaspoon dried crushed red pepper
- ½ cup crumbled feta cheese
- 3 bacon slices, cooked and crumbled

PREPARE pasta in a large Dutch oven according to package directions; drain. Return pasta to Dutch oven. Stir in tomatoes and next 5 ingredients; cook over medium heat 2 minutes or until thoroughly heated. Sprinkle with cheese and bacon. Serve immediately. **MAKES** 4 servings.

CURRIED VEGETABLES WITH COUSCOUS

family favorite

Prep: 15 min., Stand: 5 min., Cook: 15 min.

- 2 cups chicken broth
- 1 (10-ounce) box plain couscous
- ¼ cup golden raisins
- ¼ cup pine nuts, toasted
- 2 garlic cloves, minced
- 1 teaspoon grated fresh ginger
- 1 tablespoon olive oil
- 2 (15-ounce) cans VEG•ALL Original Mixed Vegetables, rinsed and drained
- 2 teaspoons curry powder
- ½ teaspoon salt
- ½ teaspoon sugar
- ¼ teaspoon ground coriander
- ¼ teaspoon ground cinnamon
- ½ cup coconut milk

BRING chicken broth to a boil in a medium saucepan; stir in couscous and raisins. Remove from heat, cover, and let stand 5 minutes. Fluff with a fork, and stir in pine nuts.

SAUTÉ garlic and ginger in hot oil in a large nonstick skillet over medium-high heat 2 to 3 minutes or until golden. Stir in canned vegetables and next 5 ingredients. Stir in coconut milk, and bring to a boil; reduce heat to low, and simmer 5 minutes. Serve immediately over couscous. **MAKES** 4 to 6 servings.

SPEEDY SKILLET PECAN RICE

family favorite • fast fixin's

Prep: 10 min., Cook: 15 min.

- 2 (3.5-ounce) bags SUCCESS White Rice
- ½ medium-size red bell pepper, chopped
- ½ small onion, chopped
- 1 cup sliced fresh mushrooms
- 2 tablespoons vegetable oil
- 1 garlic clove, minced
- 1 teaspoon Cajun seasoning
- ¼ teaspoon salt
- ½ teaspoon freshly ground pepper
- 3 tablespoons chopped pecans, toasted

COOK rice according to package directions. Set aside.

SAUTÉ bell pepper, onion, and mushrooms in hot vegetable oil in a large nonstick skillet over medium-high heat 5 minutes or until tender. Add garlic; sauté 2 minutes. Stir in cooked rice, Cajun seasoning, salt, and pepper; sprinkle with pecans. Serve immediately. **MAKES** 4 servings.

VEGGIE-BEAN SALAD

make ahead

Prep: 15 min., Chill: 2 hrs.

- 1 (15.8-ounce) can BUSH'S BEST Blackeye Peas, rinsed and drained
- 1 (15-ounce) can BUSH'S BEST Black Beans, rinsed and drained
- ¼ cup diced celery
- ¼ cup diced red onion
- ¼ cup diced green bell pepper
- 1 garlic clove, minced
- ¼ cup red wine vinaigrette
- 1 tablespoon hot sauce
- 1 jalapeño, seeded and minced
- ½ teaspoon seasoned pepper

COMBINE all ingredients in a large bowl; cover and chill at least 2 hours. **MAKES** 4 to 6 servings.

Tricks From the Test Kitchens

Do you dream of a kitchen that runs like clockwork, where nothing is ever spilled, where the chrome sparkles, and you never break a sweat? Dream on, darlin'! Every smart cook knows that a kitchen is a place where real life happens—and that it's not always going to be clean or tidy. Not to worry. With these hints and tips from our Test Kitchens Professionals, your kitchen will work harder for you, and you'll enjoy it more.

■ **Enjoy those last herbs of summer:** To store fresh herbs for maximum flavor and to extend their shelf life, rinse and dry them in a salad spinner. Wrap herbs in dampened white VIVA Towels, place in a zip-top plastic bag, and seal; place in the refrigerator's crisper. Use the cleaned fresh herbs as needed. This trick also works well with fresh lettuces and greens.

- **Grease with ease:** To grease or butter a baking pan, simply grab a piece of butter or shortening with a VIVA Towel, and thoroughly coat the pan. Baked goods won't stick, and your hands will be grease free. And speaking of grease, when we call for greasing a pan in our recipes, we use butter or shortening. When we say to "lightly grease," use vegetable cooking spray.

- **Popeye would be proud:** Frozen spinach adds color and flavor to many dishes, but too much liquid can make your prize recipe soggy. To remove excess liquid, place frozen spinach in a colander, and press absorbent VIVA Towels against the spinach, squeezing out moisture.

- **Take it from the top:** If you've ever tried to remove that extra bit of fat from the edge of soup, we have a solution. Dampen a white VIVA Towel, and place it in the freezer for a few minutes. Remove the cold towel, and gently skim the edge or top of hot soup with it. The chilled towel encourages excess fat to congeal more quickly, and the absorbent nature of the towel soaks up the fat.

- **One skillet, two uses:** Eliminate the time you spend washing cookware by wiping a skillet clean in between cooking steps. For example, cook bacon, and drain; hold a VIVA towel with tongs, and wipe the skillet. Now add fresh produce to sauté.

- **Nick Prevention 101:** To help prevent scuffs on nonstick finishes and enamelware, line pots and pans with VIVA Towels when you stack them. The same approach works for fine china and glass or copper mixing bowls.

Sweet Indulgences

Check out our collection of recipes for some scrumptious handheld treats, from brownies to peanut butter candy cups. And for good measure, we've also included an Apple-Berry Cobbler recipe and a Sweet Potato Pie that are sure to become family favorites.

CHOCOLATE ICE-CREAM SANDWICHES

freezeable • make ahead

Prep: 45 min., Bake: 12 min. per batch, Freeze: 1 hr.

    1¼ cups butter or margarine,
        softened
    2 cups DOMINO Granulated Sugar
    2 large eggs
    2 teaspoons vanilla extract
    2 cups all-purpose flour
    ¾ cup unsweetened cocoa
    1 teaspoon baking soda
    ½ teaspoon salt
    2 pints vanilla ice cream, softened

BEAT butter at medium speed with an electric mixer until creamy; gradually add sugar, beating well. Add eggs and vanilla, beating until well blended.

COMBINE flour and next 3 ingredients; gradually add to butter mixture, beating at low speed until blended after each addition. Shape dough into 1½-inch balls, and place on lightly greased baking sheets.

BAKE in batches at 350° for 12 minutes or until edges are crisp. Cool in pan 1 minute; remove to wire racks to cool.

SPREAD ice cream evenly on bottom side of half the cookies; top with remaining cookies. Wrap in plastic or wax paper sandwich bags, and freeze at least 1 hour. **MAKES** about 2 dozen.

PEANUT-TOFFEE SHORTBREAD

Prep: 30 min., Bake: 20 min., Stand: 5 min.

The word "short" in shortbread describes a pastry dough that's rich, crisp, and melts in your mouth due to the high proportion of butter to flour in the recipe.

    1 cup butter, softened
    ⅔ cup firmly packed light brown
        sugar
    ⅓ cup cornstarch
    2 cups all-purpose flour
    ¼ teaspoon salt
    2 teaspoons vanilla extract
    2 cups coarsely chopped honey-
        roasted peanuts, divided
    2 cups (12-ounce package) NESTLÉ
        TOLL HOUSE Semi-Sweet
        Chocolate Morsels

BEAT butter at medium speed with an electric mixer until creamy. Combine brown sugar and cornstarch, and gradually add to butter; beat well. Gradually add flour and salt to butter mixture, beating at low speed just until blended. Add vanilla and 1 cup peanuts, beating at low speed just until blended.

TURN dough out onto a lightly greased baking sheet; pat or roll dough into an 11- x 14-inch rectangle, leaving at least a 1-inch border on all sides of baking sheet.

BAKE at 350° for 20 minutes or until golden brown. Remove baking sheet to a wire rack; sprinkle shortbread evenly with chocolate morsels. Let stand 5 minutes; gently spread melted morsels over shortbread.

SPRINKLE with remaining 1 cup peanuts, and let cool completely. Cut or break shortbread into 2- to 3-inch irregular-shaped pieces. **MAKES** about 2½ to 3 dozen pieces.

ROCKY ROAD-PEANUT BUTTER CANDY CUPS

Prep: 30 min., Chill: 1 hr.

- 1⅔ cups (11-ounce package) NESTLÉ TOLL HOUSE Peanut Butter & Milk Chocolate Morsels
- 2 tablespoons smooth peanut butter
- 1 cup crisp rice cereal
- 1 cup miniature marshmallows
- ¾ cup chopped unsalted roasted peanuts

MICROWAVE peanut butter-and-chocolate morsels in a large glass bowl at HIGH 2 minutes or until melted, stirring every 30 seconds. Stir in 2 tablespoons peanut butter until well blended.

STIR in rice cereal, marshmallows, and chopped peanuts. Spoon mixture evenly into miniature paper candy cups. Chill 1 hour or until firm. **MAKES** about 3 dozen.

APPLE-BERRY COBBLER

family favorite

Prep: 15 min.; Bake: 1 hr., 15 min.

- 1 (16-ounce) package frozen cherries, unthawed
- 1 (16-ounce) package frozen blueberries, unthawed
- 1¼ cups sugar, divided
- ½ cup all-purpose flour
- 1 Granny Smith apple, peeled and chopped
- 5 slices SARA LEE Classic White Bread
- ½ cup butter or margarine, melted
- 1 large egg
- 2 tablespoons all-purpose flour
- 1 teaspoon vanilla extract
- 1 teaspoon sugar

STIR together cherries, blueberries, ¼ cup sugar, ½ cup flour, and chopped apple. Place in a lightly greased 8-inch-square baking dish.

TRIM crusts from bread slices; cut each slice into 5 strips. Arrange bread strips over fruit mixture.

STIR together butter, 1 cup sugar, egg, 2 tablespoons flour, and 1 teaspoon vanilla; drizzle over bread strips. Sprinkle bread strips evenly with 1 teaspoon sugar.

BAKE at 350° for 1 hour and 15 minutes or until golden and bubbly. **MAKES** 4 to 6 servings.

CREAM CHEESE BROWNIES

family favorite

Prep: 30 min., Bake: 45 min.

- 4 (1-ounce) unsweetened chocolate squares
- 4 (1-ounce) semisweet chocolate squares
- ⅓ cup butter or margarine
- 1 (8-ounce) package PHILADELPHIA Cream Cheese, softened
- ¼ cup butter or margarine, softened
- 2 cups sugar, divided
- 6 large eggs, divided
- 3 teaspoons vanilla extract, divided
- 2 tablespoons all-purpose flour
- 1½ cups (9 ounces) semisweet chocolate morsels, divided
- 1 cup all-purpose flour
- 1 teaspoon baking powder
- 1 teaspoon salt

MICROWAVE first 3 ingredients in a 1-quart glass bowl at HIGH 2 minutes or until melted, stirring once. Cool.

BEAT cream cheese and ¼ cup butter at medium speed with an electric mixer until creamy; gradually add ½ cup sugar, beating well. Add 2 eggs, 1 at a time, beating until blended. Stir in 1 teaspoon vanilla. Fold in 2 tablespoons flour and ½ cup chocolate morsels; set aside.

BEAT remaining 4 eggs in a large bowl at medium speed with an electric mixer. Gradually add remaining 1½ cups sugar, beating mixture well. Add melted chocolate mixture and remaining 2 teaspoons vanilla; beat mixture until well blended.

COMBINE 1 cup flour, baking powder, and salt; fold into chocolate batter until blended, and stir in remaining 1 cup chocolate morsels.

RESERVE 2 cups chocolate batter; spread remaining batter evenly in a greased 13- x 9-inch pan. Pour cream cheese mixture over batter in pan. Top with reserved 2 cups chocolate batter, and swirl mixture with a knife.

BAKE at 325° for 40 to 45 minutes. Cool and cut brownies into squares. **MAKES** 1½ dozen.

CHEWY PRALINE-CHOCOLATE FUDGE BARS

family favorite

Prep: 20 min., Bake: 25 min.

While the bars bake, begin making the rich, nutty icing.

- 1 cup butter, softened
- 1 cup firmly packed DOMINO Light Brown Sugar
- 1 teaspoon vanilla extract
- 2 cups all-purpose flour
- 1 cup chopped pecans, toasted
- 1 (12-ounce) package semisweet chocolate morsels, divided
- Praline Fudge Icing
- 2 tablespoons milk

BEAT butter at medium speed with an electric mixer until creamy; gradually add sugar and vanilla, beating until light and fluffy. Stir in flour and pecans. Press dough into an ungreased 13- x 9-inch pan.

BAKE at 350° for 20 to 25 minutes or until brown around the edges and bars pull away from sides of pan. Sprinkle 1½ cups chocolate morsels evenly over warm bars. Pour warm Praline Fudge Icing over chocolate morsels; spreading to edges with a spatula.

MICROWAVE remaining ½ cup chocolate morsels and milk in a small bowl at HIGH 20 to 30 seconds. Stir until smooth. Drizzle over bars. Cool completely. Cut into 1¼-inch pieces. **MAKES** about 7 dozen.

Praline Fudge Icing:

fast fixin's

Prep: 5 min., Cook: 5 min., Stand: 5 min.

- ½ cup butter
- 1 cup firmly packed DOMINO Light Brown Sugar
- ⅛ teaspoon salt
- ½ cup milk
- 2½ cups DOMINO 10-X Confectioners Sugar
- ½ teaspoon vanilla extract
- ¾ cup chopped pecans, toasted

MELT butter in a saucepan over medium heat. Add brown sugar and salt; bring to a boil, and cook, stirring constantly, 2 minutes. Remove from heat.

STIR in milk slowly. Return to heat; bring to a boil, stirring until smooth. Remove from heat; let stand 5 minutes. Add confectioners sugar and vanilla; beat at medium speed with a hand-held electric mixer until smooth. Stir in pecans. **MAKES** about 2 cups.

SWEET POTATO PIE

family favorite • make ahead

Prep: 15 min., Bake: 45 min.

- ½ (15-ounce) package refrigerated piecrusts
- 2 cups cooked, mashed sweet potatoes (about 2 pounds)
- 2 large eggs
- 1 cup EQUAL Sugar Lite
- 1 tablespoon all-purpose flour
- 1 teaspoon lemon juice
- 1 teaspoon vanilla
- ½ teaspoon ground cinnamon
- ¼ teaspoon ground nutmeg
- ½ teaspoon salt
- 1 (12-ounce) can fat-free evaporated milk
- Garnishes: reduced-fat whipped topping, grated nutmeg

ROLL 1 piecrust into a 10-inch circle on a lightly floured surface; carefully fit into a 9-inch pieplate. Fold edges under, and flute or crimp.

BEAT sweet potatoes at medium speed with an electric mixer until smooth. Add eggs and next 8 ingredients; beat at low speed until combined. Pour mixture into prepared piecrust.

BAKE at 400° for 40 to 45 minutes or until filling is set and a knife inserted in center comes out clean. Cool completely on a wire rack. Cover and refrigerate. Garnish, if desired. **MAKES** 8 servings.

NOTE: To cook sweet potatoes, arrange 2 or 3 sweet potatoes 1 inch apart on paper towels in microwave oven. Microwave at HIGH 8 to 10 minutes or until done, turning and rearranging after 5 minutes. Or cook 2 to 3 sweet potatoes in boiling water to cover 30 to 35 minutes.

APRICOT-OATMEAL BARS

make ahead

Prep: 15 min., Bake: 40 min.

- 1¼ cups all-purpose flour
- ¾ cup uncooked quick-cooking oats
- ½ cup EQUAL Sugar Lite
- ½ teaspoon ground cinnamon
- ¼ teaspoon baking powder
- ⅛ teaspoon salt
- ½ cup cold butter, cut into pieces
- 2 tablespoons water
- 1 teaspoon vanilla extract
- Vegetable cooking spray
- ¾ cup apricot or peach spreadable fruit

COMBINE first 6 ingredients. Cut butter into flour mixture with a pastry blender until mixture is very fine in texture and begins to stick together slightly. Stir in water and vanilla until well blended.

RESERVE ¾ cup flour mixture. Press remaining mixture firmly and evenly onto bottom of an 8-inch square pan lightly coated with cooking spray.

BAKE at 375° for 12 to 15 minutes or until mixture is lightly browned at edges.

REMOVE from oven; cover evenly with fruit spread. Sprinkle with reserved flour mixture, pressing gently into fruit spread.

Bake 20 to 25 more minutes or until flour mixture is lightly browned on top. Cool completely on a wire rack. Cut into bars. **MAKES** 16 bars.

NOTE: For testing purposes only, we used Smucker's Simply 100% Fruit for apricot spreadable fruit.

NOTE: Bars can be stored in a tightly covered container at room temperature.

HOLIDAY SUGAR COOKIES

family favorite

Prep: 20 min., Chill: 45 min., Bake: 12 min. per batch

- ¾ cup EQUAL Sugar Lite
- ½ cup butter, softened
- 1 large egg
- 1 teaspoon vanilla extract
- 1⅓ cups all-purpose flour
- ¾ teaspoon baking powder
- ¼ teaspoon salt
- ¼ cup strawberry or raspberry spreadable fruit

BEAT sugar/no-calorie sweetener blend and butter at medium speed with an electric mixer until well combined. Add egg and vanilla, beating until blended. Combine flour, baking powder, and salt. Add flour mixture to butter mixture; beat until blended. Cover with plastic wrap, and chill 45 minutes.

SHAPE dough into 1-inch balls, and place on lightly greased baking sheets; press thumb in center of each ball to make an indentation.

BAKE at 350° for 10 to 12 minutes. Cool cookies on baking sheets on wire racks 1 minute; remove to wire racks. Press thumb in center of each cookie to form an indentation, and let cool completely. Spoon ¼ teaspoon strawberry spreadable fruit into indentation of each cookie. **MAKES** about 3 dozen.

NOTE: For testing purposes only, we used Polaner All Fruit Strawberry for strawberry spreadable fruit.

Brunch Anytime

M̲ake your next gathering a breeze with this delectable mix-and-match menu. Some of these favorites can be prepared in advance to save you time in the kitchen on the morning of the brunch. With a bounty of irresistible sweet and savory selections, your guests are sure to go back for seconds.

SOUTHWESTERN GRITS WEDGES

family favorite

Prep: 10 min., Cook: 20 min., Chill: 2 hrs.

- 2⅔ cups chicken broth
- 2 tablespoons butter or margarine
- ⅔ cup quick-cooking grits
- ½ (8-ounce) loaf pasteurized cheese product, cubed
- 1 (10-ounce) can RO*TEL Original Diced Tomatoes and Green Chilies, drained
- 1 tablespoon butter or margarine, melted
- Toppings: sour cream, chopped fresh cilantro

BRING broth and 2 tablespoons butter to a boil in a large saucepan over medium heat; add grits, and cook, stirring often, 5 minutes or until thickened. Remove from heat, and add cheese, stirring until melted and combined. Stir in tomatoes and green chilies. Pour mixture into a lightly greased 9-inch pieplate. Cover and chill 2 hours.

UNMOLD grits, and cut into 6 wedges; lightly brush each side with melted butter.

COOK wedges on a hot, lightly greased griddle 4 minutes on each side or until golden. Dollop wedges with sour cream, and sprinkle with cilantro. **MAKES** 6 servings.

TOMATO FLORENTINE QUICHE

Prep: 20 min., Bake: 1 hr., Stand: 20 min.

Shredded cheeses, diced tomatoes, and chopped spinach combine to make Tomato Florentine Quiche simply divine.

- 1 (10-ounce) package frozen chopped spinach, thawed
- 1 (14.5-ounce) can HUNT'S Petite Diced Tomatoes, drained
- 2 tablespoons Italian-seasoned breadcrumbs
- 3 large eggs, lightly beaten
- 1 cup half-and-half
- 4 bacon slices, cooked and crumbled
- ½ cup (2 ounces) shredded sharp Cheddar cheese
- ½ cup (2 ounces) shredded mozzarella cheese
- 1 teaspoon pesto seasoning or dried basil
- ¼ teaspoon ground red pepper
- 1 unbaked (9-inch) frozen, deep-dish piecrust*
- Garnish: Italian parsley sprig

DRAIN spinach in a wire-mesh strainer, pressing with several paper towels in order to remove excess water. Set spinach aside.

TOSS together diced tomatoes and breadcrumbs.

STIR together spinach, eggs, and next 6 ingredients in a large bowl. Gently fold in tomato mixture. Pour mixture into frozen piecrust, and place on a baking sheet.

BAKE at 350° for 50 to 60 minutes. Remove from oven, and let stand 20 minutes before cutting. Garnish, if desired. **MAKES** 6 to 8 servings.

*Substitute ½ (15-ounce) package refrigerated piecrusts, if desired. Place in a deep-dish pieplate.

SAUSAGE-HAM BREAKFAST CASSEROLE

family favorite • make ahead

Prep: 20 min., Chill: 8 hrs., Bake: 45 min.

For a larger crowd, make two recipes of this beloved brunch dish.

- ½ (1-pound) package hot ground pork sausage
- 3 slices SARA LEE Classic White Bread
- 1 (8-ounce) package shredded sharp Cheddar cheese, divided
- 3 large eggs
- 1 cup milk
- 1 teaspoon prepared mustard
- ⅛ teaspoon pepper
- 2 cups chopped cooked ham

COOK pork sausage in a large skillet over medium-high heat, stirring until sausage crumbles and is no longer pink. Drain well.

ARRANGE bread slices in a lightly greased 8-inch square baking dish. Sprinkle sausage over bread. Sprinkle half of cheese over sausage.

WHISK together eggs and next 3 ingredients. Pour over cheese in baking dish. Sprinkle with chopped ham; top with remaining cheese. Cover and chill 8 hours.

BAKE casserole at 350° for 45 minutes. **MAKES** 4 servings.

CHIVE-AND-CHEESE MUFFINS

family favorite • fast fixin's

Prep: 10 min., Bake: 18 min.

- 2 cups all-purpose baking mix
- ¾ cup KRAFT 100% Grated Parmesan Cheese, divided
- 1 tablespoon sugar
- ¼ cup chopped fresh chives
- ½ teaspoon freshly ground pepper
- 1 large egg
- 1¼ cups milk
- 2 tablespoons vegetable oil

STIR together baking mix, ½ cup Parmesan cheese, sugar, chopped chives, and pepper in a large bowl; make a well in center of mixture.

STIR together egg, milk, and vegetable oil until blended. Add to dry ingredients, stirring just until moistened. Spoon batter into lightly greased muffin pans, filling two-thirds full. Sprinkle with remaining ¼ cup Parmesan cheese.

BAKE at 400° for 15 to 18 minutes or until golden. Cool slightly in pans; remove from pans, and cool completely on wire racks. **MAKES** 1½ dozen.

SOUR CREAM COFFEE CAKE

family favorite

Prep: 30 min., Bake: 40 min.

- 1 cup chopped walnuts
- ½ cup firmly packed dark brown sugar
- 2 teaspoons ground cinnamon
- 1 cup butter or margarine, softened
- 1 cup granulated sugar
- 2 large eggs
- 2 cups all-purpose flour
- 1 teaspoon baking powder
- 1 teaspoon baking soda
- 1 (8-ounce) container sour cream
- 1¾ teaspoons vanilla extract, divided
- PAM for Baking No-Stick Spray
- 1¼ cups powdered sugar
- 3 tablespoons milk

COMBINE walnuts, brown sugar, and cinnamon, and set aside.

BEAT butter at medium speed with an electric mixer until creamy; gradually add granulated sugar, beating well. Add eggs, 1 at a time, beating well after each addition.

COMBINE flour, baking powder, and baking soda in a medium bowl; add to butter mixture alternately with sour cream, beginning and ending with flour mixture, beating at low speed until blended after each addition. Stir in 1 teaspoon vanilla.

SPREAD half of batter evenly into a 10-cup Bundt pan coated with baking spray; sprinkle batter evenly with half of walnut mixture. Repeat layers.

BAKE at 350° for 40 minutes or until a wooden pick inserted in center comes out clean. Cool in pan on a wire rack 10 to 12 minutes; remove from pan, and let cool completely on a wire rack.

STIR together powdered sugar, milk, and remaining ¾ teaspoon vanilla; drizzle glaze evenly over cake. **MAKES** 10 to 12 servings.

MONKEY BREAD BITES

family favorite

Prep: 15 min., Cook: 5 min., Bake: 18 min.

- ½ cup DOMINO Granulated Sugar, divided
- 1 tablespoon ground cinnamon
- 1 (12-ounce) can refrigerated buttermilk biscuits
- 1 (6-ounce) can refrigerated buttermilk biscuits
- ½ cup plus 2 tablespoons butter
- ¼ cup firmly packed DOMINO Light Brown Sugar
- 1 teaspoon vanilla extract
- ½ cup chopped pecans, toasted
- Extra-large foil muffin cups

COMBINE ¼ cup granulated sugar and 1 tablespoon cinnamon in a large bowl. Cut biscuits into fourths, and add to sugar mixture; toss to coat. Set aside.

MELT butter in medium saucepan over medium heat. Add brown sugar and remaining ¼ cup granulated sugar, stirring until sugar dissolves. Remove from heat; stir in vanilla and pecans.

ARRANGE 5 coated biscuit pieces in a lightly greased foil muffin cup; place in a muffin pan. Repeat with remaining biscuit pieces. Drizzle evenly with pecan mixture.

BAKE at 400° for 18 minutes or until golden. **MAKES** 1 dozen.

NOTE: For testing purposes only, we used Pillsbury Golden Layers Buttermilk Biscuits.

CREAMY FRUIT SALAD

family favorite • fast fixin's

Prep: 20 min.

- 1 cup HELLMANN'S Real Mayonnaise
- 1 teaspoon grated lemon rind
- 2 tablespoons orange juice
- 1 tablespoon fresh lemon juice
- 1 tablespoon honey
- 3 bananas, sliced
- 3 medium-size red apples, chopped
- 3 small oranges, peeled and sectioned
- 3 cups seedless grapes
- Romaine lettuce leaves

STIR together first 5 ingredients in a bowl. Cover and chill until ready to serve.

TOSS fruit with half of mayonnaise mixture just before serving. Arrange fruit salad over lettuce leaves; serve with remaining mayonnaise mixture, if desired. **MAKES** 6 servings.

SPICED MOCHA LATTE

fast fixin's

Prep: 5 min., Cook: 10 min.

- 1 cup (6 ounces) NESTLÉ TOLL HOUSE Semi-Sweet Chocolate Chunks
- 2 cups half-and-half
- 1½ cups water
- 1 cup milk
- 3 tablespoons instant espresso or instant dark roast coffee
- ½ teaspoon vanilla extract
- ¼ teaspoon ground cinnamon
- Sweetened whipped cream

BRING first 4 ingredients to a gentle boil in a large saucepan over medium heat, whisking constantly until chocolate melts. Whisk in espresso, vanilla, and cinnamon, and serve immediately with sweetened whipped cream. **MAKES** 6 servings.

Metric Equivalents

The recipes that appear in this cookbook use the standard United States method for measuring liquid and dry or solid ingredients (teaspoons, tablespoons, and cups). The information on this chart is provided to help cooks outside the U.S. successfully use these recipes. All equivalents are approximate.

METRIC EQUIVALENTS FOR DIFFERENT TYPES OF INGREDIENTS

A standard cup measure of a dry or solid ingredient will vary in weight depending on the type of ingredient. A standard cup of liquid is the same volume for any type of liquid. Use the following chart when converting standard cup measures to grams (weight) or milliliters (volume).

Standard Cup	Fine Powder	Grain	Granular	Liquid Solids	Liquid
	(ex. flour)	(ex. rice)	(ex. sugar)	(ex. butter)	(ex. milk)
1	140 g	150 g	190 g	200 g	240 ml
¾	105 g	113 g	143 g	150 g	180 ml
⅔	93 g	100 g	125 g	133 g	160 ml
½	70 g	75 g	95 g	100 g	120 ml
⅓	47 g	50 g	63 g	67 g	80 ml
¼	35 g	38 g	48 g	50 g	60 ml
⅛	18 g	19 g	24 g	25 g	30 ml

USEFUL EQUIVALENTS FOR DRY INGREDIENTS BY WEIGHT

(To convert ounces to grams, multiply the number of ounces by 30.)

1 oz	=	¹⁄₁₆ lb	=	30 g
4 oz	=	¼ lb	=	120 g
8 oz	=	½ lb	=	240 g
12 oz	=	¾ lb	=	360 g
16 oz	=	1 lb	=	480 g

USEFUL EQUIVALENTS FOR LENGTH

(To convert inches to centimeters, multiply the number of inches by 2.5.)

1 in					=	2.5 cm			
6 in	=	½ ft	=		=	15 cm			
12 in	=	1 ft	=		=	30 cm			
36 in	=	3 ft	=	1 yd	=	90 cm			
40 in					=	100 cm	=	1 m	

USEFUL EQUIVALENTS FOR LIQUID INGREDIENTS BY VOLUME

¼ tsp	=							1 ml	
½ tsp	=							2 ml	
1 tsp	=							5 ml	
3 tsp	=	1 tbls			=	½ fl oz	=	15 ml	
	=	2 tbls	=	⅛ cup	=	1 fl oz	=	30 ml	
	=	4 tbls	=	¼ cup	=	2 fl oz	=	60 ml	
	=	5⅓ tbls	=	⅓ cup	=	3 fl oz	=	80 ml	
	=	8 tbls	=	½ cup	=	4 fl oz	=	120 ml	
	=	10⅔ tbls	=	⅔ cup	=	5 fl oz	=	160 ml	
	=	12 tbls	=	¾ cup	=	6 fl oz	=	180 ml	
	=	16 tbls	=	1 cup	=	8 fl oz	=	240 ml	
	=	1 pt	=	2 cups	=	16 fl oz	=	480 ml	
	=	1 qt	=	4 cups	=	32 fl oz	=	960 ml	
						33 fl oz	=	1000 ml	= 1 l

USEFUL EQUIVALENTS FOR COOKING/OVEN TEMPERATURES

	Fahrenheit	Celsius	Gas Mark
Freeze Water	32° F	0° C	
Room Temperature	68° F	20° C	
Boil Water	212° F	100° C	
Bake	325° F	160° C	3
	350° F	180° C	4
	375° F	190° C	5
	400° F	200° C	6
	425° F	220° C	7
	450° F	230° C	8
Broil			Grill

Menu Index

This index lists every menu by suggested occasion. Recipes in bold type are provided with the menu and accompaniments are in regular typeface.

MENUS FOR SPECIAL OCCASIONS

Commander's Palace Sunday Brunch
Serves 8
(page 66)
Rémoulade Sauce and shrimp
Garden District Eggs with asparagus
Pain Perdu   Bloody Marys

Texas-Style Celebration Menu
Serves 8 to 10
(page 118)
Longhorn cheese, grilled smoked sausage, and crackers
Beer-Can Chicken   Marinated Flank Steak
Creamy Lime Sauce   Warm flour tortillas
Chipotle Caesar Salad   Spicy Black Beans
Radish-Cucumber Salsa   Tomatillo Sauce
Pecan-Peach Cobbler   Vanilla ice cream
Texas beer and wine

Summer Cookout
Serves 10
(page 132)
Hot 'n' Spicy Chicken Wings   Ribs McCoy
Grilled Marinated Vegetables
Dianne's Southwestern Cornbread Salad
Pink Lemonade-Lime Dip with sugar cookies and fruit

Starlight Supper
Serves 6
(page 142)
Stuffed Focaccia With Roasted Pepper Vinaigrette
Green Bean-Potato Salad   Amaretto-Walnut Brownies
Iced tea or lemonade

Backyard Pool Party
Serves 8 to 10
(page 162)
Buried Treasure Snack Mix
Creamy Pineapple-and-Ham Rollups
Chicken-and-Bean Slaw Wraps
Lemonade Cupcakes   Emerald Sea Punch

Tasty Tailgate
Serves 8
(page 198)
Marrow's Famous Dogs
Hot Dog Chili
Sweet-and-Tangy Slaw
Southern-Style Potato Salad
Purchased cookies and brownies

Southwestern Supper
Serves 6 to 8
(page 206)
Taquitos With Pork Picadillo
Gonzales Meat Loaf
Mac and Texas Cheeses With
Roasted Chiles
José Falcón's Slaw
Spoonbread With Simple Chorizo
Rancher's Buttermilk Pie

Farmhouse Thanksgiving Feast
Serves 10
(page 230)
Pecan-Cornmeal Shortbreads
Roast Turkey With Sage and Thyme with
Muscadine Sauce
Caramelized Onion Macaroni and Cheese
Turnip greens with
Miss Kitty's Chili Sauce
Bakery rolls with
Honey-Lemon Butter
Sweet Potato-Apple Cobbler

Light Pork Roast Dinner
Serves 6 to 8
(page 236)
Orange-Glazed Pork Roast
Onion Rice Pilaf
Asparagus With Ginger
Apple-Cranberry Compote
Strawberry-Lemon Cheesecake

Game Night
Serves 6
(page 240)
Lemon-Rum Slush
Chipotle-Marinated Quail
Chile-Blue Cheese Grits   Mixed green salad
Almond-Orange Flan

Progressive Supper Club Menu
Serves 12
(page 244)

Appetizers in Icy Canada
Endive With Herbed Goat Cheese
Beggar's Purses With Smoked Salmon
Blanc De Noirs Gruet

Salad in the Big Apple
Winter Waldorf Salad   Zenata Pinot Grigio

Dinner in Johnston County, NC
Johnston County Crown Pork Roast With
Cranberry Stuffing
Bourbon-Sweet Potato Stacks
Garlic-Tarragon Green Beans
Lytton Spring Vineyard Red Ridge

Tropical Desserts From Panama
Piña Colada Crème Brûlée
Grilled Pineapple Skewers With Rum Sauce

Hanukkah Celebration
Serves 8
(page 247)
Spicy Apricot Brisket
Quick Potato-Chive Pancakes
Green Beans With Shallots
Chunky Chocolate Brownies

Ladies Reindeer Luncheon
Serves 8
(page 252)
Blitzen's Baked Salmon With Caribbean Fruit Salsa
Dasher's Dill Mini-Muffins
Cupid's Creamy Peppermint Punch
Rudolph's Chocolate Truffle Cake with **Chocolate Truffle Filling**
Chocolate Rudolph Reindeer
Vixen's vices (coffee and store-bought chocolates)

Holiday Open House
Serves 24
(page 256)
Grilled Parsleyed Shrimp and Vegetables
Lemon-Vinaigrette Marinated Antipasto
Hummus with pita bread rounds
Pork Tenderloin on Cornmeal Biscuits
Georges Duboeuf Beaujolais Nouveau, France;
Goats do Roam White or Red, South Africa
Beer and water
Gingerbread Bites With Orange-Cream Cheese Frosting
Sparkling white wines and liqueur sampling

Christmas Tea
Serves 8
(page 258)
Olive-Nut Spread Sandwiches
Shrimp Butter on Crostini
Chicken-Mandarin Orange Spread Sandwiches
Banana-Nut Bread with Lemon Curd
Assorted hot teas

Holiday Gathering
Serves 8
(page 270)
Old-Fashioned Roasted Turkey With Gravy
Piglet's Stuffing   **Bell's Sweet Potato Casserole**
Fruited Rice Pilaf
Fresh Cranberry Sauce
Pecan Squares

Appetizer Party
Serves 12
(page 272)
Hampton Place Beef Tenderloin with bakery rolls
Goat Cheese-Olive Sandwiches
Cranberry-Nut Triangles
Cupcake Cookies   **Ground Pecan Torte**

Holiday Gathering
Serves 12 to 15
(page 286)
Pork Tenderloin Sandwiches With
Cranberry-Coriander Conserve
Blue Cheese-Bacon Dip with grapes and assorted crackers
Raspberry-Brie Tartlets
Pecan Crescents   **Spritz Cookies**

MENUS FOR SPECIAL OCCASIONS (continued)

Casual Christmas Menu
Serves 6
(page 296)
Bourbon-Glazed Ham
Out-of-This-World Scalloped Potatoes
Bing Cherry-and-Cranberry Salad
Julienned Orange Carrots   Pumpkin Roll

Tex-Mex Sampler Party
Serves 6
(page 322)
Ranchero Catfish
Black Bean-Corn Salsa
Roasted Vegetable Quesadillas   Fiesta Chicken Soup
Margaritas   Store-bought pralines or brownies

MENUS FOR THE FAMILY

Easy Chicken Supper
Serves 4
(page 81)
Oven-Fried Chicken Cutlets
Speedy Garlic Mashed Potatoes   Steamed sugar snap peas
Pudding-and-Cookie Cups

Weekend Supper
Serves 6
(page 172)
Grilled Maple Chipotle Pork Chops
on Smoked Gouda Grits
Steamed broccoli   Dinner rolls
Mocha-Chocolate Shortbread with vanilla or coffee ice cream

Cozy Celebration
Serves 6
(page 82)
Grilled Pork Tenderloins With Rosemary Pesto
Lemon Rice Pilaf   Steamed green beans
Ice Cream-Toffee Dessert

School Night Supper
Serves 4 to 6
(page 182)
Chicken Casserole D'Iberville
Tossed salad   **Caramel-Apple Grahams**

Try This Combo
Serves 6
(page 127)
Stuffed Border Burgers   **Seasoned Steak Fries**
Turtle Dessert

Festive Italian Menu
Serves 6
(page 194)
Tapenade
Spicy Vegetables With Penne Pasta
Mixed gourmet greens with vinaigrette   Italian bread
Tiramisù Toffee Trifle Pie   Merlot

Family Dinner on the Patio
Serves 6
(page 138)
Grilled Pork Tenderloin With Gingered Jezebel Sauce
Grilled Yellow Squash Halves   **Fresh Tomato Biscuits**
Candy Wrap Cookies

Dinner on the Deck
Serves 4
(page 218)
Steak-and-Vegetable Kebabs over mixed salad greens
Orphan's Rice
Apple-Gingerbread Cobbler

Delta-Style Dinner
Serves 6
(page 164)
Lela's Hush Puppies
Jack's Fried Catfish   **Grilled Andouille Grits**
Tomato-and-Crabmeat Cream Gravy   Ice cream

Quick Chili Supper
Serves 4
(page 242)
Chili-Corn Chip Stack-Up Salad   **Quick Apple Bundles**

Family Gathering
Serves 8 to 10
(page 250)
Peach Holiday Ham
Bell's Sweet Potato Casserole
Winter Waldorf Salad
Garlic-Tarragon Green Beans
Rudolph's Chocolate Truffle Cake
Pecan Squares

Mediterranean Night
Serves 6
(page 282)
**Herbed Turkey Strips
With Roasted Peppers and Beans**
Roasted Sweet Onions
Roasted Garlic-and-Cheese Risotto
Grecian Tossed Salad
Blueberry Sherbet

St. Nick Supper
Serves 8
(page 298)
Cheeseburger Soup with
Easy Breadsticks
BLT Wrap
Mexican Hot Chocolate and
Chocolate-Dipped Orange Cookies

Dinner on the Grill
Serves 4
(page 320)
**Grilled Salmon With
Tangy Dill Sauce**
or **Lime-Grilled Chicken**
Grilled vegetables
**Rice-Cabbage Salad With
Honey-Dijon Vinaigrette**
Lemon or raspberry sorbet

WHEN COMPANY IS COMING

Weekend Menus for Feasting With Friends
Serves 8
(page 32)

Friday Supper
Easy Burritos with toppings
Pico de Gallo   Purchased brownies with ice cream

Saturday Breakfast
Pound Cake French Toast
Maple-Mint Cream   Raspberry Sauce
Juice and fresh fruit

Saturday Supper
Chicken Marbella   Wild rice
Tossed salad   Crusty French bread
Purchased dessert

Sunday Lunch
Purchased baked ham   **Colorful Vegetable Salad**
Purchased rolls

Elegant Couples' Party
Serves 12
(page 52)
Garlic-and-Rosemary Shrimp
Beef Tenderloin With Henry Bain Sauce and rolls
**Steamed Asparagus With
Tomato-Basil Dip**
Blue Cheese Logs and crackers
Purchased cheesecake

Keep It Casual
Serves 6
(page 71)
Zesty Feta Dip
Marinated Olives and Peppers
Crunchy Tuna-and-Almond Salad with
crackers or multigrain bread
Peanutty Spicy Noodle Salad
Banana Pudding With Sugar Biscuits
Iced Hibiscus Tea

Company Supper

Serves 6

(page 90)

East-West Flank Steak
Asparagus Pasta With Toasted Pecans
Crusty French bread
Pineapple-Cherry Dump Cake   Iced tea

Down-Home Dinner

Serves 8 to 10

(page 100)

Fried Catfish
Best Barbecue Coleslaw
Potato Salad With Roasted Red Peppers
Double-Chocolate Brownies

A Sensational Summer Menu

Serves 6

(page 168)

Tomato-and-Goat Cheese Crostini
Fruit Salsa   **Bourbon-Marinated Pork Tenderloin**
Stuffed Red Peppers With Cheesy Polenta and Green Chiles
Green Bean Salad With Feta   **Georgia Peach Trifle**

Cookout Menu

Serves 10

(page 178)

Barbara's Big Juicy Burgers   **Sweet-Hot Ketchup**
Grilled Corn With Jalapeño-Lime Butter   **Grilled Tomatoes**
Homemade ice cream

Fall Gathering for Friends

Serves 4 to 6

(page 186)

Goat Cheese Torta With Garden Pesto   **Saffron Butternut**
Squash Soup   **Barbecued Pork Quesadillas**
Kettle Corn

Small Dinner Party

Serves 6

(page 250)

Cheddar cheese and fruit appetizer tray
Apple-Sage Stuffed Pork Chops
Steamed baby carrots and pearl onions   **Fruited Rice Pilaf**
Mocha Mousse Torte

Supper Club Menu

Serves 6

(page 250)

Goat Cheese-Olive Sandwiches
or **Endive With Herbed Goat Cheese**
Citrus-Strawberry Salad
Cranberry-Glazed Pork Loin
Couscous with toasted pecans
Steamed broccoli
Piña Colada Crème Brûlée

Holiday Supper Club Menu

Serves 8 (page 290)

Orange Thing
Bacon-Stuffed Eggs
Baked Pimiento Cheese
Okra-Walnut Salad
Crabmeat-and-Spinach Lasagna
Red Velvet Cheesecake

Festive Fiesta

Serves 6

(page 274)

Fresh Salsa with colorful tortilla chips
Chicken-Sour Cream Enchiladas
Fiesta Coleslaw
Chocolate Wedding Cookies   **Vanilla Ice Cream**
Merry Margaritas

Post-Shopping Supper

Serves 6

(page 294)

Unforgettable Chicken Casserole
Orange-Ginger Peas   **Toasted Herb Rice**
Peppery Cheese Bread
Baked Lemon Pudding

Fall Supper Club

Serves 6

(page 321)

Turkey Scaloppine or
Smothered Swiss Steak with
mashed potatoes or rice
Broiled Parmesan Tomatoes
Mixed Greens With Creamy Garlic Dressing
Bakery pecan pie à la mode

Recipe Title Index

This index alphabetically lists every recipe by exact title.
All microwave recipe page numbers are preceded by an "M."

Month-by-Month Index

This index alphabetically lists every food article and accompanying recipes by month. All microwave recipe page numbers are preceded by an "M."

General Recipe Index

This index lists every recipe by food category and/or major ingredient.
All microwave recipe page numbers are preceded by an "M."

Shrimp *(continued)*

Salads
Artichoke Salad, Shrimp-and-, 50
Grilled Shrimp, Orange, and Watermelon Salad With Peppered Peanuts in a Zesty Citrus Dressing, 308
Shrimp Salad, 147
Spinach Salad With Grilled Shrimp, Tropical, 51
Sauce, Shrimp, 147
Sautéed Shrimp With Country Ham and Capers, 241
Spicy Shrimp and Grits, 176
Yogurt-Cucumber Sauce, Shrimp With, 216

SLAWS
Apple-Bacon Coleslaw, 181
Barbecue Coleslaw, Best, 100
Buttermilk Dressing Coleslaw, 24
Fiesta Coleslaw, 275
José Falcón's Slaw, 207
Soy Slaw and Dipping Sauce, Grilled Chicken With Sweet, 123
Soy Slaw and Dipping Sauce, Grilled Salmon With Sweet, 123
Sweet-and-Tangy Slaw, 199
Wraps, Chicken-and-Bean Slaw, 163

SLOW COOKER
Burritos, Easy, 32
Chili, Big-Batch, 242
Sandwiches, Easy Spanish Pork Dip, 312

SOUFFLÉS
Gingerbread Soufflés With Lemon Cream, 300
Vidalia Onion Soufflé, 167

SOUPS. *See also* **Chili, Chowders, Gumbos, Jambalayas, Stews.**
Bean-and-Ham Soup, 325
Butternut Squash Soup, Saffron, 187
Cheeseburger Soup, 298
Chicken-and-Wild Rice Soup, 26
Chicken Soup, Fiesta, 323
Garlic-and-Potato Soup, Golden, 214
Gazpacho, Yellow Tomato, 158
Lamb Soup With Spring Vegetables, 108
Mushroom Soup, Wild, 203
Onion
French Onion Soup, 243
Mexican Onion Soup, 243
Tomato-Onion Soup, 243
Squash and Leek Soup, Cream of, 42
Tomato-Beef-Wild Rice Soup, 42
Tomato-Onion Soup, 243
Tortilla Soup, 26
Turkey Soup With Green Chile Biscuits, Fiesta, 233

SPAGHETTI
Salad, Chicken-and-Veggie Spaghetti, 129

SPINACH
Florentine Quiche, Tomato, 332
Pastas
Lasagna, Crabmeat-and-Spinach, 292
Lasagna, Won Ton Spinach, 129
Penne With Spinach and Feta, 328
Pie, Super Special Spinach, 60

Salads
Southern Spinach Salad With Cheese Grits Croutons and Vidalia Onion-Balsamic Vinaigrette, 316
Tropical Spinach Salad With Grilled Chicken, 51
Tropical Spinach Salad With Grilled Pork Tenderloin, 51
Tropical Spinach Salad With Grilled Shrimp, 51
Sauté, Fresh Spinach, 285
Sauté, Tomato-Spinach, 23
Tomatoes, Spinach-Feta Stuffed, 285

SPREADS
Cheese
Bacon-Olive Cream Cheese, 196
Garlic-and-Dill Feta Cheese Spread, 238
Goat Cheese Torta, 186
Pimiento Cheese, Baked, 291
Pimiento Cheese, Chile-, 325
Chickpea Spread, Creamy, 146
Lime Dressing, Creamy, 46
Olivata, 159
Olive-Parsley Spread, Cream Cheese-and-Olive Biscuits With, 238
Tapenade, 194

SQUASH. *See also* **Zucchini.**
Soup, Cream of Squash and Leek, 42
Soup, Saffron Butternut Squash, 187
Yellow
Casserole, Squash, 126
Casserole, Two-Cheese Squash, 126
Grilled Yellow Squash Halves, 138

STEWS. *See also* **Chili, Chowders, Gumbos, Jambalayas, Soups.**
Black-Eyed Pea Stew With Rice, 19
Collard 'n' Black-Eyed Pea Stew, 24
Turnip Greens Stew, 24

STRAWBERRIES
Margarita, Strawberry, 107
Slush, Strawberry Tea, 63
Desserts
Cake, Strawberry-Lemon Sheet, 137
Cake, Triple-Decker Strawberry, 55
Cheesecake, Strawberry-Lemon, 237
Filling, Strawberry-Lemon, 137
Freeze, Strawberry, 141
Frosting, Strawberry Buttercream, 55
Ice Cream, No-Cook Strawberry, 179
Pops, Strawberry, 141
Salad, Citrus-Strawberry, 249
Salad, Strawberry-Chicken, 50

STUFFINGS
Cranberry Stuffing, 246
Piglet's Stuffing, 270

SWEET-AND-SOUR
Chicken, Sweet 'n' Sour, 311
Ribs, Sweet-and-Sour Baby Back, 87
Sauce, Sweet-and-Sour 'Cue, 87

SWEET POTATOES
Bourbon-Sweet Potato Stacks, 246
Casserole, Bell's Sweet Potato, 271
Cobbler, Sweet Potato-Apple, M232
Pancakes, Quick Sweet Potato-Chive, 248

Pie, Sweet Potato, 331
Spicy Island Sweet Potatoes, Caribbean Catfish With, 310

TACOS
Catfish Tacos, Baja-Style Fried, 311
Fish Taco Appetizers, 324
Skillet Tacos, Easy, 180

TASTE OF THE SOUTH
Ambrosia, 233
Ambrosia, Kitchen Express, 233
Breads
Rolls, Icebox, 70
Spoonbread, 58
Spoonbread, Memmie's, 57
Gumbo, Chicken-and-Sausage, 213
Muffuletta, 27
Salad, Olive, 27
Squash Casserole, 126
Squash Casserole, Two-Cheese, 126

TEA
Iced
Blackberry Iced Tea, 158
Cranberry Tea, 63
Hibiscus Tea, Iced, 72
Mint Tea, Fruity, 143
Passion Tea, 63
Punch, Mint Tea, 63
Red Tea, Iced, 143
Strawberry Tea Slush, 63
Sweet Tea, Southern, 107

TOMATILLOS
Pudding, Green Tomato-Tomatillo-Corn, 103
Sauce, Tomatillo, 119

TOMATOES
Biscuits, Fresh Tomato, 138
Broiled Parmesan Tomatoes, 322
Chicken, Creamy Tomato-Stuffed, 16
Crostini, Tomato-and-Goat Cheese, 168
Dried Tomato-Basil Pesto, 101
Gnocchi With Olive Oil, Tomato, and Parmesan, 47
Gravy, Tomato-and-Crabmeat Cream, 165
Green
Fried Green Tomato Casserole, Stuffed, 145
Fried Green Tomatoes With Roasted Red Pepper Rémoulade and Goat Cheese, 144
Fried Green Tomato Sandwiches, 145
Gumbo, Green Tomato, 314
Pudding, Green Tomato-Tomatillo-Corn, 103
Journey Cakes, Tomato, Parmesan, and Kalamata Olive, 99
Marinated Tomatoes With Basil and Balsamic Vinegar, 140
Pico de Gallo, 32, 61, 89, 311
Quiche, Tomato Florentine, 332
Salad, Tomato-Red Onion, 181
Salsas
Fresh Salsa, 274
Picante, Salsa, 41
Quick Party Salsa, 146
Sandwiches, Tomato, Swiss, and Bacon, 140
Sauces
Basic Tomato Sauce, 145
Lemon Sauce, Salmon With Almonds and Tomato-, 23

Favorite Recipes Journal

Jot down your family's and your favorite recipes for quick and handy reference. And don't forget to include the dishes that drew rave reviews when company came for dinner.

RECIPE	SOURCE/PAGE	REMARKS